Praise for *The Bitter Woods*

"[The author] has reconstructed a complex series of events with a clarity and an attention to detail that are a tribute both to his hard and careful work in the sources and his personal examination of the terrain.... He has made the battle his own—and, particularly when he is dealing with small-unit actions, his account conveys an excitement that is hard to resist."
—*New York Times Book Review*

"Exceptionally interesting.... The author's exposition of Hitler's battle plan wonderfully illuminates Hitler himself."   —*The New Yorker*

"Totally engrossing... [*The Bitter Woods* is] an important addition to the literature of World War II, tightly organized, often suspensefully written, and contributing not a little fresh data of its own."
—*Saturday Review Syndicate*

"A highly professional job. It has propelled an unknown author into the leading ranks of military writers.... John Eisenhower's book will be long read."   —Washington (D.C.) *Sunday Star*

"John Eisenhower has established himself as an historian of the first rank."   —*Book World*

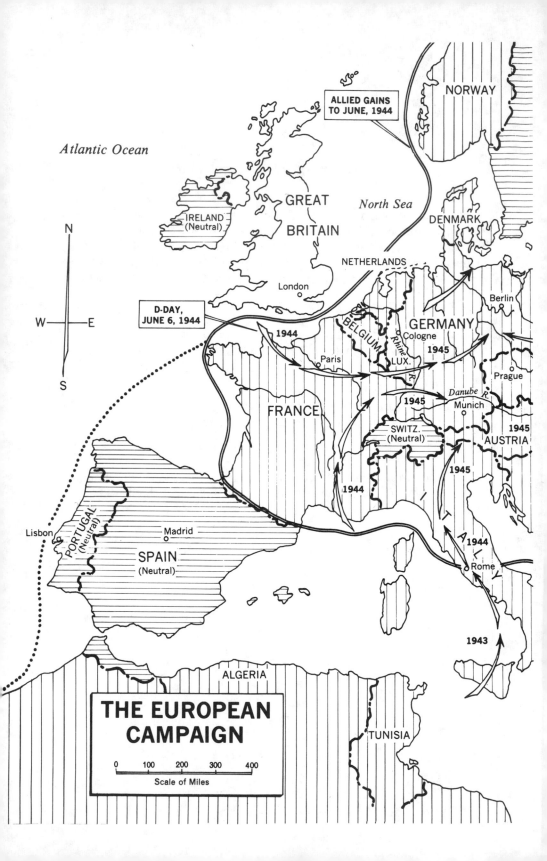

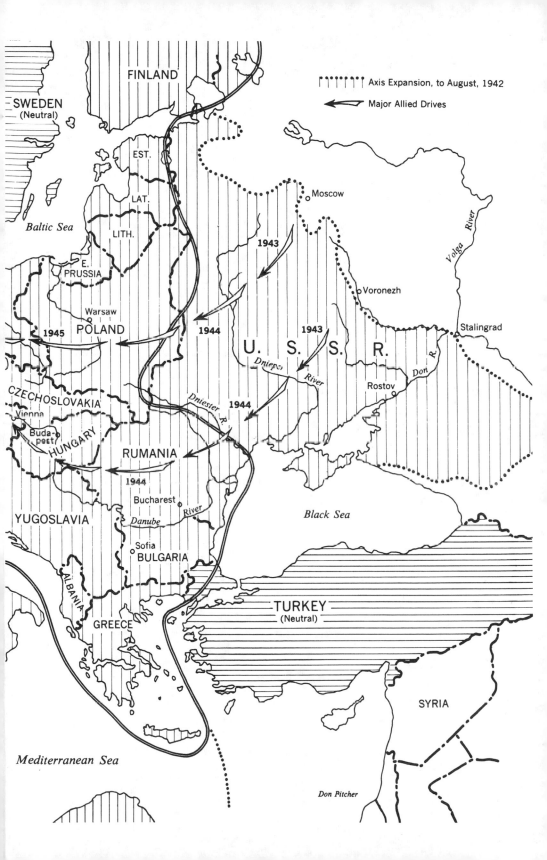

FINLAND

SWEDEN
(Neutral)

⌐⌐⌐⌐⌐⌐⌐⌐ Axis Expansion, to August, 1942

← Major Allied Drives

Baltic Sea

EST.

LAT.

LITH.

E.
PRUSSIA

Warsaw

Moscow

1943

Voronezh

Volga River

Stalingrad

1945

POLAND

1944

U. S. S. R.

1943

Dnieper

River

Don R.

Rostov

CZECHOSLOVAKIA

Vienna

Buda-
pest

HUNGARY

RUMANIA

Dniester R.

1944

1944

Bucharest

YUGOSLAVIA

Danube   *River*

Sofia

BULGARIA

Black Sea

ALBANIA

GREECE

TURKEY
(Neutral)

SYRIA

Mediterranean Sea

Don Pitcher

The Bitter Woods

The Bitter Woods

THE DRAMATIC STORY, TOLD AT ALL ECHELONS—
FROM SUPREME COMMAND TO SQUAD LEADER—
OF THE CRISIS THAT SHOOK THE WESTERN
COALITION: HITLER'S SURPRISE
ARDENNES OFFENSIVE

BY

John S. D. Eisenhower

DA CAPO PRESS • NEW YORK

Library of Congress Cataloging in Publication Data

Eisenhower, John S. D., 1922–
  The bitter woods: the Battle of the Bulge / by John S.D. Eisenhower; new
introduction by Stephen E. Ambrose.—1st Da Capo Press ed.
      p.   cm.
  Originally published: New York: G. P. Putnam's Sons, 1969. With new
introd.
  Includes bibliographical references.
  ISBN 0-306-80652-5
  1. Ardennes, Battle of the, 1944–1945. I. Title.
D756.5.A7E3   1995
940.54′21431—dc20   95-9536
                                                                        CIP

Maps by Donald Pitcher

First Da Capo Press edition

This Da Capo Press paperback edition of *The Bitter Woods* is an unabridged
republication of the edition first published in New York in 1969, with the
addition of a new introduction by Stephen E. Ambrose. It is reprinted by
arrangement with G. P. Putnam's Sons.

Published by Da Capo Press, Inc.
A Subsidiary of Plenum Publishing Corporation
233 Spring Street, New York, N.Y. 10013

To Barbara

Midway upon the journey of our life
  I found myself within a forest dark,
    For the straightforward pathway had been lost.
Ah me! how hard a thing it is to say
  What was this forest savage, rough, and stern,
    Which in the very thought renews the fear.
So bitter is it, death is little more.

> DANTE ALIGHIERI
> *Inferno,* Canto I
> (Longfellow translation)

Never in history was there a coalition like that of our enemies, composed of such heterogeneous elements with such divergent aims. . . . Even now these states are at loggerheads, and, if we can deliver a few more heavy blows, then this artificially holstered common front may suddenly collapse with a gigantic clap of thunder.

> —ADOLF HITLER
> (upon ordering the attack
> through the Ardennes)

It is not the critic who counts, nor the man who points out how the strong man stumbled, or where the doer of deeds could have done better. The credit belongs to the man who is actually in the arena; whose face is marred by dust and sweat and blood; who strives valiantly; who errs and comes short again and again; who knows great enthusiasms, great devotions, who spends himself in a worthy cause; who, at the best, knows in the end the triumph of high achievement; and who, at the worst, if he fails, at least fails while daring greatly, so that his place shall never be with those cold and timid souls who know neither victory nor defeat.

> —Attributed to THEODORE ROOSEVELT

Introduction

It was the biggest single battle ever fought by the United States Army. More than 600,000 GIs were directly involved, another 400,000 had supporting roles. That was more men than the entire U.S. Army of 1941. About 20,000 GIs were killed in the Ardennes, another 20,000 captured, and 40,000 wounded. This was more casualties than the total number of men in the Army of Northern Virginia at Gettysburg. The Americans lost nearly 800 tanks, more than there had been in the entire U.S. Army in 1941.

It was a battle fought on a scale that staggers the imagination today—and caused almost impossible problems for the commanders at the time. They had to deal with not just the enemy attack, but also extreme weather conditions, an inadequate road network made worse by snow and ice, green troops with inexperienced officers in untested regiments and divisions, shortages of artillery shells, and deficient communications. The generals had to rally beaten, dispirited troops in the face of an attack they had not expected—indeed, never dreamed possible—coming in a strength they could only guess at.

How the American commanders reacted to these challenges is John Eisenhower's theme. As a West Point graduate (June 6, 1944), veteran of World War II and the Korean War, military historian, and son of the Supreme Commander, he is uniquely qualified to tell how the generals of the U.S. Army (nearly all of them known to him personally) fought in the Ardennes from December 1944 to January 1945. Some did poorly, others fair, most well, a few brilliantly.

The creation of the U.S. Army of World War II was one of the great triumphs of the American Republic. Another was how that army was led in the Ardennes in December 1944, when it was at its peak in strength and efficiency.

The American army that fought the Battle of the Bulge had the most firepower of any army of the mid-20th century. It was the most mobile force the world has ever seen. Within days of the surprise assault the Americans had 11,000 trucks carrying 60,000 men rushing into the breach; in the first week some 50,000 trucks carried 250,000 GIs to the Ardennes. This was mobility with a vengeance, an achievement unprecedented in the history of war.

5

Not even in Vietnam, not even in Operation Desert Storm, was the U.S. Army capable of moving so many men and so much equipment so quickly.

And this was done by an army that in 1939 had less than 200,000 active duty personnel—which meant that it ranked sixteenth in the world, right behind Rumania. By the end of 1944 it numbered eight million and was second only to the Red Army, and even then second not in planes or vehicles or firepower but in gross numbers—and even there not by much.

The creation of this army was a miracle. Many men were responsible, beginning with Franklin Roosevelt and George Marshall and extending down the chain of command to those colonels and brigadier generals who had stayed with the Army in the lean years of the Depression and finally got a chance to show their abilities when the war began. The most famous of these were Dwight Eisenhower, Omar Bradley, and George Patton, but there were many others almost as gifted if not quite so lucky, men like Courtney Hodges, Troy Middleton, Leonard Gerow and Matt Ridgway. They helped to build the World War II Army, equip it, train it, and lead it into combat in Normandy in June 1944 and in the pursuit through France in the late summer.

In the fall, however, the Germans rallied and stopped the advance at their border, and on December 16 launched the counteroffensive in the Ardennes that forced Eisenhower, Bradley, Patton, and the others to fight on the defensive—a new experience. How they met the challenge and triumphed is John Eisenhower's subject. This book, as he says, is "a study in command."

Command on both sides. He follows the German generals as closely as the American. Many of them are quite fantastic characters in their own right. Their relationships among themselves and with their leader, Hitler, contrast sharply with the relationships among the American generals and with their leaders, Roosevelt and Churchill.

Strangest of all was Hitler, who gets a full-length portrait from John Eisenhower, wonderfully done. The whole idea of a counteroffensive was Hitler's—all his generals opposed it to one degree or another—and it resulted from his personal situation, rather than as a decision for the national good. Had Hitler wanted the national good, he would have surrendered after the Allies broke out in Normandy, just as Rommel urged him to do. But Hitler knew that he could not survive a surrender. He knew of his crimes. He could expect only execution for himself and the end of the Nazi Party.

Standing on the defensive on the east bank of the Rhine—as his generals urged him to do and Supreme Commander Eisenhower most feared he would do—made no sense to Hitler. Germany could never win a war of attrition. He had to gamble, to take a life-or-death risk, in order to have even the faintest hope of surviving the war. Hitler recalled Clausewitz, who said, "He who is hard pressed will regard the greatest daring as the greatest wisdom."

Within the context of his decision to fight to *win* the war, not just prolong it, Hitler's plan for the counteroffensive was a work of genius. It gave him a chance—less than 10%, as one of his generals noted—but still a chance. In briefest form, it was to strike in the Ardennes (where the Americans were badly stretched out), achieve a breakthrough, cross the Meuse River with armor, capture fuel stocks from the Allies, and drive on to Antwerp. In the process he would split the British and American forces and capture the port on which the Allies depended for most of their supplies.

Success depended on six factors: surprise; the strength of the blow; the speed of the advance; a slow American response; poor performance by the GIs; and bad weather to neutralize U.S. air superiority.

Through superhuman effort Hitler and his generals were able to gather a force big enough to have a real shot at achieving the objective. He gained surprise through a combination of skill, secrecy, incredibly tight security, and audacity. Speed of advance depended on the field commanders; for that reason, Hitler chose Josef ("Sepp") Dietrich, a former SS bullyboy, to command the Sixth Panzer Army. His qualifications for his crucial assignment were fanaticism and unquestioned personal bravery.

Hitler assumed a slow U.S. response. He believed that Eisenhower's superiors, Churchill and Roosevelt, controlled him as tightly as he, Hitler, controlled German field commanders. He therefore figured that before Eisenhower could call off the major attacks to the north and south to build a defense in the Ardennes, he would need Churchill's and Roosevelt's approval. Hitler told his people that it would take Eisenhower at least two days to comprehend the seriousness of the situation, then two or three more days of wrangling with his bosses before he could react. By that time, the Germans would be across the Meuse River, if not already in Antwerp.

Even when Eisenhower was free to react, Hitler believed, his forces would be slow to move. For one thing, Americans were unaccustomed to fighting on the defensive and would find it difficult to adjust their thinking and operations. Further, in spite of the terrible pounding the Wehrmacht had taken in France, Hitler was contemptuous of the American army. He thought the Allies had won in France only because of overwhelming air and material superiority. He believed the average GI was soft, poorly trained, badly led, and liable to panic. He was certain that kids brought up as Hitler Youth would always outfight kids brought up as Boy Scouts.

As for the final factor—bad weather was simply a question of waiting. It was certain to come sometime in the late fall in northwest Europe.

Of the six factors, Hitler got three working for him: He achieved surprise, he had sufficient strength, and the bad weather came. But he was wrong about the Hitler Youth vs. the Boy Scouts. The speed of the advance was insufficient from the first day on because the GIs held their ground in the face of overwhelming superiority in numbers. Some of the finest parts of this book are the accounts of ordinary GIs and junior officers performing feats of arms that no one had thought possible.

Hitler was equally wrong about the American command structure. When Eisenhower told Bradley to detach an armored division from Patton's Third Army to reinforce the First Army in the Ardennes, Bradley protested that Patton would be furious.

"Tell him," Eisenhower replied, "that Ike is running this damn war."

To indulge in a bit of hyperbole, with that sentence Eisenhower won the battle. First because he was absolutely correct in his immediate and instinctive judgment that getting the Seventh Armored into St. Vith was critical to keeping Dietrich from breaking through on the northern flank on the direct road to Antwerp. Second, Hodges was preparing a major offensive against the Ruhr River dams and Patton was about to launch one in the Saar. Before night fell on the first day of the Battle of the Bulge, Eisenhower decided to switch both armies from offensive missions outside the Ardennes to defensive missions. He thus undercut Hitler's assumption that Eisenhower's response would be slow and hesitant because Eisenhower would not dare to act until he had cleared his decisions with Churchill and Roosevelt. In fact, it never occurred to Eisenhower to check with the two leaders, nor with the Combined Chiefs of Staff, his immediate superiors.

He set hundreds of thousands of troops into motion. He made the battle his. He put his finger on Bastogne on the map and declared that it had to be held. On the third day of the battle he met at Verdun with his immediate subordinates. They were glum, depressed, embarrassed. They kept their faces bent over their coffee cups. Eisenhower walked in, looked disapprovingly at the downcast generals, and boldly declared, "The present situation is to be regarded as one of opportunity for us and not of disaster. There will be only cheerful faces at this conference table."

This set exactly the right tone. How it worked out in practice is told in this book in a vivid and understandable way. Like his father, John Eisenhower knows how to get to the heart of the matter. *The Bitter Woods* will be read so long as the Republic lasts.

STEPHEN E. AMBROSE
University of New Orleans
May 1995

Stephen E. Ambrose is Boyd Professor (Emeritus) of History and Director of the Eisenhower Center at the University of New Orleans. He is also the highly respected author of D-Day, June 6, 1944: The Climactic Battle of World War II; Eisenhower: Soldier & President; *and* Crazy Horse and Custer: The Parallel Lives of Two American Warriors, *among others.*

Contents

Book IV

CRISIS

Book V

DECIMATION OF THE WEHRMACHT

Allied Leaders and German Leaders, *p. 16*

Illustrations follow p. 256

Maps

Acknowledgments

A BOOK of this nature cannot possibly be the product of the efforts of an individual man. Indeed, on reviewing those who made a contribution I am startled by the number of people who were invaluable in helping me gather the material from which this manuscript resulted.

This fact is probably accentuated in the case of a new writer, to whom the prospect of writing a full-length book presents an unusual challenge. For the individual who gives encouragement to the neophyte and assures him that the job can be done is as valuable as the one who supplies him with vital information.

Of those persons invaluable to the writing of this book three stand out. First is my wife, Barbara, who not only put up at home with the temperament of a first-time author but also went to a special business school to "jump into the breach" and complete typing the so-called "final" manuscript when my regular secretary, for maternity reasons, was forced to leave before the job was completed.

The second is my father, General Dwight D. Eisenhower, who took the time to check over and supplement with new material those parts of the narrative that applied to his own thoughts and reactions. I am appreciative not only of his time and effort but even more of his frank and cheerful recognition that this book is mine alone, even though in places our viewpoints may somewhat differ.

Third, it is impossible to conceive a successful completion of this book without the encouragement and the guidance of Colonel Carroll V. Glines, USAF, Office of the Assistant Secretary of Defense for Public Information. C.V. guided me to the proper places for information and never let me forget that the Department of Defense was interested in my receiving all the cooperation humanly possible.

With these recognitions, I would like to add the rest, arranged alphabetically.

Martin Blumenson. An author in the Office of the Chief of Military History, headed by Brigadier General Hal D. Pattison, the one office that supplied the greatest amount of help by far. Martin, like others, became a warm personal friend. As one who writes such popular military books as *Kasserine Pass,* he possesses great insight into the problem of writing military history for the lay reader. I drew heavily, in the first few chapters of this book, on his excellent official Army history, *Breakout and Pursuit.*

Lieutenant Colonel Charles Burtyk, USA. C. V. Glines' able assistant, who did much to ease my arrangements with the administrative people in the Army.

Detmar Fincke. An expert on the German Army, also in the Office of the Chief of Military History. Not only did Detmar provide invaluable material on the Germans (service records, R-series manuscripts, etc.), but he acted as a sort of point of contact with others of OCMH. Associated closely with him in work and in our occasional pleasant luncheon gatherings were Charles von Lüttichau, Dr. Lida Mayo, Mrs. Magna Bauer, and the late Dr. John Miller.

Dr. Woodrow Hanson. A meticulous scholar, Woody Hanson made a major contribution by extensive research regarding the chapers on the German planning for the offensive. I am appreciative to our mutual friend, Jim Knox, for bringing the two of us together.

George A. Horkan, Jr. My lifelong friend, who just happens also to be my attorney. At the age of six the two of us, with our fathers, tramped the battlefields of World War I together, developing a consuming interest (even if not an immediate understanding) of the military history that has transpired on the soils of France, Belgium, Luxembourg, and Germany. He helped me in two ways. First, his general evaluation of the way the text was progressing gave me heart at many a low moment. Second, he made me confident always that my logistical tail was secure: "You go up to that quiet Pennsylvania countryside and write the book; I'll take care of the details!"

William James. Although Will James will be listed later as a source of information, his unusual gesture in flying to Europe at his own expense deserves special mention.

Anthony Lazzarino. A most imaginative and creative individual, Tony Lazzarino, while working on a motion picture covering much of the same general area, was the person who originally kindled an interest in me to write this book. Besides supplying me with much public domain material, he also planted the seeds of various ideas, including the book title. I trust that this book is richer for the conversations, sometimes hours on end, that Tony and I had together.

Mrs. Bastian (Bev) Leeuwenburg. Besides her unusual talents in the conventional functions of a personal secretary, her cosmopolitan knowledge gained through extensive travel enabled her to grasp the turn of events with remarkable ease. Furthermore, she possessd the balance and good humor to take difficult situations in stride.

Charles MacDonald. Chief of the World War II History Branch of OCMH and a successful author in his own right, his views on the autumn fighting of 1944, the closing of the Bulge in January, 1945, and the personalities of various commanders were invaluable. A company commander in the 2d U.S. Infantry Division on Elsenborn Ridge, he is the author of *Company Commander, The Siegfried Line Campaign, The Battle of the Huertgen Forest,* and other works.

Charles McManus. Custodian of important documents in OCMH, Charlie McManus, ably assisted by Mrs. Valerie Mecutcheon and Miss Hannah Zeidlik, saw to it that books, U.S. documents, service records, and other material were produced without delay.

Mrs. Oscar (Joyce) Mehring. My former secretary in Gettysburg, Joyce Mehring cheerfully helped in typing the final manuscript, making it possible to submit same within the limits of the deadline.

Wilbur Nigh. Head of the World War II Archives in Alexandria. Assisted by Mrs. Lois Aldridge, Bill Nigh turned his files inside out to glean information, much of it (especially combat interviews) highly dramatic.

Charles M. Sherover. Educational Resources Corporation, New York. As my agent, Charlie Sherover made this book possible. While not involved directly with the actual writing or obtaining of material, he skillfully secured such advances as to make the effort financially feasible.

Mrs. Helena Huntington Smith. A book and magazine author, Mrs. Smith supplied me with anecdotes from World War II archives that serve, I trust, to flesh out some of the impersonal material on military maneuvers.

Mrs. Judith Horvath Tegethoff. Judy Tegethoff took over as my full-time secretary after she had been helping Barbara produce the "final" manuscript. Neither Judy nor I realized at the time that she would be my right arm throughout the unexpectedly long and excruciating last stages of recasting.

Sam Vaughan. While not connected with this work, Sam Vaughan, a distinguished editor who helps my father, gave friendly personal advice and encouragement where such encouragement was most needed.

Lieutenant Colonel Robert Webb, USAF. Chief of the Book Section, assistant to C. V. Glines. After C.V.'s departure, Bob, under the supervision of Colonel Grover Heiman, Jr., served as my main point of contact with the Magazine and Book Branch. As such he was invaluable, particularly in his prompt tracking down of the "last known address" of various characters, famous and obscure.

Also helpful in securing Army photos were Miss Anna Urband, Mrs. Donna Traxler, Mrs. Annie Seily, Mrs. Myrtle Still, and Miss Bettie Sprigg.

There have been three monumental works dedicated to the Battle of the Ardennes: for perspective, Robert Merriam's *Dark December;* for human interest, John Toland's *Battle;* for completeness, Dr. Hugh Cole's *The Ardennes: The Battle of the Bulge.* In addition, Brigadier General S. L. A. Marshall's

Bastogne: The First Eight Days, and Dr. Forrest Pogue's *The Supreme Command* were invaluable. Of these authors, John Toland and Bob Merriam in particular lent me unusual encouragement. As might be expected, their views and advice carried great weight. Also four individuals, General Bruce C. Clarke, General Hasso von Manteuffel, Dr. Lyle Bouck, and William James, have all gone to unusual lengths to supply diaries and information.

EISENHOWER

General of the Army Dwight D. Eisenhower (1890–   )

Commander of the victorious Allied forces in Tunisia, Sicily, and Italy, Eisenhower was named Supreme Commander, Allied Expeditionary Forces, at the Teheran Conference in 1943. Though unknown outside the Army before 1942, he held assignments at the highest levels, associating on close terms with such generals as John J. Pershing, Douglas MacArthur, and Fox Conner. His independent, somewhat maverick outlook stemmed at least partly from his being old for his West Point class of 1915. For under the Army promotion system then in effect he early became convinced that he would never be made a general.

But this never dimmed his absorption in the Army. Those who chose to think of him as primarily a "political" general were mistaken; they overlooked his keen interest in day-by-day military operations and the fact that in 1924 he was graduated first at the Army's senior tactical school, the Command and General Staff School at Fort Leavenworth.

His enemies, the Nazis, once assessed him thus: "Eisenhower is an expert in operations of armored formations. He is noted for his great energy and his hatred of routine office work. He leaves the initiative to his subordinates, whom he manages to inspire to supreme efforts through kind understanding and easy discipline. His strongest point is said to be an ability to adjust personalities to one another and smooth over opposite viewpoints. Eisenhower enjoys the greatest popularity with Roosevelt and Churchill.*

---

* Luftwaffe Academy lecture on invasion generals, February 7, 1944. Quoted in Forrest Pogue, *The Supreme Command* (Washington: Dept. of the Army, 1954), p. 34.

MONTGOMERY

Field Marshal Sir Bernard Law Montgomery (1887–   )

Upon graduating from the Royal Military Academy at Sandhurst at the age of twenty-one, Bernard L. Montgomery made every effort—for financial reasons—to join the Indian Army. Failing to secure a commission in the Indian Army, he decided on a British unit located in India, the Royal Warwickshire Regiment, the first battalion of which was located at Peshawar. There he received the first training that led to his long and remarkable career.

During World War I, Montgomery served in France as brigade major, 104th Infantry Brigade, 35th British Division, which provided his first experience of warfare on a modern scale.

In October, 1935, when Montgomery was in command of the 9th Infantry Brigade in Salisbury, tragedy struck:

His wife died, leaving him with a nine-year-old son. Montgomery never remarried, devoting all his energy to his army duties and the care of his son.

At the beginning of World War II, Montgomery was given command of the 3d Division on the Continent, and he faced the disaster of the evacuation at Dunkirk with his comrades in the British Expeditionary Force. Later he assumed command of British II Corps, succeeding his friend and mentor, General Alan Brooke.

When the Allied invasion of Northwest Africa was in the planning stages, Montgomery was slated to command the First British Army, but the Eighth Army defending Egypt needed a commander, and he assumed command under Field Marshal Harold Alexander. The battle of El Alamein made the name Monty a household word on both sides of the water.

Entering Tunisia, in pursuit of Rom-

BRADLEY

mel, Montgomery's Eighth Army teamed up with Kenneth Anderson's First British Army and Omar Bradley's U.S. II Corps to form Alexander's 18 Army Group, all serving under Eisenhower's Allied Force Headquarters.

Known by D-Day as one of Britain's foremost soldiers, General Montgomery commanded 21 Army Group when Operation Overlord was launched.

Lt. Gen. (Later General of the Army) Omar N. Bradley (1893–   )

Marked for success from his cadet days at West Point in the star-studded class of 1915, Omar N. Bradley's peacetime career was so linked with the Infantry that he came to be known as "the infantrymen's general." Routine assignments were his, although like many others he missed overseas duty in World War I. He was commandant of the In-

fantry School at Fort Benning in 1941 and later commanded the 82d and 28th divisions.

During the Tunisian campaign General Marshall sent Bradley to Africa as an observer for General Eisenhower. Soon he was made deputy commander of the II Corps under George S. Patton, Jr.; he assumed command of the corps for the operations in Tunisia leading to the German surrender.

Bradley's success with II Corps in Sicily led to his appointment as senior U.S. ground commander for the Normandy invasion. Here he was placed in the awkward position of commanding an army group that included an army commanded by his former chief, George Patton. The way in which the two worked together was a monument to Bradley's tact and the selflessness of both. Patton once told him, "Brad, I think up all these ideas and then you analyze them."

U.S. Army Photo

HODGES

**Lt. Gen. (Later Gen.)
Courtney Hicks Hodges
(1887–1966)**

Courtney Hodges was a man who might have been practically forgotten by history. Despite his remarkable accomplishments, he had no talent for self-dramatization, which made him almost unknown to the press.

He was born in Perry, Georgia, and entered West Point in 1904, but his cadet career was cut off at his first Christmas there by a deficiency in mathematics. However, Courtney Hodges stuck to his guns, enlisted in the 17th Infantry Regiment, and won a competitive commission in the course of three years, receiving his second lieutenant's commission shortly after the rest of his West Point class.

Associated with the Infantry as much as was Omar Bradley, Hodges served on the Mexican border in 1916, accompanying John J. Pershing on his Punitive Expedition against Pancho Villa. In France in 1918 he was assigned to the 6th Infantry Regiment, 5th Division, and returned home as a lieutenant colonel, decorated with the Distinguished Service Cross.

In 1920 Hodges reverted to the rank of major, attended the Field Artillery School, and then served as a tactical officer in the Military Academy that had rejected his services some sixteen years before. He went to Command and General Staff School at Leavenworth in 1925, then became an instructor in the Air Corps Tactical School at Fort Langley, Virginia, and from there went to the Infantry Board, where he captained the Infantry Rifleman Team.

After a tour in the General Staff of the Philippine Department between 1936 and 1938, he came home to become assistant commandant—later commandant—of the Infantry School, and chief of Infantry in 1941. He soon attained command of the Third U.S. Army in February, 1943, with the rank of lieutenant general.

In June, 1944, Hodges went ashore in Normandy as deputy to Lieutenant General Omar Bradley and Bradley's designated successor.

Supporters of George Patton often conveniently overlook the fact that Courtney Hodges' First Army dashed farther across France than Patton's Third and during the bulk of the time employed more armor.

Careful and meticulous but cool under pressure, Hodges well earned the title "the soldier's soldier."

Lt. Gen. (Later Gen.)
George Smith Patton, Jr.
(1885–1945)

Though his family has its roots in Virginia, George S. Patton, Jr., was born in San Gabriel, California. Throughout his boyhood he was dedicated to joining the military profession. After one setback, he was graduated with the class of 1909, U.S. Military Academy.

One of the few members of the American High Command to see service in World War I, he was associated with tanks as early as 1917. He sailed as a member of John J. Pershing's staff and was detailed to the new Tank Corps. He commanded the 304th Light Tank Brigade in the St.-Mihiel offensive and was wounded on September 26, 1918, the first day of the Argonne offensive.

A full colonel in the war, Patton reverted to the grade of captain and then major in 1920; it was to be fourteen years before he regained the rank of lieutenant colonel. In the early 1920's he returned to his basic branch, Cavalry, and in 1931–32 attended the Army War College.

By April, 1941, Patton was back with tanks, commanding the 2d Armored Division and later the I Armored Corps at Fort Benning, Georgia.

With the command of the Western Task Force in North Africa, Patton assumed new responsibilities which henceforth lessened his direct association with armor. For from this time on, his duties in combat with the II Corps would involve command of infantry divisions,

U.S. Army Photo

PATTON

corps artillery, corps engineers, and other nondivisional units. Patton's capacity for pursuit, however, was demonstrated in Sicily. His highly emotional nature, as shown in the notorious soldier-slapping incident, nearly cost him his position and at the same time jeopardized Eisenhower's when he refused to reduce Patton.

But Patton's soldierly qualities were to pay off in the end. His greatest contributions were still ahead of him in the European campaign.

MIDDLETON

GEROW

Maj. Gen. (Later Lt. Gen.) Troy H. Middleton (1889–   )

Born and reared in Mississippi, Troy Middleton's disarming manner disguised the incisiveness of his mind.

A full colonel of Infantry in World War I, he was reduced in rank in the peacetime Army with little hope of advancement. With this prospect he retired after twenty-nine years of service in 1937 to take the position of dean of administration at Louisiana State University, where he had formerly served as professor of military science and tactics.

Recalled to active duty in World War II, Middleton rose to the command of the 45th Infantry Division in Sicily. A knee injury lost him his command and put him in Walter Reed Hospital. He was here when General Eisenhower, who had known him in the Philippines as well as in World War II, inquired of General Marshall as to his whereabouts. Upon being told of Middleton's injury, Eisenhower demanded Middleton be sent to Europe anyway. Eisenhower's feelings were summed up in one sentence: "I would rather have Troy Middleton commanding VIII Corps from a stretcher than anyone else I know in perfect health."

Middleton hurried overseas as soon as he received news of this assignment. His knee immediately showed marked improvement.

Maj. Gen. (Later Gen.) Leonard Townsend Gerow (1888–   )

Leonard T. ("Gee") Gerow, born in Petersburg, Virginia, and reared in the tradition of Robert E. Lee and Stonewall Jackson, entered Virginia Military Institute in 1907. He was graduated in 1911 with honors, and as a result received a coveted Regular Army commission, an appointment reserved for top men in all schools other than West Point.

A marked man early, Gerow became an assistant in the War Plans Division of the War Department. Later, at the Command and General Staff School, his study partner in the attic of Otis Hall was Eisenhower, who was graduated a fraction of a point ahead of Gerow, when both were graduated with honors.

After another tour of duty in Washington, Gerow went to the Philippines, and as a member of the 31st Infantry Regiment witnessed combat in Shanghai in the first phases of the Japanese invasion of China.

He returned to War Plans from 1935 to 1939, now assigned its chief, in time to absorb part of the blame for the American disaster at Pearl Harbor. While this incident reputedly cost him some of the confidence of George C. Marshall, Gerow was sent to Fort Meade in February, 1942, to command the 29th Infantry Division. In July, 1943, when V Corps was being formed, Gerow was selected to command.

Meticulous, careful, and a stickler for detail, he bore some resemblance to Courtney Hodges, under whom his corps served most of the time.

As fate would have it, V Corps was destined for the tough spots of the war: Omaha Beach, the liberation of Paris, and finally the northern shoulder of the Ardennes. Gee Gerow, one of the least known of the truly brilliant leaders of the Army, finally achieved the command of the Fifteenth Army and the four stars he so richly deserved.

U.S. Army Photo

RIDGWAY

Maj. Gen. (Later Gen.) Matthew Bunker Ridgway (1895–   )

A little older than the rest of the "airborne generals," Matt Ridgway was born at Fort Monroe, Virginia, the son of Colonel Thomas Ridgway. He was graduated from the Military Academy on April 20, 1917, and was to experience the frustration so common to other officers of the time, waiting on the Mexican border for orders overseas that never came. In September, 1918, he was sent to teach Spanish at West Point.

Ridgway's career in the ensuing years

COLLINS

MCAULIFFE

had more variation and color than most. He was executive for athletics at West Point, and in 1922 graduate manager of athletics. Then he served a tour with the 15th Infantry Regiment in Tientsin, China. Between December, 1927, and December, 1928, he was assistant to Major General Frank McCoy, then engaged in trying to straighten out problems in American relations with Nicaragua. The following month he was a member of the Commission of Inquiry and Conciliation on the Bolivian-Paraguayan boundary dispute.

Sent to Panama in 1930 and the Philippines in 1932, Ridgway then served as military adviser to a public servant also destined to make his name in the European campaign—Teddy Roosevelt, Jr. After Leavenworth and the War College, Ridgway became G-3 of the Fourth Army. He joined the War Plans Division of the War Department in September, 1939. In March, 1942,

he was made assistant division commander of the 82d Division, soon to be converted to an airborne division. In June, 1942, now commanding the 82d Airborne, Ridgway took the division to Africa, and in April, 1943, launched the first large-scale U.S. airborne assault of World War II. He remained in Italy until November, 1943. On D-Day he parachuted into Normandy. The XVIII Airborne Corps, the largest strictly American airborne formation of World War II, was his in August, 1944.

**Maj. Gen. (Later Gen.)
J. Lawton Collins
(1896–   )**

Born in New Orleans, Joseph Lawton Collins was graduated from West Point on April 20, 1917, the youngest in the class. His elder brother, who had the same initials, also served in the Army; to avoid confusion Collins went by the sobriquet J. Lawton. A major of Infantry in World War I, he missed combat duty but served a period of occupation duty in May, 1919. He spent the peacetime years from 1920 to 1932 as a captain, instructed for four years at West Point, and was graduated from the Command and General Staff School at Leavenworth in 1933 and from the War College in 1938. After instructing at the War College for a time, he was assigned to the Office of the Secretary, General Staff, War Department.

In January, 1941, Collins was appointed chief of staff of VII Corps, the unit he was later to make famous, but in the meantime he was detached to help organize the defenses of Hawaii following Pearl Harbor. Commanding the "Tropic Lightning" 25th Division at Guadalcanal, Collins soon learned that his men were taking his initials—J. L.—to stand for Joe Lightning. With VII Corps in Normandy, the brilliance of his campaign to seize Cherbourg reversed the names; for the rest of the European campaign he was known simply at Lightning Joe.

The West Point yearbook dubbed him "Optimist supreme! A man first of concentration and decision and second of rapid and hearty action."

Brig. Gen. (Later Gen.) Anthony Clement McAuliffe (1898–   )

A native of Washington, D.C., and a West Point graduate in the class of November 1, 1918, Anthony McAuliffe spent the years between World War I and 1935 as a first lieutenant discharging a series of routine assignments. He attended the Army's Command and General Staff School as a captain with the class of 1936–37. The following year he instructed at the Field Artillery

School and the next year attended the War College. Assigned to the War Department in the fields of ordnance and supply in 1942, there was little in his makeup to indicate that his name would in many ways become synonymous with the Battle of the Bulge.

In August, 1942, McAuliffe took over command of the Division Artillery, 101st Airborne Division. He parachuted into France the night of June 5, 1944, commanding the task force that captured the vital Norman town Carentan. In Operation Market-Garden, General Montgomery's effort to gain a bridgehead over the Rhine, he commanded the glider echelon of the 101st.

Taciturn and utterly matter of fact, McAuliffe's reply, "Nuts," to a German demand for surrender was typical of the man. There was nothing studied or theatrical about the statement; it simply reflected a direct man's reaction to a demand he considered ridiculous.

Maj. Gen. Norman Daniel Cota (1893–   )

The career of Norman Daniel ("Dutch") Cota parallels that of so many other regular Army officers who, though commissioned during World War I, failed to get overseas. Cota had a variegated career. A major in 1918, it took him until 1932 to regain this grade. Between 1920 and 1924, his specialty was the Finance Department, hardly a promising preparation for command in the Infantry, and during the thirties he served as instructor at West Point and attended the Command and General Staff School at Fort Leavenworth and the Army War College.

Cota's association with the 1st U.S. Infantry Division began in 1940, when he was made executive officer of the 16th Infantry at Fort Jay, New York;

COTA

HASBROUCK

he became G-3 in July, 1941, and then, as chief of staff, went overseas with the Big Red One in June, 1942.

He did not stay long. Soon he was detailed to the British Combined Operations Headquarters in London, and in the spring and summer of 1943 represented the Army Ground Forces in conferences developing American-British combined operations techniques, particularly amphibious techniques. This assignment was to bring his moment of greatest note. As assistant division commander of the 116th Infantry (29th Division) and attached to his old 1st Division, he rallied troops on the beaches of Normandy on D-Day. His outstanding qualities as a combat leader earned him the command of the 28th U.S. Infantry Division in August, 1944.

Cota marched through Paris with the 28th Division, and fought in the battle of the Hürtgen Forest, an experience he would never forget; what lay ahead—the Ardennes—was the most difficult challenge of all.

Maj. Gen. Robert W. Hasbrouck (1896–   )

The career of Robert W. Hasbrouck stands as a refutation of those who feel that all officers can be strictly categorized. Born in Kingston, New York, Hasbrouck was graduated from West Point on August 30, 1917; his branch, Coast Artillery. He sailed for France with the 62d Coast Artillery in June, 1918.

In 1919 Captain Hasbrouck was assigned to the Polish Relief Mission and sent to Fort Zegne, Poland. On his return he transferred from the relatively sedentary life of the Coast Artillery to the Field Artillery. After attending the Field Artillery School, he became an instructor there and later professor of military science and tactics at Princeton. He attended the Command and General Staff School in 1932 and 1933, and the War College in 1936 and 1937. A significant assignment in the interim was the command of the 68th Field Artillery Battalion (Mechanized) at Fort Knox, Kentucky.

The assignment that may have been the one that led him to the Armored Force came in April, 1941, when he was appointed commanding officer of 22d Armored Field Artillery Battalion, in the 4th Armored Division at Pine Camp, New York. After a brief tour with the 1st Armored Division at Fort Knox, he joined the 8th Armored in August, 1942, commanding a combat command.

His newfound role with Armor appeared to be sidetracked when he became chief of staff of 1 Army Group (later 12 Army Group) in August, 1943. But in September of the next year, relieving the former commanding general, Robert W. Hasbrouck assumed command of the 7th Armored.

Brig. Gen. (Later Gen.) Bruce Cooper Clarke (1901–   )

A graduate of West Point in the class of 1925, Bruce C. Clarke selected the Engineers as his basic branch. With a degree in chemical engineering from Cornell and a Bachelor of Law degree from LaSalle Extension University, Clarke's education was more varied than that of the run-of-the-mill officer of his day. His career included such assignments as assistant professor of military science and tactics at the University of Tennessee and district engineer in Galveston, Texas.

After graduation from Command and

U.S. Army Photo

CLARKE

General Staff School in 1940, Clarke organized and commanded the first American armored engineer organization, the 47th Engineering Troop (Mechanized) in the 7th Mechanized Brigade. When the Brigade was absorbed into the 1st Armored Division, Clarke commanded its organic engineer battalion. He became a major in December, 1940.

Shortly thereafter, Bruce Clarke joined the 4th Armored Division and early in 1942 became chief of staff; a year later he assumed command of Combat Command A, his switch from Engineers to Armor now complete.

Clarke's reputation grew with his command of CCA, 4th Armored, in Normandy and the dash across France. In early November, 1944, he was given Combat Command B of the 7th Armored and a few days later was promoted to brigadier general.

U.S. Army Photo

VON RUNDSTEDT

German Commander in Chief West, Gerd von Rundstedt was born at the town of Aschersleben in Prussia. He was one of the oldest participants in the Ardennes campaign. A general officer from the 1920's on, Rundstedt retired as a generaloberst (colonel general) in 1938 but was called back at the beginning of the war. He was promoted to generalfeldmarschall (field marshal) in 1940.

Rundstedt reached the zenith of his career when he commanded Army Group A in the victorious 1940 campaign in France, which resulted in the crushing defeat of the French and British armies. Reportedly, Rundstedt and his chief of staff, Fritz von Manstein, had induced Hitler to modify the

Generalfeldmarschall Karl Rudolf Gerd von Rundstedt (1875–1953)

Schlieffen Plan and make the main attack through the Ardennes rather than through Holland. Hitler, apparently thinking along the same lines, accepted the views of these two officers, overriding the rest of the German hierarchy.

Late in 1941 Rundstedt resigned his commission in protest over the tactics being employed by Hitler on the eastern front. Hitler accepted with rage, and Rundstedt retired to civil life.

In 1942 the austere Prussian was recalled as Commander in Chief West but was relieved again in 1944 shortly after the Allied landings in Normandy.

Recalled for a third time in September, it was to be his fate to command an operation that was destined to bear his name, perhaps permanently, though he disapproved of it totally.

Contemptuous of Hitler and the entire Nazi Party, Rundstedt made no efforts to curry favor with them, but Hitler continued to use him, as he knew that Rundstedt's rigid, nonpolitical soldier's code made him a man who would carry out orders in spite of his personal feelings.

Generalfeldmarschall Walther Model (1891–1945)

Like many others in the German High Command, Walther Model was a Prussian. Entering the Germany Army in February, 1909, at the age of eighteen, he remained on duty between the wars, rising to the command of 4th Korps. In 1938, when Germany was preparing for war, Model was promoted to the grade of brigadier general. Advancement came rapidly; on March 1, 1944, he attained the peak and was elevated to the rank of field marshal. In June, 1944, he was called to the assignment that cemented his reputation: he took over Army Group Center on the Russian front in time to resolve the confusion resulting from the massive Russian summer offensive.

Replacing Guenther von Kluge on the western front as both OB West and commander of Army Group B in August, Model found the two positions an excessive burden. He was glad when Hitler restored the respected Rundstedt as commander of OB West, leaving Model to concentrate on his own all-important army group.

With it all, Model was a torn soul, the victim of a conflict between his deeply religious nature and fealty to his Führer. This conflict he buried by throwing himself headlong into his work. He understood his soldiers, although he drove them unmercifully—as he did himself. With his officers he was less understanding.

Model was reputed to have begun to drink heavily by the end of the war, but this failed to stop him from rising daily at five o'clock to inspect his troops. Though by the time of the Ardennes Model had realized the hopelessness of the German cause, his remarkable abilities were still to be instrumenal in prolonging the agony.

National Archives Photo

MODEL

Oberstgruppenführer (General, Waffen-SS) Joseph Dietrich (1892–1966)

"Sepp" Dietrich, crony of Hitler's and practically a member of his household, was one of the rare individuals privileged to address his Führer by the familiar *du* rather than the more formal *sie*. Dietrich was a Bavarian originally, a butcher by profession. He participated in the ill-fated Beer Hall Putsch in 1923, and from then on his fortunes were tied to the Nazi Party. In 1934 he headed the execution squad that shot Ernst Röhm, another early follower of Hitler's, who had become politically dangerous.

DIETRICH

VON MANTEUFFEL

Hearty and blunt, Dietrich was a man who spoke his mind. As he made no claim to tactical knowledge, his Sixth Panzer Army was given a brilliant soldier, Fritz Kraemer, to supplement his shortcomings.

Though his status with the Waffen-SS earned him the contempt of many of the more professional German generals, those who worked with him closely still respected him as a small unit tactician. Apparently he was devoid of physical fear. Certainly he was not afraid to disagree with Hitler, sometimes interceding with his friend and chief on behalf of regular officers who would not dare such effrontery.

Through little fault of his own, Sepp Dietrich was to play a relatively minor role in the Ardennes campaign compared to his colleague, Manteuffel. The strategic planning, for which he had no responsibility, was to take him through terrain unfit for large-scale military offensives.

Military history will be kinder to Oberstgruppenführer Sepp Dietrich than were his Army colleagues, one of whom, on one occasion at least, referred to him as a pig.

General der Panzertruppen Hasso von Manteuffel (1897–   )

The youngest of the high-ranking generals, Hasso von Manteuffel, a Prussian, was noted more as a combat leader than as a General Staff officer. He served in Africa under Rommel from November, 1942, until he was evacuated across the Mediterranean in May, 1943. He was promoted to major general in February, 1944, and later that year to the rank of full general in command of Fifth

Panzer Army, completely bypassing the Corps echelon.

Manteuffel was one of the most highly decorated officers in the German Army, holding the Iron Cross of the Knights degree and Oak Leaf with Swords and Diamonds. On his efficiency report the commander in chief of Army Group Center on the eastern front wrote: "in every facet an outstanding leadership personality." Another report noted his quick capacity to judge situations and his high sense of commitment.

Manteuffel became known and admired by Model despite a bitter disagreement earlier in the war. With a capacity to inspire his troops, he was considered a "typical" cavalry officer—dashing, unconcerned in crisis, and brave.

National Archives Photo

VON LÜTTWITZ

General der Panzertruppen Heinrich Freiherr von Lüttwitz (1896–   )

Barely older than his chief, Manteuffel, and like him a cavalry officer, Heinrich von Lüttwitz volunteered for the German Army in August, 1914. By December he had been promoted to the grade of lieutenant, serving in the first Uhlans (Lancer) Cavalry Regiment. Between wars he remained in the Army.

When World War II broke out he was a lieutenant colonel, but he rose to colonel in October, 1941, and to general der panzertruppen in November, 1944. In September, 1944, Lüttwitz took command of the 47th Panzer Korps, part of which was the 2d Panzer Division, which he commanded in Normandy.

General Peter von Thoma wrote of Lüttwitz: "A passionate soldier, ambitious, sometimes more critical than necessary. With much combat experience he joined the front line fight himself. A professional soldier capable of impro-

vising. Socially courteous, he leads men by his personality and handles them well, both in theory and in practice."

Manteuffel did not consider Lüttwitz an outstanding strategist, but his most valuable quality in the fifth year of war was his understanding of the German soldier's capabilities and, more important, limitations.

Lüttwitz was destined to be the recipient of one of the most terse and publicized expressions of defiance in history.

Obersturmbannführer (Lt. Col., Waffen-SS) Otto Skorzeny (1908–   )

Originally an engineer by profession, Otto Skorzeny, Hitler's fellow Austrian, was by 1944 a great favorite of the Führer's. As a civilian he played a role in arranging the Anschluss of 1938.

SKORZENY

PEIPER

Skorzeny first donned uniform in January, 1940, in the Luftwaffe, soon rising to the grade of sergeant in the Waffen-SS. By January, 1941, he was a lieutenant of Engineers in the Waffen-SS.

Skorzeny achieved a considerable reputation as a commando. His most famous exploit occurred in September, 1943, when he and a party of picked men from his 502d Parachute Battalion rescued Benito Mussolini from his Italian captors in the mountains of Italy. From September to October, 1944, Skorzeny and his men prevented the Hungarian government at gunpoint from surrendering to the Russians.

As a lieutenant colonel in the Ardennes campaign, Skorzeny was slated for an impressive mission. By this time Skorzeny was one of the few men Hitler felt he could trust implicitly. Aware of his spectacular exploits, Allied intelligence regarded him as the most dangerous man in Europe.

Obersturmbannführer (Lt. Col., Waffen-SS) Jochen Peiper (1915–   )

Young for his grade and the degree of responsibility placed on him, Jochen Peiper was a man who had made a considerable name for himself on the eastern front. Known for his ruthlessness and professional competence, he was selected to command the lead elements of the principal drive. Peiper was objective in his evaluation of military situations and utterly contemptuous of incompetence in any form. Generals he held in little awe; wars were meant to be won, and nobody's feelings should be allowed to stand in the way.

Peiper was a strange mixture of conflicting qualities. Educated and fluent in English, yet a fanatical Nazi, he was to be associated with the most infamous of the massacres of the war on the western front—at Baugnez, near Malmédy, Belgium.

Foreword

THIS book was conceived as a study in command, an examination of the command structure on both sides in the Allied invasion of Europe during World War II. To best illustrate the many elements and stresses—even crises —that can affect command situations, it focuses largely on a single battle that, in its own way, constituted perhaps the single greatest threat to the unity of the coalition: Hitler's counteroffensive of December, 1944, in the Ardennes.

Despite the near quarter of a century since World War II, much of the world still recalls those momentous events. To those who were involved, the memories are indelible. And yet the very vastness of the operations in that conflict tend to cloud the fact that it was directed not by computers but by people.

Wars of former decades and centuries are associated in the mind of the modern reader with the names of commanders. Napoleon's marshals—Davout, Messéna, Berthier, and many others—represent the fighting forces they commanded that made up the maneuver elements of the Emperor's Grand Army. Similarly, in the American Civil War, formations were known not so much by number as by the personalities of the leaders. Thus Grant, Lee, Sherman, Sheridan, Jackson, Pickett, and scores of others are household names in America a century later; some of them still evoke strong emotions. This is partly because of more complete records and the invention of the camera, but most of all it is attributable to the writings of such authors as Douglas Southall Freeman, George F. Henderson, Kenneth P. Williams, Bruce Catton, and countless others.

Not so World War II. With the exception of top leaders with unusually flamboyant demeanor or speech, the names of the many remarkable men who directed armies, corps, and divisions have remained relatively unknown except to those who fought directly under or beside them—and even then the association is often vague.

This lack of familiarity with the personalities of World War II stems partly from the great flexibility of modern military organizations, which permit considerable interchange of commanders from unit to unit. It results, too, from the close proximity of this great conflict in point of time. Emotions have been strong; the desire has been to forget rather than study the war.

But now those on both sides of the Atlantic are beginning to view World War II with more objectivity. Twenty-three years after the end of that struggle, its personalities are becoming better known. Hopefully this trend will continue until commanders at all echelons, men like Hodges, Manteuffel, Bradley, Model, Collins, Ridgway, Gerow, Middleton, Lüttwitz, and many others will be just as familiar to the informed public as their more famous counterparts of yesteryear.

It is generally assumed that the high commander bears the ultimate responsibility for winning a campaign whereas the lower unit commander is responsible only for his own individual unit's fighting well. These pages abound with stories of commanders who did more than was expected of them. On the Allied side we see Lieutenants Lyle Bouck and Kenneth Farrens commanding platoons the actions of which had effects reaching far beyond their few troops' immediate performance; Bruce C. Clarke defending the critical road hub of St.-Vith with a handful of troops belonging to a division other than his own, impatiently ticking off the minutes until his combat command arrived and built up a reasonable defense; Major Paul J. Solis preventing Obersturmbannführer Jochen Peiper from seizing a gas dump; Creighton Abrams and George Jaques deciding on their own to attack straight through to relieve Bastogne rather than follow the prescribed route; and small units of the 51st Engineer Combat Battalion at Trois Ponts, Chevron, and Hotton vitally affecting the outcome of a great campaign.

In the higher echelons we see Troy Middleton making a decision to hold Bastogne before receiving orders from above—and J. Lawton Collins risking his career by bucking the prevalent feeling among his immediate superiors and attacking rather than withdrawing at the point of the German spearhead.

At high command level we see the breadth of responsibility that fell to General Eisenhower, who, while charged primarily with the strategic direction of a vast campaign, was obliged to cope with vexing problems of an international political nature as well.

And finally, we see Sir Winston Churchill, the great political war leader, supporting, encouraging, and giving inspiration to British and American troops and civilians.

On the German side we witness such professional officers as Walther Model, Hasso von Manteuffel and Heinrich von Lüttwitz, who, though feeling in their hearts that the ambitious offensive to Antwerp was doomed to failure, still executed their duties as soldiers with all the force of their being.

These are only a few of the names of those whose imagination, dedication, and aggressiveness led them to perform beyond the dictates of the tactical manual. In the battle for Western Europe—the Ardennes in particular—command leadership abounded. War, however, is far from a sterile chess game. It is fought against a background of death, mutilation, destruction of property, and incredible waste. Alongside these are heroism, action, indecision, nobility, cruelty, and occasional personal breakdown. Such features of war are described in these pages, but not as ends in themselves. Hopefully such combat tales will be useful primarily in contributing to the main theme: Command. The vehicle is the Allied invasion of Europe, June 6, 1944, to May 8, 1945; the spotlight, the Ardennes.

In literary drama the climax can occur long before the final curtain falls. In a Shakespearean tragedy, for example, the protagonist's doom is often sealed in the third act, though he meets his end somewhat later.

A military campaign sometimes follows the same pattern. If the combatants are determined, and reasonably well matched, the struggle builds to a point at which one side achieves decisive advantage; but considerable time and much fighting may still take place before final victory. In the American Civil War, the Battle of Gettysburg occurred in mid-1863; the Wilderness, Spotsylvania Courthouse, Cold Harbor, Chicamauga, Chattanooga, Atlanta, Sherman's march to the sea, Petersburg, and Appomattox were still to come after Pickett's shattered ranks had fallen back from Cemetery Ridge. Yet with the advantage of hindsight few historians would deny that the back of the Confederacy had been broken as of that fateful first week of July. As Stephen Vincent Benét put it: "All roads lead to Appomattox now."

So it was with the Allied invasion of the European Continent. The climax in that campaign came without question in December, 1944, when Hitler launched his great offensive known as the Battle of the Bulge. Though this bitter conflict raged in midwinter, at the turn of the year, much fighting and dying was still to come. But from the time that great German offensive was stalled, contained, and finally reduced, the outcome of the European campaign was no longer in doubt.

The final results of the battle, viewed in casualties alone, were costly for both sides (76,000 U.S., 100,000 German).[1] But, humanitarian considerations aside, the Allies could afford these losses far better than Hitler. Indeed, when the great bulge [2] in the Allied lines was finally closed and the retreating Germans were fleeing to the protection of the Siegfried Line, the Wehrmacht was practically a shell. From here on, the main resistance to the Allied advance through Germany lay in fanatic but poorly organized groups, protected sometimes by formidable terrain but more often easily bypassed and surrounded. In many ways, though Allied losses still continued and major op-

[1] Hanson Baldwin, *Battles Lost and Won* (New York: Harper, 1966), p. 438.
[2] The fifty-mile-deep penetration that gave this campaign its popular name.

erations still lay ahead, the actions following the Ardennes campaign could be considered a mop-up.

All elements of the war were present in the Battle of the Ardennes. The valor of the divisions that held the northern shoulder, the efforts of scattered American cavalrymen in the Losheim Gap, the precarious plight of the handful of engineers sent out to protect St.-Vith, the bravery of the 28th Division and the tragedy of the 106th—all represented ordeals sustained by Allied troops throughout the entire eleven months of the European conflict.

But such ordeals were far from one-sided. The hardships suffered by members of Dietrich's Sixth Panzer Army in making their way back to German lines from Stoumont; the hopeless fight of the 2d Panzer Division, out of fuel, being decimated by their American counterpart, the 2d Armored; the stubborn resistance put up in January by Germans who now knew that their last gamble had failed—all remind us that the bravery of individual soldiers was not a monopoly of the Allies.

The horrors sustained by the Belgian and Luxembourg civilians, moreover, languishing miserably for days in the basements of Bastogne or being slaughtered by SS troops in the town of Stavelot, eloquently can stand for the tragedy that befalls those who find themselves in the paths of war.

At first glance Hitler's venture into the Ardennes might seem sheer madness; yet despite the pessimism of his generals, the plan had some elements of genius. The objective, the port of Antwerp, with a capability of supporting fifty Allied divisions on a continuing basis, could be regarded as the key to the European campaign. Its loss would ruin Allied plans.

Furthermore, Hitler's forces had achieved a near miracle in this same Ardennes territory in 1940 when Rundstedt's Army Group A burst through the French lines, crossed the Meuse River at Sedan, and dashed all the way to Boulogne on the North Sea. The French and British forces were split. The French surrendered and the British evacuated what was left of their army through the port of Dunkirk.

Finally, the bad weather—and here Hitler appeared almost prophetic— would enable the Nazis to enjoy the advantage of surprise. For the first time since Tunisia, American soldiers were initially fighting the enemy without the overwhelming artillery, air, and logistical support to which they were accustomed. Thus, in a way this battle became the ultimate confrontation of the American and German soldier.

Three factors, aside from the overambitious nature of the offensive, resulted in German defeat. First was the unexpected resourcefulness of the American soldier. His lack of military bearing and his indifference to the niceties of military attitudes led Hitler and others to underestimate the way in which small American units could go into business for themselves.

Another German miscalculation was the nature of the terrain. The Ardennes region is not solid primeval forest. Approximately one third is covered by nearly impenetrable woods; the rest is land rolling in varying degrees. Nevertheless, every road leading through the Ardennes sooner or later runs into a defile, where a small group of men could act as a modern-day Horatius at the bridge and hold off large formations.

Finally, there was the unexpected swiftness of Allied reaction. As soon as news came of the breakthrough, a half million American troops were on the move to squeeze it off in a matter of two days. Such reaction Hitler had considered impossible.

One of the most interesting aspects of the Ardennes campaign, aside from the drama of individual action and confrontation of armies on new terms, was the series of events leading up to December 16. Contrary to the belief held by many, the Allied coalition in World War II was far from automatic. A basic strategic interest of the British was to maintain the "lifeline" to the Indian Ocean via the Mediterranean and Suez. The basic American objective was the quick defeat of Nazi Germany by the most direct means possible, an invasion from England. Thus, in its very conception Operation Overlord represented a compromise, agreed to only after the Allies had executed a somewhat less ambitious operation with the conquest of North Africa, Pantelleria, Sicily, and Southern Italy.

As his military thinking departed more and more from reality, Hitler tended to overestimate the magnitude of these divergencies of outlook between the two powerful Western nations. He failed to imagine either nation's submitting to the authority of a supreme commander, able to make decisions on his own and backed up equally by both governments. In Hitler's eyes the Western coalition was weak. It would hold up, he felt, only as long as the combination met unrestricted success; once an overpowering blow struck either ally, it would fall apart. Continually Hitler harked back to the exploits of his idol, Frederick II of Prussia, who during the Seven Years War successfully fought the armies of Russia, France, Sweden, Saxony, and Austria. With the advantage of interior lines (such as Germany also possessed in World War II), Frederick the Great defeated the armies of each nation in turn, breaking up the loose alliances that bound them together, finally securing a peace favorable to the relatively small nation of Prussia.

In his hope that the Western combination could be split, Hitler was doomed to disappointment. And yet he came closer to achieving this objective than most American citizens and British subjects have ever quite realized. In the ten days between December 30 and January 9, feelings between Americans and British, the latter largely represented by the personality of Field Marshal Bernard L. Montgomery, rose to unprecedented heat. Perhaps earlier in the war, when the contributions of the two Western allies were more nearly equal, Hitler could have come even closer to success. But now the coalition was taking on an increasingly American complexion. The British, having committed their last manpower and financial reserves, were able to supply only about a quarter of the forces fighting on the western front.

A coalition remains an equal partnership only when the enemy is stronger than either ally. When American strength grew to such size, the British government's influence on the conduct of the war diminished recognizably. And President Roosevelt, his mind now on matters of the future, had by this time delegated almost complete authority to the American Joint Chiefs of Staff to represent him in discussions of strategy of the European campaign. Thus one of Britain's strongest assets in the American-British relationship, Churchill's persuasive powers with Roosevelt, was largely nullified. It is a tribute to the greatness of Sir Winston Churchill that he recognized this fact, accepted it as a reality, and made the most of the situation. Churchill has described the "finest hour" of the British as the Battle of Britain; perhaps his own finest hour was this period during which he continued to carry on without flinching, forced all the while to make increasing concessions to his American comrades.

Much has been written regarding Allied dispositions on December 16, 1944, and the fact that the Americans were taken off balance. Surprise was achieved by the Nazis—of that there can be no doubt. But the Allied armies that Hitler was facing in the winter of 1944–45 were remarkable for their mobility and the flexibility of their commanders. The possibility of attack through the Ardennes had been carefully evaluated by Generals Eisenhower, Bradley, Hodges, and Middleton. Eisenhower had personally accepted responsibility for the dispositions, since the alternative, he felt, would be the cessation of the Allied winter offensives.

Actually the Allies were deceived only in two respects: they underestimated the size of the force the Germans could muster for an offensive through the Ardennes; and they expected the hardheaded, professional Gerd von Rundstedt, in charge of the German forces in the west, to do nothing rash. Instead, the Allies focused their attention on the German reserves as a force to counterattack the Allies when the latter inevitably crossed the Roer River.

But once the attack was launched, the Allied Command, having recognized the paucity of local objectives in Belgium east of the Meuse, almost instantaneously identified the offensive as a major one. Without delay, as soon as word reached Eisenhower and Bradley, two armored divisions, destined to be critical in stemming the German advance, were headed from the north and the south respectively. The next day two airborne divisions were released to Bradley's 12 Army Group and reserves in Britain were speeded up toward the Continent. Other parts of the front were thinned out to provide the forces necessary to counter this major threat.

As a military maneuver the Ardennes campaign is exceedingly difficult to follow because so much was happening in so many places at a given time. With simultaneous attacks by six German corps along a seventy-mile front— some of them penetrating deeply—it is almost impossible to visualize the entire picture as it unfolded. To convey all aspects of the Bulge, I personally scoured the terrain of the Ardennes, talked to many of the most important commanders, and studied all available records. I drew heavily on the formal histories of the U.S. Army prepared by the Army's Chief of Military History and literally lived in the piles of German manuscripts put together after World War II by American interrogators. The conclusion of this two years of research is obvious: here was the place where the European campaign was decided once and for all.

In the crucible of the Ardennes a mass of conflicting circumstances formed the climax to the drama. A possible Allied defeat was transformed into the victory that broke the back of Hitler's war machine. Those who accomplished this tremendous feat deserve to be recognized in the ever growing list of America's greats.

Book I

❧❧❀❧❧

THE ROAD TO THE ARDENNES

CHAPTER 1

❧❧

"Only Cheerful Faces"

IVAN H. ("CY") PETERMAN, veteran war correspondent for the Philadelphia *Inquirer,* flipped a small Belgian coin into the air, caught it in one hand, and flopped it on the back of the other. It was midafternoon of December 15, 1944, and he was visiting the 28th Infantry Division command post in the beautiful resort town of Wiltz, northern Luxembourg.

It was a routine decision he thought he was thus passing to the hands of fate. Heads, that afternoon he would go to headquarters of the First Army located at Spa. Tails, he would stay over in the comfortable accommodations at Wiltz, as he had been urged to do by the 28th's public relations officer, Captain Stan Horstmann. The trip to Spa would be beautiful but tiring, about a fifty-mile run. And it would be cold.

Heads. Secretly, Peterman was glad; he knew he probably would have made the trip northward anyhow. Although attached as a correspondent to the First U.S. Army, Peterman had been searching out stories of interest to the south in General George S. Patton's area near Sauerlautern. He had spent two days with Major General James Van Fleet's 90th Infantry Division, assaulting the Siersdorf mountain ridge in a drive for the Siegfried emplacements just beyond. Along with another correspondent, he had discovered 1,700 German civilians hiding in the von Papen mushroom caves. Considering the quiet, slow news of mid-December, 1944, these two stories alone were worth making the trip back to Spa to file.

Peterman and Bolton, his jeep driver, said their casual goodbyes to Horstmann and took the winding road that led up the hills to the main route from Luxembourg City through St.-Vith to Spa. This road, called the Skyline Drive by the Americans, provided a beautiful view overlooking Germany and German positions to the east and Luxembourg and later Belgium on the west. The front line, such as it was, nearly paralleled the national boundaries.

As Peterman drove along, he kept noticing movement behind the German line to the east. A feeling of ominous foreboding swept over him. In this normally quiet sector—the ghost front, as it had become known—he saw

27

signs of German activity he had never noticed when he made the trip before. He could see the Germans were moving bridging equipment to crossing sites on the Our River, the approximate national boundary and military front line. Trucks were busily running back and forth.

From somewhere back in the woods on the German side, an artilleryman had been following Peterman's progress along the ridge. He gave the order to fire. Three shells whumped in quick succession against the hillside above Peterman's jeep. Bolton needed no suggestion from Peterman; he floored the accelerator and made a quick turn into the next road to the left.

Along this road Peterman encountered three French resistance troopers. The Americans he had seen were few.

"Is this the road to St.-Vith?" he asked.

The resistance men shook their heads. *"Non,* Clervaux."

Bolton turned the jeep around, went back to the fork, and once more headed northward. He passed through St.-Vith, whose population, German before World War I, glowered as the jeep went by. Finally he reached General Courtney Hodges' First Army command post at Spa.

Cy Peterman was anxious to see General Hodges. They were old friends, and Peterman had developed considerable respect for the courtly general; he had known several of his staff from the days of the Tunisian campaign nearly two years before. However, Peterman had to wait in the general's outer office. Frankie Frisch and two other prominent baseball figures were in the briefing room making a courtesy call.

As soon as they left, Peterman hurried in and told Hodges what he had seen. Hodges, a small, spare, unassuming man, was one of the few American generals who had been decorated with a DSC for valor in World War I, and he was not easily worried. But he, too, had developed some concern over the situation in the Ardennes.

"I'll see what we can get for reinforcements," he said, "but I doubt if it will be much."

Hodges left for his office, muttering something about all he had to put into this area were a camouflage and a chemical unit.

The next morning the blow struck. In the early hours of December 16, 1944, the German armies on the western front in Europe launched an assault against thinly held American positions in the Ardennes, crossing the road that Peterman had driven the night before, and headed for Wiltz, where Peterman might have stayed, and for Clerf (Clervaux), where he nearly went in error.

This assault was to result in one of the great battles of American history— and one of the most controversial. At home it was to cause more immediate consternation and, later, more charges and countercharges than any event in World War II since Pearl Harbor. And the target of the discussion was the

Allied High Command, particularly the American, from President Franklin Roosevelt to the generals in the field down to the platoon leader.

The portents of the events in Europe that Saturday morning were not immediately recognized at home. Little wonder, for their significance was not immediately obvious even to many of the troops and commanders in Europe. Moreover, a necessary delay in release of information on the fighting did little to enlighten the home front.

On Sunday morning, December 17, twenty-four hours after the German offensive had been launched, the headlines of the New York *Times* made no mention of the Ardennes: AMERICANS CAPTURE AIRFIELDS ON MINDORO AS SAN JOSE IS WON IN 9-MILE ADVANCE: SEVENTH ARMY DRIVES DEEPER INTO REICH.

At the bottom of the page, however, under "Foreign News Summarized," the third paragraph made some offhand mention of the attack:

> On Europe's Western Front savage fighting raged as the Germans counter-attacked desperately and hurled artillery barrages at four American armies along a 200-mile battlefront. But our Seventh Army, the newest force to invade the Reich, pushed additional troops into the Bavarian Palatinate after crushing a German stand at the frontier city of Lauderbourg. General Patch's men hacked at the enemy's defenses from four crossings on the seventeen-mile front and captured the key border town of Wissembourg. In the First Army sector to the north the Germans took the offensive, but their attacks were stemmed at every point.

On page 19 of the same issue, reporter Harold Denny, then with the First U.S. Army on the western front, had written an article headlined GERMAN ASSAULTS ON 1ST ARMY FIERCE. ENEMY PAYS HEAVY PRICE IN FUTILE BLOW TO STEM THE ADVANCE OF HODGES.

> The Germans took the offensive today on much of the American First Army front. It was a new and violent move in the enemy's campaign to delay and harass us and make every yard of our advance as costly as possible.
>
> Today the assault consisted of heavy artillery fire on almost our entire line and a series of sharp counter-attacks at points in the neighborhood of Dueren along the front line for some seventy miles to the south.
>
> These counter-attacks were checked everywhere, usually after hours of severe fighting, and they cost the enemy heavy casualties.

Other newspapers reacted in much the same manner. The headlines of the Philadelphia *Inquirer* for the same morning mentioned only that General MacArthur had taken Mindoro Airfield and General Patch had captured the gateway to Bavaria. However, Peterman's article had now been revised. In place of his story on the 1,700 civilians in the von Papen mushroom caves he wrote:

> Repeated small but consistent counter-attacks, accompanied all along the First and Third Army fronts by violent artillery fire, characterized today's first widespread Nazi reaction to the precarious state of their Rhineland defenses. Striking with from 20 men to whole battalions, while throwing types of V weapons—flying bombs, rockets, and even white phosphorous artillery shells probably captured from American stock some time ago—the enemy punched everywhere from Holland to Haguenau, but gained virtually no ground.

He dubbed the counteroffensive "the liveliest show in weeks."

By the next day, Monday, December 18, the significance of the German counteroffensive was beginning to come through. The New York *Times* carried in half-inch headlines: NAZI OFFENSIVE PIERCES FIRST ARMY LINES; CHUTISTS AND LUFTWAFFE SUPPORT PUSH; AMERICANS ADVANCE 6 MILES ON MINDORO.

Now Harold Denny's article, coming from the embattled First Army, was on the first page, although not yet the lead article. In an article entitled GERMAN ASSAULT IS MAJOR EFFORT, he wrote:

> The German counter-offensive that started yesterday moved forward several more miles into our lines today with increased power. It looks like the real thing.
>
> It is too early yet to gauge its possible extent and scope and whether this is to be Germany's final all-out effort to stave off defeat. But the rate at which the Germans are throwing in divisions, including some crack ones, shows that it is a serious, major counter-offensive and serious exertions will be needed to meet it.

The Philadelphia *Inquirer,* which seemed quick to grasp the situation, headlined: YANKS DRIVEN BACK BY NAZIS ATTACKING ON 75-MILE FRONT; B-29'S BLAST NAGOYA AGAIN.

The lead article, by James F. McGlincey, summarized the situation:

> Paris, December 18, Monday, *UP*—The German Wehrmacht hurled an all-out counter-offensive against a 75-mile American front Sunday.
>
> Armored columns, supported by parachutists and the Luftwaffe's greatest effort since D-Day, blasted back United States First Army line five miles in a thrust into Belgium while two other enemy spearheads invaded Luxembourg. . . .
>
> Starting Saturday with what appeared to be a series of minor thrusts, the German drive exploded in full fury Sunday with complete divisions of tanks and infantry lunging against the American lines along the long quiet southeast Belgium and Luxembourg frontier areas.

The Philadelphia *Evening Bulletin,* December 18, had as its lead article: COOKS AND CLERKS HELP CHECK NAZIS IN ONE SECTOR.

There were even ironic sidelights, such as a report from Stockholm in the *Inquirer* on December 18 that Hitler had "lost control" of the Army as far back as the end of August. Supposedly coming from an indiscreet German official (one Fritz Brückner, Hitler's former adjutant), the report indicated that Gestapo chief Heinrich Himmler, propaganda chief Paul Goebbels, and Field Marshal Gerd von Rundstedt had forced Hitler to withdraw from military leadership and "leave the war to the generals." As events proved, nothing could be further from the truth.

At the same time the papers were full of the difficulties the British were having with elements of the partisans in Greece, the B-29 bombings of Japan, and the Russian drive toward the Luceneč rail hub in northern Hungary.

And so it went. By December 19 the *Times* headlined: GERMANS DRIVE 20 MILES INTO BELGIUM; ALLIED FLIERS POUND TANK SPEARHEADS; 742 JAPANESE PLANES SMASHED IN ONE WEEK. By December 21: NAZI PUSH MOUNTS IN POWER, 13 DIVISIONS USED; FOG BLOCKS AIR BLOWS AT RAMPAGING COLUMN; AMERICANS TIGHTEN FLANKS OF 45-MILE BREACH. The situation was "grave," and the assertion was that "the entire character of the war" had been affected.

With a necessary time lag of a few days, the news periodicals began to make their interpretations. The Christmas Day issue of *Time* described the developments along the Roer River and south of Düren as "an explosive situation," like "a gas-filled room waiting for someone to light a match." Then, "General Hodges of the First Army struck the match. . . ." Generals Omar Bradley and Hodges, according to *Time,* had been surprised and caught off balance. The magazine predicted that U.S. casualties would rise as the drive was broken. But, also prophetically, the article concluded:

> Beyond the cost, it was disconcerting that the Germans were willing and able to put on such a show at this stage of the war. It seemed to indicate more clearly than ever that they were determined to throw everything into a defense in front of the Rhine. It might make the Rhine much harder to reach than the Allies originally expected—but it would simplify, and perhaps even hasten, Allied victory in the West.

Toward the end of the month Charles G. Bolte, writing in the *Nation,* interpreted the Ardennes campaign in broad, sweeping, national terms:

> On the tactical, strategic, and psychological levels, therefore, we have committed the gravest sin [underestimating the enemy] in warfare. The only satisfactory or possible explanation of this state of affairs, it seems to me, is that we have made what might be called a historical error on a level more vital than any yet mentioned: we have, most of us, mistaken the essential nature of this war. Despite the protestations to the contrary of those of us

who have seen this war as something more than a nationalist-imperialist war of conquest and counter-resistance, our thinking has been warped by the history of past wars, in which nations quit when they were defeated. Now we are engaged in a war in which nations do not quit when they are defeated, in which there is no such thing as surrender, in which fascism is to either conquer the world or be itself utterly conquered.

The New Year's Day issue of *Time* featured Dwight D. Eisenhower, Supreme Commander, on its cover and named him Man of the Year. Inside, its editors gloomily reported:

> Nazi tanks, crunching west through the mud and sleet of Luxembourg and Belgium last week gave the U.S. two separate setbacks: one on the Western Front, one on the home front. The size of the military defeat would be measured some day in American soldiers killed, wounded, captured. The shape of the home front defeat was already obvious. U.S. civilians would begin a not-so-happy New Year by paying penance for incorrigible optimism. . . .
>
> The first impact of the German offensive in the Ardennes had been stunning. Much more so was the size of the breakthrough and the continuing spearheads. . . .
>
> So far, Rundstedt had won a substantial victory. U.S. military spokesmen said that Rundstedt was making a great gamble. What stakes was he playing for?
>
> Last week the eyes of the U.S. turned with fear and questioning to Eisenhower as he faced the greatest setback of his career. The invasion was his first great responsibility; this his second. But Eisenhower refused to admit that the battle was lost while it was still being fought.

The reactions of the press reflected the dismay of the populace in the United States. Had not the war been practically won the previous summer? Was not the Nazi already on his knees? Where had he gained the strength to hand the Allies such a defeat on the eve of apparent victory?

In Washington Colonel George A. Lincoln, at thirty-eight the chief of the Operations and Strategy Group, Operations Division, War Department (OPD), went to the office of his chief, Lieutenant General John E. Hull. As one of the joint planners of the Joint Chiefs of Staff, Lincoln felt that some guidance was needed regarding how the War Department could best assist General Eisenhower in this new turn of events. The two consulted with the Army Chief of Staff, General of the Army George C. Marshall.

A short conference clarified the situation quickly. Antwerp, the group decided, was not in danger. If the supply depots behind the Meuse were overrun, however, an attack toward the Rhine would be indefinitely delayed.

But a cold, hard fact faced them: there was nothing the War Department could do to ease General Eisenhower's problems. No reinforcements scraped up could arrive in Europe until after the battle now in progress was decided. General Marshall came to the core of the matter succinctly: "We can't help Eisenhower in any way other than not bothering him. No messages will go from here to the ETO unless approved by me."

This was only the second time Marshall had given such instructions (the other was on D-Day, the previous June). To Colonel "Abe" Lincoln this meant that no advice from the Pentagon would be sent at all.

In Atlanta, Georgia, a young infantry second lieutenant walked into a small shop to buy a gift. On the walls were pictures of Confederate generals. A sweet little lady, in her middle fifties, apparently assuming that anyone in uniform was a military authority, seized the lieutenant.

"What's going on over there in Europe?"

"Well, it looks like a pretty big deal from what I can read in the papers, ma'am," he replied.

"Where are the British?" the lady demanded. "Why don't they do something?"

"I guess they'll do what they can," the lieutenant said. "But it so happens the Germans have made this attack on the Americans."

Feeling inexplicably apologetic, the lieutenant made his purchase and left hurriedly.

In nearby Fort Benning the post commander, Brigadier General William Hobson, answered the telephone. A newspaper reporter had found out that Mamie Eisenhower, wife of the Supreme Commander, was there on a visit.

"What do you want with Mrs. Eisenhower?" Hobson snapped.

"I want to see if she has any comment on reports that her husband has been shot."

"No comment on that one," said Hobson. Then, hanging up, he turned to an aide: "See to it that Mrs. Eisenhower doesn't listen to the radio while I do some checking on something."

Major General Maxwell D. Taylor, commanding general of the 101st U.S. Airborne Division, had returned to Washington on an important mission. Striding into the War Room of the Operations Division of the Army Staff, he asked to be brought up to date on what was happening in the Ardennes. An officer looked at him quizzically. "General," he said, "you may not realize it, but your division has just been surrounded."

In Washington President Roosevelt had a conference with Secretary of War Henry L. Stimson and Major General Leslie R. Groves, the officer in charge of the Manhattan Project for the development of the atomic bomb. The German attack in the Ardennes, the President felt, might so delay the end of the war in Europe as to necessitate using this still undeveloped weapon against Germany.

"If this should become the decision," General Groves stated, "we can and will do it. However, an operational weapon won't be ready until August, 1945. If we can't test it first, the mechanism might not go off. Then the Germans might find out how it works."

Groves left the meeting sure that the President intended to drop the bomb on the Nazis if the war in Europe lasted that long.

On the morning of December 19, three days after the offensive was launched, General Eisenhower and his deputy, Air Chief Marshal Sir Arthur Tedder, began the long and tortuous journey from Versailles to a gloomy barracks in Verdun, main headquarters of General Bradley's 12 Army Group. The name Verdun was synonomous with the ghastly slaughters that had occurred there in World War I, less than three decades before. But the situation that now faced the High Command—particularly the American—made the battle of Verdun fade into ancient history.

The Allies had come a long way to reach the battle line that had been hit the previous Saturday. On the long road from Normandy to the borders of the Reich, the Allies had experienced successes, frustrations, and occasional defeats. The fighting in Normandy had at first been painstakingly slow. Then a spectacular breakout linked with landings in Southern France had hurtled the Allied armies to the borders of Germany. An unsuccessful effort had been made to cross the Rhine River in the north; American losses attempting to drive toward Cologne had been grim; supply had held up General Patton's drive toward the Saar.

But Eisenhower knew one thing: as Supreme Commander he had forged an Allied weapon of remarkable unity. Differences of strategic opinion existed between the American and British elements that constituted the two main elements of his force. His principal British subordinate, Field Marshal Sir Bernard Law Montgomery, had been particularly vociferous—even troublesome. But up to this time the views of Eisenhower's Supreme Headquarters had consistently prevailed and his plans had been executed by all.

Furthermore, this great German attack, as Eisenhower could visualize it on the morning of December 19, was primarily an American problem. So it was with American commanders he planned to confer that day in the ancient city of the Meuse.

General Eisenhower was concerned but confident. An attack in the Ardennes was something that he and Bradley, whose front had been penetrated, had considered thoroughly. Only the strength of the German attack had really surprised them.

Up the stairs Eisenhower went to a chilly conference room where a lone potbellied stove provided warmth. He surveyed the sober faces around the table—Tedder, Bradley, General Jacob Devers of 6 Army Group, the usually ebullient Patton of Third U.S. Army.

"The present situation," he said, "is to be regarded as one of opportunity for us and not disaster. There will be only cheerful faces at this conference table."

CHAPTER 2

❧ ❦

"The Results Will Be Incalculable"

THE Battle of the Ardennes—or the Bulge, as it is commonly called—constituted the climax of the Allied invasion of Western Europe, launched on June 6, 1944. At the end of the bitter battle fought in freezing weather in the dismal woods of the Ardennes, the German Wehrmacht was practically finished as an organized fighting force. And yet much could have gone differently. Conceivably the tragic suffering and losses could have been avoided. Conceivably, too, the Allied forces could have sustained a crushing defeat. That things went the way they did can be attributed to the planning and execution of military operations by commanders—humans entrusted with the accomplishment of military objectives at minimum cost in lives and substance.

Thus any study of the command decision that made the Ardennes drama unfold as it did must begin months earlier, when the breakout from the Normandy beachhead resulted in the liberation of France, Belgium, Luxembourg, and part of the Netherlands. It is here that our story begins.

On Thursday evening, July 20, 1944, a single unescorted B-25 bomber flew through the fog and rain across the Normandy beachhead and the English Channel to land at Heston Airport near London. It was practically the only plane in the air that day. Deplaning, General Dwight D. Eisenhower, Supreme Allied Commander, thanked the crew and climbed wearily into the right rear seat of his unglossed, olive-drab Cadillac. He rode in silence the few miles between Heston and Telegraph Cottage, his temporary home south of London.

During the day Eisenhower had been to the battle front to see both his senior commanders, General Bernard L. Montgomery, commanding 21 Army Group, and Lieutenant General Omar N. Bradley, commanding the First U.S. Army, which, with General Miles C. Dempsey's Second British Army, was temporarily subordinated to Montgomery.

The news had not been good. Goodwood, code name for a massive breakout attempt on the east of the line by Dempsey's Second Army, had fallen short of expectations. His three armored divisions, supported by 8,000 tons

36

of bombs and naval gunfire, had succeeded only in taking some 34 square miles and securing William the Conqueror's city of Caen. The tenacity and strength of the German defenses, together with heavy rains on July 19 and 20, had been responsible.

For these meager gains the British and Canadians had paid dearly. The British VIII Corps alone had lost 4,000 men and 500 tanks—36 percent of all such armor the British had ashore in Normandy.[1] The evening of July 20 was probably the lowest point in Allied fortunes since D-Day, June 6.

Still glum over the price the British had had to pay for Goodwood, General Eisenhower went to his main headquarters the next day. Here he found one intelligence report that interested him and which could well turn out to be good news. At Rastenburg, in East Prussia, a plot on the part of high-ranking Germany Army officers had been perpetrated against the life of Nazi dictator Adolf Hitler. A bomb had been exploded in Hitler's conference room. Though Hitler had survived, the impact of this event was yet to be evaluated. As it turned out, however, and as Eisenhower and his optimistic staff officers could not know then, the plot would strengthen rather than weaken Hitler's control of the Wehrmacht. Strong elements had remained loyal to the Führer, and the purge and torture of those responsible was immediate and thorough. The ultimate effect was to heighten Hitler's continuing mistrust of many of his generals and to kill any tendency he might have still held to allow his generals to "run the war."

After being briefed, Eisenhower asked for a report on the Germans' eastern front. The Russian summer offensive was continuing to make spectacular advances. Starting on June 23—almost a month earlier—Soviet armies had launched a gigantic attack north of the Pripet Marshes, resulting in a bulge about 200 miles deep into White Russia, including the city of Minsk. The drive was continuing all along the front, from Narva near Leningrad on the north to the borders of Rumania on the south. Soon the Soviets were expected to reach the Vistula River, and in the north would be pounding on the gates of German territory in East Prussia.

The Russian attack, however satisfying in a military sense, was causing uneasiness and impatience in the U.S. press. The Allied beachhead, by contrast, so exuberantly hailed by Allied correspondents six weeks earlier, was still only 25 to 30 miles deep along an 80-mile front. Compared to the Russian successes, the Western gains looked pitifully small on an overall map of Europe.

But these events, the Russian attack and the plot on Hitler's life, were only matters of indirect concern to the Supreme Commander. He was preoccupied primarily with the frustrations encountered by his troops in attempting to break out of the Normandy beachhead. The first objective was to seize

[1] Martin Blumenson, *Breakout and Pursuit* (Washington: Dept. of the Army, 1961), p. 193.

and consolidate the so-called lodgement area, a large part of northwestern France including both the Cotentin and Brittany peninsulas, and protected by the formidable barriers of the Loire River on the south and the Seine River on the northwest. On this solid base, including the landing beaches, Cherbourg, and the Brittany ports, the Allies would be able to pause long enough to build their logistical situation. They could then continue the advance through France to the borders of Germany. But to do so would require breaking out of the beachhead area, something the Allies had not yet been able to do.

Eisenhower's impatience was heightened by the fact that his own headquarters, still located on the outskirts of London, was not yet controlling the day by day operations of the land battle. Under the SHAEF (Supreme Headquarters, Allied Expeditionary Force) command setup, all air forces reported to Eisenhower through the Allied air commander in chief, Air Chief Marshal Sir Trafford Leigh-Mallory. A similar arrangement existed with the naval forces under Admiral Sir Bertram H. Ramsay. Eisenhower personally retained the position of overall land commander, but the Normandy front at present was not of sufficient size to warrant more than one army group. Therefore, General Montgomery's 21 Army Group was for the moment commanding both the U.S. First Army (Bradley) and the British Second (Dempsey).

All this made Montgomery a temporary overall ground commander in France. And while it was not in Eisenhower's nature or training to tell a subordinate in detail how to run the tactics of his army group, he felt some uneasiness regarding the aggressiveness—or possible lack of it—with which Montgomery had executed the Goodwood attack. But there was nothing Eisenhower could put his finger on. The Supreme Commander, described at the moment by an aide as "like a blind dog in a meathouse," could only prod his senior tactical ground commander. He sat down to his desk and composed a message:

21 July 1944

Dear Monty:

Since returning from your Headquarters yesterday I have been going over the major considerations that, in my mind, must guide our future actions. This letter is to assure myself that we see eye to eye on the big problems. . . .
You said:

1. We must get the Brittany Peninsula. From an administrative point of view this is essential.

2. We do not want to get hemmed into a relatively small area. We must have space for maneuver, for administration and for airfields.

3. We want to engage the enemy in battle to write off his troops and generally kill Germans. . . .

This is my view exactly. I think that so far as we can foresee we are at this moment *relatively* stronger than we can probably hope to be at any time of the near future. *Time is vital.* We must not only have the Brittany Peninsula—we must have it quickly. So we must hit with everything.

In late June, when First Army was cleaning up the Cherbourg Harbor area, Second Army was attempting to prevent any movement of German troops from the Eastern to the Western flank, in order that when First Army turned southward it would have the best possible conditions for a rapid advance to the base of the Peninsula. But because it had also to hold a firm defensive line, Second Army was not entirely successful in this—it could not have been done except by a definite, continuing, offensive. In any event, Bradley's advance to the southward has been disappointingly slow even though he has kept everlastingly on the attack with everything he can bring into action.

Then, a few days ago, when Armored Divisions of Second Army, assisted by tremendous air attack, broke through the enemy's forward lines, I was extremely hopeful and optimistic. I thought that at last we had him and were going to roll him up. That did not come about.

Now we are pinning our immediate hopes on Bradley's attack, which should get off either tomorrow or on the first good day. But the country is bad, and the enemy strong at the point of main assault, and more than ever I think it is important that we are aggressive throughout the front. . . .

Good luck!

As ever,
Ike

Fortunately, as the letter indicated, the Allies had another shot in the bag. Goodwood had actually been planned as part of a one-two punch, with the second punch to be delivered by General Bradley's First U.S. Army on the west. Some time earlier General Eisenhower had concluded in his own mind that since his adversary, Generalfeldmarschall Guenther von Kluge, had stacked the bulk of his armor against the British in the Caen area, the breakout would have to be made instead through the hedgerow country near St.-Lô. Nevertheless, progress in the U.S. zone also had been costly and slow. Major General Troy Middleton's U.S. VIII Corps, attacking from the Cotentin Peninsula southward, had encountered dismal failure, due not so much to enemy action as to the marshy country through which the attacks had to be conducted. By early July General Bradley had abandoned the attack on the extreme west as a bad job.

But now the new operation, code-named Cobra, a little to the east, was to jump off in a few days, probably July 24. As a partial compensation for the delays, the Allies had time to build up a force in Normandy capable of rapid exploitation. By now nearly 800,000 American and nearly 600,000 British and Canadian troops were ashore. Bradley's First Army now boasted a total of seventeen divisions. Enemy losses from D-Day (June 6) to July 23 had been estimated at nearly 120,000, of which only about 10,000 were known to have been replaced. On the front facing Bradley's VII and VIII corps, Allied intelligence estimates showed German troops to number no more than 17,000 men with less than 100 tanks, only one fifth of the American forces assembled for the attack. The only disadvantage to the overwhelming Allied forces seemed to be the heavy enemy defenses in the formidable hedgerow country.

The Allies' frustrations were minor compared to those facing Kluge. As commander of Army Group B (as well as commander in chief, western front), Kluge had two armies: the Seventh Army on the west, and an army-size formation known as Panzer Group West, commanded by General Heinrich Eberbach on the east. Eberbach had been trying to build up an armored reserve, replacing panzer [2] divisions in the line facing the British with infantry divisions scraped from other parts of France. Goodwood, on July 18, had hurt the Germans more than the Allies realized. Eberbach had been forced to recommit all his armor, leaving little now to respond to Cobra.

Furthermore, an accident of fate had deprived the German Army of one of its ablest commanders. On July 17, Generalfeldmarschall Erwin Rommel, commander of Army Group B under Kluge, had been seriously injured when an Allied fighter plane had strafed his staff car. Rommel was out of combat permanently, as things turned out. Later implicated in the July 20 plot against Hitler, he was to be invited—with aid—to commit suicide. Kluge, accordingly, as Oberbefehlshaber (OB) West (Commander in Chief West), had assumed Rommel's lesser position in addition to his own.

In spite of the tenacity with which the German soldiers had held every inch of ground in the hedgerow country, deep pessimism permeated the German Command. Much of this stemmed from Allied air superiority. Kluge expressed his own misgivings in a letter to Hitler:

> In the face of the total enemy air superiority, we can adopt no tactics to compensate for the annihilating power of air except to retire from the battle field. . . . I came here with the firm resolve to enforce your command to stand and hold at all cost. The price of that policy is the steady and certain destruction of our troops. . . . The flow of material and personnel replacements is insufficient, and artillery and antitank weapons and ammunition are far from adequate. . . . Because the main force of our defense lies in the willingness of our troops to fight, then concern for the immediate future of this front is more than justified. . . . Despite all our efforts, the moment is fast approaching when our hard-pressed defenses will crack. When the enemy has erupted into open terrain, the inadequate mobility of our forces will make orderly and effective conduct of the battle hardly possible.[3]

[2] Panzer is the term for all armor; Panther is the term for the Mark V tank; the Mark VI was called the Tiger.

[3] Letter from Kluge to Hitler, quoted in Blumenson, *op. cit.,* p. 213.

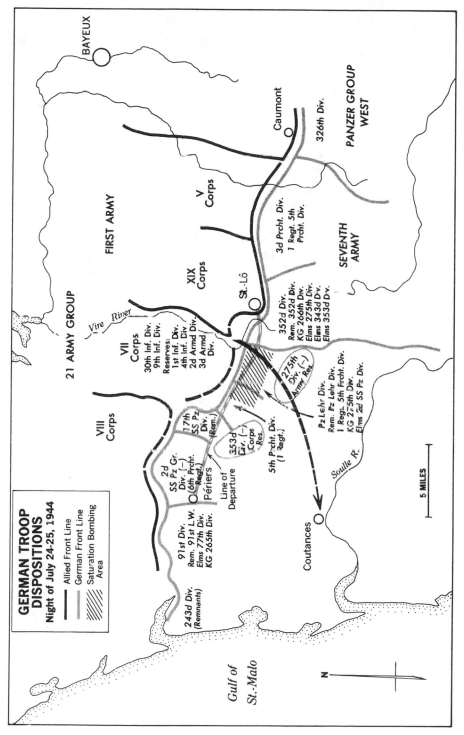

GERMAN TROOP DISPOSITIONS
Night of July 24-25, 1944

Allied Front Line
German Front Line
Saturation Bombing Area

BAYEUX

PANZER GROUP WEST

Caumont

326th Div.

FIRST ARMY

V Corps

21 ARMY GROUP

SEVENTH ARMY

3d Prcht. Div.
1 Regt. 5th Prcht. Div.

XIX Corps

St.-Lô

Vire River

VII Corps
30th Inf. Div.
9th Inf. Div.
Reserves:
1st Inf. Div.
4th Inf. Div.
2d Armd Div.
3d Armd Div.

352d Div.
Rem. 352d Div.
KG 266th Div.
Elms 275th Div.
Elms 343d Div.
Elms 353d Div.

VIII Corps

275th Div. (—)
Army Res.

353d Div. (—)
Corps Res.

17th SS Pz Div. (Rem.)

2d SS Pz Gr. Div. (—)
(6th Prcht. Regt.)

Périers

Line of Departure

5th Prcht. Div. (1 Regt.)

Pz Lehr Div.
Rem. Pz Lehr Div.
1 Regt. 5th Prcht. Div.
KG 275th Div.
Elms 2d SS Pz Div.

Souille R.

91st Div.
Rem. 91st L.W.
Elms 77th Div.
KG 265th Div.

Coutances

243d Div.
(Remnants)

5 MILES

Gulf of St.-Malo

N

Meanwhile, in his command post near Colombières, General Omar Bradley paced the floor of his personal planning room, constructed in a mess tent with board floors (a luxury heretofore unknown in his headquarters), and sketched out the detailed plans for the ground phase of Cobra. Meticulous and professional, Bradley had been earmarked for high rank in the Army from his cadet days. He had been an outstanding athlete in the class of 1915 at West Point (credited, for a time at least, with the record for the longest baseball throw in the Academy's history), and in his Army career, when he was commandant of the Infantry School at Fort Benning, Georgia, he became known as an "infantryman's general." Despite his powerful physique, he was quiet and unassuming, and more closely resembled a Missouri schoolmaster than the conventional picture of a general. Bradley made a point of avoiding personal publicity. "Any day that I can stay out of the papers is a day to the good," he once told his staff. This distaste for personal publicity, however, concealed a surprising sensitivity in professional matters, apparent only to close associates.

The key to success of Operation Cobra, the element that differentiated it from the slow-moving assaults on the west, was the planned saturation bombing of an area four miles wide and one and a half miles deep. These six square miles were to be pulverized by 200 Allied fighter bombers, 1,800 heavy bombers, and nearly 400 mediums, all protected by 500 fighters. All in all, 60,000 hundred-pound bombs were to be dropped from an altitude of 8,000 feet. Unfortunately, the might of the R.A.F. Heavy Bomber Command had to be excluded. Their aircraft could carry only larger armaments whose giant craters would delay American tank forces pouring through the gap—a lesson learned only too well in Operation Goodwood.

The air action was to be given the closest possible supervision. While directly commanded by Air Chief Marshal Leigh-Mallory, it also would be overseen by Air Chief Marshal Tedder, Eisenhower's Deputy Supreme Commander.

Even before the failure of Goodwood had been known final preparations for the air phase of Cobra had been arranged; on July 19 General Bradley had flown to Leigh-Mallory's headquarters in England for this purpose. Some disagreements had to be hashed out, such as the distance to which ground troops would fall back to avoid being hit by Allied bombs: this was resolved by compromise. But in one matter, the direction the bombers would fly, a meeting of the minds was never reached. For purposes of troop safety Bradley insisted that the attacking bombers fly parallel to the front lines—that is along the St.-Lô–Périers road. Leigh-Mallory and his assistants, on the other hand, felt that such a route was impractical. It would result in such a long stream of air traffic that the bombs could not be delivered within the given time.

Somehow Bradley left Leigh-Mallory's headquarters mistakenly feeling that he had carried his point.[4]

General Bradley's plan for the ground action was simple. He had four corps in the line. These were, east to west, Charles H. Corlett's XIX, Leonard Gerow's V, J. Lawton Collins' VII, and Troy Middleton's VIII. He would make his assault with Collins' VII, slanting off southwestward toward the town of Coutances on the French west coast. If this point could be reached, then the weak German 84th Korps on the west flank would be cut off by Collins' VII Corps and Middleton's VIII Corps, thus destroying the entire west flank of Kluge's position. To accomplish this task he assigned four infantry divisions (1st, 4th, 9th, and 30th) and two armored divisions (2d and 3d) to the colorful commander of VII Corps. Of these, the 1st Infantry and 2d Armored divisions were veterans of many battles in the Mediterranean theater.

His detailed plan completed, Bradley submitted his scheme to both Montgomery and Eisenhower, who heartily approved.

By now the Supreme Commander's customary optimism had returned. Just before the attack, scheduled for July 24, he wrote to Bradley:

> Dear Brad: My high hopes and best wishes ride with you in your attack today, which is the largest ground assault yet staged in this war by American troops exclusively. Speaking as the responsible American rather than the Allied commander, I assure you that the eyes of our whole country will be following your progress, and I take full personal responsibility for answering to them for the necessary price of victory.
>
> But a *breakthrough* at this juncture will minimize the total cost. General Montgomery's plan calls for a vigorous and continuing offensive by the other Allies in the line, thus allowing you to pursue every advantage with an ardor verging on recklessness and with all your troops without fear of major counteroffensive from the forces the enemy now has on this front. All these attacks are mutually supporting, and if Second Army should secure a breakthrough simultaneously with yours, the results will be incalculable.
>
> Good luck to every one of you.
>
> Ike

The jump-off date, July 24, arrived. The time had been set for 1:00 P.M. The infantry had withdrawn to their predesignated positions.

Bad weather forced Air Chief Marshal Leigh-Mallory to cancel the bombing at the last minute. Unknown to Collins' three assault divisions, not all the planes could be recalled, however. A few continued on their route and dropped their bombs, some of them falling on the American infantry pre-

---

[4] Omar Bradley, *A Soldier's Story* (New York: Holt, 1951), p. 347.

paring to assault. Despite the shock and the bitterness caused by this error, Collins' men reorganized and moved forward, occupying their former positions by the end of the day. Generalleutnant Fritz Bayerlein, commanding the German Panzer Lehr Division on VII Corps front, congratulated himself on repelling what he thought was the major attack.

Of all the Americans, none was more disturbed than Omar Bradley. He felt the air chiefs had let him down and so expressed himself to Leigh-Mallory.

The weather improved the next day, and on July 25 Cobra began as planned. General Bradley's violent protest of the night before, however, once again demanding that the bombers should fly parallel to the St.-Lô–Périers road, had been turned down. As a result, some of the bombs wreaking devastation on the area in front of VII Corps again fell short. Once more all three divisions were hit. One hundred and eleven American troops were killed and 490 wounded. Among those killed was Lieutenant General Lesley J. McNair, chief of U.S. Army Ground Forces in Washington.[5]

In spite of this tragic, shocking episode, the 4th, 30th, and 90th Infantry divisions bravely rallied and at 11:00 A.M. moved forward across the roughened landscape into the assault.

If the effect of the Allied bombardment was severe on the Americans, it was devastating to the Germans. No less than an estimated 1,000 German troops perished in the Cobra bombardment. By withdrawing many of his troops the night before, Bayerlein had placed them in the area of greatest bombing concentration. About one third of the total number of combat effectives died in the main line of defense, and the survivors were dazed. With a mere dozen tanks or tank destroyers remaining in operation,[6] only local and feeble resistance was now possible against the attacking American infantrymen.

Under continued pounding by Allied air during the day, the Germans were unable to reorganize and build up a new line. The three American divisions continued the attack, and by the end of the day they had advanced three miles into the German-held area, a shallow penetration on the map but spectacular compared to former actions in the hedgerow country. "As of this moment," lamented Kluge, "this evening, the front has . . . burst."

The degree of success was not immediately obvious to the Americans. General Eisenhower, who had been with General Bradley to witness the attack,

---

[5] McNair, in Europe as an observer, had taken position in a foxhole in a frontline battalion of the 30th Division. He had done so unbeknown to General Collins, who, as sector commander, would have forbidden him to take the risk, despite McNair's high official position.

[6] Blumenson, *op. cit.,* p. 240.

returned to England saddened by the repetition of the short bombing and unaware of the success that had been achieved. Thinking aloud, Eisenhower resolved impulsively to one of Bradley's aides that he would never again use heavy bombers in a tactical role. Arriving at his headquarters, General Eisenhower's gloom was deepened to learn that his friend General McNair had been one of the victims of the short Allied bombing.

Although he had not seen action in North Africa or Sicily, since D-Day Major General J. Lawton ("Lightning Joe") Collins had become a shrewd and experienced corps commander. His nickname, stemming from the days he commanded the 25th (Lightning) Division on Guadalcanal and becoming permanent after the aggressiveness he showed in capturing Cherbourg, aptly fitted him. As early as the afternoon of July 25 and despite the shallowness of U.S. penetrations, Collins noted that enemy defenses showed little or no coordination. Accordingly, he made one of the vital decisions of the Cobra operation: to commit his exploiting forces before the breakthrough forces had secured their immediate objectives. On his order, the 1st Infantry Division, and the 2d and 3d Armored divisions, moved out on the morning of July 26. By that afternoon Collins felt sure that his troops had broken loose. The next day Major General Leland S. Hobbs, of the 30th Division, exultantly exclaimed: "This thing has busted wide open."

As of the evening of July 27, Generaloberst Paul Hausser, commanding the German Seventh Army, realized that his 84th Korps in the Cotentin Peninsula was in danger of being cut off and annihilated. Without orders he began withdrawing the corps southward and setting up a strong north-south defensive line, cutting the road to Coutances; in the small corridor he stacked elements of four divisions, two of them panzer. But the withdrawal of the rest of the 84th Korps had turned into a disorderly retreat. Forty-five hundred German prisoners were taken that day, and three of Hausser's divisions had been destroyed.[7] By the night of July 29, some intermingled German units had reached a line running roughly east and west ten miles south of Coutances. Some of the 84th Korps escaped.

Meanwhile the British and Canadians were continuing to attack. On July 25, the 2d and 3d Canadian Infantry divisions and the 7th Armoured and Guards Armoured divisions had jumped off along the key National Road, leading straight from Caen toward Falaise. The results, in ground, were not spectacular. The only gain turned out to be some improvement of the Canadian position on the critical Verriers Ridge—but at the cost of over 1,000 casual-

[7] Report by the Supreme Commander to the Combined Chiefs of Staff on the Operations in Europe of the Allied Expeditionary Force, 6 June 1944 to 8 May 1945.

ties. In so doing, however, the Canadians had continued to nail down six of Eberbach's panzer divisions.

Thus was the so-called St.-Lô Breakthrough achieved by Allied forces. Besides the overwhelming effects of the carpet bombing, the energy of the attack all along the line of assault was aided by the fact that the German High Command remained convinced, in the latter part of July, that the main Allied effort in France still would be made in the Pas-de-Calais area, where the English Channel is only twenty miles across. Operation Fortitude, the deception plan that included setting up dummy headquarters, establishing a false radio net, adjusting excess Allied shipping to favor the east, a misleading pattern of Allied bombardment targets, and feeding information to known German agents, had been a magnificent success. Not until the eruption of Cobra did Kluge apparently conclude that no second invasion was forthcoming and permit the German 363d Infantry Division to cross the Seine River westward toward Normandy.

The American breakthrough now became a "breakout." General Bradley drove forward with three corps, V, XIX, and VII (from east to west), executing a powerful frontal attack. But the main effort had now shifted to Middleton's VIII Corps on the extreme west, where he had reached a spot at which tanks could roll. Sending two armored divisions (the 4th and 6th) abreast, Middleton drove twelve miles on July 29, and by the night of July 30 had entered the coastal city of Avranches. By the next night he had one column pushing eight miles southeast of this major port and another column turning westward into the Brittany Peninsula.

On August 1, 1944, a long awaited major change in the Allied Command setup was put into effect. General Omar N. Bradley stepped up from command of First U.S. Army to the command of 12 Army Group, and the American forces were now split into First U.S. Army under Lieutenant General Courtney Hodges and Third U.S. Army under Lieutenant General George S. Patton, Jr.

This new command arrangement, whereby Bradley was placed in a position equal with Montgomery as an army group commander, was far from a spur-of-the-moment arrangement. Any creation of a new army group headquarters inevitably would have had to begin back in England. Therefore—although it had not been put out to the press—General Bradley secretly had been simultaneously commanding First U.S. Army and his future army group in the United Kingdom since before D-Day.

In preparation for the command step-up, 12 Army Group Headquarters and Third U.S. Army Headquarters had been established in Normandy some time before August 1. Bradley had assigned Patton to supervise Middleton's

VIII Corps on the right and Hodges to overlook Gerow's V, Collins' VII, and Corlett's XIX, which together would comprise the future First Army.

General Eisenhower felt the secrecy in all these moves necessary; indeed, the keeping of command arrangements under wraps he believed essential to the success of the overall deception plan Fortitude. But up to this time the public had considered the invasion a single army group operation, with Montgomery acting as an overall land commander. Thus when Bradley was given a command equal to Montgomery's, it appeared to much of the press, the British in particular, that the most prominent British general had been "demoted." This impression was completely misleading. The arrangement had been agreed upon long before.

One additional circumstance complicated the matter. General Eisenhower's own Supreme Headquarters (SHAEF) was still located in England; Forward, his tactical headquarters at Southhampton, was not scheduled to move to the Continent until after mid-August. Without having his staff in the immediate battle area, Eisenhower decided not to require both army groups to report directly to his headquarters on all immediate tactical matters. Instead, until SHAEF could be established on the Continent, he arranged for 12 Army Group (Bradley) to report to SHAEF (Eisenhower) through 21 Army Group (Montgomery). Thus, General Montgomery continued some coordinating functions between the army groups, primarily in establishing boundaries of responsibility between forces. This he did with tact and consideration—and under General Eisenhower's personal supervision. Bradley felt no cause to protest this temporary arrangement.

Meanwhile General Eisenhower, finding that the constantly changing situation in Normandy made it difficult to keep matters sufficiently at his fingertips while remaining at SHAEF in London, moved personally to the Continent on August 7. There, from a tactical command post, he was able to remain in daily communication with his two principal field commanders, and major decisions were not delayed through lack of contact.

Eisenhower's personal move from Southampton to Normandy greatly facilitated his visits to both Bradley and Montgomery, so necessary to his personal supervision of the battle. The visits with Bradley were relaxed and easy; the two men had years of training and personal friendship in common. The visits with Montgomery, however, were inevitably more restrained. For although the men at this time held each other in mutual regard, their many differences, far transcending mere nationality, were great. Whereas Eisenhower was a gregarious individual, on the surface an extrovert, Montgomery was just the opposite.

Ascetic, teetotaling, and tense, Montgomery tended to be a loner. Habitually, he lived apart from his staff with only a few aides surrounding him. Later in the campaign his own chief of staff would operate miles away from the General's command post. In person, Montgomery was informal, normally eschewing the regulation British battle dress for a high-necked sweater and baggy, comfortable corduroy trousers. However, he was rarely, if ever, seen without his black tanker's beret, which had now become his trademark.

Montgomery also was a man preoccupied with his own thoughts, and often he noticed little of his immediate surroundings. He could be introduced to a person several times without recalling having seen him. This characteristic, however, was not a matter of calculated rudeness. Rather it stemmed from the fact that his mind was always with his own business—at this time, of course, on the operations of his 21 Army Group.

There was no question of Montgomery's professional competence. This he had proved in the 1940 campaign in France, later at the battle of El Alamein, through Tunisia and Sicily, and recently in the landings in Normandy. The Normandy invasion particularly had been the type of operation at which Montgomery excelled, a "set piece," carefully planned assault, with overpowering forces at his disposal. By this time, certain idiosyncrasies of Montgomery's were becoming apparent to the members of the High Command, especially the Americans. Eisenhower, Bradley, and Patton had all been associated with him since early 1943 in the Mediterranean theater. Among the more freewheeling Americans, Montgomery had achieved some reputation for caution, for requiring an almost unreasonable superiority before launching an attack. But this caution in military philosophy seemed inconsistent with his personality, which could be described as cocky nearly to the point of arrogance.

Montgomery's personal confidence and professional absorption led him to act at times somewhat as a master chess player rather than as a human being leading other human beings. However, this wiry little man with the almost birdlike voice retained a remarkable hold on the imagination of the British soldier. By August of 1944 the British nation had come to regard the name Montgomery as synonymous with success. And as time passed he would become more and more a symbol of British power and prestige.

As the two lead armored divisions of Middleton's VIII Corps rounded the corner westward at Avranches and headed into the Brittany Peninsula, Eisenhower was contemplating a new concept of the Allied operation: the Allied force would press the attack beyond the original "lodgement area," the lines of the Seine and Loire rivers. After the success of the St.-Lô Breakthrough, it now appeared that the Brittany Peninsula might be seized with only one corps—Middleton's VIII—rather than with Patton's whole army as originally planned. The German garrison on the Brittany Peninsula was known to consist mostly of fortress troops, of insufficient strength to threaten the rear of U.S. columns dashing eastward.

As early as August 2, barely a week after the launching of Cobra, the Supreme Commander was indicating this as a possibility in a message to General Marshall; the next day the concept was implemented.

Events moved rapidly. On August 3, General Bradley directed Third Army to clear the Brittany Peninsula with a "minimum of forces"; the main American effort was to drive eastward and rapidly seize the entire Continental lodgement area.

This mission that Bradley had given Patton was actually a complicated one. While Middleton was to occupy the Brittany Peninsula, the rest of Patton's forces—which first consisted only of XV Corps—were to race to the east and seize a sixty-mile stretch of the north-south Mayenne River. To protect his south flank along the Loire, Patton brought up another newly formed corps, the XX of Major General Walton Walker. Walker was to attack southward, anchor his right flank along the Loire, and continue to the east on the right of XV Corps. Thus Wade Haislip's XV Corps attacked to the east toward Mayenne as part of the first phase, while XX Corps, under Walker, was attacking south to the Loire.

Wade Haislip, known in the Army as Ham, was an old friend of Eisenhower's from the days when the two were second lieutenants thirty years before. He concealed a sharp and aggressive mind beneath a jolly, somewhat roly-poly exterior. His was a mission that called for exceptional fortitude. With no knowledge of the enemy situation to his front, he was to advance thirty miles to seize a wide stretch of the Mayenne River, while allowing his southern flank to remain exposed until Walker, on his right, could catch up.

Undaunted, Haislip moved out. By noon of August 5 he had captured the town of Mayenne. Having received orders to continue, he headed for Le Mans, forty-five miles farther to the east (see Map II). Le Mans fell on August 9. In only five days Haislip's XV Corps had gone seventy-five miles. Two hundred miles now separated Haislip's spearheads from those of Middleton's VIII Corps, moving toward the tip of Brittany. Less than one hundred miles east of Haislip's forward elements lay the Paris-Orléans Gap, the eighty-mile space between the Seine and the Loire designated by SHAEF as the 12 Army Group objective. Securing of the Gap would mark the attainment of the entire Overlord lodgement area.

Meanwhile, General Patton's other wing, VIII Corps, was rapidly occupying the Brittany Peninsula. Hitler facilitated U.S. armored movement by arbitrarily ordering all troops to retreat into the various fortress areas. Kluge had no choice; Hitler directed him essentially to write off Brittany.

By August 7, U.S. troops were engaged in combat at the approaches to St.-Nazaire, St.-Malo, Brest, Lorient, and Quiberon Bay. Aided by 20,000 French Forces of the Interior, Middleton quickly invested all the ports—but resistance of the garrisons was determined. St.-Nazaire and Lorient held out for the rest of the war; Brest was captured only on September 15. St.-Malo, the first to fall, capitulated after a hard fight on August 14.

By overrunning Brittany with minimum strength, Patton was provided with strong forces for the main drive to the east. His rear was rapidly secured. But the logistical problems involved in supplying the extensive Third Army operations without the immediate use of the Brittany ports was to haunt Allied operations for some time to come.

The British, meanwhile, had been actively engaged in slugging matches.

XXX British Corps had struck southeast toward the Orne River on July 30. Resistance on the thousand-foot Mt. Pinçon near Caen had been fierce, but the British had secured a foothold. On August 7, XII British Corps secured a bridgehead over the Orne River between Mt. Pinçon and Caen. The Canadians had conducted several holding attacks while preparing for a major drive south of Falaise.

At this time the Allied outlook was optimistic. On August 1 Colonel Benjamin A. Dickson, the normally pessimistic intelligence officer of First U.S. Army, reported: "It is doubtful that the German forces in Normandy can continue for more than four to eight weeks as a military machine. . . . In the next four to eight weeks the current situation may change with dramatic suddenness into a race to reach a chaotic Germany."

On August 4 General Montgomery wrote in a 21 Army Group directive that the German front could be made to disintegrate rapidly. The only hope the Germans had of saving their armies, he concluded, was a "staged withdrawal to the Seine." To defeat this withdrawal he planned to wheel all armies to the east—Canadian on the left; British in the center; Americans on the right, making the main effort toward Paris. Three armies would attack abreast, forcing the Germans to the east while the fourth (Patton) outran them on the south. This plan was predicated on the assumption that the Germans had no choice but to withdraw to and across the Seine.

General Bradley was not so sure of this, however. The German, he felt, might have another possibility: a counterattack to cut off the narrow corridor at Avranches through which the vast quantities of supplies necessary to support Patton were being funneled. Accordingly, although Patton was dashing east to Le Mans, and Hodges was attacking eastward on Patton's left, Bradley kept a suspicious eye on Kluge's armored forces between Vire and Mortain (see Map II).

It was well for the Allies that General Bradley sensed the possibility of such a counterattack and made provisions to meet it, for in the early morning hours of August 7, Hobbs' 30th Infantry Division in Mortain was hit by a heavy German attack from the east, with the obvious intention of driving all the way to the sea at Avranches.

This attack had been in the planning stages for four days, having been ordered by Hitler as early as August 2, when American armored units were first turning the corner at Avranches into Brittany. It was a bold move, typical of Hitler's preoccupation with offensive action. Not content to fall back by staged withdrawals to the Seine (as Montgomery had visualized), Hitler was determined to restore the front to a situation of static warfare.

As so often happened, the Führer's objective far exceeded that envisioned by the more conservative OB West, Guenther von Kluge. The latter would have been content to drive to Avranches, cut off Patton's forces, keep them isolated while destroying them, and then continue on the defensive. Hitler's plan, however, included not only restoring the line to Avranches but continuing the offensive up the west coast of the Cotentin Peninsula with the ultimate goal of throwing the Allied forces back into the sea.

Kluge had little occasion to concern himself beyond the first phase, the advance to Avranches. Taking Mortain itself, he calculated, should not be much of a problem. Leading northwest from Mortain, a good road crossed high ground directly to Avranches. True, he could attack southwest and bypass American positions, but in doing so he would split his forces. Furthermore, the German Seventh Army's plans were based on an attack northwestward through the American 30th Division. Kluge somewhat reluctantly assented.

Hitler had been silent for four days. On August 6, however, he called Kluge several times, demanding full reports on the progress of OB West's planning. In the course of one of the conversations, Hitler promised an additional sixty Mark V (panther) tanks located in reserve east of Paris, eighty Mark IV tanks, and all the armored cars of the 11th Panzer Division, currently moving up from southern France. In a later call Hitler directed that the attack be conducted not by General der Panzertruppen Hans Baron von Funck, the 47th Korps commander, but by Eberbach, commander of the newly formed Fifth Panzer Army.[8] With the reinforcements he had mentioned earlier in the day, Hitler expected Eberbach to continue his attack to the north from Avranches once that town was taken.

Compliance with Hitler's plan would require Kluge to delay at least twenty-four hours, since it had no chance of success without the additional forces Hitler had mentioned. Kluge was reluctant to wait; with every passing hour Patton's Third Army was driving deeper along his exposed southern flank, thus increasing the danger to his vulnerable rear areas. Furthermore, Kluge had intimations that the Americans were now aware of his concentration. Finally he persuaded Hitler to allow the attack to go as originally planned, leaving Funck in command. Obviously, the reinforcements Hitler had promised would not be available.

From the German viewpoint, conditions seemed to offer hope. Ground fog

---

[8] Renamed from the former Panzer Group West.

was predicted for the morning. When it lifted, 300 planes from the Luftwaffe would be allocated in support. Only the U.S. 30th Infantry and the 3d Armored divisions were thought to be located in the zone of the attack. Against them were pitted between 120 and 190 German tanks from four vaunted divisions, the 1st and 2d SS Panzer divisions, and the 2d and 116th Panzers.

The German attack jumped off in the small hours of August 7 and at first met with success. The 2d SS Panzer Division quickly captured Mortain and passed through, leaving only the 2d Battalion, U.S. 120th Infantry Regiment (30th Division), isolated on a hill east of town. The 2d Panzer to the north advanced approximately six miles eastward during the day but was stopped three miles short of its objective.

During the day, however, the Americans were able to reinforce the 30th Infantry Division at Mortain and the 9th Infantry Division on the north. General Bradley had also kept the 4th Infantry and part of the 2d Armored in the vicinity. In addition, he gave General Collins the 35th Infantry Division, scheduled for employment with the Third Army.

Then the weather broke in favor of Allied air power. The support given by the rocket-firing Typhoons of the British Second Tactical Air Force was superb. Many German tanks and soft-skinned vehicles were damaged or destroyed as ten squadrons of Typhoons flew almost 300 sorties.

The attack on Mortain was temporarily checked. Forty of the seventy tanks judged to have made the penetration were destroyed or damaged during the first day. But Hitler would not accept defeat. Apparently blaming Kluge for the losses because he attacked in good weather in the face of such overwhelming Allied air power, Hitler now began personally directing operations to an even greater degree.

During the night of August 7, the First Canadian Army, east of the Orne River, fortuitously launched a major attack that somewhat reduced the pressure on the Americans at Mortain. At 11:00 P.M. aircraft of the Bomber Command began dropping their bombs. By 11:30, the armored columns, with infantry mounted on the tanks, rolled in the darkness. Supporting artillery laid down a heavy barrage in front of the attackers. But again, the attack eventually ground to a halt. The British Columbia Regiment of the 4th Canadian Division lost 47 tanks on its first day's fighting. This operation, called Totalize, carried the Canadians about eight miles forward, or halfway from Caen to Falaise.

On August 8, 1944, one of the important decisions of the campaign was made. General Eisenhower, who had moved to the Continent the day before, was visiting General Bradley's headquarters. Kluge's attack on Mortain, begun the day before, was still continuing despite the heavy losses. Eisenhower had come to the 12 Army Group with a vaguely formulated idea—turning Haislip, now nearing Le Mans, to the north. If Haislip could reach Alençon, he might be able to trap those German forces now ranged between Mortain on the American front and Caen, held by the British.

Eisenhower found that Bradley had been thinking along the same line. They agreed that one of Patton's corps could turn northward toward Argentan from Le Mans, with Hodges' First Army turning eastward toward the same town. The basic question, however, was whether the Allies could afford to take the risk of releasing several other divisions still being held to reinforce the 30th Division struggling at Mortain. The risks, in case the 30th Division could not hold, would be serious. Should the corridor be cut off and Patton's troops have to return to reopen it, that would be interpreted as an Allied defeat.

The two discussed all possibilities. Finally Eisenhower came up with the clincher: the possibility of aerial resupply. "Even if George's rear is cut off," he said, "we can still deliver two thousand tons a day to the forward positions by air."

This was enough. "When I assured Bradley," Eisenhower writes, "that even under a temporary German success he would have this kind of supply

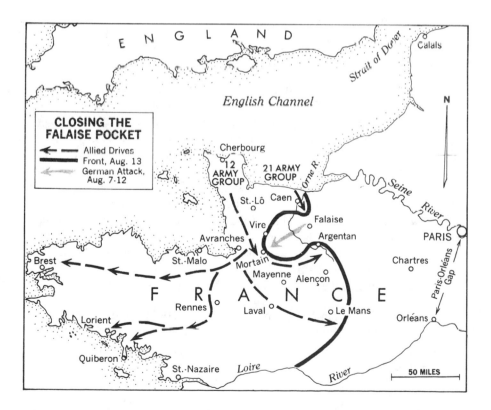

CLOSING THE FALAISE POCKET
— ← — Allied Drives
━━━━ Front, Aug. 13
⇐ German Attack, Aug. 7-12

support, he unhesitatingly determined to retain only minimum forces at Mortain, and to rush others on southeast to begin envelopment of the German spearheads." [9]

General Bradley then immediately called 21 Army Group. He explained the plan to General Montgomery, who after some hesitation agreed. With a nod of the head, Eisenhower acknowledged responsibility for the decision, and Montgomery issued a directive to implement the plan on August 11.

The episode at Mortain is significant not only because of its far-reaching results but because it illustrates the informality with which many major decisions of the European campaign were reached among the Allied commanders. General Bradley described the relationship between himself and the Supreme Commander as follows:

> Quite often the working level at SHAEF G-3 was unaware of the issues involved in these private discussions. And similarly the officers of my G-3 staff were cut off from these conversations [between the Supreme Commander and his principal subordinates]. After October Eisenhower and I were in almost daily touch by phone and he was fully informed of my every move at Group. Quite frequently our long-range plans evolved during late night conversations at Ike's C.P. or mine. Sometimes we would sit until two or three in the morning, swapping opinions and discussing plans for successive phases of the campaign. For this reason historians may find it difficult to ascribe to any individual commander his views or credits for key tactical decisions. . . .[10]

The battle at Mortain continued severe. After August 8, however, the 30th Division began to plan for a counterattack to restore the line of two days before. By August 10 it was certain that the line would hold.

Yet it took two more days before Kluge finally showed signs of abandoning his position, on August 12. Then, acting on his own responsibility, he ordered a withdrawal the next day, hoping to concentrate his armor to hit eastward and fight his way out of the pocket beginning to surround his forces. For Haislip's XV Corps was now cutting off his rear at Alençon.

On August 12 the 2d Battalion of the U.S. 120th Infantry was relieved on their isolated hill east of Mortain. Their stand resembled a modern Alamo. Between August 7 and 12, that battalion had been supplied by air, with medical supplies delivered by artillery. During that period the battalion had sustained 300 men killed or wounded, half its total strength.

The Battle of Mortain had been a costly operation. The 4th, 9th, and 30th divisions—the assault divisions for Cobra, by coincidence—lost 3,600 men, the

[9] Dwight Eisenhower, *Crusade in Europe* (New York: Doubleday, 1948), p. 275.
[10] Bradley, *op. cit.*, p. 354.

bulk from the 30th, who had borne the brunt of the fighting. German losses had been greater; close to 100 Nazi tanks had been destroyed. Far more important, Hitler's insistence on the Mortain attack and on continuing that attack after it was obviously hopeless had now set the stage for the decimation of the German Seventh and Fifth Panzer armies.

The fate of those two armies was being sealed. Wade Haislip's XV Corps, reaching Le Mans on August 9, had turned north, and by the night of August 12, the U.S. 5th Armored Division was on the outskirts of Argentan.

Kluge realized his predicament. The British and Canadian attacks from August 7 to 9 had forced German units to withdraw southward, and the Seventh Army had lost its rear installations. Supplies for the latter now had to come from the Fifth Panzer Army. Shortly thereafter, the Allied thrust northward cut off all but one of his supply routes. With the loss of Alençon— and Argentan very shortly thereafter—Kluge's original intention faded; he dared not strike at what he had hoped would be thinly held flanks of the U.S. XV Corps. He therefore deployed the 116th Panzer Division south to defend against the American attack at Argentan and sent the 1st SS and 2d Panzer divisions north against the Canadians.

With the Canadians driving south and the Americans driving north and about to meet, the complete entrapment of the two German armies seemed assured. But the gap would not be closed in time to bag them all. On August 6 General Montgomery, still coordinating boundaries for the two army groups, had established a limit of advance for U.S. forces some sixteen miles south of Falaise and a few miles south of Argentan. On August 11, however, General Patton saw fit to overlook this limit and directed Haislip to "push on slowly in the direction of Falaise." At Falaise, according to Patton's instructions, Haislip was to continue to push forward until he would "contact our Allies."

Haislip entered Argentan on August 13 and was preparing to continue to the north when he received an order directly from General Bradley. In no uncertain terms, Haislip was ordered to stop and to withdraw south to positions near Argentan. The Canadians, who were still halfway between Caen and Falaise, could not launch their next attack until August 14. This left open a gap of about twenty-five miles.

General Bradley's action has been criticized by some historians, but there were sound reasons for it. Aside from the fact that even in Argentan the U.S. forces had entered territory beyond that designated by General Montgomery, Bradley was greatly concerned with the possibility of a tragic mistake, a battle between friendly forces. In addition, Patton's forces, particularly Haislip's XV Corps, were badly stretched out. Haislip might not be able to hold against a strong counterattack by Kluge from the east. Bradley preferred, he has since written, "a solid shoulder at Argentan to the possibility of a broken neck at Falaise." [11] Eisenhower fully supported Bradley in this decision.

August 14, 1944, turned out to be an eventful day. The Canadian II Corps launched its final attack that resulted two days later in the capture of Falaise. At the same time General Patton requested permission from General Bradley to dispatch two divisions of the XV Corps for another dash farther eastward to the Seine River. A bridgehead might be available at Mantes-Gassicourt. Permission was granted.

On August 14 also, realizing the unique opportunity of the moment, General Eisenhower issued the following appeal:

> I request every airman to make it his direct responsibility that the enemy is blasted unceasingly by day and by night, and is denied safety either in fight or flight.
> I request every sailor to make sure that no part of the hostile forces can either escape or be reinforced by sea, and that our comrades on the land want for nothing that guns and ships and ships' companies can bring to them.
> I request every soldier to go forward to his assigned objective with the determination that the enemy can survive only through surrender; let no foot of ground once gained be relinquished nor a single German escape through a line once established.

The next day, at a press conference in Normandy, Eisenhower revealed that General George Patton had been commanding the fast-moving Third U.S. Army since August 1, while General Courtney Hodges had been commander of the First U.S. Army. Under a cloud before this campaign because of the notorious soldier-slapping incident in Sicily and for periodic indiscreet statements since, Patton's reputation with the public—and his spirits along with it—soared.

On August 15 General Montgomery changed the boundary between 21 Army Group and 12 Army Group to permit U.S. troops to advance farther north. Later he approved American thrusts farther east toward the towns of Chambois and Trun. From that day on, Kluge attempted to pull his forces out of the tightening trap, and the tempo of the war became increasingly frantic. The Nazis made futile efforts to fly in fuel for their panzers. By August 16 Walker's XX Corps had reached both Orléans and Chartres. An airborne drop, scheduled to seize the Paris-Orléans Gap, was obviously no longer necessary.

Hitler had given orders to fight the battle of Falaise to the last man, but the mere issuance of an order could not insure success. After the fall of Falaise on August 17, the Canadians and the Americans had slowly narrowed

---

[11] Bradley, *op. cit.,* p. 377.

the gap between the Allied pincers to a dozen miles. The German withdrawal suddenly turned into a rout, and Kluge's units lost all semblance of organization. Allied artillery and air exacted a fearful toll against the fleeing units along the packed roads and turned the entire area into a gigantic shambles of blasted German equipment, men, and horses.

At 7:20 P.M., August 19, the long-awaited contact between the Allied forces took place. The 10th Polish Mounted Rifle Regiment from the north touched Chambois, to be joined by the 90th U.S. Infantry Division, now under command of the U.S. VII Corps of the First Army. By August 22, fighting in the area of the Falaise Pocket was at an end.

The results of the Normandy campaign were dramatic. Losses in the German Seventh and Fifth Panzer armies cannot be accurately estimated. Prisoners alone totaled 50,000 in the last days; 10,000 bodies were found on the field. How many wounded escaped is unknown.[12] Despite the headlong retreat from the Falaise area, much of the German panzer strength managed to escape.[13] The less-favored infantry elements had been trapped. The panzer forces that escaped, however, did so only by abandoning large quantities of their equipment. The Germans who once faced Overlord in Western France had ceased to exist as an effective fighting force—for the moment, at least.

For Field Marshal Guenther von Kluge the campaign ended, as with so many others, in personal tragedy. Because of the abortive action at Mortain and Kluge's initiative in preparing for withdrawal from that area, Hitler's suspicions that Kluge had been implicated in the July 20 plot on his life were strengthened. Out of contact for a day with headquarters, through no fault of his own, Kluge was suspected of negotiating with the Allies for a surrender. He was relieved of his two commands, OB West and Army Group B, by Field Marshal Walther Model on August 17. He began his journey home in military disgrace two days later, with little illusion as to his fate. On the day the gap was closed at Chambois, Guenther von Kluge took cyanide.

For the Allies there were other results that would be apparent later in the European campaign. Their decision to destroy German forces between the Seine and the Loire rivers required major combat action on a large scale without first securing the use of the Breton ports. Thus, as the remainder of the Third U.S. Army continued its advance from Falaise and Le Mans toward the Seine, the most serious problem facing the Allies was that of supply, gasoline in particular. Extraordinary means of bringing in gasoline, ammunition, and troops would have to be found and found quickly.

Another, if more subtle, result was the beginning of a nagging feeling on the part of the British public that their valiant efforts had not been fully

---

[12] Blumenson, *op. cit.*, pp. 557–58.
[13] Elements of the 1st SS Panzer, 2d SS Panzer, 9th SS Panzer, 12th SS Panzer, Panzer Lehr, 2d Panzer, 9th Panzer, and 116th Panzer divisions.

appreciated by the Americans. During the days of the spectacular American advances, headlines did not mention that the bulk of the enemy armor was being nailed down by the British and Canadians at Caen. Critics in the U.S. press even went so far as to imply that the British and Canadians were lacking in drive and imagination, an opinion not shared by the American or Allied command. As General Eisenhower wrote in his report:

> From our landings in June until that day [August 17], the enemy resistance in this sector [Caen-Falaise] had exacted more Allied bloodshed for the ground yielded than any other part of the campaign. Without the great sacrifices made here by the Anglo-Canadian armies in a series of brutal, slugging battles, first for Caen then for Falaise, the spectacular advances made elsewhere by the Allied forces could never have come about.[14]

Finally some concern was developing regarding the aggressiveness of General Montgomery during this period—a feeling that began to bother some American high-ranking officers on the Continent. There were those who felt that the General was reluctant to commit large formations to full-size attacks with the necessary enthusiasm. Despite such undercurrents among some of his subordinates, General Eisenhower insisted that no such criticism become public.[15] It was essential to the combined effort that the hero of the British soldier and of the British public be treated with all the courtesy and respect due him.

But the psychological aftereffects of the spectacular role played by the Americans in this campaign were to return to haunt the Allies in the months ahead.

[14] Report by the Supreme Commander to the Combined Chiefs of Staff, *op. cit.*

[15] In a letter to the author dated January 12, 1967, General Eisenhower wrote: ". . . at the time of which you are writing, I did not agree with much of the criticism voiced by Tedder and others. Indeed when the Prime Minister and Field Marshal Brooke came to see me on this general subject one day, I told them emphatically that I hoped there would be no more dissatisfaction voiced about Montgomery anywhere."

CHAPTER 3

❧❧❧

Paris "Detour"

"AND if that series of events should come about, my dear general, I would have no choice but to go to His Majesty the King, and lay down the mantle of my high office." Thus spoke one of the world's most persuasive statesmen, Winston S. Churchill.

This remarkable statement was made early in August, 1944. General Middleton's armored spearheads were racing westward across the Brittany Peninsula, and the rest of General Patton's Third Army was proceeding with equal speed eastward toward Le Mans. Kluge was attacking the 30th Infantry Division at Mortain. Churchill and Eisenhower sat in the pleasant Norman countryside discussing not the current tactical situation but a forthcoming invasion of Southern France, an operation named first Anvil and later Dragoon—an operation that the Prime Minister fervently wanted canceled.

Churchill well knew that he had once agreed to the invasion. In Teheran, in November, 1943, when grand strategy was being discussed by Premier Stalin, President Roosevelt, and the Prime Minister, it had been established that France should be invaded from two directions—from Northern Europe (Overlord) and from Southern France (Anvil).

But much had taken place since that day nearly a year before. Upon assuming command in England in January, 1944, General Eisenhower had insisted on a five-division assault across the Normandy beaches rather than the use of only three divisions as previously planned. This increase in the size of the Overlord landing force required larger numbers of landing craft than originally estimated. These were now in short supply, and it was impossible to mount Overlord and Anvil simultaneously. As a result, Anvil had been postponed to late July or mid-August.

The unexpected successes in Normandy had now apparently convinced the Prime Minister that Anvil was no longer necessary. In Italy Field Marshal Sir Harold R. L. G. Alexander's 15 Army Group had also made substantial advances. Rome had been taken on June 4, two days before the Allied landings in Normandy. Now, the Prime Minister argued, the forces that were to have been withdrawn from Italy and employed in the southern invasion would best be left with Alexander, enabling him to continue to pursue the Germans up the boot of Italy to the Po Valley and the Alps.

Churchill seemed to be swayed by two additional considerations. He had, of course, full access to the latest military intelligence reports from SHAEF describing German weakness in Southern France, but if he read them he did not believe them. Possibly he was overinfluenced by a previous study prepared by the Allied staff in the Mediterranean, which visualized a three-month campaign to advance as far north as Lyon. In support of his view, he pictured a bloody landing against heavily defended shores, so that at best Anvil-Dragoon [1] might result in great losses to the Allies and at worst another stalemate like the Anzio bridgehead in the previous January.

One pillar of Winston Churchill's statesmanship was his generous and realistic dealings with his American allies. And yet, in this instance, it is impossible to overlook the fact that he was involved in a debate vitally affecting a theater of war, the Mediterranean, in which he had great emotional investment. Not only had he long been an advocate of attacking the "soft underbelly of Europe," but also he had come to regard the Italian campaign, which was under British overall command, as one in which the prestige of his beloved England was involved. Nearly a year before, when the command arrangements of the Normandy invasion were being settled, it was assumed that General George C. Marshall, U.S. Chief of Staff in Washington, would command Overlord rather than General Eisenhower. Then, Mr. Churchill was frank in his insistence that the Mediterranean theater should be commanded by a British officer rather than an American.

"General," he said to Eisenhower, "you know full well that we are quite happy with you and your performance. However, I am sure you realize that you will have to be removed, as it would be unfair to the British if both the European and Mediterranean theaters were commanded by American officers."

Eisenhower said that he understood perfectly, and would serve as directed by the Combined Chiefs of Staff. It was this Mediterranean theater, in which Prime Minister Churchill took such a proprietary interest, that would give up divisions to a force that would eventually come under Eisenhower's command in Northern Europe.

However, actual British participation in Dragoon was to be small. The attack was to be spearheaded by VI U.S. Corps, under Major General Lucian K. Truscott, with three of the finest divisions in the entire U.S. Army—the 3d, 36th, and 45th Infantry—to be followed up by seven French divisions destined later to form the French First Army. Except for some British in the airborne drop, any blood that might be spilled would be mostly American and French.

---

[1] When the code name was changed from Anvil to Dragoon, Churchill claimed he had been "dragooned" into it.

However the Prime Minister weighed these factors, he had firmly concluded that the operation should not proceed.

So far as General Eisenhower knew, at this late date—only a little more than a week before the scheduled operation—the matter was completely settled. The U.S. Chiefs of Staff in Washington considered the operation strictly in his hands. Accordingly, it was toward General Eisenhower that Churchill now directed most of his arguments. Earlier he had written letters to President Roosevelt and his principal assistant, Harry Hopkins, expressing his opposition to the plan.

Churchill argued that the Allies no longer needed Marseilles as a port, since Middleton's armored columns would soon release the Breton ports of Lorient, St.-Nazaire, Quiberon Bay, St.-Malo, and Brest from German control. On the other hand, a strengthened drive forward in Italy, and thence toward the Balkans, would threaten Germany from the south. Churchill apparently envisioned the entire Balkan region bursting into flames and open revolt against Hitler, thus creating a threat against Nazi Germany from yet another direction.

General Eisenhower denied, first of all, any guarantee that the Brittany ports would be available very soon. He believed that the port of Marseilles would be lightly held, with little likelihood of major destruction of docking facilities. With Marseilles secured, the Allies would soon vastly increase the rate at which additional U.S. divisions arrived. Furthermore, General Eisenhower had an eye on his own right flank (at the time of the conversation, Walker's XX Corps, under Patton, was moving south to the Loire River). Without the southern landing, so necessary to clear out all of Southwest France, the Allies would have to contend with an incredibly long, exposed right flank. Its protection would require defensive troops brought into the European theater over the beaches of Normandy and through the badly damaged ports of Cherbourg and—much later—Brittany.

Flanks such as Patton's along the Loire had to be protected by dropping off combat units, usually infantry divisions, to face the direction of potential attack. The Loire, a formidable obstacle, would help considerably, but once the Germans had recovered from the shock they were now experiencing in Normandy, Eisenhower reasoned, the price in divisions to secure that flank would still be substantial. None of the defensive forces could be used in any aggressive moves eastward. Obviously, in Eisenhower's view, all of France had to be cleared of the enemy, and this could best be done by a joining of the Overlord and the Dragoon forces.

There was an important additional factor. Seven of the divisions in the invasion were French, and it was only natural that they would desire a major role in the liberation of their homeland. General Eisenhower felt that the French would fight much more efficiently in liberating France than in operations against German forces occupying Italy.

Other arguments were brought into the discussion, but finally it was decided to continue with the plan. Eisenhower deeply regretted having to disagree with the Prime Minister, whom he admired more than any other statesman he had ever met. But what made the decision easier was the Prime Minister's insistence that his reasons were based on *purely military considerations,* with no weight given to the postwar political situation. On this basis Eisenhower had no recourse but to carry out missions that he calculated would secure the earliest victory over Hitler.

This discussion illustrates General Eisenhower's position vis-à-vis the U.S. and the British governments. He reported directly to neither. Rather, he reported to the body of the Combined Chiefs of Staff, consisting of the chiefs of the armies, navies, and air forces of both United States and Great Britain. Thus, while he normally communicated with that body through General Marshall, there was no single individual who could issue him operational orders.

The episode illustrates also a basic difference between British and American strategic views. Throughout the many Allied discussions on the conduct of the war, the Americans habitually placed a more exclusive emphasis on the Overlord operation than did their British allies. The Americans thought that if all available power were concentrated along the best avenue of approach to Germany, the war would be won with the fewest casualties and in the shortest time by fighting an intensive Overlord campaign. They added that thus the Allies would win a better postwar political position than would be gained by dividing their strength between two campaigns.

Perhaps some of the British reluctance to place all the eggs in the Northern Europe basket stemmed from the bitter experiences of World War I—at Passchendaele, Ypres, and the Somme British troops had sustained staggering casualties for pitifully small gains—and this feeling cropped up in many conversations during the planning stages of Overlord. Churchill was pessimistic. A highly successful operation, he said, would be one which simply secured the Cherbourg and Brittany peninsulas by the winter of 1944. "And if, by this time, you have secured the port at Le Havre and freed beautiful Paris from the hands of the enemy," he said to General Eisenhower, "I will assert the victory to be the greatest of modern times."

To this Eisenhower replied that the coming winter would see the Allied forces on the borders of Germany itself. In addition to the currently available 36 Allied divisions, 10 more would come from the Mediterranean, and by the end of the year 40 full divisions from the United States would pass through the captured ports.

Whatever the value of such conjecture, on August 15, 1944, in typically gallant fashion, Churchill was on board a destroyer enthusiastically observing the bombardment of Southern France in support of Anvil-Dragoon.

The friendship between Churchill and Eisenhower was close, extraordinarily so for a head of government and the commander of an expeditionary force.

Dwight Eisenhower was a West Pointer from the class of 1915. Unlike Douglas MacArthur and George Patton, both of whom were much senior to him on the regular list, Eisenhower's character was less a product of West Point than of the Kansas plains, where "Wild Bill" Hickok had tamed his town, Abilene, only a few years before Eisenhower's birth. He went to West Point almost by chance, having first heard of it as a "wonderful place that pays you to play football."

He did not find West Point much of a challenge; to a farm boy the five-fifty reveille was sleeping late. As a yearling (sophomore), he broke his knee playing football and lost much interest in his cadet's career. He smoked heavily, boxed a little, and as the yearbook says, contented himself until graduation should "set him free." However, he did not dislike the institution known as Hell on the Hudson, and he retained a great affection for the school and above all for his classmates.

Once graduated, Eisenhower resolved to make himself the best Army officer possible within the gifts he possessed. However, he remained free of many of the forms and fetishes civilians consider "military," and he never had any doubt that he could earn a living as a civilian. When an issue crossed his sense of right, his temper, a legacy of his Pennsylvania Dutch ancestry, flared.

At such times he always seemed ready to lay his military career on the line; possibly it is more correct to say that when he believed he was right it never occurred to him to think of the consequences to his career. He had on occasion differed sharply with two four-star generals, MacArthur and Marshall—once as a major and once as a brigadier general—in a manner that would have called for prompt and sharp correction from less understanding superiors. In 1932 he argued vehemently against General MacArthur's personal participation in the evacuation of the "Bonus Marchers" from Washington. In the only known instance of his speaking heatedly to General Marshall, he informed the latter that he was not in the least concerned with Marshall's power to promote him; he was merely trying to do his duty, and promotions be damned! This was scarcely a proper way for a new brigadier general to address the Army Chief of Staff.

This independence of spirit increased rather than diminished the mutual respect that Eisenhower enjoyed with relatively senior officers. Churchill was no exception.

From the military viewpoint, the Dragoon operation was a brilliant success. The vanguard of the U.S. Seventh Army, General Truscott's VI Corps, led the assault as planned. The landing took place on a 45-mile front between Toulon and Cannes. On the first day the attacking forces succeeded in sweeping aside the seven second-rate divisions of the German Nineteenth Army and 11th Panzer Division, and established a beachhead more than 20 miles in depth. Within four days the beachhead had more than doubled, and four days later—only one week after the landing—the 45th U.S. Infantry Division was as far as Grenoble, 150 miles to the north. Although a considerable part of the German Nineteenth Army escaped, 57,000 were taken prisoner.

While the Americans went in pursuit of the German forces, the French I and II corps, organized under General Jean de Lattre de Tassigny as French Army B, concentrated on seizing the ports of Toulon and Marseilles. These cities held out for nearly two weeks but finally succumbed on August 28. By this time the beachhead was of impressive size. Marseilles, a port with a capacity of 18,000 tons per day, was open by September 15. The cities had suffered little damage.

In nineteen days General Patch's Seventh Army had reached a point almost halfway between Lyon and Dijon, which happily removed Churchill's fear that the capture of Lyon would cost three months of bloody fighting. Patch continued the drive northward, determined to link up with Patton's right flank as soon as possible.

On August 19, four days after the landing in Southern France, General Eisenhower made a decision that was to have far-reaching effects on the conduct of the 1944 campaign. On that day the Falaise-Argentan Gap had almost been closed at Chambois. The efforts to reduce the ports of Brittany had been disappointing. St.-Malo had been captured two days before, but the capture of Brest was obviously weeks off (Lorient and St.-Nazaire were to hold out for the rest of the war). Cherbourg's capacity was only some 14,000 tons a day, and the lines to the front were long and tortuous. General Patton's forces had seized a bridgehead over the Seine at Mantes; to the south Patton had reached the Chartres-Orléans line and was about to plunge into the Paris-Orléans Gap. The enemy was demoralized and retreating headlong.

The question now facing Eisenhower was whether to stop and consolidate, or continue the drive east along the left bank of the Seine to Rouen and cut off elements of the Seventh and Fifth Panzer armies. Asked if he intended to chase the enemy, the Supreme Commander said, "Yes, to the very limit of supply." The Allies would pursue the routed Nazis as far as their already overstrained logistic situation would allow.[2] He told his staff, "From now on, our philosophy will be to chase the German to the very limit of our supplies. I want every plan from here on to be predicated on that premise!"

However, on the same day Eisenhower was faced with an unpleasant matter of public relations. The projected command arrangements, whereby SHAEF was to become a field headquarters and take over the direct coordination between army groups (previously performed by Montgomery), had long been scheduled to take effect on September 1. Now they were prematurely announced in a newspaper article by an American correspondent. The British

[2] General Eisenhower later stated that this decision was so easy as to be hardly a decision at all. However, military textbooks generally regard it as an important moment.

press, inferring that Montgomery had been "demoted" because of his successes in Normandy, protested immediately; at the same time the American press hailed the new command setup as evidence of American independence of action. To make matters worse, a press officer at SHAEF denied the story, later explaining the denial on the grounds that the new arrangements were not to take effect for several days.

The controversy rose to such distressing heights in the press of both countries that at one point, Eisenhower, exasperated, wrote General Marshall with some bitterness: "It wasn't enough for the public to obtain a great victory; the manner in which it was gained seemed to be more important."

The bickering in the press grew so irksome that Eisenhower made a special trip to London, where he held a press conference at the Ministry of Information and explained the entire situation. He expressed his admiration and friendship for General Montgomery and let it be known that the elevation of General Bradley's 12 Army Group to a status equal with that of 21 Army Group reflected no dissatisfaction with Montgomery whatsoever. To ease the feelings of the British public further, His Majesty's Government promoted Montgomery to the rank of field marshal, effective September 1, 1944, the day that the new command setup was to take effect.

The problem of press relations in war is a difficult one. Obviously, whatever information is released to the public is simultaneously released to the enemy. The need for security creates a conflict that can never be fully resolved, and the public information officers normally advocate telling the public far more than intelligence officers might wish. If the commanders' personality traits have an appreciable influence on the conduct of battle, then certainly announcements about command relationships must be given a hard look.

Students of the American Civil War are familiar with the contention that General Lee's intimate knowledge of the personalities of the Union commanders gave him an advantage in his conduct of battle. Probably this was so. He could not afford to be as audacious fighting against a Grant as he could against a McClellan. The same held true to a large degree in the European campaign, particularly when such personalities as George S. Patton came into play. By mid-August Patton's zest for pursuit had become common knowledge to military and public alike. Never rated particularly high as an "infighter" in a slugging match, his talent was for pursuit, which is rarer than expertise in hedgerow operations and set-piece battles. Would Patton have been as competent as Montgomery to plan an army group's invasion of the Normandy beaches? By the same token, could Montgomery have matched Patton's performance commanding the Third U.S. Army's driving pursuit of the enemy? The logical answers are no. One can only conclude that "order of battle" information, which studies the characteristics of commanders, is of considerable interest to the enemy.

Yet in the case of the High Command in France, another factor had to be given careful consideration—feelings of national pride. Pride in country and tradition is not to be discouraged; a soldier cannot fight without it. But in the highest command echelons of nations that have combined their resources to fight a common enemy, this feeling must often be subordinated to the good of the whole.

This is not easy. Napoleon's detractors have pointed out that his brilliant campaigns were fought largely against coalitions. The coalition between the British and the Americans in World War II was not automatic. It could easily be injured, conceivably fatally, despite the fact that the two national political leaders were joint signatories of the Atlantic Charter and despite the intense admiration that Americans felt for Britain as she stood alone in 1940. For this reason, General Eisenhower ruefully concluded when writing his memoirs in 1948, the concealment of projected command arrangements was a mistake.[3]

In late August Major General Manton S. Eddy, former commander of the 9th U.S. Infantry Division, was ordered to report to General Patton to take over command of the XII Corps, then at Orléans preparing to proceed eastward through the Paris-Orléans Gap. This was a new type of warfare to General Eddy, and he keenly anticipated it after the dreary struggles in the hedgerows. But one burning question crossed his mind: What about that long open southern flank along the Loire, nearly 300 miles from St.-Nazaire to Orléans? As he gazed at the map, Eddy asked Patton, "How much do I have to worry about my flank along the Loire?"

Patton's answer was typical. With a slight twinkle he said, "Well, Eddy, that just all depends on how nervous you are by nature."

In truth, General Patton was not the least bit indifferent toward his southern flank. He knew the Loire to be a formidable obstacle. He also knew that the air forces were flying daily missions to detect and break up any formations south of the river that might constitute a threat.

On August 25, as his spearheads were entering Troyes, 90 miles southeast of Paris, he crossed Haislip's XV Corps southward behind Eddy's XII Corps at Chaumont, with the mission of making contact with the Seventh Army coming up from Marseilles.

Continuing their pursuit of the beaten German forces across France, the Allied armies inevitably found in their path the magnificent city of Paris, still held by substantial numbers of undefeated and determined enemy. From a military viewpoint its main value lay in its great number of bridges over the Seine. However, symbolic of the possession of France itself, Paris was a prize of transcendent political importance. Furthermore, practically all the nation's

---

[3] Dwight Eisenhower, *Crusade in Europe* (New York: Doubleday, 1948), p. 300.

rail and communication lines—and its channels of administration—converged on this hub.

It was its intangible importance that made Paris a problem, a problem that grew with each day to the point that, for the first time since Overlord, the Allied High Command was faced with a perplexing conflict between military and political considerations. For the first time the influence of the French and of General Charles de Gaulle made itself felt on the conduct of tactical operations. And for the first time since 1940 the French were able once more to assert themselves as a sovereign nation.

Originally the Allied High Command intended to bypass the city, basing their decision on military considerations. Despite Third Army bridgeheads across the Seine both north and south of the city, General Bradley planned, with General Eisenhower's concurrence, to leave Paris in the hands of the Germans as long as possible to avoid the administrative burden of supplying it. Once the Allies had taken responsibility for its administration, they would have to feed it. The logistic planners estimated that 4,000 tons a day would be required—enough, as General Bradley put it, "for a three days' motor march toward the German border."

There were other reasons for temporarily ignoring Paris. One was purely tactical: any large city affords an excellent defensive position for determined troops. A street-by-street reduction of the German garrison might be necessary, which would occupy quite a few Allied combat troops that might better be employed in pursuing German mobile forces, and which might force the Germans to demolish untold architectural treasures in the process of utilizing Paris as a fortress.

Among the German High Command confusion reigned. On August 7 General Dietrich von Choltitz, formerly commander of the unlucky 84th Korps, which was destroyed by Cobra, was named military commander of Greater Paris. Choltitz, reputed to be a man who would "take orders," had little stomach for Hitler's resolve to destroy the city rather than surrender it intact. He felt he had been given similar tasks too often and was in no mood to be known as the "destroyer of Paris." However, Hitler's instructions were definite. His famous "field of ruins order" said:

> The defense of the Paris bridgehead is of decisive military and political importance. Its loss dislodges the entire coastal front north of the Seine and removes the base for the V-weapons attacks against England.
>
> In history the loss of Paris always means the loss of France. Therefore the Führer repeats his order to hold the defense zone in advance [west] of the city. . . .
>
> Within the city every sign of incipient revolt must be countered by the sharpest means . . . [including] public execution of the ringleaders. . . .
>
> The Seine bridges will be prepared for demolition. Paris must not fall into the hands of the enemy except as a field of ruins.

In compliance with this order, Choltitz pushed his forces, heavy with anti-tank weapons, toward the west of the town, where they formed a large bridge-head on the Left Bank.

The movement of the German troops to the west greatly reduced Choltitz's garrison within the city itself. Observing these reductions and assuming that Choltitz was operating from weakness, members of the Resistance began a series of uprisings within the city. A general strike was called; not even the policemen remained at their posts. The Resistance began requesting arms from the Allies to help them make a series of upheavals.

With this turn of events, General de Gaulle became concerned. Not only was the insurgency likely to cause the Germans to destroy the city, but also there was a danger that certain left-wing elements of the Resistance, politically dangerous from de Gaulle's point of view, might take control of the capital. He therefore began to urge General Eisenhower to take the city by force as quickly as possible. On August 21, de Gaulle and General Pierre Joseph Koenig [4] conferred with Eisenhower, who, for the moment, declined to change his original plans. However, it was important to secure General de Gaulle's cooperation, and the situation changed daily. By the next day Eisenhower was writing to General Marshall:

> Because of the additional supply commitment incurred in the occupation of Paris, it would be desirable, from that viewpoint, to defer the capture of the city until the important matter of destroying the remaining enemy forces up to include the Pas-de-Calais area. I do not believe this is possible. If the enemy tries to hold Paris with any real strength he would be a constant menace to our flank. If he largely concedes the place, it falls into our hands whether we like it or not.

In the meantime, leaders of the Resistance, through the Swedish consul, Raoul Nordling, entered into a truce with Choltitz which was due to last until noontime on August 23. Nordling was convinced that Choltitz would like to surrender, but not to "irregular" forces. He therefore arranged for a delegation to go through the lines. Their mission was to explain the situation to the American commanders. The small delegation, headed by Nordling's brother Rolf (he himself was taken sick) and accompanied by a German officer for safe conduct, went through the lines on August 22.

During this time, the French 2d Armored Division, commanded by Major General Jacques Leclerc, was still at Argentan, waiting for orders to move out and liberate Paris. Leclerc, conscious of a rendezvous with history, chafed at every passing minute. His was not the most accessible unit for the purpose, but General Eisenhower had long before deemed it proper that Paris be liberated by this gallant unit that had served so well for more than three years.

[4] Commander of the French Forces of the Interior.

Leclerc was now attached to Major Leonard T. ("Gee") Gerow's V Corps; but as the senior French field commander, he felt he possessed special prerogatives. At one point he sent a small task force toward Paris to insure that if the rest of his division were late the French would be represented when the city was entered. His superior, Gerow, had received no orders for the move. Thoroughly military in his attitudes, Gerow angrily recalled the task force: "I desire to make it clear to you that the 2d Armored Division is under my command for all purposes and no part of it will be employed by you except in the execution of missions assigned by this headquarters." [5]

Learning that Eisenhower and Bradley were considering his early employment, Leclerc contented himself with complying and biding his time. Late in the afternoon of August 22 the ordeal of waiting came to an end; his French 2d Armored was alerted for movement to Paris. Although he experienced unforeseen difficulties in locating all his men in the Norman countryside, Leclerc had got his division on the road by the evening; but on the way to Paris his troops ran into some islands of German resistance, and as a result, it was the morning of August 24 before he was in a position to attack Paris from the direction of Versailles, southwest of the city. Gerow assigned the U.S. 4th Infantry Division to support him by seizing bridges over the Seine to the south of the city, on Leclerc's right.

When Leclerc's attack began early on August 24, it proceeded very slowly, partly due to the obstruction made by the crowds, intoxicated somewhat prematurely in welcoming the liberators. Situation reports previously reaching the Allied High Command had been based mostly on reports coming from the main part of the city, where Germans were now scarce. These failed to take note that far from fleeing to the east, Choltitz's troops had moved west, and therefore the slow progress convinced the American Command that Leclerc was procrastinating. The fact was that the French lost 300 men that day—evidence that they had done some hard fighting. Impatient with Leclerc's progress, General Bradley now ordered the U.S. 4th Division to move into the city on Leclerc's right. Leclerc, possibly spurred on by the unwelcome presence of the Americans, reached the Hôtel de Ville at 10:00 P.M.

The next day, August 25, the Allied hold on Paris was consolidated by both units. Choltitz and his entire staff were captured by the French at the Hôtel Meurice and were driven to the Gare Montparnasse, where Choltitz formally surrendered Paris to the French. When Major General Raymond Barton of the U.S. 4th Division met with Leclerc that day, he found the Frenchman apparently quite irritated that American troops were in the city.

Relations between the American tactical commanders and the French lead-

[5] Martin Blumenson, *Breakout and Pursuit* (Washington: Dept. of the Army, 1961), p. 601.

ers remained cool, sometimes strained. To exacerbate Leclerc's annoyance, he had now begun to receive conflicting orders. Technically his immediate military superior remained Gerow of U.S. V Corps, but at this point General de Gaulle, now arrived on the scene, began to issue instructions of his own. On August 26, the day after the liberation, de Gaulle ordered part of Leclerc's division to participate in a parade. Gerow objected, desiring Leclerc to continue in pursuit of the enemy northward. De Gaulle carried his point. Leclerc was inclined to obey the orders of his country's leader, and Gerow, in the final analysis, declared it would be unwise "to try to stop the parade with the use of U.S. troops."

Three days later Gerow, doubtless with a sigh of relief, moved his headquarters eastward and formally turned over control of the city to French General Koenig. Koenig announced, to Gerow's surprise, that French authorities alone had been handling the administration of the city of Paris since its liberation.

On the High Command level, however, the atmosphere was far more cordial. On August 27 General Eisenhower decided to pay an official call on General de Gaulle in Paris. He took General Bradley with him. General Montgomery had been invited to accompany them, representing the British, but had turned down the invitation. He was too busy. Eisenhower took along his British military assistant, Colonel James Gault, to lend British presence to the occasion.

The results of the call, which symbolized Eisenhower's de facto recognition of de Gaulle as provisional president of France, were far-reaching. De Gaulle's gratitude was profound. In the many years of public service left to the two men de Gaulle never failed to remember this gesture whenever they met.

During the meeting of August 27 General de Gaulle had a request to make. Still not entirely sure of his position, he asked for a contingent of U.S. troops to be stationed temporarily in Paris as a show of force. Eisenhower could not spare any U.S. divisions from their immediate task—headlong pursuit of the Germans—but he rerouted an infantry division that Bradley had available and had them march through the streets of Paris in parade formation on the way to the front.

The division that marched down the Champs Elysées that August day on the way to close with the enemy was the 28th "Keystone" Division, originally from Pennsylvania. It was photographed with the Arc de Triomphe in the background, and the picture immediately attained wide publicity. Some of the British press, unaware of the reason for the march, protested, regarding it as an attempt on the part of the Americans to steal the entire credit—much of which belonged to British forces—for the liberation of Paris and therefore of France. Once again an innocent gesture had been misconstrued. But the pride of the British press and public sustained another, if minor, injury.

For the 28th U.S. Infantry Division the "victory" parade down the Champs Elysées was only a detour. The division marched through the city in combat gear, straight into battle. Ahead of them lay the Hürtgen, the Ardennes, and finally victory.

As for Paris, its liberation had been accompanied by confusion, misinformation and some conflict of Allied interests. But history must record that the city was spared; there was a minimum of lives lost. And the French, now an independent ally, were in a position to make an inspired contribution to the overthrow of Hitler. August 25, 1944, was a great day for Paris. By French reckoning, now complete victory could not be far away.

CHAPTER 4

❦

Antwerp Is the Key

ON August 23, 1944, the day after fighting had ceased in the Falaise Pocket, General Montgomery urgently requested General Eisenhower to visit him at his 21 Army Group headquarters. Montgomery, along with everyone else, was elated with the results that had been achieved in the Normandy campaign, which culminated in the virtual decimation of the German Seventh and Fifth Panzer armies.

What Montgomery had on his mind was no small matter; it involved a complete and radical departure from the previously agreed strategy for the conquest of Europe, strategy that had been worked out in detail before D-Day.

Assuming that the Nazi armies were now completely defeated, Montgomery argued that a force of some thirty divisions, given all the resources in the European theater, could now stab eastward, across the German border and the Rhine, and dash on to Berlin. It was his opinion that the European war could be won in September of 1944 with a single, all-out push. He added urgency to his arguments by calling attention to the nearly depleted state of the British manpower resources and economy after five years of conflict. The British nation, he felt, might thus be spared another winter of the European war.

General Montgomery claimed that this task could be achieved either by his own 21 Army Group or by General Bradley's 12 Army Group to the south. Naturally, he said, he preferred that it be done by his own. For one thing, his forces were located north of the Ruhr, where the terrain was more favorable than in the south; furthermore, the northern route could be supported by overwhelming Allied naval strength along the English Channel and the North Sea. But, he concluded, Bradley's army group, likewise if given all the resources of the theater, could also do the job, in which case he himself would be willing to stop.

General Eisenhower was never one to stick rigidly to a strategic plan simply and solely because it had been agreed to before D-Day. He had altered the original concept early in August by sending the bulk of the U.S.

72

Third Army eastward rather than into Brittany. He had authorized the risk entailed in the encirclement of the German forces in Normandy, under the shadow of the threat of a breakthrough by Kluge at Mortain. But the Supreme Commander could not agree to Montgomery's proposal, dramatic though it seemed on the surface. The Allies were now pursuing a beaten enemy across a broad front. Forcing Patton and Hodges to halt in place would allow many enemy troops to escape to fight another day. Furthermore, until the right flank of Patton's army could join hands with Patch, coming up from Marseilles—which would not take place for another two weeks—the Americans on the south would continue to have a long, exposed, open flank. The amount of resources that the Germans retained available in the heartland was still unknown.

Eisenhower's big problem was supply. The decision to burst out of the lodgement area without stopping to secure the Breton ports was paying dividends. Patton's XII and XX corps were both, on this date, south and west of Paris. Leclerc's French 2d Armored was preparing to assault Paris the next day. But before the forces could go much farther, the Allies would need ports, particularly Marseilles and Antwerp. Capturing these two ports and opening them to Allied use were absolutely necessary, in Eisenhower's view, before his forces could drive into Germany itself.

Despite his insistence on continuing pursuit along two axes, he agreed with Montgomery that *priority* of resources should be allocated to those forces moving northeastward across the Seine. He had several reasons. Besides the overriding need for Antwerp, located in the north, intelligence reported that the bulk of the German Army was headed in the direction of the Lower Rhine; greatest dividends could be obtained by pursuit in that direction. Furthermore, many airfields and flying-bomb sites were located in Belgium and Holland; Eisenhower needed the airfields to provide forward bases for his relatively short-range fighters, and the flying-bomb sites had to be overrun to put a stop to the destruction they were working on the city of London. Finally, the area of the Lower Rhine offered the best avenue to future isolation of the Ruhr.

Eisenhower reached an understanding with Montgomery that priority of Allied logistical support should, for the moment, go to Montgomery's 21 Army Group. Within Bradley's 12 Army Group priority of supplies would be given to Hodges' First Army to facilitate protection of Montgomery's right flank. This meant that Patton, then driving toward Nancy, Metz, and eventually the Saar, would have to make do on a shoestring.

Despite Eisenhower's willingness to give priority to 21 Army Group in the north, Montgomery was not satisfied. As the discussion came to a close that August afternoon, Montgomery felt that Eisenhower was being motivated not by military but by political reasons, that he was unwilling to stop either American forces driving in the south or British forces driving in the north because of public opinion in both countries. But returning to Supreme Headquarters,

Eisenhower found the British members of his own staff in full agreement with his decision to continue the pursuit on both fronts. His deputy, Air Chief Marshal Tedder, could not credit even Montgomery's really believing he could drive to Berlin without first taking Antwerp. The SHAEF deputy chief of operations, Major General J. F. M. Whiteley, put it differently, asking pointedly why we should have 75 percent of our troops "sitting on their hind ends" while 25 percent pursued the Germans. The SHAEF intelligence officer, Major General Sir Kenneth W. D. Strong, also doubted the success of a pencil-like thrust at that moment. As long as Hitler remained in control and people like Model were in charge of the German armies, Strong reasoned, it was essential for the Allies to consolidate their logistical situation before advancing even to the Rhine.

The decision has been debated considerably since the end of the war. Montgomery seems to have had few supporters, even among the British officers actually engaged. The principal exception was the chief of the Imperial General Staff, Field Marshal Sir Alan Brooke. In contrast, British officers at SHAEF agreed with Eisenhower's views, finding the decision reasonable.

But the most convincing refutation of Montgomery's argument comes from his own chief of staff, Major General Sir Francis de Guingand, a brilliant and personable man whose loyalty to Montgomery has never been questioned. He sums up his arguments in his book *Operation Victory:*

> It is only fair to say that throughout the war, this was the only major issue over which I did not agree with my Chief. I have always held the contrary view, and in the event, I am more than ever convinced that I was right. . . . In general, Eisenhower was agreed that the major effort should be North of the Ruhr, but *he did not believe that the strength of forces which we could maintain without the use of Antwerp would be sufficient to finish the war—especially in view of the nearness of winter.* He also could not agree to relegating a large portion of the American armies to a purely static role—virtually without the means to manoeuvre. He, therefore, agreed to Patton's Army advancing toward Verdun. Montgomery felt that it should be halted protecting Paris from the east. There were, I think, certain factors that the Supreme Commander had to take into account which Montgomery did not perhaps fully appreciate. . . . I feel myself that even if we had been able to get a sizeable force across the Rhine into Germany in the autumn, the Germans, after a period of crisis, would have produced sufficient troops to strangle its effectiveness. The flanks of our salient would have been particularly vulnerable. . . . *My conclusion is, therefore, that Eisenhower was right when in August he decided that he could not concentrate sufficient administrative resources to allow one strong thrust deep into Germany north of the Rhine with the hope of decisive success.* If he had not taken the steps he did to link up at an early date with "Anvil" and had held back Patton, and had

diverted the administrative resources so released to the north, *I think it possible that we might have obtained a bridgehead over the Rhine before the winter—but not more.*[1]

There the matter lies, for the judgment of future historians.

From the viewpoint of the Americans, Bradley and Patton in particular, it can hardly be said that the decision to give 21 Army Group priority of supplies was received with joy. At the end of August, Patton's Third U.S. Army had reached a position 35 miles from Metz and 70 miles from the Saar, with nothing visible in the way except the fortifications of the Siegfried Line, currently reported empty. On August 30 Patton requisitioned 400,000 gallons of gasoline, receiving on that day only 31,000 in his forward dumps. He was never one to make modest claims. In this instance he blustered that had he received 400,000 gallons (a request that even Bradley admitted was fantastic) he could have gone all the way into Germany.

Nobody contests that Patton's Third Army could have gone farther than it did—had it been provided with more gasoline. But going farther would have cut into the supplies sent to the main effort in the north. On neither front, in General Eisenhower's judgment, could decisive results—that is, a termination of the war in the early fall—be obtained. Patton protested, deadlined some of his vehicles, and moved forward as best he could.[2]

Bradley sympathized. He, also, hated to see prizes untaken because of a famine in supply. But he tried his best to be objective. At first he urged that only one corps of Hodges' First Army be sent north of the Ardennes on Montgomery's south flank. Nevertheless, on looking at the problem with maximum possible detachment, Bradley could see the overall virtues of giving priority to the main effort northward.

The communications zones behind the army groups were faced with a formidable task. A prodigious amount of supply was required to maintain the pursuit. A division in battle normally needed up to 600 or 700 tons of supplies per day; thus, with 36 divisions in action, the Allies were required to deliver to forward areas considerably more than 20,000 tons of supply daily. Also, the type of supply to be delivered had to be calculated in all planning. Generally the amount of ammunition expended in a combat action is inverse to the amount of gasoline consumed, depending on whether the force is engaged in heavy fighting or in pursuit. During early September, of

[1] Francis de Guingand, *Operation Victory* (New York: Scribner's, 1947), pp. 411–13. Italics supplied.

[2] A newspaper reporter visiting Patton's headquarters at this time reported to one of Eisenhower's aides that the Supreme Commander was being referred to as "the best general the British have." The aide was indiscreet enough to pass this on to his boss.

course, with the Allies pursuing across the Seine, the heaviest requirement was for gasoline, approximately a million gallons per day, whereas later, during the peak of heavy fighting, each field army would use about 2,000 tons of ammunition a day.[3] Obviously all units would have to operate on a minimum of supplies and perform only essential missions. It was also apparent that the pursuit would eventually come to an end, more through the overstretching of the supply lines than through enemy defensive action.

Since the American armies had now reached a line that the Allies had expected to reach in nine months rather than ninety days, the basic problem in resupply was transportation; there was no lack of supplies on the beaches. By the end of August, 95 percent of all supplies available on the European continent were in depots near Cherbourg, on beaches at Arromanches (an artificial port in the British sector), and on Omaha Beach. Virtually no supplies existed between these stocks and the army dumps which, by this time, were 300 miles distant. Turn-around time for trucking operations had now increased to five days.

To complicate the transportation problem, the Allies had to cope with the effectiveness of their earlier air assaults. The French railway system had been virtually demolished west of Paris by Allied bombing. Until these rail lines could be restored, the Allies would have to depend on motor transportation for all their resupply.

Eventually the answer to the supply problem would lie in the capture of more ports closer to the front. Antwerp was to be the foremost. Not only did Antwerp possess a tremendous capacity; it was located close to the borders of Germany, thus minimizing hauling distance. Once Antwerp was opened, its capacity to support troops on the frontiers of Germany would be dramatic. It was able to support fifty divisions, including reserve supplies, whereas Cherbourg remained limited to thirteen.[4]

Still the headlong pursuit continued. On September 2 General "Lightning Joe" Collins' VII Corps of First Army bumped into the rear of a retreating German unit in the vicinity of Mons, Belgium, and creating a pincers resembling that of a small Falaise Pocket, the VII and XIX corps trapped a total of 25,000 prisoners. British spearheads moved 195 miles in four days in early September; on September 4 the British 11th Armoured Division entered Antwerp and secured it almost without damage, an unusual exploit. On September 11 First U.S. Army units set foot on German soil in the vicinity of Aachen. On the same day Patton's right flank joined hands with the French II Corps, under Patch's Seventh Army, at Sombernon, creating a solid front from Switzerland to the Baltic.

---

[3] Leigh gives the figure of 1,000 tons of ammunition daily for ten days as the amount expended by a single corps on Metz.

[4] Randolph Leigh, *40,000,000 Tons to Eisenhower* (Washington: Infantry Journal Press, 1946), p. 38. Much of the following material comes from this source.

Now all of France was cleared except for those highly contested areas Alsace and Lorraine, where the Germans had dug themselves in at the Vosges Mountains and showed every sign of preparing for fierce resistance. In Southwest France the remnants of German forces, cut off from all German surface transportation, gave themselves up. At one point, a body of 20,000 German soldiers surrendered to an American platoon guarding on the Loire, commanded by a second lieutenant named Sam Magill, of the 83d Infantry Division.

Though seized almost intact on September 4 by the British 11th Armoured Division, Antwerp could not be used as a port for some time, for the Germans still controlled the water approach, a long neck of water known as the Scheldt Estuary. In the meantime, the expected linkup with the forces coming from the south would make Marseilles available, a splendid port with an extensive and only slightly damaged railway system running up the smooth valley of the Rhône. Rouen, near the mouth of the Seine, was captured on August 31, and the minor channel ports of Dieppe and Ostend were seized shortly thereafter. Le Havre was taken on September 12.

But pending clearance of rubble and reconstruction of piers, none of these ports could be used immediately; the advance would still be supported for a time over the ever-lengthening distances from the depots in Normandy.

The most famous and effective of the efforts to cope with the supply problem was an operation known as the Red Ball Express. This was the longest one-way truck artery in the world, consisting of a circuit longer than 700 miles. Instituted as an emergency expedient on August 25, 1944, it was manned by a motor transport brigade of the Transportation Corps and was designed to rush more than 80,000 tons of supply to the Chartres-Dreux area by September 1, a week away. All other traffic was excluded from the route. On its peak day, August 29, the 5,400 trucks delivered 12,342 tons from Normandy to the front. The daily average tonnage was more than 5,000. It stayed in operation until November 16.[5]

The Red Ball Express had its drawbacks. It was expensive because of accidents and increased use of gasoline. It caused excessive loss of vehicles from improper maintenance. The emergency atmosphere it engendered later caused a psychological hangover in the form of some breakdown in respect for orderly driving rules. But without the Red Ball Express the advances across France could not have been made.

The logical successor to long-haul supply by truck was delivery of freight by rail. The process of rehabilitating the railway lines began as soon as the

[5] There were other highways besides the Red Ball. The White Ball Highway, which went into operation on October 6, reached from Le Havre, after its capture on September 12, finally extending to Reims. On September 16 the Lions Express began to operate between Bayeux on the beachhead and Brussels.

Normandy beachhead was secure. Trains were actually in operation before Cobra. During the pursuit in August the railroaders, like the truckers, performed titanic jobs. As General Haislip's XV Corps headed northward toward Falaise from Le Mans, General Patton wanted the Avranches-Laval-Le Mans line rebuilt immediately. Five engineer regiments built the new line within 48 hours, including the construction of seven railroad bridges.[6] In mid-August Patton predicted that he could take Paris in two weeks given thirty trains of ammunition and gasoline. Thirty-six trains were delivered to him in five days. As it turned out, First U.S. Army rather than the Third actually took the city, but the first Allied supply train went into Paris on August 30.

During all this time the Allies maintained the ability to deliver some supply by air.[7] Much of the time theater troop carrier aircraft were used for this purpose. Since such missions conflicted with the various airborne attacks being planned, each one required a decision by the Supreme Commander. As it turned out, the advances on the ground were so swift that each planned airborne assault was found unnecessary before it was even launched.

But despite the all-out effort of the supply services it was impossible to avoid the inevitable stretch-out. The supply trucks and trains had to travel two miles more for every mile advanced. The helter-skelter pursuit across France and Belgium was coming to an end.

On September 10, the day before Patton's Third Army linked up with Patch's Seventh, General Eisenhower, accompanied by his deputy, Air Chief Marshal Tedder, and Lieutenant General Sir Humfrey M. Gale, traveled to Brussels for another important meeting with newly promoted Field Marshal Montgomery. Three days earlier, returning from a visit to the front, Eisenhower had come close to personal disaster. The pilot of his light aircraft had decided that because of a local storm they could not land on the strip near Eisenhower's forward headquarters. The only alternative was a neighboring beach, formerly mined by the Germans. With some apprehension they had landed safely and jumped out. While pulling the plane to a spot where it would be safe from the surf, the Supreme Commander had wrenched his bad knee severely and was now a temporary cripple. As a result, this meeting with Montgomery was held in Eisenhower's plane.

The purpose of the conference was to discuss Montgomery's scheme for a dramatic operation northward from the Second British Army positions in the Escaut Canal, the objective being to seize a bridgehead across the Lower Rhine River, some 60 miles away.

With the attachment of the First Allied Airborne Army to 21 Army Group

---

[6] Leigh, *op. cit.*, p. 50.

[7] It will be recalled that Eisenhower's promise of 2,000 tons a day by air made it possible for Bradley to continue the drive toward Argentan in early August despite the threat of German counterattack at Mortain.

and with a top priority in supplies, there was hope, held by General Eisenhower and Field Marshal Montgomery alike, that this ambitious goal could be reached. At the very least, large areas of Holland would be liberated, and quite possibly elements of the German Fifteenth Army to the west could be cut off and eventually destroyed.

As they discussed the various possibilities, Eisenhower rather reluctantly conceded that this plan, named Operation Market-Garden, would temporarily constitute the main effort of Montgomery's 21 Army Group. This meant that the First Canadian Army, whose task it was to clear the Scheldt Estuary, would have to make do with extremely limited fire support and supplies. However, he remained adamant in refusing to accept Montgomery's renewed appeal for all the resources in the theater.

"No," he said flatly. "I will do everything possible to aid you in getting the necessary bridgehead from which a deeper invasion of Germany can be launched, but that once done, the port of Antwerp *must* be opened."

The target date for Operation Market-Garden was September 17, a week after the meeting. However, on return to his headquarters Montgomery had second thoughts. The next day he concluded that supply would require the operation to be postponed to September 26. Immediately General Eisenhower sent Lieutenant General Walter Bedell Smith, his chief of staff, to see the Field Marshal and to promise him an additional 1,000 tons per day from U.S. truck companies and theater aerial resupply. Montgomery, seemingly content, rescheduled the operation for September 17.

The allocation of this much additional supply from U.S. and theater resources was no small item. It meant that three U.S. infantry divisions arriving in the Cherbourg area were to be deprived of their transportation, the trucks rather to be used to carry supplies for Market-Garden. By giving this support to the airborne thrust, Eisenhower was temporarily depriving General Bradley of the use of a sizable part of his force.

Operation Market-Garden was to be the first opportunity since D-Day for the airborne forces to prove their worth. For the airborne experts, anxious for employment, the pursuit had been a frustrating period. The rapidity of the ground advances across France had caused the cancellation of eighteen different plans for drops in the course of forty days, the most ambitious of which was planned to secure the Paris-Orléans Gap in early August.

All echelons of command were anxious to test the usefulness of the airborne arm, but Operation Market-Garden was not just a stunt. General Bradley, who opposed it, later called it "one of the most imaginative plans of the war." In essence, the plan involved airborne seizure of bridgeheads over a series of five obstacles in a northward path of advance. This airborne portion of the operation was known as Market. At the same time, the follow-up phase (Garden) under the command of British XXX Corps (Lieutenant General

Brian G. Horrocks) and spearheaded by the Guards Armoured Division, was to advance along a single road following the path of the airborne units. The final objective was still in Holland, a bridgehead over the Lower Rhine at Arnhem.

This axis, though relatively remote from the Ruhr, had the advantage of outflanking the Siegfried defenses while remaining within favorable operating range for the airborne forces. Furthermore, it was possible to achieve tactical surprise.

The operation jumped off on schedule, September 17. All three airborne divisions dropped on time. German reaction was unexpectedly strong, but by midnight the 101st and 82d U.S. Airborne divisions were well established in their prescribed zones near Eindhoven and Nijmegen (see map below). The 1st British Airborne "Red Devils" Division had dropped off target—nearly eight miles west of Arnhem—and had lost the effect of surprise. Regardless of this mishap, the division took the north end of the Arnhem highway bridge during the day.

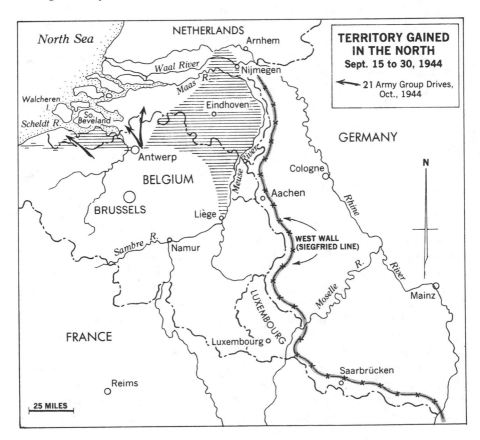

TERRITORY GAINED IN THE NORTH
Sept. 15 to 30, 1944

← 21 Army Group Drives, Oct., 1944

The attack of the XXX British Corps, however, ran into unexpectedly heavy opposition. It soon became obvious that Field Marshal Walther Model's reorganization of the defeated German forces in his short tenure of command was highly effective. In this Arnhem area he had gathered a respectable force of parachute and SS panzer troops.

The Guards Armoured Division, nevertheless, continued attacking north. It did not reach the Lower Rhine in force until September 24, a week after the start of the operation.

By this time the situation of the 1st British Airborne Division across the Lower Rhine had become desperate. Communications were virtually lost for three days following the drop. The part of the 1st British Airborne that had taken the northern end of the bridge across the Lower Rhine was cut off from the rest of the division. Unpredictable bad weather starting on September 18 rendered resupply efforts only 30 percent effective. On September 21 the group holding the Arnhem highway bridge was forced to surrender.

With all these eventualities, British Second Army realized by September 23 that the situation was grim. General Miles Dempsey gave General Horrocks permission to withdraw the Red Devils back across the Rhine. Horrocks would not give up yet, and did everything he could to relieve the division on the twenty-fourth, but by now the perimeter had shrunk to an area of about a half mile square, and on the next night Horrocks ordered the withdrawal of all forces.

By 6:00 A.M., September 26, when intense enemy fire made further crossings impossible, about 2,400 men of the 1st Airborne Division, the Polish Parachute Brigade, and the 4th Battalion of the Dorsetshire Regiment made their way back across the Lower Rhine to friendly territory. Other battalions of the Dorsets covered the operation from the north bank. The effort to cross the Rhine by taking a long chance had failed.

Some of the strongest fighting was yet to come. Between September 19 and October 4, no fewer than twelve German attacks of divisional or greater strength were launched against the Eindhoven-Arnhem salient. The Allies, for their part, gradually reinforced the corridor and widened it. British forces pushed west, eventually establishing a firm line running along the Waal and Maas rivers. To the east, the corridor was widened to bring 21 Army Group in line with the 12th.

Operation Market was the largest airborne operation by Allied forces so far in the war. More than 20,000 troops were dropped by parachute, and nearly 14,000 landed in gliders. Nearly 35,000 troops and more than 5,000 tons of material were transported by air, including 2,000 vehicles and 568 artillery pieces. Air forces flew more than 7,800 sorties.[8] Its cost was heavy.

---

[8] Report by the Supreme Commander to the Combined Chiefs of Staff on the Operations in Europe of the Allied Expeditionary Force, 6 June 1944 to 8 May 1945.

British airborne troops lost more than 7,000 killed, wounded, and missing. The U.S. 82d Airborne lost more than 1,400, and the 101st U.S. Airborne lost more than 2,000. Including the 1st Polish Parachute Brigade, American glider pilots, and air transport units, the airborne phase cost 11,850 Allied casualties. In the ground phase, it is estimated that the British lost nearly 1,500.

Compared to the most ambitious hopes for it, Market-Garden was a failure. It had not turned the Siegfried Line or secured a bridgehead over the Lower Rhine. Field Marshal Montgomery has attributed the failure to achieve ultimate gains to a couple of tactical mistakes on his own part, to bad weather, and—despite his willingness at the time to go ahead—to a lack of sufficient logistical support.

These are second guesses. The fact is that the Allied High Command, particularly Eisenhower and Montgomery, considered the effort a worthwhile gamble. They took it, and lost, even though with the losing they achieved a salient 60 miles into enemy territory. Market-Garden was at a close.

With the failure to secure a bridgehead over the Lower Rhine River, it was now obvious to the Allies, even to the most optimistic, that the Germans had recovered a very considerable amount of fighting strength and were still a force to be reckoned with. The gamble lost, the Allies' main concern now had to be the establishment of a firm logistical base from which to defeat a determined enemy.

No one felt this need more keenly than the Supreme Commander. On September 22, 1944, while Market-Garden was nearing is unhappy climax, General Eisenhower called a meeting of his top commanders in Brussels. Field Marshal Montgomery excused himself from attendance on the basis of the degenerating situation at Arnhem. He sent in his place his chief of staff, Major General "Freddie" de Guingand.

Much of the Brussels meeting concerned plans for future operations, but highest on Eisenhower's list of priorities was the protection of the city of Antwerp, seized more than two weeks before, and the clearing of the Scheldt Estuary.

The port of Antwerp is located in a somewhat unusual geographical position. Though the city itself is Belgian, the estuary that provides its access to the North Sea passes mainly through Dutch territory. On the south is a thin sliver of Holland, containing the cities of Terneuzen and Breskens, which is not connected by land with other Dutch territory. To the north is the peninsula of South Beveland, which extends to meet the island of Walcheren about 40 miles northwest of Antwerp. Both were still occupied by the Germans. Thus possession of Antwerp itself was only the beginning of the process of its rehabilitation for use as a port.

Montgomery could no longer regard the clearing of the Scheldt Estuary as a second-priority task. He gave Lieutenant General Henry D. G. Crerar's First Canadian Army, whose mission it was, priority of supplies. Crerar employed the I British Corps (attached to First Canadian Army) along the north bank and the II Canadian Corps along the south, both heading almost westward. The operation called for several amphibious landings.

On October 2, 1944, the 2d Canadian Division (II Canadian Corps) began its thrust west to clear the south bank. The attacks farther east went slowly, and it was October 24 before I British Corps was in a position to move westward along South Beveland. Progress was now rapid, and by October 26 British troops were only six miles short of the Beveland Canal.

On October 16 Montgomery shut down all offensive operations except those in the Scheldt. He instructed General Dempsey to deploy Second British Army in support of Canadian First Army. To help Dempsey do so, Montgomery requested and was granted help. First U.S. Army took over part of Dempsey's territory.

Meanwhile operations of the II Canadian Corps continued along the mainland to the south of the Estuary. By November 3 all German troops on the south bank of the Scheldt were cleared.

With the clearing of South Beveland peninsula on the north, the problem was reduced to the subjugation of Walcheren Island. The British had good historical reason to remember this piece of ground. In 1809 a force of 40,000 men was dispatched to Walcheren against Napoleon. Half the British force became casualties. This was the last British expedition against the Continent (except for Spain) until Waterloo, six years later. In 1944 the island was garrisoned by remnants of a German division and other elements of the German Fifteenth Army, the total estimated at between 6,000 and 7,000 men.

The difficulties of landing on the island were heightened by previous air strikes against the dike system intended to flood out the island positions and defensive batteries. Dikes had been blown in four places. These bombings had not wiped out the positions endangering Allied shipping, even though they put much of the island waist-deep in water, thereby making operations all the more difficult for the attacking forces.

Operations against Walcheren Island began on November 1. Early in the morning troops of the Royal Marine 4th Special Service Brigade (Commandos), followed by two battalions of the 2d British Infantry Division, reached the waterfront near Flushing (Vlissingen) without heavy casualties. Meanwhile another force approached the coast supported by naval units, landing at Westkapelle. As these two amphibious assaults were launched, the Canadians crossed the narrow neck of water from South Beveland to Walcheren Island. On November 2 Flushing was captured; only mopping up was left. To the surprise of the Allies, the number of prisoners taken exceeded the number of German troops previously estimated to be on the island.

British and Canadian casualties were heavy. Anyone tempted to consider the Scheldt Estuary operation a minor one might note that Commonwealth casualties exceeded 27,000 men, more than the total number of Allied casualties sustained in the invasion of Sicily a little more than a year before.

The Scheldt Estuary was now free of enemy, but the long channel was yet to be swept. Sixteen sweepings were required before the channel was usable. As a result it was November 28, 1944, before the first Allied convoy was safely berthed at Antwerp. Of the 40,000 tons of supplies that Antwerp was to unload per day, more than half would be scheduled for American forces operating in the northern half of the Allied front.

Immediately the Nazis began to hit Antwerp with V-1 rockets, well knowing its incalculable worth to the Allied strategy.

CHAPTER 5

❦

"We Can Still Lose This War in Europe"

WHILE the logistical bases of the western Allied forces were being consolidated by the opening of the ports of Marseilles, Antwerp, Le Havre, and others, the eyes of the Allied High Command quite naturally were focused on the east, where Nazi Germany would make a final stand to protect its homeland.

The momentum of the pursuit across France, Belgium, Luxembourg, and part of the Netherlands had carried the Allies past two great obstacles: the Seine River and its tributaries flowing northwest across France and the formidable Meuse River, whose winding gorge stretches from Alsace-Lorraine northward into Belgium and Holland, where, as the Maas, it empties itself into the North Sea.

Two more great obstacles still remained to be crossed. The first, the German "West Wall," commonly known as the Siegfried Line, was an artificial barrier running essentially along the borders of prewar Germany. This powerful defensive position took advantage of all available accidents of terrain. Fallen into disuse after 1940, it was hastily refitted by a frantic Hitler in the summer of 1944. For the Führer, while screaming to his generals that not one inch of territory should be given up, was prudent enough to foresee the possibility that the Germans might yet be defending their 1939 borders.

The usefulness of fixed fortifications has often been derided. The term Maginot Line Complex has become a common, if little understood, part of the layman's military lexicon. But properly used, a fixed fortification such as the Siegfried Line is a potent device. It enables the defender to hold great distances with minimum strength while concentrating mobile forces for powerful offensive action. It was the failure of the French in 1940 to employ the Maginot Line *in conjunction with mobile forces* that led to the widespread condemnation of the line itself.

Behind the Siegfried Line lay the final obstacle between the Allied armies and the heart of Germany: the Rhine River. From its headwaters near Basel, Switzerland, the Rhine heads northward between the Vosges Mountains in

85

France and the German Black Forest; the Franco-German border turns west at Karlsruhe, and the Rhine cuts into German territory, flowing into the North Sea in Holland near the mouth of the Maas. It is Western Europe's most powerful river, and even before D-Day plans for crossing it were being made in England. It was General Eisenhower's fervent hope that Hitler, unwilling to give up any German territory, would fight desperately to hold the Rhineland, subjecting his major forces to destruction west of this formidable obstacle.

Fighting in the autumn of 1944, therefore, consisted of a series of fairly limited attacks on the part of the Allies, in preparation for major offensives to be launched in midwinter and the early spring of 1945. Once Walcheren Island was secured, Montgomery's 21 Army Group turned its attention to clearing the west bank of the Rhine, moving south from the bridgehead over the Maas secured in the Market-Garden operation. Inundation of the lowlands by heavy rains brought progress virtually to a standstill.

For the moment, the main effort of the theater, farther south, consisted of a drive toward Cologne across the Cologne Plain by the newly arrived Ninth U.S. Army (under General William H. Simpson) on the left and part of First U.S. Army on the right. The German city of Aachen (Aix-la-Chapelle), which is in this area, was in Allied hands. Hitler had ordered a bitter, last-ditch defense of the city where Charlemagne was crowned emperor and thus instituted what Hitler liked to call the First Reich. To no avail. The attack eastward from Aachen, preceded by a heavy air bombardment on November 16, finally reached as far as the Roer River. There it was forced to halt temporarily, pending Allied seizure of a complex of dams on the Roer in the vicinity of Schmidt. To cross the Roer downstream (to the north) with these dams still in possession of the Germans would invite disaster. Were the dams to be blown, the resultant flooding would completely cut off those forces already across: there they would sit, without reinforcement, vulnerable to being cut to pieces in detail. The dams had to be taken or destroyed.

An effort was made in October to seize these dams by a surprise attack. The attempt failed. Attacks by Allied airplanes, even with heavy bombs, barely seemed to scratch them. The only recourse was ground attack through the dense and heavily defended Hürtgen Forest. Though the dams were still in German hands at the end of November, the forest itself was cleared in a battle that four gallant U.S. divisions—the 1st, 4th, 9th, and 29th—found the most difficult of the European war. It stands in history comparable to the Argonne in World War I. The 1st Division (reinforced) alone sustained nearly 4,000 battle casualties. Eight thousand men of the First Army in the Hürtgen were lost to combat exhaustion and exposure to the elements. Another 23,000 were killed, wounded, or missing. The attack was to be resumed on December 13.

Farther south, General Patton was finding the going slow. Fighting against stubborn resistance with minimal supplies, Third Army had crossed the Moselle by the middle of November and captured Metz on November 22. While denying the industry of Lorraine to the Reich—and picking up 35,000 prisoners in the process—Patton was now in position to threaten the Saar. Eagerly he looked forward to a strong attack in that region south of the Ardennes. He was to move on December 19, 1944.

The great territorial gains, however, fell to Lieutenant General Jacob L. Devers' 6 Army Group in the south, consisting of U.S. Seventh Army (Patch) and French First Army (de Lattre). In late November Devers' men burst out of the rugged Vosges Mountains, seized Strasbourg, and developed a nearly continuous line along the Rhine from Basel to Karlsruhe, penetrating the Siegfried Line at Wissembourg, west of Karlsruhe, about halfway to the Saar.

One sizable area on the west bank of the Rhine remained in German hands: the Colmar Pocket, named after the most important town in the area. Extending from a point south of Strasbourg upstream (southward) to Mulhouse, a distance of fifty miles, it was about fifty miles deep, and reached all the way to the foothills of the Vosges (see map, p. 397).

This pocket was a matter of deep concern to General Eisenhower. Reviewing the situation, he directed with some heat that no major northward movements toward Bitche and the Siegfried defenses should be attempted until the Colmar Pocket was reduced. He specifically instructed General Devers to this effect, stating further that once this was accomplished Devers should hasten to support Patton's right. Devers optimistically believed that the Colmar Pocket could be promptly reduced by the First French Army without the assistance of the U.S. VI Corps. Consequently he sent the VI Corps northward to assist the XV Corps in attacking on the right of Patton's Third Army.

As it turned out, the French First Army had been seriously weakened by the campaign through the formidable Vosges Mountains and by the detachment of some of its units to contain German holdings in southwest France. At mid-December, General Devers had failed to reduce the Colmar Pocket, which still stood as a thorn in the side of the Allied southern positions.

In many ways these operations from the end of Market-Garden to the middle of December resembled the operation in Normandy nearly half a year before. Attrition was heavy, far heavier on the German side than on the Allied; key terrain positions for future Allied attacks were being seized; the logistical base from which another Cobra could be launched was being solidified for the strike; the Allied war machine was again coiling. And yet to the press, to the people at home, and even to certain members of the governments, the results of the autumn fighting were disappointing. Certainly not everything hoped for had been gained. Market-Garden had failed to achieve a bridgehead over the Lower Rhine; fighting in the Hürtgen Forest had been cruel and not as productive as had been hoped; certain industrial parts of the Saar region remained available to Germany; finally, the Colmar Pocket remained, west of the Rhine. In light of all this, although the situation was improving every day, the optimism of the previous summer was giving way on the domestic fronts to a feeling of some puzzlement.

Meanwhile, the Combined Chiefs of Staff in Washington were considering means by which they could aid an all-out offensive, conceivably to close the war before the end of 1944. One of the means contemplated was the use of the heretofore secret proximity fuse.

General Marshall wrote to General Eisenhower that a CCS memorandum concerning an all-out offensive was being drafted. To this Eisenhower was agreeable but reminded Marshall that the logistical problems, including ammunition, infantry replacements, and so forth, required clearing the approaches to Antwerp as a requisite to waging any final all-out battle. Marshall, soon concluding that no good could come from it, withheld the projected memorandum.

Further, a proposal was being studied by the Chiefs of Staff to shift the priority of bombing targets in Germany from oil refineries to transportation systems, on the theory that this would assist in the immediate battle. Both the air forces and Supreme Headquarters joined in the discussion that went back and forth. The long-range bombers were, as of September, no longer under SHAEF's direct control, and so this was an argument in which General Eisenhower did not have the ultimate responsibility. Nevertheless his preference for the German oil refinery system as the first priority strategic target was accepted.

While these events were taking place, Allied leaders up to the head-of-government level were engaging in a reevaluation of the strategy for the final campaigns to advance into Germany.

In an examination of a map of the German frontiers one's attention is drawn at once to the route of approach to the north, along a line from Brussels northeastward across the Rhine. This northern area is amply supplied with road nets that could handle many divisions, and the country is ideally suited to mobile warfare. With the full concurrence of Field Marshal Montgomery and the less enthusiastic assent of General Bradley (the bulk of whose forces were located to the south), General Eisenhower selected this route as the primary avenue for attacking the Ruhr.

But there is another major avenue also, running almost directly eastward from Paris through the historic cities of Verdun (on the Meuse River) and Metz (on the Moselle) to a secondary industrial area of Germany, the Saar.

This route continues from the Saar past Mainz to a relatively open area known as the Frankfurt Corridor, which, like the northern German Plain, points toward Berlin. If both routes into Germany could be used, an opportunity for a rapid reduction and complete envelopment of the Ruhr would later present itself.

The directive from the Combined Chiefs of Staff to General Eisenhower, on his assumption of office in early 1944, was couched in general terms: "You will enter the continent of Europe and, in conjunction with the other Allied nations, undertake operations aimed at the heart of Germany and the destruction of her armed force." The term "heart of Germany" was left for the Supreme Commander to define, but the meaning of "the destruction of her armed force," a military fundamental, was obvious.

In his own mind Eisenhower defined the heart of Germany as twofold: the political heart was Berlin, the seat of Hitler's government; the industrial heart was the Ruhr, where much of Germany's munitions industry was concentrated. There was no conflict between these two targets; for the main avenue to the Ruhr, the northern avenue, led also to Berlin. In any event the Ruhr would have to be captured or isolated before further decisive measures could be taken.

Since SHAEF planning recognized the preeminence of the northern route to the Ruhr, Eisenhower always visualized the employment of maximum usable forces along that route. Allowance had to be made, however, for seizing other objectives instrumental in the vital mission of destroying enemy armed forces.

The general plan, then, described by General Eisenhower in referring to planning before D-Day, was as follows:

Land on the Normandy coast.

Build up the resources needed for a decisive battle in the Normandy-Brittany region and break out of the enemy's encircling positions. (Land operations in the first two phases were to be under the tactical direction of Montgomery.)

Pursue on a broad front with two army groups, emphasizing the left to gain necessary ports and reach the boundaries of Germany and threaten the Ruhr. On our right we would link up with the forces that were to invade France from the south.

Build up our new base along the western border of Germany, by securing ports in Belgium and in Brittany as well as in the Mediterranean.

While building up our forces for the final battles, keep up an unrelenting offensive to the extent of our means, both to wear down the enemy and to gain advantages for the final fighting.

Complete the destruction of enemy forces west of the Rhine, in the meantime constantly seeking bridgeheads across the river.

Launch the final attack as a double envelopment of the Ruhr, again emphasizing the left, and follow this up by an immediate thrust through Germany, with the specific direction to be determined at the time.

Clean out the remainder of Germany.[1]

Of these phases of the overall plan, the first three had now been accomplished. The fourth, building a new base along the western border of Germany, was well under way. The battles in the autumn would accomplish the fifth, wearing down the enemy and gaining advantage for the final fighting. The stage would then be set for the sixth—completing the destruction of German forces west of the Rhine.

This sixth phase, the destruction of German forces west of the Rhine *before crossing in strength,* was the one with which Field Marshal Montgomery took issue. Not even the conduct of the Market-Garden operation deterred him from continuing to insist that the bulk of the theater's entire resources be allocated to his own forces north of the Ruhr. This was the issue that was being settled while the fateful Arnhem operation was approaching its gloomy climax, and that instigated the meeting at Brussels on September 22, which Montgomery declined to attend. The subsequent failure of the Arnhem operation seemed to dampen his ardor for his own views but little.

Communications between the two high commanders were voluminous and largely repetitive. General Eisenhower felt that in essence they were thinking much alike: the *priority* of resources should be allocated to the forces north of the Ruhr until that area should be isolated, *to the extent that the region could support.* Forces driving to the south toward the Saar would be given a secondary priority. Montgomery differed: he contended that *all* resources necessary for offensive action should be allocated to the north, rendering any simultaneous attack toward the Saar impossible. In this, Montgomery had one staunch ally, the British chief of the Imperial General Staff, Field Marshal Alan Brooke, who appears, on the evidence of his diary, to have been even more vehement on the subject than Montgomery.[2]

However, the Supreme Commander persisted in his plans for the First and Ninth U.S. armies to drive toward Cologne, south of the Ruhr, while the Third attacked also toward the Saar. Meanwhile 21 Army Group set about the clearing of its sector west of the Meuse (Maas) River, and began a drive southward between that stream and the Rhine, in an effort to secure the Rhine at least from Cologne northward. While Montgomery conducted these operations, his disappointment rankled. His protests, along with those of Brooke, came to a new crescendo. On November 28 Brooke took his case to the Prime Minister. He records the interview as follows:

---

[1] Dwight Eisenhower, *Crusade in Europe* (New York: Doubleday, 1948), pp. 228–29.

[2] This is difficult to judge, as Montgomery has not made his own diary public. In an interview on October 1, 1966, he told the author in a jocular manner that publication of his diary would "start World War III."

At 12.30 I went to see the P.M., having asked for an interview with him. I told him I was very worried with the course operations were taking on the Western Front. I said that when we looked facts in the face this last offensive could only be classified as the first strategic reverse that we had suffered since landing in France. I said that in my mind two main factors were at fault, i.e.,

(a) American strategy;

(b) American organization.

As regards the strategy, the American conception of always attacking all along the front, irrespective of strength available, was sheer madness. In the present offensive we had attacked on six Army fronts without any reserves anywhere.

As regards organization, I said that I did not consider that Eisenhower could command both as Supreme Commander and as Commander of the Land Force at the same time. I said that I considered Bradley should be made the Commander of the Land Forces, and the front divided into two Groups of Armies instead of three, with the Ardennes between them; Montgomery to command the Northern and Devers the Southern.[3]

Brooke received no encouragement at this moment.

On the same date General Eisenhower was visiting with Field Marshal Montgomery, who was expressing his views more moderately: "Of course I am primarily concerned with the operations of my own army group," he said, "but Brad's disposition don't look very well balanced tactically to me."

Montgomery went on to suggest that some of Patton's divisions be moved north to restore the "tactical balance," another way of saying: Cancel all offensives except the one in the northern sector. Two days later, however, he wrote the Supreme Commander a letter dubbing recent operations a "strategic reverse." He continued by offering his solution:

> ... 3. We now require a new plan. And this time *we must not fail.* The need to get the German war finished early is vital, in view of other factors. The new plan *must not fail.*
>
> 4. In the new plan we must get away from the doctrine of attacking in so many places that nowhere are we strong enough to get decisive results. We must concentrate such strength on the main selected thrust that success will be certain. It is in this respect that we failed badly in the present operations.[4]

This brought on a rather irate reply:

> I am not quite sure I know exactly what you mean by strategic reverse; certainly to date we have failed to achieve all that we had hoped to by this time, which hopes and plans were based upon conditions as we knew them or estimated them when the plans were made. The Ruhr is an important place,

[3] Arthur Bryant, *Triumph in the West* (New York: Doubleday, 1959), p. 257.

[4] Forrest Pogue, *The Supreme Command* (Washington: Dept. of the Army, 1954), p. 312.

but let us never forget for one second that our primary objective is to defeat the Germans who are barring our way into Germany. The Ruhr itself was always given as a geographical objective, not only for its importance to Germany, but because it was believed that in that region the German forces would be largely concentrated to meet our attacks.

Specifically, I agree to the following:

a. We must determine how much profit there is in the continuation of our current attacks in the 12th Army Group area, and whether they give real promise of reaching the Rhine.

b. We must recast our future general plans in the light of conditions as they now exist.

c. We must choose the best line of attack to assure success, including the maintenance of deception lines. . . .

I do not agree that things have gone badly since Normandy, merely because we have not gained all we had hoped to gain. In fact, the situation is somewhat analogous to that which existed in Normandy for so long. Our line as late as D plus 60 was not greatly different than what we hoped to hold in the first week, but I never looked upon the situation then existing as a strategic reverse, even though out of the circumstances of our long confinement in the narrow beach head have developed some of our greatest later difficulties. If we had advanced from the beginning *as we had hoped,* our maintenance services would have been in a position to supply us during the critical September days, when we actually reached the limit of our resources.

Moreover, I do not agree that more strength could have been thrown to the North than was actually maintained there during early September. Lines of communication in the north were so stretched that even delivery of five hundred tons to you at Brussels cost Bradley three divisions, the possession of which might have easily placed him on the Rhine in the Worms area.

We gained a great victory in Normandy. Bradley's brilliant breakthrough made possible the great exploitation by all forces, which blasted France and Belgium and almost carried us across the Rhine. Had we not advanced on a relatively broad front, we would now have the spectacle of a long narrow line of communication, constantly threatened on the right flank and weakened by detachments of large fighting formations. In addition, we would have had a similar picture in the south, stretching all the way from Marseilles to Dijon. As it is, we now have a rear that is cleared of the enemy. We can look to the front.

I have no intention of stopping Devers' and Patton's operations as long as they are cleaning up our right flank and giving us *capability of concentration.* On the other hand, I do not intend to push these attacks senselessly. . . .

I most definitely appreciate the frankness of your statements, and the usual friendly way in which they are stated, but I beg of you not to continue to look upon the past performances of this great fighting force as a failure because we have not achieved all that we could have hoped.

I am quite sure that you, Bradley, and I can remain masters of the situation and the victory we want will certainly be achieved. But we must look at this whole great affair stretching from Marseilles to the lower Rhine as one great theater. We must plan so when our next attack starts we will be able to obtain maximum results from all our forces, under the conditions now existing. IKE.[5]

The Field Marshal quickly answered. He assured General Eisenhower that when he had referred to "failures," he did not mean failures of the entire campaign but rather failure specifically to implement the current strategic plan, issued formally on October 28.

Apparently the gloomy outlook of Brooke and Montgomery soon communicated itself to the Prime Minister. On December 6 Churchill wrote to President Roosevelt, saying, "The time has come for me to place before you the serious and disappointing war situation which faces us at the close of this year." While conceding the fine victories on the western front, he pointed out that the Allies had not yet reached the Rhine in the northern sector and feared that it would be many weeks before they could hope to reach that river and establish bridgeheads. He reviewed the Allied military situation in Italy (meanwhile squeezing in a remark about the adverse effects that the execution of Anvil was having on the Italian theater). He expressed disappointment at not being able to withdraw five British and British-Indian divisions from Europe to send to Mountbatten and deplored the escape of a large part of the German forces in the Balkan Peninsula. Finally he feared China's elimination as a combatant.

The Prime Minister now proposed another meeting of the Big Three, or at least a meeting between himself and President Roosevelt with their respective staffs. Churchill asked that if Roosevelt were unable to come to London before February, he send his Chiefs of Staff to Europe where "the whole stormy scene can be calmly and patiently studied with a view to action as closely concerted as that which signalised our campaigns of 1944." [6]

When he learned of this communication, for one of the few times in their long, close association General Eisenhower was irked at his friend Churchill. He recalled the early spring of 1944, during the preparations for Overlord, when he personally had constantly assured the Prime Minister that the Allied forces would be on the borders of Germany by early winter. His optimism at the time was gently but invariably derided by Churchill. He recalled Churchill's often expressed doubts about the advisability of executing Overlord at all, and Field Marshal Brooke's arguments at the conference at Algiers in June, 1943, when Brooke had gone so far as to urge Eisenhower to abandon any thought of major land operations in Europe during the next year.

Now, with things going almost exactly as he had predicted, Eisenhower

---

[5] Pogue, *op. cit.,* pp. 313–14.
[6] Winston Churchill, *Triumph and Tragedy* (Boston: Houghton, 1953), p. 270.

found himself harassed by outside pressure to change his basic plan radically. He flatly refused.

President Roosevelt's answer to Churchill reflected the basic American viewpoint: "On the European front," he wrote, "I always felt that the occupation of Germany up to the left bank of the Rhine would be a very stiff job. Because in the old days I bicycled over most of the Rhine terrain, I have never been as optimistic as to the ease of getting across the Rhine with our joint armies as many of the commanding officers have been.

"However," the President went on, "our agreed broad strategy is developing according to plan." He visualized himself and the Prime Minister in the position of commanders in chief who had committed their resources to battle, and he expressed confidence in the outcome. "I cannot see clearly just when, but soon a decisive break in our favor is bound to come." He wound up by tactfully refusing to send his Chiefs of Staff away from their posts, "since no requirement exists for broad strategic decisions to guide our field commanders. . . ."

Mr. Churchill took the rebuff with good grace.

Concurrent with all the discussion of the "broad front" versus the "single thrust," Montgomery continued a campaign for the appointment of a single, overall ground commander. Implicit in this campaign was an assumption that the land commander to be named would be himself, as he had been the one previously charged with detailed coordination between the army groups. At times his argument favored merely a single commander for the two army groups operating north of the Ardennes, with another commander for the army group located south of that area. On occasion, to strengthen his argument, he offered to serve under General Bradley if such was the Supreme Commander's preference. (As Montgomery ranked Bradley by two grades, this offer was unlikely to be implemented.) However, he visualized that no matter what the arrangement, he would retain command of his own army group, even if exercising coordinating responsibilities for others. Eisenhower refused to take such action, which he considered ridiculous.

Montgomery resorted to other avenues. On the occasion of a visit by General Marshall on October 8, Montgomery informed the U.S. Chief of Staff that since the Supreme Commander had taken personal command of the land battle, the armies had become separated "nationally and not geographically," and that "grip and operational direction" were lacking.

Receiving no encouragement from Marshall, Montgomery continued the argument in a series of communications with Field Marshal Brooke. Brooke seems to have been equally convinced—though perhaps for other reasons—that an overall ground commander in Europe was a necessity. Their correspondence, as outlined in Brooke's memoirs, reads something like the minutes of a meeting of the Conway Cabal.[7] They were not, of course, advocating Eisenhower's outright removal, but rather a device for lessening his influence on tactical ground operations.

One of Brooke's opinions, however, could hardly have given Montgomery much comfort. Recognizing that American strength in Europe now vastly overshadowed that of the British, he mentioned in a letter to Montgomery the view he had expressed to the Prime Minister on November 28: the Americans would never accede to the permanent assignment of 12 Army Group under command of Montgomery. If an overall ground commander were appointed, he feared, that individual would have to be Bradley rather than Montgomery.[8] The issue was closed, for the rest of the autumn at least, only to crop up virulently later—in the Battle of the Bulge.

General Eisenhower concluded that a conference to achieve some meeting of minds was necessary. Accordingly, he joined his principal commanders, Montgomery and Bradley, and his deputy, Air Chief Marshal Tedder, at Maastricht on December 7, 1944. It was a historic meeting. The pictures of the principals going to and from the meeting show them all wreathed in jovial smiles. But the discussions themselves were serious, even tense. Montgomery was given the opportunity to speak his piece in full.

His argument contained little that was new. Once more he declared the current operational plan of October 28 obsolete, stating that it was impossible to attack both the Ruhr and the Saar at the same time. A new plan was needed, he said, envisaging the continuation of the battle all through the winter months, gaining intermediate objectives toward the Ruhr, wearing down enemy strength, and placing the Allies in a good jump-off position for a mobile campaign in the spring. (This last point had long been Eisenhower's basic objective in the autumn campaign.)

By his account Montgomery suggested that to implement his scheme both 12 and 21 Army groups operate north of the Ardennes, with the right flank of 12 Army Group resting on the German town of Prüm (in the Eifel, north of the Moselle). Two armies of Bradley's, consisting of about thirty-five divisions, would drive toward the Rhine, one from Prüm to Bonn, the other from Düren to Cologne. The left, or northern, army in 12 Army Group (in this case the Ninth Army), comprising about ten divisions, would operate northward toward the thrust of 21 Army Group, which was currently moving southward to clear the area between the Meuse and the Rhine. These two converging armies would receive "all support." Target date for the jump-off would be January 1.

[7] A plot instituted by Brigadier General Thomas Conway, in 1777, to replace Washington at Valley Forge with General Horatio Gates. Bungled, it came to naught.

[8] At this time Brooke was apparently discounting the prospect of a ground deputy to Eisenhower coming from outside the European theater.

Then came the hooker. One commander, Montgomery contended, should be in operational control of all forces north of the Ardennes. He asserted once more that if it should be so directed, he would willingly serve under Bradley.

In answer to this presentation, General Eisenhower warned against neglecting everything except the Ruhr; the Ruhr was merely a geographical objective, which did not directly involve the destruction of enemy armed forces. Until these forces were eliminated, all plans had to consider the entire front and all our assets. Eisenhower disagreed with moving the entire 12 Army Group so far to the north. The right wing should be strong, he felt, and should advance south of the Ardennes to the Rhine at about Worms, later developing a strong thrust on the axis from Frankfurt to Kassel.

On the other hand, he was ready to place the Ninth U.S. Army, consisting of ten divisions, under temporary command of 21 Army Group and to locate Montgomery's southern boundary on the Rhine near the northwest corner of the Ruhr. The task of the reinforced 21 Army Group, therefore, would be to cross the Rhine and outflank the Ruhr from the north. First U.S. Army (Hodges) of 12 Army Group, operating south of 21 Army Group, would constitute a containing force, and make feints and threats in the Bonn-Cologne area and south of it. On the southern flank the right wing of 12 Army Group (Patton) would develop a strong thrust through the Saar toward the approaches to the Frankfurt-Kassel corridor. The general pattern would therefore include two offensives, one around the north of the Ruhr and one in the south. In between would be threats and feints.

The divergence between the two commanders' viewpoints did not lie in the direction of the main effort; both were agreed that maximum practical force should be brought to bear in the north. The point at issue was still—as it had been for some time—whether there should be, in addition to the northern thrust, a secondary thrust in strength south of the Ardennes. To Eisenhower this still did not represent a fundamental divergence of opinion; to Montgomery it still did.

When Eisenhower stuck to his guns, Montgomery concluded that he had achieved nothing at the Maastricht conference. For his own part, Eisenhower believed that he had made substantial concessions in attaching Simpson's Ninth U.S. Army to Montgomery. But Patton's attack south of the Ardennes was to go on; Patton would not be bereft of all his offensive capability in order to send unneeded reinforcements to the northern attack. The significance of this decision was to be borne out a little more than one week later.[9]

---

[9] The Maastricht meeting practically terminated the discussions. But Brooke made at least one more effort with the Prime Minister, who was now apparently reconciled to the Supreme Commander's strategy. Brooke's diary, quoted in Bryant, *op. cit.*, p. 266, gives this account:

> At 6 p.m. met Ike and Tedder with P.M. in the latter's Map Room, with the whole Chiefs of Staff. Ike explained his plan which contemplates a double advance

In evaluating the pros and cons of these arguments, it is well to consider first of all whether the final plan agreed on at Maastricht was a good one. Taken as a whole it is difficult to see how a better one could have been devised. The plan placed maximum weight in the north while continuing relentless pressure throughout the winter against an enemy with dwindling resources. It provided for the entire strength of 21 Army Group plus a U.S. Army strength of ten divisions—twenty-five divisions in all—to clear the near side of the Rhine in the north and later to cross the river in that area. It allowed for encirclement of the Ruhr before proceeding with the advance across Germany. It maintained strength south of the Ardennes, not only to threaten the Saar but also to prevent concentration of German forces against the major thrust in the north.

The logic that Montgomery and Brooke used in attempting to force cancellation of Patton's attacks south of the Ardennes is difficult to support. They themselves admitted that the conditions for immediate exploitation in the north toward the heart of Germany—if indeed those conditions had ever existed—had passed. Market-Garden should have helped drive this home. It might be noted that while they were insistent on a tactical concentration of *all* resources in one area *within Northern Europe,* Montgomery and Brooke took a different view on a global scale. Brooke, for one thing, vigorously objected to the reduction of forces in Italy to reinforce Overlord, the decisive thrust into Germany.

True, a concentrated narrow thrust in the north had an appealing note to the British. It gave hope of a quick end to the war. Americans were anxious to get the war over as soon as possible, but American feelings on this point could hardly be expected to parallel those of the British, who had thrown their last military resources into the European effort. By one account, the British were 85,000 men short in meeting their military demands for the year 1944, and prospects of closing the gap seemed slim.[10] Add to this the realization that the nation had been at war for five years, and many of its troops had been overseas for nearly the whole time. The appeal of any plan, no mat-

---

into Germany, north of Rhine and by Frankfurt. I disagreed flatly with it, accused Ike of violating principles of concentration of force, which had resulted in his present failures. I criticized his future plans and pointed out impossibility of double invasion with the limited forces he has got. I stressed the importance of concentrating on one thrust. I drew attention to the fact that with his limited forces any thought of attack on both fronts could only lead to dispersal of effort.

Quite impossible to get the P.M. to understand the importance of the principles involved. Half the time his attention was concentrated on the possibility of floating mines down the Rhine! He must get down to detail. . . .

Finally dined at 10 Downing Street with P.M., Ike, Tedder, Cunningham, Portal and Ismay. Conversations again to the same topic of the strategy, but I got no further in getting either Winston or Ike to see that their strategy is fundamentally wrong.

[10] Bryant, *op. cit.,* p. 216.

ter how risky, that would give a prospect of early victory is understandable. To the political leaders of Britain this factor would carry particular weight.

However, it seems apparent that Brooke and Montgomery were, consciously or unconsciously, utilizing this argument as a device to discredit the current command arrangements, with which they were dissatisfied. Montgomery never seemed reconciled to turning over the coordinating powers he had exercised in France between himself and 12 Army Group. As far back as early August he had been urging some kind of continuation of that arrangement. And yet it is too much to assume that officers of this stature were attempting to alter the command arrangements from purely petty motives. The concept of an overall ground commander under a supreme commander was standard procedure with British forces. Doubtless the British commanders were conscious of the considerable wartime experience they had accumulated. In 1940, when General Eisenhower was a lieutenant colonel with a reputation largely confined to his colleagues in the U.S. Army, Field Marshals Brooke and Montgomery were both corps commanders in the British Expeditionary Forces and took part in the evacuation at Dunkirk.[11] El Alamein had made Montgomery's name a household word at a time when Eisenhower was still virtually unknown. Considering that self-assurance is one of the qualities that make a good commander, it would have been unnatural for these officers to feel they deserved less than the maximum control they could retain over the conduct of operations.

General Eisenhower, on the other hand, regarded each army group as a land force in itself. The size of the region in which each operated made this view reasonable. With that in mind Eisenhower refrained from interfering personally in the detailed tactics of the various army group commanders within the broad missions he assigned them. Moreover, despite a long history of much fighting, neither the British nor the Americans had ever conducted operations on so vast a scale and with such weapons and mobility. Each group of armies comprised in itself a land force larger than any British commander had handled before. And each was supported by its own separate tactical air force.

Sometimes overlooked in these discussions was the necessity for keeping the Supreme Commander's power as great as possible. General Eisenhower remained acutely conscious of the handicaps under which Marshal Ferdinand Foch had labored in World War I, when he acted as a coordinator with no administrative power over any of the national forces. By contrast the strength of Eisenhower's position in World War II is illustrated by the fact that his will was carried out despite the occasional protests of subordinate commanders and some individual members of the Combined Chiefs of Staff. That this position was maintained was due in large part to the unswerving sup-

---

[11] Montgomery took over Brooke's II Corps in the last days of the Dunkirk bridgehead.

port Eisenhower received from General Marshall and through him from President Roosevelt. But it also reflects a sound measure that Eisenhower always insisted on: the supreme commander of any coalition force must, at the same time, be the *administrative commander of the largest force in the field*. In this case the U.S. Army was by far and away the largest force, and so Eisenhower had power to allocate needed resources to whomever he wished to accomplish a given task. This proved to be an extremely potent weapon in enforcing the authority of the Supreme Commander.

The weakness of coalitions in warfare is notorious. Those who would tear down the reputation of Napoleon are quick to point out that in the majority of his battles he was fighting against alliances, and sometimes alliances that were loosely organized. But the American-British coalition operated essentially as one nation. The discussions that took place in the autumn of 1944 were conducted in a friendly atmosphere, with only a minimum of national considerations. It is remarkable that the harmony was so great and the disagreements so few. Most important, such disagreements as came into the open were never allowed to interfere with cheerful and loyal execution of the Supreme Commander's plans, once decided.[12]

Whatever the differing tactical views of the various Allied commanders, there was always one point on which they were virtually unanimous: nobody proposed concentrating forces for an attack through the Ardennes. The reason for this was simple: nothing in that region constituted a suitable military objective. The Saar lay to the south; the Ruhr lay to the north; and opposite the Allied front in the Ardennes nothing seemed to exist but the nearly impassable Eifel, a piece of terrain that the Allies would just as soon have let

[12] Pogue, in his excellent U.S. Army history, *The Supreme Command*, felt it necessary to preface the book with these remarks:

> A word of caution is necessary for the reader who may be unduly impressed by the accounts of controversy and difference of opinion which arose between commanders of the same nationality, officers of different nationalities, and heads of government. . . . When the discussions of the participants in Allied conferences are seen in cold print, without the benefit of the smile which softened a strong argument or the wry shrug which made clear that the debate was for the record, and when there is no transcript of the friendly conversation which followed the official conference, the reader may get the impression that constant argument and heated controversy marked most meetings between Allied leaders. . . . It is inevitable that a study of such discussions will emphasize the disagreements and spell out the problems in reaching accords. The numerous basic decisions which were reached with only minor debate attract less attention. . . .
>
> The success of . . . an alliance is to be judged . . . not by the amount of heat which may be engendered between the powers in their attempts to find a course of action which will most nearly preserve their individual aims while gaining a common goal, but rather by the degree to which the powers, while frankly working on a basis of self-interest, manage to achieve the one aim for which their forces were brought together. On that basis the Western Powers forged a unity seldom, if ever, achieved in the history of grand alliances. Their commanders, while striving to preserve national identity and gain individual honors for their forces, still waged a victorious war.

the Germans keep. The Ardennes and the Eifel together were regarded never as "critical terrain features" to be seized, but rather as obstacles. In World War I Foch referred to the "almost impenetrable massif of the Ardennes."

Nevertheless, the Allied commanders were not unmindful of the history of these bitter woods during the past seventy-five years. In the span of a lifetime the Germans had sent forces of varying size against the French through the Ardennes, twice scoring decisive victories. The last time this had occurred was in May and June, 1940, when the Nazi armor, commanded by Gerd von Rundstedt,[13] the man Eisenhower was now facing in 1944, traversed the Ardennes, crossed the Meuse River at Sedan, and raced along the high ground to the French coast. The results were the British evacuation at Dunkirk and the surrender of France.

But the Allied commanders in 1944 were also aware of other facts. The four and a half years since that 1940 attack had been long years; they had taken a great toll of the German Wehrmacht. The Allies, on the other hand, had built up a war machine of unprecedented power, possessing a quality that the French had lacked in 1940—mobility. U.S. Army units, to both the north and the south of the area, were heavily equipped with tanks and trucks and could move with lightning rapidity.

The possibility of the Germans' taking action here was never discounted. On occasion, when Eisenhower scanned the war map with its markers designating each division in the line, he remarked on the thinness of U.S. positions in that area. Once he observed that we could find a "nasty little Kasserine" on our hands. But General Bradley had already considered the situation soberly. He made a special trip to the Ardennes to discuss the length of frontage with the man responsible on the ground, General Troy Middleton, whose VIII Corps was now located at Bastogne.

Together Bradley and Middleton toured the wooded front. At first Bradley thought Middleton somewhat unduly concerned about his 88-mile front's being held by three divisions. "Don't worry, Troy. They won't come through here," he said.

"Maybe not, Brad, but they've come through this area several times before."

But Middleton was willing to concede that a German attack in the Ardennes would fall short of any strategic objective. With an eye to the Meuse River to his rear, Middleton finally concluded, "If they do come through here, we can fall back and fight a delaying action to the Meuse. Certainly we can slow them down until you hit them on the flanks." [14]

---

[13] Rundstedt replaced Model as OB West on September 5, with the latter's hearty concurrence. Model retained the command of Army Group B, the command formerly held by Field Marshal Erwin Rommel.

[14] Omar Bradley, *A Soldier's Story* (New York: Holt, 1951), p. 453.

Bradley was satisfied. For morale as much as anything else he provided Middleton with part of the new 9th Armored Division and arranged for a "rubber duck" deception unit to operate in the area. Middleton put an infantry battalion of the 9th Armored on the line to give them their first, easy battle experience.

They also agreed that there was nothing within the Ardennes territory east of the Meuse River, a formidable obstacle, to constitute a worthwhile objective for a German attack.

Then General Bradley carefully reviewed the situation with General Eisenhower. Discussing the First Army dispositions with the easy informality of two men who had played football together at West Point some thirty-two years before, they slumped on a couch facing a large situation map. Holding an overlength pointer like a fishing rod between his knees, Bradley outlined his estimate of what the Germans might be able to do if they launched an all-out offensive. With Allied concentrations on both flanks, he reasoned, the enemy could never cross the Meuse without broadening the base of the penetration into the areas of Allied concentrations. In the meantime, should Rundstedt attack in the Ardennes, the quarter million troops under Patton's command to the south and the quarter million in the remainder of First Army to the north could close in and choke off the penetration at the neck and "clamp the invader in a vise."

Eisenhower weighed the alternatives that presented themselves. In the final analysis they boiled down to an unforgiving choice: either he would have to take the risk of holding the Ardennes front thinly, or else he would have to give up all hope of continuing the winter offensives that were in the process of wearing Germany down. He accepted the former and wholeheartedly approved Bradley's dispositions along the front.[15]

There were other matters of concern to Bradley at the moment. Foremost of these was the depletion of the American infantry units. The difficult battles of the autumn had created casualties among the Queen of Battles, and they were not being adequately replaced. To make matters worse, the War Department had recently cut back the total monthly allotment of replacements from 80,000 to 67,000 men, apparently diverting some of these to the Pacific. (Obviously none of Mr. Churchill's occasional pessimism had rubbed off on the American authorities in Washington.)

---

[15] General Eisenhower has written: "The responsibility for maintaining only four divisions on the Ardennes front and for running the risk of a large German penetration in that area was mine. At any moment from November 1 onward I could have passed to the defensive along the whole front and made our lines absolutely secure from the attack while we awaited reinforcements. My basic decision was to continue the offensive to the extreme limit of our ability, and it was this decision that was responsible for the startling successes of the first week of the German December attack." *Crusade in Europe, op. cit.,* p. 340.

As they mulled over this cutback, Bradley growled in near exasperation, "Don't they realize that we can still lose this war in Europe?"

And yet really losing the war in Europe was far from the mind of either man. All thoughts were directed toward the Allied offensives into Germany that would begin the coming month.

Book II

PREPARATIONS FOR THE
"MASTER STROKE"

CHAPTER 6

❦

"Watch on the Rhine"

O N July 30, 1944, Baron Hasso von Manteuffel, division commander of the elite German Grossdeutschland Division, reported to Rastenburg, East Prussia. Rastenburg was the site of Hitler's elaborate headquarters. The Nazi Government had located the Oberkommand Wehrmacht (OKW) [1] there during the first phase of the invasion of Russia in 1941. It was designed to provide Hitler a location from which he might control operations more effectively than from the Reichschancellory in Berlin.

Generalleutnant Manteuffel, as he preferred to be called, was unaware of the reason for this summons. Though a relatively junior officer and young—only forty-seven at the time—he had been in Hitler's presence more than once before. His most recent visit had been in May of that year at Berchtesgaden, and on that occasion Hitler had sent his personal plane to transport Manteuffel from Rumania.

Hasso von Manteuffel was the kind of soldier Hitler liked. True, he came from the class Hitler mistrusted, the Junker aristocracy; but Manteuffel was not a typical, arrogant product of the German General Staff. Frontline combat was his specialty. He had lived in the bitter cold of Russia and had trudged through the thick mud of Rumania. And his greatest pride was that he understood his troops.

Standing barely five feet four inches tall and extremely spare, the Baron held himself with a rigid erectness, noticeable even among his contemporaries, themselves generally considered models of military bearing. His face showed the effects of the battles he had fought, battles that had strengthened and disciplined him rather than worn him down. No Nazi, he held his Führer, in his position of Commander in Chief, in high respect, but in common with most highly experienced combat soldiers who had seen so much of death in

---

[1] The Wehrmacht was the entire German armed force, including the Heer (army), Kriegsmarine (navy), and Luftwaffe (air force). Hitler was the Comander in Chief of both the Wehrmacht and the Heer.

war, he lacked the awe and fear of Hitler that haunted so many others in the Heer at that time.

Manteuffel was conducted into the headquarters through the complex of concrete shelters and wooden barracks. In earlier years, when the announcement of triumphs had set the tone for the Rastenburg headquarters, the place had carried a more cheerful atmosphere. But after the reversals of fortunes in the east, with Russian forces pushing the front ever closer to home, the appearance of the camp had become progressively grimmer. Now barbed wire entanglements and mine fields surrounded the bleak barracks and bomb shelters, the latter being constantly reinforced and improved by the installation of more modern equipment.

From the outer enclosure, occupied by the Operations Staff of OKW and by various subordinate units, Manteuffel entered the smaller one reserved for the top commanders. Inside was the Führer's private command post, the Wolfsschanze (Wolf's Lair). Into this small compartment only ten days earlier the conspirators had brought the bomb intended to remove Hitler from the positions of Head of State and Commander in Chief of the Wehrmacht.

Manteuffel was naturally curious to see what the Führer's condition would be after the attempted assassination. To his eyes, Hitler showed remarkably few effects. True, his left arm was wounded and his left eardrum was reportedly burst. But the courteous way in which he habitually greeted respected field commanders was still there. He made light of resentment in the Heer over Göring's recent order substituting the Hitler salute for the Army's traditional touch of the cap.

Hitler soon got down to cases. He had called Manteuffel to the Wolfsschanze, he said, to discuss a recent action by the Grossdeutschland Division in East Prussia. Transferred to that region from Rumania by railroad, Manteuffel had received a cable directly from Generalfeldmarschall Wilhelm Keitel, Wehrmacht chief of staff, instructing him to counterattack the Red summer offensive before all his troops had arrived. The order from Keitel, which superseded previous personal instructions from Hitler, had resulted in heavy losses in new tanks. Hitler wanted the situation clarified.

The meeting was brief. Manteuffel took the proper leave of his Führer and left to return to his division. His status had not been injured. It had, in fact, grown. A month later he was to be given command of the Fifth Panzer Army, with rank of General der Panzertruppen.

What Manteuffel did not realize was that Hitler, the master actor, had put on a great performance for his benefit. Except for his left arm, his slight injuries had healed by now; but he remained weak. He was confined to bed for most of the day by order of his personal physician, leaving it only occasionally to receive important visitors.

This confinement was the culmination of Hitler's progressive removal from a life that had once been almost completely public. The withdrawal actually began soon after the coming of the war. After 1940 he made fewer and fewer appearances, leaving the speechmaking largely to Josef Goebbels. Preoccupied with the details of the conduct of military operations, he saw only the highest officials. Now, at Rastenburg, the process was complete. The Wolf did not leave his lair, and his life had narrowed down to the manipulation of symbols on a map, representations that progressively were less associated with units made up of human beings. Reality was rapidly being replaced by a sort of dream.

Though Manteuffel had not noticed, Hitler gave a shocking appearance to others who knew him better and who had not seen him in some time. He was fighting a stomach ailment, which some of his advisers regarded as the effect of his personal physician's medical treatment. It had recently become increasingly noticeable that his left hand and leg made spasmodic movements. He was stooped, his gestures normally slow. His eyes, except when he was excited, were lusterless; they seemed to lack the startling blueness that previously had transfixed anyone permitted to come close to him. But observers also noted that his intellect was as acute as ever.

Despite his physical infirmities, he seemed in no way depressed (although his thirst for revenge against anyone remotely connected with the plot on his life was unquenchable).[2] On the contrary, in his mystical way he regarded his phenomenal survival as a sign, a confirmation of his mission to lead Germany to greatness. With this belief he listened in comparative calm to the adverse operational reports that were brought him daily by his closest subordinates. And it was perhaps after these visits, when he could lie back in bed and reconstruct the world, that he began to dream of bringing victory out of defeat.

Hitler remained personally in control of the disposition of Germany's military forces on all fronts—and he never ceased to nurture the concept of some offensive in the west that would restore the strategic initiative to the Heer. Reports were brought to him daily by Field Marshal Keitel and by Generaloberst Alfred Jodl, chief of the Wehrmacht Operations Staff. Though Jodl was subordinate in rank to Keitel, it was Jodl, not Keitel, whom Hitler consulted on all strategic questions.[3] Jodl had become indispensable to Hitler, who had in 1941 assumed the role of Commander in Chief of the Heer.

As a German General Staff officer Jodl cut a fine figure. His bearing was

[2] "Hitler himself was now quite obviously a sick man. His actual injuries on 20 July had been minor, but it seemed as if the shock had brought into the open all of the evil of his nature, both physical and psychological. . . . On the slightest occasion he would demand shrilly that 'the guilty' be hunted down." Walter Warlimont, *Inside Hitler's Headquarters, 1939–45* (New York: Praeger, 1964), p. 462.

[3] Keitel's position was predominantly that of administrator, absorbing the functions performed by the Minister of War during World War I. He seems not to have had a decisive voice in the planning of operations.

dignified, and his expression serious and sensitive. Though many commanders and even some staff officers in the Oberkommand Wehrmacht thought him nothing more than Hitler's tool, he was respected. No one questioned his knowledge or his intelligence.

The confidence that Hitler placed in Keitel, and even more in Jodl, was not shared by the other members of the German High Command. Early in the war Hitler came into conflict with the General Staff Corps officers in positions of command and carrying out planning and operations duties. The decision to attack Poland in 1939, precipitating as it did a second world war, seemed rash and unrealistic to his military advisers who knew the thinness of Germany's military preparation. Later, when the decisions were made to take the offensive in France in 1940 and to attack Russia in 1941, the General Staff objected that the Wehrmacht was not equal to the demands that Hitler continually placed upon it. But Hitler got rid of the generals opposed to his military policies, surrounded himself with generals who would take orders.

After the attempt on Hitler's life on July 20, of course, the situation was greatly exacerbated. Now not the field marshals or the commanding generals of the Heer or the officers of the General Staff Corps could be entrusted with strategic operations. What had been dislike of the officer class turned into bitter distrust. Only to associates of proven loyalty such as Jodl and Keitel were Hitler's plans revealed, and to them only gradually.

By the summer of 1944 many surviving German officers of the highest rank had come to believe, or had convinced themselves, that Hitler possessed keen insight into the nature of war and could produce strategic concepts of striking originality. This was, of course, Hitler's view of himself: "A war leader," he said after his Russian victories, "is what I am against my own will. If I apply my mind to military problems, that's because for the moment I know that nobody would succeed better at this than I can." [4]

The fact is that Hitler had an unusual memory, and because of his extensive reading and continual discussion with experts, he had acquired a fund of knowledge in specialized areas often superior to that of the majority of the senior staff officers. Even Generaloberst Heinz Guderian, one of the few who disagreed openly with Hitler on occasion and survived, continued to respect Hitler's military learning.

But it is one thing to acquire a fund of information; it is another to apply that tool with common sense, reason, and discipline. Herein lay the basic cleavage between Hitler and the members of the professional German Officer Corps. The qualities of hardheaded reason and thoroughness that the General Staff embodied carried little weight with Hitler. The quality most important to a leader, at least to the top leader of a great nation, was the mystical quality that he termed "fanaticism."

[4] Adolf Hitler, *Hitler's Secret Conversations* (New York: New American Library), p. 67.

The conception Hitler had of "fanaticism" has little to do with the English or American definition of the word. Americans would agree that Hitler was a fanatic, but they would not understand what he meant by calling *himself* so. To Hitler a fanatic was a man who believed in the wonder-working providences of his own will. And the fascinating feature of Hitler's personality, the quality that converted skeptics into followers, was precisely power of will. To this his associates attributed the rise and the eventual triumph of Nazism out of obscurity and disgrace:

> The experiences he had acquired during his revolutionary ascent are reflected in his manner of thinking. Had his thinking been schooled according to General Staff standards, he would have estimated at each step he had climbed that reaching the next one was an impossibility. Then he would never have undertaken any attempt to seize power since according to sound calculations it seemed hopeless from the beginning. *He had remained a revolutionary in his thinking even after he had seized power.*[5]

What made Hitler a "revolutionary" in his thinking was a perversion of German romantic idealism, e.g.: man discovers the truth of existence whenever he molds the outside world into conformity with an idea. To live most deeply is to overcome obstacles, to give shape to the recalcitrant world in which one finds oneself.

Thus during his rise to power Hitler set himself and his followers objectives that seemed impossible to realize, believing that while premeditated calculations would immediately jump the rails, the impossible could always be reached through the energies generated on one's own side and the general paralysis on the enemy's. Hitler held that we must *make* a dream work—then it will be as real as a panther tank.

When Hitler's obsession with the "primacy of the will" is taken into consideration, many of his attitudes and actions can be better understood. It accounts for his supreme confidence in himself as a military leader and for two of the chief tenets in his military doctrine: (1) "Attack is the best defense," a notion that he praised Clausewitz for expressing, and (2) "Troops should never be made to feel uncertain by withdrawal." If only the will to resist is inflexible, most requests for withdrawal are superfluous. The German military found that preparing a precautionary defensive line behind the line of present contact was usually impossible, for Hitler normally refused to allow any commander to look over his shoulder. Commanders were defeatists unless they looked for new forward positions to which to *advance*.

But to Hitler fanaticism had implications extending far beyond the planning of battles and inflexible determination to achieve victory. He spoke of these implications frequently to a small group of secretaries, advisers, and visitors, who were privileged to join him after the last of his daily situational

---

[5] Percy Schramm, MS # A-862. Italics added.

conferences (usually beginning after midnight and ending toward morning) as he sat over his supper of vegetables and cold water. In this table talk, with a secretary sitting discreetly in a corner recording his words for posterity, Hitler ranged over a body of historical, political, anthropological, geographical, scientific, humanist, and military material. Bits of common and uncommon information and scraps of knowledge were processed through his preconceptions, hatreds, and prejudices, cast in the form of either sallies of wit or aphorisms, and presented as considered judgments. In one of his table talks early in the war, he boasted in one of his characteristically expansive moods: "If I am reproached with having sacrificed a hundred or two hundred thousand men by reason of war, I can answer that thanks to what I have done [in building an empire] the German nation has gained up to the present, more than two million five hundred thousand human beings. . . . I am creating conditions favorable to growth." [6]

He had no second thoughts when he ordered thousands of his countrymen to their death. A prophetic note recurs in these "conversations." In the inevitable struggle between the "races of the East" (for he set Germany apart from the decadent capitalist democracies of the West), either the Germans or the Russians must survive, not both. That Germany would win out he had no doubt, for Germans possessed not only superior intelligence but also power of will—something unknown to the brutish Russians. And as that German among Germans who possessed the power of will in its highest, most undeniable development, Hitler was the providential leader of the German people. In fact, in a mystical way Hitler embodied the will of his people. "The conviction that by obeying the voice of duty one is working for the preservation of the species helps one [the Führer] to take the gravest decisions." [7]

In directing Germany in its struggle for survival, Hitler, the embodiment of German will and purpose, saw himself guided by "intuition." He brushed aside the disciplined reasoning of his General Staff, confident in the validity and reliability of intuition, the handmaiden of the will. Intuition directed the absorption of Austria and Czechoslovakia, the occupation of Norway and Denmark, the attack on Russia at that precise moment in 1941 when he decided to move. At the height of his power, intuition told him that Russia was to be utterly destroyed, Moscow and Leningrad leveled, their names and records blotted out of geography and history alike, the Russians peonized. Intuition gave him the confidence to order the holding of ground in the face of overwhelming odds and the faith to order audacious attacks in the face of defeat. Intuition gave him his trust in the German common soldier and his distrust of the General Staff officers.

And—after the losses in France—intuition told him that a gigantic counter-

6 Hitler, *op. cit.,* pp. 24, 37.
7 *Ibid.*

offensive in the west would divide the Allies and free forces for stopping the Russians.

Hitler was now ready to gamble the lives of thousands of Germans on the turn of a card out of a deck that he had reason to believe might not be stacked as it had been before. He had convinced himself that a successful offensive in the west would drive a wedge between the Americans and the British, or the British and Canadians, who would have become tired of a hopeless war. He had long held to the belief that the Western Alliance was a weak, or at best a temporary, coalition. Two years earlier he had expressed the view that England might withdraw from the war. He reasoned that in the event of Allied victory only America would gain; if the Allies were defeated, only England would be destroyed. He went so far as to visualize a bitter war between England and America. He could even see England and Germany marching together against the United States.

A giant offensive might turn the trick.

On July 31, 1944, the day after the Manteuffel visit, Hitler called a meeting with Jodl and a few selected members of the Operations Staff. The purpose was to begin planning Kluge's ill-fated counterattack against American forces at Mortain—the "master stroke" that was to drive the Allies into the English Channel. However, Hitler had come to realize that in a succession of "battles of movement" Allied superiority in the air and Allied resources in tanks and men might eventually force him to conduct operations from the protection of the German frontier. At the conclusion of the meeting, while still instructing Kluge to hold all French seaports and every inch of ground, Hitler also gave the order that the commander of the German Replacement Army was to refit the Siegfried Line.

But a more significant revelation was made that day. In an apparent fit of pique Hitler gave a hint of the dream that had presumably preoccupied him when he was recovering from his wounds: a great offensive, which would decide the outcome of the war, would be undertaken in the west. Perhaps Hitler was thinking only of the Mortain attack, insisting that it be driven home to what he hoped would be a final conclusion. It has been suggested that his outburst was mere bluster, a reaction to the American breakthrough at Avranches. But the order to refit the Siegfried Line at the same time suggests something more.

During the first week in August, immediately after his outburst on July 31, Hitler set the pattern that governed his operations on the western front for the next four months: the ground west of the Siegfried Line was, naturally, to be held at any cost; the enemy was to be slowed down by repeated counter-thrusts despite the difficulty of assembling forces in the face of Allied air superiority. The reasoning here was that the Heer must maintain some initiative at all times.

But it was not to be. The attack at Avranches failed; thousands of men and vehicles were needlessly lost at Falaise; the Allies took Paris and crossed the Seine. In early September OKW had a faint hope that a defense line running north to south through Belgium might be established. This line, beginning at Antwerp, would follow the Louvain Canal to the city of Louvain, which was only about 30 miles from the Meuse, a formidable obstacle to the south. If the Heer could not hold this line, a retreat to the Siegfried Line, with bastions in the Netherlands and Lorraine, would be inevitable. The line did not hold, Antwerp itself being captured on September 4. Rundstedt, now reinstated as commander in chief, was instructed that all attempts to stop the Allied advance in front of the Siegfried Line were being abandoned.

In the meantime, however, Hitler ordered a series of heavy counterattacks by Manteuffel's Fifth Panzer Army to try to turn the Allies' southern flank. All failed. Still the Führer clung to his belief that a reversal of events was possible. If the September defeats had shown that an offensive launched from a position forward of the West Wall was no longer possible, "then," Hitler reasoned, "the change in the situation will have to be brought about by an attack originating from the West Wall." [8]

On September 6 General Jodl made a special report to the Führer in the Wolfsschanze. There was nothing unusual about Jodl's making a periodic briefing. What made this briefing different was that the chief of the Operations Staff was reporting on conditions he had previously been instructed to study: the conditions for an all-out offensive in the west.

Jodl reported that there were certain explicit features common to all plans for a counteroffensive in the west. First of all, Allied air superiority made it essential that a date be set that took advantage of bad weather to eliminate temporarily the dreaded Allied air forces. Also to be considered was the status of military production on the home front. The German home front, apparently not impressed with the attempt on Hitler's life on July 20, had rallied behind their government in a remarkable manner and in some areas, despite Allied bombings, production was reaching a new peak. However, the military destruction of the summer was such that time was necessary to allocate the matériel now running off the assembly lines. Another fact to consider was increased requirements in personnel. "It will take," Jodl said, "an operational reserve of twenty-five divisions. Part of this reserve will have to be filled out with men combed out of other services." Furthermore, he concluded, an overwhelming superiority in men and supplies would have to be focused at

[8] Schramm, *op. cit.*, p. 26.

the sector that was chosen for the attack. He did not have to remind the Führer that secrecy in a situation like this was of first importance.

With these considerations in mind, Jodl gave Hitler his own conclusions: "A major offensive of this type will not be possible before November 1."

During the next three weeks Hitler and Jodl took time out from the day to day conduct of the war on its several fronts to draft a preliminary, very general plan. A concrete move toward its execution was made on September 14, when Hitler ordered the organization of the staff of a new panzer army. It was to be designated the Sixth Panzer Army and was to be commanded by SS-Oberstgruppenführer Josef ("Sepp") Dietrich, a longtime Nazi and early associate of Hitler's—a man utterly free of the stigma of the German General Staff Corps.

The next stage was estimating the strength and disposition of Allied forces on the western front. Obviously the offensive had to avoid an encounter with the full strength of the Allies—and yet it had to upset enemy plans at the least, if it was to stabilize the situation in the west.

At that moment Hitler and Jodl estimated British and American forces on the Continent at approximately sixty infantry, airborne, and armored divisions, with thirty-two still in England and Scotland. Thirty-nine divisions were still in the United States and five more apparently on the way. Even with the fall of Antwerp, they calculated, the Allies would find it slow going disembarking on the Continent those troops in England and the U.S., especially if the German Fifteenth Army could continue to block the Scheldt Estuary.[9] They could assume, therefore, that at the moment the Allies had no major strategic reserves on the front in Europe. The assumption was correct.

A moment arrived at one of the daily conferences in the Wolfsschanze when Hitler reportedly began to detect the emphasis on the Allied left wing, with secondary concentrations on both sides of Aachen and a lesser emphasis on the battle area of Nancy and the southern Vosges front. Between the Nancy battle area and Aachen he noted a relative weakness, particularly from Nancy along the Moselle to the confluence of the Moselle and Sauer rivers east of the city of Luxembourg, and thence along the Sauer and Our rivers, which form part of the border between Luxembourg and Germany. In essence this area of Allied weakness included the regions of Lorraine to the south and the Ardennes-Eifel to the north.

From this data Hitler and Jodl attempted to diagnose Allied intentions. The British and Canadians, they concluded, would attack from the Scheldt Estuary on the west to Nijmegen on the east. The American First Army could be expected to try to break through the Siegfried Line in the Aachen sector, preparatory to a large-scale offensive toward the Ruhr industrial area. The American Third Army could be expected to attack northeast of Nancy, to-

---

[9] Antwerp was not opened to full Allied use, it will be recalled, until November 26.

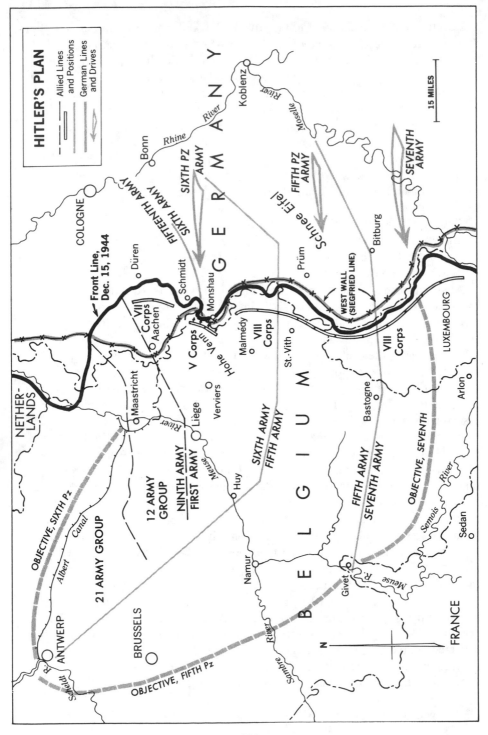

HITLER'S PLAN

Allied Lines
and Positions

German Lines
and Drives

15 MILES

Koblenz

Rhine River
Moselle River

Bonn

SIXTH PZ ARMY

FIFTH PZ ARMY

SEVENTH ARMY

G E R M A N Y

FIFTEENTH ARMY

Schnee Eifel

COLOGNE

Front Line, Dec. 15, 1944

Düren

Schmidt

Monschau

Prüm

Bitburg

WEST WALL (SIEGFRIED LINE)

VII Corps

Aachen

V Corps

Höfen

Malmédy

VIII Corps

St.-Vith

VIII Corps

LUXEMBOURG

NETHER-LANDS

Maastricht

Liège

Verviers

SIXTH ARMY

FIFTH ARMY

Bastogne

Arlon

12 ARMY GROUP

NINTH ARMY

FIRST ARMY

Huy

Meuse River

FIFTH ARMY

SEVENTH ARMY

OBJECTIVE, SEVENTH

Semois River

Sedan

Albert Canal

21 ARMY GROUP

OBJECTIVE, SIXTH Pz

Namur

B E L G I U M

Givet

Meuse R.

FRANCE

N

ANTWERP

BRUSSELS

Sambre River

OBJECTIVE, FIFTH Pz

Scheldt R.

114

ward the Saar industrial area. It was thought that in the south the Allied right wing, consisting of American and French forces, would attempt to break through the Vosges to the Upper Rhine.

These were the clues. Hitler studied them. Finally he put his finger on the map in the region of the Ardennes-Eifel and announced that through that area the great offensive would take place.

On September 25, 1944, Hitler called together a meeting of a few members of Jodl's Operations Staff. The general concept of the offensive he had been discussing with Jodl for the past three weeks had jelled in his own mind. He was well enough along in his own planning to include such officers as General Walther Buhle, chief of the Army section of OKW, and Major I. G. Buechs, Jodl's assistant. The circle had widened to include those who were going to do the detailed, high-level planning.

To their astonished ears Hitler presented the general picture of his projected offensive, discussing its location, method of execution, allocation of forces, and timing.

The most suitable area for the penetration, Hitler had concluded, was the sector of the western front that lay between Monschau—a picturesque little German town, a favorite of his, twenty miles southeast of Aachen—and Echternach in Luxembourg, on the Sûre River about fifty miles as the crow flies south of Monschau. The First U.S. Army, responsible for a big stretch of the front from both sides of Aachen to the boundary between southern Luxembourg and France, was covering the wide sector selected for the attack with but four infantry divisions and one armored division. Not only were the Allied forces very thin in this area, but also the wooded area of the Eifel at the rear of the German line would camouflage the assembly of German troops, a vital consideration. After the Nazi forces had achieved a breakthrough in this area, the thrust was to continue in a northwesterly direction across the Ardennes, and cross the Meuse River between Liège and the Namur corner. Its objective: Antwerp! [10]

In general the attack would be conducted in a conventional manner. Infantry troops in the assault would force a rupture in the Allied front as rapidly as possible in order to give panzer units freedom of movement in the unoccupied ground beyond. Bridgeheads across the Meuse between Liège and Namur would be seized before the Allies could demolish the bridges; and Antwerp was to be reached by a further thrust from the southeast, the main effort passing to the north of Brussels. Once the Germans reached the Brussels area, all rear communications of the Allied 21 Army Group would be severed. "If all goes well," Hitler boasted, "the offensive will set the stage for the annihilation of the bulk of twenty to thirty divisions. It will be another Dunkirk."

[10] Schramm, *op. cit.,* p. 62.

Hitler next addressed himself to the allocation of forces, estimating that in general a minimum of thirty divisions would be required, at least ten of which should be panzers. Here he was touching on a matter that would become a critical issue between the OKW and the commanders in the field. Even at this moment his commanders were crying for reinforcements, but from the beginning he had decided to strip all other sectors of the western front, risking the defense in other areas. He was confident that once the attack was launched the Allies could be depended upon to relinquish any intended attacks of their own, "taking up the defense on all sectors, committing all available forces in the breakthrough areas." [11]

Speed was the key to success, and therefore two panzer armies would spearhead the offensive. One was Dietrich's new Sixth Panzer Army, which was to command all SS panzer divisions in the offensive. The other was the Fifth Panzer Army, commanded by Manteuffel. The two panzer armies were to advance abreast and both were to cross the Meuse and drive to Antwerp. Two other armies, consisting mainly of infantry and blocking units, were to be responsible for protection of the flanks, one north and one south.

Since surprise was to be an important element in the success of the attack, artillery preparation was to be brief, though powerful. After the panzers had passed through the assault infantry forces and had rapidly fanned out in the Allies' rear, surprise and consequent confusion should reign among the enemy, making it possible to establish vital bridgeheads across the Meuse by the second day of the attack. At this point the second wave of panzer units would be committed. The advance to Antwerp would be resumed on a broad front. Infantry units, following as closely as possible, would pour in rapidly and occupy favorable defensive sectors, particularly along the northern flank, since the first counterattacks could be expected from that direction.

In this rapid war of movement, all leaders must concentrate on thrusting deeply into each zone of operations and refuse to be diverted from the original objective by threats of Allied counterattacks on flanks. Hitler reminded his officers of the way in which surprise had worked to the German advantage in Russia in 1941. "Any tendency toward prematurely turning off—for example against the flank of Allied forces around Aachen—*must be strictly opposed from the outset*," he said. "Any turning off can only run into enemy strength. Never in this way can we obtain a complete success." [12]

These tactics had been proven in Poland in 1939, in France in 1940, and in Russia. Hitler cited instances in every case in which the General Staff Corps had opposed his own conceptions of warfare. Russia had borrowed the tactics, and so had the Western Allies. Had not the Allies, after the Normandy breakout, crossed France with a southern flank along the Loire held by

---

[11] Horst Wilutsky, MS # B-034; see also Schramm, *op. cit.;* Fritz Bayerlein, MS # A-977.

[12] Bayerlein, *op. cit.;* Schramm, *op. cit.*

minimal forces? Experience had shown that, in contrast to accepted tactics of World War I, there was no need to secure the flanks on every breakout operation.

The all-important question of timing came next. The offensive had to be executed during the onset of "favorable" weather, which meant nonoperational flying weather. Hitler considered that six to eight weeks would be needed for reorganization of the panzer units; for activation of the volksgrenadier (VG) divisions, volks artillerie corps, and volks werfer (rocket projector) brigades; for procurement of the necessary ammunition and fuel; and for assembly of all units. Therefore the attack could be launched between November 20 and 30—the most suitable time with respect to weather conditions.

Hitler was banking on one belief: the attacks would catch the Allies off guard. Considerable time would elapse before the Allies could mount large counterattacks. First they would have to realize the *extent* of the offensive. Then they would have to consider whether to stop any of their attacks already under way. Then they would have to begin considering the withdrawal of forces and their transport to the breakthrough area.

These, Hitler believed, would be difficult and time-consuming decisions. Since his opponent consisted of an alliance, the allied nations would have to reach agreement at the political level before countermeasures could be taken. The threat of immediate Allied reaction could therefore be dismissed. And during this interval adequate German reserves would be brought up to reinforce the threatened flanks.

At this meeting on September 25 General Jodl was asked to prepare the first draft of an operations plan, including accurate calculations of all forces —infantry, panzer, artillery, werfer, and others—that would be required. He was also to draft an order providing for security measures to maintain secrecy and to give camouflage for the troops. Field Marshal Keitel was to prepare an overall estimate of the ammunition and fuel requirements. OB West, Field Marshal Gerd von Rundstedt, was to be ordered to withdraw 1st and 2d SS Panzer corps, whose units included the 1st SS, 2d SS, 9th SS, and 12th SS Panzer divisions, as well as the Panzer Lehr Division. He was not to be told why. These units were to be moved to Westphalia, east of the Rhine, for reorganization and training. Orders were to be given to the Luftwaffe to estimate the maximum fighter protection the attacking troops could expect for support over the zone of operations.

At the end of his lengthy monologue, Hitler directed that those concerned present the drafts of these orders at the earliest opportunity.

Hitler had set the stage. It was now up to the staff of OKW—still without benefit of the field commanders' views—to come up with a more concrete operational plan and statistical data on availability of troops and resources. By October 8, about two weeks after the Operations Staff meeting, General Buhle had estimated that the Heer could scrape together twelve panzer divisions (six of which were not yet rehabilitated) by November 15. Ten volksgrenadier divisions would be available by November 20, three more by November 30, and a total of 20 VG divisions operational by December 10. Organized in mid-August as part of the "general reserve," these new divisions were coming off the production line rapidly enough to make a November 20 deadline.[13] Artillery and werfer units were being organized even more slowly than the divisions. It would be December 15 before seven werfer brigades were ready. Thirteen antitank and assault gun brigades would be available early in December, with more to come later.

On October 9, apparently for the sake of formality, the Operations Staff went through a rather remarkable exercise of determining "by systematic examination," General Staff style, which of five alternative offensive possibilities —or combinations thereof—was preferable. The areas considered ranged from Holland all the way to Lorraine. Hitler was present at the conference and had probably directed that it be conducted.

Of the areas considered at this conference—(1) Holland toward Antwerp; (2) Liège-Aachen, northwest from northern Luxembourg; (3) Luxembourg; (4) Lorraine; (5) Alsace—the last three were quickly ruled out, owing partly to anticipated changes in the front in the ensuing weeks. This conveniently left the area preferred by Hitler.

It turned out, however, that the General Staff Operation Number 2, Operation Liège-Aachen, was not precisely the same as the one Hitler had previously outlined. Operation Liège-Aachen did call for a main attack from the northern corner of Luxembourg toward the northwest, later pivoting to the north to meet a secondary thrust from the area northwest of Aachen, but it did not include Antwerp as an objective. Surprisingly, Hitler concluded the conference by expressing his tentative approval: "A further development [of the Liège-Aachen operation] would perhaps pay dividends if the available data were consulted." He gave Jodl two days to study the "available data."

Jodl wasted no time; he consulted the "available data." Obviously the material most pertinent was the operations plan for the attack on France conducted in May, 1940. Put in Jodl's hands barely in time for the presentation on October 11 of his draft operations plan, it was sent from the Army archives, which had been located at Liegnitz since a fire in 1941. Many relevant

---

[13] There were two types of units sharing the designation Volksgrenadier Division. One type received the name in recognition of exceptional service. In this category was the 12 Volksgrenadier Division. The other type came into existence with Goebbels' Fortress Germany program. The personnel of these units consisted of men from broken divisions, recruits produced by the more stringent draft laws of 1944, and men scraped together from the Luftwaffe and Kriegsmarine.

records had been lost; those submitted were burned at the edges, some being so fragile that the archivist had to send photostat copies. However, the material proved valuable.

The plan that Jodl presented embodied ideas expressed in previous discussions of the offensive, defining them more precisely and incorporating more accurate statistical data. It also reflected ideas that had been developed since the map exercise held two days earlier. For in this report the Aachen-Liège operation, which called for a secondary thrust from the area northwest of Aachen, was combined with the Holland operation, which called for a thrust to Antwerp. Hitler "accepted" the change (perhaps having insisted on it) and settled on a revised plan that included double envelopment. One prong was to be launched to the north of Aachen; one to the south. The objective still was to be Antwerp. The main emphasis was to be placed on the prong emerging south of Aachen from the Ardennes. With the northern prong relegated to a secondary attack, the plan had now practically evolved to Hitler's original concept of September 25. Jodl then gave the details of the offensive. The attack sector was to be broad, some fifty miles in width. The newly constituted Sixth Panzer Army, with the Fifteenth Army on the right, was to launch the main attack out of the West Wall between Monschau on the north and Prüm on the south. It was to cross the Meuse on both sides of Liège; then, taking advantage of the protection of the Albert Canal (Maastricht to Antwerp) on the right and a flexible boundary shared with the Fifth Panzer Army on its left, it was to advance to its objectives.

The Fifth Panzer Army, attacking from an area between Prüm on the north and a line running through Bitburg and Bastogne, was to bypass Bastogne on the south. It was then to turn in a northwesterly direction and, crossing the Meuse at Namur and bypassing Brussels, converge on Antwerp.

This was Hitler's concept, only couched in more concrete terms.

Jodl's report included a description of the main topographical features of the area between the West Wall and Antwerp, based on the material sent by the archivist at Liegnitz. The Meuse would present a considerable barrier; its steep banks would make bridge construction almost impossible under fire. Even where bridges were seized intact, crossing in the face of resistance would be difficult. The southern flank of the Fifth Panzer Army, crossing south of Namur where the Sambre joins the elbow of the Meuse, would have to cross both rivers. However, once crossed, the Meuse would afford protection when the Allies began their counterattacks. East of the Meuse the terrain of the Ardennes was hilly, in places reaching 2,500 feet. The plateaus were cut by numerous deep gullies and small rivers. Forests were everywhere.

At the beginning of the attack, Jodl explained, the Sixth Panzer Army faced the most difficult terrain, over a dense elevated swamp known as the Hohe Venn; however, Dietrich would jump off from a position only about 25 miles from the Meuse. The Fifth Panzer Army to the south would find terrain and resistance easier at first, but it would later find the terrain more difficult, and the distances to be covered far greater. To reach the Meuse, Manteuffel would have to traverse the whole width of the Ardennes, which ran straight across his line of advance.

As always planned, the breakthrough was to be executed by infantry divisions along the whole length of the attack front. The selection of suitable breakthrough points was to be left to the armies concerned.

Following the breakthrough by infantry, the panzer divisions were to be launched. The Sixth Panzer Army was to attack in two waves in its sector. The first was to thrust to the Meuse as quickly as possible to occupy bridgeheads. With these consolidated, both panzer corps were to be committed abreast and start the attack on Antwerp. Protection of Sixth Panzer Army's right flank would be the responsibility of Army itself; the corps on the left wing of the Fifteenth Army, therefore, was to be attached to it.

Jodl paused in his exposition to underline a point: *Nothing should be allowed to delay the panzer armies in their thrust toward the Meuse.* They were to bypass strongly held positions and villages that could not be taken by the first attack. They were to make some effort to cover their flanks, but these missions, as well as the defense against counterattacks, were to be left to the infantry divisions following in their wake. Advance detachments led by resourceful men should be formed, whose task was to secure bridges before the enemy had time to destroy them.

As for the all-important question of reserves, some of these were to be at the disposal of Army Group B (Model), others at the disposal of OB West (Rundstedt). A third portion (almost all of them, Jodl might have added) remained under control of the OKW.

Jodl finally turned to the "prerequisites for success," calling attention once more to the delicate balance of forces that Hitler had emphasized on September 25. It was a balance upon which Hitler's plans depended. Would developments between now and the moment when the offensive was to be launched alter conditions so drastically that the offensive would have to be called off? Could the Germans hold Holland and continue to blockade the Scheldt Estuary? Would the Russian front stabilize? Would Germany continue to increase its war production? Would the western front be able to receive a flow of men and matériel, or would the Allied air forces interrupt German lines of communication? Would bad weather set in at the right moment, and would it last, compensating for the enemy's superiority in the air?

Hitler was more interested in the tactical details than in the potential hazards. He expressed himself "in general agreement" with Jodl's draft, but he altered certain important details. He broadened the front; he concentrated artillery firepower; he provided more reserves from the Aachen front—all to support Sepp Dietrich's Sixth Panzer Army.

Hitler had fewer suggestions for the Fifth Panzer and Seventh armies, which seemed to interest him less than his specially anointed Sixth, its composition dominated by the SS. He declined to allot a panzer division to the Seventh Army.

Hitler also opposed the use of parachute troops in attempting to establish bridgeheads over the Meuse. The Luftwaffe, he felt, was not equal to the task. He agreed on the chain of command. Field Marshal Walther Model, on whose front the offensive would be executed, should be given responsibility for the attack—theoretically, at least, reporting to OB West, Field Marshal Gerd von Rundstedt.

After being informed by Keitel that the necessary quantities of fuel and ammunition could be obtained by the end of November, Hitler said that he now considered November 25 the earliest possible date for the beginning. This would be a favorable time because there would be a new moon and the assembly of troops would be protected against air reconnaissance. All officers initiated into the plan were to work with speed and fervor, since in December flying weather would improve. Fuel, ammunition, and other supplies sent into the area were to be camouflaged.

Hitler agreed that troops should be located in assigned assembly areas so that they could be used in emergency at any critical point along the front. However, measures were to be taken to guarantee that they would not be committed except with Hitler's approval. They were to be designated OKW Reserves, *not* available to Rundstedt.

In closing, Hitler went back to his favorite subject: secrecy. The success of the offensive depended upon complete surprise. In the interest of secrecy the preparations were to be carried out under a misleading code name. Even Rundstedt was subject to this concealment until the time should come when the Führer was ready for him to be initiated into the real objective. For the benefit of OB West Rundstedt, and all others among the uninitiated, the operation was given the code name Wacht am Rhein (Watch on the Rhine).

CHAPTER 7

⁂

Hitler Overrides His Generals

H ITLER'S meeting with Jodl's staff at the Wolfsschanze on October 11, 1944, completed what might be called the stage of general planning. Myriad details had now to be worked out by the Operations Staff. While this was going on, the German OKW was involved in a kind of double duplicity. Not only from the enemy was the massive enterprise concealed; in order to insure airtight security Hitler insisted that the only people made privy to the plan were to be the staff working with him at Rastenburg and the necessary secretaries, clerks, and typists (all of whom were given oaths of secrecy carrying a penalty of death).

Keitel supplemented the Watch on the Rhine cover story. As soon as the October 11 meeting was finished, he announced to commanders on the western front that it was not possible to stage a German offensive at this time, and that it was therefore all the more important that the reserves be assembled to guarantee success against the Allies in the imminent defensive battle. The mobile forces to be withdrawn from the line within the near future were to be assembled behind the northern sector of the western front; they were to be considered OKW reserves—under direct control of the Führer.

To commanders in the west this announcement primarily meant that they were to lose certain units and that they could expect no replacements or relief for their embattled divisions. Keitel's order gave preliminary directives for the regulation of movements behind the front. Simultaneously certain divisions were withdrawn and plans were laid to build up supplies.

On October 21, 1944, ten days after the meeting, Sturmbannführer (Major, Waffen-SS) Otto Skorzeny reported to the Wolfsschanze, flushed with the success of his latest daring exploit. Skorzeny, described as Hitler's favorite commando, was the blond Nazi giant whose miraculous rescue of Mussolini from his Italian captors in the Alps had electrified the world a year earlier. With a group of 108 men he had snatched the Fascist dictator from the Albergo Campo Imperatore Hotel, a veritable fortress manned by superior numbers of Italian guards. He had then delivered Il Duce out of this desolate spot in a small, overloaded Fieseler plane.

But this exploit was now ancient history. Skorzeny was reporting on a new operation, code-named Mouse, that rivaled the Mussolini rescue in daring and probably exceeded it in importance: he and his men had seized the citadel in Budapest, Hungary, thus temporarily allaying a period of great governmental crisis; his troops had, at gunpoint, prevented the Hungarian government from signing a separate peace with the Allies.

Skorzeny was met warmly. Greeting his visitor with an enthusiastic handshake, Hitler elatedly exclaimed: "Well done, Skorzeny! I have promoted you to Obersturmbannführer [lieutenant colonel, Waffen-SS] with effect from the sixteenth of October, and awarded you the German Cross in gold. No doubt you want decorations for your men, too. You have only to speak to my aide-de-camp. It's all arranged. Now tell me all about this operation Mouse." [1]

Skorzeny gave the details of the operation, to the Führer's obvious delight. Having finally finished his story, he prepared to go. "Don't go, Skorzeny," said the Führer in haste. "I have perhaps the most important job of your life for you. So far very few people know the preparations for a secret plan in which you have a great part to play. In December Germany will start a great offensive which may well decide her fate."

Hitler then proceeded to give his protégé a lengthy and detailed picture of the operation in the West, continually harking back to his theory that the Western European Allies could not (or would not) see that by barring Asia's path to the west, Germany was fighting and bleeding for Europe. The governments of the Western powers, he told Skorzeny, considered Germany virtually prostrate, but if the "corpse" should rise and strike them with a crushing blow, pressures within the Western nations would force their governments to make a favorable armistice. He then explained the alternatives discussed in the planning sessions with relish and animation.

"I am telling you all this," he said, "so that you can consider your part in it and realize that nothing has been forgotten. One of the most important tasks in this offensive will be entrusted to you and the units under your command, which will have to seize one or more of the bridges over the Meuse between Liège and Namur. You will have to wear British and American uniforms. The enemy has already done us a great deal of damage by the use of our uniforms in various commando operations. Only a few days ago I received a report that the use of our uniforms by an American force had played no inconsiderable part when they captured Aachen, the first German town in the west to fall into their hands. Moreover, small detachments in enemy uniforms can cause the greatest confusion among the Allies. They can

[1] This and all other quoted conversation in this interview between Hitler and Skorzeny quoted from Otto Skorzeny, *Skorzeny's Special Missions* (London: Robert Hale, 1957), pp. 146–50.

give false orders and upset their communications, sending bodies of troops in the wrong direction. Your preparations must be complete by the second of December, and you can settle all the details with Colonel-General Jodl."

Skorzeny was in a position where he could afford to speak his mind: "Mein Führer, the short time available will make necessary a great deal of improvisation. What is to be done about the other commando projects? I cannot manage them all together!"

Dismissing the objections, Hitler insisted: "I know that the time is very, very short, but you must do all that is humanly possible. . . . I forbid you to pass beyond the front line in person. In no circumstances must you let yourself be taken prisoner!"

The interview completed, Skorzeny was taken to General Guderian, now chief of staff of the Army High Command, Oberkommando des Heeres (OKH), and later to General Jodl, who outlined the details of the plan concerning the Sixth Panzer Army, to which Skorzeny's brigade was assigned.

Concerned about the view international law takes of wearing enemy uniform, Skorzeny consulted a "specialist" in this field. He was satisfied with the outcome of the conversations. His small commando units, the Einheit Steilau, who were going to disguise themselves in Allied uniforms and spread confusion in the American rear areas, risked being treated as spies and brought before a court-martial if captured. The larger units of his so-called 150th Panzer Brigade were going to act as an advance guard and, posing as Allied soldiers, seize bridges over the Meuse. International law forbids *only the use of arms* by a soldier wearing the enemy uniform; so if the advance guard wore German uniforms underneath their disguises and removed their false uniforms before actually opening fire, the dictates of international law would be met.[2] Satisfied, Skorzeny went back to his own headquarters.

---

[2] Legal opinion on this issue by R. Stuart Jenkins, Esq., Media, Pennsylvania, August 25, 1967:

THE ISSUE is whether or not the use of enemy uniforms [by Skorzeny in December, 1944] to penetrate enemy lines for action behind the lines is improper and contrary to the Laws of War.

THE CONSIDERATIONS, in determining the answer to the foregoing *Issue* are as follows:

1. Paragraph 23 (f) of the Hague Regulations of 1907 prohibits improper use of *** Military insignia and uniform of the enemy as well as the distinctive badges of the Geneva Convention. There is no indication in the Hague Regulations as to what constitutes "improper use."

2. Writers on International Law have expressed themselves variously on the use of enemy uniforms as follows:

a. There is clear agreement that the use of the enemy uniform for the purpose of deceiving the enemy by concealing hostile status is unlawful when done in combat.

cf., Bluntschli, Das Moderne, Voelkerrecht 318, 319, (3rd ed. 1878); 3 Calvo Le Droit International 152, 154, (1880); 2 Westlake International Law 80 (2nd ed. 1913); Lawrence, Principles of International Law, 552 note 18.

Finally the day came when Hitler had to bring even his field commanders into his plans; reluctant as he was to let the word out of OKW, he realized that his commanders needed time for their own planning. Hitler kept his generals under close rein—in contrast to Nazi gauleiters, whom he allowed great latitude in making local decisions and from whom he tolerated much that was politically embarrassing—scrutinizing details of the command decisions made by subordinates and other matters that are ordinarily avoided by planners of strategy, to say nothing of heads of state. However, with the date of attack (code name: Null-Day) set at November 25, time was growing short. Accordingly, on October 22, the day after Jodl submitted his finished

---

    b. Some writers take the position that the wearing of enemy uniforms for camouflage purposes is prohibited under all circumstances.
        cf., Winthrop, Military Law and Precedents Section 1223 (2nd ed. 1896, reprinted 1920).
    c. Other writers maintain that enemy uniforms may be worn on occasions other than open combat, i.e., when approaching enemy lines prior to battle.
        cf., Bordell, The Law of War, 283, (1908); 2 Westlake, International Law, 80, note 21.
    d. Certain writers maintain that the distinction between the use of enemy uniform in open combat and otherwise is a spurious one.
        cf., 3 Hyde, International Law 1811, 1812, (2nd rev. ed. 1945); Jobst II, Is the Wearing of the Enemy's Uniform a Violation of the Laws of War? 35 Am. J. Int'l L. 435, 440, 441, (1941); Lawrence, Principles of International Law 552, (6th ed. 1915); Hall, Treatise on International Law, 649, (8th ed. 1924); Spaight, War Rights on Land, 104, 105, (1911).
    3. It is to be noted, however, that none of the writers has considered the specific situation in the Skorzeny case in which enemy uniforms were used as a stratagem to penetrate enemy lines for the purpose of action behind those lines, ie., seizure of one or more bridges over the Meuse River between Liege and Namur.
    4. The settled distinction between ruses and stratagems of war that are allowed and the acts of treachery and perfidy that are unlawful must be kept in mind in determining when the use of the enemy's uniform is unlawful.
        cf., Lawrence, Principles of International Law 551, (6th ed. 1915) "that they may be used at all is due to the fact that war is a conflict of wits as much as a conflict of arms." Stowell, International Law, 515, (1931) "To prohibit them would be to arrest progress and to favor mere brawn at the expense of brains." Holland, The Laws of War 45 note 20, (1908). (Article 24 of the Hague Regulations does not authorize acts of treachery); 2 Wheaton, International Law 208, (7th ed. Keith 1944) Article 24 is subject to prohibition of treachery as well as that contained in Article 23 (f). Spaight War Rights on Land, 106, (1911) Ruses of law are recognized provided they do not involve treachery; Jobst II, Is the Wearing of Enemy's Uniform a Violation of Laws of War? 35 Am. Int'l L. 435, 440, (1941) While ruses of law are legitimate, devices which involve perfidy or treachery are unlawful; Spaight, War Rights on Land, 104, 105, (1911) "The quiddity of the rule is difficult to follow. When the disguise has done what it is intended to do, there is little virtue in discarding it. If it is improper to wear the enemy's uniform in pitched battle it must surely be equally improper to deceive him by wearing it up to the first shot or clash of arms."
    5. So far as can be ascertained the formation and use of the brigade did not contemplate actual combat in American uniforms.
    6. The Department of the Army has taken the position (subsequent to the

operations plan to Hitler, the chiefs of staff of Field Marshals Rundstedt and Model were invited to Rastenburg. Rundstedt's chief of staff, General der Kavellerie Siegfried Westphal, had formerly held the same position under Feldmarschall Albrecht Kesselring on the Italian front. His youth, vigor and intelligence were expected to compensate for Rundstedt's advanced years. Model's chief of staff, General der Infanterie Hans Krebs, had been attached to the Russian Embassy during the period of German-Soviet "friendship." He had always held staff assignments and therefore lacked the experience with troops that Model possessed, but he had remained with his exacting superior for the past two years, and this may be taken at least as proof of his adaptability.

Reporting at Wolfsschanze on October 22, Krebs and Westphal expected the cool reception Hitler customarily accorded his General Staff officers. Aachen had just fallen into Allied hands, and they brought a request from Rundstedt for troops with which to protect the Ruhr. This, like so many earlier requests by OB West, was categorically turned down. They were not, however, prepared for the reception they actually received: upon reporting for a briefing session before seeing the Führer, they were required to sign a pledge of secrecy concerning an operation about which Rundstedt himself was still ignorant, and told that the secret must be kept or they would be shot.

At noon they were brought into the Wolfsschanze, and heard Hitler personally explain the objectives of the offensive—the destruction of enemy forces, not the acquisition of territory, and the attack to Antwerp, which seemed the best method of achieving this end. After Hitler had described the disposition of the attacking armies, Jodl discussed details, though Westphal and Krebs were not let in on the whole extent of the projected operation.

Before they returned to their headquarters, Westphal was instructed to make clear to Rundstedt that he was to hold his front without committing any of the formations earmarked for withdrawal and participation in the offensive. He was also told that OB West was to draft a plan for the first phase of the offensive (as far as the Meuse) and forward it within the next few days.

Skorzeny trial) that Article 23 (f) of the Hague Regulations does not prohibit deceptive use of enemy's uniforms under all circumstances but merely deceptive use in combat action.

cf., U.S. Army Field Manual, The Law of Land Warfare, 23, (1956) The use of enemy uniforms as a ruse is forbidden during combat, but their use at other times is not forbidden.

IN CONCLUSION there is no common agreement among authorities in International Law that the use of enemy uniforms for camouflage purposes is a violation of the Laws of War. The only principle in this area on which all agree is that the use of enemy uniforms in open combat is a violation of the Laws of War. It may, therefore, be concluded that Skorzeny's mission which contemplated the use of enemy uniforms to penetrate enemy lines for action behind the lines was not contrary to the Laws of War.

Meanwhile, Field Marshal Rundstedt was waiting in his command post in Ziegenberg Castle near Frankfurt for an explanation of this mysterious call to Rastenburg.

Rundstedt had been a soldier for fifty years. He was an old man now—his seventieth birthday was only days off—but although Hitler had replaced him on July 3 with Field Marshal Kluge, he had now returned Rundstedt to the command of OB West. The old soldier was not as agile as he had been once. He visited the front only when he had to and did not like his staff to be away from his headquarters. But Hitler, like everyone else who knew Rundstedt, respected him. He was self-contained. Unlike other commanders, who used their traditional privilege of calling Hitler by phone, he refused to enhance his standing with the Führer by this means. Once Hitler wished to talk with him and ordered him to his personal headquarters. "Hitler was pacing up and down for a quarter of an hour before von Rundstedt's arrival, putting on and pulling off his gloves, and as soon as von Rundstedt arrived he left everything just as it was and went to meet the car of the Field Marshal." [3] He never behaved like this with any other officer.

On the other hand, Generalleutnant Günther Blumentritt, Rundstedt's chief of staff from 1942 until September, 1944, saw in his chief a softened version of the prototype of the Prussian officer: "He was excessively modest," said Blumentritt, "too reserved. He led a simple life and was indifferent to money or possessions." Though he had no particular indulgences, he was no abstemious Prussian. He smoked too much and enjoyed drinking. Besides, he liked the French. He felt at home in France during the occupation, and even "chose to speak in French with visiting dignitaries who had expressed a wish to see 'The Field Marshal.' " Everywhere he went he was regarded as a nobleman soldier of the old school, "affable to inferiors, extravagantly polite to women . . . but also to all insignificant people."

Blumentritt recognized in Rundstedt what the Germans call *ein mensch,* a man of sympathy and with a deep knowledge of human nature. And he had a fine wit, which sometimes developed a saber-sharp edge: open in his disenchantment with "the state," he was fond of "uttering bitingly sarcastic historical and political judgments, and had an intuitive presentiment of things to come." His visits with Hitler did not dampen his perception. "Coming from the Führer," said Blumentritt, "he always expressed himself very sharply, saying that the officers of the higher command were all idiots."

Two days after the meeting with Hitler, General Westphal returned to Ziegenberg Castle to report the astonishing news to his chief. Rundstedt, of course, understood its full implications. He had put himself on record two

[3] Günther Blumentritt, MS # B-344.

months earlier as believing that only a stiff German offensive would relieve the pressure on retreating German forces and allow the Heer to set up a more effective defense of the homeland; but an offensive of this magnitude, with Antwerp as its objective, struck him as unrealistic—though he conceded that the plan itself showed a touch of genius.

Still, attempting to change Hitler's mind about the extent of the offensive would be unrealistic, too. All he could do was convert Hitler's injunction to draw up an operational plan for the first phase of the attack into an occasion for submitting an alternative plan—one that matched the situation at the front and could be carried out realistically with the current German strength in men and matériel. Any operation that hoped to succeed, he believed, must recognize the fact that the Allies held a two-to-one superiority over German forces. It must also recognize the strong possibility that divisions earmarked for the German offensive might at any moment have to be used to relieve exhausted units at the front—especially if the Allies were to launch an attack of their own in the meantime, as intelligence reports indicated was likely.

In response to Hitler's order for an operations plan for the "first phase of the attack," Rundstedt and Westphal set about drafting a plan for an offensive to be launched from a front sufficiently narrow to guarantee a considerable concentration of forces.

Under the Rundstedt plan, the Fifth and Sixth Panzer armies would advance with the Sixth Panzer Army on the right on a 25-mile front between Simmerath (near Monschau) and Bleialf, just southwest of the Schnee Eifel. They would achieve a rapid breakthrough and drive toward the Meuse at a point north of Huy. Simultaneously a secondary, heavily armored thrust by the Fifteenth Army from the north in the bulging Roermond sector (on the Meuse twenty-five miles north of Aachen) would meet with the main thrust near Liège, enveloping the concentration of Allied troops preparing for an attack on the Ruhr. Flank protection would be given by the advance of the Seventh Army in the south and by the advance of the Fifteenth Army in the north.

At his command post in Krefeld-Fichtenhain (formerly a hospital for alcoholics), Field Marshal Model also received word of the coming offensive. The thickset but spruce field marshal was a favorite of the Führer. Not only was he respected for his brilliant defensive achievements in Russia and now in the west, but also he was apparently more at home wtih the Nazi regime than the average German field marshal. A product of the German Staff School, he had proved himself a forceful leader. And if Oberst Günther Reichhelm's evaluation of his personality is accurate, small wonder. Reichhelm, Model's operations officer, recollected that it could be said of his chief, *"Den lieb ich, der Unmögliches begehrt"* (I love him who craves the impossible). Model was the embodiment of Hitler's "fanatic leader."

Yet even Model had grave misgivings about Antwerp as an objective. When first told of the offensive by General Krebs, his reaction was frank: "To me the whole affair seems damned moldy."

At about the time that Field Marshal Model was apprised of Hitler's plan for the grand offensive, his Army Group B took over command of Manteuffel's Fifth Panzer Army, now withdrawn from the line where it had been fighting under Army Group G to the south. Manteuffel reported to his new superior with some misgivings. Besides having totally different personalities, the two men had already experienced difficulties. In 1942, when Manteuffel was commanding a combat team of the 7th Panzer Division on the eastern front, Model ordered an attack that Manteuffel, in view of the waist-deep snow, held up. In a rage, Model told Manteuffel that he should be court-martialed. The division commander, General Freiherr von Stroke—incidentally, Model's uncle—backed Manteuffel's decision. Since that dispute there had been no contact between them.

Now, two years later, when Manteuffel reported with a sharp, formal salute, he was greeted brusquely.

"Do you remember our conversation on the Russian front in 1942?"

Manteuffel nodded.

"That is now finished. We two now have the same task. We are good friends."

"Good."

This episode was hardly the last difficulty that Manteuffel was to experience with the fanatic who was the real tactical commander of the forthcoming attack, but the atmosphere of mutual respect in which they now operated enabled them to work in relative harmony.

During the next six weeks, all the time that was left to him, Model would invest all of his charm, personal force, and persuasive powers in an effort to convince Hitler that the goal of Antwerp was beyond the capability of German forces as they stood in the fall of 1944. Yet to his subordinates he gave no indication that anything short of Antwerp had ever entered his mind.

Nor did Model's unenthusiastic reaction to the proposed offensive affect the manner in which he undertook a study of Jodl's operations plan. Having studied it, he outlined his conception of the first phase of the offensive in response to Hitler's order. In contrast to Rundstedt, Model held that the northern pincer advocated by OB West could not be made strong enough to be of any use. All forces would be badly needed in the main action (the Ardennes); therefore, such a secondary attack meant wasting forces. He insisted that it would be better to use the armored formations assigned by Rundstedt to the secondary attack in a general reserve, or throw them in as the secondary wave of the main drive.

The attack outlined by Model (given the code name Herbstnebel—Autumn Fog) was to be carried out along a forty-mile front running south from the Hürtgen Forest. Attacking forces would be led by two panzer armies, as in the other plans, with the Seventh Army pouring in after the breakthrough on the left.

In Model's plan, the main effort was to be made not by Dietrich's Sixth Panzer Army but by Manteuffel's Fifth. Not only was the Fifth Panzer Army attacking through the easier terrain, but also Model considered Manteuffel, despite their cool personal relationship, the best man to be entrusted with the responsibility. Model's views fell on deaf ears.

On November 2 Rundstedt and Model each received copies of Jodl's latest version of the OKW's operations plan for the offensive, dated the day before. The latest version left Jodl's basic draft of October 11 unchanged, but introduced a significant modification: in addition to widening the attack area north and south, the plan was enlarged by a secondary attack. Army Group H in the north was to throw in a second thrust as soon as the Allies began to throw stronger forces against the Sixth Panzer Army.[4]

Hitler apparently was able to predict what his more conservative generals might propose. In case the inclusion of a secondary attack should evoke thoughts of a plan terminating in a pincer movement closing at the Meuse, Jodl made it clear in his covering letter that Hitler would accept nothing less than a thrust to Antwerp: "The venture for the far flung objective is unalterable although, from a strictly technical standpoint, it appears to be disproportionate to our available forces. In our present situation, however, we must not shrink from staking everything on one card."[5]

But Hitler was willing to get his generals' views once more. His plan was sent as a plan only, not an order. This he did purposely "to give them first an opportunity to express their opinions and submit the result of their deliberations."

The very day Rundstedt received the plan he left for Model's headquarters, having arranged for Model, Westphal, Manteuffel, Dietrich, and General der Panzertruppen Erich Brandenberger to be present—and Jodl there also to explain the plan. When the group had gathered, Jodl covered the details. Then he asked for questions.

"General von Manteuffel will speak first," said Rundstedt.

Manteuffel was frank. "General, I think under your plan that we can

[4] Percy Schramm, MS # A-862.
[5] *Ibid.*

reach the Meuse—but only if certain conditions are met." He then went on to list those conditions:

1. The units promised must be made available before the attack with personnel and matériel, including support from the Luftwaffe;
2. All supplies must be made available at the start of the attack, especially fuel, ammunition, and equipment;
3. The plan must offer improved mobility of all units and improved bridgeheads;
4. The movement of the Seventh Army (on Manteuffel's left) must be strengthened.
5. The diversions in other sectors must proceed as Jodl stated.

The meeting resulted in no alteration to the plan: the concept, according to Jodl, was "irrevocable." But it did serve to bring the commanders of the field armies into the picture. The meeting on November 2 was the first time they had been apprised of the plan. Manteuffel, for one, was astonished at the detailed planning that had been done at such a high level as OKW and was based on such risky assumptions.

During Manteuffel's arguments Model said little and appeared absorbed in his subordinate's reasoning. The meeting over, Rundstedt and Manteuffel stayed for dinner at Model's invitation. He wanted to talk the whole thing over in a more confidential, relaxed atmosphere.

"General," he said to Manteuffel, "I agree on the whole with what you said in the meeting. But please go into more detail how you have come to the conclusion that seizing the bridgeheads over the Meuse is as far as the Army can go." [6]

Manteuffel expanded his comments, including his estimate of Allied strength and capabilities. He repeated the prerequisites for an attack against them. Only under unusually favorable conditions, he felt, could the German forces continue the attack after reaching the Meuse. More likely, allowing for losses due to the difficult terrain, bad weather, and Allied resistance, the Germans would be feeling the wear and tear by the time the panzer armies reached the Meuse.

At this point, Manteuffel continued, the attack would have to be reinforced in depth. But with what forces? All fronts had critical shortages. Where would the reinforcements come from? "I drew the conclusion," Manteuffel wrote later, "that our forces would not be sufficient for the successful continuation of the attack across the Meuse, where, if not sooner, we had to expect strong enemy forces." [7]

Manteuffel was an avid bridge player. Borrowing from the lexicon of that

[6] Interview by author with Manteuffel, October, 1966.
[7] Hasso von Manteuffel, MS # B-151; Schramm, *op. cit.*

game, he pushed his argument one step further: "What we are planning here, General, is a 'grand slam' in attempting to go all the way to Antwerp. I do not think we hold the cards. I would like to see the bid reduced to a 'little slam.' After a penetration of the thin American lines in the Ardennes, the two panzer armies could wheel north. My own left flank could be protected by the Meuse on the west and we could cut off all of the First American Army north of the penetration. We could inflict tremendous damage. Furthermore, I do not see how we can launch this attack before December ten."

Model was impressed with these views but decided to go into the matter further before submitting his recommendations.

The next day, November 3, Model and Manteuffel met again at Krefeld-Fichtenhain. There they worked further on Manteuffel's "little slam," a plan that was destined to crop up from time to time, always to be disapproved by the Führer. From that day on, not Rundstedt, or Model, or Manteuffel made any plans for operations beyond the Meuse. But, despite their growing mutual confidence, none of them ever mentioned this fact to any of the others.

Model was now convinced that planning for the "first phase" of the attack was quite enough. Accordingly, he modified his Herbstnebel plan to include two sets of suggestions, one calling for the "small solution," which he preferred, and the other for the "large solution." In his recommendations to his superiors he incorporated Manteuffel's concept of a wheel north upon reaching the Meuse. The Seventh Army would cover the left flank of the thrust; the Fifteenth Army was to support it by a secondary thrust from the Sittard area to the north; the two limbs of the pincers would meet in the vicinity of Tongres, northwest of Liège. The pocket thus formed would catch some twenty to twenty-five American and British divisions.

In the event the Führer insisted on his own plan, Model preferred the Fifteenth Army, in the north, not to be committed in the offensive; the forces earmarked for it should be used to reinforce the Fifth and Sixth Panzer armies.

Model's recommendations were duly sent through channels to Rundstedt, whose perception of the situation was different from both Hitler's and Model's. Having both OKW's operations plan and the commentary by Model at hand, Rundstedt held to his initial conviction that so long as Hitler insisted on Antwerp as an objective, a secondary thrust (which Model desired canceled) from the Venlo-Roermond area had to be made simultaneously with the main thrust. The double envelopment, Rundstedt argued, would be the first phase of the drive to Antwerp. The Allies would not be able to mass for a counterthrust, and the real purpose of the attack—the destruction of Allied forces—would be best realized, for American and British forces would be encircled.

The suggestions by Rundstedt and Model regarding Jodl's developed operations plan of November 1 were received, noted, and ignored at OKW. The

Führer had already made up his mind in favor of the "grand slam," or "large solution." He continued to insist that the deeper the German thrust into Allied rear communications, supply lines, and supply centers, the more feasible the destruction of enemy forces in the Aachen-Maastricht-Liège area. If German forces pivoted to the right immediately after the breakthrough, turning toward the area of concentration of enemy forces, then conditions would be the same as those governing a frontal attack. The "large solution," on the other hand, met the requirement that forces be destroyed and, in addition, looked forward to depriving the enemy of his only good port, rolling up *the entire front* between the line of departure and Antwerp.

Hitler's design for the offensive had prevailed over that of his generals. It remained for him to *will* it to "reality." That he should be able to reject the opinion of men in close touch with the front was explained by some of his subordinate officers as another example of his conception of himself as an authority in all spheres of life. Others attributed it to Hitler's *Frontfremdheit*— failure to appreciate the front. Doubtless it was a combination of both. For despite efforts to rotate staff officers, the OKW had steadily lost contact with true battle conditions as the war progressed, especially following on the centralization of all executive powers in Hitler's hands. He seldom left headquarters; and as his distaste for unfavorable news became more evident to his generals, the information he received regarding the situation at the front and the industrial output on the home front become increasingly unreliable. Since all decisions had to be made by Hitler personally, they were inevitably delayed, and in a fast-moving situation, countermeasures directed by Hitler's headquarters were often based on circumstances which in reality no longer existed.

General Staff Officer Günther Reichhelm, ordered from the eastern front to become Model's operations officer during the last weeks of October, did not suffer Hitler's handicap of aversion to fact. Before reporting for his duties with Army Group B, Reichhelm took the opportunity to make a tour of the western front to get a personal idea of the condition of the whole area—the roads, the formation of ground and terrain, and especially the condition of the troops. He visited nearly every corps and division headquarters and several regimental and battalion headquarters from the mouth of the Scheldt to the Moselle ports.

On the long 280-mile front Reichhelm seemed to find only a few units he could call fully organized. "All the rest were improvised units of all kinds, mostly under strange, not familiar, staff command and with even troopless headquarters among them." However, the miracle of defense then being achieved by Field Marshal Model before the Siegfried Line and the failure of the Allied parachute attack at Nijmegen gave Reichhelm "a new start, restored the balance of his mind, and filled him with new hope for further action." [8]

Reichhelm had inspected a beaten and demoralized army that was still fighting.[9] It was miraculous, he observed, considering the damage to cities and to railway systems and essential war industries, that German resistance continued. But he also said, "It could be foreseen that as early as spring, 1945, Germany would break down if something extraordinary, some miracle, did not take place." [10]

That there was still faith in "last possibilities" was a product of German propaganda. Goebbels had been permitted to go ahead with his idea of a "Fortress Germany" and draw upon every ounce of German man (and woman) power to bolster the Heer and restore losses in the industrial plant. The many propaganda agencies of the Nazi Party kept telling Germans that they were succeeding, that it would not be long before a fantastic new weapon would reverse the trend of the war and bring victory to Germany. As Reichhelm recalled: "The propaganda . . . led to false suppositions, especially as to the strength of Germany's home reserves and as to new units and outfits, etc. Overstatements of this kind formed the material for many decisions and orders of higher and highest commands." [11]

So, says Reichhelm, thoughts of surrender were rejected. But there was something more. In the throes of the *Götterdämmerung* fever that engulfed him after the July assassination attempt, Hitler regarded any inclination toward retreat at the front or despair at home as evidence of sedition. Germans were held in terror by the realization that as long as Hitler lived reprisals would be taken against any person declared to be a "traitor," and against his family also. And when Hitler proved indestructible they lost their nerve.

So that was the relationship between "idea" and "reality." It was tragic, and it was absurd. Hitler and the great mass of Germans whom he had prom-

[8] Günther Reichhelm, MS # A-926.

[9] At this time (October, 1944) Field Marshal Model had unsuccessfully made the following request for men and matériel:

1. At least one volksgrenadier division for the Dutch area;
2. Three or four VGD's for the Aachen region;
3. About 200 tanks—Panzer IV's or Panzer V's—or armored storm artillery guns in order to fill up the motorized units at hand and the antitank detachments of the infantry units;
4. 20,000 recruits with small arms to fill up all units as to be directed by Army Group;
5. A fuel reserve of at least 1,500 cubic meters (300,000 gallons) additional to the current supply. Schramm, *op. cit.*

[10] Reichhelm did not know that Allied bombing, though extensive, had not knocked out German war production; that in fact war production reached a peak during the fall of 1944.

[11] Reichhelm, *op. cit.*

ised to lead into "the new order" were mutually trapped in the myth that Hitler and the Nazis had created.

As the planning stage of the offensive drew to a close, all responsible German commanders concentrated their attention on the preparation of the attack forces. To this end the western front was favored over the eastern front, and Army Group B over Army Groups G to the south and H to the north. Immediately after Rundstedt and Model were initiated into the plan it was announced that the 2d, 9th, and 116th Panzer divisions and the 10th SS Panzer Division were to be rehabilitated close to the front. Jodl informed the Army General Staff that fourteen volksgrenadier divisions (including the five already ordered) were to be assembled in the west by November 20. Other units were expected soon from the Russian front.

OB West, Field Marshal Rundstedt, set out to meet his responsibility for selecting the divisions for the various tasks and starting their special training. He had already recommended a strong, simultaneous attack on the right wing north of Aachen to meet with the main effort, the Ardennes, in order to encircle and destroy the U.S. First Army in the area between Liège and the front on either side of Aachen. At this moment he was contemplating a target date of November 25; however, he feared an Allied attack might come before this date, in which case all planning would have to be temporarily canceled. Rundstedt had pointed out that the forces to be employed were weak compared with those of the Allies. It would be very difficult to hold the captured area unless the enemy was completely annihilated. He therefore forwarded a request for additional units to be made available from the Zone of the Interior.

OKW rejected Rundstedt's requests for additional troops, just as it rejected his plan for a pincers movement. But he had pointed to the possibility of a prior attack by the Allies, and his warning did not escape OKW notice. On November 5 Rundstedt was instructed to organize his front to conform with the OKW plan of attack. The Sixth Panzer Army was assigned to him effective November 10. Fifth Panzer Army, at the moment defending on both sides of Aachen, was to be withdrawn later, and its sector from Düren to the north of Roermond taken over by the Fifteenth Army. The divisions that had been set aside for the offensive, it was emphasized, were to be committed *only* in the sectors assigned to them. The divisions left over were to be assigned directly by the Führer (OKW reserves).

The most welcome news to come to Rundstedt in early November was the announcement that the Sixth Panzer Army had begun its movement. Transporting the 1st, 2d, 9th, and 12th SS Panzer divisions (and at this time the Panzer Lehr) had required 800 trains. Having reached the command area of OB West, the units were to be immediately "withdrawn" for "rehabilitation" to the Cologne-Rheydt-Jülich-Düren-Bonn region.

Despite continued Allied air attacks against rail centers, the movement of the Sixth Panzer Army, of the volksgrenadier divisions, and of the general headquarters troops was carried out almost according to schedule—all now began to arrive in increasing numbers.

The problem of secrecy remained. To give an excuse for the troop concentrations—which would inevitably be detected—an order intended to mislead both the enemy and subordinate commands was issued: ". . . the German command expects a major attack by the enemy against the line Cologne-Bonn to take place this year. One northwest of Cologne, and the other in the Eifel."

On November 7 General Jodl placed the total number of divisions available for Watch on the Rhine at 38, plus 9 artillery corps and 7 werfer brigades. This would have been an impressive increase over previous estimates had it not included six divisions, four of them panzer, still pinned down in defensive battles now developing—and all the divisions of the Fifteenth Army, two of which had been merged. Self-deception in OKW achieved a new high. The inflated troop list of November 7 was attached to the final operational directive, Watch on the Rhine, signed by Hitler on November 10.

Hitler's official directive of November 10 set November 27 as the date for completing operational concentration of troops, so the attack was postponed until December 1. This, Rundstedt found, meant that he shared a dilemma with OKW: each week of delay saw German attack forces growing stronger, yet it also meant that the Allies were growing stronger at the same time, and it lessened the chance of keeping the attack secret. The commanders of the attacking armies, faced with a thousand loose ends, wanted time. Model could have used more time also but preferred to adhere to the December 1 deadline.

Hitler continued to dispense a stream of specific instructions, repeating in detail what he had already directed. Even a slogan was supplied; once the breakthrough was achieved, the watchword was to be "Thrust on and across the Maas."

Now that everything was set—on paper—the success of the projected offensive depended upon maintenance of the status quo on the front. The enemy had to be held, especially from making a breakthrough, without compromising the creation of a formidable attacking force. This might not be easy.

On November 2 Rundstedt estimated that the Allies were employing about 17 armored and 40 infantry and airborne divisions, with 3 armored and 5 infantry divisions in reserve. Out of approximately 80 units, less than a fourth, he calculated, were not engaged.

He predicted that Allied attacks could be expected to begin within two weeks, those in the vicinity of Metz before those at Aachen. He could hardly have been more accurate. On November 8 the Allied attack he had foreseen began in Lorraine, where the First German Army was defending in front of the Siegfried Line from north of Metz southward to Nancy and Strasbourg.

South of this line the German Nineteenth Army was trying to hold hastily prepared positions west of Vosges against French and American forces driving toward the Belfort Gap and the Swiss border.

The next day the Third U.S. Army attacked north of Metz, just as Hitler was signing the order putting the Ardennes "large solution" into effect and forbidding Rundstedt from touching divisions set aside for the Ardennes offensive.

On November 14 Rundstedt forwarded to OKW a pessimistic appraisal of the situation in Lorraine. General Patton's Third U.S. Army, attacking north and southeast of Metz, was threatening to encircle this ancient fortress city. The First German Army at Metz had pulled back to a shortened position; Metz would have to be written off within a week.

Two days later the dreaded American offensive from Aachen against Cologne was finally launched. To meet it Hitler agreed to spread German troops thin on the Netherlands front and reinforce other fronts. By November 28 Jülich and Düren, on the Roer River, were within range of First U.S. Army's light artillery.

The First U.S. Army attack was having devastating effects. Twice during the three days following the jump-off (November 16), Model submitted a plea that a double envelopment of the new American Aachen salient be launched, using troops earmarked for Watch on the Rhine. Rundstedt was essentially in agreement. Hitler's reaction was the same as ever: "No improvisations" would be permitted.

On November 25 Jodl visited Rundstedt's command post at Ziegenberg. The crippling effect of the Allied November offensives was coming to be more fully appreciated. Of the 38 units promised for the offensive, many had been committed or would have to be held in the line. But Jodl had not come to discuss the deteriorating situation either in the south or on the Roer. Hitler had sent him to discuss details of the coming offensive and to deal at first hand with the growing heretical opinion in favor of the "small solution." The attack had been postponed once more, this time until December 10. But despite the gloomy predictions of his generals, Hitler held fast to the guiding principle of the offensive.

Soon after his visit with Hitler in October, Otto Skorzeny was startled to receive a copy of an order signed by one of the senior headquarters officers and entitled, "Secret commando operations: All units must . . . send in the names of all English-speaking officers and men who are prepared to voluntarily apply for transfer, for a special operation, to the formation commanded by Obersturmbannführer Skorzeny, in Friedenthal, near Berlin."

Skorzeny, in his own words, "almost had a fit." He knew that Allied Intelligence could not fail to learn about such a widely distributed order, and as he saw it, this piece of folly meant the end of his enterprise even before it had begun. However, his official protests in writing fell into the abyss of bureaucratic channels, and finally Reichsführer of the SS Heinrich Himmler himself expressed the general attitude: "It's idiotic, but it has been done. We cannot hold up your operation now."

Skorzeny went back to his headquarters and continued with his work. His force, the 150th Panzer Brigade, would consist of 3,300 men. The execution of Operation Greif, named after a mythical bird, was based on the assumptions that the Sixth Panzer Army would secure a clean break through the American lines on the first day of the attack and that by the second day the Meuse would have been reached and crossed. His unit, therefore, needed great mobility, but he could keep his support units to a minimum.

It will be recalled that Skorzeny's operation had two parts. The major effort of the 150th Panzer Brigade was to be made by a relatively standard tactical unit, though it was far below an actual brigade in strength. Its organization, as approved by Jodl, consisted of two tank companies, three reconnaissance companies, three motorized infantry battalions, and antiaircraft defense and fire support units. This was the group that was to accompany Dietrich's lead formations and then, in American and British uniforms, dash ahead and seize the Meuse bridges at Engis, Amay, and Huy by surprise. Skorzeny told Jodl in no uncertain terms that air photographs of the three bridges to be seized were indispensable.

The other part of the operation, that of the commando company (Einheit Steilau), would employ nine teams of German officers and men, fluent in English and American slang, who were to roam the roads in the American rear, spreading news of disaster, changing directional signs, and doing everything possible to create panic and confusion in the rear areas.

But Skorzeny had other problems besides the possible compromise of his mission by the "secret commando operations" order. Captured American tanks, scout cars, and trucks were in surprisingly short supply, possibly because the German line units who captured such equipment were reluctant to give it up. Even more disturbing was the lack of volunteers with fluent knowledge of American slang. Most of those who qualified in this respect were sailors who had spent considerable time in America. Of these he had only ten. The general linguistic ability of the troops available was so poor that Skorzeny concluded that only very few should try to talk to Americans. For most of his men, the best way of operating was simply to mingle with the fleeing Americans and pretend to be too flurried and overcome to speak. To make up for part of the deficiency of American tanks, Skorzeny was supplied with twelve German tanks, camouflaged in their guns and turrets to make them look like Shermans. "All I can say," he commented dryly, "is that they can deceive only very young American troops, viewed at night from very far away."

He made no secret of his difficulties. He carried his problems to Jodl, to Model, to Rundstedt, and even to the Führer himself. At a meeting in the Reichschancellory in Berlin, he told Hitler of the various deficiencies, including the lack of air photographs, which he had been promised weeks before. Wrathfully, Hitler turned on the chief of the Luftwaffe, Hermann Göring, in such violent terms as to embarrass Skorzeny, who with all his bravado was conscious that his rank was only that of lieutenant colonel.

But the preparations had at least one light side, the speculation among the men of the 150th Panzer Brigade as to what their missions would be. The mere seizure of bridges over the Meuse River and spreading of chaos behind enemy lines was far too modest for the imagination of some. One man, a lieutenant in the commando company, informed Skorzeny that he had figured out their real mission: to go straight to Paris and capture the Supreme Allied Commander, General Eisenhower. Skorzeny listened with interest but neither agreed nor disagreed. At the end of the confidential conversation he merely admonished his speculating lieutenant "to keep as silent as the grave." The nonsilent grave was unwittingly to work havoc in the Allied rear within the next few days.

The impact of the Allied offensive throughout November continued severe. The Heer had been driven back to the Siegfried Line from the Luxembourg border to Switzerland in the south. In the center, north of the Ardennes, the West Wall had been penetrated as far east as the Roer. On the northern flank the Heer had retreated to Roermond. In Holland it had given up Nijmegen. Divisions earmarked for the Ardennes offensive had been left in the line, and others brought up as a part of the Ardennes concentration had been committed. Replacements from the interior counted on to fill out decimated units had been fed into the line. The date of the offensive was confirmed as December 10.

Even the Führer was impressed with the losses and delays, but he did not relinquish his determination to go on with the concentration of forces for the Ardennes offensive. Accordingly, on November 29, 1944, Field Marshal Model issued his formal orders. Based on the OKW order on November 10, the order embodied the concept of the "large solution." The code name at Army Group B remained Herbstnebel.

As time went on and the situation during November continued to degenerate along the whole German front, Manteuffel became more and more convinced that the "large solution," or "grand slam," as he personally referred to it, was infeasible. Furthermore, he was highly dissatisfied with some of the detailed tactics that had been dictated to the army commanders by Hitler and

OKW. In late November he decided to visit the front, where he would later attempt to penetrate American lines, even though his own Fifth Panzer Army was still defending around Aachen.

Disguising himself as a colonel of infantry, Manteuffel pretended that he was reconnoitering for a routine relief of a division in the Siegfried Line overlooking the Our River. He reported to the division commander holding the sector and went to see the battalion commanders on the front. Here he stayed for twelve hours, questioning officers and men, especially those returning from combat patrols. "What are the habits of the Amis?" he asked.

The results of the visit were enlightening. The Americans in the sector, he learned, considered this area a "quiet sector," almost a rest area. Every night the Americans would remain on the alert until about an hour after darkness. Then they would retire to their huts for the night. An hour before dawn they would rise, shave, and come into position. In the meantime, during the night, German patrols could penetrate miles into American territory with relative impunity.

The habits of the troops on the Eifel front gave Manteuffel considerable pause. It would be silly, he reasoned, to wake these people up and alert them with a massive artillery preparation as directed by the Führer. Perhaps such a preparation would apply elsewhere, but in this area far better results could be achieved by letting the Americans sleep and crossing the Our in rubber boats during the hours of darkness. When the Amis came into position in the morning they would find their foxholes already occupied by the Germans.

But such a change of method would require the approval of the Führer himself. Besides, pugnacious Manteuffel wanted one last say regarding the "grand slam," and this at the highest level. He went to his immediate boss, Field Marshal Model.

Model was in sympathy with Manteuffel's views; he also wanted to speak his own piece one more time. Together they went to Ziegenberg Castle, command post of OB West. Field Marshal Rundstedt, by now personally disenchanted with the whole operation, received the two officers cordially. With a wave of the hand he gave them permission to ask for an audience with Hitler in Berlin. He would not attend; if the audience were granted his chief of staff, General Westphal, would represent him.

The resulting conference, held in the Reichschancellory on December 2, was hardly an intimate one. Attending were Jodl, Keitel, Buhle, and Köhler from OKW, as well as Model, Manteuffel, Dietrich, and Westphal. Rundstedt's deliberate absence was noted. Altogether, about fifty officers were present.

One other significant absentee was Brandenberger, recently appointed commander of Seventh Army. Possibly Model thought it necessary that only the commanders of the main attacking armies be present. However, it was generally recognized that Model did not like Brandenberger, a "typical" product of the General Staff Corps, with the "features of a scientist," not the sort to appeal to Model. Their ways of thinking showed such fundamental differences that "they talked over one another's head." [12]

Sepp Dietrich, though present, hardly opened his mouth throughout the entire five-hour meeting. Indeed, he played as insignificant a part in the development of Army Group B's operations plans as the absent General Brandenberger, but for different reasons. Dietrich was the kind of Bavarian Germans like to think of as "typical." Hearty and bluff, he was liked by fellow SS officers for his joviality, his native cunning, and his bravery as a commander. Associated with the Nazi Party from its early days, he had risen step by step from the rank of technical sergeant to commander of large SS units. His exploits and personality had gained him popularity with the public, who knew scarcely anything about other commanders. He was a favorite with Hitler, who did not realize that Dietrich's abilities were probably limited to that of division commander at most. His rise had continued.

But the higher Dietrich had risen, the more noticeable his reliance on others became. Evidently, according to one witness, Dietrich "was sensible enough to realize that by now more was being expected of him than he was capable of doing." He relied completely upon his chief of staff, the capable Brigadeführer der Waffen-SS Fritz Kraemer, in all matters pertaining to higher command functions. Furthermore, Dietrich was reportedly beginning to lose some of his "enthusiasm for self-sacrifice." He still enjoyed drinks and companionship, but now he was thinking of himself more and "no longer capable of inspiring his divisions with the enthusiasm [that had] formerly emanated from him and which the Führer still presumed unchanged." [13]

The conference, which went on for hours, dealt chiefly with the hard realities of the attack, particularly with the means necessary to exploit the initial breakthrough. Behind the discussion was the unexpressed hope of the field commanders that Hitler, while intending to reach Antwerp, might provide enough wherewithal to reach the Meuse. But if reaching the Meuse was to be anything more than a "bulge" in the front, as Model expressed it, there would have to be an enveloping action this side of the river. And *that* meant the "small solution" that Hitler had rejected several times already.

Model, ably assisted by his operations officer, Reichhelm, made the first presentations; his speech was short and clear, the concise language of the experienced, aggressive soldier. Everybody in the large conference room listened with respect. He gave his position frankly, courageously, and vigorously. Hitler also was strongly impressed.

It required art and courage to report unpleasant facts to the Führer in these days, unless he was in one of his rare expansive moods. But at this late date the commanding generals had no choice but to let him know that

[12] Interview by author with Manteuffel, October, 1966.
[13] Schramm, *op. cit.*

units and training were still deficient. Each had his special anxieties. Supplies showed large gaps. "In all," recalled Reichhelm, "it appeared necessary and inevitable to procrastinate the attack for at least three weeks."

At one point Model questioned the supply situation as given by Buhle. Hitler, who enjoyed such details, thereupon tried to telephone Minister of War Production Albert Speer to get first-hand information about the amount of equipment and the possible date of delivery.

Model and Manteuffel, sitting opposite Hitler at the narrow table, were the only officers to make formal presentations. When Manteuffel's turn came, he reviewed his "conditions" as before. He expressed his misgivings about the German infantry's ability to effect a quick breakthrough against American troops during daylight. He wanted to advance the hour of attack, to catch the enemy unaware. He described the American activities that invited infiltration.

Model had previously cautioned Manteuffel "not to be too abrupt" in explaining to Hitler his lack of confidence in the German infantry's ability to break through without cover of darkness—yet Model was apparently glad for Manteuffel's support. Dietrich, however, entered the debate against a night attack, knowing of Hitler's faith in heavy artillery preparations, which was based on his own experiences in World War I. Finally a compromise was reached. The two armies would use different tactics: Dietrich would use heavy artillery preparation and attack at dawn; Manteuffel would begin infiltration a bit earlier.

Manteuffel had one more recommendation. The forests on the east side of the Our River were extremely black, he observed. He was concerned that a mass of searchlight batteries would give away German positions and intentions prematurely. He would like to use artificial moonlight, created by bouncing heavy searchlight beams off the clouds. This measure, usually associated with the defense, would light the way sufficiently for his troops to move into position while causing no suspicions among the Americans.

"How do you know you'll have clouds?" Hitler demanded.

"Mein Führer, you have decided everything on the prospect that the weather will be bad."

Manteuffel obtained approval of his scheme for surprise—the artificial moonlight and infiltration of American lines. It applied to his army only.

Toward the end of the conference, Model made a final attempt to bring about the adoption of the "little solution," only to hear Hitler reject it once more, along with what by now must have become a dreary repetition: the origin and development of the concept of the offensive, the anticipated destruction or capture of enormous amounts of matériel, the annihilation of 25 to 30 divisions, and the thwarting of the Allied High Command's plans. The Allies would have to agree politically before they could respond. The Western alliance might shatter. Hitler would gamble all because Germany needed a breathing space. (Manteuffel observed that this last point was consciously directed at Model.)

The commanding generals should have left enthusiastic at the conclusion of the conference. During former times, when they still had faith, they would have been elated over Hitler's statement regarding the buildup of strong forces; furthermore, on the all-important question of air support, the Führer had promised 800 to 900 sorties a day.

By contrast, Manteuffel left the long meeting disappointed. He would later recall, "I do not remember any conference so clearly as this one. . . . Nothing was changed in the concept of the operation. The objective was still Antwerp. No decision was made as to the secondary attack to be launched from the northern wing of the Fifteenth Army. The Seventh Army did not get reinforcements as envisaged in the original plan. . . . The result of the conference as a whole was consequently unsatisfactory." [14]

The fact that Hitler kept him for a few moments after the meeting to assure him that the Third Reich had committed 80 percent of its tanks, artillery, and trucks gave him small comfort. He returned to headquarters, Fifth Panzer Army, at Manderscheid in the Eifel, at noon on December 4.

[14] Manteuffel, *op. cit.*

CHAPTER 8

❧❧

The Fog and Mists of the Eifel

ADOLF HITLER and Oberstgruppenführer Josef ("Sepp") Dietrich had developed a rather peculiar relationship. Dietrich was Hitler's darling —the loyal Nazi, Hitler's follower from the early days. And yet, even though Hitler planned his operations to give "staunch old Dietrich" the greatest opportunities for glory, still he seemed to sense what Dietrich himself was beginning to sense, that the former butcher was over his head in charge of the major attacking army of the forthcoming offensive to Antwerp.

The hard core of the Sixth Panzer Army, the four SS panzer divisions, had been withdrawn from the fighting line early and sent to Westphalia, east of the Rhine, for refitting and training. Despite Dietrich's pleas that delays in obtaining necessary equipment were holding up reorganization, Hitler had become dissatisfied with his progress. On November 6 Hitler moved the Sixth Panzer Army across the Rhine to its strategic assembly area, which was roughly bounded by Cologne, Jülich, and Düren. There, under the watchful eye of the driving Field Marshal Model, Dietrich might make more progress. The concentration of troops behind Army Group B in the vicinity of Cologne was but part of a larger plan for the concentration of Sixth Panzer Army. The concentration in the north was to be conducted fairly openly with a display of troop movements by day. The larger concentration of the army was to take place in another area farther south, its center of gravity in the region known as the Eifel, the extension of the Ardennes eastward into Germany. This operation would be conducted with utmost secrecy and until the time for the jump-off of the offensive it had to remain undetected.

By and large, it was the panzer units that would assemble in the concentration area to the north. These units, of course, would be the most visible. They were also the units best known to the Allies and the ones Allied intelligence took special pains to keep track of.

The volksgrenadier divisions, easier to camouflage than armor and of lower priority in Allied intelligence activities, were to be concentrated in the Eifel, which was ideal for the purpose. Here, secrecy was all-important. While officers of senior rank had to be let in on the secret during the month of November, all were sworn to silence on pain of being shot. Radio blackout of the assembled divisions was enforced; nighttime patrols and artillery registration were forbidden.

The Seventh Army continued to hold the front to the south and indeed, up to the last few days, to direct the movement of supplies into the Eifel area. But the major ace Hitler held in his effort to keep the operation secret was the wooded terrain, and much depended on the bad weather that could reasonably be expected at this time of year—the fog and mists of the Eifel.

A more difficult problem was secrecy and camouflage for the reorganization and assembly of Manteuffel's Fifth Panzer Army, to the south of Dietrich's infantry elements in the Eifel. The reason was timing. The Fifteenth Army could not relieve Manteuffel's army from the vicinity of Aachen until November 27 to 30; elements of the 2d Panzer Division and the 26th Volksgrenadier, both scheduled for employment on Manteuffel's south, would have to stay on until the last moment.

During this period a great burden lay on the shoulders of a man who, though he held the highest German military title (other than Hitler himself), had been relegated to the realm of supply and logistics. This officer, Field Marshal Wilhelm Keitel, has been described as a "pliant toady." [1] Fairer, perhaps, is the estimate of Generaloberst Heinz Guderian, a man not given to false praise. Guderian considered Keitel a "basically decent individual who did his best to perform the task allotted him." However, even Guderian admitted that Keitel had early fallen under the spell of Hitler's personality and, as time progressed, became less and less able to shake off the hypnotic powers emanating from the Führer. [2] Hitler realized that he could place unlimited confidence in Keitel's loyalty, and the task performed in November, 1944, by Keitel (who was a weak man but a capable administrator) is little short of startling.

It was up to him to assemble quantities of ammunition and fuel sufficient for an offensive of the scale proposed. At this time the Allied air forces were concentrating on the German oil industry, and the effects could be seen in the figures for crude oil production. The sole outside source of crude oil was now Hungary. There was a continual drop in production of oil by Germany's decentralized coal distillation plants.

But despite Allied attacks, the German Reichsbahn performed the truly remarkable feat of hauling some 500 trainloads of troop equipment, fuel, and ammunition across Rhine bridges and unloading it at varying distances from the front without being discovered. In the face of continuous Allied air attacks against Rhine rail bridges, and the general destruction of railroads,

[1] Chester Wilmot, *The Struggle for Europe* (New York: Harper, 1952), p. 84.
[2] Heinz Guderian, *Panzer Leader* (New York: Dutton, 1952), p. 464.

the delivery was accomplished quickly and in time. Delays resulting from Allied attacks lasted no longer than one or two days. An attack on Koblenz on December 10 left a hundred bomb craters, yet twenty-four hours later the trains were in full operation. On December 11 the main double-track line from Cologne to Euskirchen, which supported Sixth Panzer Army's assembly, was hit. All traffic was stopped; yet the line was running again the next day. Altogether the destruction was light, and supply shipments during the buildup were on schedule in the actual concentration area.[3]

At first, supplies from east of the Rhine were stored by the chief of staff of the Heer, who was responsible for supply services in the so-called Zone of the Interior. Here they were secure from air attacks during the preparation period. But eventually they had to be moved. By early December, when the transfer of supplies reached the crucial stage, eight reinforced railway bridges were functioning behind the assembly area, and in addition, eight highway bridges and twelve Rhine ferries capable of handling locomotives.[4]

Keitel estimated that a hundred trainloads of ammunition had to be accumulated in order to insure the success of the offensive. And despite the drain upon the reserve resulting from defense against the Allied ground offensive of the autumn, the stocks were replaced.

Keitel promised that an adequate supply of fuel would be ready for the offensive. On October 28 he issued an order whose objective was 660,000 gallons of oil and nearly 4,000,000 gallons of gasoline. The Allied offensive in the Jülich-Düren area threatened the reserve, and he was urgently requested to release fuel stocks in order to avert a disaster, the daily consumption on the western front being some 170,000 gallons. Reluctantly, very slowly, and in small quantities, Keitel granted these requests. By December 15, however, he had accumulated the 4.6 million gallons of fuel, though because of the difficulties of delivering it to the panzer units, perhaps half remained stored on the east bank of the Rhine.[5]

Null-Day, the date on which the offensive was to be launched, was tied to the speed with which the concentration and final assembly of troops and matériel could be accomplished. By December 15 the main concentration area in the Eifel had received 1,502 troop trains and approximately 500 supply trains whose freight amounted to 144,735 tons. Most of this was earmarked for the offensive.[6]

The effectiveness of the troops would depend in part upon their training for the offensive during the period of concentration. This meant movement into the assembly areas in minimum time. Troop deployments for the Sixth

[3] Percy Schramm, MS # A-862; Hugh Cole, *The Ardennes* (Washington: Dept. of the Army, 1965), pp. 64–66.
[4] Cole, *op. cit.*, pp. 66–68.
[5] Schramm, *op. cit.*
[6] Cole, *op. cit.*

Panzer Army went according to schedule, and Dietrich was able to complete the transfer of most of his troops by the date specified by Hitler, November 20. From early in November the efficiency and ingenuity of the Reichsbahn enabled OB West and Seventh Army,[7] the responsible commands, to direct a steady stream of men and equipment into the two centers of gravity of the Sixth Panzer Army assembly area. Rail lines running westward from Cologne to Düren and from Bonn to Euskirchen carried the bulk of combat troops, tanks, motor vehicles, artillery, rocket launchers, and service and supply troops gathered from East Prussia, Poland, Austria, the Netherlands, Denmark, and Norway. Billeted in villages and sheltered in the forests of the Eifel, men and equipment of the armored divisions and some of the infantry divisions were ready in good time for extensive training.

Still the utmost degree of secrecy was maintained, partly by a clever ruse. Taking a page from the Allies' book on their invasion of Normandy, the German High Command, in assigning the Sixth Panzer Army to Army Group B, ordered Model to make preparations for the assembly of a fictitious Twenty-Fifth Army in the area northwest of Cologne. This dummy headquarters consisted of small working parties and radio stations. Quarters were prepared for new units and villages, and roads leading to the billeting area were marked with direction posts showing names mentioned in deceptive radio messages.

Early in December the German High Command received a scare. About December 2 a strong American reconnaissance patrol penetrated to the observation posts of a battery of the 1st SS Panzer Korps, which was scheduled to lead Dietrich's main effort. Two men belonging to this battery were found to be missing. When the Allies showed no reaction, however, the Germans began to relax: maybe the two men were dead when they were captured by the Americans or maybe they refused to give any information; perhaps they knew nothing and were therefore unable to give anything of value.

To make the spread of information about the projected attack only gradual, a scheme was followed by which officers from OKW downward were initiated in successive stages as preparations progressed. Only as many commanders and staff officers were brought into the picture as were absolutely necessary. Even within the army staffs, only the commanding general, the chief of staff, the operations officer, and one additional person were informed. Each officer was told only as much as he needed to know to perform his part in the operation.

But the German commanders and staff officers, accustomed as they were to defensive fighting, needed retraining. To accomplish this, the staffs were given extensive map exercises based on a projected German flank attack

[7] Seventh Army, responsible for the sector, was given responsibility for moving troop trains, etc., in the area.

against a motorized Allied breakthrough on the Roer River. From the middle of November Army Group B headquarters planned precise training regulations and issued them under the title "Leading Counterattacks." Night maneuvers and map exercises were conducted to instruct commanders and leaders in forming up troops, regulating traffic, and leading mixed units in attack. Officers received instruction in winter warfare. Road service during snow and ice, traffic regulations, and sanitary service also were stressed.

Günther Reichhelm, who had recently reported to Army Group B headquarters disillusioned and despairing, found his spirits immediately lifted. Model, he could see, had committed himself completely to the offensive and to the training and instruction of his officers and his new units. As Model's operations officer, Reichhelm accompanied his chief as he visited the various headquarters of his three main armies. Here Model discussed Allied military dispositions, consulting detailed operational and intelligence maps and listening to reports given by each commander. During this period Model held a map exercise with each of the attacking armies.

For some reason the leader of the main attack, Sepp Dietrich failed to attend very many of Model's discussions with the staff of Army Group B. Normally he was represented by General Willi Bittrich of the Waffen-SS, the prospective commander of the 2d SS Panzer Korps. He was absent even from the map maneuver of his own Sixth Panzer Army.

Indoctrination and training of members of the General Staff was one thing. The organization of the armies themselves, dependent as it was on gathering together the units as they came into the Eifel, was more difficult. Training, long neglected on both eastern and western fronts, had to be reestablished. It was particularly necessary to reindoctrinate panzer units, now used to holding defensive positions, in the spirit of the offensive; they had to be reminded that armored formations were designed principally for aggressive conduct in battle. Panzer leaders' thinking once more had to emphasize maneuverability and speed. Tank drivers and all troops were further trained in the techniques of night fighting. Combined arms offensive training among tanks, infantry, and artillery had to be learned once again. Furthermore, the tank drivers' quality had degenerated; many drivers had been taken out of their vehicles and committed as infantrymen—only to become casualties—and new ones had to be trained overnight to negotiate the hilly and dangerous terrain.

This task was far more easily said than done. Not even the Sixth Panzer Army was able to keep all its divisions intact for training purposes. Manteuffel's Fifth Panzer Army had even less of a chance. As the Fifth was defending against terrible Allied attacks north and south of Aachen, its commander was unable to withdraw divisions for training.

Ruefully Manteuffel compared his current situation with that of Erich von Ludendorff in 1918, when the Heer was preparing its large-scale spring offensives that were to be Germany's last great effort of World War I. At least Ludendorff was able to pull men out of the line for retraining; the Wehrmacht of 1944 was unable to do this. "To my special regret," Manteuffel has recalled, "I hardly got time to take care of my troops, which were indeed my tools."

Reorganization and training of the volksgrenadier divisions, such as the 18th and 26th, were particularly difficult, since these units were required to defend broad sectors of the front; only small, local reserves could be detached —and for insufficient training at that. Manteuffel, always in the forefront of the fighting, was used to commanding seasoned troops. He had his doubts about using the new volksgrenadier divisions, which were going to be sent in for the first time. They had too high a percentage of personnel with little if any combat infantry experience. Furthermore, adequate means and time were lacking for training them under competent subordinate commanders.

On the whole the panzer troops were better off. Manteuffel, a veteran tanker, observed that his tankers were being trained by experienced men. They enjoyed a kind of glamour, too. They "attracted more talent and volunteers," said Manteuffel, with a slight touch of smugness, "than the other units of the Wehrmacht." [8] Thus, the 2d Panzer Division, despite its long time in the line, was in better condition than the rest of Manteuffel's troops.

The Führer Begleit (Escort) Brigade, once Hitler's bodyguard, was commanded by Colonel Otto Remer, formerly a member of Manteuffel's command. While this division-strength brigade was still being held under Hitler's control, Manteuffel had hopes of obtaining it, in good condition, as part of his reserve after battle was joined.

Training of artillery and engineering units went on. Army Group B included seven volks artillerie corps, a number of separate battalions, and three volks werfer brigades. These, under the senior artillery commander, were distributed so as to make the most effective use of firepower. Command posts were to be established two days before the start of the attack. Instructions were issued on infantry-artillery cooperation, on approach roads, and on expected weather. Fire support for the great offensive would be adequate.

The Wehrmacht went into the final phases of preparation for the attack in the second week of December, 1944. The strength of the forces provided for the offensive was less than Jodl's initial astonishing figure of 32 divisions— Army Group B would begin the offensive with only 22, of which 7 would be panzer—but despite this shortfall from the most optimistic estimates, an

[8] Hasso von Manteuffel, MS # B-151.

amazing job had been done. Spirits were high. A formidable force had been assembled.

On December 11 a group of German commanders belonging to Army Group B assembled at Ziegenberg, Field Marshal Rundstedt's command post. They were soon joined by some of the major field commanders for the forthcoming offensive: Rundstedt himself, Model, Manteuffel, and Dietrich. Late in the afternoon they boarded buses and were taken on a journey by circuitous routes designed to confuse anyone unfamiliar with the area, winding up only a few kilometers from where they had started.

Before their departure from Ziegenberg Castle the Generals were stripped of their weapons and briefcases, and when the bus stopped this normally proud group was led between a double row of SS storm troopers into a deep bunker, which turned out to be Hitler's command post, known as the Adlerhorst (Eagle's Nest). It was from here that the victorious Ardennes campaign of 1940 had been directed.

Ushered into the meeting room, the generals were soon joined by Keitel, Jodl, and the Führer.

It was a strange meeting, although strange meetings were far from unusual in Hitler's headquarters.

Hitler began by paying special honor to the commanders of two battle-tested divisions, Generalmajor Harald Baron von Elverfeldt of the 9th Panzer Division and Generalmajor Siegfried von Waldenburg of the 116th Panzer. Both were decorated with the Knight's Cross and were invited to express their views about the condition of their troops and the offensive in general. They spoke openly and frankly about their misgivings regarding the far-reaching objectives of the offensive. A smaller but more certain success seemed preferable, they said, and would lessen the danger of again exhausting and decimating the panzer divisions. Discussion of this viewpoint, the ghost of the "small solution," was terminated by Hitler. The small solution would not be considered; the "grand plan" was still "irrevocable."

The meeting took place in a large room. About sixty officers were present. Hitler sat at a narrow table scarcely thirty inches wide with Keitel on his right and Jodl on his left. Opposite Hitler sat Rundstedt; Model sat on Rundstedt's left, and Manteuffel on Model's left.

Manteuffel, sitting within inches of the Führer, was disturbed. As he later described the meeting: "Among the generals reporting was a great number of battle-tried veterans of all ranks who had a name at the front and knew their job." Compared to these men, whom Manteuffel respected, the highest military commanders of the Wehrmacht showed to poor advantage. What shocked Manteuffel, however, was that Hitler himself now seemed "a broken man, with an unhealthy color, a caved-in appearance in his manner, with trembling hands; sitting as if the burden of responsibility seemed to oppress him, and compared to his looks in the last conference in the beginning of December, his body seemed still more decrepit and he was a man grown old." [9]

Manteuffel noticed another feature of Hitler's deportment: his left arm was by now completely limp. And yet, by careful manipulation, reaching for it under the table with his right hand, Hitler could put his left hand on the table and move maps and papers. Manteuffel was sure this manipulation escaped the notice of all the officers in that large room except for the three facing Hitler—Rundstedt, Model, and Manteuffel himself.

Once begun on his presentation, the Führer seemed to derive additional strength from within. He raved for two hours, covering the political situation for forty or fifty minutes, stressing the weakness of the Allied coalition and reminding those present of the strategy and triumphs of his idol, Frederick the Great of Prussia, over the coalitions against which that ancient warrior had fought. Hitler's face lit up and he became alive. Manteuffel was sure that by the time the meeting was over, 90 percent of the officers in that room, many of whom were seeing Hitler for the first time in their lives, were under the impression that Hitler was in excellent condition.

Many assurances were given at that meeting—assurances of the weaknesses of the Americans, assurances of unprecedented air support for the offensive. The Führer himself informed the officers that Reichsmarschall Göring was counting on committing 1,000 out of the 3,000 available planes in serviceable condition. He added wryly that he realized the generals distrusted Göring's overoptimistic figures, but in this instance he himself felt they could count on 800 planes, a number that guaranteed the success of the coming offensive. All available tanks, artillery, self propelled assault guns, and other matériel had been brought up. The newly activated volksgrenadier divisions, now to be committed, were outstanding in their morale and equipment. Down to the last gallon of gasoline, everything not absolutely essential to operations in the eastern front had been withdrawn.

True, not all the news was favorable. When Hitler confidently inquired about civilian morale, he was diplomatically told that the local population who lived behind the lines were now afraid they would be destined to lose even their last possessions, and for this reason, the German people seemed to desire that the fighting be brought to an end, whatever the outcome.

Despite this, Hitler confidently expected a decisive turn in the war. He appealed to all to do their best in the coming struggle in view of the suffering being experienced on the home front. He made one concession: in order to allow time to bring up men and equipment, he postponed the offensive once more, to December 15.

The next day, December 12, he repeated the eerie exercise for those com-

[9] Manteuffel, *op. cit.*

manders who missed the meeting of the eleventh, making a final postponement: Null-Day would be December 16, a date that stood.

Oberst Friedrich August Baron von der Heydte, commandant of the German Parachute Army Combat School at Alten, received word, completely without warning, to report without delay to his superior, Generaloberst Kurt Student, at Parachute Army headquarters. It was December 8, 1944. General Student, commanding general of Army Group H, had exciting news, and he began at once: "The Führer has ordered a parachute attack within the framework of a powerful offensive. You, my dear Heydte, are ordered to carry out this task."

Understandably, Colonel von der Heydte would have liked more details; none were forthcoming. Student himself was unable at this moment to divulge even the general location of the mission, whether it was to take place on the eastern or western front. He was specific, however, as to the composition of von der Heydte's command. It would be a newly organized kampfgruppe with 900 to 1,000 men. Each regiment of the 2d Parachute Korps was to give up its hundred best and most experienced parachutists to form this new unit.

Von der Heydte demurred. Certainly he could have no objection to the mission he was training men to perform. But he objected to the "pickup" nature of the kampfgruppe itself. Why could he not instead utilize the entire 6th Parachute Regiment, which he had formerly commanded in Holland? It could not be, he was told; the movement of an entire regiment would jeopardize secrecy. However, von der Heydte was permitted to choose his platoon and company commanders personally.

Friedrich August Baron von der Heydte was in some ways an unlikely prospect for this type of operation. Besides holding the titles Baron and Oberst (Colonel), he was once a professor of international law.[10] He was one of the early members of the great July 20 conspiracy against the Führer's life and was a cousin of Count Klaus von Stauffenberg, who actually made the attempt and paid with his life. Von der Heydte was fortunate that he had escaped the same fate.

But there was no time for such thoughts now. Time was exceedingly short. Accordingly, after departing from Student's headquarters, von der Heydte spent the rest of the evening sketching out the organization of the new kampfgruppe. It was essentially of battalion size, and he planned to establish four light infantry companies, one heavy weapons company of heavy machine guns and mortars, a signal platoon, and a supply platoon. Officers available that evening were called together for a briefing after being pledged to strictest secrecy. To provide a cover, von der Heydte let it be known within

[10] Von der Heydte, a veteran of the Crete campaign, was also the former holder of the $16,000 Carnegie Fellowship for study of international law.

the kampfgruppe that a large-scale field exercise, including a parachute drop, was to be prepared as a demonstration for the Army Combat School.

The next morning von der Heydte was dismayed to receive the various "picked" troops from the regiments of the 2d Parachute Korps. In common with other armies, each unit had taken full advantage of the opportunity to send their sick, lame, and lazy. "Never during my entire career," von der Heydte wrote later, "had I been in command of a unit with less fighting spirit." By quick action he was able to get rid of the 150 worst and replace them with volunteers from the parachute school, some of whom lacked any previous experience in jumping.

Von der Heydte continued his tasks with energy—assigning clothing and arming, equipping, and vaccinating his troops. Miraculously, by the evening of December 9, the day after he first received word of the enterprise, he had his unit essentially organized.

Veteran that he was, he realized from the very beginning the difficulties he was up against. Although the Wehrmacht had in past years done well in developing techniques of airborne warfare, in 1944 the bulk of the paratroopers were inadequately trained.[11] Qualified personnel were fairly evenly distributed among the available 100 so-called parachute battalions, but of these experienced people, about one third had not jumped for several years, in most cases since the Crete landings in 1941. Others in von der Heydte's kampfgruppe had not jumped since the invasion of Holland, a year before Crete. Barely half his men had been trained to jump with weapons, and only a few had ever jumped at night or in forests.

Like Skorzeny, von der Heydte was not one to keep his concerns to himself. After wrestling with his problems for four days he went, on December 12, all the way to the commander of Army Group B to state his objections to the commitment of inadequately trained plane crews and paratroopers.

Field Marshal Walther Model had worked all through the night, but he was not annoyed to be awakened early in the morning to see von der Heydte. After listening to the Baron's protests, however, he asked a blunt question: "Do you give the parachute drop a ten percent chance of success?"

"Yes," von der Heydte answered quickly.

"Then it is necessary to make the attempt," Model said, "since the entire offensive has no more than a ten percent chance of success. It must be done, since this offensive is the last remaining chance to conclude the war favorably. If we do not make the most of that ten percent chance, Germany will be faced with certain defeat."

Model then assigned von der Heydte to the Sixth Panzer Army. He departed to report to Sepp Dietrich.

[11] General Student has estimated that in December, 1944, Germany had not more than 3,000 paratroopers fully trained and ready for employment.

Dietrich, located a few miles south of Army Group headquarters at Münstereifel, emitted a faint odor of whiskey. He was also less considerate than Model.

As von der Heydte walked in, he was greeted with the words, "What can you paratroopers do, anyhow?"

"Give me the mission, General, and then I can evaluate the feasibility."

"I can't give you a mission until I know what you're able to do."

Finally, after some more discussion, Dietrich turned to his chief of staff, Fritz Kraemer, who assigned von der Heydte the following mission:

> On the first day of the attack, the Sixth SS Panzer Army will take possession of Liège or the bridges across the Meuse River south of the city. At early dawn on the first day of the attack, Kampfgruppe von der Heydte will drop into the Baraque Michel mountain area, eleven kilometers north of Malmédy, and secure the multiple road junction at Baraque Michel for use by the armored point of the Sixth Panzer Army, probably elements of the 12th SS Panzer Division. If for technical reasons this mission is impracticable on the morning of the first day of attack, Kampfgruppe von der Heydte will drop early on the following morning into the Amblève River or Amay area to secure the bridges there for the advance of the Sixth SS Panzer Army's armored points.

But von der Heydte's exchange with his superior did not end at that point. When he reported the low state of training from which both the Luftwaffe crews and the paratroopers suffered, Dietrich snorted, "I am not responsible for the deficiencies of the German Luftwaffe."

Asked for information concerning the locations of American strategic reserves, Dietrich gave an equally brusque answer: "I am not a prophet. You will learn earlier than I what forces the Americans will employ against you. Besides, behind their lines there are only Jewish hoodlums and bank managers."

Two things von der Heydte was successful in accomplishing: a boundary was fixed between his area and that of Skorzeny, and he secured the services of an observer from the 12th SS Panzer Division, equipped with a radio, who was to jump with him. However, when he asked that carrier pigeons be provided for use if the radio equipment was broken, Dietrich almost exploded: "I am leading my panzer army without pigeons; you should be able to lead your kampfgruppe without pigeons."

Other high-ranking officers with whom von der Heydte dealt in the next few days were cooperative, but the means for correcting all deficiencies simply were not available. However, von der Heydte was able to produce some 300 dummy parachutists, which were to be dropped in the areas of Eupen, Spa, Stavelot, and Elsenborn. The provision of these dummies was no mean task, but by mid-December it had been accomplished.

And, more important, von der Heydte had put together a unit that could at least be employed. With what success remained to be seen.

As Manteuffel left the December 11 meeting and headed back to his command post, he knew his feelings were probably much the same as those of the other generals. Although they were unable, of course, to share their apprehensions, the majority, as Manteuffel recalled, seemed disappointed in Hitler's presentation. His own apprehension was particularly acute. True, in the meeting ten days earlier in Berlin, Manteuffel had received no comfort when he pleaded for the "small solution," but he had left the meeting with a feeling that everything possible would be done to remedy the deficiencies in equipment and troops that still existed.

Albert Speer, in charge of armament production, had done miracles already, and Manteuffel had continued to hope for miracles in the time left to them. Obviously now they were not to be forthcoming.

At this time Manteuffel's headquarters was located at the hamlet of Manderscheid, which nestles in the steep canyon of the small Lieser River about 13 miles northeast of Bitburg. The distance from Ziegenberg is only about 70 miles in a direct line, but by the tortuous, twisting roads of the Eifel it was much longer. He had time to think. Perhaps he was too pessimistic. There was always the possibility that Hitler alone had intelligence information regarding the enemy situation that promised success in spite of the obvious difficulties.

As Manteuffel turned things over in his mind, a certain rationale developed. One thing was certain: Despite the doubts, despite the maddening tangle of loose ends in the order of battle and supplies, the impending "decision-seeking offensive" would go on. He had no choice in this. He would have to act in the name of the thousands under his command. Small wonder he fell back on traditional military attitudes: "These were matters of so high a level that I was unable to judge, because of the military, political, overall situation, the situation of enemy forces." All these, in a general sense, were neither known nor accessible to him.

By the evening of December 12, 1944, most of the divisions being assembled for the attack were in the general attack area, a region that reached from the small town of Gemund, ten miles east of where the Siegfried Line ran through Monschau, to Bitburg on the south. The units being assembled were held east of a "base line" some twelve miles behind the current front until such time as Hitler gave the order for final assembly. Though Seventh Army had handed over control of its long sector to the Fifth and Sixth Panzer armies on December 10, its frontline units were to remain in position under their command until the last possible minute.

The next day Hitler gave the order. All three armies moved in to occupy the next phase of assembly areas closer to the front. In this phase the infantry was held behind a restraining line six miles east of the front. The armor, scheduled to follow the infantry in the first day's attack, remained behind the original twelve-mile line.

By the night of December 13 all three armies had closed into these assembly areas. Guns and howitzers of army and corps artillery moved into final assembly positions about five miles to the rear of their ultimate firing emplacements. Werfers, easier to camouflage, moved up just to the rear of their planned firing positions. Horses belonging to the Seventh Army were used to pull the batteries into position; the wheels were wrapped with straw to muffle the sound.

The following night, December 14, the infantry divisions moved quietly into their last attack positions, only two and a half miles behind the front. Luftwaffe planes traversed the front, providing a cover of sound that supplemented the noise made by the normal artillery activity. Remaining Seventh Army units in the area selected for the Fifth Panzer Army attack were withdrawn and moved south where, under General Brandenberger, they could protect Manteuffel's left flank.

In all these movements security remained intact by dint of drastic measures. Attack units were forbidden to make reconnaissance until after December 13, and even then only regimental commanders and higher officers, carrying special identification cards and accompanied by an officer of the current front-line divisions. In the southern Eifel concentration area, assigned to Fifth Panzer Army, Manteuffel issued charcoal for cooking so that smoke from fires would not betray the presence of his troops.

A special road service was set up, supplied with sand, prime movers, winches, and recovery equipment at the more difficult points. Movement was to be only at night. To enforce this order, Manteuffel gave instructions that the tires be shot on any vehicles on the roads during the daytime, regardless of the protests of the occupants. Wrecked motor vehicles, tanks, and artillery were camouflaged, so that even if Allied air reconnaissance discovered them, photo interpreters would find it difficult to draw conclusions. Horse-drawn artillery was used to the maximum extent possible; straw was placed through the horseshoes to stifle the noise further.

Strictly forbidden in the concentration area was the marking of the roads of march or side roads into shelter areas, as well as signs indicating shelter of troops, command posts, and telephone and radio stations. Officers called road commanders were put in charge of camouflage measures and were ordered to see that they were strictly carried out.

Despite all this, in the bitter cold, the German units moved on schedule and with negligible losses in men and morale.

This was the situation on the evening of December 15 as U.S. correspondent Cy Peterman, a few miles west, was driving up the "Skyline Drive" from Wiltz to Spa. The troops were moving into position; the stage was set. Three German armies, consisting of 22 divisions, were prepared to launch an assault against a sector held by an estimated four and a half U.S. divisions. In addition to these 22, Hitler was holding out as OKW reserves four division-size units: the 3d Panzer Grenadier Division, the 9th Volksgrenadier Division, the Führer Begleit Brigade, and the Führer Grenadier Brigade. The last two, nearly up to strength, were considered elite.

In mobile equipment Army Group B had an estimated total of 1,800 tanks and self-propelled guns, which usually seem to have been lumped together in German calculations. Of these, however, a large number were tied down by the Fifteenth Army around Aachen as the offensive started, so the combat vehicles available for the offensive to Antwerp came to about 900.[12]

The forces assembled were weak in one respect: bridging equipment and trained engineers to operate it. The Todt Organization, composed of volunteer labor groups, was to furnish much engineering support, but it was never even nearly adequate, despite the cries of the field commanders.

Army Group B fell short of the 32 divisions promised by Jodl on October 11, but it was a powerful force nonetheless.

The commanders of the three armies, ready in their command posts, each had his own particular problems. Sepp Dietrich, Sixth Panzer Army, would seem to have had the least. He had the narrowest front—from Rötgen to Losheim—the shortest distance to travel, and the greatest strength. Of the 22 divisions assigned to the armies, he had 9, and the 4 SS panzer divisions were completely up to strength and considered second to none in the Wehrmacht. He had the 12th Volksgrenadier Division, one of those so designated for exceptionally meritorious service in combat. The 3d Parachute Division was also considered elite. Only the 277th, 246th, and 322d were largely unknown quantities. His tank and self-propelled gun strength came to 450.

Dietrich's overall mission was unchanged: to break through the thin American lines with his infantry elements and to drive the 26 miles to the Meuse River, bypassing Liège on both sides, and on to Antwerp. To be sure, he had an obstacle of some significance on his immediate front, the Hohe Venn, a large rugged territory, covered with very heavy woods and remarkable for its swampy ground despite its height. Furthermore, the U.S. units defending in this area were not believed to be spread out quite so widely as the U.S. VIII Corps in its sector to the south.

Dietrich's projected timetable was considerably more realistic than Hitler's. Whereas Hitler visualized reaching and crossing the Meuse in two days, Dietrich was figuring that a day would be consumed in penetrating and breaking out, a second day in getting his armor over the Hohe Venn, and a third

---

[12] Estimates vary. These figures come from Schramm, *op. cit.* Charles von Lüttichau, in the R series manuscripts, gives higher figures.

day in reaching the Meuse. His chief of staff, Kraemer, calculated that a fourth day would be required for securing the bridgeheads over the Meuse.

To accomplish his first, difficult job of breaking through the American lines and crossing the Hohe Venn, Dietrich—with ample supervision from Model and OKW—organized his army with the 1st SS Panzer Korps, under Generalleutnant der Waffen-SS Hermann Priess; the 2d SS Panzer Korps, under General der Waffen-SS Willi Bittrich; and 67th Infantrie Korps, under General der Infantrie Otto Hitzfeld. The main effort of Priess' 1st SS Panzer Korps was to be made in the south of the sector, where the Losheim Gap, an area of relatively rolling terrain, provided better country for armored exploitation than the Hohe Venn to the north. Here the 3d Parachute Division on the left, and the 12th Volksgrenadier Division on the right, were to tear open a hole, to be followed through by Hitler's own 1st SS Panzer Division (Leibstandarte Adolf Hitler), under Wilhelm Mohnke.

The 277th VG was to attack north of the Losheim Gap, to be followed through by the 12th SS Panzer Division (Hitler Jugend).

About fifteen miles north of the Losheim Gap in the vicinity of Monschau, the 67th Infantrie Korps was to attack with the 322d Volksgrenadier and the 246th Volksgrenadier divisions abreast. Upon achieving a breakthrough in that area, this infantry corps, along with the infantry from Priess' 1st SS Panzer Korps, was to wheel north and protect Dietrich's right flank. The panzers were to continue to the Meuse, where Bittrich's 2d SS Panzer Korps, consisting of the 2d SS (Das Reich) and 9th SS (Hohenstauffen) Panzer divisions, was to continue through to Antwerp, using the Albert Canal between Maastricht and Antwerp to protect the right flank. The Fifteenth Army attack, a couple of days after Null-Day, was to help by occupying the bypassed Americans and British.

Farther to the south, Hasso von Manteuffel had a somewhat different problem. His Fifth Panzer Army was receiving less support (350 tanks and self-propelled guns)—and less supervision—from Hitler and the rest of the chain of command. Manteuffel had no SS divisions under his command, which was highly to his liking. The units assigned to him, while good, were generally considered only 60 to 80 percent reorganized. Of these, Oberst Meinrad von Lauchert's 2d Panzer Division was in the best condition, having had a chance to do some reorganizing even though it had come fairly recently to the line.

Manteuffel had brought with him his own proven corps commanders. The two selected to make the main efforts, Generaloberst Walther Krüger (58th Panzer Korps) and General der Panzertruppen Heinrich Freiherr von Lüttwitz (47th Panzer Korps), were his own men. Lüttwitz was considered the more aggressive. Indeed, despite his unprepossessing, supercilious, and rather porky appearance in his standard photograph, he was known as a hard-driving commander and one who cooperated well with adjacent units. Manteuffel admired one of Lüttwitz's characteristics more than any other: he understood his men, a valued quality in this sixth year of the war.

Thus it was to Lüttwitz's corps that Manteuffel assigned the longest and most difficult objective. His corps, consisting of the 2d Panzer Division, the Panzer Lehr Division, and the 26th Volksgrenadier Division, was to cross the Our River in the vicinity of Dasburg and Gemund, seize Clerf, overwhelm the important road center of Bastogne, and move on to seize crossings over the Meuse River south of Namur.

Krüger's 58th Korps, on the north, was to cross the Our River near Lutzkampen, take the town of Houffalize, and continue past the Ourthe River to seize crossings over the Meuse between Namur and Andenne.

To the north of this sector lay the Schnee Eifel, a heavily wooded piece of terrain branching off the rest of the Eifel and running northeast to southwest. On this piece of ground the 106th U.S. Infantry Division had relieved the 2d some five days before the attack, occupying a position that poked its nose through the fortifications of the Siegfried Line. This was the piece of ground that had bothered the U.S. VIII Corps commander, General Troy Middleton, who had wanted to evacuate it.

But if the Schnee Eifel was a source of concern to the Americans, it was every bit as much one to Manteuffel. Elsewhere along the static part of the front, German troops, spread thin to provide the weight of this counterattack, were able to defend from positions of strength in the Siegfried Line. Here no such protection existed. An attack from the south, with the Schnee Eifel still in American hands, would leave a dangerous open flank for the Fifth Panzer Army on the north.

Manteuffel decided, therefore, to bite off the Schnee Eifel with his 66th Infantrie Korps, under General der Artillerie Walther Lucht, push on to the important road hub of St.-Vith, and in that area establish a blocking position to hold open the northern shoulder.

The terrain features of the Schnee Eifel made a beautiful target for a double envelopment. Two main roads following the Losheim Gap came through the lines in the thinly held northern sector. On the south another road, originating at Prüm and running along the valley of the Alf River, turns northwest and joins the roads from the north at Schönberg. They all branch out again and lead to the town of St.-Vith. To make a double envelopment of the Schnee Eifel even more tempting, Manteuffel knew that the areas north and south of this long, rugged piece of ground were lightly held.

A desirable scheme for attacking the Schnee Eifel would have been to place one division north of the position and one division south, with adequate defensive forces between. But Manteuffel's situation was anything but conventional. The 18th VG Division was holding the line in front of the Schnee Eifel, but Lucht's other division, the 62d VG, would not be available until the last minute. Manteuffel made a daring decision: to attack and surround the bulk of a U.S. division with the power of a single rebuilt volksgrenadier division of only six battalions. Two regiments of the 18th VG Division, the 294th and 295th, were to attack around the Schnee Eifel to the north, and the third regiment of the division, the 293d, was to attack up the Alf Valley to the south, thus completing the encirclement. Manteuffel was gambling on the premise that the Americans would not attack forward out of the Schnee Eifel. He left that area along the long six-mile front to be held by only the very meager replacement battalion of the 18th VG Division.

Now, on December 15, it seemed that the 62d VG would soon arrive. The plan was unchanged; but the 62d VG would follow the 293d regiment.

On the south Erich Brandenberger, Seventh Army, had a yet different problem. His mission was to protect Manteuffel's flank by crossing the Our River near Vianden and driving along the south of the Panzer Lehr Division, gradually fanning out his infantry elements to face what was believed to be a negligible force in the south. He was also to threaten the city of Luxembourg if the opportunity afforded itself.

To perform this mission he selected the 85th Korps, under General der Infantrie Baptist Kniess, to whom were assigned the 5th Parachute Division and the 352d VGD. His other two corps, the 80th and 53d, between them shared three volksgrenadier divisions and were scheduled to demonstrate and hold the line.

In general, these tactical plans were made difficult by the terrain that was faced. To begin with, Manteuffel was to go through thinly held American lines and somewhat better terrain than Dietrich—but with fewer forces. On the whole the Ardennes constituted an obstacle in itself, leading as it does to the cup of the Meuse and Semois rivers, and cut by the Amblève, the Ourthe, and the Salm, all of which flow generally northward toward Liège.

As noted, the area is not solid forest; in fact, only about a third is forested. The country is cut up, and therein lay the difficulty. The many small streams and rivulets made every road a winding, twisting trail, and although the road net was impressive—considering the number of villages—(due to the heavy tourist trade in peacetime years), the area was such that determined resistance could do much to slow down formations of vastly superior forces. Armor would be painfully roadbound in the winter season.

But the difficult nature of the Ardennes was why Hitler had decided to make his gamble in this area. Had it been considered good tank country—rolling, hard-surfaced, with a minimum of streams and sharp valleys—the

Allies might well have been attacking through this area rather than defending it with fewer than 80,000 troops.

Through the night of December 15 panzer and infantry units moved into their assault positions. When it appeared certain that all units would be in place and another postponement would not be necessary, Hitler placed a telephone call to Field Marshal Model.

"I have now," he said, "made my final decisions. All prerequisites for the success of the operation have been established. The results now solely depend upon the leadership of you and your subordinates during the course of the attack. There will be no deviation by the panzer units east of the Maas [Meuse] toward the north. The Sixth Panzer Army must keep clear of the covering front to be built up by the 66th Infantrie Korps between Monschau and Liège. Do not let Dietrich become involved in the fighting along his northern flank. Furthermore, Dietrich has rights to the entire road net on Manteuffel's right even as far as Namur. If these instructions are followed, a great success is assured."

Model renewed his pledge of loyalty to the plan. Later that night he called back: "I have given your instructions to Sepp Dietrich. All the efforts of Army Group B will be directed toward the thrust to Antwerp."

The next morning Operation Herbstnebel would begin.[13]

[13] Schramm, *op. cit.*

CHAPTER 9

❧❧❧

Allied Intelligence Is Befuddled

THE assistant chief of staff (G-2) is the general staff officer at any Army headquarters who is expected to possess a crystal ball. Engaged in what can at best be called an inexact science, the "gumshoe" is required to wade with unerring accuracy through a sea of obstacles—conflicting reports, bad weather, and just plain absence of information—and to keep his chief warned of any eventualities that may befall the command.

Particularly during the years leading up to World War II, intelligence technique in the U.S. Army suffered to a marked degree. The American Army was not planning an aggressive war, and it was deployed almost exclusively in the United States and the Philippines, where intelligence was remote from everyone's mind. Understandably, other problems took precedence, and intelligence was too often relegated to the background. As a result intelligence officers suffered greatly in prestige.[1] The unlucky G-2 or S-2 [2] had to confine his activities largely to security matters (such as locking safes), clearances, and if he was lucky, study for the day when combat intelligence would become a real need. The unit G-2 had little to do with supplies (the province of the G-4), with operational and training missions (the G-3), or with assignment of personnel (the G-1), so he was ripe for selection, "in addition to his other duties," as post exchange officer, club officer, and officer for the control of social diseases.

During World War II the American intelligence system made remarkable progress, with much help from the British. With the development of aerial reconnaissance, particularly photo interpretation, the capabilities of the intelligence officer improved immeasurably.

After the American disaster at Pearl Harbor, Allied Intelligence had some signal successes. It broke the Japanese radio code, to provide a great assist at

[1] This did not hold true with the British, whose forces were deployed all over the world, often in touchy situations. Consequently the British maintained an intelligence system of considerable competence.

[2] Intelligence officer below division level.

Midway. Later, Operation Fortitude, in support of the D-Day landings at Normandy, succeeded in deceiving the Germans as disastrously as Pearl Harbor had the Americans—though Fortitude has been less publicized than Pearl Harbor.

Traditionally the intelligence officer is supposed to be a pessimist. Rarely has G-2 been called to account for pointing up possibilities that have failed to materialize. But woe to the man who neglects to call attention to an enemy capability that, once exercised, will come back to haunt him.

In early December, 1944, this traditional pessimism had all but evaporated on the German front. Caught up in the tide of buoyant optimism engendered by the dash across France, Allied Intelligence at all echelons contributed a chorus of happy news.

And well they might. For the information coming in was optimistic indeed. Most dramatic was a flood of stories—from deserters and prisoners—about vastly lowered German morale. Entries in the periodic intelligence reports of the various units bear this out:

Numerous captured documents of recent date [September and October] demonstrate the enemy's constant, it might even be said frantic, preoccupation with his troops' morale (VII Corps).

Today the German soldier knows that he is no longer the legendary "superman" of the early days of the war. His Nazi fanaticism and unshakeable belief in German victory has disappeared. As a result security among German soldiers is also steadily decreasing (V Corps).

After the terrific artillery and air bombardment in the Argentan-Falaise pocket and all along the roads of retreat, the general tone of letters from soldiers was much less confident and much more critical of the situation than in preceding days. It is particularly worth noting that of all our weapons the fighter bombers are the most dreaded and are obviously the most effective destroyers of morale. . . . All soldierly pride goes by the board when the bombers arrive and the only thought of the individual is to save his own life even if he throws himself in the gutter.

The majority of letters written after the Normandy breakthrough in the battle of the Seine then speak of real flight, headquarters staff and whole units simply running away. The belief that something was rotten in the leadership occurs often. Many writers blame the defeats on the betrayal which went on behind the backs of the front soldiers, specifically the plot of the generals' clique against Hitler (Third U.S. Army).

On October 26 VIII Corps issued a report on the interrogation of a prisoner of war, a staff officer of the 17th SS Panzer Grenadier Division. It was called "The Odyssey of Goetz von Berlichingen," the subject being the devastating impact of the Allied Jabos (fighter-bombers) on German morale and effectiveness.

There was evidence that German efforts to counteract the effects of this low morale showed signs of desperation. On November 12, 1944, VIII Corps had the following to report:

> 1. 12th Army Group . . . reported that a story had been circulated in the German Army to the effect that President Roosevelt and Marshal Stalin had agreed that all German PW's would be sent to Russia for reconstruction work. In order to prevent desertion a new catch word had been adopted: *"Sieg oder Siberien"* (Victory or Siberia). PW's stated that another deterrent to desertion came in the form of a warning that arrangements had been made with the Americans to have deserters exchanged through neutral Switzerland.
> 2. The same source stated that PW had reported a rumor that mines had been sowed behind their lines to prevent retreat. . . .
> 4. First U.S. Army reported PW stated: "We are living under constant coercion. It's easier to earn a bullet than a piece of bread."

This gloomy picture was amplified by the publication of a captured letter written by Heinrich Himmler:

> *Reichs Führer SS*—10 September 1944
> Certain unreliable elements seem to believe that the war will be over for them as soon as they surrender to the enemy.
> Against this belief it must be pointed out that every deserter will be prosecuted and will find his just punishment. Furthermore, his ignominious behavior will entail the most severe consequences for his family. Upon examination of the circumstances they will be summarily shot.
>
> [Signed, Himmler]
>
> Cognizance of the above will be acknowledged by signature on the back of this sheet.

On the back of the order was written: "I have been informed about desertion, and I am aware of the fact that I will bring disaster upon myself and my kin if I desert."

On December 10 VIII Corps dubbed this one "All Things in Moderation": "*Scorpion West,* morale-building news propaganda sheet of the German Army, enlightened its readers a few days ago with this statement: 'Troops are authorized to liquidate commanders who order them to retreat. However, this privilege must not be abused.' "

Stories were also circulated about Hitler. A report by VII Corps, for example, noted Hitler's strange absence from public events—an astute observation—and remarked that this "is causing some wonder among those who customarily wonder about such things." It added that Hitler had made no public appearances since July 20, and his failure to appear on November 8 marked the only time since coming to power that he had not made an address in commemoration of the Beer Hall Putsch.

Stories were told about the atmosphere inside the Führer's headquarters; some PW's were convinced that Hitler was mad. *"Mami,* will the big lunatic chew up our carpets too?" was the story told with some relish by one prisoner.

Even more encouraging to intelligence staffs, the tremendous battles of attrition during November were bringing the Wehrmacht practically to the breaking point. German casualties on the 12 Army Group front alone were estimated at approximately 100,000 men. On December 15, 12 Army Group estimated as follows:

> At no time since September has such a critical dilemma confronted the enemy. It would seem doubtful that the enemy can hold in the Aachen area without committing the Sixth Panzer Army. It also seems doubtful that he can hold the West Wall in the south without additional reinforcements including armor. The enemy may have to divide the Sixth Panzer Army, thus risking defeat both in the north and in the south, or if he holds Sixth Panzer Army in the north, run a good chance of the Third and Seventh U.S. Armies reaching the Rhine this year in the area of Mainz. Finally, to solve this problem with reinforcements from the Russian front is to invite disaster in the east.[3]

There is no doubt that in the fall of 1944 the traditional G-2 pessimism was put on the shelf.

To be sure, there were also disquieting bits of information. One item of recognized significance was the capture on October 30 of a document sent out by the 86th Korps directing the establishment of a new unit under Otto Skorzeny:

> (1) The Führer has ordered the formation of a special unit of a strength of about two battalions for employment on reconnaissance and special tasks on the western front. The personnel will be assembled from volunteers of all arms of the Army and Waffen-SS and must fulfill the following requirements: (a) physically A-1, suitable for special tasks, mentally keen, strong personality, (b) fully trained in single combat, (c) knowledge of the English language and also the American dialect, especially important is the knowledge of military technical terms....
> (2) Captured U.S. clothing, equipment, weapons and vehicles are to be collected and reported for the equipment of the above special troops. Personal

[3] Two days later VIII Corps wrote, showing how G-2 sections paraphrase each other:

At no time since September has he [the enemy] been in such a critical condition. It is doubtful that he could hold in the Aachen area without committing the Sixth Panzer Army, and it is also doubtful that he can hold the West Wall in the south without additional reinforcements including armor. He may have to divide the Sixth Panzer Army, thus risking defeat both to the north and south; or if he holds the Sixth Panzer Army in the north, runs a good chance of the Third and Seventh Armies reaching the Rhine this year in the area of Mainz. Finally, to solve this problem with reinforcements from the Russian front is to invite disaster in the east.

wishes of the troops to make use of this kind of captured equipment must take second priority. Details will be notified later.

(3) Divisional Q Staffs are entirely responsible for the collection of captured equipment and will render a report by 1 November to Corps Q Branch.

Wissman, Chief of Staff

This was the order that almost gave Skorzeny a fit.

Furthermore, certain puzzles began to present themselves to the Allied Intelligence chiefs. One was the location and contemplated employment of Sepp Dietrich's Sixth Panzer Army, which Hitler had ordered to be organized on September 13. The first indications that the Germans were withdrawing armor from the front came about October 1, when Major General Kenneth Strong, the SHAEF G-2, noticed that armor was being drawn from the line of the Seventh German Army. Up to this time Model's Army Group B, on the north, had lacked armored support such as the Fifth Panzer Army provided Army Group G on the south. In a series of counterattacks against U.S. Third Army's right flank in the south, Fifth Panzer Army had been providing Army Group G with a genuine armor capability.

Guenther von Kluge, back in Normandy, had continually attempted to form an armored reserve—the British and Canadian attacks around Caen, it will be recalled, had been largely successful in thwarting this effort on his part— so it was hardly surprising to the intelligence chiefs that the Germans should attempt to form some sort of armored reserve, and conjecture centered on its location and the area where it would be employed. At the end of the first week in September, Sixth Panzer Army was mentioned by a deserter, and at the same time General Strong pointed out that the Fifth Panzer Army as well as the Sixth had been withdrawn from the line and could not be located.

The Allies were less interested in finding the Fifth Panzer Army than in finding the Sixth. The Fifth was known to have been badly mauled, and it was thought to have been withdrawn for rehabilitation. By November 20 intelligence staffs had generally agreed that Sixth Panzer Army had been forming in Westphalia, but now it appeared that the Army had moved to west of the Rhine. It was almost unanimously assumed that its mission would be to defend the Roer River line against the attack that the First and Ninth U.S. armies were conducting in that direction, the attack that was expected to advance to the Rhine once the Schmidt Dams were in Allied hands.

The intelligence chiefs were never quite able to agree on the exact location of the bulk of the Sixth Panzer Army. Most were of the opinion that Dietrich's headquarters was in the vicinity of Cologne, but Brigadier General Edwin L. Sibert, G-2 at 12 Army Group, thought Dietrich's army was concentrating somewhere to the northeast. First Army declined to go further than to place it in the general area between the Roer and the Rhine rivers, whereas Third Army felt it was located between Düsseldorf and Cologne. On December 10

SHAEF reported: "There is no further news of Sixth SS Panzer Army beyond vague rumours." [4]

The Allied camp had just learned that the designation SS had been awarded to the Sixth Panzer Army. (In actuality the SS designation was unofficial and seems not to have been used much by Hitler.) The Third U.S. Army came out with the following remarkably accurate report:

Strategic Order of Battle:

(1) Sixth SS Panzer Army: (a) a cooperative and well-informed PW stated that the army controlling 130 Panzer Lehr Division, while in Westphalia, was designated Sixth SS Panzer Army. PW also stated that I SS Panzer Corps, 9 SS Panzer Division "Hohenstaufen," 10 SS Panzer Division "Frundsberg," were also under control of Sixth SS Panzer Army. . . . PW also stated that SS Obergruppenführer [Lieutenant General] "Sepp" Dietrich commands Sixth SS Panzer Army.

(2) It has been suspected that the Panzer Army which reformed in Westphalia was designated Sixth SS Panzer Army, but this is the first concrete evidence of the SS designation. Logically, this title would be appropriate since the army is commanded by an SS general and includes at least four SS Panzer divisions (1, 2, 9, and 12) and two SS Panzer corps (I and II). Further, the fate of Nazism rests with the success of this new army. Under these circumstances, it would seem logical for Nazis to honor the new army with the elite SS title.

On December 13, as Hitler gave the order to move forward to the twelve-mile restraining line, VIII Corps, which was holding the thin Ardennes front, believed it had the situation figured out:

Order of Battle Note, 13 December 44, Headquarters VIII Corps:

Sixth SS Panzer Army: Since the move of the Sixth SS Panzer Army from its reforming and retraining area in Westphalia to its present location, much has been said about the dispositions of the divisions under its command. The vast majority of reports regarding these locations have been furnished by interrogation of PW's who had either recently passed the areas in question or picked up information concerning the whereabouts of these units by hearsay. Interrogation of civilians also supplied a number of clues which were helpful in solving the puzzle of Sixth Panzer Army.

The Army as a whole occupies the area between the Roer and the Rhine Rivers. The northern boundary of this sector probably runs from München-Gladbach to Neuss. From this line south, SS troops are to be found in almost every town and village, and much of their armor and heavy equipment such as artillery is thought to be stored in buildings, while the rest is no doubt camouflaged in wooded areas. These concentrations of men and matériel continue south to a line extending from Remagen to Blankenheim. The pattern of rail and road movement observed by tactical reconnaissance confirm

[4] Hugh Cole, *The Ardennes* (Washington: Dept. of the Army, 1965), p. 58.

the presence of at least four armored divisions in the area described above.
At least four SS Panzer divisions are accepted as part of the Sixth SS Panzer
Army. They are probably grouped under I, II SS Panzer Corps. It is thought
likely that another panzer division, and possibly two, may yet be added to
this army. I SS, 2 SS, 9 SS, and 12 SS Panzer Divisions are the divisions
accepted under Sixth SS Panzer Army, and it is thought that 2 Panzer Division and 5 SS Panzer Division may yet appear.

The intelligence officer's job goes far beyond playing sleuth in pursuit of an
elusive Sixth Panzer Army. Indeed, identification of enemy units is little more
than an academic exercise except as it contributes to the G-2's main chore:
advising the commander what the enemy is capable of doing and, if possible,
providing him an intelligent estimate of which course of action the enemy is
most likely to adopt.

The intelligence officer is truly useful only if he can give the commander
judgments based on concrete observations and definite enough to influence
the disposition of his own forces. This accounts for the rather sensitive attitude exhibited by those charged with watching the enemy during early December, 1944.

It is neither necessary nor desirable to examine in detail all the clues observed by intelligence, pointing in one direction or another. However, it is
safe to say that all, commanders included, were so imbued with the current
spirit of optimism that their judgment was clouded.

This predetermination of enemy intentions was particularly harmful to sur-
veillance of the Wehrmacht in mid-December. For Hitler had been lucky—
he got his days of bad weather—so when the Allies searched for evidence,
they were forced to look where they *believed* they might find something. This
was particularly so in the case of a most important source of information,
air intelligence. During the first half of December, according to one account,
the 67th Tactical Reconnaissance Group, supporting 12 U.S. Army Group
fairly consistently, included on the daily mission orders targets located in the
Eifel. However, since these targets were given low priority, they were dropped
when poor weather made it necessary to fly only high-priority missions, which
were primarily targets in the Saar and around Aachen. From December 10 to
15, the critical five days before the attack, the 67th Tactical Reconnaissance
Group flew a total of 71 missions, and on only one day, December 13, were
all U.S. airplanes grounded. However, again the matter of priorities came in.
On December 14, for example, the 30th Photo Reconnaissance Squadron
flying over Trier reported the weather clear. But the pilot of a second mission,
only two hours later, found visibility very poor, and he reported he was unable
to see much.[5]

[5] Cole, *op. cit.,* p. 61.

One of the difficulties facing Allied aerial reconnaissance was the extremely thorough security measures exercised by the German units moving through the Eifel, and these measures were facilitated by the nature of the vegetation—coniferous trees, which do not lose their cover in winter. Units of the three Nazi armies moving into position were simply not seen in the limited number of missions flown. Many of the conclusions drawn by the Allies were dependent on interpretation of train movements: on December 10 First U.S. Army reported that no sightings had been made on two days during the week because of poor weather conditions; the rail lines in the army zone had been well covered on the remaining days. There had been train movement at some time during the week on all rail lines in the V and VII U.S. corps zones, including the Rhine Valley. However, such trains as had been sighted opposite VIII Corps were interpreted as moving either north or south—or stopping over in the Eifel area en route to one of the two other critical fronts.

As a result, all aerial observations fitted into a neat preconceived pattern: German units were being switched back and forth between Aachen and the Saar with periodic stopovers in the Eifel area opposite the Ardennes.

Colonel Benjamin A. ("Monk") Dickson, G-2 of First U.S. Army, was a tall, strapping, moustached man who, though son and brother of West Point graduates, had spent most of his career in civilian life. He was graduated from West Point in one of the abbreviated World War I classes, the class of 1918, and became a member of one of the American expeditionary forces in Siberia. Assessing the prospects of peacetime promotion, he decided to resign from the Army.

After graduation from Massachusetts Institute of Technology as a mechanical engineer in 1922, Dickson settled in Philadelphia in 1925, where, besides his civilian activities, he kept a commission in the Army Reserves. His business took him abroad, and unlike many Americans, he was highly proficient in French and German, so he was not surprised when he was called up to duty as a captain in military intelligence in October, 1940.

Dickson was not to remain a captain long; nor was he to stay long in the United States. In June, 1942, he went to Africa with the II U.S. Corps, and throughout the Tunisian campaign served as intelligence officer to Generals Fredendall, Patton, and Bradley. Bradley had confidence in Dickson, and when he moved up the ladder from commander of II Corps to First Army, he took Dickson with him from the Mediterranean to Bristol, England.

Their ways parted on August 1, 1944, when Bradley, with a ready-made staff at 12 Army Group, left Dickson (now a colonel) as G-2 to his successor, General Courtney Hodges.

By this time his wealth of experience, in the Army and out, had made Monk Dickson a "pro"—for our Army—in the intelligence game. Known as an extrovert and a raconteur, he was also considered something of a pessimist—not a fault in a G-2; veterans like Cy Peterman who, in his own words, "had been chased around by Rommel's tank elements" in Tunisia, were "willing to pay attention to him."

And Dickson the pessimist, G-2 of the army most concerned—the First—began to get uneasy concerning this newly identified Sixth Panzer Army's buildup in the vicinity of Cologne.

Nevertheless, he tended to wax hot and cold in his reports. A little earlier, on November 20, as Sepp Dietrich was crossing the Rhine River bridges to the Cologne area, Dickson wrote, "the enemy's capability of a spoiling attack is now lost," reasoning that the American attack launched on November 16 would nail down the Nazi reserves. The enemy's strategic plan, he continued, appeared to be based on a counterattack rather than a planned offensive on his own initiative. With some insight Dickson predicted that the key to German strategy would probably be found in the whereabouts and activity of Sixth Panzer Army. But he ended on a cheerful note: "The enemy's over-all strategy in the Western Front can be summed up as the defense of the Reich west of the Rhine. . . . It is not unreasonable to believe the defense of the Reich west of the Rhine will be unsuccessful, that he will soon be forced into retirement behind the Rhine which, if not skillfully executed, may lead to another military disaster comparable to the battle of France."

But by the end of the first week of December, Dickson had become concerned over what he saw in the target subsection of his G-2 office; he prepared a document entitled "Study of Enemy Armored Reserves," which included a fairly detailed analysis of the location of Sixth Panzer Army units, especially those close to railheads. It listed 48 targets, broken down into three categories:

> (A) List One (Red Bomb [first priority])—Troop concentrations close to railheads and rail junctions.
> (B) List Two (Blue Bomb [second priority])—Rail junctions and regulating joints through which the troops and supplies are known to pass.
> (C) List Three (Brown Bomb [third priority])—Troop concentration areas.

The study concluded that the trouble with aerial bombardment in the past in most cases had been concentration of damage in *one* place at *one* time; repair crews rushed to the spot had been able to keep the through lines open; the trains were rerouted to undamaged and repaired lines. If all the switch points and rail crossovers were taken within a period of four to five days, there would be more damage than the repair crews could handle at once. Trains could not be rerouted, and isolation would last many times longer.

Dickson duly submitted his study to General Hodges and Major General Elwood Quesada, commanding from Normandy the 9th Tactical Air Command supporting First Army. They were enthusiastic, and the request was forwarded, but to Dickson's disgust the mission was washed out by higher Air Force headquarters as "not sufficiently remunerative."

Two days later Monk Dickson published one of his periodic estimates. This, destined to become famous and controversial, was Estimate 37, December 10, 1944.

> It is plain that his [the enemy's] strategy in defense of the Reich is based on the exhaustion of our offensive to be followed by an all-out counterattack with armor, between the Roer and the Erft, supported by every weapon he can bring to bear. . . . It is very probable that his current production of V-1's is being routed to new sites in the Black Forest and elsewhere east of the Rhine, where they can be brought to bear in support of his all-out counterattack by interdicting and bombarding our supply installations and artillery areas. . . . A captured order for a comb-out of selected personnel speaking the American dialect to report to Hq Skorzeny at Friedenthal, near Oranienburg, by 1 November, obviously presages special operations for sabotage, attacks on CP's, and other vital installations by infiltrated or parachuted specialists. *An extremely intelligent PW whose other observations check exactly with established facts stated that every means possible is being gathered for the coming all-out counteroffensive.* It is notable that morale among PW's freshly captured, both in the Army cage and at Communications Zone cage, recently achieved a new high. This has been expressed by attempts to escape and avowed eagerness on the part of the prisoners to return and rejoin the battle *for Germany. It is apparent that von Rundstedt, who obviously is conducting military operations without the benefit of intuition, has skilfully defended and husbanded his forces and is preparing for his part in the all-out application of every weapon at the focal point and the correct time to achieve defense of the Reich west of the Rhine by inflicting as great a defeat on the Allies as possible.* Indications to date point to the location of this focal point as being between Roermond and Schleiden,[6] and within this bracket this concentrated force will be applied to the Allied force judged by the German High Command to be the greatest threat to successful defense of the Reich.[7]

Unfortunately Colonel Dickson, like the rest, was looking at the Roer River. He believed the restoration of the West Wall was still a probable strategic objective. "Von Rundstedt," he wrote, "apparently is accepting defeats in the south rather than compromise his hope of a decisive success in the north. . . . During the past month there has been a definite pattern for the seasoning of newly-formed divisions in the comparatively quiet sector opposite VIII Corps prior to their dispatch to more active fronts."

But Estimate 37 weakened its own case: The concentrated counterattack *"is to be expected when our major ground forces have crossed the Roer River,*

---

[6] Schleiden, Dickson points out, is east and slightly south of Monschau. However, Estimate 37 shows Schleiden as the southern rather than the northern shoulder of the attack.

[7] Italics supplied.

and if the dams are not controlled by us, maximum use will be made by the enemy of flooding of the Roer in conjunction with his counterattack." [8]

Dickson had come close. He had correctly foreseen the German capability for a major counteroffensive. But this estimate fell victim to the line of thinking that was prevalent: the reserves were being husbanded for a counterattack against Allied crossings of the Roer River.

As the situation developed during the next several days, Dickson watched the Ardennes front with more apprehension. He began to have an uneasy feeling that this was the area where the attack could come. On December 14 he received a report that made his eyes pop:

> A German woman, whose statements are believed reliable according to VIII U.S. Corps, has given the following information of her observations behind the German lines during the three days beginning 10 December. She saw many horse-drawn vehicles, pontoons, small boats, and other river-crossing equipment coming from the direction of Bitburg, and moving toward Geichlingen. In Bitburg she overheard some military personnel saying that it had taken them three weeks to get there from Italy. There were also troops in town with gray uniforms and black collar patches. She also stated she had seen many artillery pieces, both horse-drawn and carried on trucks. (Comment: A very interesting report. Build-up of troops has been confirmed by Tac/R and PW statements. Presence of large numbers of engineers with bridging equipment suggests preparation for offensive rather than defensive action.)

That night Dickson's impetuosity got the better of him. At a meeting with General Hodges and other members of the First Army General Staff, he struck the operations map in the area between Monschau and Echternach. "It's the Ardennes!" he exclaimed.

But Colonel Dickson had slapped maps before, and he had little of a concrete nature to back up his hunch. Furthermore, the word had come discreetly from as high a level as SHAEF [9] that perhaps Colonel Dickson should be toned down a bit, and on December 12, in a document designed bluntly to nullify the effects of Estimate 37, Sibert, G-2 at 12 Army Group, had published his own estimate:

> It is now certain that attrition is steadily sapping the strength of German forces on the western front and that the crust of defenses is thinner, more brittle and more vulnerable than it appears on our G-2 maps or to the troops in the line. Two outstanding facts support this unqualified statement:
> (a) The first is that there is ample evidence that the strength of the infantry divisions that have been in the line on active sectors since the beginning

[8] Italics supplied.
[9] Letter, General Kenneth Strong to the author, dated November 25, 1966.

of our offensive has been cut at least fifty per cent and several other divisions are known to have been virtually destroyed. . . .

(b) The second fact is that while the enemy's minimum replacement need in the face of our offensives is twenty divisions a month, the estimated total available to him from all sources, for the foreseeable future, is fifteen a month. Recently the enemy has not even been able to keep up this rate—its replacement rate for several weeks being only two or three a week.

These two basic facts—the deathly weakness of the individual infantry division in the line plus the inevitability of the enemy falling still further in replacement arrears—make it certain that before long he will utterly fail in his current attempt to withdraw and arrest his tactical reserve so that he will be forced to commit at least part of his panzer army to the line. . . .

All of the enemy's major capabilities, therefore, depend on the balance between the rate of attrition imposed by the Allied offensives and the rate of infantry reinforcement. The balance at present is in favor of the Allies. *With continuing Allied pressure in the south and in the north, the breaking point may develop suddenly and without warning.*[10]

On the morning of December 15, the day after his outburst, Dickson, with the hearty consent of his chief, left for Paris on his first four-day leave since landing in Normandy the previous June.

General Strong, at SHAEF, shared 12 Army Group's optimism regarding the overall weakness of the Wehrmacht. Strong, it is true, was concerned about the thin Allied lines in the Ardennes early in December and mentioned this to General Walter Bedell Smith, the SHAEF chief of staff. Smith was so impressed with Strong's misgivings that he asked him to visit General Bradley, and Bradley, as has been mentioned, studied the situation carefully; Strong's presentation merely reinforced Bradley's knowledge of the calculated risk he was taking. But in the overall picture, things did look good.[11]

Other headquarters were expecting a German attack at that moment no more than was SHAEF. Field Marshal Montgomery, for one, could hardly have been anticipating an attack anywhere along the front when he wrote to General Eisenhower requesting permission to be absent at Christmas to visit with his son in London. Montgomery's own chief of staff, Major General Francis de Guingand, was actually in the United Kingdom on December 15. General Bradley, writing after the war, seemed still to harbor some pique:

[10] Italics supplied.

[11] SHAEF's *View of the Enemy Situation:* The problems still facing the enemy are naked enough. The longest term problem is to find enough men and equipment to stand up to the present rate of attrition. It is estimated that the present allied offensive has been costing the enemy 3,000 permanent or long-term casualties a day in each of the three major battles, i.e. 9,000 a day since 16 November: this is something like three-quarters of a (German) division a day, or up to five a week. . . . It cannot be met indefinitely, even by sending to the west all reserves becoming available.

During the middle of November G-2 reported that the Sixth SS Panzer Army may have been moved from its assembly point in Westphalia to an area nearer Cologne. Another panzer army, the Fifth, was reported to have massed its tanks a little farther north. So conspicuous were these telltale signs of von Rundstedt's apparent intent to nab us astride the Roer, that we should probably have sifted them for evidence of deception. But if anyone on that Western front sniffed in those preparations an intent to mislead us on a German offensive elsewhere, he certainly did not share his suspicions with me.[12]

Those seeking explanations for Allied inability to detect German intentions often mention the frame of mind that dominated Western leaders and intelligence officers alike. Fixed on the idea that any counterattack would be executed to counter the forthcoming Allied main attack in the north toward the Rhine, the Allies gave little consideration to any other possibility.

This mental attitude was enhanced by an interesting misinterpretation. On September 5, 1944, Field Marshal Gerd von Rundstedt was restored to the command of OB West, replacing Field Marshal Walther Model in that capacity, although Model remained commander of Army Group B. Well aware of this change in command, Allied officers instinctively expected Rundstedt, a respected professional soldier, to conduct his operations in a sensible, conventional manner: Rundstedt would of course do what other professionals would do. An attack through the rough Ardennes, bereft of objectives of any consequence short of the Meuse River, just did not make hardheaded military sense. The Allied commanders were far from realizing that Rundstedt himself was not really in charge. Hitler conceived this plan, and the man executing it, Model, while admittedly advocating the "small solution," was sufficiently devoted to Hitler to execute any operation with energy and zeal.

Despite the almost unanimous condemnation of Allied Intelligence for those days of December, 1944, one has to sympathize: little, it would seem, of a concrete nature could be gleaned from the evidence that was presented. It is difficult to place oneself in the position of any of these intelligence officers, who received large numbers of false and conflicting reports daily, and visualize putting one's finger on the map and saying, "Sixth Panzer Army under Dietrich and Fifth Panzer Army under Manteuffel are poised in the Eifel."

The fact is the Allies were surprised.

While higher headquarters were debating the significance of recent German moves, the VIII U.S. Corps also showed little concern. On December 9, 1944, Colonel Andrew Reeves, G-2 of VIII Corps, estimated the enemy forces

[12] Omar Bradley, *A Soldier's Story* (New York: Holt, 1951), p. 447.

available for reinforcement in the corps zone to be four infantry divisions, three of them volksgrenadier, averaging 6,000 men each, making a total of 24,000. On the front the enemy was expected to continue the active defense of his present positions, and this situation was not expected to change until VIII Corps went on the offensive:

> The enemy's present practice of bringing new divisions to this theater to receive front line experience and then relieving them out for commitment elsewhere *indicates his desire to have this sector of the front remain quiet and inactive.* Capabilities No. 2 and No. 3 [counterattack and reinforcement] will doubtless never be implemented unless the enemy feels that VIII Corps is preparing to mount an offensive.[13]

Little unusual enemy activity was observed by the corps divisions. The 106th Infantry Division replaced the 2d on the Schnee Eifel on December 10. The 106th Division G-2 journal entry for 7:28 P.M., December 12, reads, "At 1830 tanks were heard . . . moving northeast." Typical of a new outfit, the reporting unit was uncertain: "Reported by Company H, 2d Battalion. Not sure they were tanks. Two white flares seen . . . at 1815 by Cannon Company."

The next day, December 13, noises of vehicles were heard by the more experienced 4th Division to the south.

The 28th Division, which had come to the Ardennes by way of the Hürtgen Forest since the day they had marched through Paris, was also reporting motor vehicle travel in five different locations on December 14.

But motor vehicle noises were common. As pointed out later by Colonel Gustin M. Nelson, commanding officer of the 112th Infantry, 28th Division, this traffic was considered normal, necessary for the relief of troops within the sector. Three weeks previously the Germans had made such a relief, giving the same signs of movement.

About this time an incident occurred that added some interest to the otherwise dull task of the G-2 Operations Office. The 107th Field Artillery S-2 picked up two civilians, a man and woman, who had come through the lines in the vicinity of the battalion observation post. The couple had been part of a work party in Germany. They were immediately sent to an interrogation team. It was Lieutenant Muchnick whom they startled with the news of a considerable enemy buildup across the Our River.

Muchnick was on the phone with Major Hurwitz of the Division G-2 section in little more than an hour. Hurwitz demanded, "Find out the following information":

1. Direction of traffic from Geichlingen.
2. Types of boats and equipment mentioned.

[13] Italics supplied.

3. How did she get back so quick on her return trip?
4. How did she know traffic was going where she said it was?
5. What did she see between Oberweist and Bitburg?
6. Did she know what effect our artillery shellings had on Bauler?
7. Where did she spend each day?
8. Any movement or anything in Bauler on return trip.
9. What does she mean by "many" [boats, pieces of bridging equipment, etc.]?

The major obviously did not believe much of what he had heard. But this was the report that, transmitted to First Army, touched off Colonel Dickson's outburst: "It's the Ardennes!"

The news was passed back; the interrogation of the woman went on sporadically for another day. Nothing more is mentioned about the man, but the woman was held. Finally, on the evening of December 15, 28th Division decided to send her back to the First Army G-2 for further interrogation. Colonel Dickson was now in Paris. Cy Peterman was driving from Wiltz to Spa, the woman's destination. She arrived at Spa on December 16.

A final piece of unusual information came out of the 28th Division. An observation post reported something new that evening: for the first time German soldiers in the vicinity of pillboxes were dressed in overcoats. "The bearing of these soldiers," the report continued, "was more soldierly than heretofore. Guards were relieved in double time and much saluting was observed. Digging of many small holes and stringing of wire, type unknown, were also observed."

This report was sent to VIII Corps headquarters, which had also received similar information from some infantry units of the 9th Armored Division squeezed in between the 28th on the north and the 4th on the south. First Army's comment: "Very likely a recently arrived VG division coming in to relieve 212 VG Division."

Despite these minor routine reports, all was quiet. The 4th Infantry Division journal reported at 9:00 A.M., December 16: "G-2 left CP for a three-day pass to civilazation [sic]."

How far the G-2 ever got on his trip to "civilazation" is not shown in the records.

Book III

ASSAULT

CHAPTER 10

❦

"We March!"

O N the eve of December 16, 1944, a member of the Waffen-SS penned
a letter to his sister:

> Dear Ruth:
>
> My daily letter will be very short today—short and sweet. I write during
> one of the great hours before an attack—full of unrest, full of expectation
> for what the next days will bring. Everyone who has been here the last two
> days and nights (especially nights), who has witnessed hour after hour the
> assembly of our crack divisions, who has heard the constant rattling of
> panzers, knows that something is up and we are looking forward to a clear
> order to reduce the tension. We are still in the dark as to "where" and "how"
> but that cannot be helped!
>
> Some believe in big wonders, but that may be shortsighted! It is enough
> to know we attack, and will throw the enemy from our homeland. That is
> a holy task! I do not want to talk or write much now—but wait and see what
> the hours ahead will bring!
>
> Overhead is the terrific noise of V-1, of artillery—the voice of war. So long
> now—wish me luck and think of me. . . .

A postscript was hurriedly scribbled on the back of the sealed envelope:
"Ruth! Ruth! Ruth! WE MARCH!!!"

The storm trooper who wrote his sister was a member of one of the elite
SS panzer divisions assigned to General Sepp Dietrich's Sixth Panzer Army.
Farther south all troops in the Fifth Panzer Army had read to them a message
originating from Field Marshal Gerd von Rundstedt, endorsed by the commander of Army Group B, and finally endorsed by the commander of the
Fifth Panzer Army. Each of these officers expressed his view of the significance of the coming venture in his own way:

> *OB West:*
>
> Soldiers of the West Front!! Your great hour has arrived. Large attacking
> armies have started against the Anglo-Americans. I do not have to tell you

179

anything more on that. You feel it yourself: WE GAMBLE EVERYTHING! You carry with you the holy obligation to give everything to achieve things beyond human possibilities for our Fatherland and our Führer!

von Rundstedt, C in C West
Generalfeldmarschall

Army Group B:

In addition to the daily order of C in C West: We will not disappoint the Führer and the homeland. . . . Advance in the spirit of Leuthen. Our password will remain now more than ever: No soldier of the world can be better than we soldiers of the Eifel and Aachen area.

Model, Generalfeldmarschall

Fifth Panzer Army:

Forward double time! Remember the heritage and the ardor of our dead comrades as well as the tradition of our proud Wehrmacht.

von Manteuffel,
General der Panzertruppen

The sixteenth of December—Null-Day, the day Hitler had designated for the Nazi infantry to punch holes through the American lines and create gaps through which the panzer formations could pour westward—defies simple overall description on the fronts of the German Army Group B and the U.S. V and VIII corps.

On an operations map showing the entire front, the German infantry attacks against U.S. lines running from Monschau on the north, southward through Udenbreth, the Losheim Gap, Bleialf, and Dasburg, to Vianden were individually unimpressive. In only rare cases did a local American commander realize that his unit was facing part of a major attack.

The story of December 16, 1944, then, is the story of a series of apparently disconnected small unit actions. The large red arrows on the maps and the massive movements of troops would come another day. The story of Null-Day is the story of individuals and small units.

The great German offensive started out inauspiciously. At Lippspringe, his planned point of departure, Parachute Colonel Friedrich von der Heydte was pacing the floor impatiently. The previous morning he had received his combat orders: the air drop of Kampfgruppe von der Heydte was to take place on December 16 between 4:30 and 5:00 A.M. Motor transport columns provided by Army Group B were to convey the troops from their billeting area to the Paderborn and Lippspringe airdromes. The arrival of these columns had been promised for 7:00 P.M. the previous evening.

Von der Heydte had briefed his officers on the conduct of the operation and had driven ahead to Lippspringe to await the kampfgruppe. At 4:00 A.M. on December 16, it became apparent that his troops would not arrive on time; not even half the kampfgruppe had shown up at the airdrome. Von der Heydte had no choice but to postpone his airborne mission, at least for a day.

Major General Walter Lauer, commanding the newly committed 99th U.S. Infantry Division on the south of General Gerow's V Corps, realized that his command was in an uncomfortable position. He had a front extending more than twenty miles along the Siegfried Line, from the Losheimergraben cross-roads in the south to Monschau in the north. His troops were deployed in dense terrain, where fields of fire were difficult to achieve, and the miserable road net would make it difficult to maneuver the one battalion he was hold-ing out as division reserve.

The situation was mitigated to some extent by the presence of the veteran 2d U.S. Infantry Division, recently relieved from the Schnee Eifel, attacking through Lauer's center. Gerow, whose V Corps had been assigned the task

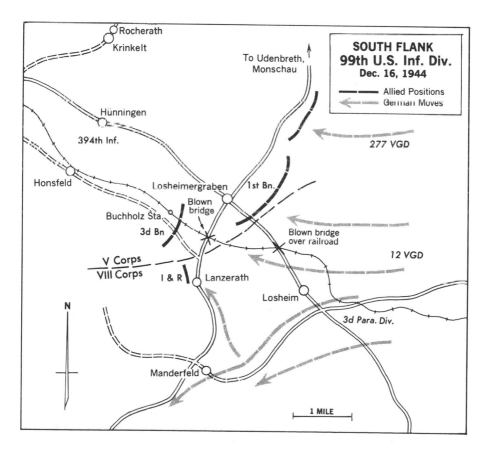

SOUTH FLANK
99th U.S. Inf. Div.
Dec. 16, 1944

Allied Positions
German Moves

of seizing the Roer River dams, had elected to attack along a road from Krinkelt-Rocherath in Lauer's center running northward to Wahlerscheid, where it veered to the northeast. This time he hoped to bypass the Monschau and Hürtgen forests. Thus the 2d Infantry Division was attacking northward through Lauer's northern regiment, the 395th. The 395th was supporting the effort with two of its battalions.

The territory in the north was less worrisome to Lauer than that on the south. On the southern flank his 394th Infantry was spread over a distance of nearly five miles. And through the southern part of that regiment ran the main hard-surfaced road between the German positions and the Meuse River. This road, running from Losheim to Losheimergraben, to Hünningen, Büllingen, and Butgenbach (Lauer's own command post), led on to the west.

Other roads led into Lauer's position, to be sure, including a main road that ran from the south through the village of Lanzerath to Losheimergraben, the position of the flank of the 394th. There a fork led to both Lauer's rear and the right flank of his southernmost battalion. Troops that turned west on that fork could cut the 99th from the rear practically without meeting a soldier from the 394th. Unfortunately, the responsibility for the area of the road through Lanzerath was not his. It belonged to the 14th Cavalry Group, attached to the 106th Division of VIII Corps.

Lauer studied his south flank situation. There, four towns, Buchholz Station, Losheimergraben, Losheim, and Lanzerath, formed a quadrangle with each town well joined by passable roads (see map, p. 181). Losheim was in the hands of the Germans. Lanzerath was in the area of the 14th Cavalry Group. The vital road junction at Losheimergraben was defended by the 1st Battalion of Colonel Don Riley's 394th Infantry Regiment.

Lauer did all he could to protect his south flank. Behind the 1st Battalion at Losheimergraben he positioned the division reserve, Riley's 3d Battalion, in such a location as to protect his right at Buchholz Station. Riley had only two battalions left under his command.

Riley went one step further. Suspicious of the route leading north through Lanzerath, he positioned his Regimental Intelligence and Reconnaissance (I & R) Platoon just northwest of Lanzerath, mainly to give warning of enemy attacks from that area.

It was fortunate for the 99th Division that the commanders took these precautions. For it was in this small quadrangle that the critical battle of the northern shoulder of the Bulge broke loose on the morning of December 16. Through the area of the 99th Division—indeed, through the regimental area of the spread-out 394th Infantry—ran the main roads designated to carry the main effort of Sepp Dietrich to the Meuse.

Like the other villages and hamlets throughout this region, historically Lanzerath belonged to Germany. It became part of Belgium only after World

War I, by the Treaty of Versailles. The town itself was rather unimpressive, consisting of fewer than ten houses, probably five on the east side of the road and three or four on the west. These houses, mostly of frame construction, offered little protection against fire of any kind, so in itself Lanzerath was useless as a defensive position. And yet this village was to become the scene of one of the bitterest small-unit struggles of World War II.

The significance of Lanzerath derived from its location. It lay about 300 yards south of a vitally important road junction from which a left fork ran westward to Buchholz Station and a right fork to Losheimergraben. Running northwest from Losheimergraben, as mentioned, was the major road of the area, the best route between Dietrich's army and Liège.

Lanzerath sat on the side of a hill. West of the town a knoll, although it was not high, gave troops occupying the position a dominant location from which to rake the highway to the south. East of the town the ground dropped off steeply. Thus Lanzerath at once afforded the Americans a magnificent observation post into German territory and made maneuver of troops difficult on the east (German) side of the road. Away from the town, on the opposite side of the knoll, was a thick wood, difficult enough for infantry and virtually impenetrable by armor.

Following a patrol on December 10, eighteen men of the Intelligence and Reconnaissance Platoon of the 394th Infantry Regiment of the 99th Division moved into position onto this hill dominating Lanzerath and its highway.

The unit that had previously occupied it, rumored among the men to have been a full company of the 2d Infantry Division, had dug it in well, protecting the foxholes with overhead cover.

The I & R Platoon, small as it was and new to combat, was a proud unit. The men were convinced they were protégés of the regimental intelligence officer, Major Robert L. Kriz, a veteran of the North African campaign. They knew for sure that their platoon leader, First Lieutenant Lyle J. Bouck, Jr., had been handpicked by Kriz. Though the second youngest man in the platoon, Bouck had already finished six years of military service. Enlisting in the 35th Infantry Division (National Guard) at St. Louis before legally of age, Bouck had been commissioned a second lieutenant at eighteen. Sandy-haired, he stood a fairly stocky five feet nine inches, and though informal in manner, he was sharp, incisive, and determined.

Bouck's platoon sergeant was a soldier of a different vintage. Technical Sergeant William Slape was a tall, professional enlisted man from Oklahoma. When the war was over, Slape, in contrast to most of the rest, would stay on as a thirty-year man—a "lifer."

The only man in the platoon younger than Bouck was Pfc. William James Tsakanikas,[1] barely nineteen years old. Tsakanikas, or James—inevitably his

---

[1] He has since dropped the last name and is now William James.

nickname was Sak—was one of the most aggressive soldiers in the platoon. Serving as Bouck's runner and, more important, as the point man for the platoon, always volunteering for patrols, always anxious to do more than his part in every kind of action, James was a soldier Bouck felt he could count on for any job.

James liked being a frontline infantryman no more than anyone else who could calculate the percentages of getting through the war without at least a "million-dollar wound." However, he was proud of the platoon and even more proud of the confidence Bouck obviously had in him. He had resolved to do more than his best to serve his country.

But in the small hours of the morning, December 16, 1944, James, like other men along the front, was feeling uneasy. Too many things had happened that added up to trouble. For one thing, the platoon knew that the 2d Division was attacking through the 99th Division to the north. Further, they had been informed that G-2 expected this attack to call for some sort of a "spoiling" attack by the Germans, and the logical place for such action was the south flank of the 99th Division, where Bouck and his men were in position.

Other goings-on had convinced James that the higher-ups were being a little oversolicitous. The day before, a generous liquor ration had been delivered (both Bouck and James, nondrinkers, gave their shares to other men)—obviously the condemned men's last treat. Extra ammunition had been recently issued in large quantities. A jeep with a mounted .50-caliber machine gun had been brought into position the day before. James did not know that the extra ammunition and the machine gun were simply equipment that Bouck had been urgently requesting for days and that Major Kriz had finally secured for him. He was also unaware that the liquor ration was a relatively routine thing. But one item could not be denied: The night before, Bouck had ordered every man to remain alert at his battle station all night long. Not a man had gotten a wink of sleep. All during their vigil the platoon had heard unusual noises to their front.

Lieutenant Bouck reviewed his platoon's situation. It was being employed on an unusual mission. Probably he hardly realized that his men were located outside 99th Division territory, across a corps boundary. In the town of Lanzerath, only about one hundred yards forward of Bouck's foxholes, was located a section of guns from Company A, 820th Tank Destroyer (TD) Battalion, attached to the 14th Cavalry Group, in whose sector they were. Bouck had wire communication with the TD's, but they had talked little. Both units had gone about their own business. Atfer all, they worked for different people.

I & R was trying to get along as comfortably as possible. A heavy layer of snow covered the ground, and the weather was damp and cold. Normally, except when all were on alert as during the previous night, the members of the platoon took turns warming themselves in two shacks to the rear. At the edge of the woods near the shacks hung a deer carcass. They would have a feast of venison in a couple of days.

Just before dawn the men of I & R Platoon witnessed an awesome sight. Above German positions on the ridge north of Losheim and extending all the way to directly in front of the platoon the sky was lit up by the muzzle flashes of what must have been a hundred artillery pieces. The flash of the barrage silhouetted great numbers of tanks and self-propelled guns on the German skyline.

The platoon dove into their foxholes before the heavy shells could reach their position. This was their first time under really heavy artillery. When the shells arrived, the fright was something new. It was just as they had told him in basic training, James thought. He reeled in a state of momentary shock, and he could feel the fright in his bowels. Fortunately the barrage was a rolling one, proceeding northwestward from the I & R position up the road toward Buchholz. Quickly the men picked up the pattern. The "overs" and the "shorts" were wasted so far as they were concerned. But whenever the concentrations crashed around their position the psychological effects were stunning. James and Bouck, together in a machine gun foxhole, were thankful that all the men had splendid overhead cover and were almost completely safe from anything except a direct hit.

The artillery preparation continued for about an hour. When it was raised, Bouck prepared for an immediate infantry attack. But as he looked out, he could not figure where the German infantry would come from. Possibly they would come directly from the northeast down the road from Losheimergraben (see map, p. 181). The men waited, but no German infantry came. It was now light enough for them to see a little, although the valley between their position and the ridge where they had seen the silhouetted vehicles a few moments earlier was still covered with mist. The tops of the Losheim houses could be seen a little more than a mile away, but not the streets.

But within ten minutes after the barrage had lifted, James and Bouck saw to their horror and disgust the tank destroyers of the 14th Cavalry Group pull out, heading to the rear along the Buchholz-Honsfeld road.

"If they can't sign off on the phone, they might at least wave goodbye as they leave," James growled.

Bouck was more charitable. "If we didn't have any more cover than those guys down in Lanzerath, we'd be pulling out too," he muttered as the TD's disappeared into the woods.

Bouck picked up his radio and called the 394th Regiment, located at Hünningen. He told the extent of the artillery preparation and the negligible damage to his position, and asked for instructions.

"Send a patrol down to Lanzerath, observe, and report," came back the answer.

Bouck looked around him. Four men would be enough. "Okay, come on, Sak, Pop, John."

"Pop" Robinson (so named because of his advanced years—he was thirty-five) and John Creger joined the other two; they took a circuitous route—all the way north to the Buchholz road and then southward down a ditch—to Lanzerath.

Bouck knew which building the tank destroyers had used—probably, he reasoned, the best observation post in town. The four men scrambled out of the ditch to the front door of the house and charged up the stairs. As they reached the second floor, they were astonished to see a large man in civilian clothes sitting next to the window facing Germany, talking on a civilian telephone line.

Instantly James pulled his bayonet from its scabbard and stuck it against the big man's belly. "Reach!" he growled. Whether or not the man understood English, his hands went up. James was sure he was a spy. His first impulse was to drop the bayonet and pull the trigger on his M-1, but reason stopped him. This was no place to start a fire fight. And if the group were to be captured, surely this was no place for a dead German.

"Let him go," Bouck snapped.

James gestured toward the stairs, and with a big grin, the man thundered down and out to the street.

All this action had taken only about twenty minutes. But as the patrol looked over the valley, they could see German troops en masse pulling out of Losheim and, as far as they could tell, given the undulating ground, heading toward the southwest. This meant that the masses of German troops they could see would be coming up the road behind them, through Lanzerath, and toward the right flank of I & R Platoon—apparently, an attack northward into the right flank of the 394th. The Germans seemed to be marching single file in close formation.

This observation was enough for Bouck. "Sak, you come with me. Robinson, you and Creger stay here in this house and observe down the road. As soon as that Kraut column comes into the home stretch, about a mile down the way, come back on up to the platoon."

Back in the platoon position, Bouch tried to telephone 1st Battalion, 394th. The lines were out from the shelling. He could reach regimental headquarters by radio. The officer at the other end was incredulous.

"Damn it," Bouck hollered. "Don't tell me what I don't see! I have twenty-twenty vision. Bring down some artillery, all the artillery you can, on the road south of Lanzerath. There's a Kraut column coming up from that direction!"

He waited, more and more disappointed, but no artillery came. "If we could only use that new proximity fuse we could sit inside these foxholes and never be hurt."

There was little time for thinking. Robinson and Creger, using the wire left behind by the tank destroyers, were on the line. "The Krauts are already downstairs," Robinson yelled in fright. "What shall we do?"

Bouck hesitated, wondering how to extricate the men he had left behind. But it was for a moment only. At one yell from their platoon leader, a group of men jumped out of their foxholes, ready to charge the few yards to Lanzerath to save their buddies. But heroism was unnecessary; in an instant both Robinson and Creger had appeared on the hill. The "Krauts," it turned out, had been Belgian civilians heading for their cellars. The German column was still a short distance away. But the two men had done their job. They had confirmed a German column coming north toward Lanzerath, and all were back safely.

Having seen the size of the force coming up the road, Robinson and Creger were ready to keep moving to the rear. So was everyone else. Bouck, however, grabbed a couple of men, shoved them into their foxholes, and ordered the rest of I & R Platoon to take up fighting positions.

A major attack seemed in the making. The members of the platoon were not sure from which direction the attack would come, but it made little difference. The platoon was disposed in a beautiful tactical position, a perimeter defense at the edge of the wood line. At the point nearest Lanzerath was the foxhole occupied by Bouck and James. A couple of .30-caliber light machine guns were covering the Honsfeld road junction to the north, and many of the men had Browning automatic rifles. James had a special weapon of his own. He had taken the liberty of appropriating a "grease gun" (submachine gun) from supply after the last patrol six days earlier. The .50-caliber machine gun on the jeep, protected from direct fire, could put down devastating fire, but whenever artillery came in, whoever was manning the .50-caliber would have to hop into a foxhole.

They waited for the German troops to arrive. They were not disappointed.

When the Germans approached, the Americans gasped in amazement: two columns marching on both shoulders of the road in close order, weapons slung, looking to neither side; no security had been put out on either flank. James, waiting with the rifle he had kept (along with his grease gun) let a group go past. The Germans were in mottled uniforms. James was surprised at this regalia, but Bouck, having been an instructor for two years at the Infantry School, Fort Benning, recognized them as paratroopers' uniforms and later reported this to the Regimental S-2 section, now much concerned.

When to open fire? Sergeant Slape, sharing a foxhole on the left flank with Bouck, picked up his rifle and took aim on the lead German as he entered Lanzerath. "Your mother's going to get a telegram for Christmas," he mumbled.

Bouck knocked the rifle aside. "Maybe they don't send telegrams. Besides," Bouck went on, "I don't want to get the point. I want to get the main body." Slape chuckled.

James, in the forward platoon foxhole, watched the Germans pass his position. He calculated that the formation would continue northward along the road toward Losheimergraben. But if the front of the column turned left along the Honsfeld road, he reasoned, this would cut off the rear of the I & R Platoon. He, for one, had made up his mind that he would open fire at that time.

The Americans waited. The German paratroopers took the right fork and continued northward toward Losheimergraben. At least the rear of the platoon would not be cut off. James, like Bouck, decided that he would wait for a good group to get past before letting go. About 300 men went by. Up the road came three figures, separate from the rest, obviously the commander and a couple of his staff. It was these James selected to open fire on. The time was ripe.

As James drew a bead on the center figure, a little blond girl of about thirteen—James even noticed the red ribbons in her hair—suddenly dashed out of a house on the other side of Lanzerath, ran up to the officers, pointed quickly to the I & R position, and ducked back inside. James was not overconfident of his marksmanship. If he fired at the officer, he might hit the girl. He held his fire for an all-important split second; in that moment the German officer gave a shout and signal; the German paratroopers dived into the ditches. The chance of ambush was gone.

The fire fight began; the Germans were pinned down. Fortunately for Bouck's men, the road to the south was exposed, and the parachutists could never reinforce this isolated battalion without coming under heavy .50-caliber fire from the Americans some distance off.

The fire fight never ceased all day. James dashed back to man the .50-caliber machine gun and, staying down on his knees for protection, fired by observing the strike of the bullets in the snow. He began raking the ditches and woods to the north and south. He took an inventory of his grease gun: five magazines of nineteen rounds each.

By noon some of the I & R men were wounded, but none seriously. Repeatedly, James screamed at Bouck to bring in artillery with the new proximity fuse. Bouck, in turn, kept screaming to Regiment over his radio. But for the moment no artillery came in.

"What shall we do then?" Bouck demanded of Regiment.

"Hold at all costs."

Lieutenant Edward A. Buenger, assistant S-2, 394th Infantry, in Hünningen, was on the radio talking to the I & R Platoon leader, who Buenger knew was dug in somewhere barely northwest of Lanzerath. Bouck's position, Buenger learned, was being surrounded by Germans. It seemed that Bouck was too busy fighting to think about retreating; he seemed to be anxious to get back in the fight with his men. Buenger was in a position to be a little more objective. This was an *intelligence* platoon; besides fighting, it was up to them to supply information on the enemy situation in their sector of the front lines.

Bouck confirmed that he was to "hold at all costs," but just as Buenger was demanding more information on the nature of the German attack, Bouck's radio receiver emitted a loud thud. Buenger heard no more.

Lieutenant Lyle Bouck was lucky. The bullet that destroyed his radio missed him entirely. True, he had been knocked to the ground, but a couple of men picked him up and dragged him to a foxhole, where he gathered his wits. Upon examination he found he was unhurt.

Still the attack continued. James was bewildered. "Whoever's ordering that attack," he mumbled to himself, "must be frantic. Nobody in his right mind would send troops into a position like this without more fire support."

Wave after wave of Germans in mottled uniforms came up the hill, and James, firing continuously, felt a certain sickness as the tall, good-looking "kids" climbed the snow fence from the road and houses. As the waves came up, all were cut down. No Germans broke or retreated. The range was so close that James could see their faces. He tried to divorce his mind from the faces. With his grease gun, his .50-caliber machine gun, and occasionally his M-1, he tried to imagine himself firing at movement, not at men.

At midmorning a white flag appeared. The Americans raised their fire, and German medical corpsmen moved about the hill, pulling out the wounded. The Americans checked their own situation and found the casualties surprisingly light. Louis Kalil was severely wounded in the face by a rifle grenade. James saw no reason why sparing the German medics should prevent his firing long distances away toward Losheim and Manderfeld. After all, there were probably Germans in those towns. He therefore stood on the jeep and fired away, allowing the Germans in the immediate front to haul off their wounded.

As soon as the German medics were finished another assault came. This time the attack was supported. Hearing the hollow sounds of mortars from the valley behind Lanzerath, the men of I & R jumped into their foxholes. When the mortars lifted, Bouck and Slape rolled out and went up and down the position, checking the condition of the men.

James went back to the .50-caliber. Three paratroopers crawled up close enough to threaten Risto Milosevich, whose .30-caliber light machine gun was protecting the left flank. The .50 could not swing fast enough; James reached for the grease gun hanging ready at his neck and cut the Germans down. In a frenzy, he stumbled over to the bodies and emptied an entire magazine of nineteen rounds into the corpses lying there looking at him. The impact of one of the .45-caliber slugs rolled one body clear over.

Thus it went all afternoon, but eventually the spirits of the I & R Platoon began to sag. The men were tired, and they were well aware that the 3d Battalion, 394th, was right behind them only a mile to the northwest at Buchholz Station. False rumors were circulating of enemy paratroopers in their rear at Honsfeld. Somewhere an artillery forward observer appeared. The rounds he brought in had psychological effect at least. But still no reinforcements. In front of the platoon the German dead lay in heaps. (Four hundred men, Bouck finally estimated, but James thought there were rather more—though who could tell under such conditions?)

Finally a lull came. Bouck called James over to him. "Sak," he said, "I want you to take the men who want to go and get out."

"Are you coming?"

"No, I have orders to hold at all costs. I'm staying."

"Then we'll all stay," said James.

As they talked, two German helmets popped over the hill. Both Americans fired at the same time, and James' muzzle, close to Bouck's ear, made the latter's eardrum ring. James allowed himself a moment to pout as his friend, the lieutenant, turned around and gave him the very devil.

As the light began to fail—which was quite early in Northern Europe in December—Bouck's men were nearly out of ammunition. Some ammunition for the M-1 rifles remained. James had one last clip in his grease gun.

Bouck sent word to the men to report when all ammunition was gone. When it was gone he would feel justified in pulling out. Nobody knew how the end would come.

A German soldier with a white flag came within shouting distance. "Americans, give up!" he shouted. An American—nobody knew who—began to amuse himself by shooting near the German's feet. The man dashed back down the hill, followed by a torrent of obscenities. At dark artillery started coming in again, the heaviest since morning.

The mission had been accomplished, as far as Bouck could see. Two men had to go to Regiment to get orders or reinforcements. He sent for Corporal Jenkins and Private Preston.

"Sam," he said to the NCO, "you and Bob take off down the Buchholz road and go to Regiment. See if you can find Major Kriz and get us reinforcements or orders to pull out. We can't hold out much longer."

Both men departed; neither returned.

Bouck now felt justified in planning a retreat. Miraculously, although there were some wounded, only one man had been killed outright during the day. Bouck figured he might be able to move back in three groups, two at a time covering as the third traveled.

The Germans, however, were infiltrating the position in the darkness. Figures could be seen in outline no farther than a few feet away. Hole by hole the platoon position was being taken.

Those Americans left continued to fight. Suddenly Slape lost his restraint —he could not give up while the .50-caliber machine gun still had a few rounds of ammunition. Up to the jeep he leaped and fired, cursing roundly. Small arms knocked out the weapon.

Finally the Germans made a frontal assault on Bouck and James. James was out of M-1 ammunition, and his grease gun was nearly empty. An explosion picked him off his feet and seemed to send him into the next world; he had been hit in the face by a German burp gun. Yet through the haze he could still hear boots tramping by.

Bouck grabbed him. "Sak, I'll get you out of here," he said, and he pulled him out of the foxhole into the night.

In the dusk Bouck could see the extent of James' wound. The right side of his face had been shot away, and his right eyeball was hanging limply in the cavern where his cheek had been. A German officer within a couple of feet took a quick look at Sak's face, and gasped under his breath, "*Mein Gott.*"

Two other Germans closed in, ready to shoot, one, weeping and muttering to himself, "*Ach, meine kameraden!*" Bouck knew he was finished for sure. The German officer, however, jumped between the Germans and the two Americans, shouting "*Nein!*" At that point James passed out. (Later he was to wonder if this was the officer he had fixed in the sights of his M-1 that morning.)

Shortly thereafter James regained consciousness. Bouck had been wounded in the leg but could walk. He and a German soldier were practically carrying James down the hill to a café in Lanzerath. The whole platoon had been captured. Bodies were so thick it was impossible to avoid stepping on them.

In the café, James thought he was dying. He thought of the mothers of the boys he had mowed down and of his own mother. He passed out again. The next thing he knew, he was lying on the floor being treated by a German aidman. From a distance he could hear an interrogation and the words, "name, rank, serial number"—no particular name, rank, or serial number, merely those words. As consciousness returned, he realized that it was he who was being interrogated and was saying the words. The German, giving up the interrogation, leaned over and whispered in English, "*Ami,* you and your comrades are brave men." In spite of everything James felt good for a moment.

The cuckoo clock in the café struck midnight. Lieutenant Lyle J. Bouck, also lying wounded on the floor, had turned twenty-one years old.

"What a hell of a way to become a man," he mumbled to himself.

The action of the I & R Platoon, 394th Infantry, was remarkable for the contribution that a handful of men—eighteen in all—was able to make on December 16. Their story is only typical of the experience of scores of American platoons along the overextended VIII and V corps fronts. All along the front the Americans were surprised by the attacks that hit simultaneously at 5:30 A.M. Small American units, situated in isolated positions, found themselves quickly surrounded.

In most cases the American forces did not realize that day the magnitude of the offensive being launched against First U.S. Army. Most infantrymen were sure the assaults on their own position were local.

Many Americans were astonished by the lack of normal caution on the part of the attackers as they approached the American positions. This was noted not only by units of the 394th Infantry, but also by the commanding officer of the 112th Infantry (28th Division) to the south and by the 14th Cavalry troopers in the Losheim Gap. It probably stemmed from the lack of time afforded the German commanders to train the raw volksgrenadier troops adequately. Responsible, too, were Hitler's stringent secrecy measures in the last fateful days in the Eifel which made it impossible for commanders to reconnoiter. As a result, in more cases than one, German units moving down the road in almost parade-ground formation found themselves suddenly mowed down by an enemy that they did not suspect was there.

But in other respects, the experience of the units on the front line was to vary. On the two shoulders of the penetration—the northern one occupied by the 2d and 99th Infantry divisions and the southern one by the 4th Division—the battle would shape up into strictly defensive operations facing great but not impossible odds.

Experience in World War I had established that holding the shoulders is the most effective tactical response to a dangerous enemy penetration. If the enemy's drive can be contained between two unyielding shoulders, his next objective—that of widening the breach, preparatory to exploiting the advance —will be forestalled. Eventually the penetration can be choked off. In the Ardennes offensive some of the fiercest, if most thankless, fighting was the heroic efforts of the American forces to hold the two shoulders, commonly thought of as Elsenborn in the north and Echternach in the south. These were to prove critical to the prevention of an Allied defeat. Between them, the highly overextended 106th Infantry Division (14th Cavalry Group attached) and the 28th Infantry Division to their south would suffer the heaviest losses.

In this sixty-mile gap there would be plenty of problems. Lieutenant Kenneth Farrens would hold Krewinkel, a small town, against overwhelming numbers. Colonel Mark Devine would see his 14th Cavalry Group temporarily destroyed as a fighting unit. Farther south two U.S. Infantry regiments, the 422d and 423d, would be surrounded by a single German volksgrenadier division. A lieutenant of the 423d, Oliver Patton, would find himself sent on a hazardous mission to find two lost artillery battalions. Colonel Gustin Nelson's 112th Infantry Regiment would hold with some success. Colonel Hurley Fuller of the 110th Infantry, which was in the middle of the 28th Division, would find himself out of contact with his surrounded units on the Skyline Drive. To the south Lieutenant Colonel Earl Rudder, an unperturbed ex-ranger, would fight with no intention of giving up ground.

The story of these units cannot be told as an entity—the picture of December 16, from the American point of view, is exasperatingly confused. But the story of each unit bears telling individually.

Action of 99th Division

The I & R Platoon, 394th Infantry, had successfully blocked the Lanzerath road against a force of at least a battalion, maybe more, of the 3d German Parachute Division. They had protected the south flank of the 394th against a powerful attack, which might well have meant a collapse of the American position if it had been delivered in the early morning. The main German effort now became a matter of two frontal attacks by the 12th VGD: the 48th Grenadier Regiment on the north attacking Riley's 1st Battalion at Losheimergraben, and the 27th Füsilier Regiment attacking the 3d Battalion, supposedly division reserve, at Buchholz Station a mile west and slightly south.

The terrain crossed by the German regiments differed. The 48th Grenadier had to traverse dense woods to reach its objective; the 27th Füsilier, following the axis of the railroad from Losheim to Buchholz, was in more open country and actually hit 3d Battalion first. General Lauer no longer had a reserve.

The experiences of the Americans in other positions along the 99th Division front resembled those of Bouck's men except that the odds were more even.

First came the unexpectedly heavy barrage, assumed by most Americans to be merely a diversion from the 2d Division attack. Then came the delay after the barrage lifted about 7:00 A.M. Then the infantry attacks.

At Buchholz Station, Company L, 3d Battalion, was lining up for breakfast when a German assault company was sighted approaching through the fog, marching along the railroad track two abreast. The Americans were perplexed. Who would attack in such fashion? But as the Germans came on, the men of Company L abandoned breakfast and began shooting. The Germans scattered and took refuge behind the boxcars outside the station; a close-quarters fight began that lasted all morning. Finally, with the support of some tank destroyers and mortars, Company L, now reinforced by Company K, was able to drive the remaining Germans back by about noon, leaving 25 German bodies behind.

The main threat in the southern sector, however, came shortly after the 3d Battalion battle commenced. The 48th Grenadier Regiment finally made its way through the thick woods to the north and struck the 1st Battalion, 394th. Company B of that battalion lost sixty men and was forced back about 400 yards. There it formed a position and held. With this exception the position of the 394th was kept fairly intact during the day of December 16. The 2d Battalion of the regiment, on the left of the two threatened battalions, was never in serious trouble.

But though the ground had been largely held, there was no cause for complacency. Not only was this an attack in great strength, but also, and more serious, contact between the 394th Infantry and the 14th Cavalry Group to the south had been lost early in the day, to say nothing of Bouck's platoon, which had not been heard from since its radio went out.

As a result of these ominous signs, Lauer took further action to protect his division. He appealed to General Gerow and received the attachment of Lieutenant Colonel John M. Hightower's 1st Battalion, 23d Infantry Regiment, one of the battalions of the 2d Division that was not yet committed to the Wahlerscheid battle. Fortunately Lauer had earlier possessed the foresight to prepare a blocking position at Hünningen; Hightower's 1st Battalion, 23d, occupied that position during the course of December 16. At the same time Lauer moved the 394th Regimental CP.

Farther north in the 99th Division center the 393d Infantry Regiment received the brunt of the German 277th VG attack aimed to seize the twin towns of Rocherath-Krinkelt. In heavy fighting of company-sized units, this regiment finally was able to restore its positions in the areas of the 1st and 3d battalions, and by the end of the day the American front was only slightly to the west of the original position. The 2d Battalion, 393d, on the north had received very little attack. However, in the afternoon, General Lauer, having secured the 3d Battalion of the 2d Division's 23d Infantry also, placed that battalion in the line along with the 1st and 3d of the 393d. Here they were at the end of the day.

In the north of the division sector the 326th VG, under the 67th Korps, was attempting to make a penetration to secure the right flank of the Sixth Panzer Army. The fighting was severe, hampered to a large extent by abominable visibility. The 3d Battalion, 395th, with the 38th Reconnaissance Squadron attached, had remarkable success in holding. As the Germans came through the woods at point-blank range, they were mowed down by riflemen and tank destroyer gunners in such close quarters that sometimes the bodies of the Germans toppled into the very foxholes from which the fire came. At the end of the action, reports of German dead in front of Höfen varied from 25 to 200, whereas the 3d Battalion, 395th, had lost only 4 killed, 7 wounded, and 4 missing.

In retrospect the day's battle on the front of the 99th U.S. Infantry Division was a phenomenon. The Sixth Panzer Army was attacking in full force in three places on the division front: the south flank of the 394th (12th VGD); the center toward Rocherath-Krinkelt (277th VGD); and the north flank of the 395th Infantry at Monschau-Höfen (326th VGD). And yet, at the same time, the 2d U.S. Infantry Division was still attacking through the 395th, supported by two battalions of that regiment. American commanders considered the attack to Wahlerscheid going well; the first objectives had been taken.

The size of the German attack had become evident, but its significance had not been recognized. As December 16, 1944, came to a close, the 2d Division was still planning to attack eastward through the 99th Division the next day.

The 14th Cavalry Group Collapses in the Losheim Gap

As events turned out, General Lauer's concern for his south flank was more than justified. In this area Colonel Devine's 14th Cavalry Group, consisting of only two squadrons, the 18th and 32d, was screening an area 9,000 yards wide, nearly the frontage prescribed by the "book" for a full infantry division (see map, p. 196). The 99th Division was on the north; the 106th Division, to which Devine was attached, was on the south.

In order to keep some element of mobility, Devine had placed one of his two squadrons, the 18th, in strongpoints along the line from Lanzerath to Kobscheid. The 32d Armored Cavalry Squadron was located in reserve twenty miles back at Vielsalm. Devine was reinforced by Company A from the 820th Tank Destroyer Battalion, but his B Troop had been taken away from him to perform a similar mission of screening south of the Schnee Eifel between the 423d Infantry and 424th, both also of the 106th Division.

Devine split the 18th Squadron into small pieces holding various strongpoints. To Company A of the 820th TD's he gave the towns of Lanzerath, Merlscheid, and Berterath. To C Troop he gave the center, with detachments at Krewinkel and the nearby town of Afst. On the south he placed the bulk of A Troop in the town of Roth, with a detachment at Kobscheid to tie in with the 422d Infantry Regiment of the 106th Division. His own command post, plus that of the 18th Squadron, was located in Manderfeld, a town on a ridge about the center of the sector.

All this constituted a peculiar deployment for a normally "mobile" unit, but Devine had little choice. Three main avenues probed into his position, all branching off the main north-south route on the German border from Prüm to Losheim. These avenues were the road from Losheim to Berterath, the road to Krewinkel, and the road to Roth. Each of these main approaches was covered by a different troop.

What Devine did not know was that the Losheim Gap, which he was screening, was the main breakthrough area in the German plans. In the north the attached tank destroyer company and two platoons of his Troop C would have to contend with the entire German 3d Parachute Division. His Troop A lay across the German boundary in Manteuffel's area. Here this one troop would be standing in the way of two regiments, the 294th and 295th of

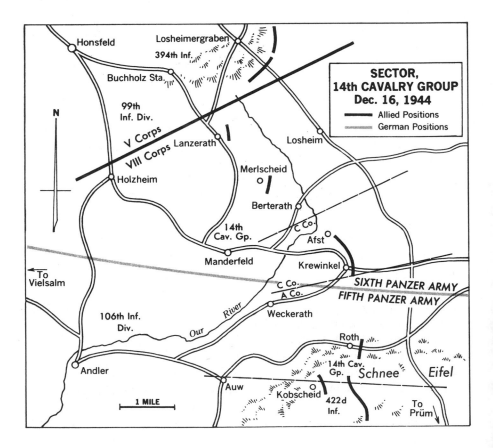

Manteuffel's 18th VGD, with which Manteuffel planned to encircle the north of the Schnee Eifel. Here lay the all-important road running southwest from Roth to Auw.[2]

As in the 99th sector to the north, the first indication of attack came around 5:30 A.M., when a robot bomb flew in low, seemingly just clearing the Schnee Eifel ridge, bobbled directly over Manderfeld, and continued to the northwest. The duty observer at the Manderfeld command post, Captain Robert Gies, did not consider this of particular importance, for the sector had been nicknamed Buzz Bomb Alley, because of the continuous traffic of V-1 bombs over the area for the past two or three weeks. However, before the bomb had passed directly over Manderfeld, the eastern horizon exploded in violent flickerings of light that heralded momentarily large concentrations of artillery. Border and rocket fire were reported by frontline strongpoints, and at least two enemy bombers droned over the area, dumping medium and light fragmentation bombs. Apparently German artillery did not know the exact position of the squadron's garrisons, for the fire did not fall exclusively on positions occupied by Devine's troopers. The first fire fell on the forward positions, and then the artillery was "walked" up to Manderfeld, where it was thickened for the second time.

Lieutenant Farrens' 2d Platoon of C Troop, 18th Squadron, garrisoned in the important town of Krewinkel, quickly lost communication with outpost positions as a result of the barrage. But the established procedure in such instances was to man all battle stations, and the garrison went on total alert. It was fully half an hour after the barrage lessened before the cavalrymen saw the first enemy troops. Germans came from the northeast, east, and southeast, the principal thrust coming along the road from the Schnee Eifel in the east.

The troopers were amazed to see a German column boldly marching along the road, four or five files abreast, talking, whistling, and singing. Farrens was luckier in his ambush than Bouck, up north. He waited until the unwary men of the German 3d Parachute were about 20 yards from the garrison's outer strands of barbed wire and then gave the signal to fire.

The sudden, devastating fire from the cavalrymen's automatic weapons

---

[2] "The boundary between the Fifth and Sixth Panzer Armies bisected the 14th Cavalry Group area by an extension south of Krewinkel and Manderfeld. North of the line elements of the 3d Parachute Division, reinforced by tanks, faced two platoons of Troop C, 18th Cavalry Squadron, two reconnaissance platoons and one gun company of the 820th Tank Destroyer Battalion, plus the squadron and group headquarters at Manderfeld. South of the boundary the 294th and 295th Regiments of the 18th Volks Grenadier Division, forty assault guns, and a reinforced tank destroyer battalion faced Troop A and one platoon of Troop C, 18th Cavalry Squadron. On no other part of the American front would the enemy so outnumber the defenders at the start of the Ardennes counteroffensive." Hugh Cole, *The Ardennes* (Washington: Dept. of the Army, 1965), p. 145.

struck the marching Germans full force, dispersing them at once. One squad broke off from the column and tried to breach the barbed wire, where they were cut up by the booby traps that had been planted there. Thereupon, in a rigid battle drill, a three-man mortar team, covered by two flanking riflemen, split off from the right of the column and began to set up. This attack carried 50 to 75 of the enemy into the interior of the village defense system, and by six fifteen the Germans were screaming, "Surrender, Americans! You are surrounded!"

Each outburst brought concentrated machine gun fire in reply. In the northern sector three light machine guns had an ideal position from which to fire on a snowy ridge that the Germans had to cross, where they were silhouetted near the top. When daylight came, the machine gun sergeant, Donald Forney, commented on the vivid pattern made by the blood streaks of the slaughtered Germans as their bodies slid down the snowy incline. Just before dawn the enemy withdrew from the town. Among the last to leave was a bold one who yelled at Farrens' command post, "Take a ten-minute break, soldier. We'll be back."

"And we'll be waiting for you—you son of a bitch," Farrens screamed back.[3]

Remarkably, 2d Platoon troopers sustained only one casualty in this first enemy attack: a sergeant, assistant to a forward observer in the 275th Field Artillery, had been shot in the jaw.

Shortly after 7:00 A.M. a second artillery concentration came down on the garrison. This time the bombardment was augmented by direct fire from enemy self-propelled guns that had approached the town from the southeast. One of the flat trajectory shells blasted into the second story of a house that held the observation post for the 275th's forward observer. The observer was wounded in the right leg and foot.

Fifteen or twenty minutes after the second barrage, the Germans attacked the town again, and now Farrens realized he needed extra ammunition. The Germans were jamming transmissions on radio circuits, and so the Krewinkel garrison could not call the troop command post at Weckerath. However, the transmissions were routed through the garrison at Afst, and the network functioned despite the jamming. Ammunition was delivered by 8:00 A.M.

At about this time, more German troops began approaching from the east. The troopers could see through their field glasses that the Germans were dressed in snow camouflage suits. Apparently they were bicycle troops; they were carrying their bicycles under their arms, with rifles slung at right shoulder. Now the self-propelled vehicles were firing with greater accuracy into the command post and the artillery observation post.

[3] Combat interviews, World War II Archives, Alexandria, Virginia.

Miraculously, none of the cavalrymen (except for the artillery forward observer party) had yet been wounded. The garrison settled down. They were well supplied with ammunition. Around the northern and eastern approaches of the town were scattered 150 to 200 enemy bodies; none of the members of the garrison could venture an estimate of how many men had been killed at their positions.

But in other sectors the fight was going less favorably. At Roth, Captain Stanley E. Porché of A Troop reported that he was being attacked by one tank and 75 to 80 infantry troops. In accordance with Manteuffel's tactics, Porché's position had been infiltrated and surrounded early in the morning. At 8:00 A.M. three tanks came out of the woods southeast of Manderfeld and started on the road toward Auw, completely bypassing the 18th Squadron's strongpoints. At 8:30 A.M. the last message came from Porché: "Tiger tank seventy-five yards from CP, belting us with direct fire. Out." Troop A, soon to be overwhelmed, would not be heard from again.

Strangely, German formations bypassing A Troop in Roth saw no American troops at all. The visibility was so bad they thought the American lines had been pulled back to the Manderfeld ridge.

By 11:00 A.M. Colonel Devine realized that those of his garrisons not already overwhelmed soon would be. Earlier he had secured permission to move his other squadron, the 32d, from its assembly position near Vielsalm up to the Manderfeld ridge, the location of his present headquarters and of the pre-planned "second delaying position." Devine sent the order to the frontline strongpoints to evacuate.

All garrisons withdrew with difficulty except for the particularly fortunate ones at Krewinkel and Afst. However, these garrisons withdrew just in the nick of time—before a major attack. By 1:00 P.M. various intermingled cavalry units had reached the Manderfeld ridge.

Meanwhile, Devine was in contact with headquarters of 106th Division at St.-Vith, asking for a counterattack north of the Schnee Eifel area to restore his position. Major General Alan W. Jones, commanding the 106th, was powerless to do so for lack of sufficient reserves. At this time Jones apparently considered the situation less serious than Devine did.

Early in the afternoon it became apparent to Devine that the Germans were pushing west around both his flanks. The Our River valley ran to the rear of his position on the Manderfeld ridge. This valley was wide open to encirclement, and contact with 99th Division had been lost. By now the German attack had bypassed Manderfeld, and its troops were moving toward a bridge over the Our River at Andler.

Devine obtained permission shortly after 4:00 P.M. to withdraw to the line Andler-Holzheim, a series of ridges with some protection on the east afforded by the Our. Manderfeld was evacuated.

The last elements to leave Manderfeld were the headquarters of the 32d Cavalry Squadron. At the last minute seven men were destroying records in the house that had been occupied by the 32d Squadron's command post. Among them, Captain Reed (the S-2) and the commanding officer of the 32d Squadron, Major Kracke, were in different parts of the house busy pouring gasoline from five-gallon cans when a dull, thudding explosion sent Kracke hurtling out of the cellar door—he escaped with a singe, minor cuts, and abrasions; Reed dove out of the second-story window unhurt. Both men estimated the time of their blazing departure at about 3:30 P.M.; they said the landscape was "crawling with Germans" working in toward the town.

By early evening, the 14th Cavalry Group was forming a defensive position along the Andler-Holzheim line; it was going to have to regroup so as to re-establish the identity of the two squadrons. The 275th Armored Field Artillery Battalion, in direct support, was in the process of moving to new positions near St.-Vith. There was no sign of enemy pursuit.

Two American Regiments Are Surrounded on the Schnee Eifel

With the collapse in the Losheim Gap, the northeastern flank of the 422d Infantry (the left regiment of the Schnee Eifel position) was wide open. Late in the day, as Devine's cavalry group was moving into Andler-Holzheim positions, General Jones reassessed the situation. His reserve consisted of the 2d Battalion, 423d Infantry. Having decided to commit that unit, Jones sent the 2d Battalion through St.-Vith to Schönberg (see map, p. 201). He intended to close the gap between the 422d and the cavalry at Andler and cover the open northern flank of the 422d. But in the "fog of war," Jones' intentions seem to have been misconstrued by the battalion commander, Lieutenant Colonel Joseph F. Puett. The result was more confusion.

Second Lieutenant Oliver B. Patton, a recent graduate of West Point (1944) had come overseas with the 106th Division, having been graduated from the Infantry School at Fort Benning a few weeks before. Although the 106th Infantry Division had been on the line since December 12, "Ollie" Patton had not been in action, as he was assigned to Puett's 2d Battalion, 423d Infantry, in division reserve near Born, north of St.-Vith. Patton was the platoon leader of the 2d Platoon of Company F, commanded by Captain Frank Kullig.

Early in the afternoon of December 16 the 2d Battalion, on orders from division, quickly mounted trucks and bounced and jostled its way to an assembly area east of St.-Vith. At about 3:00 P.M. they mounted up again and moved to the vicinity of Schönberg, where the main roads from north and south converge behind the Schnee Eifel. Although little had been said, the speed with which the 2d Battalion had been moved forward gave Patton the feeling that something unusual was happening.

Immediately on arrival at Schönberg, Patton was told to report to Colonel Puett. Puett gave Patton a fairly simple order. Patton was given a location on the map and told to go out and find the 590th Field Artillery Battalion and then find the 589th, which was somewhere beyond the 590th to the southeast. Puett interpreted his job as finding and protecting the exposed field artillery battalions. The 590th, he said, was probably not more than three miles away.

Ollie Patton selected a driver and jeep and took three men with him. He started down the main road, which ran southeast toward Bleialf, where unbeknown to him part of the German 18th VG Division had already overrun American positions that morning. However, about a mile north of Bleialf the main road made an extremely sharp bend to the east, and Patton discovered a second corduroy (log) road running eastward to the point where the 590th was supposed to be. This road he took.

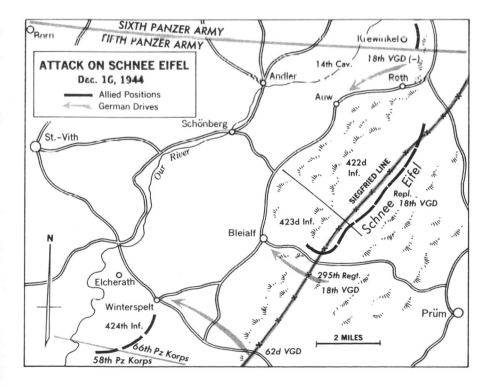

All around him Patton could hear scattered small-arms fire. Though Puett had been calm, Patton was beginning to suspect that this was not a routine road march. Then he heard above the noise of his jeep motor the cacophonic racket of a tank unit up ahead, accompanied by guttural shouts.

Patton wasted no time. The jeep was driven into a ditch, Patton spread his men out, and they lay there as a sizable German unit passed.

"If that's a patrol," Patton muttered, "It's the biggest damn patrol I ever heard of in my life."

The German unit having passed, Patton and his men pulled the jeep out of the ditch and, though they had to push it to get the motor running again, eventually were able to move on down the road toward the coordinates where the 590th Field Artillery Battalion was supposedly located.

By this time Patton had surmised that the outposts of the 590th might be just a little jumpy. He made no mistake. He approached the outpost cautiously and whispered the password: "Armored." He was relieved to get the correct answer: "Knight."

Safely within the perimeter of the 590th Field Artillery Battalion, Patton paused only a moment before proceeding to the 589th, the other "lost" battalion. On his arrival, Patton was taken immediately to the commanding officer, who was delighted to see him. "I sure am glad the infantry has finally reached us."

"I'm sorry to say, Colonel, the infantry hasn't reached you. What you have here is a patrol of one jeep. I've only come to find your location. I'm to go back and tell Colonel Puett where you are."

Patton called back. "Bring a guide so we can can find them later," Puett said. Patton picked up a warrant officer from headquarters, took him along in his jeep, and without further incident returned to Schönberg and the 2d Battalion, 423d Infantry.

That night Puett moved out the 2d Battalion and soon successfully had made contact with the 589th. This mission accomplished, temporarily at least, the 2d Battalion prepared to move north along the road toward Auw the next morning. But the gap at Losheim continued to grow during the night.

Meanwhile, during the afternoon of December 16, the commanding officer of the 422d Infantry Regiment, Colonel George L. Descheneaux, Jr., sent a task force to try to recapture Auw and cut off the Germans attacking to the south. The task force started out in a snowstorm and made contact with the Germans near Auw, at which point it received orders to return to protect the regimental command post, now threatened by Nazi infantry advancing along the draw from the east.

The German attack in the Losheim Gap was going according to plan. The 294th Regiment, spearheading the division's main effort in the north, had advanced as far as Auw the first day, about two and a half miles behind the line of contact, achieving a definite breakthrough. North of the 18th VGD, the 3d Parachute Division continued its advance during the night, marching northwest of Manderfeld and consolidating Lanzerath.

Meanwhile the German attack around the south corner of the Schnee Eifel had gone a little less well, and was to go worse at Bleialf. At 6:00 A.M. on December 16, Colonel Charles C. Cavender, the regimental commander of the 423d U.S. Infantry Regiment, received word that his antitank company was under small-arms fire at Bleialf. Here, almost two miles behind the lines, some thrown-together elements of the 423d were holding their own as best they could in poor defensive positions. He had asked for the return of Puett's 2d Battalion but had been refused. Service Company, Cannon Company, and later Company B, 81st Engineer Combat Battalion, were thrown into the fight at Bleialf. By 3:00 P.M., these units had ejected the Germans from the town. Cavalry Troop B, 18th Cavalry Squadron, on the south of the 423d, was separated from the regiment and finally got permission to pull back in the early afternoon. At the end of the day Bleialf remained in American hands.

Across the line, Generalmajor Frederich Kittel, commanding general of the 62d Volksgrenadier Division, which had followed and then branched off to the south of the 18th VGD spearheads, got word at midday on December 16 that his regiments had reached a spot overlooking the vital road to Winterspelt. He ordered into the attack along this road his reserve of one battalion mounted on bicycles and supported by self-propelled assault guns. This battalion struck the American Cannon Company of the 424th Regiment, who fought a delaying action all the way to Winterspelt. By midnight a company of Germans were inside the village. By the end of the day the 62d VGD had taken some heavy casualties, but all the American reserves in the area had been committed. The American artillery was low on ammunition, and the Germans had made a dent toward Winterspelt. Kittel had made progress.

Thus the 106th Division, like the 99th on the north, gave very little ground in the areas occupied by its combat troops on December 16. But penetrations had been made as far as Auw in the north, and as far as Bleialf in the south; the Germans were still moving. Very little American resistance lay in the path of the three regiments of the 18th Volksgrenadier Division.

The picture was beginning to clarify for General Jones and his staff back in St.-Vith. That evening, intelligence section of the 106th Division staff wrote: "The enemy is capable of pinching off the Schnee Eifel area . . . at any time."

The Keystone Division Is Decimated

Despite the dramatic circumstances surrounding General Hasso von Manteuffel's double envelopment of the 422d and 423d U.S. regiments on the Schnee Eifel, the main effort of the Fifth Panzer Army was directed against the highly extended 28th U.S. Division to the south of the 106th. This division, the "Keystone," originally from Pennsylvania, had marched down the Champs Elysées; it had been battered in the Hürtgen Forest in the middle of November; now it had been sent to this quiet sector to refit. It was up to strength, the new replacements were being assimilated, and morale was good. In common with the other divisions in the VIII Corps sector, however, its frontage was excessive.

Major General Norman D. ("Dutch") Cota had deployed his 112th Infantry Regiment in German territory, in a position east of the Our River, its left joining with the 424th Infantry of the 106th Division. These two regiments held a bridgehead over the Our, which was sustained by two main bridges in the vicinity of the town of Ouren (see map, p. 206). Understandably, these bridges were much coveted by the commander of the German 58th Panzer Corps, General Krüger. South of Ouren the 112th Infantry line ran west of the Our River to a point where it joined the 110th Infantry Regiment, commanded by Colonel Hurley Fuller. This regiment, which was holding a line along the Skyline Drive, was recognized as "overextended" even in a corps where this condition had come to be considered commonplace.

To the south of the 110th, occupying a somewhat narrower sector in good defensive terrain, was the 109th Infantry Regiment, which recently had been taken over by Lieutenant Colonel James E. Rudder, a hero of D-Day, whose rangers had scaled 100-foot cliffs on June 6 to seize Pointe-du-Hoc, a critical spot between Utah and Omaha beaches.

Against this long front manned by the 28th Division, Manteuffel planned to employ two entire panzer corps. On the north Krüger's 58th Korps was to employ the 116th Panzer Division to try to take those two bridges at Ouren held by the U.S. 112th and 424th Infantry regiments. Part of the 560th VGD, the other division in Krüger's corps, was to cross the Our in the same general vicinity. These plans faced the Americans with stern odds indeed.

But it was to the south, in the sector of the 110th Infantry Regiment, that the main weight was to be thrown. Against this one American regiment, spread out for ten miles along the Skyline Drive—and with one of its battalions held some ten miles to the rear as division reserve—Manteuffel would hurl Lüttwitz's entire 47th Panzer Corps, with the 2d Panzer and the 26th VG in the assault. The Panzer Lehr Division would follow in the footsteps of the 26th VG. For good measure, part of the 560th VG Division of Krüger's corps in the north would cross in the sector of Hurley Fuller's 110th Infantry.

It is ironic that it should have been Fuller's regiment that was selected to face such impossible odds. Fuller was an old soldier who had seen combat in the Argonne Forest in World War I. As his classmates at Fort Benning had noted, he still harbored bitter memories of that bloody engagement as late as the mid-1920's. Since then, Hurley Fuller had been known for two things: his fighting qualities and his cantankerous disposition. Commanding a regiment of the 2d Infantry Division during the Normandy campaign, Fuller's irascibility had come to overshadow his virtues in the minds of his superiors. He had been relieved. Fuller had then gone to his old friend, Major General Troy Middleton at VIII Corps, near Cherbourg, to state his plight. Middleton, also a veteran of World War I, had retained confidence in Fuller and asked General Bradley to give Fuller another chance for action. Only recently Fuller had joined the 110th Infantry, holding the thinnest sector of the VIII Corps line.

When the 28th Division had moved to the Ardennes, Fuller had established his command post in the town of Clerf, which besides being an ideal location for a command post also happened to be the location of the main crossings over the critical Clerf River. He had done all a commander could under these circumstances: he had stationed strongpoints in company strength along the Skyline Drive at critical road junctions and had placed thin outposts farther east along the line of contact with the Germans.

Thus it was that the towns of Heinerscheid and Marnach (in 1st Battalion area) were held by A and B companies respectively. To the south (in the 3d Battalion area) Hosingen was held by Company K, and Weiler was held by Company L. Each battalion held its third rifle company in reserve. Between these towns there was little by way of friendly forces. A man in a jeep could travel along the Skyline Drive for nearly four miles between strongpoints without encountering any of Fuller's troops (Cy Peterman had found this out). And yet the Luxembourg mountains, forested as they were, made it necessary for the Germans to reduce these strongpoints before large forces, particularly panzer, could be supported in an all-out offensive.

Colonel Fuller's 2d Battalion was held by General Cota as division reserve at Donnange, about eight miles behind Marnach. As usual, a small reserve was all that Dutch Cota could afford to hold out.

For the 110th Infantry, the battle began much as it did for other units along the Ardennes front. K Company, in its strongpoint at Hosingen, habitually kept an observation post (OP) on the town water tower. Usually this OP saw little of a disturbing nature, but at 5:30 A.M. it reported back: the entire German line was a series of "pinpoints of light." The message delivered, the first shells began landing. Wire communication was immediately severed. The artillery preparation lasted forty-five minutes, but intermittent fire was received for the rest of the day. Several houses in Hosingen were set on fire; as K Company put it, the town was "pretty well lit up."

But it was soon discovered that elements of the German 26th VG Division had infiltrated across the Our River even before the preparation had begun and were already very near the American positions. Manteuffel's reconnaissance had served his troops well.

Almost immediately Fuller, back in Clerf, found himself out of contact with his two frontline battalions, but word soon got through to him about what had happened. He was skeptical at first, but by 9:00 A.M. he had become convinced that the men coming through the lines between the American positions were Germans, not Americans.

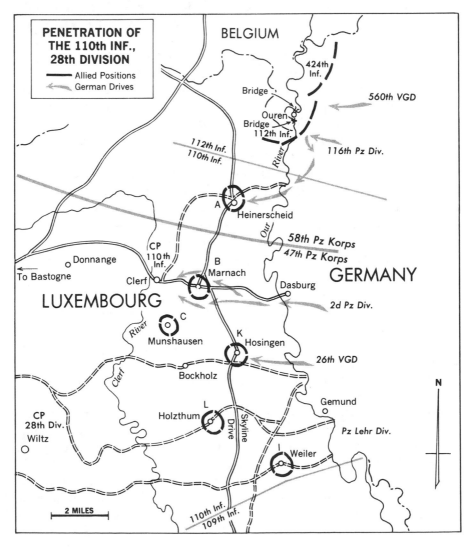

As a result of the German infiltration, the American companies were all isolated almost instantly. In the 3d Battalion on the south, Company L in Holzthum was unable to move to the aid of either I or K; in the 1st Battalion, Company C was likewise immobilized in Munshausen. Indeed, these supposed "reserve" companies were hit almost simultaneously with the "frontline" companies on the Skyline Drive, so that Fuller's two frontline battalions had all their companies committed.

During the morning Fuller sent Lieutenant Colonel Daniel Strickler, executive officer, to the 3d Battalion to see what was taking place. Strickler tried to go to 1st Battalion later but was unable to get through. However, the defending companies seemed to be keeping the Germans occupied and from all reports seemed to be doing fairly well.

Nevertheless, as the morning progressed, the 26th VGD attack in the Hosingen area simply bypassed the town. Soon lead troops had penetrated two or three miles and reached U.S. artillery positions near Bockholz. Despite the efforts of the 110th Infantry—and of the division commander—the day saw American units forced farther and farther back into the little towns they had been occupying.

The story in the 1st Battalion zone was the same as that in the 3d. By 8:00 A.M., the 2d Panzer Division had reached the strongpoint of Marnach, a crossroads needed by Colonel Lauchert of the 2d Panzer. By midmorning Lauchert had become involved in a battle to knock out Marnach, but he was sending other elements past the village on the road toward Clerf—all that stood in Lauchert's path to Bastogne.

At dusk the Americans in the zone of the 110th Infantry Regiment were still holding their original positions but, like other VIII Corps units, had been infiltrated and bypassed. The 2d Panzer Division failed to reach Clerf on December 16, and even Marnach remained in American hands. The Germans had suffered severely. The regimental commander of the German 304th Regiment was a casualty, and one battalion had been badly scattered during piecemeal counterattacks by American tank platoons.

During the day Cota, at 28th Division headquarters in Wiltz, realizing the seriousness of the situation, ordered his commanders to hold their positions at all costs. At 10:00 A.M. he ordered Companies A and B of the 707th Tank Battalion to reinforce the 110th Infantry, hoping to sweep the Skyline Drive clear. He met with some local successes only, but refused to release the last of his division reserve, Fuller's 2d Battalion.

At nightfall the garrison at Weiler (Company I) broke into two groups and made its way westward. Company B sent the last report from Marnach: German half-tracks were moving in. By midnight the German 3d Panzer Regiment had consolidated the village.

The 2d Panzer Division had been identified on the Clerf-Bastogne road in the zone of the 110th. Shortly before dark Lüttwitz completed sixty-ton bridges across the Our River at Gemund and Dasburg. These were a prime necessity for the chunky monacled commander of 47th Panzer Korps, for unlike Krüger to the north, who had two ready-made, permanent bridges waiting for him at Ouren, Lüttwitz had to construct his own after seizing adequate space on the American side of the river.

Once these were in place, he would be able to cross his vaunted panther and tiger tanks and pour through the gap now widening in the zone of the U.S. 110th Infantry.

To the south of the 110th Infantry, the 109th had its share of hard fighting during the day, but because of the strong terrain and the relatively narrow front it was able to hold its own. Colonel Rudder later described the action in matter-of-fact terms:

> When the first report came in of the attack all units were alerted and Division was notified of the fact. All the battalions reported company strength attacks of infantry but not tanks. Everyone was holding and I saw no cause for alarm. We were in a good position and had a distinct advantage of terrain. As the attack progressed it became apparent that it was in great strength. We did not even consider giving up any ground, and the division order was to hold as long as the position was tenable.

Actually the situation was more difficult than Rudder's taciturn report would indicate. By the time the day was over the reserve battalion had been committed and the regiment was holding off three German infantry battalions that had crossed the Our River in the regimental sector. While the 3d Battalion, 109th, held its original positions, Company E was out of contact with the rest of 2d Battalion. The unit was well aware of the penetration that had been effected in the 110th Infantry zone.

On the extreme north of the 28th Division, the 112th Infantry, which was also defending a relatively narrow sector, had likewise been able to hold, even though its positions were heavily infiltrated and its reserves were all committed by the end of the day of December 16. The bridges in the vicinity of Ouren, however, remained in American hands throughout the day. The 112th's greatest concern was that it was being separated from the rest of the division by penetrations in the 110th Infantry to the south.

Reviewing the day's action, Colonel Nelson had reason to be proud of his regiment's work. He estimated that it had cost the German 116th Panzer Division more than 400 men killed and at least 89 prisoners. Like many others on that first day, Nelson remarked on the German tendency to move against prepared positions in almost close-order column formation. Many Germans paid with their lives to machine gun fire from the dug-in positions of the 112th Infantry.

On his side of the river, Lüttwitz was not pleased with the progress made by his attack divisions. However, he had his two heavy tank bridges, and the Americans appeared to be weakening. The 2d Panzer was moving, and Lütt- witz believed that the Clerf River could be crossed by the evening of De- cember 17.

The Southern Shoulder Holds—Precariously

Erich Brandenberger, commanding general of the German Seventh Army, had a limited mission. To protect the south flank of the Fifth Panzer Army at- tack, he was to cross the Our River and push forward on Manteuffel's south— if possible in the direction of Luxembourg at the same time (see map below).

But his means were limited. Along his attack front, which faced the U.S. 109th Infantry Regiment (28th Division), the 60th Armored Infantry Battal- ion (9th Armored Division) near Beaufort, and the 12th Infantry Regiment (4th Division), Brandenberger had a total of four volksgrenadier divisions organized into two corps, the 85th and 80th. Manteuffel's efforts to secure Brandenberger a panzer division had been to no avail.

The critical fighting in this area revolved around Brandenberger's efforts to crack the southern shoulder of the penetration, held by the 12th U.S. Infantry

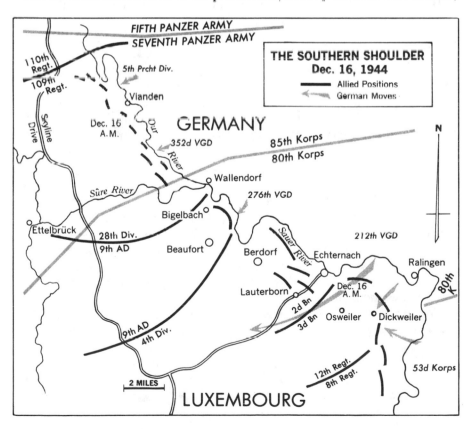

Regiment of the 4th Division. Like the 28th Division, the 4th Infantry Division had been placed in this quiet zone for refitting. It had suffered more than 5,000 battle casualties in the Hürtgen Forest plus nearly 2,500 nonbattle casualties as the result of exposure. Like its sisters to the north, the 4th Division was rehabilitating, resting, and giving its tired infantry a chance to live in houses for a while after the icy Hürtgen foxholes.

In common with the other units, the 12th Infantry Regiment, with 3,000 troops, was destined on December 16 to fight against overwhelming odds: 14,000 men of the German 212th Volksgrenadier Division. The Americans had tank support, however; Brandenberger had none.

As elsewhere, the attack began at 5:30 A.M. Still, it was shortly after noon before the 12th Infantry Regiment realized that the attack was something more than a raid. The Germans were having difficulty in crossing the Sauer, because the river increases in size below the confluence of the Our with the Sûre. It was almost 10:00 A.M. before the German 320th Infantry Regiment advanced on the outposts of the 3d Battalion, 12th Infantry, where the Sûre, having joined the Our, makes a right angle south at Ralingen, about five miles east of Echternach.

Detachments had been sent across the Sûre earlier, however, and a German patrol had reached the rear of Osweiler and Dickweiler, two towns behind the U.S. front, by the time the 320th launched its attack. While an American company commander of this 3d Battalion was reporting the assault to his battalion commander, he was startled by an interruption; a voice with a heavy German accent announced on his line: "We are here."

Strangely enough, the Germans continued to listen in on the American telephone line; they never cut it. The 3d Battalion treated the line like a radio. Encoded messages continued to flow, even though the Americans knew the Germans were listening.

Typical of the confusion was the situation at the 2d Battalion on the left. Lieutenant McConnell, of Company F, reported a possible enemy patrol moving on Berdorf. This news reached the 2d Battalion headquarters about 9:00 A.M. and was reported to headquarters, 12th Infantry Regiment, at 9:45, reaching 4th Division command post at ten twenty. Nobody was particularly concerned until Lieutenant Feinsilver tried to drive through Berdorf. Feinsilver hurried back to battalion headquarters with his driver wounded in five places. The 2d Battalion concluded that F Company had been besieged by an entire German battalion.

From then on, swift action was taken. The 2d Battalion executive officer was sent to investigate the situation and to open communications with Companies E and G. It was 2:00 P.M. before he was able to get a message back from Company G. By 11:00 A.M. the division commander, Major General Raymond O. Barton, knew that both the 2d and 3d battalions of the 12th Infantry were under strong attack. He released his reserve (consisting of 1st

Battalion, 12th Infantry) to Colonel Robert H. Chance, commanding the 12th Infantry, and instructed the 70th Tank Battalion, which was with the 4th Infantry Division, to attach one of its companies to the 12th Infantry. During the day Chance attacked one place after another in the areas of the 2d and 3d battalions. Dusk saw the 12th Infantry still holding five main centers of resistance: Dickweiler, Osweiler, Echternach, Lauterborn, and Berdorf. All five were besieged by superior numbers.

There were no attacks on the other regiments of the 4th Division, but General Barton realized that the Germans had launched a major effort. Next morning he reinforced the 12th Infantry with the reserve battalion of the 22d Infantry Regiment, moving it by truck from the opposite flank of the division. Borrowing a company of tanks from the 9th Armored Division, he succeeded in establishing a relatively strong infantry-tank reserve.

Wedged between the 28th U.S. Infantry Division on the northwest and the 4th U.S. Infantry Division on the southeast was a new battalion from the 9th U.S. Armored Division (Major General John W. Leonard), the 60th Armored Infantry Battalion. Unlike the two weary units on its flanks, it had been placed in a strong, narrow sector just south of the confluence of the Our and Sûre rivers. Its commander, Lieutenant Colonel Kenneth W. Collins, had been concerned that the sector was too quiet, that the battalion would not obtain sufficient experience here to be of much value when they later joined the other elements of the scattered 9th Armored to fight as a unit.

Collins was in an enviable position compared to that of his colleagues on his flanks. His infantry battalion was being supported by a whole field artillery battalion, the 3d Armored. More units, including the 19th Tank Battalion, were available from Combat Command A (CCA), located to his rear. Collins was to need all the help he could get.

When the attack began in the early hours of the morning, Collins' battalion was hit by nearly a whole volksgrenadier division, the 276th. With two companies on the line, Collins' men were able to exact a fearsome toll.

But penetrations were made, and during the day German infiltrators came up the ravines to occupy the hamlet of Bigelbach, behind Collins' front; so Collins, now reinforced by some tanks from CCA, committed his reserve Company B, which he brought up from Beaufort. By the end of December 16, the 60th Armored Infantry Battalion had restored the front along the Sûre River with three companies abreast. From the next day on, Collins' battalion was to fight as a component of Colonel Thomas L. Harrold's Combat Command A.

The salient feature of the fighting on December 16, 1944, is the fact that the American units generally held their ground, though sizable penetrations were made between their positions.

Most of the American units thought they were sustaining intensive local attacks. Unable to see what else was happening across the U.S. V and VIII corps fronts, few of the frontline troops suspected that a major offensive was being staged.

Actually, the German gains, viewed on a small-scale map, were relatively unimpressive. They consisted, on the whole, of penetrations of two or three miles. By and large they were comparable to the gains made by the 4th, 9th, and 30th U.S. Infantry divisions on the first day of Operation Cobra, five months earlier.

But German bridges were being built over the rivers; tanks were being brought across; and preparations were being made for the greatest blows yet to come.

The Allied High Command Reacts

Field Marshal Sir Bernard Law Montgomery was feeling in need of relaxation. After months of directing the operations of 21 Army Group without letup, he had hopes of spending Christmas back in England. His chief of staff, Major General "Freddie" de Guingand, was already there.

This period, when the Allies were in the process of preparing for the next offensive, would be a relatively quiet one. Montgomery's intelligence officer was estimating the German situation in these terms:

> The enemy is at present fighting a defensive campaign on all fronts; his situation is such that he cannot stage major offensive operations. Furthermore, at all costs he has to prevent the war from entering on a mobile phase; he has not the transport or the petrol that would be necessary for mobile operations, nor could his tanks compete with ours in the mobile battle.[4]

A prospect appeared that Montgomery could not pass up. The headquarters of the Royal Air Force Group supporting British Second Army just happened to be located in the clubhouse of a golf course at Eindhoven. The great professional, Dai Rees, was presently on duty there, and December 16 seemed a perfect day for a few holes of golf with Rees.

Some time after they had teed off, a plane landed and a message was delivered to Montgomery. "A hell of a row," it seemed, was going on in the area of Bradley's 12 Army Group to the south. On receipt of the news, the disappointed Field Marshal "chucked" the game and proceeded to return to his headquarters at Zondhoven.

Shortly thereafter, Montgomery called together his eight trusted liaison offi-

---

[4] Intelligence Estimate, 21 Army Group, 16 December 1944, quoted in Omar Bradley, *A Soldier's Story* (New York: Holt, 1951), p. 460.

cers—his personal eyes and ears—and gave them their instructions: they were to proceed to Spa next morning, report in to General Hodges' First Army Headquarters and then, presumably with Hodges' blessing, fan out to predesignated command posts to find out what was going on; they were to report personally to Montgomery exactly what the situation was. His own front had not been hit, so this was all he could do on December 16, 1944.

Otto Skorzeny, at the head of his 150th Panzer Brigade, was poised behind the lead elements of the 1st SS Panzer Regiment waiting for an opportunity to pass through the lines and attack. Skorzeny himself, having been admonished once more by Hitler that he must never be taken prisoner, had arranged with the staff of the Sixth Panzer Army to join the battle station of the 1st SS Panzer Korps at Schmittheim.

Immediately after the attack had jumped off, Skorzeny began to receive reports which as early as 7:00 A.M. he felt were not too favorable. Apparently Dietrich's artillery bombardment had not wrought sufficient damage on American positions at Losheimergraben, and the Americans were defending themselves stoutly; the attack was progressing slowly. By noon the news was of violent fighting without much gain of ground. "The intended collapse of the whole front," he wrote later, "had not been achieved."

Skorzeny drove to Losheim to get a clearer picture of the situation. He found the roads crammed with vehicles of every kind; officers were trying to keep the traffic flowing by getting out of their cars and walking beside them. He himself walked six miles.

Skorzeny could see the handwriting on the wall. The success of the plan rested on a clean breakthrough on the sixteenth. The logical action now was to cancel Operation Greif. But Skorzeny had put too much of himself into this effort to call it off quite so lightly. Young Colonel Jochen Peiper, commanding the 1st SS Panzer Regiment, was to be committed at midnight. There was still a chance. Skorzeny stole a few hours' sleep in hopes that December 17 would bring his operation into full play.

For the Supreme Allied Commander, every detail of the day of December 16, 1944, was indelibly stamped in the memory. On the light side, General Eisenhower received a letter from Field Marshal Montgomery requesting permission to return to the United Kingdom to spend Christmas with his son. Montgomery also laid claim to have won a bet made fourteen months previously in which Eisenhower predicted the end of the war in Europe by Christmas of 1944. Eisenhower wrote that he envied Montgomery's opportunity to visit his family in England, but as to the wager, there were still nine days to Christmas.

Eisenhower had just received notification of his promotion to the rank of

General of the Army, the five-star rank equivalent to Field Marshal in foreign armies.[5]

There were other items of a personal nature. The wedding of Eisenhower's orderly, Mickey McKeough, to Pearlie Hargrave, a WAC at SHAEF, took place in a beautiful chapel at Versailles in a frigid temperature. Later in the day, the Government of Free Poland presented decorations to both the Supreme Commander and his chief of staff, Lieutenant General Walter Bedell Smith.

Aside from these activities, General Eisenhower had something to look forward to that afternoon. Brad was coming back from 12 Army Group Headquarters in Luxembourg to talk to him and his staff about the problem of infantry replacements. This procedure was not a normal one; Eisenhower always preferred to go forward to visit his commanders in their own areas. But in this case General Bradley was sending his personnel officer, Brigadier General Joseph J. ("Red") O'Hare, back to Washington to argue the case against diverting too many trained replacements to the Pacific. In order to impress on all the seriousness of the situation, Bradley was making a special trip to Paris. After the conferences were over, the two men could settle down to a pleasant dinner, and Bradley would return to Luxembourg the next morning.

Recently Eisenhower had been traveling a great deal to visit frontline troops. He enjoyed it. In his own headquarters in Paris he led a lonely life. Comfortably situated in a villa formerly occupied by Field Marshal Gerd von Rundstedt, he ate at home, served with simple but good food by competent messboys. On occasion he would have a couple of people in for dinner; normally an aide lived with him in the house. But to have a visitor come and spend the night was something of a special occasion.

And Eisenhower had prepared a special treat: Steve Early, President Roosevelt's genial press secretary, had thoughtfully taken advantage of a plane flying from Washington to Paris to send the Supreme Commander a bushel of oysters. Eisenhower adored oysters and, assuming that Bradley did also, had made up detailed plans for his friend's enjoyment. The repast was to begin with oysters on the half shell, to be followed by oyster stew, and to be concluded with fried oysters, a treat to satisfy anyone denied this delicacy for more than two years.

General Bradley had to drive the whole way from Luxembourg because of the bad weather. At dusk, when the two commanders and some of their staff officers were seriously discussing the problems at hand, a colonel from the G-2 section tiptoed into the briefing room and handed a message to General Strong, SHAEF intelligence chief. Strong interrupted the proceedings to refer

[5] Others promoted at the same time were General George Marshall, General Douglas MacArthur, Fleet Admiral William Leahy, Admiral Ernest King, Admiral Chester Nimitz, Admiral William Halsey, and General Henry Arnold.

to a map, and then solemnly announced that the Germans had secured penetrations along five points on the U.S. VIII Corps front. The attack had begun early in the morning, and the size and extent were as yet undetermined, but most threatening was the curving finger penetrating between Gerow's V and Middleton's VIII corps in the Losheim Gap, north of the Schnee Eifel.

As the briefing progressed, General Eisenhower reviewed in his mind the extensive conversations he had held in the previous days and weeks with Bradley. With eight German divisions already identified and spread out over such a wide front, he suspected strongly that something large was afoot. Further, as he and Bradley had agreed, there were no immediate objectives in the Ardennes area—indeed anywhere in Belgium or Luxembourg east of the Meuse—to merit the launching of such an effort. "That's no spoiling attack," Eisenhower declared.

General Bradley was apparently less convinced. What did Ike have in mind? Eisenhower sent for another operations map that showed two U.S. armored divisions out of the line, the 7th in the Ninth Army sector in the north, and the 10th in the Third Army sector to the south. "I think you had better send Middleton some help," he answered. "These two armored divisions."

Bradley agreed that such a precaution would be wise but reminded his chief that the 10th Armored would have to be taken from an irate George Patton, whose heart was set on his offensive to be launched in the Saar in three days.

"Tell him," Eisenhower snarled, "that Ike is running this damn war."

Soon Bradley had Patton on the line and was telling him the news: The 10th Armored Division was to head immediately north for Luxembourg and report to Troy Middleton at Bastogne. Patton was not convinced. This German attack, he howled, was being conducted only to weaken his own attack in the Saar.

The situation required all of Bradley's tact and determination. Eventually, after hearing out Patton's arguments, he laid down the law: The 10th Armored Division was ordered to move to the north.

Then Bradley instructed his staff in the city of Luxembourg to send orders to the Ninth Army for the 7th Armored Division to head immediately south from Holland. Unlike with the headstrong commander of the U.S. Third Army, it was unnecessary to make personal explanations to the steady General Simpson.

As Bradley hung up the receiver, Bedell Smith recalled the times that Bradley had wished the Nazis would come out of the defenses and fight in the open. Smith laid his hand on Bradley's shoulder. "Well, Brad, you've been wishing for a counterattack. Now it looks like you've got it."

"A counterattack, yes, but I'll be damned if I wanted one this big."

These moves were all the redeployment ordered for the moment. To be sure, there were two more divisions readily available, the 101st and the 82d

Airborne, both recuperating and reequipping in training camps near Reims, France. There were others available in varying degrees: the 17th Airborne, the 11th Armored, and the 87th Infantry, all in England. But movement of these divisions could wait for further evaluation.

The German attacks cast a new light on the entire situation facing the senior commanders of the European theater. As Eisenhower and Bradley debated the ramifications at dinner, bare notice was given to the fact that Bradley was allergic to oysters and had to be provided with scrambled eggs instead.

CHAPTER 11

❧ ❧

Breakthrough

SHORTLY before midnight, December 16, 1944, Obersturmbannführer Jochen Peiper strode into a café in the Belgian town of Lanzerath. Here, he was told, he could discuss with the colonel commanding the 9th Parachute Regiment (3d Parachute Division) plans for passing his panzer kampfgruppe through the parachutists in order to break out through American lines and begin the real drive to the Meuse.

The café was a dismal place. A bar stood against one wall; a cuckoo clock sounded the hour from another. Sprawled on the floor were a number of soldiers, German and American. In one corner an American lieutenant, wounded in the leg, was holding a young soldier who had lost a part of his face. The soldier's blood was flowing freely, despite the bandage, drenching the lieutenant's field jacket. Many other men seemed merely asleep.

Peiper noticed none of these details; he simply gained the impression that the whole front "had gone to bed instead of waging war."[1] Acutely conscious that he was to lead the 1st SS Panzer Division in the main effort of Dietrich's Sixth Panzer Army, Peiper's mind was focused completely on Huy—on the Meuse. As far as he was concerned, Lanzerath did not exist.

Finding his map awkward to handle, he finally solved the problem: he held the sheet up against the wall, stabbed the corners with bayonets, and, thus prepared for business, turned his wrath on the commander of the 9th Parachute Regiment.

Peiper was an ideal man to lead the advance elements of the SS formations. Tough, arrogant, and hard-core Nazi, he was another who possessed what Hitler admired as "fanaticism." But he was also a competent soldier. A few nights earlier he had personally driven a tank over a fifty-mile trial run during hours of darkness to test the possibilities of a one-day drive to the Meuse at night.

He was famous for his ruthlessness. Formerly an adjutant to Heinrich

---

[1] Letter, Jochen Peiper to Lyle Bouck, December 9, 1966.

217

Himmler, he had performed notable feats of daring with his tanks in Russia —where he allegedly burned two villages and killed all the inhabitants.[2] Some of the SS troops he was to lead in the Ardennes campaign had served for a long time on the eastern front, where brutality of all sorts was commonplace. Others were boys, but fanatic believers in the Führer. Softheartedness would have no place in this offensive, a most difficult assignment for which Jochen Peiper was a natural selection.

But the failure of the 3d Parachute Division to open the way for his tanks had already, in Peiper's estimation, thrown off the Nazi timetable. If the infantry had punched their hole through American lines at 7:00 A.M., according to expectation, he might at this moment have been astride the Meuse River. But the infantry had failed; and here he was, still at Lanzerath.

Circumstances had conspired to give Peiper a frustrating day. It had been difficult enough to get his kampfgruppe into position to attack. In the original plans, his route from Losheim was through Losheimergraben and Hünningen, but these two towns were still in the hands of the Amis. Worse, a bridge over a railroad on the route to Losheim, blown in the German retreat some weeks earlier, had not been repaired, and so he had not even reached Losheim until 7:30 P.M. At Losheim he had received a radio message from his division commander, SS-Oberführer Wilhelm Mohnke, informing him that a second railroad bridge, northwest of Losheim, was also blown and the engineers would be unable to repair it in time; so he had to change course and go to Lanzerath in the 3d Parachute Division sector, which lost him at least five tanks to American mines.

Even movement on the roads had been difficult. The 12th VG's horse-drawn artillery was clogging the roads. It was doing no firing anyway, and Peiper had ordered his vehicles to push through rapidly, ruthlessly cutting down anything that got in their way.

Now, with a regiment of the 3d Parachute Division temporarily attached to him, Peiper was considering the tactics for making the breakthrough himself. Certainly Buchholz Station and Honsfeld would have to be taken. Afterward, the route assigned to him ran west from Honsfeld to Schoppen, generally north of the Amblève River, through Ligneuville, then south of the Amblève to Stavelot, where he should have a choice of routes for crossing the Salm River at Trois Ponts. From Trois Ponts on he would have easier going and be able to make a dash to Huy on the Meuse by way of Werbomont (see map, p. 236, and back endpaper).

This route possessed only one advantage: it crossed few bridges. In other respects, the roads assigned to the division to the north, the 12th SS Panzer Division, and the 2d Panzer Division in Manteuffel's army farther south, were

---

[2] Hugh Cole, *The Ardennes* (Washington: Dept. of the Army, 1965), p. 263.

far superior. His own road, he complained, was "not for tanks but for bicycles." The protests he had made earlier had fallen on deaf ears; the higher command would not even discuss the matter. The Führer himself had ordered that Peiper should take this specific route, designated Route D, that had been assigned to him.

Peiper had two somewhat conflicting requirements to fill in his planning. At a briefing two days earlier, the corps commander, Hermann Priess, and the division commander, Mohnke, had both admonished him not to concern himself with his flanks. His task was to drive rapidly to the Meuse River, making full use of the element of surprise, avoiding all temptation to stop along the way to mop up local resistance. There was nothing difficult about this requirement in itself. But he had also learned at the same time that two trainloads of gasoline, urgently needed for the offensive, had not arrived. This meant that somewhere he would have to deviate from his westward drive to capture American gasoline. He believed some might be found north of his route at Büllingen, Stavelot, and possibly Spa. This made these three locations, north of his axis of advance, of critical importance to him.

The 9th Parachute Regiment attached to Peiper was commanded by a full colonel, a grade above him, and giving the parachute commander instructions would have worried an officer who had greater respect for military rank. But Jochen Peiper was an officer in the Waffen-SS and, like Otto Skorzeny, a favorite of Hitler's, and so automatically he held an advantage over any run-of-the-mill colonel. Furthermore, the colonel of the 9th Parachute Regiment was a man of no combat experience, just skimmed out from the Ministry of the Luftwaffe.

The quality of the 9th Parachute Regiment soon became apparent. Requesting all the information available on the enemy situation, Peiper was told that the woods above Lanzerath were heavily fortified, full of fiercely fighting Americans. Scattered fire from prepared pillboxes, plus mines in the road, were holding up the regiment's advance; it was impossible to attack under the circumstances.

"Have you personally reconnoitered the American positions in the woods?" Peiper asked.

"No. I got my information from one of my battalion commanders."

Peiper immediately got in touch with the battalion commander, who admitted he had gotten the information of the heavy fortifications from one of his captains. A call to the captain revealed that the captain had not personally seen the American forces; they had been reported to him.

In utter disgust, Peiper ordered the parachute regiment to give him one battalion; he would lead the breakthrough with his own kampfgruppe. At 1:00 A.M. on December 17, he began to organize his attack formations. Two panther tanks would lead the column, followed by a series of armored half-tracks, and then a mixture of panthers and Mark IV's. The battalion of paratroopers would ride the tanks. One parachute company would provide flank security. Further delay was caused by the difficulties encountered by the paratroop officers in finding their men, who were comfortably ensconced in houses.

Launching the attack at 4:00 A.M., Peiper discovered that no American troops were in position short of Buchholz Station. The two American platoons still left at that location gave his panzers little resistance. Only a radio operator remained; taking refuge in a basement, he kept American forces informed of the size of Peiper's column. By 5:00 A.M. he had notified General Lauer at 99th U.S. Division that 30 German tanks, 28 half-tracks, and long columns of foot troops had passed through Buchholz.

Heading westward toward Honsfeld, Peiper found the roads filled with American traffic traveling in the same direction. This made it simple. The Nazi vehicles simply fell into column and entered Honsfeld with the American traffic. Most of the Americans there were caught asleep. Two antitank guns were in position but not manned. When the garrison discovered the situation they scattered like a disturbed ant heap. Route D, the axis of advance of the 1st SS Panzer Division, was now open to the west. The booty Peiper picked up at Honsfeld included 50 reconnaissance vehicles, half-tracks, and trucks, and 15 or 16 antitank guns.[3]

Having taken Honsfeld, he turned to the commander of the battalion from the 9th Parachute: "Stay here and mop up," he commanded. "Await further orders from your regimental commander." Peiper was now traveling alone.

Peiper had to decide on his next move. His orders dictated that he travel directly west along a bad secondary road toward Schoppen; but he had not forgotten the gasoline in Büllingen to the north, and a reconnaissance party sent toward Schoppen showed the road to be in deplorable condition.

Banking on the assumption that the 12th SS Panzer Division was a considerable distance behind him, he took his life in his hands and disobeyed Hitler's command. He went north along the road to Büllingen outside his allotted territory. Encountering almost no resistance, he overran a small American garrison, destroyed 12 American liaison planes on the ground, and appropriated about 50,000 gallons of gasoline, ordering 50 American prisoners to work at filling the tanks. He was fortunate, for the mountainous terrain around the Schnee Eifel had made him use up as much gasoline in fifteen miles as normally would have taken him thirty.

At about nine thirty, shortly after capturing Büllingen, the kampfgruppe was hit by some American artillery, which caused some casualties. Undaunted, Peiper continued to the southwest to pick up his assigned road before the 12th SS Panzer Division could catch up with him. He sent a small reconnaissance party toward Hünningen. Americans from the 99th and 2d divisions, their rear areas exposed, were spared, for Peiper's orders were to push on to

[3] MS Ethint # 10, Jochen Peiper interview, p. 15.

the west. He had turned the flank of the critical shoulder of the penetration, but his eyes were fixed on his objective: the Meuse.

In the early morning of December 17, American plans on the northern shoulder of the penetration underwent a radical change. Major General Leonard T. Gerow, commanding V Corps at Eupen, sensed the significance of the previous day's attack before Courtney Hodges, his chief. Gerow had been urging that the 2d Division's projected attack toward Wahlerscheid scheduled for that day be canceled; First Army had stalled on this decision. But at 7:30 A.M. Hodges gave Gerow permission to defend his corps front as he saw fit. Gerow canceled the attack immediately.

It was plain to Gerow, a careful, meticulous infantryman (who had studied with Eisenhower their whole year at Command and General Staff School, Fort Leavenworth), that the situation of the 99th and 2d divisions was an embroiled mess. Moreover, the front lines of the corps stuck too far out in the thick woods, making them nearly impossible to supply under the circumstances. As General Robert E. Lee, in whose tradition Gerow had been reared, had selected a defense line on Marye's Heights at Fredericksburg, so Leonard Gerow selected a position called Elsenborn Ridge about six miles behind his present line of contact. He would fall back and defend on that line.

But to extricate this force would be a difficult task requiring direction by one man on the spot. For this responsibility he chose Major General Walter M. Robertson, commanding the 2d Division; units of the 99th would be temporarily under his command. The choice was logical, even inevitable. Robertson not only was one of the most experienced and respected division commanders in the Army (having been committed in Normandy only a couple of days after D-Day), but also he possessed the only uncommitted reserve, the 23d Infantry Regiment (although two battalions of that regiment had been farmed out to strengthen General Lauer's 99th Division the day before). Robertson would get the two divisions back to the Elsenborn Ridge if anyone could.

Gerow had one more ace up his sleeve. On the night of the sixteenth General Hodges had released to him the vaunted 1st U.S. Infantry Division. This veteran of North Africa, Sicily, Omaha Beach, Coutances, Mons, Aachen, and the Hürtgen Forest was on the way from Verviers to Camp Elsenborn. One regiment was to report to General Lauer without delay. The mission: to block the main road leading west from Büllingen, the road known as Route C in Hitler's plans.

General Robertson found himself faced with what was probably the most complex maneuver encountered by any division commander in World War II. In twenty miles of terrain Robertson had under his temporary command 18 intermingled infantry battalions. Some were under heavy attack; others were extended far to the north. His road net was strained by the presence of tanks, tank destroyers, artillery, and logistical units. Frontline units for the most part poked out into thick woods where fighting was difficult on both sides.

Robertson's two divisions were being hit by the might of the 12th SS Panzer Division and the 12th and 227th VG divisions. Furthermore, he could look over his right shoulder and see that his main road to the rear was cut by Peiper's troops.

This was a situation that would have unnerved a lesser commander. Quiet, soft-spoken, and methodical, Robertson had commanded his 2d Infantry Division without flourish but with unusual competence from the day of its landing in Normandy. He made a quick and decisive estimate.

The withdrawal of troops under heavy enemy pressure is a hazardous operation under ideal conditions. It becomes nearly impossible when the troops being withdrawn are new to combat, as those of the 99th Division were. This, plus the extension of two thirds of his own 2d Division to the north toward Wahlerscheid (see map below), made it logical that he should execute his withdrawal in two phases. First he would employ the extended regiments of the 99th Division (the 395th on the north, the 393d in the center, and the 394th on the south) to protect the withdrawal of his two attacking regiments, the 9th and the 38th infantries. These two regiments would then protect the vital towns

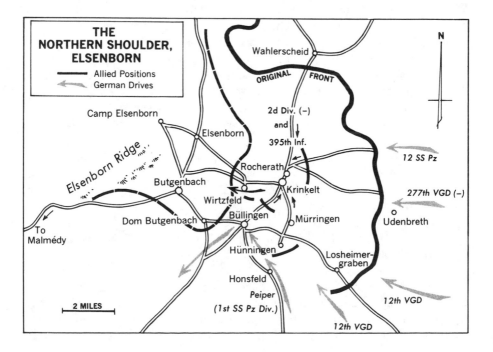

of Krinkelt and Rocherath, known as the "twin towns," being so close together as to be in reality one. Their importance lay in the fact that with the route to Büllingen cut, they formed the eastern terminus of the only secondary road running back to Wirtzfeld and Elsenborn Ridge, where V Corps would make its stand. From these twin towns roads spoked out toward Wahlerscheid (north), Udenbreth (east), Hünningen (south), and of course Büllingen (southwest). If these two towns could be held, the disparate battalions of the two divisions could be funneled through them and make their way to their final positions. Thus, with the 9th and the 38th infantries of the 2d Division holding the twin towns, the less experienced 99th Division units and the 23d Regiment of the 2d Division could pass through to the rear.

Robertson's principal problem lay on the south. Here the 394th Infantry, which had fought so well throughout December 16, had been practically decimated by the blows of the elite 12th VG; the 394th had assembled at Mürringen. The 23d Infantry had temporarily ceased to exist as a unified tactical unit, for its three battalions had been parceled out on the sixteenth to bolster the regiments of the 99th Division. Therefore, Robertson's principal working tools for the moment were the 9th and 38th regiments to the north.

The withdrawal of these two regiments from the north was executed with remarkable success. The 395th Regiment, in position in the woods, protected the single road along which they fell back. The first unit to arrive at the twin towns was the 2d Battalion of the 9th Infantry. It was followed by the rest of the regiment and the 395th. The 395th Infantry covered the withdrawal.

All of this was executed in the shadow of bitter fighting to the east of Rocherath-Krinkelt. One battalion after another, regardless of its parent unit, was shoveled into place to stop the attacks of the 12th SS Panzer Division and the 227th VG. Fortunately for the Americans, the 12th SS Panzer on the north was bogged down in mud. Nevertheless, the American lines gradually gave way. In one case a battalion of the 38th Infantry, placed in blocking position east of the twin towns, was practically annihilated. As a precautionary measure Robertson put a battalion from the 38th to protect Wirtzfeld from Peiper's troops in Büllingen.

During the night of December 17–18, 1944, the now shattered 394th Infantry made its way northward through the twin towns and westward toward Wirtzfeld. Ironically, one battalion, hearing the savage fighting at the twin towns, abandoned its vehicles and slogged on foot across country to Wirtzfeld. A following battalion found the vehicles and proceeded to drive through Krinkelt, Rocherath, and westward unmolested. Hightower's battalion of the 23d Infantry covered the withdrawal. During the night Krinkelt and Rocherath remained in American hands.

The next morning, December 18, General Robertson turned over defense of Rocherath-Krinkelt to Colonel Francis H. Boos, commanding officer of the 38th Infantry Regiment. Boos was far from alone in his task, however; he had substantial elements of the 99th Division, and of the 9th and 23d regiments attached to him. He had, furthermore, two battalions of tank destroyers, one battalion of tanks, and the artilleries from both divisions. The fighting remained severe; advance elements of German tanks and infantry actually penetrated the twin towns during the day. Nevertheless, he succeeded in holding the towns and in evacuating all elements of the 99th Division. These units fell back to Elsenborn Ridge, where they were turned over to their own commanding general, Walter Lauer. Here they would organize the defense of the new position.

By the morning of the nineteenth, Robertson and Boos were faced with the problem of withdrawing the 2d Division to Elsenborn. As in so many other places on the front, they were aided by a German High Command decision. Sepp Dietrich, disgusted with the lack of progress of the 12th SS Panzer Division, decided to withdraw it and move it around to the south. The Nazi corps commander, Hermann Priess, demurred, but Dietrich insisted, so the U.S. 2d Division was now faced on the east with only the 277th, an untried VG division. During the day the 2d Division made a successful withdrawal to the Elsenborn Ridge.

During the next few days Nazi elements were to continue to make desperate attacks, but with the arrival of the 1st and 9th U.S. Infantry divisons—two of the most experienced divisions in the Army—the northern shoulder was safe. To avoid disaster it had been necessary for two divisions to make enormous sacrifices. The 99th Division alone lost 2,200 men.

But the action of the 2d and 99th divisions on the northern shoulder could well be considered the most decisive of the Ardennes campaign.

Baron Friedrich von der Heydte and his airborne kampfgruppe were proceeding on their mission at 3:00 A.M. on December 17. After the cancellation of their drop the day before, the troops had gone back to rest, but during the day word had come through that Sepp Dietrich's main attack had not gone off well—the 99th Division had not broken and fled as it should have—so Kampfgruppe von der Heydte was to be dropped on the morning of December 17 south of Eupen, the same spot as originally ordered.

Von der Heydte was in bad shape for a drop. He was jumping with injuries sustained earlier: a shattered left forearm and a damaged right arm. In addition he had been practically without sleep since he had first received his orders nine days before.

Thus far he had accomplished all that was expected of him. At the moment, however, he was concerned about the wind velocity on the ground, for if it was higher than twenty feet per second, the reported present velocity, he would not make a jump at night in the forests. The wind report, he suspected, was erroneous. In fact, the velocity was more than fifty feet per second.

The operation ran into difficulty from the beginning. Many of the untrained and inexperienced jumpmasters, not realizing the amount of headwind that the great Junker aircraft were bucking, gave the jump order according to clock time. About 200 men jumped into the Bonn area on the Rhine River rather than into the Hohe Venn Mountains. The following waves also had great difficulty locating the landing place. When the planes got to the main American defensive area, antiaircraft guns opened up with heavy fire. Several planes were shot down, and the formation was dispersed.

Von der Heydte jumped at precisely the right place. However, only 10 other planes out of a total 105 dropped their men in the same area. On reaching the assembly point he found that the formation had been scattered. Only 6 men had been gathered by 3:50 A.M.: by 4:50 A.M. he had only 26. Baron von der Heydte realized that the drop had failed.

With the American northern shoulder holding but bypassed, Gerow's V Corps and Hodges' First Army directed their efforts to building the lines to the west, even while the withdrawal to the Elsenborn Ridge was simultaneously in its most desperate stages. The 1st SS Panzer's drive through Büllingen and southwest, for example, had threatened the command post of the 99th Division at Butgenbach early on December 17. The only sensible reaction was to close down the V Corps truckhead, which was also in that town, and evacuate rations and gasoline to the west.

The 99th Division command post was preparing to pull out that morning as well. Division Commander Lauer, together with most of the high-ranking officers, had already moved back to Elsenborn. The division intelligence officer, Lieutenant Colonel Howard B. St. Clair, and the operations officer, Lieutenant Colonel Dan C. Norman, still remained. Both had final communications duties, and as a parting shot Norman was desperately trying to bring down air strikes on the passing German vehicles he could sight.

As the last group was preparing to leave, a jeep pulled up outside the slate-roofed farmhouse. In strode a balding, wiry man with an impressive red handle-bar moustache. He was wearing the proud patch of the 1st U.S. Infantry Division, known through the Army as the Big Red One. On his shoulders were the blue spades of the 26th Infantry Regiment. Lieutenant Colonel Edwin Van V. Sutherland, executive and acting commanding officer of the 26th, had come to look over the situation. His troops were not far behind.

When advised of the situation, Sutherland seemed completely unperturbed. "Don't worry about a thing," he said. "The First Division is here now and everything is under control."

Then Sutherland went about the business of preparing to move his men to protect the main road toward Büllingen, for which he would have to shove forward to Dom Butgenbach.

Sutherland's men soon arrived, marching along both sides of the road —2d Battalion, commanded by Lieutenant Colonel Darrill Daniel, in the lead—and Sutherland directed them into place.

Despite his assurance, "Van" Sutherland and his men were tired. The 1st Division had been refitting after its experience in the Hürtgen Forest, but had been alerted to move on the night of the attack, December 16. He and his men had put in a difficult and sleepless twenty-four hours. During that wild night of travel from Eupen to Elsenborn, Sutherland had obtained some idea of the confusion on the 99th Division front—impressions strengthened by the flares from German aircraft and the sight of von der Heydte's men plunging from the doors of their planes toward scattered drop zones.

Holding a good piece of defensive ground, however, Sutherland was glad to be joined on December 17 by the other two battalion commanders of the 26th and by Lieutenant Colonel Hugh Brown of the 33d Field Artillery Battalion. While Brown placed the artillery, one gun at a time, Sutherland picked up stragglers who had decided they were "sticking," though their only weapons were makeshift. Heartened by the bravery of tired men who still wanted to stay and fight, Sutherland and the rest of the 26th Infantry Regiment settled down for their most difficult defensive battle since Normandy.

Major General John F. M. Whiteley, the British chief of the SHAEF Planning Staff, studied the operations map pensively. Like many others, he had now concluded that the German attack was a major offensive. The only thing that SHAEF could do at the moment, since the two armored divisions in 12 Army Group were already on the move, was to release the SHAEF reserve, the U.S. 82d and 101st Airborne divisions, to General Bradley.

Picking up the telephone, Whiteley called Major General Leven C. Allen, chief of staff of 12 Army Group at Luxembourg, and reminded him of the availability of the two divisions. He got a quick affirmative answer.

"I'll put it up to Ike, if you wish," Whiteley said. "But where do you want them sent?"

Allen thought the road center of Bastogne would be a logical place to send them.

Rarely had there been such unanimity of opinion. Whiteley had little difficulty with his bosses. Before the morning was out General Hodges was trying to reach General Bradley, who was still at Versailles, to ask to have the two divisions released to him. The 82d and 101st Airborne divisions at Reims were alerted to move. The details of their destination could be worked out by Generals Bradley and Hodges later.

In his command post on the first floor of a schoolhouse in St.-Vith, Major General Alan W. Jones, commanding the U.S. 106th Infantry Division, was aware by the morning of December 17 that his 422d and 423d regiments on the Schnee Eifel were about to be surrounded, at which time little would be left between the attacking German columns and his own command post. His third regiment, the 424th, was also on the line to the south. As if this were not enough for any division commander to bear, Alan Jones had a personal burden—his son was serving in the headquarters of one of the regiments about to be cut off.

However, things were not all black. Brigadier General William M. Hoge's Combat Command B of the 9th Armored Division had been attached to Jones the day before. Jones had sent Hoge to Winterspelt early that morning to make contact with the 424th. And the 7th Armored Division should arrive at any time. Then an attack to the east could relieve the two surrounded regiments. Jones continued to hope.

Far to the north Brigadier General Bruce C. Clarke, commanding general of Combat Command B, 7th Armored Division, was in a happy mood the evening of December 16. He had received his promotion only a few days earlier, and he had just returned from a dinner at the command post of the division commander, Brigadier General Robert W. Hasbrouck, during which General Hasbrouck had suggested that Clarke take several days of rest leave in Paris.

Clarke, a large bear of a man with a powerful frame, was ready for that rest. He had been in continuous combat since he had led Combat Command A of the 4th Armored Division through its fighting in the St.-Lô breakthrough in Normandy. A shift to the 7th Armored had afforded him no respite. In addition, he was suffering from a severe case of gallstones, and only the medication his doctor supplied enabled him to conceal his condition from his troops and keep fighting. A trip to Paris would not cure the gallstones, but it would give him a welcome change of scenery.

General Clarke changed into his most formal uniform available under these circumstances, an "Ike" jacket, and started for his old borrowed Mercedes-Benz. Just then the telephone rang. It was the division commander.

"Bruce," said Hasbrouck, "the 7th Armored has just been ordered to move to Bastogne. I have no idea why. Maybe we are going down to try to draw off some German troops from the Roer River area. At any rate, I want you to get your combat command going as soon as road clearance can be obtained. In the meantime I'd like you to go to Bastogne yourself. Find out what you can from General Middleton. Take a radio jeep so you can let me know what's happening."

"Well, there goes Paris," said Clarke. "I'll be on my way to Bastogne within the hour."

By 9:00 P.M. Clarke had secured his radio jeep, rounded up his driver, his aide, and his operations officer, Captain Owen Woodruff, and started off through the rain and the muck, destination Bastogne. The trip was a long one, made even longer by a buzz bomb that struck a block ahead of Clarke's party as they drove through Liège. Finally, at nearly 4:00 A.M., he arrived at VIII Corps command post. Immediately he proceeded to the G-3 operations room where he talked at some length with the chief of staff and the operations officer, informing them that the 7th Armored Division was already on the move.

The staff of the VIII Corps told him that the Germans had attacked, and attacked in force, but nobody was quite sure what it was all about. The 106th Division, they informed him, had been hit hard, as had the 28th on the south, but nobody knew at the moment whether this was a local attack or a major offensive.

General Middleton had been waiting up for Clarke to arrive, and his news was about the same as the staff's. Middleton seemed to think, however, that the major problem on the front was in the 106th Division area, where a breakthrough of some proportions had occurred in the Losheim Gap. "I intend to use you in that area, Clarke," he said, "but first go and get some sleep. Then you can go up and report to Jones and work out some way you can help him."

After informing Middleton that his own Combat Command B (CCB) was leading the march, Clarke took him at his word and stole a few hours of sleep. Immediately after breakfast he radioed the 7th Armored Division. He specified his column should leave the original route and turn east toward St.-Vith when it reached Vielsalm. Bastogne was out. During this conversation Clarke learned for the first time that his combat command had not left their assembly area near Heerlen, Holland, until nearly 5:00 A.M. Obtaining road clearance had held them up. CCB would not arrive until much later in the day.

There was no reason for Clarke himself to delay, however. Traveling by way of Houffalize, he arrived at General Jones' command post in St.-Vith at about 10:30 A.M. The news Jones gave him was far from encouraging. Two regiments had been surrounded on the Schnee Eifel, and Jones had completely lost contact with them. The 14th Cavalry, in very doubtful combat condition, was up to the north, but otherwise there were only scattered friendly units between where they were sitting and the surrounded units on the Schnee Eifel.

"Well, we've got to get word to your regiments," said Clarke. "If you can't get them by telephone, how about getting them on the radio?"

"They don't answer," said Jones.

"Well, I'll put my radio on. Maybe I can raise them."

"Well, as a matter of fact, in our training we haven't paid much attention to the use of radio."

Jones' statement was borne out. Clarke's own radio was unable to obtain a response from the Schnee Eifel. Wire communication invariably would be knocked out under heavy artillery shelling—as well as by German sabotage.

"There's a lot of advantage in not having to depend upon wire," Clarke reflected. Armor was fortunate to be able to transport heavy radio equipment as its primary means of communication.

But the worst shock was reserved for Alan Jones: "I want you, Clarke, to take your combat command and counterattack toward Schönberg about seven miles to the east of us, and break that ring that these people have closed around the Schnee Eifel."

"General, I have no idea when my troops will arrive. We didn't get road clearance to leave from Heerlen until five o'clock this morning. And I have no idea what the conditions will be between here and there."

The forces that General Jones had been counting on would not arrive for hours.

For the next four hours there was little the two generals could do. In General Clarke's own words, both were "fit to be tied." The morning wore into early afternoon. At about 1:30 P.M. the door burst open, and in rushed Colonel Mark Devine, commander of the ill-fated 14th Cavalry Group.

"General, we've got to run," Devine gasped. "I was practically chased into this building by a tiger tank, and we all have to get out of here."

"I suggest we send Colonel Devine back to Bastogne," said Clarke. "Maybe he could give General Middleton a first-hand account of the conditions up here."

Devine, in Clarke's opinion, had gone through too much; he was in no state to be particularly useful to his command at the moment. The colonel left and did not reappear at the command post at St.-Vith.

Throughout the waiting, General Jones' spirits seemed alternately to rise and fall.

"I've lost a division quicker than any other division commander in the U.S. Army," he said at one point. "I've two regiments out on the Schnee Eifel, and my son is in one of them. I don't know whether we'll get to him at all."

Clarke, who was still not certain of the magnitude of the German offensive, assured Jones that when his combat command arrived he would attempt a rescue if at all possible.

Shortly thereafter, on the wire with General Middleton, Alan Jones was reassuring: "Don't worry about us, General. We'll be in good shape. Clarke's troops will be here soon."

From his headquarters in Bastogne, Troy Middleton was somewhat surprised that Jones was not more anxious to pull his two regiments off the Schnee Eifel. However, he was a firm believer in the man on the spot being in the best position to judge, and actually he rather admired Jones' spirit in holding to his positions. Moreover, in World War I, he had seen the result of withdrawing green troops under fire: it is almost impossible to stop them from continuing to the rear. "Those regiments might just keep going all the way to Paris," he mused. Satisfied, Middleton hung up his phone.

Clarke, however, hearing only Jones' end of the conversation, was somewhat taken aback by Jones' show of optimism.

By 2:30 P.M. the suspense was interrupted by the sound of small-arms fire to the east. Jones and Clarke stumbled to the third floor of the schoolhouse. In the direction of Schönberg, a German patrol appeared to be coming out of the woods about two miles away.

"General Clarke," said Jones, "I've thrown in my last chips. I haven't got much, but your combat command is the one that will defend this position. You take over command of St.-Vith right now."

"All right, General," said Clarke. "I will. I'll take over—but with what?"

There was very little to fight with. The headquarters and service companies of two engineer battalions were the main forces available, those of the 81st Engineer Battalion, commanded by Lieutenant Colonel Thomas J. Riggs, and of the 168th Engineer Battalion, attached from corps and commanded by Lieutenant Colonel W. L. Nungesser. In addition, Jones had the "palace guard," a platoon assigned to protect the division command post. That was all. And these troops were already committed on the Schönberg road east of St.-Vith.

Lieutenant Colonel Tom Riggs, located about a mile east of St.-Vith in the tiny village of Prümerberg, was busy trying to organize some sort of defense against the German forces that had already occupied Schönberg. Riggs, a big man and former football star from the University of Illinois, had been given command of the heterogeneous defense forces of the 106th Division at 10:00 A.M., just before Clarke's arrival at St.-Vith. His mission was to proceed two miles along the road to Schönberg and set up a defense through which, it was supposed, CCB of the 7th Armored would later attack.

Hardly had Riggs' task force gotten out of town when they met scattered German resistance. Pushing on, Riggs found that Prümerberg was as far as he could go, but at least he had reached the crest of the hills and could set up something of a defense line cutting that all-important mountain road.

Riggs had available to him only a limited amount of antitank defense, consisting of a couple of 57-mm. antitank guns and some bazookas, most of which came from the 106th Division Headquarters defense platoon. These he placed in locations where they could be most effective, covering an open field to his left and a fifty-foot fire brake in the woods to the right. Fortunately a platoon of six tank destroyers from the 822d TD Battalion showed up.

At about 3:00 P.M. Riggs' position was hit. Four German tanks, supported by infantry estimated at a battalion, appeared about 1,000 yards to the front. One 57-mm. gun opened up; it was soon knocked out in an uneven fight. The tank destroyers had more luck. Without sights for the weapons, the gunners adjusted fire by observing over the gun barrels; nevertheless their fire was effective enough to force the German tanks to take cover.

To protect his north flank and consolidate the position, Riggs then instructed the tank destroyer platoon leader to move his guns to the woods just to their rear. The TD's turned north to take position but were never heard from again.

Fortunately for Tom Riggs' task force, the Germans did not push their attack. The tanks sprayed the American lines with fire but did not move forward. Miraculously, an observation post ahead of Riggs' position spotted the German location and the division air-ground liaison officer contacted a P-47 fighter, which was in the air despite the weather. After several passes, the P-47 knocked out one German tank.

The fight continued in small groups, but for the moment the Germans did not push a coordinated attack.

The defense of St.-Vith had begun.

Meanwhile, trying to move eastward from Vielsalm to St.-Vith, CCB, 7th Armored Division, was struggling through volumes of traffic heading west. On the narrow roads, which had barely two-lane capacity under good conditions, the 7th Armored was finding it impossible to make more than a couple of miles an hour.

At this time Major Donald P. Boyer, S-3 of the 38th Armored Infantry Battalion, was struggling to break a way for the 7th Armored's tanks to come through. His own account:

> My driver and I arrived at the road junction at Poteau about 1230, 17 December. We were about an hour ahead of the 38th Armored Infantry Battalion which was the lead unit in the Reserve Command's march column. As we arrived at the road junction, we were hit by a sight that we could not comprehend, at first; a constant stream of traffic hurtling to the rear (to the west) and nothing going to the front (to the east). We realized that this was not a convoy moving to the rear; it was a case of "every dog for himself"; it was a retreat, a rout.
>
> Here would come a 2½-ton, with only a driver, then another with several men in it (most of them bareheaded and in various stages of undress), next perhaps an engineer crane truck or an armored car, then several artillery prime movers—perhaps one of them towing a gun, command cars with officers in them, ¼-tons—anything which would run and which would get the driver and a few others away from the front. It wasn't orderly; it wasn't military; it wasn't a pretty sight—we were seeing American soldiers running away.
>
> About a mile farther up the road at the little town of Petit-Thier, all traffic had stopped. In fact it was the most perfect traffic jam I have ever seen. We had run into this hopeless mass of vehicles fleeing to the rear on a narrow road which would barely support two-way traffic at slow speeds. Vehicles streaming to the rear had attempted to pass each other in the intervals be-

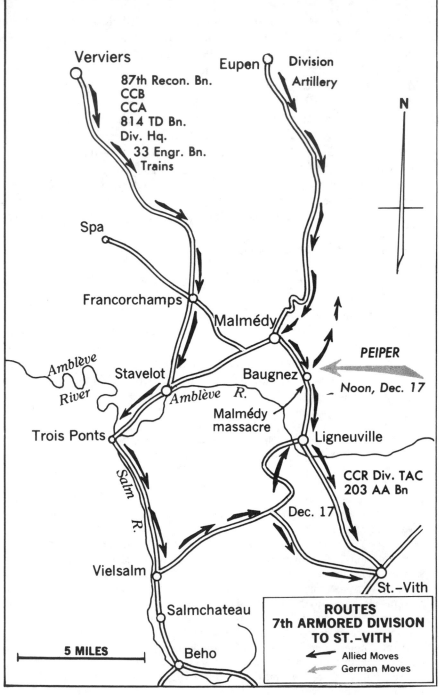

Verviers

87th Recon. Bn.
CCB
CCA
814 TD Bn.
Div. Hq.
33 Engr. Bn.
Trains

Eupen — Division Artillery

N

Spa

Francorchamps

Malmédy

Amblève River

Stavelot

Amblève R.

Baugnez

PEIPER

Noon, Dec. 17

Malmédy massacre

Trois Ponts

Ligneuville

Salm R.

CCR Div. TAC
203 AA Bn

Dec. 17

Vielsalm

St.–Vith

Salmchateau

5 MILES

Beho

**ROUTES
7th ARMORED DIVISION
TO ST.–VITH**

Allied Moves
German Moves

232

tween the tanks of the 31st Tank Battalion, which was leading CCB, and now no one could move. . . .

It was already 1515 and from the looks of the road jam, neither the tanks nor anything else was going to reach St.-Vith for a long time. Lieutenant Colonel Fuller, Corporal Cox, and I took over the job of clearing a path for the tanks, and we started getting vehicles to move over to the sides. Slowly a path was beginning to open and the tanks began to roll along at a snail's pace with halts every 50 to 100 feet. Several times we had to wave the lead tank forward at full speed when some vehicle refused to pull over. Usually the sight of 30-odd tons of steel roaring down on him was all we needed to get the driver to move over.

Several times senior officers in command cars attempted to pull out into a space which I was opening up, and each time I told them to get back, that I didn't care who they were, nothing was coming through except our tanks and anything else which was headed for the front, and to get out of the way. (One company commander, Captain Dudley J. Britton, Company B, 23d Armored Infantry Battalion, said, "That day I saw the highest ranking traffic cops I have ever seen.")

Now in command of the St.-Vith sector, General Bruce Clarke calculated that his Combat Command B should be arriving at any time. He sent his operations officer, Woodruff, to the crossroads just west of St.-Vith to guide them in and to keep the road clear of westbound traffic. He was to let Clarke know when somebody from CCB arrived. However, having little to do, Clarke soon went out to see how Woodruff was getting along. What he saw shocked him. Woodruff was standing dejectedly by the side of the crossroad, and a medium field artillery battalion, having abandoned its howitzers, was moving to the rear and monopolizing the road.

"What's happened here, Woody? How come you're letting these people use this road?"

"General, this lieutenant colonel told me he was going to use the road anyway and he'd shoot me if I got in his way."

Clarke felt his blood pressure rise. He soon had the lieutenant colonel before him: "You get your trucks off this road so my tanks can get up here. If there's any shooting done around this place, I'll start it."

The lieutenant colonel, faced with the choice of obeying orders, shooting a brigadier general, or having the honor of being shot by one, chose the first alternative, and the artillery trucks were run off the road.

General Clarke stayed by the crossroads for most of the afternoon.

At one point he was accosted by a diminutive lieutenant colonel, standing barely five feet one, named Maximillian Clay.

"General, my name is Clay and I came to report to you. I have a separate battalion of self-propelled 105's, the 275th, and I want to shoot."

"God bless you, Clay. You're the only artillery support we have. Head out and shoot in support of those engineers, on the ridge east of town."

For the next few days, until the 7th Armored Division artillery, now cut off by Peiper's men, could make their way to St.-Vith, the 275th Armored Field Artillery Battalion (formerly supporting the 14th Cavalry Group) was to be the only artillery support Clarke had. On occasion parts of the 275th actually held a sector on the line.

About 4:00 P.M. the great moment arrived. Caked with mud, the lead unit of Troop B of the 87th Cavalry Reconnaissance Squadron drove up to General Clarke's crossroads, the rest of CCB behind them. The captain in command dismounted and reported.

Clarke's orders were simple: "Keep going down this road. You'll run into a great big lieutenant colonel. His name is Riggs. Tell him that you're attached to him and he'll tell you what to do."

Late that afternoon General Clarke's superior, General Hasbrouck, reached Vielsalm. Like Clarke, he had preceded his troops and had come to St.-Vith by way of Bastogne. There he learned that Clarke had been sent to Jones at St.-Vith.

By the time General Hasbrouck had arrived at St.-Vith the first elements of CCB were on the spot and the hour was growing late. Calling a conference with Jones and Clarke, Hasbrouck reluctantly decided that a counterattack to relieve the 422d and 423d Infantry Regiments in the Schnee Eifel was out. The problem had resolved itself into holding St.-Vith itself with the forces available.

Hasbrouck could not help feeling sorry for Jones. General Jones had been led to expect the 7th Armored to arrive at seven o'clock that morning; he had been counting on this when he sent Hoge's CCB, 9th Armored, to Winterspelt rather than to Schönberg. Perhaps, Hasbrouck reflected, Jones would have employed Hoge's force differently had he known that Clarke's troops would be held up.

The decision to settle for holding the vital road junction at St.-Vith having been made, Hasbrouck again wended his difficult way through the double-banked traffic, largely the 14th Cavalry, from St.-Vith to Vielsalm, the new headquarters location of the 7th Armored Division. From here the overall divisional battle would be directed.

During the day and evening of December 17, CCB, 7th Armored, rolled into St.-Vith and began to build up a position in the form of a large horseshoe on the high ground to the east. By eight o'clock that evening Clarke had his forces disposed: two companies of the 87th Cavalry Reconnaissance Squadron were on the north; next were two companies of the 38th Armored Infantry Battalion in the center; south of them was Troop B of the 87th Cavalry Squadron (the first CCB unit to arrive) and the two engineer companies that had been the first in contact with the Germans; and finally, on the extreme south, Company B of the 23d Armored Infantry Battalion. Strangely, nothing was said to Riggs about the 7th Armored's having assumed responsibility for the sector. For the next two days he handled his command independently, on the assumption that he was working for General Jones of the 106th. He was too busy fighting to worry much about the chain of command anyway.

However, the show was now the 7th Armored's. Clarke spent the entire night placing his troops in position. The forward element on the high ground to the east was supported by a reserve consisting of parts of the 38th Armored Infantry Battalion and Company A of the 31st Tank Battalion. West of the town, Clarke now had a respectable combat command reserve, consisting of a tank battalion (the 31st), an armored infantry battalion (the 23d), and B Company of the 33d Engineers.

By four o'clock the next morning, Clarke was able to tell Jones that the defense of St.-Vith was in fairly decent shape. At one point, irritated by Jones' occasional tendency to give suggestions in the form of orders, Clarke offered to turn the command back over to either Jones or one of his brigadiers (all of whom were senior to himself). But Jones still insisted that this was completely a 7th Armored Division fight. A little later the command post of the 106th Division pulled back to Vielsalm, in the same town as that of the 7th Armored but still some distance away.

As time passed, Jones would be able to augment his truncated division with other units and hold a sector in the horseshoe-shaped front that was building up. But General Middleton declined to put one man in charge of the sector, without doubt influenced by the fact that Hasbrouck, who commanded the bulk of the troops, was junior by one grade to Jones. But Middleton's preference for cooperation rather than unity of command caused less confusion than might be imagined. In the critical eastern sector, for example, two brigadier generals—Clarke and Hoge—simply cooperated on an equal basis. Indeed, true unity of command was not to be achieved until five days after St.-Vith sector had been occupied. In the meantime, Hasbrouck plugged the gaps in the line with his own troops regardless of the location of units attached to the 106th.

One item was settled, however. Bruce C. Clarke was now in sole command of the St.-Vith sector of the 7th Armored Division's front.

By noontime on December 17 Jochen Peiper was back on his prescribed axis of advance heading westward well beyond Moderscheid. Things were going well; the breakthrough was complete. He was now approaching the crossroads of Baugnez, between Malmédy and Ligneuville. Had Peiper arrived some time earlier, he would have encountered Combat Command Reserve (CCR) of the 7th Armored Division moving southward from Malmédy to St.-Vith on a road roughly parallel to that being used by Clarke's CCB (see map, p. 232). Such an encounter would have altered the history of the battle. As it was, CCR had passed by, and in the gap between CCR and the

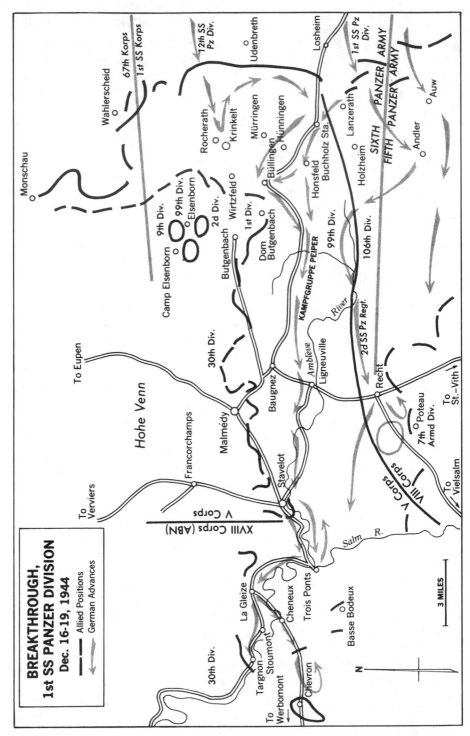

BREAKTHROUGH, 1st SS PANZER DIVISION

Dec. 16-19, 1944

Allied Positions
German Advances

3 MILES

N

next unit of the 7th Armored Division, Battery B, 285th Field Artillery Observation Battalion, had inserted itself on the road. As soon as Peiper's troops saw Battery B, they opened fire.

Complete confusion ensued within the American column. Vehicles were abandoned in panic and left on the road, some of them burning. Some of the men of the observation battalion threw their arms away while others sought cover in the ditches; a third group tried to reach the nearby forest. Peiper himself had little time to worry about the survivors. Those who had not escaped were rounded up and left under light guard while Peiper himself, with his advance formations, continued southwest toward Ligneuville.

Shortly thereafter, as a second panzer column approached, some of the 150 prisoners were headed into a meadow by SS troopers and mowed down by machine gun and pistol fire. A few escaped by feigning death. Those who were detected as still alive were shot through the head with pistols. Approximately 80 men survived out of the total 150 in the PW group. This was the infamous Malmédy Massacre.

The stories surrounding the circumstances of the Malmédy Massacre are varied. One version is that the prisoners were left unguarded and were beginning to scatter when they were mowed down by fire. One of the survivors later testified, "The firing started the moment when I had almost reached the edge of the forest." But this is not the only crime that has been laid at the feet of Peiper and his battle group. The official U.S. Army history estimates that by December 20 Peiper's command had murdered approximately 300 American prisoners of war and at least 100 unarmed Belgian civilians from twelve different locations along Peiper's line of march.[4]

At the site of the massacre stood a small café operated by Madame Adel Bodarwé. A widow whose son, Louis, had been pressed into the German Army, Madame Bodarwé, unfortunately for her, was a witness to the crime. She disappeared that day and has not been heard of since.

The Malmédy Massacre was like an electric shock throughout the U.S. commands. The bodies of the slain were discovered by a patrol from the 291st Engineer Combat Battalion at about two thirty in the afternoon the same day. Three hours later the inspector general from First Army was aware of the atrocity. That evening Major General William Kean, chief of staff of First Army, wrote in his diary: "There is absolutely no question as to its proof— immediate publicity is being given to the story. General Quesada has told every one of his pilots about it during their briefing."

By late evening of the seventeenth the word that the enemy was killing

---

[4] Cole, *op. cit.*, p. 262. The Malmédy Massacre was the subject of extensive hearings after the war. A U.S. military tribunal at Dachau sentenced 73 former members of Kampfgruppe Peiper—43 to death, 22 to lifelong imprisonment, and 8 to prison terms ranging from ten to twenty years. Many of these sentences were commuted.

prisoners had spread throughout the American divisions on the front. Surrendering to the Americans was now a riskier business for any German, and for SS men in particular.

Jochen Peiper had gone from Baugnez to Ligneuville, spurred on by word that an American command post was located there. So it was, but the command post had also received word that Peiper was on the way. He arrived in time to capture only their lunch. Some of his men, however, took time to shoot a group of eight American prisoners. The lives of fourteen others were saved only by the bravery of Peter Rupp, the owner of the Moulin Rouge Hôtel, and the intervention of an SS officer with more inhibitions than his junior, who had already given the order.

Just outside Ligneuville Kampfgruppe Peiper ran across American tanks for the first time since achieving the breakthrough, tanks belonging to the supply trains of CCB of the 9th Armored Division. In the ensuing engagement Peiper lost one panther and two other armored vehicles; American losses were two Shermans, one M-10 tank destroyer, and a few machine guns. At about 4:00 P.M., Peiper continued the march westward.

Following the strict orders he had received from higher headquarters, he did not send reconnaissance troops into Malmédy. His trained ear could tell that the 12th SS Panzer Division on the north was still far behind him; his northern flank was exposed. But the Americans were thus far reacting to only a minimal degree, and Peiper felt he had to save his gasoline. Most of all, he had to stay on his prescribed route; the few troops of the 291st Engineer Combat Battalion holding Malmédy were not molested.

Having missed the American command post at Ligneuville, Peiper's objective was now Stavelot (with its gasoline stores to the north at Francorchamps) and beyond it the important road and bridge intersection of Trois Ponts. Taking a southward bend across the Amblève River, the head of Peiper's column approached Stavelot at dusk.

The road bent around a gigantic rock and funneled into the single stone bridge over the Amblève. His Mark IV's and half-tracks were confined to a single defile leading to the bridge. Stavelot itself looked like a little fortress—the buildings formed the walls, the Amblève its moat.

Peiper did not pause. His first vehicle rounded the rock and attempted to approach the bridge, only to be knocked out by an American antitank mine. Since the restricted road made it impossible for him to deploy his armored vehicles, he quickly dismounted his available infantry—sixty in all—and tried to seize the bridge on foot. He was met by antitank and sniper fire, and pulled his advance troops back to safe positions.

Checking the map, he discovered a road winding its way south of the Amblève to Trois Ponts. He dispatched a tank company without delay to see if this road could be used; word soon came back that the route was impassable.

Peiper looked about him. Most of his men were asleep; they had had no rest since December 14, three days earlier. He had no food to speak of and was nearly out of fuel. Just then his lead task force was hit by an unidentified American platoon. Admiring their courage, he drove them off with ease. But the platoon had made a real contribution to the battle, if only psychological. Peiper was becoming increasingly aware that his flanks were open. American traffic moving westward north of the river was heavy. And finally, at about midnight, he received a visitor, a naval lieutenant from Skorzeny's Einheit Steilau, who had made his way to Stavelot by hitchhiking. All the German rear, the lieutenant said, was one big traffic chaos. Infantry and trucks following some of Peiper's shortcuts through the woods—secondary roads that Peiper had selected to gain surprise—were bogged down in mud between Honsfeld and Ligneuville.

Peiper had a sinking feeling. His original discouragement at Lanzerath had for a while been converted to elation after his breakthrough at Honsfeld. Now he sensed once more that "the big strike was over." [5]

During the night, therefore, Peiper closed up his units, shelled the American traffic on the north bank of the Amblève, and prepared to launch a coordinated attack on Stavelot early the next morning. Even if he could not reach the Meuse, he might at least extricate himself from the mousetrap he was in and regain territory more useful for tanks.

But in so delaying Peiper lost a few hours, hours that would be precious to the American defense.

General der Panzertruppen Hasso von Manteuffel was concerned with the lack of progress in his attack beyond the Schnee Eifel toward St.-Vith. That night he left his command post at Waxweiler to spend the night with the 18th VGD at Schönberg. Walking to avoid the delays in the jammed-up traffic, Manteuffel encountered his superior, Generalfeldmarschall Walther Model, a man nearly as short as he but much stockier.

"Good evening, Marshal."

"Heil Hitler," Model said. "And how is your situation, Baron?"

"Mostly good."

"So? I got the impression you were lagging, especially in the St.-Vith sector."

"Yes, but we'll take it tomorrow."

"I expect you to. And so that you'll take it quicker, tomorrow I'm letting you use the Führer Escort Brigade. You disagree?" Model said casually.

"Not really. We've got to take St.-Vith tomorrow. And," he added a bit reluctantly, "the brigade may swing the balance. I turn off here, Marshal," Manteuffel said. "Good night."

"Heil Hitler," Model said. "And good luck tomorrow." [6]

[5] Letter, Jochen Peiper to author, April 4, 1967.

[6] John Toland, *Battle* (New York: New American Library, 1959), p. 78. Confirmed in interview with Manteuffel by author, October 12, 1966.

Twenty-two years afterward, Manteuffel was amused to recall that on the evening of December 17, 1944, two opposing generals—he and General Bruce Clarke—were both directing traffic on opposite sides of the small town of St.-Vith.

Colonel "Monk" Dickson was enjoying his two-day respite in Paris; but on the evening of December 16 he received word indirectly from Brigadier General Edwin Sibert, G-2 of 12 Army Group, that he should come to Luxembourg. Sibert would give no details. Dickson got the impression that all hell had broken loose; he was off at dawn.

Arriving at General Bradley's headquarters, Dickson was shown a confused situation map reflecting nightmarish and disastrous reports. Like everyone else, he was deeply concerned, but he would have been less than human not to feel a moment of vindication. "If you look at my Estimate Number Thirty-seven from last week, you'll find the key to this situation," he said.

From Luxembourg Dickson went by way of Arlon to Bastogne, where he found the situation among the staff of VIII Corps chaotic. He conferred with General Middleton and his G-2 at 5:00 P.M., then headed up the main highway through Houffalize toward Liège, feeling very lonely indeed. Small wonder. Just a few miles east Jochen Peiper had stopped for the night at Stavelot; a little farther east, Bruce Clarke was building up his force at St.-Vith. Dickson passed the crossroads at Werbomont, not realizing that he was perched atop Peiper's immediate objective, beyond which the panzer commander expected to have easy going across good country to the Meuse.

About ten miles north of Werbomont, at the crossroads of Aywaille, Dickson normally would have turned right to First Army Headquarters at Spa. At Aywaille, however, he encountered a cavalry reconnaissance force, 12 Army Group's T Force, commanded by his friend Colonel Francis P. Tompkins.

Tommy Tompkins was just getting ready to pull ahead along Dickson's planned route to protect Spa from Nazi columns reportedly nearby at Malmédy and Stavelot. But he was worried. "If I were you," he warned Dickson, "I'd go all the way north, then turn back to Spa by way of Theux. It's longer but safer."

Dickson knew that Tompkins' force was a small, specialized unit of only 300 men at most, hardly the type designed for heavy combat.

"If 12 Army Group is using its T Force for this kind of job," Monk Dickson reasoned, "then they're really scraping the bottom of the barrel."

He thanked his friend for the advice and took the circuitous route to the north. On the way he noted the traffic congestion and saw truck convoys removing gasoline from the Francorchamps dump north of Stavelot. At Spa he went straight to General Hodges and told him what he had learned at Luxembourg and Bastogne, and what he had seen on the way. He concluded with a recommendation:

"General, I think you ought to move this CP out of this place tomorrow."

The same evening, December 17, a council of war was held at the headquarters of 1st SS Panzer Korps in Manderfeld, former command post of the U.S. 14th Cavalry Group. Sepp Dietrich was present. The situation on the capture of Büllingen was reviewed. Peiper was known to be at Stavelot, and an attack was supposedly in progress but meeting strong enemy resistance. Surprise had been complete, but the idea of a sweep to the Meuse in a single unopposed rush had to be abandoned—there was no hope of setting the Americans into the panicked flight necessary to make Operation Greif possible. The Meuse could not be reached at that battle sector the next day, or even the day after that.

On consideration Otto Skorzeny recommended, with regrets, that Dietrich renounce his original intention of using Skorzeny's men to seize crossings over the Meuse. Dietrich approved. Skorzeny's 150th Panzer Brigade was to remain attached to the 1st SS Panzer Korps as an ordinary combined arms team. Except for the command operations, Operation Greif, as such, was finished.

Meanwhile, other plans were being executed. The commando team (Einheit Steilau) sent out by Skorzeny on December 16 and 17 had shown results. Of the nine teams sent, Skorzeny estimated that six to eight got behind American lines, two teams eventually were captured. Newly laid telephone cable had been torn up, signposts used by American supply units had been removed, and considerable intelligence had been brought back. One team got into the American back areas and actually reached the Meuse without encountering opposition. In one instance a team leader, wearing the uniform of an American sergeant, had been accosted by an American officer who wanted to know something about the situation at the front. With great ingenuity the "sergeant" invented a story that caused the officer to withdraw from the town he was occupying.

But most significant were the wild stories that had now begun to circulate in the American rear areas. The disruptive effects of the rumors begun by Skorzeny's commandos, combined with the mystery engendered by von der Heydte's scattered paratroopers, caused chaos and delays among the Americans. Everyone was under suspicion. This phase of the operation, at least, was a great success.

During the night of December 17–18 First U.S. Army did indeed, in Monk Dickson's phrase, "scrape the bottom of the barrel" to bolster the defense of the Amblève River line. If Peiper could be kept south of the Amblève and east of the Salm, he would be denied access to any strategic objectives. A company of the 526th Armored Infantry Battalion, under the command of Major Paul J. Solis, with a platoon of three-inch towed tank destroyers, was accordingly sent to Stavelot, where the head of Peiper's column lay. Just before daybreak, Major Solis began moving this detachment into position, placing two platoons on the south bank of the river, a section of tank destroyers at the old roadblock, and one platoon with three 57-mm. antitank guns and a second section of tank destroyers in reserve around the town square north of the river.

Before the U.S. troops could get completely organized, the Nazi infantry attacked. The Americans, taken by surprise, failed to destroy the bridge. Two panther tanks, supported by a panzer grenadier company, charged around the protected curve and clanked across the bridge at top speed. The first panther was hit and burned, but it still had sufficient momentum to crash through the antitank obstacle and damage two American Shermans. The second panther used this opportunity to drive through and seize the bridge. The breakthrough was followed by other vehicles, and in short order the Americans were driven back to the center of Stavelot.

Major Solis' defenses held out in the town square for some time. A fierce tank battle, lasting two hours, caused heavy losses to both sides. Odd American units—antiaircraft artillery batteries from the 7th Armored Division and a company from the 202d Engineer Combat Battalion—joined the battle. But by the end of the morning the Americans were driven out of Stavelot.

In the confusion of pulling back slowly to the top of the hill above Stavelot, Solis' detachment moved eastward along the Malmédy road instead of northward with its main body toward the Francorchamps gas dump. The American commander was well aware of the significance of the dump—originally it contained two million gallons of gasoline.[7] Solis came up with an ingenious gambit. He had his men pour some of the fuel into a deep road cut and set it ablaze. Peiper's lead tanks, unable to bypass the conflagration, turned back. At the cost of 124,000 gallons of gasoline, Solis had denied the Nazis the fuel that could have carried them all the way to the Meuse. Peiper's delay on the night of the seventeenth had been costly indeed.

Jochen Peiper did not wait to mop up all resistance around Stavelot. Even as the fight was still raging in the town square, he turned the bulk of his tanks toward the vital crossing of the Salm River at Trois Ponts. If he could get that bridge and a resupply of gasoline, he might be on his way to the Meuse. But unknown to him—although "Axis Sally" was smugly announcing it on the air—the 30th U.S. Infantry Division was heading south to meet him.

During the day of December 18, General Robert Hasbrouck of the 7th Armored was concerned about the situation on his north flank. Clarke, he calculated, could probably hold for a while at St.-Vith against the 18th VGD. But at two o'clock that morning, troops from the 1st SS Panzer Division had struck from the north and seized Recht, vital to the north flank of Clarke's CCB.[8] Hasbrouck immediately scraped together a team of a tank battalion

---

[7] This was the dump that Monk Dickson saw being evacuated the night before. How much was removed is unknown.

[8] These German SS troops were part of 1st SS Panzer Division but not part of Kampfgruppe Peiper, which was driving farther north at this time in the vicinity of Stavelot. These came from the 2d Panzer Grenadier Regiment.

and an armored infantry company. Though the team could not retake Recht, it could at least protect Clarke's flank. At 8:00 A.M. the Germans continued their attack through the cold mist with well-coordinated infantry assaults. The tiny town of Hünningen was lost temporarily but was regained by an aggressive counterattack.[9]

Later in the day the same Nazi tank and infantry forces that had forced CCR out of Recht during the early morning hours pushed on to the southwest and took the crossroads town of Poteau, also vital to Clarke's left flank and rear. This threat was serious enough for Hasbrouck to decide that a whole combat command, CCA, would have to retake Poteau (they had taken it once already). He employed a tank company to delay and then ordered CCA, nine miles to the south, to move to Poteau without delay by way of St.-Vith. Just as dark fell, CCA launched its second attack on Poteau and this time was successful. Bitter fighting raged in the dark, and a stand to the last man by the Germans proved that the units of the Leibstandarte Adolf Hitler Division were of as good a caliber as any that the Germans had put in the field during the war.

Fortunately for General Hasbrouck and his men, the St.-Vith salient was located astride the boundary between Dietrich's Sixth Panzer Army on the north and Manteuffel's Fifth Panzer Army on the south. The two armies had different missions. Manteuffel's troops, attacking St.-Vith from the east, were interested primarily in taking this road junction; 1st SS troops in the Sixth Panzer Army to the north were bent on moving to the west.

General Hasbrouck, like others, later admitted that his best ally that day was Adolf Hitler. The Führer's obsession that nobody in the Sixth Panzer Army should deviate from the drive westward meant that the main Nazi effort had insufficient maneuver room and roads for even one panzer division, much less an army.

Major General Matthew B. Ridgway, commanding general of the U.S. XVIII Airborne Corps, was sleeping through the early hours of December 18 at his main command post in Wiltshire, England, where one of his three airborne divisions, the 17th, was located. His other two divisions, the 82d and 101st, were on the Continent near Reims, still recuperating and training after their recent tough fight in Holland. At 2:15 A.M., Ridgway was awakened by a call from First Army, at Spa in far-off Belgium. The Germans were smashing through the Ardennes in great force, he was informed, and the previous day General Eisenhower had released his XVIII Airborne Corps from theater reserve to First Army. Both the 82d and the 101st Airborne divisions had been ordered to proceed with the utmost speed to the general area of Bastogne.

Ridgway had no time to lose. While two of his divisions were in France, much of his corps headquarters was in England. It was essential, if his corps

[9] This town should not be confused with the larger town of the same name in the sector of the 99th Division on the northern shoulder.

was to function properly, that he move as much of his staff and equipment as possible to the Continent. Immediately he contacted Troop Carrier Command and lined up every C-47 available. By dawn, 55 aircraft had taken off, carrying Ridgway and his entire staff contingent.

They made it in the nick of time. As the last planes cleared the runway, a heavy fog rolled in over the English Channel. Ridgway's group was the last to leave England for forty-eight hours. They flew through the fog over France to Reims, where by some miracle of navigation Ridgway's pilot found a deserted airstrip. Immediately Ridgway headed for his forward command post to find the 82d and 101st Airborne divisions. The last elements of the 101st were clearing as he arrived at their bivouac areas; the 82d had already moved out.

At about dark, after a harrowing drive through the fog and rain, he pulled into General Middleton's command post, which was still located at Bastogne. In contrast to the commander, who was calm and optimistic, Ridgway found the other members of the VIII Corps staff fraught with gloom and foreboding, primarily because communications to the front were out. Middleton had been ordered out of Bastogne by Hodges, but was determined to stay the night until the 101st Airborne could get into position.

Ridgway was of a mind to push on that evening. Once again, as with Clarke, Middleton persuaded a guest to stay overnight and get a few hours' sleep.

On the morning of the nineteenth Ridgway awoke to hear a conversation between two soldiers:

"We'd better get the hell out of here," said one man.

"We can't," said the other. "They've got us surrounded."

Ridgway, who as an airborne soldier was trained to fight surrounded by the enemy, found this hard to comprehend. But his own job was elsewhere. By this time First Army had decided on the employment of Ridgway's troops. The 101st Airborne was of course to stay in Bastogne, but the 82d was already headed for Werbomont, where Ridgway's XVIII Airborne Corps was to take command of Major General James Gavin's 82d Airborne Division and whatever else became available.

Before leaving, Ridgway was warned by Middleton about the enemy movements: "Matt, if you go up that Noville road, you might get captured. It would be a shame to lose a good corps commander. I think you ought to go to Werbomont by the northwest road, all the way west to Marche."

Anxious as he was to reach his command, Ridgway agreed. When he reached Werbomont, where the 82d Airborne was being dispatched to block the westward advance of Jochen Peiper, he set up his XVIII Corps command post, only about eight miles airline from the Salm River crossing at Trois Ponts. As elements of the 82d arrived, plus units of the 3d Armored Division he had been lucky enough to locate, Ridgway began the job of building a defensive position over a distance of nearly 65 miles. Eventually his corps would take command of the 7th Armored and 106th Infantry divisions, which were fighting desperately to the southeast at St.-Vith and Vielsalm.

The situation at First U.S. Army headquarters at Spa on December 18 was complicated not only by the foggy tactical situation but also, since Peiper was descending in force on Stavelot, by a threat to the safety of the headquarters itself. General Hodges was conferring with Major General J. Lawton Collins (whose corps he was planning to pull out as reserve) when a report came that the Germans were only a couple of miles down the road. Hodges, though realizing his "palace guard" could not hold back a sizable force, calmly finished the conference. Collins remained equally calm on the surface, but once Hodges was through with him he did not delay his departure.

The report turned out to be false. Hodges nevertheless concluded that Monk Dickson's advice had been good; First U.S. Army TAC pulled back to "Main" at Chaudfontaine, near Liège, that day.

Two officers from the 7th Armored Division who had been on rest leave reported to their former command post at Maastricht. There they found no trace of their unit. They headed south and finally made their way to Spa. It was a ghost town. But on the walls of the former First Army Headquarters were a couple of operations maps which, in their haste, the departed staff had failed to remove. The officers took down the maps, put them under their arms, and eventually made their way to St.-Vith, where they turned them over to Brigadier General Bruce C. Clarke. Clarke took a long, hard look at the situation maps—and realized the confusion that must have reigned in First Army headquarters.

"Hell, when this fight's over, there's going to be enough grief court-martialing generals," he said. "I'm not in the mood for making any more trouble." He destroyed them on the spot.

For the first half of December, 1944, the 51st Engineer Battalion had been assigned a relatively soft job for a combat unit. Part of the 1111th Engineer Group, this battalion was engaged primarily in the First Army winterization and bridge timber cutting program. From December 1 to 17 it had done itself proud: the battalion, with headquarters at Marche, was operating with an average of 28 mills every day, encountering such routine difficulties as labor troubles, financial delays in line of payment, breakdown of machinery, transportation shortages, frequent snows, scarcity of suitable timber, and long hauls from logging sites to mills.

A picture of the uneventful life led by the battalion before the panzers struck can be gathered from the operations reports and histories of December 15 and 16: Sergeant Pringle was sent to Ordnance to get a jeep, Lieutenant Lee was conducting tests for patching potholes on roads in cold weather, the mills were turning out approximately 50,000 board feet daily. Major Robert B. Yates, the battalion executive, rejoined the unit after being hospitalized for nonbattle injury three and a half months earlier, and was given a royal welcome. On December 15 Lieutenant Colonel Harvey R. Fraser, who had assumed command of the 51st the day before, called all the officers of the battalion together to introduce himself, and the next day he went off on a tour of the sawmills to become acquainted with their owners and civilian personnel.

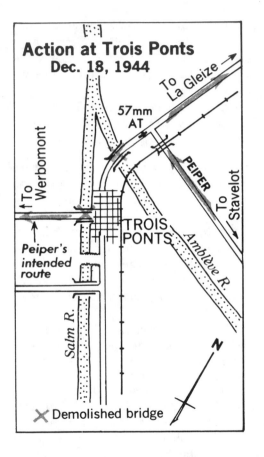

Action at Trois Ponts
Dec. 18, 1944

To La Gleize →

57mm AT

PEIPER

To Werbomont ↑

To Stavelot

TROIS PONTS

Ambléve R.

Peiper's intended route

Salm R.

N

✕ Demolished bridge

The idyll was shattered at 5:30 P.M. on December 17: the battalion received an alert to move out to various defensive positions to blow bridges and execute a delaying action in the face of an enemy attack.

Of this group, Company C was given a mission destined to have a major impact on the campaign in the Ardennes: it was ordered to proceed from its campsite near Marche with demolition equipment to a small town named Trois Ponts. Located about 25 miles east by road, this town, at the confluence of the Ambléve and Salm rivers, was thus named because it boasted three bridges, one over the Ambléve and two over the Salm (see map at left). At eleven thirty that night an advance section of 75 men arrived in Trois Ponts, set up a command post in the railway station, and began preparations to blow up two of the bridges at Trois Ponts—the one entering the town over the Ambléve and the major bridge to the west over the Salm. Major Yates, in charge of the task force, ordered roadblocks to be set up to protect both demolitions.

By eight o'clock the next morning, as Peiper was attacking Stavelot in earnest, Company C had taken position on the west bank of the Ambléve River, which skirts the edge of Trois Ponts. By singular good luck, it had commandeered an ally, a wandering 57-mm. antitank gun and crew lost from their parent unit, Company B of the 526th Armored Infantry Battalion, 7th Armored Division. As the company continued to prepare the bridge for demolition, the gun and crew were placed forward of the bridge over the Amblève. All told, the company had 120 men, armed with eight bazookas, four .50-caliber machine guns, and .30-caliber machine guns in addition to M-1 rifles.

All morning David waited on the east side of the river for Goliath. (A 57-mm. antitank gun can scarcely be counted much more than a slingshot against the heavy armor and 88-mm. gun of a tiger or panther tank.) Then at 11:15 A.M., nineteen tanks, the advance guard of Kampfgruppe Peiper, rumbled down the road from Stavelot, took the turn under the railroad underpass, and roared toward the Trois Ponts bridges, river crossings which led to Basse-Bodeux and Werbomont, and then, with better tank country all the time, to Liège and the Meuse.

The lead German tank fired first. The 57-mm. antitank gun answered, knocking off a tread and immobilizing the tank. Soon, however, the fire from the panzers was too much: the small antitank gun was knocked out. Four of its crew members were killed. The rest, now weaponless, withdrew.

But the sacrifice of the courageous gun crew was not in vain. The engineers back at the Amblève had been alerted, and literally in the face of Peiper's lead tank the bridge was blown. Major Yates withdrew his outposts to the west bank of the river and placed the men in buildings where they had good observation of developments along the high east bank.

Peiper now reconsidered. He had no way of knowing the strength—or lack of strength—of the force facing him. The Amblève and Salm presented formidable obstacles to armor. He turned right (north) to bypass Trois Ponts by way of La Gleize.

C Company now settled down to hold their defensive positions at all costs, repelling reconnaissance patrols coming across the river and simulating armored reinforcements during the night by putting chains on a four-ton truck and running it up and down through the town—they even took bazookas into the woods and fired them to simulate artillery. The ruses were effective enough to fool Jochen Peiper, one of Germany's most experienced tank commanders. The company stayed in position for several days.

The blowing of the bridges over the Salm and the Amblève was a bitter disappointment to Peiper. As he later said, "If we had captured the bridge at Trois Ponts intact and had had enough fuel, it would have been a simple matter to drive through to the Meuse River early that day."

But there was no time for remorse. Finding no bridges adequate to carry the 72-ton royal tiger tanks, Peiper still hoped to cross the Amblève River (now combined with the Salm) at La Gleize, whence he could drive on in his preferred direction toward Werbomont. This, admittedly, was a circuitous route and led through the steep gorges of the Amblève, but Peiper had to get south of that river if he was going to get on his Werbomont axis. In his view, he had no choice, so northward to La Gleize he continued.

He had an easy trip to La Gleize, meeting little or no resistance. Upon reaching the town he sent out a reconnaissance party and found that he had indeed been lucky enough to seize a bridge intact a little more than a mile southwest of town at Cheneux. This, then, would bring him back onto the Werbomont road that had been denied him at Trois Ponts.

However, crossing the Amblève at Cheneux, Peiper ran into a second piece of bad luck. American Cub airplanes flying underneath the cloud cover had discovered his location and had called in fighter-bombers which, on December 18, were partly operational.

Between two and four o'clock that afternoon American fighter-bombers attacked Peiper's panzer column as it was crossing the Amblève River. Caught in an area that offered little cover, to seek safety, his tanks had to disperse. Not until daylight began to fail at about 4:30 P.M. could the advance toward Cheneux and Werbomont be resumed.

Peiper had lost two hours and ten vehicles, three of them tanks. More important, however, the location of Peiper's column was now known to First U.S. Army headquarters. In the north the element of surprise, on which Hitler's counteroffensive had been based, was now compromised.

Once again able to move, Peiper continued with his kampfgruppe toward Werbomont, only four miles away. But standing between him and his objective was Lienne Creek, which despite its small size was unfordable. Just before the kampfgruppe arrived, a squad from the U.S. 291st Engineer Combat Battalion blew another bridge in his face, and once more Peiper was blocked.

It was now about 8:00 P.M., and Peiper had to keep trying to push. He sent a reconnaissance party north to find another bridge; again the bridges located were unsuitable for the heavy tiger tanks. One detachment managed to advance with its half-tracks over a newly discovered bridge only to be ambushed and nearly annihilated. When the remnants of the unit returned, Peiper, frustrated, decided to retrace his steps to the bridge at Cheneux and continue on the northern road through La Gleize and Stoumont toward Aywaille. This route, though less desirable for armor, could still get him to Liège.

The unit that had ambushed Peiper's reconnaissance force across Lienne Creek was the 2d Battalion of the 119th Infantry—part of the 30th U.S. Infantry Division—a unit, commanded by Major Hal D. McCown, that had barely got into position the evening before Peiper arrived. Had he not been delayed by the engineers at Trois Ponts and on the Lienne, Peiper might still have found his way through to Werbomont and the Meuse River.

Bivouacked for the night in the vicinity of Stoumont, beyond La Gleize,

Peiper was now the object of a manhunt conducted by two first-class U.S. divisions, the 30th Infantry, heroes of the Mortain action, and the 82d Airborne Division.

On December 17 the 30th Division had been ordered to move as rapidly as possible to the vicinity of Eupen for employment in Major General L. T. Gerow's V Corps. That same night, after the lead regiment, the 119th Infantry, had gone into position to back up the 1st Infantry Division at Butgenbach, the mission of the entire division was changed. Gerow was now aware of the swift and determined westward drive on the part of the 1st SS Panzer Division —a drive that could turn northward and cut off his rear at any one of several crossroads. (Actually Hodges and Gerow were far less concerned with the continuation of a drive to the west than with a turn to the north, the "small" solution that the German generals had tried to advocate to Hitler.)

To counter this northward-turning movement Gerow would have to build up a line running east and west, holding the vital roads going through Waimes on the east, Malmédy in the center, and Stavelot farther west. Even with these towns secured, First Army still would be forced to build up to the west to prevent the Leibstandarte Adolf Hitler from reaching the Meuse River or turning north to capture Liège.

The task of blocking the roads north from Malmédy and Stavelot fell to the 117th Infantry, still on wheels from the move the night before. At dawn on December 18, after a difficult road march through heavy traffic, the regimental commander, Colonel Walter M. Johnson, after conferring with officers of 12 Army Group, General Gerow, and General Leland S. Hobbs of 30th Division, decided to leave one of his battalions, the 3d, at Malmédy and to send the 1st to reinforce Major Solis' detachment at Stavelot.

The 1st Battalion, under Lieutenant Colonel Ernest Frankland, relieved Major Solis' task force on the road between Spa and Stavelot shortly after Peiper's tanks had given up trying to go through Solis' burning gasoline. The objective, however, was not merely to hold in place but to counterattack and regain the town with its vital bridge across the Amblève River.

Frankland's veteran 1st Battalion was up to full strength in both personnel and equipment, and heavily reinforced by two reconnaissance platoons, a platoon of tank destroyers, three 75-mm. self-propelled guns, and the promise of a platoon of Sherman tanks. With one infantry company on each side of the road, he moved past the inferno of burning gasoline toward Stavelot. To the surprise of all, little German resistance was encountered until just north of town. There Frankland's men came under rather ineffective fire, and by nightfall the 1st Battalion had recaptured half of Stavelot.

After darkness, as Peiper was pausing at Stoumont, three Sherman tanks from the 743d Tank Battalion arrived in Stavelot, and the 118th Field Artillery Battalion had been set up and registered. Contact was established with the 2d Battalion of the 117th, which was covering the east flank on the Malmédy-Stavelot road. Frankland prepared to attack. If he could consolidate Stavelot the next morning, he would cut off Jochen Peiper from the rear.

Ernest Natalis, the schoolteacher of the small town of Stoumont, could see that portentous events were in the offing around his town. Medium-sized, erect, and extremely thin, the professor, one of the town's most respected citizens, had seen armies come and go over this part of his native Belgium from as long ago as World War I, when the Kaiser's cavalry had passed through. Since then, the Germans had come westward in 1940 and the Americans eastward in the fall of 1944. But never before had Stoumont itself been the scene of a pitched battle.

On this night of December 18, 1944, a large German column, reportedly SS troopers, equipped with many tanks, half-tracks, and self-propelled guns, was reported to be in bivouac between Stoumont and La Gleize, only a mile and a half to the east. The Nazis had arrived fairly late in the evening.

Earlier an American unit had moved in from the west, and the American commander was using the kitchen of Natalis' schoolhouse as headquarters. On inquiry, the professor learned that this unit was the 3d Battalion, 119th Infantry, 30th Division, and it was commanded by Lieutenant Colonel Roy G. Fitzgerald.

During the night the entire battalion staff stayed up, poring over maps in the badly lighted schoolhouse. Natalis watched in fascination as American patrols came in and out of the headquarters to report on the enemy situation.

The seriousness of the Americans'·plight became progressively more apparent. Nazi parachutists were reported to be in the hills north of the town, and Nazi infantry was heading up the gentle slopes of the Amblève River valley.

As the news filtered in, Colonel Fitzgerald looked at the situation soberly. "Gentlemen," Natalis overheard him say, "it looks as if we may all be prisoners by tomorrow morning."

While the 7th Armored Division was building up the St.-Vith horseshoe and the 30th Infantry and 82d Airborne divisions were moving on Jochen Peiper to the west, a time of reckoning and soul-searching was taking place far to the east, along the Schnee Eifel, the original American positions inside the German Siegfried Line. Major General Alan Jones' two regiments, the 422d and 423d Infantry, without aerial resupply or relief, had decided to fight their way back to the west. It would be hard: the 106th Division front, as General Jones has since pointed out, extended over a distance nearly as great as that from Baltimore to Washington. Coordinated action among the surrounded units would be difficult to achieve. But the effort would be made, battalion by battalion, if necessary.

Early in the morning on the eighteenth, Lieutenant Oliver Patton was once more called from his own company to Headquarters, 2d Battalion, 423d Infantry. Colonel Puett told him he was to take 27 men, some from his own platoon and some from the Intelligence and Reconnaissance Platoon of the 423d, and head west to find a way out of the 423d's surrounded position. "Patton," Puett said, "you are leading the battalion. Get out and make contact with somebody—anybody. The 7th Armored Division is attacking up here to join up with us. Go ahead and make that contact."

About this time "Ollie" Patton was beginning to wonder why he was so often selected the lead man of the 2d Battalion. Maybe because he was a West Point graduate Puett expected some little extra from him; but regardless of source of commission, Patton would have been noticed among any group of lieutenants. Tall, solid, and athletic, with dark eyes and hair and a heavy beard, Patton was a soldierly individual. He was also aggressive and imaginative.[10] Being new to combat, he would make mistakes; nevertheless, he was obviously a man who would take action. But Patton had little time to conjecture why he got so many of the tough jobs. He organized his patrol and started westward.

After a short distance he and his men found a commanding position on the main road somewhat north of Bleialf—quite close, in fact, to the spot where he had encountered the German unit a couple of nights before. Here he could set up a small command post in a farmhouse and send out detachments to develop the situation. He broke up his patrol: the men from I & R he sent west toward Schönberg; of his own eleven he sent six south toward Bleialf and three north toward Auw. Two men he kept with him. He had no communication with any of the other three groups, although an SCR-300 (walkie-talkie) enabled him to maintain communication with Colonel Puett at battalion headquarters.

At 11:00 A.M. Patton got bad news: a getaway man from I & R reported in that the platoon had been ambushed. Before either of his other patrols returned, Patton spied a group of four Germans sauntering southward down the road. He immediately radioed battalion.

"Colonel Puett," Patton said, "there are four Krauts walking up and down between me and you and acting as if they owned the place. What do you want me to do?"

"Capture them."

Rapidly Patton made his plan. He told one man to shoot the first German and another to draw a bead on the fourth. Obviously if the first and last were killed, the two in the middle would surrender.

Both Americans did their job with deadly accuracy, but instead of surrender-

---

[10] Patton now has an important position on the Joint Staff in the Pentagon.

ing, the other two Germans plunged into the bushes and disappeared. Patton had lost his prisoners.

Disconsolate but determined to retrieve what he could, Patton searched the bodies of the two dead Germans, removing documents and discovering a new type of German weapon that was unfamiliar to him. About this time he heard the sound of rifle and machine gun fire to the south and went down the road to investigate. Here, to his amazement, he found Colonel Puett and the advance guard of the 2d Battalion.

"I thought you were supposed to be coming along behind me, Colonel," Patton halfway demanded.

Puett said little but asked about the prisoners. His disappointment turned to praise when Patton gave him the papers and the new German weapon.

His contact completed, Ollie Patton rejoined his group to find the two reconnaissance patrols had returned. Satisfied that the I & R men would never come back, Patton took the remainder of his men south to rejoin 2d Battalion where he was relieved of his special mission.

When Patton rejoined Company F he found his company commander, Frank Zullig, gone, and the 423d about to make its major attack southwestward to beat their way across the Bleialf-Schönberg road to join the 7th Armored Division. During the late afternoon Patton's company attacked, meeting only light resistance.

As they approached the main Bleialf-Schönberg road, Patton picked up a German position, well dug in, spitting fire with a light machine gun. Patton thought back quickly to his days at Fort Benning, and with eight men in his immediate vicinity, moved forward, using the standard "fire and movement," part of the force pinning the Germans down while the others charged forward, periodically flopping on their bellies. Soon they were within a few yards of the hole. Patton pulled out a grenade, and with an accuracy that caused him a certain pride, he dropped it right into the German foxhole.

Patton had always stayed awake in the bleachers of Fort Benning. One thing he remembered: Once you get the grenade in the foxhole, charge forward and follow it up. This he did. He dashed the few remaining yards, jumping feet first into the foxhole.

But in his excitement he had been too fast. A grenade explodes five seconds after the pin is released; Ollie had made it in four. He landed in the foxhole as the grenade went off. Fortunately, the sloppy mud at the bottom plus the impact of Patton's drop almost negated the effect of the grenade. The only casualty was Patton himself, who suffered a few lacerations on his hands. Quickly recovering his senses, he discovered he was in a hole with two terrified German boys—only kids—who were completely untouched by the explosion. Peering over the edge into the hole were eight bewildered faces of Patton's other men. The young volksgrenadiers were duly taken prisoner, and Patton's hands and forearms were patched up by an aidman.

Patton and what was left of his platoon continued their attack to the west and at dark reached the main road. By now they were mixed in with Company G. A German flak-wagon was sweeping the road clean, methodically cutting down any American who stuck his neck out to cross over.

Patton pulled back into the ditch to check out his platoon, and sent a runner to the company command post to report the situation: The road could not be crossed. He was ordered to pull the platoon back and, with what was left of F Company, join the rest of the 2d Battalion.

Patton moved back to the main road to make sure that he had brought all his men with him. In the darkness he could see figures moving. One man along the road seemed in a daze, and Patton yelled out to him: "Get the hell back to your position."

The man, unfortunately, was not from his platoon but a member of the 18th Volksgrenadier Division; Patton was shot by a burp gun through both thighs just below the hips. Patton's runner, miraculously unscathed, pulled the lieutenant back to the corduroy road, placed him on the hood of a jeep, and drove him back to the battalion aid station in a dingy basement in Radscheid. Patton's operations, which stretched over a period of three days, had taken place in a triangle with roughly three-quarter-mile sides.

That night—the night of December 18—it was obvious that the entire 2d Battalion and its aid station would have to move on. Patton, who had never lost consciousness, talked with the battalion chaplain and Colonel Puett and the surgeon, "Doc" Sutherland. No ambulances were available, and all were sure that Patton would freeze to death if they carried him any length of time in the cold, so he was left with Lieutenant Brownell, severely wounded, and an aidman. They were to remain in the basement until the Germans picked them up.

South of the 106th Division, the situation in the middle sector (110th Infantry) of the 28th Division was becoming critical. The problem, as General Norman Cota at division headquarters saw it, was how to delay the Germans as much as possible. Every effort had to be made to prevent their seizing the critical town of Clerf, just a few miles behind the Skyline Drive (Map IV). But the Germans had cleared the approaches to Clerf through Marnach.

During the night of December 16–17, Lüttwitz's 47th Panzer Korps had continued to press the attack with the aid of large searchlights turned against the sky (the reflected light was equivalent to that of a three-quarter moon). A great number of pyrotechnics were also used. By 9:00 P.M. Cota had released his division reserve, the 2d Battalion, 110th, under Colonel Fuller, though he withheld Company G, which was moved to defend the division command post at Wiltz.

Early next morning, December 17, Fuller's 2d Battalion jumped off to try to retake Marnach. His force was woefully inadequate.

Approaching a wood, the battalion was met by strong resistance, supported by twenty tiger tanks and self-propelled artillery from the 2d Panzer Division. The battalion dug in and stayed there until after midnight, when it broke up into small squad-sized groups and attempted to infiltrate back through the German lines.

With his 1st and 3d battalions both pinned down, there was little Hurley Fuller could do to stop the German push toward Clerf. His attached tanks, tank destroyers, and artillery could not stop a German detachment with burp guns from creeping into Clerf under cover of darkness. At first the attackers engaged the Headquarters Company troops in and around the château to the east of town, a forbidding structure that had dominated the Clerf River since the twelfth century. The pressure seemed to relax just before noon, and a tank company from the 9th Armored Division arrived in Clerf with nineteen Shermans. These Fuller parceled out to his troops south of town, his 2d Battalion, and his 1st Battalion at Heinerscheid. For a time things seemed to improve; the American armor appeared to have discouraged the German infantry.

Meanwhile, Fuller continued to receive instructions from General Cota to hold his ground. However, at six o'clock that afternoon, German tanks broke into Clerf, rolled up to the front of the 110th Infantry command post in the Claravallis Hotel (some distance from the château housing Headquarters Company), and opened fire through the window at point-blank range. Fuller's staff engaged the German infantry for a short time, but the tanks were rapidly wrecking the hotel. At 6:25 P.M. Fuller phoned the 28th Division chief of staff to say that his command post was under tank fire. He and his staff escaped by way of the rear of the hotel, hoping to join Company G, which was supposed to be coming in from the west.

From this time on, the 110th Infantry ceased to function with any semblance of control. No contact existed between battalions, and Colonel Fuller, one of the last to leave Clerf, was missing in action and later captured.

One hundred and two men from the 110th Infantry Headquarters Company in the château held out until the morning of December 18; however, the Americans left in the château were of no particular hindrance to the Germans going through Clerf.

The way to Bastogne along the hard-surfaced Clerf road was now clear.

Along the more southerly route to Bastogne lay Wiltz, where the command post of the 28th Division was situated. The headquarters was trying to hold out against the German onslaught on Wiltz with its own troops and an engineer combat battalion, under the supervision of Lieutenant Colonel Linus T. Hoban, the division headquarters commandant. In addition Hoban had G Company, 110th Infantry, plus some antitank guns, six medium tanks, and four towed tank destroyers.

That night service and rear echelon personnel were going to move the division records out of Wiltz, but all troops not essential to this movement would stay to defend the village.

The 112th and 109th Infantry regiments, in the north and south of the 28th Division, respectively, faced some difficult fighting but were able to maintain their tactical integrity. Colonel Gustin Nelson's 112th Infantry wheeled back and later joined the remnants of the 106th Infantry Division farther to the north. Colonel Earl Rudder's 109th Infantry was able to fall back across the Sûre River, where it formed part of the defense of the southern shoulder.

But the principal significance of the 28th Division defense was the delay it imposed on Lüttwitz, whose timetable was tight. Lüttwitz cared little for the towns as such on his immediate fronts; his first main objective was Bastogne, and his drive toward that road center was being delayed by the tenacious American resistance in insignificant towns. Time had been lost, and now the U.S. 101st Airborne Division was on the move from Reims and was racing him to Bastogne.

General Hasso von Manteuffel had blasted a gap some ten to twelve miles wide by the evening of December 17. Pouring through the gaps were troops of both the 58th and the 47th Panzer corps, with three panzer divisions, the 2d, the 116th, and the Panzer Lehr, and two infantry divisions, the 26th and 560th Volksgrenadier. Only Bastogne stood between Manteuffel's Fifth Panzer Army and the Meuse River.

On the night of December 18, Field Marshal Gerd von Rundstedt, correctly anticipating that the Allies would withdraw forces from the Aachen salient, decided this was the opportune moment for a previously planned attack by the northern wing of the German Fifteenth Army. This thrust, if successful, would encircle and contain the Allied forces grouped in the Aachen salient and at the same time interfere wtih the systematic transfer of reserves to counter the German offensive. He ordered preparations for the attack, which was to begin on December 19.

To Rundstedt's dismay, Hitler canceled his plans. Thinking differently from Rundstedt, Hitler not only anticipated strong Allied resistance at Aachen, but also, and more important, he wanted to use all available units to exploit the breaches already made in the gaps in the American lines. The Fifteenth Army was given a defensive mission. Two armored divisions were transferred from Fifteenth Army to OKW reserve, where they would probably be used with the Sixth Panzer Army.

Rundstedt felt that Hitler, and with him Keitel and Jodl, had passed up a good chance of encircling significant Allied forces. For as Rundstedt saw the picture on the evening of December 18, progress was satisfactory in the center of Manteuffel's Fifth Panzer Army and in some units of Dietrich's Sixth, primarily Peiper's. Continued stubborn resistance was being encountered in the north in the Monschau area. However, as of this evening, Rundstedt had confirmed his view that the operation could never make it to Antwerp.

On the same evening, December 18, General Eisenhower, realizing that this was truly a major German effort, had decided it was time to deal with it—not passively but by counteraction, first from the south, later by attack from the north.

That night he called a meeting of his staff and senior American commanders, to be held at Verdun the next morning, December 19, 1944.[11] And in view of the unexpected strength of the enemy, the confusion and uncertainty, it is no wonder he felt it desirable to admonish his commanders that there would be "only cheerful faces" in that room.

As it turned out, Eisenhower had little to worry about. The situation was tense, yes, but by and large the American commanders were thinking like him, not of retreat—not even of holding the line—but of attack. The Americans could hit the soft underbelly of what had now become a sizable bulge. If they could squeeze the penetration to a mere 25 miles between Bastogne and St.-Vith, they would inevitably limit the distance the penetration could go by the very shortage of supply routes.

At the time of the meeting, no one knew whether Bastogne was yet surrounded, but there was no doubt in anybody's mind that surrounded it soon would be.

Essentially there were two problems to be worked out. The first was the distance that Lieutenant General Jacob Devers' 6 Army Group could move its northern boundary, taking over responsibilities from Patton's Third Army. This problem was complicated by the continued existence of the Colmar Pocket, the German bridgehead west of the Rhine that made it impossible for Devers to stretch as far north as Eisenhower would have liked. Recognizing this, the Supreme Commander shifted the boundary between 21 Army Group and 6 Army Group to a point about halfway between Sauerlautern and Saarbrücken. This gave Devers the Saar region formerly designated for Patton's attack that was originally scheduled to jump off on the day the group was meeting.

That much settled, the discussion turned to timing. How soon could Patton's Third Army on the south of the Bulge launch a counterattack toward Bastogne? Turning to his longtime friend, who was unusually subdued that day, General Eisenhower said, "George, I want you to command this move—under Brad's supervision, of course—making a strong counterattack with at least six divisions. When can you start?"

"As soon as you're through with me," Patton answered.

[11] Present in addition to Eisenhower were Bradley, Patton, Tedder, Devers, Strong, and other staff officers.

General Eisenhower visits General Montgomery in Normandy on July 26, 1944, the day after launching Operation Cobra.

General de Gaulle is greeted in the town of Laval, France, three days before the fall of Paris.

A grim Adolf Hitler strides through an undesignated town with a cortege of solemn-faced Nazi officers.

German film captured by U.S. Army Signal Corps on the western front

Jochen Peiper's men on the march after having achieved their breakthrough, December 17, 1944.

American victims of the massacres near Malmédy, Belgium.

M. Henri le Joly, one of the few surviving civilian witnesses to the Malmédy Massacre.

The bridge over the Amblève River at Stavelot, seen from the American (northern) side.

St.-Vith, Belgium, looking eastward toward Schönberg and the Schnee Eifel.

Field Marshal Bernard L. Montgomery and Major General Matthew B. Ridgway check situation maps in Belgium.

Wrecked vehicles of Team Cherry, CCB, 10th Armored Division, along the Longvilly Road near Bastogne.

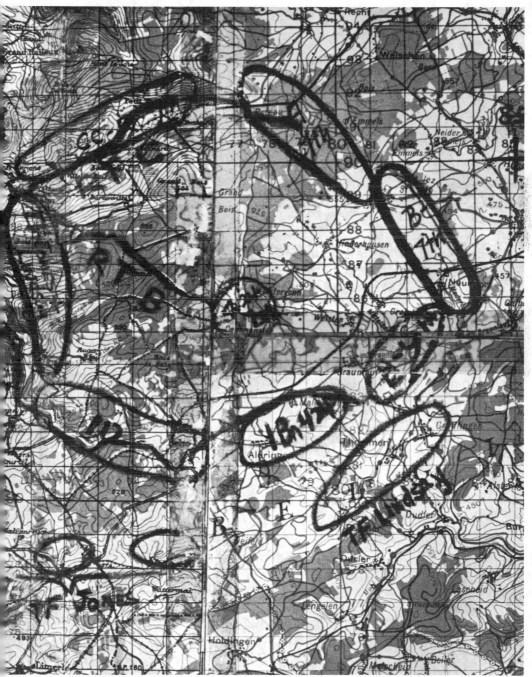

Courtesy General Bruce C. Clarke

XVIII U.S. Airborne Corps plan for last-ditch defense
of the St.-Vith Goose Egg.

Two exhausted infantrymen from Hurley Fuller's decimated 110th Infantry Regiment, after having made their way to the perimeter of Bastogne, December 19, 1944.

Wiltz, Luxembourg, where the command post of the 28th Division held out until the morning of December 19, 1944.

U.S. Army Photo

Christmas service in Bastogne.

Wreckage of the town square, Bastogne.

U.S. Army Photo

Two youthful Hitler Jugend storm troopers captured by the
U.S. 6th Armored Division.

Lieutenant General Omar N. Bradley and Lieutenant General George S.
Patton, Jr., meet in Bastogne.

General Eisenhower and Prime Minister Churchill witness the crossing of the Rhine, March, 1945. General Simpson and General Bradley are in background.

Lieutenant General Courtney Hodges, commanding general, U.S. First Army, makes contact with the Russians on the bank of the Elbe River.

Lieutenant General Walter Bedell Smith signs the document of German surrender in the early morning hours of May 7, 1945.

General Eisenhower accepts General Jodl's surrender. General Ivan Susloparov, representing the forces of the Russians, stands on his right.

U.S. Army Photo

SS leaders tried at Dachau for the Malmédy Massacre. *Front row, left to right:* Dietrich, Kraemer, Priess, Peiper.

Thirteen years after the Ardennes campaign, General Maxwell D. Taylor, then Chief of Staff of the U.S. Army, greets former paratrooper Baron Friedrich August von der Heydte, University of Würzburg.

U.S. Army Photo

Baron Hasso von Manteuffel and General Bruce C. Clarke revisit the St.-Vith battle scene twenty years later.

The author's wife, Barbara, chats with Viscount Montgomery of Alamein, October, 1966.

The only vestige of Kampfgruppe Peiper at La Gleize: a lone tiger tank occupies the town square.

Asked what he meant, Patton said he had left his household in Nancy in perfect order. He could proceed to Luxembourg straightaway at the end of the meeting.

"When will you be able to attack?"

"The morning of December twenty-first," said Patton. "With three divisions."

"Don't be fatuous, George. If you try to go that early, you won't have all three divisions ready and you'll go piecemeal. You will start on the twenty-second and I want your initial blow to be a strong one! I'd even settle for the twenty-third if it takes that long to get three full divisions."

Witnesses to the occasion testify to the electric effect of this exchange. The prospect of relieving three divisions from the line, turning them north, and traveling over icy roads to Arlon to prepare for a major counterattack in less than seventy-two hours was astonishing even to a group accustomed to flexibility in their military operations.

Patton was truly ready to get under way. That morning he had held a meeting with his staff and had come up with three concepts of how the Third U.S. Army might be employed. Each concept had been assigned a code word, which he had left with his chief of staff, General Hobart Gay, so by merely uttering a single word over the telephone, Patton could launch his army according to anticipated orders.

Eisenhower thereupon issued formal verbal instructions for the attack, repeating that the Third Army was to jump off no earlier than December 22 and no later than December 23, and with a strength of at least three divisions. When Patton's forces reached the Bastogne area, they should be prepared to move on, probably in the direction of Houffalize. Eisenhower promised ample air support once flying conditions improved. He further informed the group that he would begin arrangements for offensive actions on the northern flank as soon as the Nazi attack against Hodges had spent itself.

The decision made, George Patton moved from the conference table, telephoned his headquarters, and issued the code word. The 4th Armored was to start rolling on Arlon by way of Longwy; the 80th Infantry Division in the direction of Luxembourg via Thionville; the 26th Infantry Division was alerted pending orders to move.

When Patton excused himself from the meeting, Eisenhower strolled to the door with him. Referring to his promotion of three days before, the new five-star general grinned a little. "Funny thing, George, every time I get another star I get attacked." [12]

Patton's impish nature returned. "And every time you get attacked, Ike, I have to bail you out."

[12] Referring to the attack at Kasserine Pass in Tunisia, just after Eisenhower had received his fourth star.

Book IV

CRISIS

CHAPTER 12

❧❧

St.-Vith Stems the Northern Tide

FIELD MARSHAL Sir Bernard Law Montgomery could see that the German penetration through the U.S. VIII Corps south of him might have severe repercussions on his own 21 Army Group. Should the Nazi effort cross the Meuse at Namur and continue through open country to Brussels and beyond, his own supply lines and rear areas would be torn asunder. The seizure of Antwerp might result in the destruction, or at best the evacuation, of not only First and Ninth U.S. armies, but of his own command as well.

Montgomery was not so concerned that he lost all his sense of humor. At the end of a detailed report he was sending to a worried War Office in London, he concluded: "We cannot come out through Dunkirk this time as the Germans still hold that place." The message was passed on to the Prime Minister with the last sentence deleted.

But besides penning light words to London, there were concrete measures the Field Marshal could take to protect his command. In the process of preparing for his attack south through the Rhineland (a measure agreed upon a long eleven days earlier at Maastricht), Montgomery was withdrawing and refitting a reserve consisting of the XXX British Corps, under Lieutenant General Sir Brian Horrocks, for employment in his extreme north. Horrocks' corps could be used to protect the south flank of 21 Army Group farther south. Then, when the mess in the Ardennes was over, XXX Corps could return to its mission in the north.

General Horrocks himself was on leave in Brussels, having left the withdrawal of his corps to his chief of staff. While visiting Queen Elizabeth of the Belgians, he received word to rejoin his corps and concentrate it in the Louvain–St.-Trond area, about halfway between Brussels and Maastricht. Weather delayed him overnight, but by December 19 XXX British Corps, with the Guards Armoured Division and the 43d, 51st, and 53d British Infantry divisions assigned (together with three armored brigades) began its

261

concentration just a few miles north of the Meuse. Montgomery also sent reconnaissance troops into First U.S. Army zone to help cover the Meuse bridges—if necessary, all the way from Liège on the north to Givet on the west.

On that same morning, December 19, the American 30th Division was beginning to tighten its stranglehold on Kampfgruppe Peiper. Of far-reaching consequences to this action was the early morning attack of Frankland's 1st Battalion, 117th Infantry, from the hills above Stavelot to recapture the town.

Frankland jumped off early. Companies A and B, operating abreast, pushed into the town rapidly, and by noontime all of Stavelot north of the Amblève River was cleared of Germans, with the exception of a fringe of houses on the western edge, where a tiger tank fought off all efforts to knock it out. The Germans had not built up any sizable reinforcements during the night, presumably because Peiper's spearhead column had turned west on its primary mission, according to instructions. The 3d Parachute Division—on which Peiper had banked so heavily—had not arrived. Peiper, whose kampfgruppe comprised approximately half of the 1st SS Panzer Division, was now cut off from the rear. He learned that Stavelot had fallen to the Americans shortly after the town had been cleared.

Follow-up German units began arriving, determined to recapture the town. During the afternoon of December 19, other elements of the 1st SS Panzer Division launched two fierce counterattacks. None achieved success.

The most dramatic of these efforts to relieve Peiper's rear occurred at 4:00 A.M. on December 20. Two companies of German infantry attempted to recapture Stavelot by wading across the Amblève River and assaulting the town frontally from the south. The swift current and the icy cold water made the assault difficult to coordinate. As a result the Germans came under American fire before reaching the north bank, many of them before they had even got into the water. The American unit holding the line of houses along the Amblève was the 1st Platoon of Company A. To enable them to see what they were shooting at, Frankland's battalion sent up flares, and then the tanks of the 743d Tank Battalion, under Lieutenant Jean Hansen, set fire to the houses on the south side of the river. The swimming Germans silhouetted against the light were easy targets. Half were killed in the water or forced back to the south bank. The rest, supported by direct fire, finally managed to reach the north bank and made the 1st Platoon retire to the second row of houses. However, now the direct tank fire by which the Germans had been supporting their attack from the south was masked, and Lieutenant Murray, commanding the 1st Platoon, launched a counterattack with the help of B Company and drove the remnants of the Germans back into the river. Only a small fraction of the attackers succeeded in reaching the south bank. The

American line was completely reestablished along the north side by 7:30 A.M., December 20. It was not to be lost again.

Madame Regine Heuser Grégoire, thirty, was alone with her two small children in her house along the road about a mile west of Stavelot. She had spent the night before, Monday, December 18, at home, without being bothered, despite the columns of 1st SS Panzer tanks and half-tracks that had passed her doorstep.

But the battle for the town had not ceased. The Americans had retaken the town proper, to be sure, but the Nazis on the south side of the Amblève were making it dangerous for civilians to be above ground. On Tuesday, December 19, as the German armor was holding Frankland's battalion in the town, Madame Grégoire decided to go with her children across the street to the house of Monsieur Legaye, which had a basement that would afford more protection.

Madame Grégoire was not a native of Stavelot; her original home was Manderfeld, on the German border, and this was later to save her life.

She found huddled in the Legaye basement 23 persons, most of them women and children who, like herself, had not been molested up to this time. About noontime the civilians were startled by the appearance of an American soldier. Glancing quickly around the basement to assure himself that none of his buddies were hiding out, he left. Toward nightfall another American soldier came in. As best he could, he explained to the refugees that the Germans were making an attack through the hills toward the hamlet of Ster but the column had been checked. His advice was to stay in the cellar and make no noise.

Shortly thereafter the terrified refugees heard exchanges of shots over their heads. Obviously either the Americans or the Germans—probably the former —were using the building as a strongpoint in a house-to-house fight. The firing went on for about an hour.

A little after 8:00 P.M. a grenade was rolled into the basement by SS troopers. Miraculously, no one was hurt. Several moments later the Nazis threw a second. Again the grenade was relatively ineffective, the only casualty, Madame Grégoire, wounded slightly in the leg. Then came the shout into the basement, *"Heraus!"*

Madame Grégoire became the spokesman for the group. Calling up the stairway, she told the Nazis that the basement was occupied only by civilians. "Have mercy," she pleaded.

The Nazis refused to listen. Fearing another grenade, the wounded Madame Grégoire decided to lead the group out. Accompanied by her two children she accosted the first German she saw, and repeated once more: "The basement contains nobody but civilians."

Immediately she found herself surrounded by a dozen SS troops who demanded that the rest of the refugees come out of their hiding place. She called down the steps, and they stumbled single file into the garden.

One of the SS men approached Madame Grégoire, demanding if everyone was present. She pretended to count, knowing that three persons had made their escape a short time ago, but she made her bluff good and affirmed that all were there.

After some discussion, the Nazi troopers told Madame Grégoire to instruct the civilians to crouch or sit in the garden against the hedgerow. Then she and her children were removed to the rear and told to tend the injuries of a German—probably wounded by the exchange of fire in the house earlier. Despite the darkness, she could see that two soldiers, each armed with a revolver and a rifle, were methodically and coldly shooting the civilians, one by one. She did her best to stop the slaughter. "There are none here but innocent civilians," she pleaded to one of the SS men.

The man was unperturbed. "It is necessary that the innocent pay for those guilty. The people of Stavelot have been hiding American soldiers," he said.

After the SS finished their slaughter, they marched Madame Grégoire and her children to the basement of a house nearby, Monsieur Massotte's, where she was forced to act as interpreter between Germans and French. The SS behaved as though convinced that all civilians were guerrillas. One made the remark, "I know what the people of Stavelot are. I'll flatten them all."

Madame Grégoire realized bitterly that the SS troopers did not honestly suspect the civilians of firing on the German columns. The SS conducted no search for firearms; indeed, they made no inquiries of any kind.

As she lay in the basement of the Massotte house through the night of December 19, Madame Grégoire heard the storm troopers boasting about the atrocities they had committed—or pretended to have committed. One SS man told how he decapitated a civilian, stuck the head on a pike, and used it for target practice. One returning patrol claimed to have assassinated American soldiers. In the dim light Madame Grégoire recognized one of the SS men who had participated in the massacre at the Legaye house. "There is a good pile of victims in that garden," he boasted, "and it will be even more beautiful tomorrow." Some of the bodies, he admitted, had moved after they were shot, but after a while all movement had ceased.

Madame Grégoire was fortunate. She and her children were rescued several days later by the Americans. But Madame Grégoire's experience and the murders at the Legaye house are not the whole story. About a mile north of the small hamlet of Parfondruy stands the Chapelle Sainte Lucie, built in 1629. By the chapel a monument has been erected in memory of 26 civilians similarly slaughtered. They ranged in age from nine months (Bruno Klein-

Terf) to seventy-eight years (Josephine Grosjean-Hourand). Farther up the hill, at Ster Parfondruy, a monument contains another 30 names.

In all, 138 civilians were killed at Stavelot by Peiper's troops.

Pfc. Robert F. Hall, from the Ammunition and Pioneer Platoon of the 3d Battalion, 119th Infantry, was by now a veteran. Having joined the U.S. 30th Division before the St.-Lô breakthrough, he had been decorated with the Silver Star and had been twice wounded in the autumn fighting. He could look around him and see that not many men present had been with the outfit as long as he had.

This night, December 18, while his battalion commander, Colonel Roy Fitzgerald, was poring over his maps in the schoolhouse, Hall and two other men were summoned by his platoon leader, Lieutenant Walter J. Goodman. Goodman ordered a difficult mission: "I want you three to go up to the top of that hill to the north, set up an observation post, and don't leave."

The men began trudging through the cold night toward a small farmhouse along the dirt road that leads from Stoumont to Spa. At the top of the hill they settled down to await developments.

At daybreak their suspense ended. A massive attack of both tanks and infantry was on the way. Hall's two companions disappeared instantaneously, but Hall, remembering his lieutenant's instructions, stayed as long as he could.

Which was not long. The tanks were firing tracers and coming close. Hall turned tail and dashed for a stone house about 300 yards to his rear toward Stoumont. He stumbled down the steps into the cellar and was astonished to discover 25 or 30 other Americans, also taking refuge. Looking around, he saw a potato bin: it flashed across his mind that this might be a place to hide, but he soon rejected the idea. Going to the cellar window, he peered out of the broken pane only to discover black boots marching past the house. A little to the rear he saw a tank with American markings, obviously being used by the German SS.

Hall had seen enough combat to know that he had better get out of the cellar, especially since the presence of the Americans apparently had not yet been discovered by the Krauts. Too many times as a precautionary measure when going through villages he himself had dropped grenades in open windows. Up the steps he went. Out in the street he was surprised to find about 200 Americans standing with their hands up. An SS man motioned him to join them, searched him, and removed a new fountain pen just sent him by his family; then the prisoners were marched along the road toward a spectacular castle overlooking the Amblève River valley. On the way, Hall glanced at the SS troopers waiting to move forward; they were young and cocky, not like the veterans he had been up against in Normandy. But his greatest concern at this moment was the prospect of a shelling by American artillery. For the moment, none came.

Soon Hall and his companions were crowded into the castle, which was being utilized by this German force as a command post and hospital. Hall was put to work handling the German dead and wounded. He was to stay here at the Château Froid Coeur only about six hours. The Germans then moved his group of unwounded prisoners back to the town of La Gleize.

The Nazi attack that swallowed Private Hall and his 200 comrades was Jochen Peiper's main effort in his attempt to break out to the west. Opposing Peiper, the 3d Battalion, 119th Infantry, had set up a perimeter defense of Stoumont, backed by eight towed tank destroyers and two 90-mm. anti-aircraft guns, in addition to three 57-mm. antitank guns. The regimental commander, Colonel Edward M. Sutherland, had pressed higher authority for tank support and had been promised a company of Sherman tanks.

The terrain around Stoumont was more open than that farther east, which made the town a difficult place for the Americans to defend. Nevertheless, from a tanker's viewpoint the terrain was far from ideal; Peiper felt he was still confined too much to the roads, with inadequate room to maneuver his tanks.

Employing a battalion of infantry and the technique he had used at Stavelot —sending two or three tanks at maximum speed past the American road-blocks—Peiper attacked. The promise made to Sutherland was fulfilled: ten minutes after the assault was launched, ten Shermans arrived from the 743d Tank Battalion. Colonel Fitzgerald committed four to support I Company on the east, four more were attached to L Company on one of the flanks, and two were held in reserve. As at Stavelot, the Americans retreated to the middle of town under the weight of Peiper's attack and delayed his advance for almost two hours, principally with tanks and 90-mm. antiaircraft guns. By 10:00 A.M., however, the now decimated 3d Battalion had retired from Stoumont, covered largely by the tank support and a barrage of smoke.

But Peiper's interest did not lie in the 3d Battalion, or in the whole 119th Infantry, for that matter. Twice the day before—at both Trois Ponts and Chevron, when bridges over unfordable streams had been blown practically in his face—he had been frustrated in his effort to reach Werbomont. If he could now break out of Stoumont and reach Targnon, a small town about a mile to the west where the Lienne Creek flowed into the Amblève, he could turn southwest on a fairly major road along the west bank of the troublesome little Lienne and take Chevron (see map, p. 284). Hoping finally to break out of the Amblève River valley, Peiper drove ahead.

The Americans were driven before his onslaught to a short distance beyond Targnon, but Peiper could not use the Targnon road without driving the 119th slightly farther, for at Stoumont Station they could still look down his throat as he traversed the Targnon-Chevron road.

Help came to the Americans in the form of a fresh tank company from the 740th Tank Battalion. This unit, rushed in under emergency conditions, had just cannibalized an ordnance depot in the vicinity of Aywaille; some, equipped with British radios, were for all practical purposes bereft of communication. Nevertheless, the tanks had guns and the men had courage, and it was largely because of the efforts of these tanks, some manned by ordnance people and some by the 740th, that the 119th survived as well as it did. Nevertheless, Company I, which sustained the assault from the east, had been reduced to 24 men; Company K was down to 55; Company L to 80; and the Heavy Weapons Company had one hundred.

At this point Jochen Peiper decided he had insufficient gasoline to continue. He halted, beat off some American counterattacks, and finally ordered his forces west of Stoumont to withdraw to the town itself. His 1st Battalion, 1st Panzer Regiment, was to hold positions in Stoumont; his 2d Battalion was to hold positions in La Gleize. The 84th Light Flak Battalion, supported by the 2d Grenadier Regiment, was to hold the crossing over the Amblève at Cheneux. Meanwhile his exit to the north along a secondary road from La Gleize, which had previously been occupied only by American engineers, was now occupied by the battalion from the 118th Infantry that had formerly been in Malmédy. Thus Peiper's force was confined to the occupation of two towns, La Gleize and Stoumont, barely a mile and a half apart. Peiper's drive had been halted on December 19.

On the evening of December 19, General Eisenhower, Air Chief Marshal Tedder, and Eisenhower's military assistant, Colonel James Gault, had just returned to headquarters at Versailles from the Verdun meeting. Eisenhower was satisfied with the arrangements for Patton's counteroffensive, but the journey back had been long. New reports were coming in from the front including the fall of Wiltz, the imminent surrounding of Bastogne, and the dangers, such as were known, to the American position at St.-Vith. The Supreme Commander sat down to ponder on them.

The same evening Major General Sir John F. M. Whiteley, who was billeted with SHAEF's British intelligence officer, Kenneth Strong, was also pondering. The enemy thrust, it was now obvious, was being directed toward Namur and northward. How could Bradley, who was determined not to leave Luxembourg, protect the Channel ports and give the northern shoulder of the Bulge the detailed, personal supervision that it required? Furthermore Hodges' signal facilities at Chaudfontaine had been disrupted, and communication between First Army and SHAEF was bad.

Whiteley checked with Strong and found they thought the same: Field Marshal Montgomery should be given command of the entire northern sector of the Bulge. By 9:00 P.M. Whiteley had called General Bedell Smith and asked if he and Strong could come to Smith's office.

"Jock" Whiteley was by now a veteran associate of Bedell Smith. They had worked together for two and a half years as members of Allied Force Headquarters in the Mediterranean and had never had a quarrel. Knowing Bedell Smith's short-fused temper, Eisenhower himself had noticed and remarked on the smoothness of their relationship.

This occasion marked the end of Whiteley's winning streak with Smith. When Whitelely outlined his concept of a split in the command, giving the First and Ninth U.S. armies to Montgomery, his superior's eyes burned: Whiteley, Smith barked, had been one he had always counted on to maintain a completely Allied outlook. Now, he snarled, Whiteley was talking like a damned British staff officer.

This remark hurt Whiteley considerably, but he tried to control his temper. He had, he retorted, given his best advice based on military considerations only. He reminded Smith he was no partisan of Montgomery's—quite the opposite. Smith could fire him the next day, but his recommendation stood.

Smith settled back, paused for a moment, picked up the telephone, and called Eisenhower, who was still in his office. He outlined Whiteley's recommendation. Smith put down the telephone: "General Eisenhower says we can decide this matter after our staff meeting tomorrow morning." It was now 11:00 P.M.

Without a word, General Whiteley stalked out of Smith's office.

Smith's call confirmed what General Eisenhower had strongly suspected all along—indeed, all doubt had practically disappeared from his mind before the phone call: this was a major offensive aimed northward where the objectives were lucrative. It intensified Eisenhower's concern about General Bradley's headquarters, located way to the south and east at Luxembourg, too far removed from the point of greatest danger, the northern shoulder, for Bradley to exercise the close personal supervision over the critical part of the battle that the Supreme Commander would have liked. Just the day before, Bradley had gone to see Courtney Hodges; the round trip, besides being dangerous, had taken the entire day. Eisenhower had admonished Bradley that this was expensive in both time and risk. In addition Eisenhower was aware that direct communication between Bradley's headquarters and the northern sector had been cut; it was necessary for them to go through an elaborate series of relays, in which service was poor, to maintain signal communications.

Besides the matters of communication and Bradley's inaccessibility to the north, however, another factor had to considered. At the moment the only sizable reserve out of the line in the north was Horrocks' XXX British Corps, which could be employed anywhere along the northern battle line from Holland to the flanks of the penetration itself.

As Supreme Commander, Eisenhower had the legal authority to order that

British reserve to be employed in the American sector under American command. Montgomery might appeal against such action, but in all likelihood Eisenhower would be backed up by the Combined Chiefs of Staff and by the heads of governments. Far preferable would be the employment of Horrocks' corps under its own commander, Montgomery, in charge of a single battle line at the point of the greatest threat.

Eisenhower sensed the pitfalls inherent in this action. He was aware that this arrangement, though temporary, would be taken amiss by much of the American command, to whom it would appear a surrender to the arguments of Montgomery and Brooke that Eisenhower had been fighting off for weeks. And yet he regarded these considerations as surface, almost normal, irritations of a coalition command. Basically he had strong faith in the team that he had developed in the European campaign. He believed that, despite its difficulties, any temporary command scheme would work.

General Eisenhower went to his map and with a pencil drew an east-west line straight across the center of the Bulge, running from Givet on the Meuse River to Prüm in the Siegfried Line. All the forces to the north of this line, including elements of the First and Ninth U.S. armies, and the British Second and the Canadian First armies, would fall temporarily under the command of 21 Army Group, Field Marshal Montgomery.

His decision made, Eisenhower telephoned his chief of staff with the request that he call General Bradley and discuss the temporary change with him. Smith's call took Bradley by surprise. During the morning he had detected no concern on Eisenhower's part over his communications to the north; and communications were being laid in across the western tip of the Ardennes, with still another for safety's sake behind the Meuse.[1]

Bradley questioned the wisdom of the switchover; he was thinking primarily of the counterattack phase. He felt it would be easier to keep all troops in the Ardennes campaign under one army group command, since one army group could coordinate the counterattack phase better than two, with the overall control exercised by SHAEF in Paris.

But Bradley felt a certain conflict in his mind. He feared that his objections were based too much on personal considerations. He would have been less disturbed, he told Smith, had the command been turned over to another American on the north, or even a British officer other than Montgomery. Keenly aware of Montgomery's earlier demands for a single thrust under his own command, Bradley shared Eisenhower's concern that the arrangement would

---

[1] Merriam asserts that the buried cable and the radio link were cut on December 23, and the open circuit cable on December 25. "Only sporadically could the repeater station at Jemelle hear the noise of its operation because of the noise of battle, and even this channel was cut off altogether on December 26. A roundabout telephone circuit from Verdun to Reims to Namur, and then to Liège was kept open the entire time, but the circuits were few and the connections poor." Robert Merriam, *Dark December* (Chicago: Ziff-Davis, 1947), p. 123.

appear to discredit the American command. However, Bradley did agree with the assumption that Montgomery's temporary takeover would make available XXX British Corps, which was a welcome addition.

Mistrusting his own motives and being assured by Bedell Smith that the changeover would be temporary only, Bradley silenced further objections.[2]

During the night Eisenhower received a phone call from the Prime Minister; Churchill was calling to ask how the battle was going. Eisenhower told him what he had decided and explained his temporary command setup. Churchill remarked that this plan would make the British reserve instantly available for use wherever needed, regardless of previously defined zones. "I assure you," he said, "that British troops will always deem it an honor to enter the same battle as their American friends."

The next morning, December 20, the usual small group of staff officers reported to the Supreme Commander's briefing room. Whiteley was still angry at Smith's outburst the night before. Usually he walked to the briefing room with Smith; today he saw to it that he made his way there by himself.

Whiteley's formal assignment was Chief of Planning Section for SHAEF G-3; it had become habit at SHAEF for him to act as spokesman in the briefings. Unaware of what had happened late the night before, he had barely begun the briefing when he was interrupted by Eisenhower: "Jock, I think you had an idea last night to give the northern half of this battlefield to Monty. What about that?"

Whiteley was perplexed. He had said his piece the night before and, being a loyal staff officer, felt it improper now to go over the head of his superior. Hesitating, he glanced in Bedell Smith's direction. Smith did not let him down. "Yes, sir, that is so."

Eisenhower grunted, said no more, and the briefing was completed. A few moments after all had returned to their offices, Whiteley received instructions from Smith to write an operation order, splitting the battlefield between Givet and Prüm, with all areas north of this line to go to 21 Army Group, and all areas south to remain with 12 Army Group.

At the same time Eisenhower was on the phone to Montgomery, giving him instructions regarding his new responsibilities.

Whiteley immediately put his planning staff to drawing up the written order. It happened he was being visited that day by a senior British officer from the War Office, London. While they were conversing, Bedell Smith entered the room. He walked up to Whiteley, held out his hand, and in front of his high-

---

[2] To insure that his action would not be interpreted as a reproof to Bradley, whom he considered faultless in his handling of the Ardennes situation, Eisenhower recommended to General Marshall that Bradley be promoted to four-star rank without delay.

ranking guest made a complete and sincere apology for what he had said the previous evening.

At noontime on December 19, XVIII U.S. Airborne Corps became operational, taking responsibility for all territory west of Stavelot, with emphasis on operations to reduce Peiper's lead kampfgruppe of the Leibstandarte Adolf Hitler. At first the corps had only the 82d Airborne Division and the 119th Regimental Combat Team of General Hobbs' 30th Division, though during the next sixty days the corps would command nine different divisions plus Combat Command B of the 9th Armored. In the meantime General Ridgway sat down and wrote a note to Hobbs, who he knew would be annoyed at having a third of his division taken from him:

> Dear Leland:
> Delighted to have your CT119. Know how you feel about detachments. Meanwhile, we will take best care of them, and I know they will deliver the goods.
> Warm regards,
>
> Matt

Meanwhile, the Americans of the 117th Infantry were discovering what kind of enemy they were up against in Peiper's men. In the process of cleaning out the western edge of Stavelot and the small surrounding villages of Parfondruy and Ster, the troops found evidence of the killings. In homes and outlying buildings north of the Amblève, Americans counted the corpses of 117 men, women, and children, all killed by small-arms fire.[3] When the chief of police, Monsieur Armould, showed them the bodies, the Americans found it difficult to restrain themselves.

Captain John Kent, commanding Company A, 117th Infantry, found himself confronted by infuriated American soldiers. They were escorting nine prisoners from the 1st SS Panzer Reconnaissance Battalion who, it was affirmed, had taken part in the atrocities. "Sir," they asked, "do you want to bother with them?"

Kent had little feeling for the prisoners, but he paused. In the hopes of securing some valuable intelligence, he ordered the prisoners to be turned over to the division cage for interrogation.

In Stoumont Professor Ernest Natalis was beginning to be concerned over the safety of the people. News travels fast, and the professor felt these Germans would not hesitate to perpetrate another massacre.

By 11:30 A.M. the town was occupied by Peiper's troops and Americans were being brought out of hiding. The SS troopers, largely fanatic youths, were in a fury of frustration. The professor asked an officer for a doctor to

---

[3] Some of the killings mentioned above occurred south of the river, at the bridge.

come and treat a dying American soldier. The officer went into a rage, and immediately the professor found himself surrounded by twenty angry SS troopers. "All the people around here," said one, "are terrorists."

The SS officer snatched the professor's hat and hurled it to the floor. When the professor bent over to pick it up the SS man jammed the muzzle of his pistol on the back of his neck.

But now Natalis had a stroke of luck. The officer removed the pistol and said, "Here comes the commander. Speak to him."

The professor changed his tactics. This time, instead of asking for a doctor for American soldiers, he asked if someone would treat the children. Again he was refused. "All you people in the region," the Nazi colonel repeated, "are terrorists."

The professor played his trump card. "Sir," he said, "you are, as a professional officer, well versed in matters such as order of march and tactics. But let me ask you a question. Do you know the nature of the population around this region?"

A shade of doubt flicked over the Nazi officer's face.

Pressing his point, Natalis pulled out of his pocket a small booklet, a pocket calendar for the year 1944. He turned the pages to January 21, where there was marked the diagram of an airplane—a stick representing a fuselage, a stick of equal size crossing it, and two smaller sticks representing a tail.

"What possible connection can there be between your people and this silly diagram?" the Nazi demanded.

"Colonel, I made this mark in my book as a reminder. For this last January twenty-first a German plane from Bremen, destined for Chievres, crashed a couple of kilometers north of Stoumont. Thirty-five German soldiers were aboard. All the people from Stoumont turned out, and although the plane was burning, saved as many of the soldiers as they could. Though they greeted us with pistols, we hauled them out of the plane and sent them to the hospital in Spa. Our people are humanitarians, not terrorists."

Jochen Peiper paused for a moment, bowed slightly, and turned to give orders that the population of Stoumont be protected. The population of Stoumont took what refuge they could. Seventy people hid out in the basement of Dr. Robinson's house (he was a Belgian despite his English name), 120 people huddled in the basement of the church; there were 200 (patients and civilians) in St. Edouard's Sanatorium about a kilometer northwest of town.

Even so, the next few days were to be full of danger and discomfort for the people of Stoumont. The refugees had neither food nor water. American artillery from the 30th Infantry Division closing in on Jochen Peiper was devastating the town. Once a German soldier, about twenty years old and slightly wounded, came into the basement of Dr. Robinson's house. Seeing the condition of the children, he offered to go out to the field and milk a cow.

He never returned. The professor later learned he was killed in the field, presumably by American artillery.

The American squeeze on Jochen Peiper began in earnest. The bulk of the American strength lay to the west, particularly after Combat Command B of the 3d Armored Division had been attached to the 30th Division. The American troops were now organized as Task Force Harrison, after the assistant division commander, Brigadier General William K. Harrison, who was commanding operations against both Stoumont and La Gleize. Attacking from the west of Stoumont was 1st Battalion, 119th Infantry, supported by a company of the 740th Tank Battalion.

The most dramatic part of the battle for Stoumont entailed the St. Edouard's Sanatorium for sick children and aged people that sat on prominent ground along the road to the northwest. Several platoons of the 1st Battalion decided that it would make an excellent place for their command posts. The sanatorium was full of Germans, but they were driven out in the early stages of the fighting on December 20; three or four platoon command posts were set up in the building. Companies B and C deployed north of the road, while Company A set up south of the road. Father Hanlet and those who had sought shelter in the basement of the building now thought they were safe, but plans for evacuating them had to be postponed until daylight.

Unfortunately, this was not possible; at eleven o'clock the evening of December 20, the Germans launched an aggressive counterattack, supported by several tanks, from the road north of the sanatorium. They recovered the building from which they had been evicted after a bloody fight lasting several hours. At the end only one group of eleven Americans held out in an adjoining building, while B and C companies built up a line along a hedge not more than 30 yards away. The reconstituted 3d Battalion of the 119th was in position north of town, and the 2d Battalion was preparing to cut the road between Stoumont and La Gleize.

The next day the American attack on the building continued. Tank destroyer fire was placed with precision on the sanatorium, thanks to the American troops still holding down the annex of the main château. By afternoon the front of the sanatorium presented nothing but a series of gaping holes and the American infantry were able once more to work into two rooms. At this point a panther tank moved to the rear of the building, firing round after round of 88-mm. fire right through the ground floor. No further advance was possible. A bazooka team tried and failed to knock out the panther. Finally, by constructing a corduroy road the 1st Battalion was able to get several American tanks to the side of the building on a level with the sanatorium. Three Shermans and a tank destroyer moved right up to the sanatorium, sneaked around the right side, and knocked out the panther. The tank destroyer and the tanks then covered the withdrawal of 22 men who had been pinned down in the building. German possession of the sanatorium was still preventing the 1st Battalion from taking Stoumont from the west.

However, Jochen Peiper's problems were becoming severe. True, American efforts to attack from the east into La Gleize had been thwarted by the terrain characteristic that had frustrated German armor: steep road cuts that "canalized" the tanks. But supplies were running lower all the time, and the morning of the twenty-first the main hard-surfaced road from La Gleize to Stoumont was cut by a battalion of the 119th Infantry. Peiper still had a route open between the two towns, but it was a secondary dirt road, well to the south.

Major Hal D. McCown was now a prisoner of war, a prisoner of Jochen Peiper, whose command McCown's battalion had stopped near Chevron the evening of the eighteenth.

After Peiper had withdrawn to La Gleize that evening, McCown's 2d Battalion, 119th Infantry, had remained in place until relieved the next morning by Major General James M. Gavin's 82d Airborne Division. McCown and his troops had then been released to rejoin his regiment closing in on Peiper from the west and north.

The morning of Thursday, December 21, the day of the heavy fighting around St. Edouard's Sanatorium at Stoumont, was to be the time of the 119th's heavy punch. Elements of the 2d and 3d battalions had been ordered to hit Stoumont and the connecting road to La Gleize at dawn. Of the three battalions of the regiment, McCown's 2d was in by far the best condition.

The 2d Battalion jumped off on schedule in the morning, and McCown was successful in cutting the main road. He did not know it at the time, but the attack of the 3d Battalion on the right for some reason failed to go, and his unit was left astride the Stoumont-La Gleize road alone.

Concerned about lack of contact with the 3d Battalion, McCown, with a runner and radio operator, moved out beyond his right company to reconnoiter. All of a sudden, he sighted three Germans from a strong combat patrol. He dropped one; the other two disappeared in the bushes.

Then from his rear came the warning: *"Kommen sie hierher."* The Americans turned to see a whole line of Nazi infantry. Major McCown and his two men came out with their hands up.

McCown was escorted by his captors first to Stoumont, where he was interrogated briefly by an authoritative Nazi lieutenant colonel who bore all the earmarks of being in charge of the operation. Getting no information, the officer, ignoring the presence of his new prisoner, turned to the task of ordering a counterattack against McCown's battalion to the east.

Then McCown was moved down the circuitous dirt road to La Gleize, where he was questioned by a group of junior officers and later by a group of noncommissioned officers. None used violence; however, the threats of the sergeants were less subtle than those of the lieutenants. Both groups finally wearied of the effort, being well versed by now in McCown's name, rank, and serial number.

Eventually McCown found himself in a cellar adjoining a schoolhouse. Concluding that the safest place to rest would be against the wall, he leaned back and discovered a bookshelf over his head. In the dim light he found a book in English. He tried to pass the time by reading a battered edition of E. Phillips Oppenheim's *Great Impersonation.*

Around noon Peiper called his unit commanders together for a conference in the kampfgruppe's command post at the Château Froid Coeur. He had received a radio message from 1st SS Panzer Division headquarters that the division intended to advance to Trois Ponts to relieve him, but obviously neither Stoumont nor Cheneux could be held under prevailing conditions.

Peiper decided to pull back all available elements of the kampfgruppe around La Gleize and to keep open the bridge at Cheneux. With these dispositions he would be in the best position to make contact with the rest of the division if they could break across the Salm and Amblève rivers. Peiper's own command post in the castle and the prisoner of war cage were outside the new German perimeter, so all German walking wounded and the remaining unwounded prisoners were marched back to La Gleize late in the afternoon of December 21, preparing for the German forces' withdrawal. About 80 wounded Germans and all wounded Americans were left in the castle under the care of a German medical sergeant and two American medical privates.

Late in the afternoon American artillery began to pound La Gleize in earnest. Hal McCown, in his basement with four junior American officers and four German guards, ceased reading and pressed against the wall.

A large shell hit just outside the window above his head. Fragments were scattered through the basement; McCown's wall bulged inward and he was stunned.

He came to moments later to find a German guard, mortally wounded in the head, slumped over his body. Most of the other eight men in the room were either killed or wounded. McCown was unhurt, but the German's body lay heavily on him and only with great effort was he able to extricate his left arm. Once freed, he discovered that he had lost his wedding ring. A sentimental man despite his hard-boiled exterior, McCown was determined to find the ring. While he was searching frantically in the darkness a German warrant officer appeared. McCown grabbed him and, using his flashlight, finally located the ring in a pile of straw.

That evening Jochen Peiper ordered his senior American prisoner to be brought to his command post cellar in La Gleize. Confident that McCown could never get away, and apparently eager for some companionship, Peiper began to discuss his own plans. McCown noted that Peiper had given up trying to elicit information.

McCown was primarily concerned about what Peiper would do to the 149 prisoners, 15 of them wounded, still in the Nazi's custody. Although fairly certain that his captor was the leader of the unit that had committed the already infamous Malmédy Massacre, he kept his own counsel. The presence of many young toughs in Peiper's command did little to alleviate his worry. He told the obersturmbannführer that he himself was a professional soldier and realized his responsibility as senior PW for the welfare of his men, and demanded whether Peiper would abide by the Geneva Convention; Peiper declared that he would.

In the course of the long nocturnal conversation, McCown found Peiper to be an educated man, who spoke fluent English. Younger than most of the men of his staff, he even showed signs of some sense of humor. "When I get you back to Germany," Peiper said at one point, "I want to take you to the Russian front. You have no idea how fine it is to fight in a tiger tank, and how easy it is to kill Russians."

McCown continued to dig for intelligence information. Peiper, especially at first, exuded supreme confidence, uttering all of Hitler's line about new weapons, full commitment of the Luftwaffe in this operation, and the claim that the Nazi forces would most certainly take Antwerp. But before long it became apparent that Peiper really knew Germany could not win the war.

As the morning approached, McCown's concern for the safety of the American prisoners eased somewhat. Jochen Peiper had been saying that on the Russian front both sides treated each other like beasts; the Russians had been first to break the Geneva Convention, and the Germans retaliated. But the Germans fought by different rules on the eastern and western fronts. Then he asked if McCown had been treated fairly thus far. When he said he had, Peiper promised he would continue to be treated well.

So far as McCown could observe, Peiper's behavior toward his American prisoners at Stoumont and La Gleize was correct. Only once did he violate the rules by compelling some prisoners to load trucks under artillery fire. However, Peiper warned McCown that a few Americans had tried to escape and seven had been shot, and said he should instruct the American prisoners not to try to escape. This McCown refused to do.

The Americans were slow in detecting Peiper's withdrawal from Stoumont on Thursday, December 21. At 10:00 A.M., December 22, General Harrison once more came to the front line to assess how to attack the town. He noticed that nothing was happening near the sanatorium; then two civilians from the area reported that the Germans had vacated during the night. A reconnaissance patrol found the place deserted; 1st Battalion, 119th Infantry, occupied the town of Stoumont without firing a shot. Miraculously, none of the 200 people who had cowered in terror in the basement of St. Edouard's Sanatorium for several days was hurt. Two or three seriously wounded Americans had been left behind when the Germans pulled out.

As the Americans moved cautiously into Stoumont, Professor Ernest Natalis huddled in his basement with three other civilians. Suddenly he found himself confronted by several Americans, rifles at the ready. "There is no one but civilians here in the cellar," the professor cried out quickly in English.

The American in charge, mistaking Natalis' hasty pronunciation of "cellar" for the German word *keller,* thought the professor was a German civilian. It turned out that the soldiers had been shipped by truck so rapidly from their former front in Germany that they imagined they were still in that country rather than in Belgium.

Finally, when he had half convinced the Americans of his true nationality, Natalis broke out a bottle of his best wine. Before joining in, the soldiers made him take the first drink. Then, as they were all drinking heartily, Ernest Natalis departed on an errand to the doctor's house. Later he returned home to find that his entire wine supply had vanished.

Jochen Peiper's situation in La Gleize continued to deteriorate. Never one to sanction incompetence, he was seething over an order from division headquarters immediately to report the location of his dressing stations for the wounded. He had been admonished further: "Unless you report the amount of gas still on hand, you cannot hope for any additional gasoline." Maddeningly, his communication with headquarters was one-sided only. He could not contact Mohnke by radio, but all the German high command knew his whereabouts by listening in on American radio nets.

Fighting had now developed in each of the thirty houses in La Gleize. American artillery never ceased its merciless pounding; even during the night the fire progressively increased in intensity. At 2:00 P.M. on December 22, U.S. forces launched a concentric attack along both sides of all roads leading to the town. Peiper's men were able to repel these assaults, though during the day several houses changed hands. Several others were set afire by American incendiary shells, and the smoke screen added to the confusion.

General Harrison, anticipating a hard battle to reduce La Gleize, decided to wait a day and try to take it by surprise on the morning of Sunday, the twenty-fourth, coming in from the north out of heavily wooded territory. Patrols had found those woods clear of the enemy. For the main attack he planned to employ his still best-fitted unit, the 2d Battalion, 119th. During the twenty-third he contented himself with pounding the town. The 740th Tank Battalion poured heavy direct fire into the buildings of La Gleize from positions near the Château Coeur Froid (now occupied by Harrison and the Americans).

Peiper now concluded his situation was hopeless, and during the afternoon of the twenty-third decided to break out of the extremely restricted pocket. He held a discussion with his subordinate commanders. No food supplies had arrived since the first day of the attack. Three airplanes had dropped ammunition and fuel on December 22, but only 10 percent had reached the target area.

At 5:00 P.M., confirming his decision, Peiper received a message from higher headquarters ordering him to break out toward the east with his vehicles and men. Peiper realized that he could probably do so, but he would have to abandon all vehicles, all heavy equipment, all prisoners of war and wounded. He sent for Major Hal McCown.

He told McCown his orders and said he wanted to make a deal. If he agreed to turn loose all the American prisoners, except for McCown himself, who was to be kept as hostage, would McCown guarantee that the American commander who took La Gleize would release all German wounded? He would leave a German medic with those wounded; and upon their return to Peiper, McCown would be released.

"Colonel," McCown snapped, "that proposal is a farce. For one thing, I have no power to bind the American command regarding German PW's. All I can do is sign a statement that I heard you make this offer. I can't do anything more."

Peiper produced another captured American officer, Captain Bruce Crissinger, formerly commanding Company A, 823d TD Battalion. The two Americans signed McCown's statement, and the document remained with the captain.

Between two and three o'clock the following morning, the remnants of the once proud and arrogant Kampfgruppe Peiper, now down to 800 men, moved out in a southerly direction.[4] Of all the prisoners of war, Major Hal D. McCown was the only one Peiper took with him. According to McCown, the group moved so silently that they could have passed within 200 yards of an outpost without detection. Two hours after their departure, the column heard the first German tank blow up inside La Gleize. Within thirty minutes the entire area formerly occupied by Peiper's command was a holocaust. From La Gleize the remains of the kampfgruppe went south to the La Gleize railroad station, crossed the Amblève River over a small bridge, and struggled their way to the wooded areas of the U.S. 82d Airborne Division, which, spread out over 25 miles and in the process of withdrawing on orders of higher

---

[4] The exact strength of Peiper's battle group is unknown. However, as it was the largest of the four columns that constituted a 22,000-man division, it is likely that his original strength was considerably greater than 5,000 men.

headquarters, could hardly guard every crossing point over the Salm in strength.

McCown marched with Peiper through fourteen inches of snow. As they trudged along, bone tired, the sun came out and the skies cleared. Pausing for a moment, Peiper pointed to a fir tree, brilliantly lighted by the sun's reflection on the snow. Smiling somewhat sardonically, Peiper said, "Major, I promised you the other night I would get you a tree for Christmas. There it is."

Shortly after dark on Christmas Eve, the remains of Peiper's kampfgruppe crossed the road between Trois Ponts and Basse-Bodeux. Heading southward, the German unit surprised U.S. outposts just north of Bergeval—only about three miles south of Trois Ponts—at midnight. During the fight, McCown ducked into the bushes and escaped in the darkness.

Swimming across the icy and turbulent Salm River, Kampfgruppe Peiper made contact with German elements four miles east of the Americans. On December 26, the 1st SS Panzer Regiment was transferred to an area due west of St.-Vith for rehabilitation.

In the attack on La Gleize on December 24, the Americans of Task Force Harrison encountered only some 50 Germans who had stayed behind. The SS men fought fiercely, either because they had not received evacuation orders from Peiper or because they preferred to die rather than surrender.

Few survived. No Americans were killed in the engagement, and the 119th, to its surprise, found that many of the vehicles Peiper had left behind were in perfect working condition.[5] The U.S. prisoners, most of them from the 3d Battalion, 119th Infantry, were in good condition, shaken up mainly by the terrific pounding the U.S. artillery had given La Gleize while they were captive. Robert F. Hall, for example, recalls that the German guard simply set down his gun and surrendered.

The spearhead of the Sixth Panzer Army had failed. By nightfall of Christmas Day the 30th Division held an unbroken line north of the Amblève River, all the way from Stoumont Station to Malmédy.

Jochen Peiper, despite occasional errors, can hardly be blamed for the failure of his offensive. Its demise was due primarily to the inability of the 1st SS Panzer Division follow-up echelons to provide him with vitally needed fuel. Hitler apparently realized this; at the end of the war Peiper was a temporary division commander fighting on the Russian front.

After the war Peiper was tried for the atrocities committed by his men.[6]

[5] Thirty German tanks and more than a hundred half-tracks, however, had been put to the torch.

[6] Peiper was sentenced to death, but because of faulty evidence a mistrial was declared and he was set free on probation. Major Hal McCown, having been treated properly at Stoumont and La Gleize, was one of the chief witnesses for the defense.

In the process of intensive interrogation by American military historians, he was asked what he would do differently if the Ardennes offensive were to be conducted again. Peiper was specific:

1. Institute a speedier system of supplying gasoline.
2. Have no artillery preparation and keep the horse-drawn artillery from clogging the roads.
3. Attack with combat teams and tanks at the same time as the infantry. An unsupported infantry attack wastes too much time.
4. Reduce the length of each column, and instead of three columns, use twenty; then upon finding the softest spot, all columns should concentrate on this point.
5. Use more infantry on tanks.
6. Take along a bridging unit with each armored point.
7. Make each combat team completely self-sufficient.
8. Put a general at each street corner to regulate traffic. [Interviewer's note: Peiper indicated that there were two good reasons for such a move and one of them was not traffic control!] [7]

Baron Friedrich von der Heydte had come to the end of his rope. With the scattering of his drop early Sunday morning, December 17, he had realized he could never seize his objectives. Nevertheless, he had taken up positions in concealed areas near Malmédy and sent reconnaissance parties to Stavelot, Malmédy, Verviers, and even Werbomont, where one of his patrols observed the arrival of the 82d Airborne Division. Powerless, hiding by the road, he and his group had watched elements of the 1st and 30th Infantry divisions and the 7th Armored Division head southward. All this was intelligence of the highest potential use to Field Marshal Walther Model, but since von der Heydte's radio had been smashed in the drop—and since he had been denied carrier pigeons—he had no way of getting this information back to his superiors.

Eventually von der Heydte had decided to take his tiny group and try to make his way back through American lines toward Monschau and beyond. But he had run into several patrols that had obviously been dispatched to find him, so he decided to split up his group into smaller groups of three, and with his own executive and orderly, he set out eastward on December 21.

By now von der Heydte was in bad condition. Besides his broken arm, he feared his feet were frozen, and he had not eaten since leaving Germany. Mentally and physically exhausted, he turned to his two companions: "Go on without me. I'm too weak to continue."

The next day he stumbled into Monschau, found an occupied house, and

[7] MS Ethint # 10, Jochen Peiper interview, p. 24.

sent word of his whereabouts to the Americans. Baron von der Heydte surrendered.

Von der Heydte did not know what major contribution his paratroopers had made to the near panic rampant in the Allied rear areas. In the first couple of days, four men from Skorzeny's Einheit Steilau had been captured. Unaware still of their true mission, they had repeated the rumor current in their unit: the Skorzeny force was earmarked to assassinate Eisenhower, Montgomery, and Bradley. Now, with paratroopers scattered all through the Malmédy region, the rumors spread like wildfire. Americans were wasting valuable time quizzing each other to get proper identification; as for the three commanders involved, Allied concern resulted in considerable restriction of movement. General Bradley was hedged with elaborate security precautions, and his C-47 aircraft moved from the Luxembourg airport to a night fighter base forty minutes away from his command post. Field Marshal Montgomery was forced to obtain an American identification card, since the soldiers demanding identification were unfamiliar with British documents. In the middle of the battle at St.-Vith, General Clarke was held prisoner by American MP's for five hours on December 21: after all, under interrogation Clarke had placed the Chicago Cubs in the American League. (On being released, Clarke was asked by an MP for his autograph.)

But the victim who suffered most was General Eisenhower. For several months he had been driving everywhere around France with no more protection than that provided by an orderly and an aide. He found his greatest emotional release in his visits to the front lines to talk to Allied soldiers, and he made such visits as often as possible in light of his other responsibilities. But since December 20, he had been a virtual prisoner in his own command post. That day, an American colonel came to him certain of the existence of a plot on Eisenhower's life. He outlined it in great detail; his conclusions were supported by other members of the staff. Agreeing it was necessary to conform reasonably to the desires of the security people, Eisenhower remained in his headquarters for several days, leaving only when necessary but with the proviso that the protective detachments be held to a minimum.

On December 23 "General Ike" was visited by his naval aide, now a member of the Public Information Office, Captain Harry C. Butcher. Butcher, like others, automatically associated Skorzeny with the paratroopers. A group of about sixty men was said to have passed through the lines intending to assemble at the Café de la Paix in Paris, just around the corner from Butcher's own office at the Scribe Hôtel. There a force of German sympathizers and agents were supposed to meet with them to furnish information about General Eisenhower's living arrangements and habitual movements. Skorzeny's men were reported to be completely ruthless, prepared to sacrifice their lives, and all spoke fluent English.

Eisenhower was angry and frustrated by his imprisonment. He had, he confided, derived some satisfaction the day before by giving the slip to his guards and taking a walk around the snow-covered yard of his Versailles villa. Harry Butcher, a genial man on informal terms with his chief, chided Ike. "Now you know how it must feel to be President and always under the watchful eyes of the Secret Service," he joked.

Before Butcher left, he gave his chief a slightly ominous piece of news regarding Eisenhower's decision to split the Ardennes battlefield between Montgomery and Bradley. London papers were already referring to Montgomery's new responsibilities, implying that the British had been forced to come to the rescue of an American army in serious trouble. Eisenhower, however, realized this danger. Butcher recorded the conversation:

> Ike felt that such inferences were deplorable from the standpoint of Allied relationships, but his decision to give Monty temporary command of the two American armies was dictated by the exigencies of the battle. If we were to be so generous as to tell the German High Command that Monty commanded on the northern flank of the bulge and Bradley on the southern, the Germans, being familiar with Monty's and Bradley's different types of fighting, would be greatly pleased to have the information and could better plan their tactics. The command arrangement could be announced later, but not now.[8]

General Courtney Hodges, in his new command post at Tongres behind Liège, had a difficult human decision to make, not directly connected with his military operations.

The four men from Otto Skorzeny's Einheit Steilau who had been captured in American uniforms had been tried and condemned as spies. One, who had informed on the rest, was granted a stay of execution; and Hodges had been given verbal authority by Eisenhower through Bradley to proceed with the execution of the other three.

Too old and experienced a soldier to take such action without written authority, Hodges delayed twenty-four hours until the written authority arrived on Saturday the twenty-third. General Hodges gave the word.

In Eupen, about forty miles to the east, the condemned Germans awaited their fate. When the decision arrived, the three men took the news bravely.

"Do you have a last request?" they were asked.

"Yes. You have some German women prisoners. We would like to hear Christmas carols."

The request was granted. With the sound of the women's voices still in their ears, Skorzeny's three spies were shot.

For the troops of the U.S. 7th Armored and 106th Infantry divisions defending that large area to which St.-Vith has given its name, Tuesday, Decem-

[8] Harry Butcher, *My Three Years with Eisenhower* (New York: Simon & Schuster, 1946), p. 730.

ber 19, presented a situation similar to that faced by the 2d and 99th Infantry divisions to the north: consolidating new positions—several miles behind the original front line on the border.

Some order was emerging from the chaos that had reigned two days before. The area being defended by these two units, plus their attachments, was beginning to take the form of a large horseshoe, its axis running approximately northeast-southwest. The rounded, or forward, part of the horseshoe encompassed a fairly strong position, with Colonel Dwight Rosebaum's CCA, 7th Armored, on the north between Poteau and Rodt; Clarke's CCB, 7th Armored, in the center protecting St.-Vith; and Hoge's CCB, 9th Armored, tying in with Clarke on the south (see map, p. 284). The northern prong was also fairly secure along the road from Poteau and Vielsalm (on the Salm River). This part of the line was held by CCR of the 7th Armored and faced dense forests which protected it from concerted armored attack. As the prongs later were forced together, the horseshoe came to resemble and be called the "goose egg."

It was in the south, where the weakened 424th Infantry (106th Division) tied in with Hoge and bent back protecting Burg Reuland, that the danger existed. The regiment's flank was hanging in the air, vulnerable to attacks by the 116th Panzer Division to the south. The distance from Burg Reuland on the southeast to Poteau on the northwest was about ten miles, through dense woods cut by a single secondary road, the only line of retreat for thousands of men defending the partially completed horseshoe against attack from three directions.

The Germans did not attack the St.-Vith salient fiercely on the nineteenth. The reason for the comparative respite was hardly an indifference to the town's importance: the roads to the German rear were completely jammed.

At this point General Hasbrouck of the 7th Armored began to notice a probing tactic on the part of the Germans. During the day they exerted some pressure on every portion of his perimeter; whenever they found a point of the line strongly defended they would try another. At 9:30 A.M., for example, an attack was made toward St.-Vith from Hünningen on the north, apparently an effort to envelop Clarke's left flank. They fought for more than three hours, and finally withdrew, leaving one burning tank and 150 German dead.

Failing to find a soft spot in the north, the Germans proceeded to hit the southern flank, where they moved against Hoge's CCB of the 9th Armored. Before this attack even got going, three enemy tanks were knocked out and the rest of the force withdrew.

By now Hasbrouck knew that the forces attacking CCB of the 7th Armored Division consisted of the 18th and 62d Volksgrenadier divisions, according to Manteuffel's original plan; while northwest of CCB, in the Recht-Poteau area, there was at least a regiment from the 1st SS Panzer Division. Kampfgruppe Peiper had passed on to the north, and Krüger's 116th Panzer

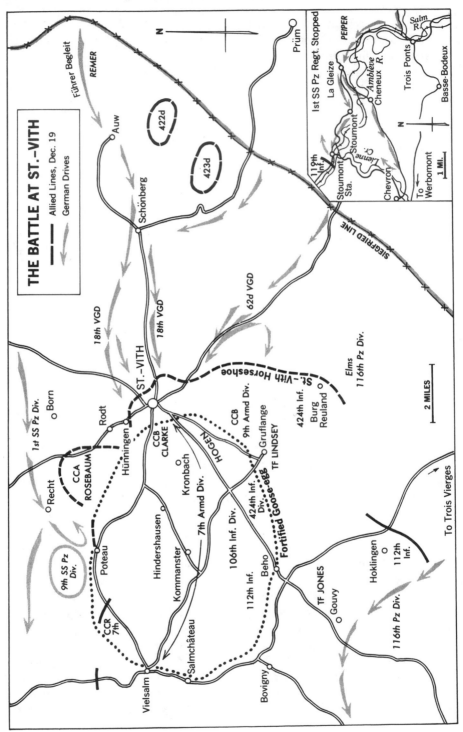

THE BATTLE AT ST.-VITH

Allied Lines, Dec. 19
German Drives

Prüm

Führer Begleit

REMER

Auw

422d

423d

Schönberg

SIEGFRIED LINE

62d VGD

18th VGD

18th VGD

St.-Vith Horseshoe

Elms
116th Pz. Div.

ST.-VITH

1st SS Pz. Div.

Born

Rodt

Hünningen

CCB
CLARKE

424th Inf.

Burg
Reuland

424th Inf.
Div.

CCB
9th Armd. Div.

Gruflange

TF LINDSEY

2 MILES

Recht

CCA
ROSEBAUM

Kronbach

HOGEN

7th Armd. Div.

106th Inf. Div.

Fortified Goose-egg

9th SS Pz.
Div.

Poteau

Hindershausen

Kommanster

Beho

112th Inf.

TF JONES

Gouvy

Hoklingen

112th
Inf.

To Trois Vierges

CCR
7th

Salmchâteau

Bovigny

116th Pz. Div.

Vielsalm

PEIPER

Salm
R.

1st SS Pz Regt. Stopped

La Gleize

Amblève
Cheneux R.

Trois Ponts

Basse-Bodeux

N

Stoumont

Stoumont
Sta.

Cr.
Lienne

Chevron

119th
Inf.

To
Werbomont

1 MI.

Division was bypassing the St.-Vith salient to the south. However, 19 enemy dead from the Führer Begleit Brigade had also been picked up by Clarke's men. On the south, elements of the 560th Volksgrenadier Division, part of Krüger's 58th Panzer Corps, were also identified as pushing against elements of the St.-Vith salient.

On the nineteenth Brigadier General Bruce C. Clarke was in his command post at Kronbach, two miles southwest of St.-Vith, when in strode Brigadier General William M. Hoge, commanding general of CCB, 9th Armored Division, the unit directly to Clarke's south. Despite his stony features and imperturbable demeanor, Hoge was in a state of some exasperation. He had withdrawn his positions over the Our River, where he had been sent to make contact with the 424th Infantry, and then tied in his left flank with Clarke. But he still had no idea of the overall situation.

"Who do I work for?" Hoge demanded. "I was sent down here by First Army to be attached to Jones and the 106th Infantry Division. Where is Jones? Now I don't know what the situation is. Maybe I had better go back to Bastogne and find out."

"Don't do that," Clarke blurted out. "Stay here. There's a lot of good fighting going on, and you're needed south of St.-Vith a lot more than you're needed in Bastogne."

This agreed. Clarke got through by radio to Hasbrouck in Vielsalm, informing him that CCB of the 9th Armored was working in cooperation with himself. No effort was made to decide who was in charge of whom. Until the situation could be clarified, they agreed that they would fight their own fight and work together.

One problem had to be solved, and solved quickly. A glance at the map made it obvious to both men that Hoge's command, jutting out to the east on the exposed side of a steep railroad bank, would be unable to withdraw on his own axis, should that become necessary. This eventuality was of concern to Clarke as well as to Hoge.

"Bill," Clarke said, "I know that there's a big buildup on my front and I'm going to be hit hard pretty quick. And when that happens I'm going to have to give up St.-Vith sooner or later. My suggestion is that you'd better get back to the west side of the railroad track. You'll have to do it at night, and you'll have to come all the way north to St.-Vith and back down again with your tanks."

This made sense to Hoge, who had been looking at his position with a jaundiced eye himself. That evening CCB, 9th Armored, made the move, which turned out to be a fortunate one, for Hoge later admitted that had he not pulled back behind the railroad track that evening he would have become a guest of the Germans for the rest of the war.

General Hoge's perplexity regarding the command setup between the 7th Armored Division and 106th Infantry Division was typical of the confusion that reigned. Although General Jones and his staff had pulled out of St.-Vith on the morning of the eighteenth, the roads between that town and Vielsalm had been so difficult that the 106th Division command post had not opened in Vielsalm until six o'clock that evening. Apparently direct communications between Jones and Hoge did not exist, even though Hoge's combat command had theoretically been attached to the 106th. Hoge's readjustment of his lines was done without consultation with the 106th Division; Clarke informed 7th Armored Division headquarters what was happening.[9]

One of the basic difficulties of the divisional situation was that Jones was senior to Hasbrouck, who had not yet received his second star. On the other hand, the bulk of the troops in the area were organic to the 7th Armored Division; the 106th had only one regiment left of its three, the 424th.

General Middleton had done little to clarify the situation when he had talked to General Hasbrouck on the subject the previous day.

"You two carry the ball up there for me," he had said. The two command posts were to be operational in the same town, Vielsalm, with neither in charge of the other.

But regardless of the confused command setup, the force in the St.-Vith position continued to grow. On the nineteenth Colonel Gustin Nelson's 112th Regimental Combat Team from the 28th Division was contacted by a patrol of the 7th Armored Division. The regiment withdrew to a position on the right of the 424th, forming a more or less continuous line on the south prong of the fortified horseshoe. The American line now ran nearly to Trois Vierges. Although spaces existed between units, particularly between the 424th and 112th, at least the main roads leading northwestward into the position were defended. Between Trois Vierges and Vielsalm, however, the open end of the horseshoe was undefended and would remain vulnerable until U.S. units to the west could drive forward and contact Hasbrouck's rear.

But Hasbrouck regarded the 106th, with its pickup, decimated units, as shaky. On the nineteenth, having learned of attacks by the 560th Volksgrenadier Division on his southwest flank as far west as Gouvy, he formed Task Force Jones, named after Lieutenant Colonel Robert B. Jones, commander of the 814th Tank Destroyer Battalion.[10] With this task force he garrisoned Gouvy, Deifeld, and Chérain. In addition he was finally able to constitute a task force from the remnants of the 14th Cavalry Group, and he stationed the unit, Task Force Lindsey (named for Captain Franklin P. Lindsey) behind the 424th Infantry as a backup. In addition to these units, 7th Armored Division picked up the 434th Armored Field Artillery Battalion on the after-

---

[9] Confusion was not limited to combat command level. On the hill east of St.-Vith, Lieutenant Colonel Tom Riggs of the 81st Engineers considered himself under command of the 106th Division until the evening of the nineteenth when Lieutenant Colonel H. G. Fuller, 38th Armored Infantry, took command of the sector.

[10] Other elements came from the 17th Tank Battalion, the 440th Armored Field Artillery Battalion, and armored, infantry, tank, engineer, and cavalry elements.

noon of the nineteenth and two batteries of the 965th Field Artillery Battalion. Up to this time artillery support had been furnished principally by Lieutenant Colonel Roy Udell Clay's valiant 275th Armored Field Artillery Battalion.

Thus, at the end of Tuesday, December 19, the St.-Vith salient was beginning to show signs of order though it consisted of only one armored division, a truncated and shaken infantry division, a separate regiment and armored combat command—and was provided minimum field artillery support and reinforced with such miscellaneous units as Task Force Jones and the small Task Force Lindsey. But already Manteuffel's attack on St.-Vith was three days behind schedule.

On December 20 it was becoming apparent that the Germans were determined to take St.-Vith soon. In addition to the 18th and 62d Volksgrenadier divisions assigned the original task, many other units were identified that day. The 2d Panzer Grenadier Regiment of the 1st SS Panzer Division was still attacking on the north at Poteau. The attacks of the 18th and 62d Volksgrenadier divisions were spending themselves against Clarke at St.-Vith and against Hoge on the south. In addition, elements of the 116th Panzer Division were attacking against the 424th Infantry at Burg Reuland, and two regiments of the 560th VG Division and elements of 2d Panzer Division were bypassing far to the west. Word was received that a motley collection of stragglers, under Lieutenant Colonel Robert O. Stone, had formed a task force at Gouvy. When incorporated into Task Force Jones, Stone turned over 350 prisoners and the stores at the railhead.

Even the trains—the rear elements—of the 7th Armored Division, fighting as infantry, were beating off other German attacks as far west as Samrée, 13 miles beyond the Salm River. At this time General Hasbrouck considered the 424th Infantry Regiment 20 percent effective and the troops at St.-Vith about 50 percent effective. Hasbrouck concluded correctly that the Germans on the north were bypassing westward; but on the south Krüger's corps was trying to turn the flank and destroy the position of the horseshoe.

Amid all this Hasbrouck still had no idea where First Army headquarters was located. He remained out of contact with friendly troops to his rear.

Hasbrouck dispatched his division chemical officer, Lieutenant Colonel Fred Schroeder, to try to clarify the situation, his task being to locate First Army CP. Schroeder carried with him a letter to Hasbrouck's friend, Major General William B. Kean, chief of staff of Hodges' First Army:

Dear Bill:

I am out of touch with VIII Corps, and understand XVIII Airborne Corps is coming in.

My division is defending the line St.-Vith–Poteau inclusive. CCB, 9th Armored Division [Hoge], and 424th Infantry Regiment of the 106th Division [Reid], and the 112th Infantry Regiment of the 28th Division [Nelson] are on my right, and hold from St.-Vith (exclusive) to Holdingen. Both infantry regiments are in bad shape. My right flank is wide open except for some reconnaissance elements, TD's, and stragglers we have collected into Two German divisions, 116 Panzer and 560 Volksgrenadier, are just starting defense teams at road centers as far back as Cheram [Chérain], inclusive, to attack northwest with their right on Gouvy. I can delay them the rest of today *maybe* but will be cut off by tomorrow.

VIII Corps has ordered me to hold, and I will do so, but need help. An attack from Bastogne to the northeast will relieve the situation and, in turn, cut the bastards off in the rear. I also need plenty of air support. Am out of contact with VIII Corps so am sending this to you. Understand 82d Airborne Division is coming up on my north and the north flank is not critical.

Bob Hasbrouck [11]

After a long hard ride, Colonel Schroeder finally located First Army command post, then at Chaudfontaine. When he entered the office of the commanding general, an important conference was in progress: Field Marshal Montgomery, who had just taken over the First and Ninth U.S. armies, was having his first meeting with General Hodges.

Montgomery had come to First Army headquarters with an attitude, as one aide put it, of "Christ cleansing the temple." Hodges, on the other hand, was understandably weary. But he was well acquainted with the situation and had his wits about him. Montgomery, in British fashion, was used to supervising the actions of subordinates very closely. He had developed the habit—which many American commanders disliked—of sending liaison officers practically to the front and using them as a direct channel for information. He ran his battles in great detail.

But with all his "peacock" attitude, Montgomery was basically more conservative than the self-effacing Hodges. Hodges was concerned about holding the road junction of St.-Vith as long as possible and of rescuing the 7th Armored and 106th Infantry divisions from their isolated position. Montgomery was primarily concerned with the plight of the two American divisions. He had decided that Ridgway's XVIII Airborne Corps could not attack successfully toward Vielsalm and contact the 7th Armored rear. As Montgomery expected the Germans to turn north and try to cross the Meuse at Liège, his solution to the problem was simply to send a message through to Hasbrouck telling him to withdraw the 7th Armored—somehow. Hodges demurred.

When General Kean read Hasbrouck's letter aloud, Hodges stiffened his position. "In the light of this new information," he said, "Ridgway will *have* to keep driving forward to St.-Vith to Hasbrouck's relief."

[11] At this time General Hasbrouck had no idea of the situation at Bastogne. He has since been amused at his request for reinforcements from that area in view of what actually was happening to the south.

Hodges' quiet logic was indisputable, and Montgomery agreed. Ridgway would attack to the southeast until he could reach Vielsalm and insure an escape corridor for Hasbrouck's men. Then, as soon as possible, the 7th Armored and 106th would withdraw to the northwest, thus straightening and shortening First Army's defense line.

"After all, gentlemen," Montgomery concluded, "you can't win the big victory without a tidy show." [12]

When Schroeder arrived back at General Hasbrouck's command post in Vielsalm, he brought with him a message which, of course, was welcome news: "Ridgway, with armor and infantry, is moving from west to gain contact with you. When communication is established you come under command of Ridgway. You retain under your command units of 106th Infantry Division (R.C.T. 112) and CCB 9th Armored Division. Ridgway has command post vicinity of Werbomont. He holds Malmédy-Stavelot-Trois Ponts."

This message sought to clarify the command relationship by placing elements of the 106th Division under the command of the 7th Armored Division. That such action was taken is not surprising. The view from First Army is recorded by General Kean:

> At 1:30 this afternoon General Montgomery arrived for his first conference with General Hodges. . . . During General Montgomery's stay a Lieutenant Colonel arrived from the 7th Armd Div to report that the 7th and 9th Armd Divs together are holding firm at St.-Vith along the approximate line: St.-Vith–Holdingen. Contact between the 82d and 7th Armd and between the 82d A/B and what remains of the 106th was made tonight although not in strength. The two regiments of the 106th are still cut off and there is no word from them. The 112th Inf which has performed magnificently under Colonel Rudder [13] is now attached to the 7th Armd Div.

Word of the 7th Armored Division's situation rapidly reached SHAEF. That same day General Eisenhower sent a message to General Hasbrouck: "The magnificent job you are doing is having a great beneficial effect on our whole situation. I am personally grateful to you and wish you would let all of your people know that if they continue to carry out their mission with the splendid spirit they have so far shown, they will deserve well of their country."

The records of the evening of December 20 are notable for two examples of the valor commonly being displayed along the front. That night 68 men and two officers, led by Lieutenant Long of the I & R Platoon, 423d Regiment, having passed through the German lines, arrived at the command post

---

[12] John Toland, *Battle* (New York: Random, 1959), p. 162.

[13] This was an error in General Kean's diary. The 112th was commanded by Colonel Nelson.

of CCB, 7th Armored Division. Long informed his questioners that the commanding officers of the two 106th Division regiments on the Schnee Eifel were preparing to surrender. Orders were being given to destroy arms and equipment, though anyone wishing to make his way back to friendly lines was authorized to leave; this the 70 men had done. The news from the Schnee Eifel was black. General Clarke, admiring the spirit of these infantrymen, established an assembly point in a schoolhouse, where they were given rations and supplies and rest. They were back in the line within twenty-four hours.

That same night the Germans penetrated a portion of Clarke's sector, and Troop B of the 87th Cavalry Reconnaissance Squadron, constantly engaged since Clarke had met them at the crossroads the night of the seventeenth, were isolated. About midnight, Sergeant L. H. Ladd brought back 46 men, all that remained of the troop. Obviously exhausted, Ladd nevertheless insisted on seeing General Clarke.

"General," Ladd demanded, "I want to get it from you personally that Troop B was ordered out of the positions we were holding. Me and my men had decided we were not leaving and I just want to get it straight that we were ordered out by you."

Clarke assured Ladd that he personally had issued the order for withdrawal. The sergeant, satisfied, moved out into the darkness to occupy a new position in the defense line building west of St.-Vith.

Lieutenant Oliver Patton, formerly of the 423d Infantry, was lying in a basement in Radscheid, ten miles east of St.-Vith, when the Germans arrived. Soon the room was full of Germans and American prisoners. Patton and Lieutenant Brownell, who was the more seriously wounded, were carried on a litter by American prisoners to a blacktop road.

All of a sudden a captured American jeep appeared, driven by a furious German officer, who was frantically trying to shift out of "low-low" gear. In a rage, the officer asked if anybody could help him. Someone who could speak English—Patton could never remember who—struck a bargain. If Patton would show the German officer how to get the jeep into operation, the officer would deliver Patton and Brownell to a German aid station. This proposition seemed all right: the prisoners who had been carrying him were exhausted, and he was in pain. Ollie demonstrated how to shift the gears of the jeep and was duly placed prone on the hood.

Before the jeep pulled away, Patton happened to spy a sergeant from his former platoon, and for some reason gave him all the money in his pocket. Patton felt somehow that the sergeant would be in a better position to dispose of the money than he himself.

Patton and Brownell were taken to the small, picturesque town of Prüm. The aid station was so full that many wounded—German and American alike —were lying outside on the ground in the falling snow. After some time on the ground, Patton was moved inside the aid station and questioned. He knew little of the tactical situation and what he knew he would not tell. Evacuated through German medical channels,[14] Lieutenant Oliver B. Patton was to spend the rest of the war as a prisoner of the Third Reich.

Not knowing that the 7th Armored and the 99th Infantry divisions were fighting for their very lives, he long remained bitter that those two units had failed to come to the rescue of the two regiments of the 106th on the Schnee Eifel. But, though wounded, in a way Patton was lucky. He was spared the humiliation that befell the 422d and 423d Infantry regiments, the largest surrender of American troops since Bataan in 1942.

Early in the morning on December 18, Lieutenant Colonel Joseph Puett was ordered to report to Colonel Charles Cavender's command post, 423d Infantry. He took with him his executive officer, Major William J. Cody Garlow. Garlow, a grandson of the famed Buffalo Bill, was a rugged young man of thirty from Wyoming who, in civilian life, often wore cowboy clothes, a habit that belied the fact that he was a graduate of Harvard Law School.

On arrival at Colonel Cavender's CP, Puett and Garlow found the rest of the battalion commanders of the 423d prepared to receive a field order. Cavender had just received a message two and a half days old, couched in dramatic terms, implying that the eyes of all America were focused on the regiments in the Schnee Eifel. The message went on to order the 422d and 423d to attack west toward Schönberg and fight their way out of the ring of Germans.

But when Cavender came to issuing the order, Garlow was jolted. The time was about 8:00 A.M., and Cavender apparently expected to launch a full-scale attack by nine thirty. How, Garlow reasoned, could such an attack possibly be organized and coordinated with Descheneaux's 422d?

Garlow was in the habit of speaking his mind: "Don't you think—" he began.

"You're not supposed to think," came the curt reply.

Puett and Garlow departed, puzzled but resolved to do their best to get the attack under way.

Later in the day, the 2d Battalion attacked toward Schönberg, but by this time, with the German 62d VG in place, Puett found movement impossible. He sent a message to regimental headquarters to ask for the 1st Battalion to attack on his left. Garlow was sent to guide the battalion into position, but to no avail. The two battalions were withdrawn; they were molested little during the night.

Just before daylight on the morning of the nineteenth, Colonel Cavender once more assembled his three battalion commanders and his staff for a

[14] Patton later learned, to his sadness, that Brownell died somewhere near Prüm.

council on the next action. They were all in a small, open field, and German artillery was pouring in. The commanding officer of the 1st Battalion, standing next to Bill Garlow, was killed instantly by a shell fragment in his chest. Resisting the tendency to run for the woods—where they all would be in danger from artillery bursts in the trees—Garlow stood up between incoming volleys and shouted to the rest to stay where they were. At least, lying flat on the ground, the group was comparatively safe—exposed only to direct hits.

Once the immediate danger was past, Garlow, in command of the 2d Battalion now that Puett had been separated from the unit, went to Cavender and advised that the two regiments coordinate their attack westward. This meant that the 423d would have to make its way north across the hilly Schnee Eifel to join the 422d.

"O.K.," Cavender said. "Take your battalion and lead us to the 422d."

As was his habit, Bill Garlow moved out at the head of the 2d Battalion, and in the course of the morning joined Descheneaux's 422d. On counting heads, however, it turned out that those following behind were only remnants. Descheneaux's command in essence consisted of the 422d and one battalion and other bits of the 423d.

On its way toward Schönberg the whole command found itself in a large depression in the side of the hill, extremely vulnerable to artillery. Soon reports came in that the Germans were preparing to lay in that heavy artillery, so in the early afternoon, Descheneaux called together all the field-grade officers. They met in a bunker in the Siegfried Line—some sprawling, some sitting, while the wiry, peppery little colonel stood dramatically on his feet.

"Gentlemen," he said, "we are in a bad fix. We are miles behind enemy lines and our food and ammunition situation is bad. I would like to have your views on what we should do."

After listening to some discussion on the possibilities of continuing the attack, Descheneaux came to his conclusion: "My opinion, gentlemen, is that we should surrender. Does anyone disagree?" Not one officer raised an objection. The opinion of all—as Garlow was to recall later—was that the force should surrender. Painful as it was, only thus could they save countless lives from the German artillery.

But Descheneaux offered another out. Those who wanted to try to make it back through the German lines were free to do so. Few took advantage of the opportunity.

But Garlow began conferring with a sergeant and a lieutenant, and the three plotted their escape. Garlow was confident that with the confusion in the German lines, they could make it through.

However, his plans were upset when Descheneaux asked for a volunteer to go through the German lines to negotiate the surrender. Descheneaux seemed to look straight at Garlow—or so Garlow thought. "O.K., Colonel, I'll go." So saying, he handed over his .45 pistol to Descheneaux, borrowed two white handkerchiefs, and took off by himself, darting on a zigzag path down the side of the hill, waving his handkerchiefs wildly.

He did not think to bring a man with him who could speak German. As Bill Garlow entered the German position, he suddenly found himself engulfed by enemy soldiers scrambling out of their foxholes. In a moment, Garlow's prized possessions—his watch, several candy bars, and a pint of bourbon whiskey—had been stripped from him. Not speaking German, he was unable to explain that he had come to negotiate a surrender, so he was relieved to be approached by a short, spare, erect German lieutenant—with crew-cut hair. As the lieutenant stepped up to him, stopped, clicked his heels, and gave the Hitler salute, the soldiers fell back. Garlow dropped his arms—they had been raised in surrender—and returned the salute.

"Major," the lieutenant said, "aren't you glad the war is over for you?"

Garlow's voice choked with emotion. "It doesn't look much like it, does it?"

But, almost at once, Garlow pulled himself together. He snapped at the lieutenant: "Quite obviously you are a regular army officer. I demand that your men return my property." A sharp bark from the lieutenant, and back came the watch, the candy bars, even the pint of bourbon.

In the course of a brief conversation—the lieutenant spoke perfect English Garlow admitted to representing 400 to 500 men who wished to surrender. He was afraid to admit that the figure was about ten times that many, including the artillery battalions, for fear the Germans might be tempted to continue the fire. Above all, the crucial thing to Garlow was preventing a heavy artillery barrage; even as they spoke, fire was taking lives of the exposed Americans.

Recognizing Garlow's sense of urgency, the German lieutenant pointed to a spot about three fourths of a mile away, where, he said, the German fire direction center was located. They started out together, but Garlow, a fast runner and an expert fence jumper, soon outdistanced his young companion. When the German caught up, he laughed. "You are in better shape than I am, Major." They went into the bunker in the fire direction center.

As it turned out, the German major in command also spoke English and agreed to raise the fire until surrender could be negotiated. Turning to the lieutenant, he snapped some orders in German which, Garlow soon learned, charged the lieutenant with conducting a patrol of nine or ten men to accompany Garlow back to the American positions.

Faced with a tense situation, the young volksgrenadier's personality instantly changed. He jabbed Garlow viciously in the back with his Schmeisser burp gun. "If this is a trick, Major, you're dead." Garlow winced under the painful blow; later it turned out that his chivalrous enemy had broken two of his ribs.

But the lieutenant's former friendly attitude returned. Keeping Garlow covered, he let the American guide his patrol back up the hill to Descheneaux's CP on the Schnee Eifel, where they found that Descheneaux had prepared everything. Weapons were already broken.

The German lieutenant looked around him and observed the number of American troops milling around. "Major, you told me you had only four hundred to five hundred men here."

"Well, there may be a few more."

"I understand," the lieutenant said quietly.

Without delay, the lieutenant marched up to Descheneaux and gave the Hitler salute. Descheneaux returned a salute of his own. With many Americans in tears, Colonel Descheneaux sealed the fate of most of the American command on the Schnee Eifel.

"The troops are ready to surrender."

By the evening of December 20, the German High Command was feeling the effects of the St.-Vith salient intensely. This "thumb in the throat" was preventing a linkup of the Fifth and Sixth Panzer armies, both of which had driven far to the west. Furthermore, with St.-Vith denied the Germans the resultant road jams had caused an acute shortage of gasoline and ammunition in units well to the west. Both Model and Manteuffel wanted Lucht's 66th Korps, as well as Remer's Führer Begleit Brigade, free for other missions. Accordingly that evening Sepp Dietrich issued orders to the 2d SS Panzer Korps to move to the south so that parts of that corps could assist Manteuffel in taking St.-Vith without delay.

Lucht was ordered to make an all-out attack on the twenty-first. During the night of December 20–21 American troops in St.-Vith could hear vehicles massing to the northeast and to the south. The time was coming near.

On December 21 at 11:00 A.M., the assault was launched. A German artillery barrage fell on the northern and eastern portions of Clarke's and Hoge's combat commands. By 1:00 P.M. the entire line was aflame with German artillery, rockets, tanks, and infantry. The situation on the right flank of the division was also critical. Hoge's CCB, 9th Armored, requested assistance, and General Hasbrouck committed Task Force Lindsey, the only reserve he had thus far been able to hold, who restored the line and were quickly recovered by Hasbrouck. He needed some reserve for this mobile type of warfare.

But even in the midst of the heaviest fighting there were matters of human relations to consider. Major General Alan Jones, incensed that his 106th Infantry Division was generally considered to consist of only a collection of remnants, protested to Hasbrouck. To correct this impression, Hasbrouck, always a gentleman, wrote again to his friend at First Army:

Major General W. B. Kean
Chief of Staff, First Army

Dear Bill:

Upon receipt of operational instructions of the XVIII Corps a few hours ago which attach elements of the 106th Infantry Division to my Division it occurs to me that my hurried note of yesterday may have given you an erroneous impression of the status of the 106th Division. It, with its own 424th RCT; Combat Command B, 9th Armored Division; and the 112th RCT of the 28th Division attached is on my right and is holding the line from St.-Vith (exclusive) to a point approximately 2000 yards south of Holdingen. Two regiments of the 106th were cut off south of Schönberg and we arrived too late to help them out. Major General Alan Jones commands the 106th and has his CP in the same town with me, Vielsalm. He has control of his command and he and I have been cooperating and getting along alright.

Inasmuch as I have more troops available than Jones, I have put what I could scrape up in his zone along our south flank to try to protect our open flank. General Jones is a Major General and I am a Brigadier. His being attached to me makes it look as though he had failed in some respect and I want to put myself on record as saying he is in the saddle in control of his outfit and that we are cooperating in the best possible way. If my note gave any other impression, I want to correct it at once before an injustice is done.

Sincerely,
R. W. Hasbrouck
Brigadier General, USA
Commanding

On the copy he sent to General Jones, Hasbrouck added the following P.S.:

This is being dispatched at once with a copy to General Ridgway. I hope it will correct any misimpression my note to General Kean may have caused. However I believe the telegram I got from First Army was dated at 1253 while the note I sent was not dispatched from here until 1230 and could not have reached there prior to that time.

Hasbrouck

In the meantime another development proved a great comfort to Hasbrouck: a representative of Field Marshal Montgomery arrived in his area and was now reporting all the action in detail to his chief. In addition, regular communication had been established with General Ridgway's XVIII Airborne Corps. Hasbrouck no longer felt out of communication or lost.

The Germans were not to be denied St.-Vith on December 21. Late in the day they launched three major attacks, each directed along a main road leading into the town. At about 5:00 P.M. they attacked along the Schönberg road from the east; at 6:30 P.M. they came down the Malmédy road from the north; at 8:00 P.M. an attack started from the southeast along the Prüm road. Each was preceded by an intense artillery barrage, lasting from fifteen to thirty-five minutes, closely followed by infantry and tanks.[15]

General Clarke had divided his front into two sectors. The critical eastern sector along the Schönberg road was being held by various units—reconnaissance, tank destroyer, and engineer—attached to Fuller's 38th Armored Infantry Battalion. Fuller had established his forward command post in a stone house beside the road, about 800 yards behind the front. Tom Riggs was with him, serving as executive. Communications were good. Fuller's front was organized into several task forces, of which Major Don Boyer's was one.

Finally came the all-out assault. In Major Boyer's words:

> The Krauts kept boring in, no matter how fast we decimated their assault squads. As fast as we would kick back one assault wave, another would return.... It certainly looked as if the Germans were determined that they were coming through, but their spirit alone was not enough to sustain them against the merciless hail of small arms fire which we were hurling at them.
>
> All machine guns were employing swinging traverse and taking a deadly toll.... But again and again there was a flare of flame and smoke (the explosion could not be heard over the general din) as some Kraut got in close enough to heave a grenade into a machine gun crew or to launch a dread Panzerfaust. (One caliber .50 squad which heretofore had been dishing out a deadly hail of fire all along the front, was hit by a Panzerfaust which struck the barrel halfway between the breech and the muzzle. The gunner fell forward on the gun with half his face torn off; the loader had his left arm torn off at the shoulder and was practically decapitated; while the gun commander was tossed about 15 feet away from the gun to lie there quite still.)
>
> The men were magnificent, and as long as there were targets, their fire never ceased. Whenever a machine gun was silenced by having its crew killed off, other men leaped from their holes to take over the gun so that its devastating fire could be continued. Artillery: we were using it like mortars and never before had I seen artillery do such damage with almost no casualties because of "shorts." As fast as Higgins, Holland or Rogers (new CO of B trp, after Stewart was wounded Tuesday night) called for fire, I relayed the request to Shanahan (FO from 275th, who had reported to me just as the noon attack

---

[15] This description centering largely on the problems of CCB, 7th Armored Division, should not give the impression that other units were not under the same sort of punishment. On December 21, 1944, Corporal Horace M. Thorne of Troop D, 89th Reconnaissance Squadron, from General Hoge's CCB, 9th Armored, earned the Congressional Medal of Honor. Attempting to clear German forces out of the heavily wooded area, Thorne cut down two of the enemy, left his position, and crept forward to kill two more Germans with hand grenades. Moving his machine gun to the rear deck of a knocked-out German tank, he fired rapid bursts, killing or wounding eight of his enemies. Finally his gun jammed, and Thorne was himself cut down by German small-arms fire concentrated upon him. His action, while outstanding, was representative of that occurring all across the front.

started). Within 2–4 minutes we could hear the shells whistling over our heads. . . .

Frankly, I didn't see how our men could stand up to this pounding without any cessation and no replacements. . . . And always there were more Germans, and more Germans, and then more Germans! Where they were all coming from, I did not know but it looked as if battalion after battalion must have been massed up behind the original assault waves. That's the only way they would be able to keep on attacking, attacking, and reattacking for better than 1½ hours.

At ten minutes to seven, Boyer called Colonel Fuller to report that his lines were still holding, that a few Germans had gotten through but his men could take care of them. He thought he could hold through the night, although he must have relief in the morning. But at 7:00 P.M., the werfers starting coming in again. Once more a systematic raking of the entire area began, and knowing that before long he would have more tanks and infantry on him, Boyer no longer felt that he could hold back an assault such as this promised to be. This looked like *it*.

The German attack continued. For an hour the 38th Armored Infantry kept the Schönberg road under heavy machine gun and bazooka fire. Although a tiger tank was destroyed and German dead lined the ditches on both sides of the road, their comrades still kept pressing forward to follow their tanks. Boyer's men were unable to stop all of them, and the Americans, in their turn, were paying a terrific price. No machine gun or bazooka team lasted more than ten or fifteen minutes; each gun had already been manned by at least several teams. As soon as one team was wiped out it was replaced by another, which was killed in turn a few minutes later.

Finally Boyer refused to pay the price any longer. He directed B Company to cease replacing bazooka teams along the road. An hour later, at 10:00 P.M., he learned that Colonel Fuller's forward CP had been wiped out and Fuller evacuated. At least eight panther and tiger tanks had entered St.-Vith, and German infantry were reportedly pouring in after them. Boyer attempted to send patrols across the Schönberg road to learn the situation in A Company of the 23d Infantry and A Company of the 38th Infantry, but they could not make it across the road.

Major Boyer was now with Lieutenant Colonel Tom Riggs, who had come up to the thick of the fighting. Using the radio of the field artillery forward observer, Riggs reported to General Clarke: "Road cut. At least eight heavy tanks and infantry in town. What are our orders?"

About forty-five minutes later he received an answer: "To Riggs or senior officer present: Reform; save what vehicles you can; attack to the west to St.-Vith; we are forming a new line west of town."

Boyer called his company commanders together and told them the gist of Clarke's orders. The company commanders demurred. Their men, they insisted, were in no shape to launch such a westward attack. Boyer agreed; he decided to peel off to the right, heading the command south so as to avoid the town. The men were to carry all personal and crew-served weapons, and he sent a messenger to the mortar platoon with word to destroy their vehicles but keep their mortars and bipods. Some of the tank units in support of the forward infantry companies had already left, and there was hope that they had passed through St.-Vith ahead of the German tanks. One infantry company had five men so severely wounded that they could not be moved. An aidman volunteered to stay with them; in the morning he would try to surrender the group to a German medical detachment.

Giving his orders to move out, Boyer worked his way down to the right, informing each platoon leader along the way. When he reached one company, he learned that their right flank had vanished. The Prüm road, over which his command would have to pass to make it south of St.-Vith, had been cut. German tanks and infantry had been pouring up the road into St.-Vith and westward for more than two hours.

By this time snow had been falling for more than an hour, giving every indication it would be almost knee-deep by morning. When the column came down the hill, Boyer swung out through the trees, heading west. Progress was slow through the thick forest. Of the estimated 150 men that Boyer had left, more than half were wounded, and all were suffering from the pounding they had taken all day. Occasionally German patrols passed within only a few feet; as the gray light of dawn began to come, Boyer's troops were still not across the Prüm road.

Now Boyer issued orders to destroy all but personal weapons, break up into small groups of five to ten, and attempt to infiltrate back to the west.

Few were successful. The town of St.-Vith was lost. Riggs, Boyer, and a force of no fewer than 600 officers and men had to be written off as prisoners.

With the American position east of St.-Vith broken, General Lucht's 66th Korps continued to press its attack. Fortunately for the Americans, the German units within the town became jammed up, temporarily immobilized. But Remer's Führer Begleit Brigade was in a position to avoid St.-Vith and launch a tank attack from the north toward the town of Rodt. At 2:00 A.M., December 22, Remer launched his assault. Resistance by American service troops was fierce, but by 11:35 A.M., the town was captured, splitting Rosebaum's Combat Command A from Clarke's Combat Command B. The nine-hour battle was a grim affair in which every possible man—cooks, drivers, radio operators—was employed to augment the defense.

With Rodt fallen, Clarke pulled back his left flank to protect Hinderhausen, a key position on the emergency exit route to Kommanster and Vielsalm. But the two combat commands were out of contact, and Clarke had moved his command post back to Kommanster and sent all unessential vehicles to the rear. By nightfall his line was being held by the 87th Cavalry Reconnaissance Squadron on the left, the 31st Tank Battalion in the center, and the 17th Tank Battalion on the south.

In his command post in Vielsalm on the morning of the twenty-second, Brigadier General Hasbrouck was preparing a message to Major General Matthew B. Ridgway, commander of XVIII Airborne Corps. Hasbrouck was disturbed about a document he had just received from Ridgway's headquarters: a plan for a perimeter defense of the presently occupied area between St.-Vith and Vielsalm. The basic assumption was that both the 7th Armored and 106th divisions would remain in place, surrounded and cut off from other friendly forces and supplied by air, and the gap to the west would be held by Task Forces Jones and Lindsey. The division reserve, located at Kommanster, was to consist of the depleted 424th Infantry, minus its 1st Battalion. On the bottom of the sheet of paper on which the plan was pasted were scribbled the words: "XVIII Corps (Airborne) order for final defense of area 21 Dec 1944."

Hasbrouck had talked to Clarke about this tentative plan, and neither officer wanted any part of it. Their troops were exhausted and spread out; they needed relief. Furthermore the circle (nearly ten miles in diameter) contained a mass of forest and only one decent road, running northwest-southeast. This was no place to conduct a mobile defense. Whoever had drawn up the plan, they concluded, was thinking in terms of supply requirements for the lighter airborne divisions, not for armor. The outspoken Clarke had irreverently renamed the plan Custer's Last Stand. (See photo of XVIII Corps plan.)

For the moment, at least, Clarke and Hasbrouck were becoming somewhat exasperated with their immediately higher headquarters. This attitude toward senior commands is hardly rare in the Army; it tends to be a rule. But in this case there were reasons. Although Corps plan for an encircled "goose egg" was becoming almost a reality, the plan undoubtedly confirmed the tankers' suspicions that infantrymen, particularly the airborne, were unaware of or unsympathetic to the problems of armor. Furthermore, some of the difficulty lay in the personality of Matthew Ridgway.

Ridgway was by any yardstick a strong commander. A large, tough, athletic man, somewhat older than the airborne troopers of his day (class of 1917 in West Point), he prided himself on being a soldier's soldier. And although a capable, rounded professional—one of the few in the Operations Division Eisenhower had relied on in the early days of the war—he set aside his rather quiet, almost courtly manner when he went into combat.

Ridgway did not indulge in developing a glamorous image for himself, unlike his parachuting junior James Gavin, but he wore a harness with grenades fastened to the front and seemed to derive relaxation from going on frequent personal hunting expeditions in search of enemy tanks. Sometimes his bazooka bagged one. This was dangerous business, but Ridgway lived by a lighthearted philosophy regarding the safety of generals: "A general is no less expendable than anyone else. In fact it might be good for morale if the troops saw a dead general now and then." His men revered him as the toughest of the paratroopers and spoke of him in hushed tones.

However, Ridgway's positive, powerful personality was somewhat detrimental to his effectiveness in commanding his corps, for his relatively inexperienced XVIII Airborne Corps staff held him in such awe that when he was absent from his command post—which was frequently—they tended to become immobilized. Even routine decisions had to await the return of the General. This served to exacerbate the confusion that existed with Jochen Peiper still at large in La Gleize and the corps front grossly overextended.

In the early morning hours of December 22, Ridgway's headquarters sent a message to Hasbrouck and Jones that Ridgway, years after the war, could not account for. In one paragraph it seemed to put Hasbrouck in command of what was now called a "fortified goose egg"; the second paragraph contradicted the first, placing the 7th Armored under Jones.[16] Hasbrouck, however, did what he considered necessary in the desperate situation in midmorning; he sent his message directly to the commanding general, XVIII Airborne Corps:

> . . . Unless assistance is promptly forthcoming I believe our present position may become serious for several reasons, namely:
>
> a. Our supplies must come in through a bottleneck over a bridge near Vielsalm.
>
> b. We may become subjected to enemy artillery fire from practically any direction.
>
> c. The road net within our position is totally inadequate to the troops and vehicles concentrated therein. The map shows many roads, but on the ground, the majority of these are mere tracks on which even a jeep bogs down if more than two or three travel on it.
>
> d. If the 2d SS Panzer Division attack should succeed in driving back the two RCT's of the 82d Airborne Division now between Salmchâteau and

16

Hq XVIII Corps (Airborne)
APO 109, U.S. Army
220635 December, 1944

To CG 7th Armored Division, CG 106th Infantry Division

1. Following message sent you at 0100 is repeated for your information: "Confirming phone message to you, decision is yours. Will approve whatever you decide. Inform Jones he is to conform. Report decision when made."

2. In addition to his force, Major General A. W. Jones will command 7th Armored Division effective receipt of this message.

M. B. Ridgway, Major General
U.S. Army, Commanding

Hebronval even as little as 3,000 yards we will be completely severed from any source of supplies.

Since the chances of assistance in the immediate future do not seem bright, I would like to suggest that consideration be given to withdrawal of the 7th Armored and 106th Divisions to a position to the right (west) of the 82d Airborne Division where they may be of assistance in halting a possible advance north by the 2d SS Panzer.

The withdrawal of CCB, 7th Armored Division, last night from St.-Vith was expensive. So far we are missing at least one half of Clarke's force. Of course many of them will show up, but they will be minus weapons, ammunition, blankets and rations as well as at a low physical level. I don't think we can prevent a complete break-through if another all-out attack comes against CCB tonight due largely to the fact that our original three infantry battalions have at present melted to the equivalent of only two very tired battalions.

P.S. A strong attack has just developed against Clarke again. He is being outflanked and is retiring west another 2,000 yards refusing both flanks. I am throwing in my last chips to halt him. Hoge has just reported an attack. In my opinion if we don't get out of here and up north of the 82d before night, we will not have a 7th Armored Division left.

RWH

In the meantime, Field Marshal Montgomery's liaison officer at 7th Armored Division had reported the situation in detail to his own chief. Unwilling to risk sacrificing the division, Montgomery sent a message to General Hasbrouck: "You have accomplished your mission—a mission well done. It is time to withdraw."

In early afternoon of December 22, General Ridgway, now notified of the Army Group commander's order, came to Hasbrouck's headquarters to plan the withdrawal.

The 82d Airborne and 3d Armored divisions had just beaten their way eastward to make a fairly decent contact with the 7th Armored along the Salm between Vielsalm on the north and Salmchâteau on the south, about two miles apart.

From Vielsalm, Ridgway and Hasbrouck made their way to Clarke's CP at Kommanster. Ridgway wanted to get a personal feel of the situation for himself.

But he was also anxious to talk to a man in whom he had supreme confidence, Brigadier General Bill Hoge. Double-talking his identification over the radio with allusions to West Point football days, Ridgway gave Hoge a location at which to meet him. The other commanders he left behind.

Ridgway found Hoge skeptical. His command was fighting hard and the mud had mired him down. Told that his command would be pulled out, Hoge asked how it could be done. Matt Ridgway did not know exactly. He simply answered, "Bill, we can and we will."

On his return to Vielsalm that evening Ridgway found General Alan Jones in his command post. In Ridgway's eyes the commander of the 106th Division seemed listless and hardly interested in the next day's operation. Since the withdrawal would have to be conducted under the direction of one man, Ridgway placed the command of the horseshoe—now known as the "fortified goose egg"—under Hasbrouck, at the same time appointing Jones his own deputy corps commander.

Unknown to General Ridgway, Jones' heart was troubling him. Shortly after midnight, under the strain of the previous week, he was stricken with a heart attack. One of the unluckiest commanders of World War II, Jones was evacuated to Liège.

The withdrawal from the "fortified goose egg," scheduled to begin the morning of Saturday, December 23, was far from an easy task under these conditions. After Ridgway left on the evening of December 22, Hasbrouck called Clarke once more and asked about the road conditions. His answer resembled Hoge's: the mud had made the roads impassable for armored vehicles. Hasbrouck warned that the bridge at Vielsalm might have to be blown by noon on the twenty-third, in which case few of the vehicles, certainly no tanks, would be able to make their way out, and possibly a portion of the men would be left behind. "The mud makes it pretty difficult," said Clarke. "I don't know how we're going to do it. However, I'll go down and see Bill Hoge again."

"We'll never make it out," Hoge told Clarke. "Let's just stay and fight. We've got our jeeps in up to our hubcaps. We haven't got a chance."

Clarke went back and reported to General Hasbrouck that they would have to stay.

At five o'clock the next morning, however, Hasbrouck got through again to Clarke. "Bruce," he said, "do you think you can get out?"

"A miracle has happened, General!" Clarke exclaimed. "That cold snap that's hit us has frozen the roads. I think we can make it now. At 0600 I'm going to start to move."

One hour later Clarke was standing at the crossroads in the village of Kommanster, once more directing traffic. There had been no time for such formalities as operations orders; Clarke had simply sent out word that all vehicles were to start down the road. He personally would decide which was to go first. The lead unit was Hoge's CCB, 9th Armored, and by 10:00 A.M. the bulk of all the troops had passed through Kommanster. At this time Clarke told Lieutenant Colonel Vincent L. ("Moe") Boylan that his task force, consisting of reconnaissance elements, tanks, infantry, and tank destroyers, should cover the rear. Then, mounting his own vehicle, Clarke followed the column west, with Boylan's unit behind.

CCB of the 7th Armored Division went into assembly area that afternoon in the vicinity of Xhoris, well behind U.S. lines, and by evening some semblance of organization had been restored. Along with others, Bruce Clarke had not slept lying down for seven days.

But the escape of Clarke's and Hoge's commands was only the beginning of the withdrawal of the whole force; the plan was to peel off the forward elements first. Task Force Boylan had done a superb job in delaying Remer's Führer Begleit Brigade as it pressed down from Rodt to Hinderhausen to Kommanster. Now, miraculously, the pressure on Boylan was released, for Remer's interest lay to the south, and he continued in that direction.

The other route of withdrawal—Clarke had gone from Kommanster northwest to the Vielsalm bridge—lay to the south through Maldingen, Beho, and Bouvigny, thence north along the Salm Valley road to Salmchâteau bridge. This was the route followed by the 112th Infantry and the 424th, their rear being covered by Task Force Jones, assembled at Bouvigny. At about 1:00 P.M. this withdrawal was completed, although for a while severe German attacks required the southern force to fight their way to the Salmchâteau bridge.

Early in the afternoon General Hasbrouck sent the signal for Colonel Rosebaum's CCA to pull out on the extreme northern route. The last CCA vehicle crossed the Vielsalm bridge shortly after 4:00 P.M., followed by CCR. It was long after dark on December 23 by the time the entire 7th Armored Division task force had crossed the Salm River, but it did cross with a negligible loss of vehicles and personnel.

Considering this episode, it is necessary to balance what was lost against what was gained. In the 7th Armored Division, with the 14th Cavalry Group attached, nearly 3,400 officers and men were killed, wounded, or missing. In addition, known losses were 59 medium tanks, 29 light tanks, and 25 armored cars. As the division crossed the Salm River, Ridgway was told that about 100 usable tanks remained in the forces that came out of St.-Vith.[17]

For the Germans the loss was a valuable six days in securing this objective so vital to their drive to the Meuse.

After the war, in 1964, Bruce C. Clarke had the opportunity to meet with Hasso von Manteuffel and discuss the operations against St.-Vith that took place twenty years before. Clarke was interested in the early part of the action.

"Why in the world," he asked Manteuffel, "when I had only twenty-five hundred men available to my command on December seventeenth, did you not just execute a powerful frontal assault and overrun me?"

[17] Hugh Cole, *The Ardennes* (Washington: Dept. of the Army, 1965), p. 422.

Manteuffel's reply solves much of the riddle of the entire Ardennes campaign. "We estimated," he said, "that we were up against a division, and perhaps against an entire corps. We made several probing attacks, and every time we went into your position, we encountered armor. Our preliminary briefings had told us that there would be no armor in our path. When you get surprised like this, you become cautious."

Manteuffel, like the rest of the German High Command, had underestimated the mobility of the U.S. Army.

Thus on the evening of December 23, three separate, vital actions were coming to an end. On the northeast shoulder of the Bulge—at Monschau, Elsenborn, and Butgenbach—the efforts of Sepp Dietrich's Sixth Panzer Army to crack the Elsenborn Ridge position had come to naught. The 1st, 2d, 9th, and 99th divisions had frustrated his attempt to drive the shortest distance to Liège.

That same night, approximately twenty miles west of Butgenbach, Jochen Peiper's 800 men were abandoning their heavy equipment and making their way southeastward to cross the Salm River, eventually to be rehabilitated in the vicinity of St.-Vith.

Also that night the 7th Armored Division (reinforced) had crossed the same river in the other direction, just south of Peiper's force, and was assembling for further action near the area in which Peiper had operated only a few days before.

In effect, the Allied lines had solidified along a front, from Monschau to the Salm River, perhaps forty miles in length. To use one of Field Marshal Montgomery's favorite terms, the battlefield along this distance had been "tidied up."

In these three actions the significance of the St.-Vith salient cannot be overestimated. Not only did the presence of an armored division in the south of the Sixth Panzer Army remain a continual threat that Dietrich could not ignore, but by choking off the highways through the possession of this vital territory, it prevented Mohnke and Priess from resupplying their one successful drive, Kampfgruppe Peiper's.

The northern shoulder of the Allied positions had held; the main effort of the German counteroffensive had failed. True, to the south and west, Model's other effort, that of Manteuffel's Fifth Panzer Army, was achieving spectacular success; but Manteuffel had great distances to travel in his final run to the south. As at Elsenborn, Hitler's "master stroke" had suffered a critical defeat.

CHAPTER 13

❧❧❧❧

"I Am Mighty Glad to See You!"

MAJOR GENERAL Norman D. Cota, commanding the unlucky 28th Infantry Division, was an outstanding combat leader, highly experienced and possessed of an ideal temperament for command. Since his West Point days Cota had been known as "Dutch," not because of German ancestry but probably because of his personality—deliberate, methodical, and pragmatic. He came from Chelsea, Massachusetts, and his New England accent was clearly discernible.

Dutch Cota had seen a great deal of combat, starting with the North African invasion. During the landings in November, 1942, he had served as chief of staff of the 1st US Infantry Division, and then the fortunes of war had taken him to the beaches of Normandy, where as a brigadier general in the 29th Infantry Division, he had stormed the hills behind Omaha Beach beside his old comrades of the Big Red One. His staunch performance and heroism there later earned him the command of the 28th, a proud Pennsylvania National Guard division badly in need of leadership at the top.

Major General Cota had injected new life in the 28th, commanding it through the campaign of the Hürtgen Forest. Now, supposedly refitting in a "quiet" sector of Luxembourg, he was seeing his spread-out division decimated by the power of Manteuffel's Fifth Panzer Army, reinforced with two divisions of Brandenberger's Seventh.

General Cota and his staff were still in their original command post at Wiltz on Monday night, December 18, after three days of Manteuffel's attack. A more timid commander would have departed sooner. Hurley Fuller's 110th Infantry had ceased to exist the day before, when his CP at Clerf was overrun; Gustin Nelson's 112th Infantry was out of contact and falling back northward where—although Cota did not know it—it would next day join the 106th Division in the St.-Vith horseshoe; James Rudder's 109th Infantry was pivoting rearward to the south, linked with Raymond Barton's 4th Infantry Division. Cota's own command post, whose defense he had assigned to Task Force Hoban, was precarious—perhaps it was surrounded.

That same night, about 15 miles to the rear of Cota's beleaguered garrison, the spearheads of Heinrich von Lüttwitz's corps were approaching the environs of a town whose name was to become practically synonymous with the whole Ardennes campaign: Bastogne.

This small town was a focal point in Hasso von Manteuffel's planning for his army's role in the Ardennes counteroffensive. Boasting only about 3,500 inhabitants, it was important as the hub of a vital road net. From its town square emanated seven major hard-surfaced routes (see map, p. 314): the Houffalize-Manhay-Liège road north; the Longvilly-St.-Vith road to the northeast; a winding but still major road southeast to Luxembourg; a straighter road due south to Arlon; another southwestward to Neufchâteau; one to another road center, Marche-en-Famenne, and one to La Roche. In the cut-up, wooded terrain of the Ardennes, these roads were critical arteries for the execution of any ambitious military action.

Bastogne was one of three critical communication centers in Manteuffel's projected path, the other two being St.-Vith to the northeast and Marche-en-Famenne to the northwest. True, the Ardennes' extensive secondary road net made it possible for limited formations to bypass these centers, but during early winter no commander could count on a solid stretch of sufficiently dry or cold weather to carry adequate tonnage across these roads. Sometimes

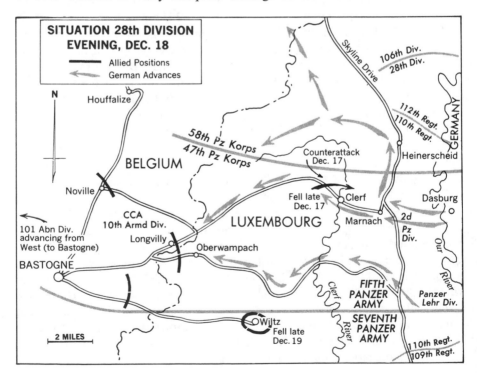

hardly more than cattle trails, they often would be mired in mud that made them impassable for wheeled or tracked vehicles.

Hitler himself early recognized the importance of Bastogne to the attack of the Fifth Panzer Army to the extent that he apparently made it a partial exception to his "always westward" rule. According to Manteuffel, after the war, he specified that although "centers of resistance where enemy was in force should be bypassed . . . at the express orders of the Führer, Bastogne was to be taken." In this Hitler had met no disagreement. Jodl, Model, and Manteuffel concurred that "the swift capture of Bastogne was essential to the development of Hitler's plan." [1] Bayerlein, talking after the war, stated with a touch of General Staff condescension: "A glance at the map is sufficient even for someone with no military training to realize that Bastogne was vital for the offensive." [2]

Having agreed that Bastogne was a vital objective for the Fifth Panzer Army, the German High Command still faced the problem of what tactic to employ in its capture. Bastogne was 30 miles west of the Our River by road, so, as at St.-Vith, success depended on the effectiveness of surprise; the town would have to be seized by a sudden *coup de main.*

The mission Manteuffel gave to his favorite lieutenant, Lüttwitz of 47th Panzer Korps, was as follows: "Panzer Lehr Division holds itself ready to advance by order of the corps following behind the 26th VGD by way of Gemund-Drauffield toward Bastogne and the Meuse in the sector Namur Dinant. It is essential for the division to take up positions . . . close to the 2d Panzer Division advancing over Noville. *In the case of strong enemy resistance, Bastogne is to be outflanked, its capture is then up to the 26th VGD. . . ."* [3]

Manteuffel's preference, naturally, would have been a quick seizure of Bastogne by December 26, permitting the Panzer Lehr Division and the 2d Panzer to bypass on the south and north, respectively, freeing both panzer divisions to seize bridgeheads over the Meuse.

But after three days of fighting, the *coup de main* had not materialized. The advance elements of Lüttwitz's 47th Korps did not reach the village of Niederwampach, more than five miles east of Bastogne, until after dark on Monday, December 18. In the meantime things had been happening on the American side.

The first phase of the historic defense of Bastogne consisted primarily of armored action. On the Longvilly road ten miles to the east was what might be considered the forward outpost of the town, Task Force Harper (named for its commander, Lieutenant Colonel Ralph S. Harper), a unit from Com-

[1] H. A. Jacobsen and J. Rohwer, *Decisive Battles of World War II: The German View* (New York: Putnam's, 1965), pp. 395, 398.
[2] Fritz Bayerlein, MS # A-941, p. 17.
[3] Hasso von Manteuffel, MS # B-151a. Italics added.

bat Command Reserve (CCR) of the new 9th U.S. Armored Division. The tankers and infantry waited in a lonely position at Allenborn, about halfway between Bastogne and Clerf. When darkness fell the evening of the eighteenth, Task Force Harper was hit by a sizable force of panther and tiger tanks. So sudden was the attack that Harper's few Shermans were quickly knocked out, and his half-tracks and armored cars set ablaze. Infantry casualties were heavy, and the roadblock soon collapsed. The survivors made their way back to Longvilly, where Colonel Joseph H. Gilbreth, the commander of CCR, gathered what troops he could muster from his own Headquarters Company and stragglers, setting up a skirmish line in front of CCR artillery positions.

In the meantime, Lieutenant Colonel Sam Tabets' 158th Engineer Combat Battalion was setting nearly 1,000 antitank mines between the towns of Foy and Neffe, only 3,000 to 5,000 yards east of Bastogne. Fortunately for the remnants of CCR and the 158th Engineers, the tanks of the 2d Panzer Division, which had crushed the CCR roadblock at Allenborn, turned northwest on a secondary road toward the hamlets of Bourcy and Noville, bypassing Bastogne, and headed for the Meuse. Reducing Bastogne was not their problem; it belonged to the 26th VGD and the Panzer Lehr.

The American buildup in Bastogne was now under way. In the middle of the afternoon the commanding officer of CCB, 10th Armored Division, came into General Middleton's headquarters, his lead troop units not far behind. Colonel William L. Roberts, older than most men in this line of work, previously had been an instructor in armored tactics at the Army's senior tactical school, the Command and General Staff School at Fort Leavenworth, Kansas. Middleton and Roberts were old friends, and there was little time for formalities. Middleton quickly outlined the situation as he saw it. Of the seven roads leading out of Bastogne, only three seemed to be threatened at the moment: Route 15, running north to Noville; the road eastward through Mageret and Longvilly, where CCR of the 9th Armored was still in place; the road southeast to Marvie and Wardin. He needed mobile outposts along these roads, and he needed them quickly.

"Robbie, how many combat units can you make out of your combat command?"

His friend looked concerned. "What do you have in mind?"

"I need a combined arms team to advance out and guard each of these three roads."

"That's no way to use armor."

"Robbie," said Middleton, "I may not know as much about the employment of armor as you, but that's the way I have to use them."

Roberts thought for a moment. Obviously Middleton had an exceptional situation on his hands. Mentally setting aside the "Do's and Don'ts of Armor" doctrine he had taught at Leavenworth, he organized CCB into three teams without further protest.

When the first arrived, Team O'Hara, Roberts sent Lieutenant Colonel James O'Hara's 500 men and 30 tanks down the road to Wardin. Orders were to hold at all costs.

Shortly, the commander of Roberts' second team, Lieutenant Colonel Henry T. Cherry, reported in, and immediately Team Cherry was sent along the road to Longvilly to back up the remnants of Gilbreth's CCR, 9th Armored. Cherry took the advance guard of his team to a point about half a mile west of Longvilly, placed it in position, and hurried back to Bastogne to report the dangerous situation facing Gilbreth.

The third task force to arrive was that commanded by Major William R. Desobry. Desobry was sent north to hold at Noville—though neither Desobry nor Roberts knew it, directly in the path of the German 2d Panzer. Before Desobry left, Colonel Roberts spoke to his young friend in a fatherly manner: "Bill, you'll probably want to pull out tomorrow morning. Remember I told you not to."

Thus each of the three main approaches to Bastogne on the east was covered by a team from CCB of the 10th Armored Division, a total force of respectable strength.

Brigadier General Anthony C. McAuliffe, division artillery commander of the 101st Airborne Division and acting commanding general, had the distinct feeling he could afford to know a little more about the tactical situation. Alerted on December 17 when General Eisenhower had released the 82d and 101st Airborne divisions to General Bradley—who had then assigned them to First Army—McAuliffe first understood that the two divisions were to head for Bastogne. Since the 82d Airborne had progressed further in its refitting after the Holland operation, that unit had been placed on the road first. (Many of the troops of the 101st Airborne were without helmets and some without weapons.) Before leaving on the eighteenth, the 82d Airborne received the word that their destination was not Bastogne but Werbomont, where that night Jochen Peiper had occupied the town of La Gleize, so McAuliffe presumed that the 101st, as part of Ridgway's XVIII Airborne Corps, would follow along with them.

General McAuliffe left by jeep from Reims and headed toward Werbomont, taking with him his division G-3, Lieutenant Colonel H. W. O. Kinnard, and his aide. Traveling ahead of the bulk of his troops, actually within the march column of the 82d, he found himself with a little time to spare. Since the route passed near Bastogne, he decided to take a right fork in the road and stop off at General Middleton's headquarters to get a new look at the situation. When he walked into the VIII Corps command post, he found Colonel Roberts and various other officers already there.

It was lucky that the stocky, taciturn artilleryman had dropped in. His mission had been changed: the 101st Airborne was to head not for Werbomont but for Bastogne. The advance party of the 101st Airborne was already approaching Werbomont, and its arrangements for the division there were going to be all for nothing.[4]

McAuliffe got the word back to his division to change their destination, then he and Kinnard took over the role of the missing 101st advance party. Their first task was to select an assembly area for the division to pull into when it arrived; almost with a sweep of the hand, McAuliffe chose a roughly triangular area northwest of town that included the villages of Mande-St. Étienne, Champs, and Hemroulle (see map, p. 314). Middleton cheerfully acceded, although the selection was slightly north of the ground he himself had visualized. McAuliffe later was to take pride in this decision. From this assembly area, each unit had to go only a minimum distance to its initial position of employment, and the 101st Division Artillery was ideally placed for defense of the area: immediately, without even moving, it could go into business.

In the meantime General Middleton had been in contact with General Bradley and had clarified certain matters. Bradley had now agreed on the importance of holding Bastogne and supported Middleton's employment of the 101st Airborne Division, plus CCB of the 10th Armored Division, for this purpose. This was a sober decision: Bradley realized full well that Bastogne might easily be cut off, but he was willing to accept the risk. Moreover, he had learned that evening that General Eisenhower would cancel Patton's attack in the Saar and turn the Third Army north toward Bastogne regardless of the situation of the garrison there.[5] But Bradley did insist that Middleton himself pull out and his VIII Corps headquarters displace back to Neufchâteau, about 17 miles to the southwest. Middleton accordingly sent advance detachments to the new location, but he would personally remain behind until McAuliffe's situation was set up.

One important matter needed to be settled. With Middleton departing for Neufchâteau the next morning, unity of command for the bastion of Bastogne became a question of prime importance. Sensing this, McAuliffe proposed that Colonel Roberts' CCB, 10th Armored, be attached to his 101st Division. Roberts bristled; he was suspicious of the way armored forces might be employed by an untutored airborne division.

McAuliffe was sympathetic toward his protest. Not only had he a high regard for Roberts, but he realized that on the Regular Army list, Roberts was nine years his senior at West Point and some pride might be involved. Mc-

---

[4] At the time of McAuliffe's arrival, General Middleton was unsure whether First Army had given him the 101st to employ as he saw fit, but there was no doubt in Middleton's mind that the vital crossroads at Bastogne had to be held.

[5] As an example of American lack of knowledge about the situation, on the night of December 18, as the Germans were approaching Bastogne, General Bradley had intended to drive to Spa by road. He was only deterred by Hodges' aide, who warned him about Skorzeny's and von der Heydte's men. Bradley was unaware that Route 15 from Bastogne to Noville (and thence to Spa) was just about cut off by the 2d Panzer.

Auliffe himself made no claims to be an expert on armor, but he was a matter-of-fact man and got straight to the point. "Do you suppose that my entire division should be attached to your combat command?" he demanded.

Middleton settled the question temporarily, much as he had with Generals Jones and Hasbrouck at St.-Vith. He simply asked the two men to cooperate, with neither in charge.

Later in the evening of the eighteenth Colonel Julian J. Ewell, commanding officer of McAuliffe's 501st Parachute Infantry, arrived to receive his instructions. His regiment would close into Bastogne that night. Ewell, a salty, incisive, outspoken character, whose "lean and mean" exterior so well represented the airborne tradition, took in the situation at a glance.[6] The members of the VIII Corps staff seemed to him "punchy," probably from lack of sleep and many hours under pressure. The situation map was a sight: it looked as if it had the measles. Reports of German tanks and troops were plastered all over it—a sobering sight. Fortunately, Ewell noted, General Middleton was completely calm and in command of himself.

Ewell listened intently, and by the time Middleton and McAuliffe were finished, he felt he knew just about all that they did. He knew the general location of Team Cherry, as well as the skimpy word regarding the situation of CCR, 9th Armored Division. Other things were showing up on the operation map. Most serious was the indication that the enemy, possibly part of the Panzer Lehr Division, was already pushing from the south toward the Longvilly road at Mageret, threatening to cut off both the advance guard of Team Cherry and Gilbreth's command. It was this danger, as a matter of fact, that Colonel Hank Cherry had already reported to Colonel Roberts.

Ewell asked for and was granted flexibility in his mission. "Move out along this road to the east," he was told, "make contact with the enemy, attack, and clear up the situation."

---

[6] Chaplain (Major General) Francis L. Sampson (then a chaplain in the grade of captain with Ewell) in his excellent book, *Look Out Below,* described something of Ewell's approach to welcoming replacements to his regiment:

> When the replacements arrived, Colonel Ewell assembled them and spoke to them in a kindly way. As he welcomed them as full-fledged members of the regiment, he told them that the men they replaced had set a very high standard of military service and that the new men were obligated to live up to that standard. His wonderfully droll wit won the men to his side immediately. Then the Colonel introduced each staff member in his own inimitably funny way. When he finally came to me, he said, "Men, this is Father Sampson. He will take care of you fish-eaters. In Alabama he lit in the Chattahoochee; in England he lit in a lake; in Normandy he lit in a creek; in Holland he lit in the canal. And I guess, if he ever jumps in the Sahara Desert, he will land in a puddle left by some cockeyed camel."
>
> Chaplain Engel was present and almost fell off his seat from laughing—until the Colonel introduced him. "Now, you left-footers, this is Chaplain Engel, the Protestant chaplain, and if I catch any of you saluting or wearing the uniform the way he does, I'll have you court-martialled."

The undramatic Ewell replied with a terse "Yes, sir!"

Ewell then went off to prepare for the next day's attack, thankful that he had recently been on leave in Bastogne and had become somewhat familiar with the terrain.

On the German side of the hill that evening, the situation looked favorable. Of course the *coup de main* had failed. And while intercepted radio messages had informed Lüttwitz that two American parachute divisions were headed toward Bastogne, he estimated that the earliest they could arrive was noon the next day, the nineteenth. Also, there was the possibility that they would be spread out on a line running northeast from Bastogne.

Lüttwitz had some real successes to crow over. The 2d Panzer Division had destroyed some forty American tanks east of Longvilly, and there was every reason to believe that the defenses at Bastogne were crumbling. Certainly a coordinated attack on the part of the 26th VGD and the Panzer Lehr Division would be sufficient to take the town the next day. Lüttwitz felt there was no reason to question orders that the 2d Panzer Division should go north to Noville and continue westward, bypassing Bastogne.

But the night of December 18 was, for the Germans and the Panzer Lehr in particular, one of lost opportunity. Their commander, General Fritz Bayerlein, was a competent man. On the one hand, Manteuffel considered him a good commander and a good General Staff officer, experienced and capable of thought and action on a grand scale; on the other, he suspected Bayerlein was not strict enough with his subordinates.

Bayerlein now had some decisions to make, the first being what route to take into Bastogne. Having reached Niederwampach by 8:00 P.M., he could advance on Bastogne either by proceeding directly westward along the secondary road through Benonchamps to the Longvilly road, or by going southwestward across a stream and railroad track to Wardin (where Team O'Hara was being placed) and move into Bastogne from the southeast. Bayerlein made what seemed like the best decision: the northern route to Mageret, thence following the Longvilly road through Neffe. In an hour he had reached Mageret and was on the main road into Bastogne.

But here Bayerlein paused and accosted a Belgian civilian for information. Two hours previously, the Belgian reported, an American combat command of 50 Sherman tanks, 25 self-propelled guns, and 40 or 50 other armored vehicles had passed through Mageret headed east; and an American general had been in Mageret. (In actuality the force reported by the Belgian was Team Cherry, commanded by a lieutenant colonel.) Bayerlein believed the Belgian. Convinced that Team Cherry was indeed the formidable force described by the civilian, he satisfied himself with cutting the road between Longvilly and Bastogne, placing tanks in position east of Mageret, and laying mines. Here he intercepted American traffic going from Bastogne toward the east, but he did not press his attack in what was actually a nearly undefended area. Bayerlein's chance to seize Bastogne had passed.

Colonel Ewell's 501st Parachute Infantry Regiment moved out of Bastogne at 6:00 A.M., Tuesday, December 19, heading directly east on the Longvilly road. Moving in heavy fog in a highly uncertain situation, he made his approach march with battalions in column, led by the 1st Battalion. He got as far as Neffe, only about two miles east of Bastogne, only to run square into the advance elements of Fritz Bayerlein's Panzer Lehr. Surveying the situation in person, he could tell that this German armored force was no ordinary roadblock to be taken head-on with infantry; the Germans were deployed in strength. He decided to try to turn the armor out of position. He sent his 2d Battalion off the road to seize Bizory, a town located to the north on a supplemental road to Mageret, and then a promontory called Hill 510, which dominated both Mageret and his present position at Neffe. When the 3d Battalion came up, Ewell ordered it to turn to the right to take the small town of Mont and the bridge over the Wiltz River south of Neffe. He was now fighting with three battalions abreast.

By noon the 501st had attained most of its objectives. Ewell found Bizory still outposted by troops of the 158th Engineer Combat Battalion, but after passing through toward Mageret, his 2d Battalion ran into some resistance and it required a major effort to take Hill 510.

The aggressiveness of Ewell's attack had a sobering effect on Fritz Bayerlein. He had decided to turn north and clean up what American armored elements were still along the Longvilly road; but when attacked by Ewell, he feared that he had been hit by a whole division. Leaving substantial forces to hold Hill 510 and the Mageret-Neffe road, Bayerlein moved on, slipping around to the south. At the end of the day, Ewell had established substantial positions and had some feel for the enemy situation at the front, but had decided it was not feasible to reach the armored elements of Team Cherry and CCR of the 9th Armored, the latter of which had now decided to withdraw to Bastogne.

At the most advanced roadblocks of CCR, 9th Armored, Colonel Gilbreth began displacing his guns to the rear some time before daybreak on the nineteenth, and the main force began to move back from Longvilly at about 8:00 A.M. However, Gilbreth's force was ambushed by part of the Panzer Lehr Division and thrown into disorder as it approached Mageret. Cherry's advance guard, Team Hyduke (named after First Lieutenant Edward P. Hyduke), fought with difficulty, hampered by the long column of stragglers from the two 9th Armored Division roadblocks and other refugees. At 8:30 A.M., Hank Cherry realized that his larger team, Team Ryerson, was cut off by the German force at Mageret and ordered Captain William F. Ryerson to punch his way back.

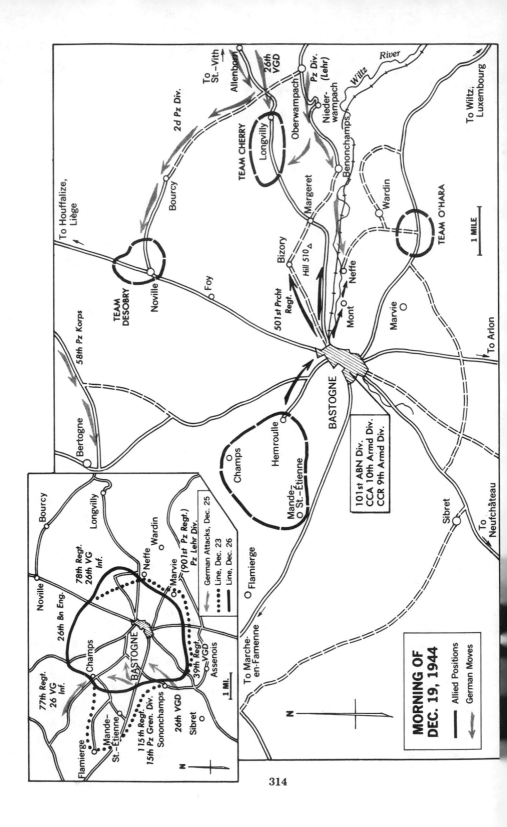

To Houffalize,
Liège

To St.-Vith

To St.-Vith

Allenborn

26th
VGD

River

Wiltz

Pz Div.
(Lehr)

Oberwampach

Nieder-
wampach

Benonchamps

To Wiltz,
Luxembourg

2d Pz Div.

TEAM CHERRY

Longvilly

Margeret

Wardin

TEAM O'HARA

1 MILE

Bourcy

Foy

Noville

TEAM
DESOBRY

58th Pz Korps

Bizory

Hill 510

Neffe

Mont

Marvie

To Arlon

501st Prcht
Regt.

BASTOGNE

Hemroulle

Champs

Mande-
St.-Étienne

Bertogne

101st ABN Div.
CCA 10th Armd Div.
CCR 9th Armd Div.

Sibret

To
Neufchâteau

To Marche-
en-Famenne

Flamierge

N

**MORNING OF
DEC. 19, 1944**

Allied Positions

German Moves

Inset map:

Bourcy

Longvilly

Noville

Neffe

Wardin

26th Bn Eng.

78th Regt.
26th VG
Inf.

Marvie

77th Regt.
26 VG
Inf.

Champs

BASTOGNE

39th Regt.

Assenois

(901st Pz Regt.)
Pz Lehr Div.

German Attacks, Dec. 25

Line, Dec. 23

Line, Dec. 26

Flamierge

Mande-
St.-Étienne

115th Regt.
15th Pz Gren. Div.

Sononchamps

26th VGD

Sibret

1 MI.

N

314

But the column between Longvilly and Mageret was the target of at least portions of all three German divisions attacking Bastogne. The Panzer Lehr Division was sending the bulk of its forces from the southwest; the 26th VGD was coming from the southeast; and the 2d Panzer Division, bypassing to the north, found the jammed road a lucrative target. The result was wreckage. Bayerlein estimated that 23 Sherman tanks, 15 self-propelled artillery pieces, 30 jeeps and 25 trucks were captured intact, and many vehicles were destroyed. Although some of the Americans escaped on foot, the portion of Team Cherry that had gone forward of Neffe was now destroyed as a combat unit. But precious hours had been bought by Team Cherry of CCB, 10th Armored Division.

At Noville, north of Bastogne, Bill Desobry also had more than his share of problems. On miserable roads and fighting dense fog, the lead elements of the 2d Panzer Division heading westward hit Team Desobry at about 7:20 A.M. One or two panther tanks reached the village itself before pulling out. Attempting to analyze the situation, Desobry sent a patrol up the road toward Houffalize; it returned to report the road open. However, the Germans now began to hit Noville with heavy artillery. Many Americans were casualties, and damage to the ambulances made it doubly difficult to get the wounded out.

By this time the northeastern defenses of Bastogne were being manned by the 506th U.S. Parachute Infantry Regiment, just south of the town of Foy, about halfway between Noville and Bastogne. Coming to Desobry's relief, a platoon from the 705th Tank Destroyer Battalion and Lieutenant Colonel James L. LaPrade's 1st Battalion ran directly into the attack the 2d Panzer had been readying since midmorning. When the fog lifted, nearly 32 German tanks appeared on the field. Fighting was fierce, though Lauchert's panzers were not particularly aggressive, possibly out of fear of bazooka fire in Noville and of the fire from the tanks and tank destroyers positioned around the town. The 90-mm. tank destroyers, as always, were worth their weight in gold; the few panzers that did approach Noville were hit by these TD's from the 705th. Five were destroyed at 1,500-yard range.

During the heavy artillery bombardment, one shell crashed near the American command post. Colonel LaPrade was killed [7]; Major Desobry was wounded. Major Robert F. Harwick, of the 101st Airborne, assumed overall command of the combined force at Noville. During the night of December 19–20, the paratroopers and tankers held the 2d Panzer Division at arm's length; the American force at Noville had accomplished a remarkable feat.

By morning of Tuesday, December 19, Major General Norman Cota had decided that there was little a division headquarters could accomplish at Wiltz

[7] General McAuliffe later called LaPrade the finest battalion commander he had in the division.

when it had lost all three of its regiments. There was only one thing to do: pull the division CP back where it could reassemble strength for a counter-attack. This meant going back a long way. Sibret was selected, a town south-west of Bastogne on the road to Neufchâteau.

During the night of December 18–19, as Middleton, McAuliffe, Roberts, and Ewell were organizing the defenses of Bastogne, Cota's defenses were being pulled in closer to Wiltz. Lieutenant Colonel Daniel Strickler, executive officer of the decimated 110th Infantry, reported in, and General Cota left Strickler in command of the town when 28th Division CP left Wiltz the morning of December 19. Strickler had available to him Task Force Hoban and others. His mission was to defend.

General Cota departed from Wiltz about 10:00 A.M. with an aide. Up to the hills on the south of town the vehicle went, turning westward along the road to Bastogne. Cota himself saw nothing along the way to concern him. Not so the MP jeep riding "shotgun" behind. Hardly had the party turned westward than through the fog Sergeant William Fellman sighted a German tank crossing the road a short distance to their rear.

Though battles were raging to the north at Neffe, Bizory, Hill 510, Mageret, Longvilly, and Noville, miraculously Cota and his party reached the defenses of Bastogne without difficulty, entering town on the only clear road, from the southeast.

As he was passing through Team O'Hara of the 10th Armored, General Cota encountered his old friend Colonel William Roberts standing along the road. Roberts appeared a little out of sorts. Pulling Cota aside, he suggested to his friend that as a major general—and therefore senior man in town—Cota take command of the defense. Cota was doubtful; after all, the troops in town, except for stragglers, belonged to another command. He asked if Roberts was in communication with General Middleton. He was.

A call to Middleton settled the matter. Middleton asked if Cota had seen McAuliffe. He had not. Middleton decided to keep his command arrangements as they were. Cota was to remain with the remnants of the 28th. McAuliffe was to retain command of the 101st Airborne in Bastogne.

Before leaving Bastogne for his new CP at Sibret, Cota thought for a moment about visiting McAuliffe, but he well knew what it was like to be a busy commander in charge of a confused situation, and instead he drove out on the southwest road from town, determined, if possible, to organize a task force of men and supplies to relieve the heroic garrison he had left 15 miles to the east at Wiltz.

Bastogne was seething with confused mobs. Frightened people were coming in from the east; some stayed to fight, but others, realizing the roads were still open to the west, went on. None of this feeling seemed to affect the paratroopers or the tankers of the 10th Armored, though Ewell's 501st was being hit hard during the nineteenth—for example, Company I, sent as part of 3d Battalion to Wardin, had been overrun in the afternoon by a German battalion task force; only 83 men survived out of the entire company.

Colonel Roberts was busy rounding up those stragglers who would stay and fight. Out of the confusion he organized a military unit as best he could. In typical sardonic GI fashion, the soldiers themselves named it Team SNAFU. The team was to prove of value in the days ahead.

On the evening of December 19 the garrison received a serious blow: most of the division's service area west of town around Mande-St. Étienne was lost to German raiding parties. The majority of the quartermaster and ordnance troops made their way southwest to VIII Corps, but the raiders captured or killed most of the division's medical company, and only 8 officers and 44 men escaped. Fortunately for the garrison, food, ammunition and other supplies were available inside Bastogne—supplies that VIII Corps had been unable to evacuate.

During that evening a soldier came in to see General McAuliffe with a gift of a bottle of bourbon whiskey. The soldier, one of the few from the medical company that had escaped, wanted to thank the general for being rescued.

As the German High Command reviewed the situation at the end of December 19, they had cause for both optimism and disappointment. Wardin, where Team O'Hara had originally been located—and where Company I of the 501st had been so badly mangled—finally had been taken that evening. No progress had been made in penetrating the 501st in the vicinity of Neffe and Bizory, however, and Team Desobry, at Noville to the north, still held out. But Lüttwitz was elated over his spectacular destruction of American armor between Longvilly and Mageret, a victory he attributed largely to the superiority of the panther tank over the 75-mm.-armed Sherman.

That night Lüttwitz was once more faced with the old problem of whether to gather all forces to capture Bastogne the next day, the twentieth, or stick with the original plan, which called for the 26th VG Division to take Bastogne and his two panzer divisions to carry on westward.

Certainly Bastogne was important; if held by the Americans, it would hinder movements to the west and constitute a danger to the flank of the Fifth Panzer Army. Lüttwitz knew Manteuffel was disappointed that the German Seventh Army had not contained the Americans in the south as originally visualized, but it seemed best to order the 2d Panzer to continue without delay to the west. The other two divisions would remain and attack Bastogne once more—the 26th VG from the north and the Panzer Lehr from the east. The Panzer Lehr at the same time would proceed to bypass Bastogne to the south, thus making forces available to advance to the west. Lüttwitz knew that Manteuffel's other panzer corps, Krüger's 58th, had already reached Houffalize on the north and had sent reconnaissance units as far west as Bertogne, and it was necessary for the 2d Panzer to exploit this success.

This decision made Fritz Bayerlein of the Panzer Lehr Division unhappy.

The first coup having failed and the second having been repelled, he insisted that all of Lüttwitz's divisions—the Panzer Lehr, the 2d Panzer and the 26th VG—should be concentrated on taking Bastogne before the German attack should continue farther west.

After a long discussion, Lüttwitz acceded to Bayerlein's views; but on consulting his chief, Manteuffel, he reverted to his original plan. This, Bayerlein later concluded, was "probably on a directive from higher headquarters, as I heard that they considered Bastogne 'child's play' and incapable of interfering with the rapid continuation of the offensive." Actually, the Fifth Panzer Army was merely following Hitler's instructions.

December 19 was critical for the Battle of Bastogne, as it was at the Battle of Elsenborn Ridge and St.-Vith. On this day American forces consisting of the 101st Airborne Division, CCB of the 10th Armored, the 705th Tank Destroyer Battalion, remnants of CCR, 9th Armored, and other miscellaneous units, were now organized in a strong position. Middleton's VIII Corps had moved to Neufchâteau but had left a clear mission: Bastogne must be held at all costs. The period of greatest confusion, on the American side at least, was over.

As the morning of December 20 began, Team Desobry, now commanded by Major Harwick, was still standing at Noville, the main obstacle in the path of Lauchert's 2d Panzer. But by this time Lauchert had brought up his entire artillery force to support an all-out attack. German guns continued to place heavy fire on the village, and at 5:30 A.M. the grenadiers of the 2d Panzer moved into Noville on three sides. In response, the U.S. 420th Field Artillery Battalion laid down protective barrages, but the eight Sherman tanks still available to Harwick had run out of armor-piercing ammunition. They were reinforced by a fresh platoon of tank destroyers from the 705th Tank Destroyer Battalion, and the attack was repelled.

By midmorning Harwick had a clue to bad news: some antiaircraft half-tracks, "quad-fifties" (half-tracks mounting four .50-caliber machine guns), were supposed to join him at Noville, and their failure to arrive indicated that the road to the south had been cut. Through the artillery net, Harwick sent the word back to Bastogne: "All reserves committed. Situation critical."

General McAuliffe and Colonel Roberts consulted, and agreed that the forces in Noville should withdraw. But they realized that the withdrawal would be difficult. The only way to rescue the Noville garrison, they concluded, was a counterattack by the U.S. forces deployed about two miles away at Foy. Brigadier General Gerald J. Higgins, assistant division commander, was commanding the sector in this area. It would be a rugged fight, for the Noville road was the one the 26th VGD intended to follow in attacking Bastogne from the north. By 2:00 P.M., however, the 3d Battalion, 502d

Parachute Infantry, had passed through the lines of the 506th, driven through Foy, and dug in to the north of town. In the late afternoon they met Harwick's column, fighting its way through the smoke and fog out of Noville, and by 5:00 P.M. the Noville garrison had passed through their lines.

The losses of the original Team Desobry were severe. Of eight Shermans remaining that morning, four had been knocked out in the battle to fight south from Noville. Thirteen officers and 199 men from the 1st Battalion of 506th alone were killed, wounded, and missing.[8]

But having taken Noville, the 2d Panzer was faced once more with the problem of where to go. It would seem the question had been well answered the night before, but some German commanders—Bayerlein and Lauchert being the most vociferous—refused to give up trying to get permission to take Bastogne.

To support his views, Lauchert did a strange thing: he appealed to Krüger of the adjacent 58th Panzer Korps. Krüger answered with some impatience: "Forget Bastogne and head for the Meuse." It was the job of the Panzer Lehr Division (Bayerlein) and 26th VGD (Generalmajor Heinz Kokott) now to take Bastogne.

Meanwhile Lüttwitz had altered his entire scheme for taking Bastogne. Faced by stiff resistance on the east and northeast, he would sideslip to the south and make his new attack on Bastogne from that direction. In order to do so he performed an intricate maneuver. Up to this moment the 26th VGD had been attacking with two infantry regiments, the 77th and 78th. These units Lüttwitz simply attached to the Panzer Lehr, whose center of gravity remained eastward. Lüttwitz then moved the headquarters of the 26th VGD south to the Arlon road by way of Wardin; the 26th VGD would now attack from Remonfosse on the south. Available for this attack were the Reconnaissance Battalion, 26th VGD (previously attached to the Panzer Lehr), and the 39th Regiment, just now arriving on the south. The Reconnaissance Battalion could not arrive, however, before evening.

Meanwhile in the east Bayerlein had sent his 902d Panzer Grenadier Regiment against Neffe, but it was caught by a roving patrol from Team O'Hara and suffered severely under heavy American artillery and the guns of American paratroopers and tankers.

On the American side, the situation on December 20 did not seem nearly so gloomy as might be imagined. That morning General Cota came into town from his temporary command post in Sibret. He found the streets still jammed with vehicles and stragglers, including some survivors of his 110th Infantry. These he rounded up and took out what men he could find, abandoning their vehicles. Then he headed for Neufchâteau, where he again conferred with General Middleton on the situation at Bastogne.

[8] Hugh Cole, *The Ardennes* (Washington: Dept. of the Army, 1965), p. 455.

That afternoon, despite the confusion in the town, General McAuliffe sent a liaison officer to Cota's headquarters to ask if the 28th could attack toward Wiltz. He had learned that the town had fallen the night before, and Colonel Strickler was sending the men out in small groups. McAuliffe was overly optimistic: Cota had nothing left to fight with.

With the loss of the field hospital, Tony McAuliffe's biggest concern at the moment was care of the wounded. Also in serious condition were the civilians, who had been crowded in unsanitary basements, some suffering from disease and hysteria.

Strangely, McAuliffe was not particularly concerned about the mere fact of being surrounded. In a way that made his job easier: trying to pull out under fire would only result in his division's being destroyed. The roads west to Ortheuville and southwest and south to Neufchâteau and Arlon reportedly were still open, although he had received word of a series of clashes with scattered units on the southern flank during the day. Finally McAuliffe was banking on the 4th U.S. Armored Division's being able to move rapidly to his assistance in a very short period of time.

Late in the day McAuliffe decided it was worth the risk to go see General Middleton. Realizing the precarious nature of the trip, he took the road still open to Neufchâteau. On his arrival Middleton informed him: "There are three German divisions in your area, and the 116th Panzer is on its way. You're going to have a rough time staying there."

"Hell," McAuliffe replied, "if we pull out now, we'd be chewed to pieces."

Middleton had some doubts that Bastogne could be held, but McAuliffe insisted that it could be done, assuming, of course, that he would not be required to hold out for any great length of time.

McAuliffe and Middleton worked out a series of code words whereby they could communicate by a radio link vehicle with some degree of security. At the end of the visit Middleton could not repress a laugh: "Now, Tony, don't get yourself surrounded."

General McAuliffe was lucky that he was able to make it back to Bastogne.

That evening General Middleton decided that the split command in Bastogne would no longer do—a tight command control by radio would be impossible to maintain. He talked to Roberts directly, and simply told him that from here on General McAuliffe "had the say" in Bastogne.[9] From now on the command in Bastogne would be unified with one man, McAuliffe,

---

[9] There is no indication that McAuliffe pressed for this in his meeting with Middleton, but Cole seems to think that General Cota, having observed conditions in Bastogne that day, advocated unifying the command when he visited Middleton in Neufchâteau the afternoon of the twentieth.

responsible. The armored phase of the operation completed, Colonel Roberts accepted his subordinate position with good grace.

That Wednesday night the picture on the German side was mixed. Some successes had been achieved on the eastern flank of Bastogne: Wardin had been captured, and so had Bizory, just a few thousand yards out of Bastogne, but for the most part the American lines were holding firm. On the other hand, the 2d Panzer, having captured Noville only that afternoon, had traveled west all the way to Ortheuville; there by midnight Lauchert would have seized a bridge intact over the Ourthe River. Hasso von Manteuffel had decided that Bastogne should be contained but bypassed. To that end, he returned the two regiments (the 77th and 78th) to Kokott's 26th VG Division and, leaving behind one panzer grenadier regiment, the 901st, ordered the bulk of Bayerlein's Panzer Lehr Division to bypass Bastogne to the south and head immediately for St.-Hubert, 15 airline miles to the west. Thus only one reinforced division, the 26th VGD, remained to invest the garrison at Bastogne, a difficult task if the Americans could be resupplied.

The German objective was still the Meuse, and Manteuffel's 58th and 47th Panzer corps were shooting in that direction with lightning rapidity.

December 21, the day St.-Vith was lost and Jochen Peiper decided to evacuate Stoumont, was a day of reprieve at Bastogne. Cool weather had frozen the ground, adding to the mobility of attackers and defenders alike. For the first time some aerial resupply to the Americans was possible; their primary need was for medical supplies. But the two antagonists were now lined up. Of McAuliffe's four regiments, less than half the battalions—only five out of twelve—had been seriously engaged in the fight thus far. He had available four light artillery battalions, reinforced by two medium howitzer battalions, whose range far exceeded that of the airborne artillery. In addition he had the 420th Armored Field Artillery Battalion, a part of Roberts' CCB of the 10th Armored. About 40 operable medium tanks were available to McAuliffe on the twenty-first, along with a number of light tanks. And he valued particularly the power of the 705th Tank Destroyer Battalion.

Surrounding him was the German 26th VG Division, consisting of the 39th Regiment, the Reconnaissance Battalion, the 901st Panzer Grenadier Regiment from the Panzer Lehr Division, the 77th and 78th regiments, and various engineer units. General Kokott was becoming interested in what he considered the "soft" southwest flank. Although to all intents and purposes the Bastogne garrison had been surrounded by the night of the twentieth, the process was certainly completed by the twenty-first.

On December 22, Major Alvin Jones, operations officer of the 327th Glider Infantry, received an emergency call from 2d Battalion at Marvie. Four Germans, he was told, had just driven up the Arlon road from Remonfosse at 11:30 A.M., and under cover of a white flag had turned themselves in to Company F. The Germans, a major, a captain, and two enlisted men, described themselves at *"parlementaires."* Unable to contact the regimental commander, Jones hurried to the F Company CP himself, after insuring that division headquarters was informed of this new twist, and found the two German officers (the enlisted men had been left at the outpost where they had been taken). The *parlementaires* delivered a written message to Jones, who headed with it to division headquarters in Bastogne.

By this time the word had circulated that the Germans had come to negotiate their surrender to the Americans. The defenders of Bastogne relaxed. But the note the Germans had brought said nothing of the kind:

> To the U.S.A. Commander of the encircled town of Bastogne.
>
> The fortune of war is changing. This time the U.S.A. forces in and near Bastogne have been encircled by strong German armored units. . . .
>
> There is only one possibility to save the encircled U.S.A. troops from total annihilation: that is the honorable surrender of the encircled town. . . .
>
> If this proposal should be rejected, one German Artillery Corps and six heavy A.A. Battalions are ready to annihilate the U.S.A. troops in and near Bastogne . . .
>
> All the serious civilian losses caused by this artillery fire would not correspond with the well-known American humanity.
>
> The German Commander

The message was delivered to General McAuliffe as he was preparing to go congratulate some men on a roadblock who had done an exceptional job in repelling an enemy attack. He looked at the message and dropped the paper on the floor. "Nuts," he said, and left.

When he returned he was reminded of the message. For the first time McAuliffe gave the matter serious thought. A man of exceptionally few words, he was perplexed how to phrase what obviously had to be a blunt refusal. He sat down to think it over, then asked helplessly, "What should I say?"

His energetic G-3, Lieutenant Colonel H. W. O. Kinnard, who had a flair for the dramatic, answered quickly: "That first remark of yours would be hard to beat."

"What did I say?"

Kinnard told him.

Colonel Joseph H. Harper, commanding the 327th Glider Infantry Regiment, was inspecting one of his frontline battalions south of Bastogne when he received a message over his jeep radio: "Report to division headquarters immediately."

Harper arrived at the dismal, single-story Belgian cantonment where General McAuliffe had set up his CP and found McAuliffe and General Higgins in the basement under the main building. A sergeant was typing up a sheet of eight-by-eleven-inch bond paper. As Harper entered, the sergeant handed it to McAuliffe, who glanced at it with amusement.

But instead of showing it to Harper, McAuliffe produced instead the message received earlier from the German emissaries and asked how Harper would reply. Harper read the message, then hesitated. With obvious pleasure, General McAuliffe produced his answer:

> To the German Commander:
> Nuts!
>
> The American Commander

"Will you see that it is delivered?"

Harper was delighted. "I will deliver it myself, General. It will be a lot of fun!"

"Well, don't go into the German lines."

Harper proceeded to the company post of F Company where the two German officers were standing in the wood, blindfolded and under guard. Harper said to the captain, who served as interpreter: "I have the American commander's reply."

"Is it written or verbal?"

"It is written," Harper answered. Addressing the German major directly, he said, "I will stick it in your hand."

The Germans were obviously unsure how to translate the reply. Their apparent assumption that the Americans were going to accept the surrender began to irritate Harper. "The reply is decidedly not affirmative," he said. "And if you continue this foolish attack, your losses will be tremendous."

Then Harper put the two Germans in his jeep and drove them about a quarter of a mile through the snow on a meadow trail to an opening in the wire fence that led to the blacktop Arlon road. Turning south, Harper delivered the two officers to the American outpost where the German enlisted men were conversing casually with the Americans. While driving along, Harper had turned the conversation over in his mind, becoming progressively angrier at what he considered Teutonic arrogance. Upon delivering the two officers to the outpost, he removed the blindfolds and said to the German major, "If you don't understand what 'Nuts' means, in plain English it is the same as 'Go to hell.' I will tell you something else—if you continue to attack, we will kill every goddamn German that tries to break into this city."

The German major and captain both saluted. "We will kill many Americans. This is war."

"On your way, Bud," said Harper, "and good luck to you."

As the Germans went down the road, Harper wondered how, by a slip of the tongue, he could wish his enemies good luck.

But Harper also realized the significance of the message he had delivered, and he spent the rest of the day in a position about a half mile behind the front. Here, overlooking the Arlon road, he waited for a German reaction in the form of some violent attack. It never came.[10]

This episode gave the 101st U.S. Airborne Division great pleasure, and it came at a time of general optimism: an air drop had been promised by General Middleton for eight o'clock on the evening of the twenty-second, and there had been a message—doubtful security, but great cause for rejoicing—that Hugh (Major General Hugh J. Gaffey, commanding the 4th Armored Division) was on his way. The G-2, Lieutenant Colonel Paul A. Danahy, in his periodic report, mentioned the "Nuts" incident with obvious relish: "The commanding general's answer was, with a sarcastic air of humorous tolerance, emphatically negative."

It is hardly surprising that McAuliffe's answer caused corresponding displeasure among the German High Command. Indeed, since the end of the war there has been considerable discussion about who was responsible for the original ultimatum. According to one account, Generals Manteuffel and Lüttwitz had decided on an ultimatum as early as December 20, but Manteuffel apparently had become disenchanted with the idea in the meantime and the message was sent on the initiative of Lüttwitz and Bayerlein.

Manteuffel was angered by the entire episode, particularly since it was going to be difficult to carry out the threat of leveling Bastogne with an entire corps of artillery. "This is crazy," he muttered. He would have to request support from the Luftwaffe to carry out the threat as best he could.[11]

The last hope for an easy surrender shattered, Fritz Bayerlein, with his Task Force 902 (consisting of the bulk of the Panzer Lehr Division), continued on to the west toward St.-Hubert, and Heinz Kokott, of the 26th VG Division, was now made directly responsible for the conduct of the Bastogne operation. There were developments to give Kokott cause for optimism. For one thing, the right wing of Brandenberger's Seventh Army had finally made its way west and seemed ready to take over the prearranged blocking position facing southwest toward Neufchâteau and south toward Arlon. The 5th Parachute Division was already across the Arlon road. The night before, Rundstedt had become convinced that the time was ripe for a concentric at-

[10] This account comes from S. L. A. Marshall's *Bastogne: The First Eight Days* (Washington: Infantry Journal Press, 1946). It has been modified by an interview with General McAuliffe in March, 1966, and by a letter, Major General Harper to the author, dated July 6, 1966.

[11] In a television interview in 1960, General Lüttwitz admitted responsibility for the ultimatum to the Bastogne garrison. See Robert Merriam, *Dark December* (Chicago: Ziff-Davis, 1947), p. 180.

tack on Bastogne. Despite his intention to move on to the west, he had told Manteuffel that Bastogne must be taken that day.

Accordingly, between seven and eight o'clock on the morning of the twenty-second, the 39th VG Regiment and the Reconnaissance Battalion, 26th VGD, launched an attack from the west (see map, p. 314). It made slow progress, and in the sector of the 1st Battalion of the 327th U.S. Glider Infantry and the 326th Engineer Battalion, the Americans were able to counterattack with tanks, actually breaking through in a couple of places east of Assenois and threatening German artillery positions in that area. About this time Kokott decided to move his 77th VG Regiment to Champs, about four miles northwest of town, thus placing it opposite the U.S. 502d Parachute Infantry. The area southeast of Bastogne was still held by the 901st Panzer Grenadier Regiment.

The failure of the attacks convinced Manteuffel that the Germans no longer had the ability to take the offensive: the Americans were too strong. Kokott decided simply to besiege the area. He took up defensive positions, hoping that the supply situation in Bastogne would turn the trick.

As it turned out, on that day the supply situation was eased somewhat by American air activity. The largest air drop, however, was canceled; and the fact that the Luftwaffe made good Lüttwitz's threat and bombed the town (whereas American air had done less than promised) put a damper on some of the optimism the Americans had felt during the morning.

Despite the decision to go essentially on the defensive, the German High Command continued to execute limited attacks on the twenty-third. General Kokott employed the 39th VG Regiment on the northwestern finger that stuck out more than five miles to Flamierge, at the same time hitting at Marvie in the southeast, and continuing to fight against the 1st Battalion, 327th Glider Infantry, with its Reconnaissance Battalion. Illustrative of the Americans' plight was the fact that the 420th Armored Field Artillery Battalion, commanded by Lieutenant Colonel Barry D. Browne, was reinforced and used as a frontline combat element (Team Browne) to absorb much of the German attack coming from the west.[12] By strange coincidence, each of the battalions of the 327th Glider Infantry, even though separated from each other by miles, seemed to be focal points of the attacks on December 23.

But December 23 will be remembered all over the Ardennes campaign as the day when the weather broke. A high-pressure area came in, freezing the ground and clearing the skies for Allied air activity. This was the "high" that permitted the forces in the "fortified goose egg" in St.-Vith to withdraw across the Salm River. It was also the "high" that permitted 240 airplanes, carrying

[12] Colonel Browne was severely wounded in these actions. He was later killed when a heavy bomb hit a building used as a hospital.

some 1,200 pounds each, to bring supplies into Bastogne. At General Bradley's headquarters in particular, Lieutenant General Hoyt Vandenberg, commander of the Ninth Air Force, had been increasingly despondent with each poor flying day. Now, on the morning of December 23, Vandenberg's meteorologist hurried into the "Eagle Tac" War Room with a forecast of good weather. "Within an hour," according to General Bradley, "the air began to pulse with a mighty roar of engines." By Bradley's account, a total of more than 1,200 sorties were flown that day across the front.[13]

At Bastogne, of course, it was impossible to hit the drop zones with every sortie, nor was it possible to recover all the supplies, but the effects were dramatic—particularly on morale.

But despite this favorable turn of events, it should not be thought that all was optimism in the command post at Bastogne. Colonel Kinnard, no pessimist by nature, telephoned the VIII Corps G-3: "In regard to our situation, it is getting pretty sticky around here. They [the 4th Armored Division] must keep coming. The enemy has attacked all along the south and some tanks are through and running around in our area. Request you inform 4th Armored Division of our situation and ask them to put on all possible pressure." [14]

Ground activity on December 24 was devoted mainly to preparations for action on the twenty-fifth. On the German side, Lüttwitz had some good news: he was to receive support in his Christmas attack from the 15th Panzer Grenadier Division. This unit could move around to the northwest side of the Bastogne perimeter and attack between Champs and Mande-St. Étienne, roll up the 3d Battalion of the 327th, and attack toward Hemroulle, about halfway between Champs and Bastogne.[15] Thence the attack could hit either the rear of the 502d Parachute Infantry north at Longchamps or directly at Bastogne. This was an exciting prospect. In addition to the 15th Panzer Grenadier Division, the Recon Battalion of the 26th VG was also to join in.

When the 15th Panzer Grenadier arrived, however, its strength did not live up to expectations: Lüttwitz had been allocated only one regimental combat team whose estimated strength was one and a half rifle battalions, a reconnaissance battalion—consisting of 25 or 30 armored personnel carriers—20 tanks or assault guns, an engineer company, and two artillery battalions. True, the 9th Panzer and the 15th Panzer Grenadier divisions had been released from OKW reserve—and word had come all the way from Hitler to Model that Bastogne should be reduced, so the attack to seize the Marche plateau had to be continued with all available forces.

On the American side also adjustments were being made. First of all, there

[13] Omar Bradley, *A Soldier's Story* (New York: Holt, 1951), p. 479. He also states that on the next day, December 24, 2,000 bombers, escorted by more than 800 fighters, went after 31 tactical targets with 4,300 tons of bombs.

[14] Cole, *op. cit.*, p. 472.

[15] It will be recalled that Mande-St. Étienne, Champs, and Hemroulle delineated the original assembly area of the 101st Airborne.

was no point in retaining that thumb sticking out westward to Flamierge and Mande-St. Étienne, so Colonel Kinnard had drawn up a new defensive plan that gave up this salient, excluding the towns of Mande-St. Étienne and Senonchamps while retaining Champs. In addition to establishing a smaller perimeter, only 16 miles in circumference, the new defensive plan placed each of the four sectors of the front under command of one of the airborne regiments— 501st, 502d, and 506th Parachute and 327th Glider. Each regiment was organized as a combined arms team: Team O'Hara and a platoon of the 705th were attached to Julian Ewell's 501st; two platoons of the 705th joined the 506th; and two platoons of the 705th Tank Destroyer Battalion went to the 502d. The 327th was reinforced by the 326th Airborne Engineer Battalion, two platoons of the 9th Armored Engineer Battalion, and four platoons of the 705th, as well as Team Browne, organized around Browne's 420th Armored Field Artillery Battalion.

For reserve General McAuliffe retained the rest of Roberts' CCB plus part of the original Team SNAFU, which by now was becoming a more effective combat unit.

The most spectacular combat action of the day was in the air. P-47's from the 512th, 513th, and 514th squadrons of the XIX Tactical Air Command flew fighter cover for C-47's carrying in supplies, and once the C-47's had gone, the P-47's were free to knock out German positions with general purpose fragmentation bombs, napalm, and machine gun fire. This they did with pleasure, and that evening fires all around the perimeter of the Bastogne defense area attested to the effectiveness of the air support American airborne troops had received that day.

But the Luftwaffe was far from inactive. The bombardment of the town that evening was severe, and civilians in particular continued to suffer. Dozens of buildings were burning inside the town; an improvised military hospital was hit directly and reduced to a mass of debris. The command post of Team Cherry was destroyed, and four officers, including Lieutenant Hyduke, who had put up such a gallant fight on the nineteenth at the Longvilly ambush, were killed in the bombing.

The day was not simply December 24; it was Christmas Eve. Accordingly, General McAuliffe issued a message to be given out in celebration of Christmas the next day:

Merry Christmas!

What's merry about all this, you ask? We're fighting—it's cold—we aren't home. All true, but what has the proud Eagle Division accomplished with its worthy comrades of the 10th Armored Division, the 705th Destroyer Tank Battalion and all the rest? Just this: We have stopped cold everything that has been thrown at us from the North, East, South and West. . . .

Allied Troops are counterattacking in force. We continue to hold Bastogne.

By holding Bastogne we assure the success of the Allied Armies. We know that our Division Commander, General Taylor, will say: "Well done!"

We are giving our country and our loved ones at home a worthy Christmas present and being privileged to take part in the gallant feat of arms and are truly making for ourselves a merry Christmas.

But the men of Bastogne, with all their heroism, did not wish to play Santa Claus alone on Christmas: they would have liked a Christmas present themselves. Earlier in the day they had received a promise of one in a message from General Patton of the Third Army: "Xmas Eve present coming up. Hold on."

McAuliffe, by now dubbed the commanding general of the Battered Bastards of the Bastion of Bastogne, said on the phone to Middleton, "The finest Christmas present the 101st could get would be a relief tomorrow."

Middleton understood: "I know, boy. I know."

Kokott's attack on the western face of the Bastogne perimeter on Christmas morning afforded one of the most dramatic breakthroughs of the entire Bastogne operation. It also broke his back. The significant battle action took place along the road from Bastogne to Champs (a distance of just slightly more than three miles); at Hemroulle, a point halfway between those two towns; in Champs itself; and in a small stretch of road barely a mile and a half long.

Kokott's intentions seem to have been twofold: He planned to attack northwest of Champs early on Christmas morning with his 77th Regiment; then he planned to break through about two miles farther south with 115th Panzer Grenadier Regiment of the 15th Panzer Grenadier Division, half of which would turn northeast as he approached Hemroulle, thereby cutting off at least the 1st Battalion of the 502d Parachute Infantry and considerable elements of Colonel Joseph Harper's 327th. The other portion of the 115th PG Regiment he planned to send through Hemroulle and down through Bastogne itself. This force was to be supported on its right by the Reconnaissance Battalion of the 26th VG Division.

The attack got off to a reasonable start. With Luftwaffe support, German infantry of the 77th VG Regiment reached Champs by 3:00 A.M. and had made penetrations into it as early as four o'clock. The American company commander at Champs notified the 502d Regiment command post only about a half mile to the southeast that he was under attack, and the regimental commander, Colonel Steve A. Chappuis, immediately moved his reserve, the remainder of the 1st Battalion, from Hemroulle to back up A Company at Champs.

At 5:30 A.M. the main effort of the 115th Panzer Grenadier Regiment jumped off, completely overrunning two companies of the 1st Battalion of the 327th Glider Regiment. These two companies fought well, and although battalion headquarters was overrun, they simply stayed in their foxholes, and stayed on to fight after the tanks had passed over their positions, capturing many German prisoners in the wake of the panzers.

Thus far all had been good news to General Kokott. He even received a report—fallacious, it turned out—that part of his force was approaching the outskirts of Bastogne. But then he heard no more. The regimental commander, Colonel Wolfgang Maucke, sent a liaison officer to try to find the tanks, to no avail.

What had happened early Christmas morning was that the two panzer grenadier columns had been destroyed. Part of the column had headed northward to cut off the American rear at Champs and in so doing had encountered Companies B and C of the U.S. 502d, who were also on the road, going to the relief of Company A. These companies fell back in good order into the woods and, taking the seven enemy tanks under fire, completely stripped off the infantry, who were riding 15 or 16 men per tank, from the backs of the armored vehicles. The German tanks turned north toward Champs, shorn of their infantry. In turning, they exposed their thin sides and were destroyed by the tank destroyer fire of Company C, 705th Tank Destroyer Battalion, and by bazooka fire.

The fate of the southern fork was just as complete. When it reached Hemroulle, it was taken under fire by tanks, tank destroyers, 57-mm. anti-tank guns, and bazookas. None of its vehicles survived. Strangely, one tank from the northern fork was captured intact.

By 9:00 A.M. of December 25, a half-mile stretch of road within the Bastogne perimeter was strewn with the ruins of 17 German tanks, and all the German infantry had been killed or captured; a force had been completely wiped out. This was all the more painful, as Manteuffel later put it, because "after December 25 the attacking divisions were no longer in a position to launch large scale attacks because of the losses suffered." [16]

But on Christmas night relief had still not arrived at Bastogne. Despite the success of the day, disappointment was strong.

As General George S. Patton, Jr., left the meeting at Verdun on the morning of December 19, uncharacteristically he rode in his jeep with only his aide and his driver, Sergeant Mims. His first destination was Thionville, on the Moselle River, where he planned to consult with Major General Walton H. Walker, Commander of the XX Corps, before proceeding to Luxembourg City.

Patton's performance that morning at Verdun had not been a piece of theatrics. His optimism regarding his projected switch in direction from east to north had been based on sound planning. To be sure, sometime earlier he had hurriedly committed the 4th Armored Division to prevent its being taken

---

[16] Some days later, General Patton visited the Bastogne area, which still had **not** been policed up. Many frozen bodies still lay where they had fallen from the German tanks. "Finest battlefield I ever saw," Patton chortled.

away from him; but when, on the evening of the eighteenth, he realized the seriousness of the situation farther north, he withdrew the 4th from the line. It would be ready to move in a short period with minimum delay.

Patton was exhibiting that day the characteristic that so often escaped the press: his dedicated professionalism. For, with all his foibles—his extravagant uniforms, his worship of the niceties of military discipline, his exaggerated military bearing (necessitated partly by an increasing tendency to gain weight), and his highly emotional nature—the fact was that Patton lived and breathed the Army twenty-four hours a day. He was a man who knew his business.

It was not through economic necessity that Patton had dedicated his life to the Army. Independently wealthy in his own right—his wife, the former Miss Beatrice Ayers, was even more so—Patton could easily have led a life of horseback riding and sailing, both of which he did with relish. But the important thing to him was to be a soldier, with all the risks that profession entailed.

General Patton was a rounded tactician, not limited to the role of tank specialist—at least not to the extent of studying and working with tanks to the exclusion of the other arms. Admittedly an expert in armored warfare, Patton was interested in the problems of the infantry as well, and had studied the military problems of all the branches with gusto. One of the problems that preoccupied him, for example, was the impact of the new proximity fuse on land warfare, particularly on the infantry. Perhaps one answer might be to equip all attacking infantry with armored personnel carriers; he was not sure. But he thought about it seriously.

Patton seemed always to regard war with a detached clinical eye and somewhat wonderingly—always seeking after new truths of his chosen art. Every tactical event seemed to hold a lesson, either for himself or for others, which he sometimes rather pedantically passed along. During the war he put together collections of "reflections and suggestions" on matters sometimes important, sometimes seemingly trivial, sometimes humorous. Examples:

> The soldier is the Army. No army is better than its soldiers. The soldier is also a citizen. In fact, the highest obligation and privilege of citizenship is that of bearing arms for one's country. Hence it is a proud privilege to be a soldier—a good soldier.
>
> *Marching Fire:* The proper way to advance, particularly for troops armed with that magnificent weapon, the M-1 rifle, is to utilize marching fire and keep moving. This fire can be delivered from the shoulder, but it is just as effective if delivered with the butt of the rifle halfway between the belt and the armpit. One round should be fired every two or three paces.
>
> *Night Attack in Woods:* It is not necessary or advisable to attack through woods at night. In the first place, the woods themselves give the cover which the darkness does in the open. In the second place, it is almost impossible to move through woods at night except in column on roads.

Tanks and Infantry: The question of whether infantry or tanks lead in attacking is determined by the character of the ground and of the enemy resistance. Whenever the ground permits tanks to advance rapidly, even with the certainty of a loss from mine fields, they should lead.

Cemeteries: Do not place military cemeteries where they can be seen by replacements marching to the front. This has a very bad effect on morale, even if it adds to the pride of the Graves Registration Service.

Length of Attack: Infantry troops can attack continuously for sixty hours. Frequently much time and suffering are saved if they will do so. Beyond sixty hours, it is rather a waste of time, as the men become too fatigued from lack of sleep.[17]

With all his study, Patton was well aware of his limitations. When General Bradley, one of his former subordinates, was named commander of 12 Army Group and his new boss, he took a seeming demotion with impressive good humor entirely in keeping with his generous nature. On the other hand, he probably would not have enjoyed a higher command, for above the level of field army, soldiering is less personal—the fronts are too broad—and politics begin to enter the picture. Pure tactics are the realm of the field army, corps, division, and regiment, and Patton considered himself primarily a tactician. He never seriously regarded himself as a strategist, no matter how free he felt to complain of policies implemented by SHAEF and even by his immediate superior, 12 Army Group.

George Patton had long been a warm, and at intervals a really close, friend of Dwight Eisenhower. Their friendship went back to the days of World War I, in which they had served with a newly invented weapon called the tank. At that time, with the tank still largely in the experimental stage, there were various theories regarding its employment. The two friends shared a common conviction: the tank was a weapon to be used in mass and, technically, should be developed as a highly mobile machine with considerable armor and firepower. This contention, strangely, was not universally accepted. Eisenhower's insistence on this principle at times had put him at loggerheads with the hierarchy in his own branch, infantry. The chief of infantry, in the early 1920's, regarded the tank not as a weapon to be used independently but simply as an infantry support vehicle.

Patton and Eisenhower served together at Fort Meade in the early twenties, where their friendship grew. Life there was less exciting than in the days of World War I. Both had been reduced in rank, and appropriations were putting a bite on the interest that the Army was showing in armored warfare. Occasionally, to combat boredom, the two would resort to a curious hobby. There was then a lonely road between Camp Meade and the main highways from Washington, and the road was a notorious site for holdups. The two young

[17] George Patton, *War as I Knew It* (Boston: Houghton, 1947), pp. 335, 339, 342, 349, 353.

officers would slowly drive up and down this road at night, hoping to be stopped—for both were loaded to the ears with several pistols and other weapons; but for all their attempts, they were never treated to the opportunity of seeing a highwayman look down the barrels of their guns.

Despite the difference in age, service, and experience—Patton was from the West Point class of 1908, Eisenhower the class of 1915—Patton always regarded the younger man as his future superior in war. Often, talking in his jocular manner, Patton would tell of the days when they would run the next war. "Ike, you will be the Lee of the next war, and I will be your Jackson."

During the thirties, Patton and Eisenhower had seen less of each other. Patton had gone back to the horse, where he commanded the 3d Cavalry at Fort Myer; Eisenhower had been pulled primarily into staff work in the War Department and returned to his original branch, infantry. But in Washington they visited on occasional Sundays in informal family gatherings, usually amid the impressive array of silver cups Patton had won for horsemanship.

At the advent of the invasion of North Africa, Eisenhower was sure he had come to know his man well during their long acquaintance: he felt Patton would be a master of pursuit. This quality, Eisenhower theorized, is one of the rarest to be found in a commander. It has been possessed by others—by Napoleon (who, incidentally, probably lost Waterloo because of his uncharacteristic failure to pursue vigorously after the action at Quatre Bras) and by Grant. On the other hand, Lincoln came within a hair's breadth of firing Meade for his failure to pursue Lee after the Union victory at Gettysburg.

The will to pursue relentlessly, even though one knows his men are dropping with exhaustion—and the pursuit will probably end in a bloody nose for his spearheads (unless he happens to win the war in this one swoop)—is rare indeed. For this Eisenhower regarded Patton almost uniquely qualified.

Thus it was not sentiment that had caused General Eisenhower to risk his own future in late 1943 when he stood up for General Patton after the notorious soldier-slapping incident in Sicily, nor friendship alone that caused him to tolerate the antics and impolitic public statements that kept Patton at odds with the press. Eisenhower stood by his old friend through a hardheaded conviction that George Patton was necessary to the Allied cause.[18]

As Patton bounced along in his jeep toward Thionville that Tuesday, December 19, he had much on his mind. Once there, he discussed the situation with General Walker, who, though not directly concerned, was someone Patton admired as a "fighting son of a bitch." The day was getting long, and

---

[18] In fact, Eisenhower had achieved a reputation in some circles for being overly severe in his handling of officers who failed in combat—he simply sent them home to the United States, reduced to their permanent rank. In one case he demoted and sent home a West Point classmate for indiscreet talk that might have jeopardized the security of the Overlord operation.

in view of the confusion on the roads Walker dissuaded Patton from continuing his trip to the city of Luxembourg. Borrowing a toothbrush and pajamas, General Patton stayed over, sending his aide back to Nancy the following day to pack things up and begin moving his headquarters to Luxembourg.

The next morning, December 20, Patton started out early to establish himself in his new location and to see General Bradley. This was the day when responsibility for the southern part of the Bulge was to pass to Third Army when it assumed command of Middleton's VIII Corps at noon.

Arrived in Luxembourg, Patton discovered that CCB of the 4th Armored Division under Brigadier General Holmes E. Dager, one of his favorite units, had been attached to VIII Corps; there was some prospect that Middleton intended to send it into Bastogne alone, without the rest of the division. The Neufchâteau-Bastogne road was still open at this time, but barely. Patton learned also that the march of the 80th Division toward Mersch had been halted at Luxembourg. With General Bradley's assent, Patton, now in command of the southern shoulder, rescinded both orders, sending Dager back to Arlon, and putting the 80th Division back on the road to Mersch.

Like Bradley, Patton viewed the command arrangement that placed the northern shoulder of the Ardennes battle under Field Marshal Montgomery with grave suspicions that the decision involved more than the mere breakdown in communications. Both regarded it as a temporary demotion for Bradley, and Patton admired the way in which Bradley took it. However, there was business to be done, and, his conference finished, Patton was soon on the road to Arlon, location of the new III Corps, whose responsibility it was to relieve Bastogne. Before leaving for Arlon, however, he sent word that he wanted Middleton to come over and see him. Middleton's VIII Corps, now in the Third Army, consisted of only the 101st Airborne Division, remnants of the 28th Infantry Division, the 9th Armored Division (minus Hoge's Combat Command), and corps supporting units. Most of these troops were within the Bastogne area, and the tenuous line between Neufchâteau and Bastogne was about to be cut.

When General Middleton reported to the Third Army Commander at Arlon, he was greeted by a typical Patton outburst: "Troy, of all the goddam crazy things I ever heard of, leaving the 101st Airborne to be surrounded in Bastogne is the worst!"

Such words from another commander might have been cause for concern. Not so with Troy Middleton and George Patton: they were in the habit of exchanging frank opinions. They had been students at Leavenworth together, and Middleton, an expert horseman, was one of the few officers excused from that august institution's equitation course and permitted to help exercise George Patton's fourteen polo ponies. But aside from their past relationship

Middleton could rely on the axiom: If General Patton is swearing at you, the chances are that you are currently rating pretty high on his list.

"George," said Middleton in his gentle Mississippi drawl, "just look at that map with all the roads converging on Bastogne. Bastogne is the hub of the wheel. If we let the Boche take it, they will be at the Meuse in a day."

Patton's kaleidoscopic face changed pattern. "Well, if you were in my position, where would you launch the attack? From Arlon down here or from Neufchâteau?"

"I'd attack with the 4th Armored from the place where our lines are closest to Bastogne. You've got to use both roads, but I'd put the weight on the Neufchâteau road. But as for the main effort of III Corps, I'd put it farther east. You don't cut troops off by pushing them in their front."

As so often happens, two honor graduates of the Command and General Staff School took the same set of facts and came up with different answers. The III Corps main attack would be made by the 4th Armored up the Arlon road.

Patton's main preoccupation at this time was indeed the attack of Major General John Millikin's III Corps, scheduled to jump off in two days, the morning of the twenty-second. The selection of the three divisions to constitute this corps had been almost automatic, since the 26th and 80th Infantry divisions and the 4th Armored had been either out of the line or in quiet sectors when the Third Army had been ordered north the day before. Indeed, the 4th Armored and 80th Infantry divisions had already been shifted to Millikin on the night of December 18, when Generals Bradley and Patton, informed of what would happen the next morning at Verdun, had begun making preparations.

The 80th Infantry was probably in the best condition. The 26th was full of replacements, having lost 2,500 men in the Lorraine campaign; the 4th Armored, with all its brilliant combat record, was suffering from lack of replacement personnel, but even more severely from worn-out equipment, much of which had been in constant combat since the days of the Normandy campaign. Patton was on the telephone much of the time arranging for self-propelled tank destroyer battalions, nondivisional tank battalions, hospitals, ammunition, and bridging materials. He directed that all three divisions of the III Corps cannibalize their antitank gun units and turn them into riflemen since all three were short of critical infantry replacements.

But while the headline attack of Third Army would be that of Millikin's III Corps to relieve Bastogne, this operation was only a portion of Patton's movement north. Middleton, on the west at Neufchâteau, could of course do little. But on the east, where the 4th Infantry Division, the 10th Armored, and elements of the 28th had held the critical southern shoulder, another attack was to be launched—indeed, had Bastogne not been held by the 101st Airborne Division, this attack from Luxembourg north to St.-Vith might well have been Patton's main effort. As it was, the first priority had to be given to relief of Bastogne.

Patton's 90-degree shift of his Third Army involved a gigantic sideslip to the left. As Devers' 6 Army Group took over Patton's former territory in the Saar, Patton moved Major General Manton Eddy's XII Corps to Luxembourg to direct operations on the right of Millikin. Eddy's corps would include the 4th and 5th Infantry divisions and the 10th Armored. By the night of December 20, Eddy had moved to Luxembourg and was preparing for his attack.

Meanwhile George Patton continued to scrape divisions from other sectors of Third Army. With the 35th Infantry and the 6th Armored divisions soon to be ready, Patton felt doubly sure of success.

These moves of divisions, complicated as they may seem, were perhaps the simplest elements in the gargantuan problem of shifting the Third Army. Besides relieving units and assembling them over long distances and icy roads, there loomed the questions of 20,000 miles of communication wire that had to be relaid and moving of ammunition supply points for five classes of supply, not to mention preparation for the attack itself through strange, rough country against a determined enemy. Patton was a busy man in these days, so busy, in fact, that his driver suggested he had no need for the rest of his staff. But Patton himself was the last man to claim all the credit for such a problem in management. Discussing the move with General Bradley, he marveled at the performance of various members of his staff. He thought they had performed miracles.

On one count, however, he was perfectly willing to take full credit. He dubbed himself the "ray of sunshine and the backslapper" for both his superiors and those serving under him.

On the night of Thursday, December 21, he held a final meeting of the corps commanders. He was at his optimistic best. To be sure, there supposedly were elements of four German divisions in the line opposite III Corps—the 5th Parachute Division and the 212th, 276th, and 352d Volksgrenadier divisions. All but the 5th Parachute had been identified previously as belonging to the German Seventh Army. The III Corps attack would have to go through a fragmentary screen of friendly troops, through uncertain positions, against an unknown enemy, and over unfamiliar terrain. The area for the III Corps counterattack extended from the Alzette River on the east to Neufchâteau on the west, a front of some thirty miles (see map, p. 339).

General Patton could not find out much about the enemy from intelligence sources. The garrison at Bastogne were experts by this time on the location of the troops hitting their own area, but beyond that they knew very little. Even the location of friendly roadblocks and outposts in the direction in which

III Corps would attack was unknown. The attack would advance north with three divisions abreast: the 4th Armored Division, attacking from Arlon directly to Bastogne; the 26th Infantry Division in the center, attacking in the direction of Wiltz; and the 80th Division on the east attacking from the vicinity of Mersch to retake Ettelbruck and the line of the Sûre River. The XII Corps, on the right of the III Corps, was also to attack northward to restore the line of the Sûre River. Unfortunately the area of the 26th and 80th Infantry divisions was the toughest country in practically the entire Ardennes.

During the meeting with the corps commanders, Patton's last instructions reflected General Eisenhower's admonition against piecemeal attack. He specified to his corps and division commanders that he favored an attack in a column of regiments, or in any case "lots of depth." Patton felt certain the Germans were unaware the attack was about to be launched, largely because of bad weather, which this time had covered the movements of the Americans rather than the Germans. He was certain the Germans could not react in less than thirty-six hours.

Of the three divisions, the one that received the closest attention from the Army commander was the 4th Armored, for several reasons. It was a pet unit of his, and although its equipment and personnel strength were not what they should have been, Patton had a right to expect a great performance. Furthermore, the command had just been assumed by his former chief of staff, Major General Hugh Gaffey. Most important, however, was the dramatic role that the division was to perform. It was to go through country relatively open (compared to that of the infantry divisions) and burst through and rescue the surrounded garrison at Bastogne.

Patton himself prescribed the tactics to be used by General Gaffey and the 4th Armored. He specified that the artillery and tank destroyers, with armored engineers, should lead off, with the main body of armored infantry kept back. Envelopment tactics rather than frontal attack should be employed when the force encountered stiff resistance, and all envelopments should be wide, begun a mile or a mile and a half back and made at right angles.[19] General Gaffey can hardly be envied for being supervised in such a careful fashion.

But above all, Patton wanted speed, and plenty of it. He closed the meeting with the corps commanders on the evening of the twenty-first with the admonition: "Drive like hell."

On the morning of the twenty-second, the day of the Third Army jump-off, General Eisenhower issued one of his rare orders of the day, addressed to every member of the AEF.

[19] Cole, *op. cit.*, p. 525.

The enemy is making his supreme effort to break out of the desperate plight into which you forced him by your brilliant victories of the summer and fall. He is fighting savagely to take back all that you have won and is using every treacherous trick to deceive and kill you. He is gambling everything, but already, in this battle, your unparalleled gallantry has done much to foil his plans. In the face of your proven bravery and fortitude, he will completely fail.

But we cannot be content with his mere repulse.

By rushing out from his fixed defenses the enemy has given us the chance to turn his great gamble into his worst defeat. So I call upon every man, of all the Allies, to rise now to new heights of courage, of resolution, and of effort. Let everyone hold before him a single thought—to destroy the enemy on the ground, in the air, everywhere—destroy him! United in this determination and with unshakable faith in the cause for which we fight, we will, with God's help, go forward to our greatest victory.

But General Patton had a different approach. In the hands of the soldiers of the attacking divisions was a prayer for good weather:

Almighty and most merciful Father, we humbly beseech Thee, of Thy great goodness, to restrain these immoderate rains with which we have had to contend. Grant us fair weather for Battle. Graciously hearken to us as soldiers who call upon Thee that, armed with Thy power, we may advance from victory to victory, and crush the oppression and wickedness of our enemies, and establish Thy justice among men and nations. Amen.

The prayer had been put together rather reluctantly some days before by Chaplain (Colonel) James H. O'Neill of the Third Army to apply to the attack in the Saar, now canceled. When reminded of this fact by General Gay, Patton said blithely: "Oh, the Lord won't mind. He knows we're too busy right now killing Germans to print another prayer."

The prayer may have seemed a bit ironic. The attack jumped off in fog and snow.

In accordance with General Millikin's request jump-off on December 22 had been delayed from 4:00 A.M. to 6:00 A.M. Despite considerable resistance and difficulties from blown roads and bridges, at first the attack went fairly well. Extensive gains were made, averaging approximately seven miles along the entire III Corps front. This was not what Patton had hoped for, but he realized that it is sometimes difficult to get an attack rolling, and normally seven miles is a fair gain for the first day. There were a couple of things he was keeping a special eye on. For one, he was somewhat concerned about his left flank, which, protected by Middleton's skeleton VIII Corps, was largely hanging in the air. He further recalled the German attack at the beginning of their assault against the French in 1940. On that occasion, in a secondary attack, they had swung southwest through Saarbrücken, penetrating the Maginot Line to seize Thionville and Metz. He was concerned that this might be repeated.

On the other side of the coin, he was encouraged when he met eight soldiers and one officer at Arlon who had escaped from Wiltz after Colonel Strickler had broken up the defense force on December 19. These men had walked straight across the southern portion of German-occupied territory, seeing only seven Germans on the way. Maybe, Patton mused, the German attack was less dense than had been reported.

On balance, Patton was pleased with the first day's effort. That night he told General Millikin that this was the chance to win the war; the attack must be kept rolling through the night.

The next morning, December 23, General Patton looked out the window in Luxembourg. He was greeted with the same sight that gave hope to General Clarke at Kommanster and General McAuliffe at Bastogne: clear, cold weather. Allied aircraft were busy. On the Third Army front alone seven groups of fighter-bombers, eleven groups of medium bombers, a division of the Eighth Air Force, and numbers of RAF planes were active. Patton, sending for his deputy chief of staff, was exultant. This was doubtless the chaplain's doings. "God damn! That O'Neill sure did some potent praying," he crowed. "Get him up here, I want to pin a medal on him."

Chaplain O'Neill was rushed from Nancy to Luxembourg City; the next day, with the weather still fine, he was warmly greeted: "Chaplain, you're the most popular man in this headquarters. You sure stand in good with the Lord and soldiers."

General Patton duly pinned the Bronze Star Medal on the breast of Chaplain O'Neill.

For the next three days the attack along the III Corps front and the XII Corps front generally went well. The infantry with the greatest distance to cover was the 26th Division—about 12 miles from its line of departure at Niedercalpach to the Sûre River line. In the XII Corps sector the distances were somewhat less. Despite the appearance on the front of a new unit, the crack Führer Grenadier Brigade, the 26th U.S. Division, the 80th Division on its right, and XII Corps on the extreme right had nearly closed in on the entire line of the Sûre by the end of December 26. The town of Echternach, sitting in a cup on the Sauer, still remained in German hands. Fighting was difficult and slow; the many valiant actions were offset by the frustrations of close combat—generally the kind of fighting of which George Patton was not particularly fond.

As the 4th Armored Division drove northward to relieve Bastogne, the situation on the left flank of the Third U.S. Army was more fluid.

In planning the 4th Armored Division's attack, it had been necessary first to select the routes over which the two combat commands would travel.

Standard procedure in the 4th Armored was to employ Combat Command A and Combat Command B as the fighting units of the division; Combat Command Reserve was rarely employed tactically.

Middleton's advice to Patton regarding the main route had much merit; his strongest argument was that elements of the 28th Division were still holding positions on the Neufchâteau road only about six miles from the Bastogne perimeter. On the Arlon route, the forwardmost U.S. positions were at a town called Martelange, about 12 miles south of the perimeter. On the other hand, the road from Neufchâteau had one very distinct disadvantage: it required the attack to be launchd from an area far to the west. The three towns of Arlon, Neufchâteau, and Bastogne form an approximate equilateral triangle, with Neufchâteau almost as far from Arlon as from Bastogne. The use of the Neufchâteau route, therefore, would place the weight of the 4th Armored Division attack so far to the west as to leave a 15-mile gap between its main effort and that of the 26th Infantry Division, attacking on its east. This, Patton felt, would be risky.

In the final scheme of maneuver Combat Command A of the 4th Armored was to proceed along the Arlon-Bastogne road while Combat Command B,

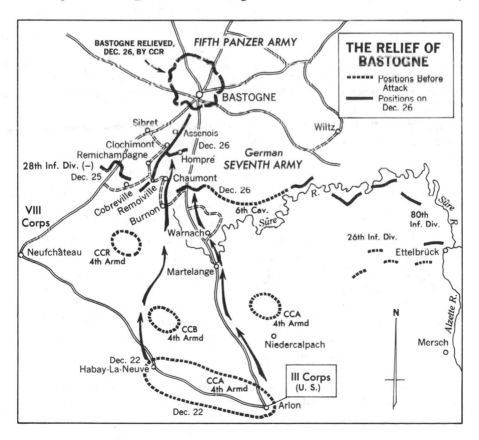

jumping off at Habay-La-Neuve about five miles west, would follow secondary routes through hilly, forested country, where little resistance was expected. The two routes would draw closer together as the units moved north; after a few miles of advance the two commands would be within mutual supporting distance, less than two miles apart.

When the attack began early in the morning of December 22, CCB under General Dager found that intelligence had been correct: only minimal resistance lay in its path. It had traveled nearly 12 miles by noontime, reaching the vicinity of the village of Burnon, only seven miles from the center of Bastogne. However, on its right CCA had been delayed by the efficiency of American demolitions, laid generously to slow the advance of the German Seventh Army. Near Martelange a large crater held up the column, and during the afternoon CCA became involved in a heavy fire fight with a rifle company of the German 15th Regiment (5th Parachute Division) guarding the demolished bridges at Martelange: a single German rifle company held up a whole combat command until about three o'clock the next morning, December 23, when it was finally driven out by an equally large unit of American armored infantry. CCA was forced to spend the whole day of the twenty-third bridging the Sûre River at Martelange. Despite the fact that CCA had hardly moved, General Millikin was optimistic. He informed Middleton that with the Sûre River bridged, he expected to be in contact with the 101st Airborne that same night.

Meanwhile, Dager's CCB had been stopped at Burnon. A bridge had been blown, and a small German party was able to hold him until the small hours of the twenty-third.

On the twenty-third CCB pushed forward a couple of miles to the tiny village of Chaumont. As the advance guard was nearing that town, German antitank guns opened up for the first time, knocking out one of Dager's Shermans. The advance guard withdrew to the main body. CCB had covered only about a quarter of a mile during the night, and now, having reached its first appreciable resistance, it was forced to deploy for a coordinated attack.

With the cold sunny weather on December 23 Allied air forces became active. Priority went to the drive of the 4th Armored, and the support was superb. Fighter-bombers from the XIX Tactical Air Command hammered Chaumont, meanwhile putting on a spectacle of dogfights with the Luftwaffe for the ground troops.

General Millikin at III Corps received a phone call. It was General Patton: "There's too much piddling around! Bypass these towns and clear them up later. Tanks can operate on this ground now."

Dager's CCB assaulted Chaumont in the early afternoon of the twenty-third. The attack consisted of a tank-infantry lunge into the village and an envelopment on the west. Unfortunately for the Americans, however, the sun had been out for long enough to thaw out the open country, and the Sherman tanks were beginning to bog down in the mud. A company of the German 5th Parachute Division, 14th Regiment, was finally driven out of Chaumont, but apparently the Germans had decided to make an issue of this town. Since the village lies on low ground surrounded by hills and connecting ridges, the Germans brought up an assault gun brigade, bearing both 75-mm. guns and infantry troops. The German assault guns knocked out what American tanks they could sight, and retook Chaumont.

American losses were heavy. Company A of the 10th Armored Infantry Battalion, the first unit into Chaumont, lost more than 60 men. CCB lost 11 Sherman tanks, and had been stopped only a couple of miles beyond the point reached at noontime on the twenty-second, more than twenty-four hours earlier.

Brigadier General Herbert L. Earnest's CCA crossed the bridge at Martelange at about the same time that CCB was beginning its assault on Chaumont. With heavy artillery support, CCA reached the village of Warnach, about two miles north of Martelange. Thinking the town clear, the American tanks rumbled past. When the thin-skinned half-tracks of the infantry came by, however, German small arms cracked from the village. Warnach, CCA learned the hard way, could not be bypassed; it would have to be reduced. General Earnest's men launched a series of tank-infantry attacks on the town but were repulsed with heavy losses. An assault was attempted the next morning from three sides, with infantry riding tanks. The result was predictable: an infantry dogfight. The German troops fought desperately, filtering back into houses that had been considered cleared. Finally, at noon, the battle ended. The Americans had killed 135 Germans and taken an equal number of prisoners, but their own losses in capturing this small village were 68 officers and men dead and wounded.[20] At noontime on Christmas Eve, CCA was still several miles behind the point reached by CCB at noon on the twenty-second.

During the day of the twenty-fourth, on the other hand, Dager's CCB was able to make some progress, reaching Hompré, just south of Clochimont and about three miles from the Bastogne perimeter.

It was now apparent that something had to be done to get the 4th Armored Division attack moving. General Millikin came up with two devices. First, since both CCA and CCB of the 4th Armored Division had taken great losses in infantry, he attached two infantry battalions from the 80th Division to the 4th Armored. One battalion went to each combat command. This, hopefully, would give both CCA and CCB added impetus.

[20] Cole, *op. cit.*, p. 530.

But more radical, perhaps, was the decision to employ the third combat command, CCR, to the west of Dager's CCB. It so happened that the new axis was the one General Middleton had recommended in the first place.

That night CCR moved to the vicinity of Cobreville. Most of the sector it had been holding to the east along the Sûre River was taken over by a battalion of Colonel E. M. Fickett's 6th U.S. Cavalry Regiment, and some was assumed by Major General Willard S. Paul's 26th Infantry Division.

CCR, commanded by Colonel Wendell Blanchard, consisted of two maneuver battalions, the 37th Tank Battalion, commanded by Lieutenant Colonel Creighton W. Abrams, and the 53rd Armored Infantry Battalion, commanded by Lieutenant Colonel George Jaques. It was supported by two 105-mm. howitzer battalions and a battery of 155-mm. howitzers.

Colonel Blanchard selected his own route, free of friendly demolitions, and assembled in an area a mile behind Cota's 28th Division at the crossroads town of Bercheux. From there, he drove on Christmas morning almost due east to Cobreville and continued on a mile to Remonville, where he hoped to turn north in the direction of Remichampagne. At Remonville something warned Blanchard of trouble. Perhaps a liaison plane or possibly a prisoner gave warning.[21] Regardless of the source of information, Blanchard ordered Remonville leveled by four battalions of artillery from CCR assisted by support from the adjacent CCB. A strong tank-infantry attack revealed a whole German battalion, the 3d, of 14th Parachute Regiment. It was dusk before the combat command had overwhelmed the battalion, taking more than 320 prisoners.

On Christmas evening General Patton again felt disappointed by the results of the day. Again he had awakened to find the morning clear and cold. "Lovely weather for killing Germans," he had said to himself (reflecting afterward that the thought was somewhat at variance with the spirit of Christmas). He had visited two combat commands of the 4th Armored, as well as elements of five other divisions. But the addition of the two infantry battalions to the 4th Armored had not turned the trick; nor had the employment of CCR on the west. Tony McAuliffe would not get his Christmas present of relief on the twenty-fifth.

That evening Patton had Christmas dinner at General Bradley's mess at Luxembourg City. Bradley had spent the day on a trip visiting Field Marshal Montgomery. After dinner the two Americans had a long talk, during which Bradley quoted Montgomery in nearly unbelievable terms. He said that Montgomery had estimated that First U.S. Army (now under Monty's command) could not attack for three months; that the only attacks possible would have to be executed in the south by Patton's Third Army—but that Third Army

---

[21] Cole, whose extensive research could bring forth no concrete answer, allows the possibility of a "sixth sense."

was too weak to have much effect. Bradley quoted Montgomery as advocating a retreat in the south to the line of the Saar River and the Vosges Mountains —or even the Moselle River—in order to gain enough force to permit Patton to continue the attack. General Patton said he found the idea "disgusting." [22]

While the two generals were talking that Christmas night, CCR, 4th Armored Division, was planning its next day's attack with the use of a map from Bastogne that had just arrived by liaison plane. It showed the American dispositions in the Bastogne perimeter, as well as the most accurate enemy situation that could be conjured up. Not surprisingly, the order of battle as it faced inward toward the perimeter was, as ever, detailed and exact, whereas enemy units identified at farther distances still tended to be vague and questionable.

The plan finally arrived at, after much consultation, called for an advance to Remichampagne, a mile and a half away, and from there to Clochimont. Then, to avoid becoming embroiled with CCB on the right and to get back on the main Neufchâteau-Bastogne road, a turn northwest to Sibret was ordered; CCR was to clear Sibret of German troops and then enter Bastogne from the southwest. Fighter-bomber support had been promised for the morning of the twenty-sixth.

The next morning, December 26, CCR started for Remichampagne. Where the ground was frozen, tank going was good. After the column had gotten under way, a number of P-47's appeared. With effective bombing only a few hundred yards in front of the lead tanks, the P-47's cleared the way past Remichampagne and the woods that covered it from the flanks. Clochimont, only three miles from Bastogne, was now open.

CCR was much under strength, not so much from this particular action as from the division's logical policy of attaching battalions to CCR that had been depleted by previous action. Colonel Abrams, for one, had no more than twenty Shermans left in operation. Colonel Jaques' 3d Armored Infantry Battalion was short 230 men. They stood at Clochimont discussing the situation.

Taken as a whole, the U.S. armored division of World War II—which has not changed drastically since—was an admirable organization. Considered a pool of diversified arms capable of being "tailored" into task forces fitted for specific situations, the armored division constituted an instrument of great

---

[22] It is difficult to imagine such a statement coming from Montgomery. However, both Americans were critical of Montgomery's performance and attitudes, particularly since Patton felt that U.S. First Army had been capable of attacking even a couple of days before, on the twenty-third. In an interview with the author on October 1, 1966, Montgomery categorically denied estimating that First Army could not attack for three months. As of Christmas, 1944, the Field Marshal described the situation as "a piece of cake." However, he agreed that withdrawal of some divisions from Alsace would have been wise, and in this Eisenhower agreed. See Patton, *op. cit.,* p. 203.

flexibility. But no organization is perfect. The Achilles' heel of the armored division concept was—and is—a downgrading of the power and prestige of the combat command commander. As his attached battalions came and went, the CC commander enjoyed far less continuing association—and therefore control—over them than did his infantry counterpart, the regimental commander. For a combat command leader to run as tight an organization, it took the personality of a Bruce Clarke or a Bill Hoge—and even then it was helpful to be operating somewhere independent of the rest of the division.

So Jaques and Abrams of the 4th Armored—who had worked together before under other combat commands but who lacked much in the way of awe for their temporary commander—standing on a hill at Clochimont, came up with their own answer to the problem that faced them. The solution, which they executed without reference to higher headquarters, shortcut the scheme prescribed for them that morning.

Supposedly CCR was to attack westward, take Sibret (teeming with Germans), and enter Bastogne from the Neufchâteau road. But why not bypass Sibret and barrel on into Bastogne through Assenois—a direct line?

At 3:30 P.M. Abrams sent for his battalion S-3, Captain William Dwight. It was approaching dusk, which would make an attack difficult. But in the distance the congregated officers could see a fleet of C-47's making a cargo drop into the Bastogne perimeter and taking heavy losses as they caught heavy flak.

"We're going in now!" said Abrams. He and Dwight selected a tank company, Jaques an infantry company. The basis for the "honor" was primarily ammunition supply: in the case of the 37th Tank Battalion it was a matter of who had the most machine gun ammunition on hand.

Dwight thus found himself the commander of Task Force C consisting of an armored infantry and tank company. He was instructed to take his force, break northeast of Assenois, and keep moving until he reached the Bastogne lines. All the artillery supporting CCR was directed to stand ready to place a concentration on Assenois.

Dwight moved out. As he approached Assenois he called for artillery fire on the town and on the woods to the north. The artillery support was so close that shells were still dropping in the town when the first tanks moved in, and they knocked out a couple of the infantry half-tracks. Five American tanks with one infantry half-track drove through the confusion and kept moving toward Bastogne. In the town, German foot troops from both the 26th VG and the 5th Parachute divisions emerged from the basements, and an infantry melee was under way again. It was nearly midnight before Jaques' men completely cleared Assenois and the woods to the north. The five tanks and the half-track that had gone through were driving toward Bastogne when a gap developed between the lead three tanks and the other three vehicles, and some enterprising Germans jumped out and strewed mines across the road.

The half-track hit one of the mines and was destroyed. Dwight dismounted with some of his men to clear the other mines away. Meanwhile, the three lead tanks kept going.

On the afternoon of December 26, General McAuliffe, who had been in contact with VIII Corps, was notified that the 4th Armored Division was only four miles to the southwest along the Assenois road. Taking his aide, Ted Starrett, with him, he drove to the sector of the 326th Airborne Engineer Battalion. There, from a piece of high ground, he could see in the distance a few tanks of the 4th Armored making their way through the minefields that had been hastily laid by the Germans between Assenois and the U.S. positions. He watched as they came on.

At 4:50 P.M. First Lieutenant Charles P. Boggess, commanding officer of Company C, 37th Tank Battalion, took the first vehicle from the 4th Armored Division into the lines of the 101st Airborne. He was followed by Captain Dwight, who had now caught up. As Dwight's bedraggled tankers passed the engineers' foxholes, Dwight noted with some surprise that, in accordance with rigid 101st Airborne discipline, the paratroopers were clean-shaven to a man.

"Well, things don't look so goddam rough around here to me," he muttered.

Soon Dwight found his way up the hill to General McAuliffe's observation post. Dwight saluted; his report was informal: "How are you, General?"

"Gee, I am mighty glad to see you," said one of the most unpretentious generals in the U.S. Army.

CHAPTER 14

❧❦

High-Water Mark

A S his westernbound panzer divisions bypassed Bastogne on the south and attacked First U.S. Army positions on the north, Generalfeldmarschall Walther Model, son of a schoolteacher, was at the height of his career. Dark, graying, blue-eyed, well-coordinated, and stocky, Model seemed shorter than his five feet ten inches. He rated high with Hitler. At least on one occasion the Führer had said of Model, *"Das ist mein bester Feldmarschall."*

Whether Model was Hitler's best field marshal was open to debate, but there was no denying his competence. He had held all the important positions in the staff and line and had developed depth of experience in all. Still, his detractors tended to regard him primarily as a "defense specialist"—with the implication that the Ardennes offensive was an undertaking out of his field. There was some basis to the charge; it stemmed from the fact that having come to his high rank late in the war—after the end of the great German offensives—it was only logical that Model's greatest services would be rendered in defensive operations. But his admirers saw no reason why he should not be as brilliant in directing a great offensive as in reorganizing shattered armies.

Above all, Model was imaginative; to do one's duty was simply not enough. What he demanded, in his own words, was "never-failing daemoniac genius, fully conscious of his own creative power of mastering everything." As such, he was a practitioner of the personal command, riding a light reconnaissance plane to assess the tactical situation personally rather than relying on reports from others. Often he was quoted as saying, "He who cannot invent anything, who cannot organize anything, who cannot shape his surroundings according to his whole being, never knew any urge of necessity and, for a lack of imagination and energy, never can lay claim to leadership."

In common with many creative people, Model was a bundle of startling contrasts. A stickler for military organization, he reorganized his units unmercifully. His subordinate officers often felt his tactlessness worst. Günther Reichhelm, the operations officer of Army Group B, has recalled how he felt it necessary to go to the front lines to smooth the ruffled feelings of Model's

346

officers—which sometimes reached such intensity that they contemplated suicide. And yet Model was sympathetic in his dealings with German soldiers,
who believed in him implicitly.

As might be expected from such a temperament, Model was a stern dis-
ciplinarian. He had a strong tendency to threaten to bring offending subordinates to court-martial—although often once such action was taken he
moderated it. This idiosyncrasy stemmed probably from a paradox in his nature—an overweening sense of duty and fiery temper combined with a softheartedness beneath. He had a reputation as a drinker, but if it was earned
it certainly failed to interfere with his habit of rising at 5:30 A.M. daily to
begin his inspections of the front.

No doctrinaire Nazi, Model was completely devoted to his profession of
arms. He allowed himself little time for leisure and recreation, and deprived
himself of the opportunity to make close friends. His admirers described him
as a deeply religious Christian, with a strong sense of family, domesticity, and
love of nature.

And yet, when Germany's armed might was to end, these qualities would
not be enough to sustain him. Within a very few months of this peak of his
career, he would be one of the German generals to take his own life.

As Model surveyed the situation on the Ardennes front the evening of December 20, he could find causes for satisfaction and causes for disappointment. He reviewed his positions from north to south.

Hitler had canceled the attack of the German Fifteenth Army two days be-
fore, thereby eliminating any chances for a double envelopment of the U.S.
First Army by the Fifteenth in the north and the Sixth Panzer Army from
Elsenborn Ridge. Even more disappointing was the fact that the main effort
of his own Army Group B—the attack of Dietrich's Sixth Panzer Army across
Elsenborn Ridge toward Liège and the Meuse—had failed. For days the
12th SS Panzer Division had been trying to budge the American position at
Elsenborn to no avail.

But at least Rundstedt and even OKW had now admitted the failure. Hitler
no longer insisted on beating Dietrich's head against a wall, and Rundstedt had
permitted the 12th SS Panzer Division to switch from the Monschau Forest
and try to open the road from Büllingen to Butgenbach. Manteuffel, farther
south, had achieved a substantial breakthrough. The Americans did not seem
to be trying to stop him; instead they were concentrating on building a defensive line facing south along the Amblève River. They still held Malmédy
and now, after the counterattack the day before, had cut off Jochen Peiper by
retaking Stavelot.

Peiper was in La Gleize and Stoumont, apparently unable to move because
of lack of fuel. His position was becoming more precarious daily. Elements
of the U.S. 82d Airborne Division had been identified on the west side of

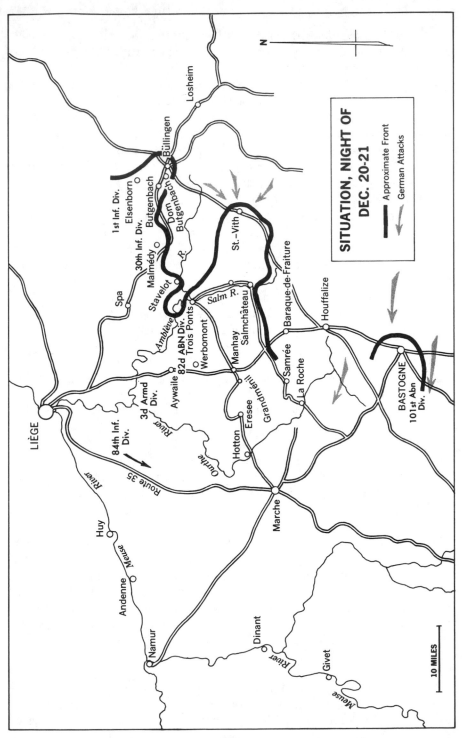

SITUATION, NIGHT OF
DEC. 20-21

— Approximate Front
↓ German Attacks

N

Losheim

Büllingen

1st Inf. Div.
Elsenborn
Butgenbach
Dom Butgenbach
30th Inf. Div.
Malmédy
R.
St.-Vith
Stavelot
Amblève
Trois Ponts
Salm R.
Baraque-de-Fraiture
Houffalize
Spa
82d ABN Div.
Werbomont
Manhay
Salmchâteau
Aywaile
Eresee
Samrée
La Roche
3d Armd Div.
Grandménil
River
84th Inf. Div.
Hotton
Ourthe
LIÈGE
Route 35
BASTOGNE
101st Abn Div.
Marche
River
Huy
Meuse
Andenne
Namur
Dinant
River
Givet
Meuse
Meuse

10 MILES

the Salm River, moving up to Trois Ponts. South of Peiper the U.S. 7th Armored Division still held the crossroads of St.-Vith, but Remer's Führer Begleit Brigade was making its way around to the north; success, Model felt, would inevitably be forthcoming in a couple of days.

South of St.-Vith the picture was more cheerful. The 116th Panzer Division of Krüger's 58th Panzer Korps had seized Samrée (see map opposite) that day and had been ordered to cross the Ourthe River, twenty miles by air to the northwest, on the twenty-first. Here was real progress.

Lauchert's 2d Panzer Division had been successful in taking the town of Noville on the twentieth from the stubborn American paratroopers and tankers. Orders had been for the 2d Panzer to bypass the town of Bastogne and to continue on in the direction of Dinant on the Meuse. On the next day, the Panzer Lehr Division would leave a regiment behind to help the 26th VGD invest Bastogne, and the bulk of the division would begin the thirty-mile drive westward to St.-Hubert.

The Seventh Army on the south had not gone so well, although the 5th Parachute Division would soon be in position to protect the southern flank of Fifth Panzer Army. Brandenberger had been unsuccessful in cracking the southern shoulder, as Dietrich had been in the north. But not much had been expected in the south anyhow. The city of Luxembourg was not a primary objective. The important thing was that Bastogne would be surrounded by the next day, and Hasso von Manteuffel's two panzer corps would be driving toward crossings of the Meuse River on both sides of Namur.

Thus did the picture across the front appear to the commander of German Army Group B. On that Wednesday evening, December 20, OB West (Rundstedt) summed up Model's situation by saying that operations thus far had made slower progress than anticipated, but that the offensive might be continued successfully, provided a number of prerequisites were fulfilled. First, Allied forces in the Elsenborn-Malmédy area would have to be destroyed; second, all available OKW and OB West reserves would have to be released to Model; third, sufficient fuel would have to be supplied.

Model could hardly have been overjoyed by this assessment. He no longer counted on success in the Elsenborn area; Hitler's releasing all reserves in Germany was unlikely; and finally, the fuel promised to Manteuffel would actually have to be delivered—an assumption that past experience made doubtful.

The area of greatest interest to Model and his superiors at this time was the long northern line extending westward from Elsenborn, a line he was trying to envelop. But as his spearheads moved westward, the American position built up at the same rate. The distance from Butgenbach, the corner of the Elsenborn Ridge, to Dinant on the Meuse was about 120 miles by air. This distance was divided into three approximately equal segments by two major rivers. The eastern, the Salm River, would have to be crossed by the defenders of St.-Vith and the "fortified goose egg" to pass through the lines of the 82d Airborne. The Salm was an obstacle of considerable proportions; but, as of the twentieth, it had been bypassed on the south by the 116th Panzer Division, which had already reached Samrée, toward the western end of the middle segment.

The next river, separating the central from the western segment, was the Ourthe. The Ourthe, more formidable than the Salm and the Amblève, could also be bypassed, but only by taking a southern route more circuitous than the 58th Panzer Korps of the Fifth Panzer Army wanted to take (see map, p. 348).

Through each of these three segments ran a major north-south road to Liège. In the eastern segment the route ran from Liège through Spa to Malmédy. In the central segment was Route 15, the Bastogne-Liège road, which ran through the small towns of Manhay, Werbomont, and Aywaille. In the western segment, on a high area known as the Marche Plain, ran Route 35 from the town of Marche to Liège; a branch of this road, starting about halfway between Marche and Liège, ran toward Huy, selected by the Germans as an important area for crossing over the Meuse.

By the twentieth Malmédy was already famous and the Americans were there in force. But Model had not quite given up trying to take it, and he had not given up Butgenbach either. There were also the critical crossroad towns of Baraque-de-Fraiture and Manhay on Route 15 in the middle segment and Marche in the western segment. Hardly less important was Hotton, some six miles northeast of Marche, where there was a good crossing over the Ourthe River. The seizure of Hotton and Marche would be a job for Manteuffel's northern corps, Krüger's 58th Panzer Korps. Lüttwitz's 47th Panzer Korps, its northern flank thus protected, would dash toward a crossing of the Meuse just south of Namur.

In these three sectors Model's men were destined to fight three nearly independent battles during the next week, the crisis week of the Ardennes campaign. He would find it impossible to unify them into one battle. The banks of the Amblève, Salm, and Ourthe would force Model to fight separate actions. He was destined to be exhausted almost simultaneously in each sector—by December 26, the day the Nazi tide began to recede.

On the Allied side on December 20, First U.S. Army was trying desperately to bring enough troops from the Ninth Army sector to build up a defensive line to the west faster than Model's swift-moving panzers (Manteuffel's) could outflank the line. This was no mean task. By the nineteenth General Hodges had 208,000 men with their tanks, vehicles, and artillery moving southward, a feat that not even those who had gambled on the mobility of the U.S. Army would have counted on.

The moves had been swift. The 1st U.S. Infantry Division had started to arrive in the Elsenborn area on the seventeenth. On the eighteenth the 30th Infantry Division had arrived in Stavelot, Malmédy, and Stoumont to begin the process of bottling up Jochen Peiper. The 82d Airborne had come into position west of the Salm, and the bulk of the 3d Armored Division was sending out task forces between the Salm and Ourthe rivers to feel out the elements of the 116th Panzer Division.

During the night of December 20, Major General Maurice Rose, whose 3d Armored Division was now west of the 82d Airborne, pushed southward in an effort to make contact with VIII U.S. Corps at Bastogne. Obviously the Germans were in strength in that area; Rose asked and received permission to hold up his advance.

But the First Army attitude was not entirely defensive. Two days before, General Courtney Hodges had instructed Major General J. Lawton Collins to pull his VII Corps out of the line near Düren to the north. Hodges' idea was for Collins to regroup his corps westward, on the Marche Plain, ready to counterattack southward.

This assignment was much to Joe Collins' liking. He was to receive Major General Alexander R. Bolling's 84th Division, which had obtained some experience in the Geilenkirchen area; the 2d and 3d Armored divisions, which he considered among the best in the Army; and a new division, the 75th, which was preparing to come into action. Bolling's 84th was expected to arrive in Marche late on the twentieth. Until Collins' VII Corps could set up in Mean (west of the Ourthe), the 84th Division was to be attached temporarily to Ridgway's XVIII Airborne Corps.[1]

But Collins felt that a counterattack from the Marche Plain would be positioned too far west: so long as the main obstacle to be denied Model was the Meuse River, the counterattack should have assembled farther eastward. In the ensuing days, as he periodically conferred with Field Marshal Montgomery, he was to repeat his conviction that his corps should be moved to Elsenborn and prepared to drive southward toward St.-Vith, cutting off the German attack at the base. Collins felt it unnecessary for the First Army to plug the gap on its west flank, as he knew that on the nineteenth Montgomery had ordered his XXX British Corps to move from Holland into the area between Liège and Brussels. Let the counterattack go eastward, Collins argued, so as to chop off the Germans in large numbers.[2]

---

[1] This arrangement extended the XVIII Corps sector to fantastic length, all the way from Marche to the Salm River, including command of the "fortified goose egg," which was not to be pulled back for three days.

[2] Since Montgomery protected the Meuse crossings only from Givet northward, Lieutenant General John C. H. Lee, of the Services of Supply, was given responsibility for protecting the river to the south. However, this part of the river was of less importance in a way, as it was expected that the German attack would be heading north rather than south of Givet. Within a couple of days four engineer combat regiments had taken up positions along the Meuse, reinforced with a field artillery battalion,

In these discussions, Field Marshal Montgomery insisted that Collins could not support his corps on a single road from Malmédy to St.-Vith. "Maybe you can't, sir," Collins insisted, "but we can.[3] If you're not careful, Field Marshal, the result will be the same as at Falaise. Rather than cut off the Germans, we will simply push them out of the bag."

Despite his protestations, Montgomery's orders stood: Collins was to assemble on the Marche Plain.

The battle on the northern sector of the Bulge, west of the St.-Vith "fortified goose egg," consisted of a series of small actions which, by reason of their very complicated nature, are difficult to visualize as a whole. Thus the battles for the three sectors must be examined as three separate actions, although by so doing the narrative must violate chronology.

At 1:30 A.M., Thursday, December 21, Lieutenant Colonel Derrill M. Daniel, commanding the 2d Battalion, 26th Infantry, 1st U.S. Infantry Division, began to receive an attack toward his position at Don Butgenbach from the direction of Büllingen to the southeast.

Daniel, known to his associates as a hard-boiled and difficult man, was also respected as a great craftsman in battle. Though his position was exposed, he had picked the strongest position in the area.

At 3:00 A.M., the German attack began in earnest. A heavy barrage of artillery, mortars, and rockets began crashing on 2d Battalion positions. Soon communications were cut between Daniel and his frontline companies. Tanks and infantry of the newly deployed 12th SS Panzer Division overran both E and F companies and, breaking into the rear, took Daniels' command post under point-blank fire at 75-yard range.

But the Americans held. Major General Clift Andrus, division commander and an old artilleryman, had seen to it that the 1st Division Artillery was tied in to that of the 2d and 99th divisions. When the attack reached serious proportions he poured it on; 10,000 rounds of American artillery were fired that night. Soon the grenadiers were separated from the panzers. Companies E and F, consisting of 90 percent replacements and even then down to 100 men each, simply remained in their foxholes with Nazi tanks in their rear, concentrating on such German infantry as escaped the artillery. The German tanks, deprived of their infantry protection, were picked off one by one by American tanks, tank destroyers, bazookas, and artillery. By 11:40 A.M. all 2d Battalion positions had been restored.

This was not the last attack to be faced by the Big Red One. The next

---

regimental antitank company, and six French light infantry battalions provided by the military governor of Metz. These troops and responsibility for the sector from Givet to Verdun were handed over to VIII Corps on December 23.

[3] Having fought through this area before, Collins knew the roads were of high quality. Besides the Aachen-Malmédy road, there was also the Verviers–St.-Vith road.

day a penetration by another regiment of the 12th SS Panzer was to force commitment of parts of all three of Andrus' regiments, the 16th, the 18th, and the 26th.

In the two-day action the 1st Division counted 44 Nazi tanks destroyed and estimated 1,200 casualties in the Waffen SS.

West of the 1st Division another attack threatening the northern shoulder was in progress. Otto Skorzeny's 150th Panzer Brigade—tough, picked men— was being employed as a straight combat unit. On the morning of December 21 Skorzeny was making a last effort to take Malmédy.

The main east-west road of the area, known on German maps as Route C, ran from Waimes-Baugnez to Malmédy and thence to Stavelot. The Germans had cut the road on both sides of Malmédy, so Skorzeny split his panzer brigade into two main wings, one to attack from Baugnez into the eastern side of Malmédy, and the other to attack from the direction of Stavelot.

The attack jumped off at dawn, but it was doomed to failure. The 120th U.S. Infantry Regiment, from Hobbs' 30th Infantry Division, was too well entrenched.

From his command post, Skorzeny heard the sounds of a powerful American artillery barrage on his right, and realized that the eastern prong of his attack was being held up. He ordered a defense line established and then traveled over to see how the left, or western, prong was progressing.

On a ridge from which he could see a substantial portion of the road system he watched six of his tanks engaged in an unequal struggle with a superior force of Americans. The attack was obviously hopeless, especially without artillery support, and so Skorzeny gave orders for the brigade to reform behind the crest, establishing a shaky defense line about six miles long.

That evening Skorzeny went to headquarters, located in the Hôtel du Moulin in Ligneuville (where Peiper's men had shot several Americans four days earlier). On his way, he and his companions were caught in long-range American artillery fire. Jumping out of their armored car into the pitch black of night, they groped their way along, trying to keep to the middle of the road. Suddenly Skorzeny felt a blow in the forehead and something warm running down his face; he discovered a bleeding piece of flesh hanging over his right eye. There were holes in his trouser leg also, and his thigh was bruised, but his leg was otherwse unwounded. An aid station was handy; Skorzeny, to keep his head clear, refused any strong anesthetics while the doctors worked on him. Then, over the protests of the doctors, he returned to his CP. This was the last combat action of the Ardennes for Obersturmbahn-führer Otto Skorzeny.

On the morning of December 21, the American positions in the center sector, between the Salm and the Ourthe, were held by elements of only two

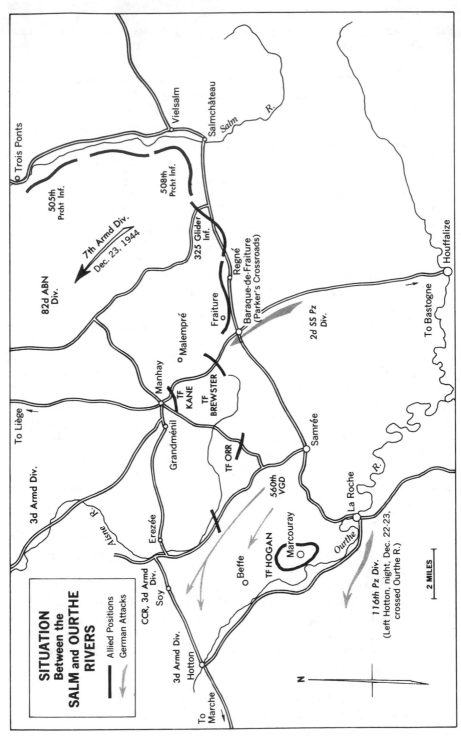

SITUATION
Between the
SALM and OURTHE
RIVERS

━━━ Allied Positions
⇣ German Attacks

Trois Ponts

Vielsalm

Salmchâteau

Salm R.

505th Prcht Inf.

508th Prcht Inf.

7th Armd Div.
Dec. 23, 1944

82d ABN Div.

325 Glider Inf.

Regné

Fraiture

Baraque-de-Fraiture
(Parker's Crossroads)

Houffalize

2d SS Pz Div.

To Bastogne

Malempré

Manhay

TF KANE

TF BREWSTER

To Liège

3d Armd Div.

Grandménil

Samrée

TF ORR

560th VGD

La Roche

Ourthe R.

Aisne R.

Erezée

Soy

Beffe

TF HOGAN

Marcouray

CCR, 3d Armd Div.

3d Armd Div.

Hotton

To Marche

116th Pz Div.
(Left Hotton, night, Dec. 22-23,
crossed Ourthe R.)

2 MILES

N

354

divisions (Map II). The 82d Airborne was now consolidated in positions running north-south for approximately seven miles along the west bank of the Salm River, from Trois Ponts (where Company C of the 51st Engineers had made their stand) to Vielsalm (headquarters of the 7th Armored Division and the 106th Infantry Division), thence westward, in a noncontinuous position just north of Salmchâteau and La Roche.

Major General James Gavin was holding a tremendously long line with 200 yards between foxholes. Nevertheless, his strung-out 82d Airborne sector covered less than half the distance between the two rivers. Responsibility for stopping the German drives west of the Bastogne-Liège road fell to one combat command, CCR of the 3d Armored Division, commanded by Colonel Robert L. Howze, Jr.[4]

Colonel Howze set up his headquarters in Soy, only three miles east of the Ourthe River and its important crossing at Hotton. Howze, too, had a vastly overextended front, and he felt it necessary, as had Roberts at Bastogne, to break his combat command into three independent task forces and send them southward to intercept the German drives along the major roads north and west.

Samuel M. Hogan, a colorful Texas lieutenant colonel, had taken the 400 men of Task Force Hogan to La Roche, a position eight miles south of Soy. La Roche not only protected a major crossing of the Ourthe River but also controlled a five-point road net.

Task Force Orr, under Lieutenant Colonel William R. Orr, was sent to another important road junction, about four miles northwest of Hogan, though a much longer distance by road.

Howze's third unit, Task Force Kane, commanded by Lieutenant Colonel Matthew W. Kane, was placed at the critical five-point crossroads of Manhay, on the Bastogne-Liège road.

Across a front eight miles as the crow flies, Howze had deployed three task forces covering the most important road junctions, with gaps of approximately four miles between them. Occupying Samrée, between Task Force Hogan and Task Force Orr, was Krüger's whole 58th Korps (the 560th VG and major elements of the 116th Panzer).

Unknown to Howze, the German 116th Panzer Division had orders on the twenty-first to cross the Ourthe River at Hotton, just three miles west of his command post. Bypassing the American task forces that morning, the 116th Panzer moved out between Hogan and Orr on secondary roads and made its way rapidly to the main artery between Soy and Hotton. From there it turned westward to try to force a crossing over the Ourthe at Hotton.

---

[4] CCB of the 3d Armored was still attached to the 30th Infantry Division farther east, closing in on Jochen Peiper; CCA was still in the Malmédy area, searching out Baron von der Heydte's paratroopers.

The 116th Panzer's advance came as a complete surprise to Howze: at daybreak that morning an American patrol from CCR had discovered Germans in the 3d Armored rear, and soon a report came in that the Germans were on the Soy-Hotton road, headed for Hotton. To protect his own command post Howze had to scrape up some headquarters and service elements.

But the Germans were turning away from Soy at the moment. The command post in real danger was that of the division commander, General Rose, located in Hotton itself. A handful of 3d Armored headquarters troops had to join with elements of the ubiquitous 51st Engineers—the battalion that had defended Trois Ponts—to form a pickup task force and defend the crossings. The engineers and tankers did well—so well, in fact, that reports reaching Manteuffel convinced him that he was up against a major force deployed along the Ourthe River. Generalmajor Siegfried von Waldenburg, the 116th Panzer commander, reported he was unable to force a crossing.

Meanwhile, Hogan, to the southeast of La Roche, had been hit hard. He held out through the evening of the twenty-first, but on the twenty-second his unit was given permission to drop back well to the rear. However, it was impossible to retreat as far as he intended, and he had to settle for setting up a perimeter defensive position in Marcouray, only three miles northwest.

By the evening of the twenty-first, Manteuffel was convinced that he was facing major forces at Hotton and gave orders for the withdrawal of the 116th Panzer Division back to Samrée. The division crossed the Ourthe River at La Roche the evening of the twenty-second. This whole operation had cost Waldenburg's crack 116th Panzer a good two days, and the buildup of Collins' VII Corps, west of the Ourthe River, was protected.

Throughout these actions, General Hodges at First Army still concentrated on guarding against the possibility of a German swing to the north toward Liège. If the shoulders of the Bulge were not widened, a continuation of the German attack west toward the Meuse at Dinant could only result in eventual starvation for supplies, but by December 21 it was becoming apparent that both shoulders, north and south, would hold. However, the possibility of a northward attack up a major road to Liège, where the Germans could capture American supplies, was always on Hodges' mind. During these days the spotlight rested not only on the "fortified goose egg" at St.-Vith, but also on the battle for the route between Bastogne and Liège.

Finally convinced of the wisdom of following up Manteuffel's success, Hitler had authorized the use of the 2d SS Panzer Korps—originally scheduled to follow in Peiper's footsteps—for this purpose. On December 21, therefore, the 2d SS Panzer moved to a position north of Houffalize, ready to attack through the vital crossroads of Baraque-de-Fraiture toward the twin towns of Manhay and Grandménil.

The episode at Baraque-de-Fraiture was another in which the ingenuity of an individual was to prove critical. Like so many local place names, Baraque-de-Fraiture was merely the name of a crossroads, the kind of position that can be expected to attract the attention of commanders at all echelons. However—possibly because the Bastogne-Liège road lay on the boundary between the 3d Armored and the 82d Airborne—it was at first neglected. It fell to a major, Arthur C. Parker III, to recognize its importance; on his own initiative he set up a defense on December 19.

Parker's original unit consisted of pickup units, but he was reinforced the next day, and his task force defended successfully against a large patrol coming northward, which they identified as elements of the 2d SS Panzer. Task Force Kane later supplied him with 11 tanks and a reconnaissance platoon.

General Gavin and General Rose finally recognized the critical nature of this position on their boundary. Gavin sent his reserve, consisting of only one battalion, to defend the nearby town of Fraiture (not to be confused with the crossroads itself) and so protect his right flank.

By this time Baraque-de-Fraiture was known as Parker's Crossroads. On December 22, Colonel Charles E. Billingslea, regimental commander of the 325th Glider Infantry, sent a company to reinforce Parker.

They were afforded some respite when the 2d SS Panzer Division had trouble with its gasoline; but on the twenty-third the main effort of the 2d SS Panzer hit. In the early morning hours the one regiment made a surprise attack on Fraiture and then settled down to pound the area with artillery. By 4:00 P.M. the barrage had reached a tremendous volume. Then a whole panzer grenadier regiment, reinforced with two companies of tanks, attacked. An hour later the commander of F Company at the crossroads was refused permission to withdraw. During the next hour, the Germans completed the reduction of the crossroads, taking all survivors prisoners and capturing armored cars, half-tracks, and howitzers. Of the original 116 men who had gone to Parker's Crossroads, 44 got out.[5]

The way was opened for a German attack on Manhay to the north. The remainder of Task Force Kane was at Manhay, and CCA, 3d Armored (now relieved of its mission of chasing von der Heydte's parachutists), arrived. At dark on December 23, as the last elements of the St.-Vith forces were being withdrawn across the Salm River, Major Olin F. Brewster was moving his 3d Armored tankers south of Manhay.

Emulating Parker, Brewster picked up stray elements—lone tanks, infantry stragglers, and even a platoon of tank destroyers. During the night he stopped the continuing attack of the 2d SS Panzer.

The withdrawal of the St.-Vith salient on the night of December 23 freed for General Ridgway a reserve of about 15,000 men and one hundred usable tanks. However, the men were exhausted, their equipment was largely un-

[5] Hugh Cole, *The Ardennes* (Washington: Dept. of the Army, 1965), p. 391.

serviceable, and their morale was low. Furthermore, the reduction of the St.-Vith salient had freed far more German troops than American.[6]

During the day of December 24, General Bittrich, of the 2d SS Panzer Korps, did little to push forward the line from Parker's Crossroads to the all-important objective, Manhay. Part of the reason, without a doubt, was the good weather, with the consequent increased Allied air support. But the American position remained precarious; wide gaps existed between some units.[7]

Though the 75th Infantry Division was on the way, General Ridgway felt that more would be necessary to stem the tide. With great regret, he ordered Colonel Dwight A. Rosebaum, commanding CCA, 7th Armored Division— still in bad condition from St.-Vith, although hurt less than the other combat commands of the 7th Armored—to prepare to go into action the next day.

By the morning of the twenty-fourth—only a few hours after the withdrawal from the St.-Vith "goose egg"—CCA of the 7th Armored was outposted in Manhay, but the detachment sent southeast between the 3d Armored and the 82d Airborne did not quite fill the gap between these two units.

On the evening of December 24, Field Marshal Montgomery made a controversial decision. He ordered the 82d Airborne, stuck out in a point in the Vielsalm-Salmchâteau area, to be withdrawn so as to straighten out the lines, the new line running as directly as possible from Trois Ponts to Manhay to Hotton. This action he took, as in the case of the St.-Vith salient, by giving orders first and persuading General Hodges afterward. General Gavin was unhappy; the 82d Airborne had never given up an inch of ground, and Gavin was in no mood to begin at this point. However, he had his orders; the withdrawal began on the night of the twenty-fourth. Morale in the 82d was not materially affected.

At the same time Generalleutnant Heinz Lammerding's 2d SS Panzer Division was moving into position. With two panzer grenadier regiments abreast, Lammerding waited for dark—indeed for 9:00 P.M.—on Christmas Eve to

[6] As Parker's Crossroads had fallen to the Germans, General Bittrich of the 2d SS Panzer Korps had not only the entire 2d SS Panzer Division at his disposal but also the advance guard of the 9th SS Panzer Division, which had been attacking St.-Vith from the north. General Walther Lucht's 66th Korps, comprising the 18th and 62d VGD's, was coming to bolster the flank held by the badly decimated 1st SS Panzer Division. Bittrich had been promised the 12th SS Panzer Division (Hitler Jugend), the 3d Panzer Grenadier, and Remer's Führer Begleit Brigade, which, it will be recalled, had traveled southwesterly around the "fortified goose egg" through Rodt, Beho, and Hinderhausen. Bittrich had a potent force to use against the U.S. 82d Airborne and the 3d Armored.

[7] Two regimental combat teams from the new 75th Infantry Division, assigned to Collins' VII Corps, were en route, but CCB of the 3d Armored was still with the 30th Division in the XVIII Airborne Corps. Effective December 23, the boundary between Collins' VII Corps and Ridgway's XVIII Airborne Corps had been moved to the Bastogne-Liège road. The bulk of the 3d Armored was now under Collins' control, rather than Ridgway's.

make his attack toward Manhay. Because of confused coordination between the 3d and 7th Armored divisions, a hole was permitted to form in the American lines, and as a result American units executing a preplanned withdrawal were cut up by German units of inferior size. Nineteen American tanks were lost, as well as 100 men. German losses were negligible.

Lammerding's 2d SS Panzer drove on. He rammed into the gap in the American lines, where the exhausted members of the 7th Armored Division withdrew in haste and confusion. Task Force Brewster was cut off, and Brewster was forced to abandon his tanks and send his men out on foot.

Late on Christmas Eve, the 2d SS Panzer had taken Manhay, and the American position was desperate. The Germans held a good road net and could reinforce the Sixth Panzer Army with units from the St.-Vith area; both Liège and the Meuse bridgehead were in grave danger.

Once again Hitler's obsession came to the Americans' rescue. For while the Americans were concerned with the danger to Liège, the Germans remained focused on the drive to the west. Bittrich had no intention of pushing Lammerding farther north. He was to go west from Manhay to Grandménil to Soy, turn the flank of the rest of the 3d Armored, and seize a bridgehead at Hotton.

In the early morning hours of Christmas, however, a regiment from the 75th Infantry Division [8] had closed into assembly areas west of Manhay. This time, the German column was stopped by a soldier on two feet who knocked out the lead tank with a bazooka round, holding up the entire unit. The man has never been identified. During the fight the 289th Infantry became disorganized, but by 8:00 P.M. on Christmas Day the regiment had pulled itself together.

Christmas Day, another good day for the air forces, found the Germans failing to enlarge the penetration they had made into the American lines. As a result, Bittrich found it impossible to employ more than one unit at a time. To make matters worse, the 9th SS Panzer Division had failed to close up on the 2d SS Panzer's right.

Major General Matthew Ridgway was furious. Without delay he ordered an inspector general's investigation of the debacle surrounding the withdrawal to Manhay. He also insisted that the gap in the lines be closed—regardless of the condition of the 7th Armored, he ordered General Hasbrouck to retake Manhay by dark on the twenty-fifth. By cannibalizing forces from CCA and CCB, as well as utilizing the 2d Battalion of the 424th Infantry, Hasbrouck finally launched an attack. He did not meet Ridgway's deadline, but by the end of December 26 Manhay was retaken. The German drives westward be-

[8] Colonel Douglas B. Smith's 289th Infantry Regiment.

tween the Ourthe and the Salm rivers were halted. American plans to drive south to Houffalize and to Bastogne were likewise frustrated, but the U.S. line was now continuous.

Pfc. Frank A. Carroll, of the 2d Platoon of I Company, 334th Infantry, 84th Division, was jubilant. So were the rest of the men in his platoon. During its month in combat, from November 18 to the morning of December 20, the 84th Infantry Division, the "Railsplitters," had made a good record. Having seized Geilenkirchen on the northern boundary of Ninth Army, the Railsplitters had pushed forward and the 334th Infantry Regiment had taken Lindern and gone on to Würm and Mullendorf. They were now almost through the Siegfried Line and were approaching the Roer River.

But that morning, December 20, the 334th Infantry had been pulled out of the line, and Carroll and his buddies had been loaded into trucks. They were heading for the rear, and it was obvious to them that they were going to a rest area.

The convoy rolled southwest, and the men of the 84th recognized the towns they were going through. First they reached Aachen, then the Belgian border; at Verviers the convoy paused momentarily, then continued southwest farther into the friendly territory of Belgium. As they rode along, the GI's of the 2d Platoon sighted men and vehicles going in the opposite direction. With the 84th going into rest area, the others had to be going to the front. In typical GI fashion, Carroll's platoon made light of the plight of the men in the passing vehicles, shouting cracks and warnings that it was pretty tough up there on the Düren front.

That evening the 334th closed into a small, quiet Belgian town. Carroll noticed a sign at the outskirts. The name was unfamiliar: Marche.

The men of the 2d Platoon were bedded down in a parochial school building, then released for the evening. Carroll looked around him curiously. This town didn't look like much of a rest area, but everything was quiet. Carroll and his friends went out to see what sights there were.

Wandering down one street, Carroll spied a bakery, a nice old-fashioned bakery shop. Sauntering in, he was amazed to see the goodies on display— rolls, tarts, and even cream puffs—he hadn't seen pastry like this since he had left the States. Having eaten his fill, he left the bakery and went on his way.

Before returning to his bunk Carroll stopped in a tavern and had a couple of drinks, talking with those Belgians who could speak English. The Belgians seemed concerned about a German breakthrough that had occurred to the east, but they were not excited and nobody was leaving. More tired than anything else, the group of men from 2d Platoon went back to the school to hit the sack for the night.

At breakfast the next morning, December 21, somebody produced a copy of the *Stars and Stripes*. Carroll glanced at the front page casually, and then let out a whoop: "My God," he hollered. "It says here that Marche has been captured by the Krauts!"

The movement of the 334th Infantry, of which Frank Carroll's platoon had been a part, to Marche actually was the start of the buildup of Collins' VII Corps, preparatory to a hoped-for counterattack toward Bastogne. But Collins' corps was not yet operational. Until it was, Major General Alexander Bolling's division was under Ridgway's XVIII Airborne Corps.

General Bolling was in Marche the morning Carroll made his discovery. His division was assembling behind the protection afforded by a small group of men from the 51st Engineers and the men from Headquarters, 3d Armored Division, who were holding off the German 116th Panzer at Hotton, five miles east (see map, p. 366).

About noontime on the twenty-first, General Ridgway ordered Bolling to use the 334th to protect the vital road between Marche and Hotton inclusive. Reports were coming in of large numbers of German tanks heading west, and there was some question whether Marche itself should be held. The threat was great, and Marche lay in a somewhat exposed position, close to the main axis of advance of the German spearheads. Nevertheless, General Hodges had decided that Marche should be held, and the 84th Division began to dig in.

During the late afternoon Bolling set up his own command post in Marche, and the question was settled. By that night he had assembled his entire division in the area, allowing him to concentrate the 334th on the left and position the 335th to protect Marche itself. The regimental sectors were wide, but no more so than the sectors being held by other divisions.

On December 22, Ridgway ordered Bolling to send a unit from the 335th to Rochefort, an important town and river crossing about eight miles southwest of Marche, to deny its use to the Germans moving westward. Bolling sent a battalion. It reached Rochefort with no difficulty. Preceded by a reinforced rifle company, the American position was built up to include most of a battalion.

That day General J. Lawton Collins arrived at Bolling's headquarters. Neither officer had much idea of what was going on, but Collins recalled later how impressed he was with Bolling's calm approach to the situation. Satisfied with the way things were being conducted, "Lightning Joe" set up his corps headquarters in the small town of Mean, just north of Marche, a corps with only one division in the line. However, the 2d Armored was coming up in the rear, as was the 75th Infantry Division. The 3d Armored, still with Ridgway, was scheduled for assignment to Collins the next day.

But General Collins' visit to Bolling on the twenty-second convinced him of one thing: counterattack for the moment was not feasible. VII Corps, like the XVIII Airborne Corps to its east, was to be engaged in a fight for its life.

On that same morning, December 22, Baron Hasso von Manteuffel considered the possibility of reaching the Meuse by December 24. The action on the twenty-first had been disappointing. Krüger's 58th Panzer Korps, still consisting of the 116th Panzer and the 560th VG, had failed to cross the Ourthe River at Hotton. He had been deceived by the heroic action of the small group of defenders into issuing orders the night before for the 116th Panzer to withdraw and cross the Ourthe farther south at La Roche, proceeding westward from there to cut the U.S. positions between Marche and Hotton near Verdenne.

Extremely discouraging to the wiry little commander of the Fifth Panzer Army was the fact that Lüttwitz's corps to the south had not progressed faster. After his spectacular dash to seize a bridgehead over the Ourthe at Ortheuville the night of the twentieth, Lauchert had done little on the twenty-first other than expand his bridgehead a couple of miles and try to bring up his tail.

One reason was that a shortage of gasoline was now making itself felt, a result of Allied air activity on the twenty-first. But the main reason for the holdup at Ortheuville was that the men of the 2d Panzer [9] simply were exhausted.

The other panzer division of Lüttwitz's 47th Korps also was making insufficient progress, disengaging south of Bastogne and moving toward St.-Hubert. The 26th VG, of course, had not taken the Bastogne stronghold, but this was not sufficient reason for delay; and during the day Manteuffel visited Bayerlein's Panzer Lehr and urged him to get moving.

Nevertheless, despite these delays, Manteuffel felt things might still break favorably. Certainly the most promising *potential* situation was that of Lauchert's 2d Panzer, sitting in the middle of the penetration where it appeared the strongest U.S. positions could be bypassed, so that Lauchert might be able to drive by way of Marche and reach Namur, his original objective.

The 2d Panzer Division started in the early hours of December 22 and headed northwestward toward Namur, following a route leading through Bolling's entrenched position at Marche, but it had hardly moved before it was delayed by a road demolition. During the day it was subjected to Allied air attacks.

Lauchert consulted Lüttwitz. Marche could be assaulted in force or bypassed. In keeping with the concept of the entire campaign, Lüttwitz turned the bulk of his forces westward, bypassing Marche but leaving the 2d Panzer's north flank exposed to Bolling's U.S. 84th Infantry Division—much to Lauchert's discomfort.

---

[9] Not to be confused with the 2d SS Panzer, fighting at Manhay.

It was obvious to Lüttwitz that the Americans considered the road line Hotton-Marche-Rochefort, 13 miles by air and not much more on the ground, a serious defense line. The attack (westward through Harsin-Hargimont) could penetrate the southern portion of this defense line. Lüttwitz left a reinforced panzer grenadier battalion to seal off Marche and advanced with all major forces south and west.

However, a major offensive could not be sustained in such a constricted area as the seven miles between Marche and Rochefort: Rochefort, still occupied by the 3d Battalion of the 335th U.S. Infantry, had to be reduced. The 2d Panzer Division continued to head straight west on December 23, while Manteuffel assigned Bayerlein's Panzer Lehr the job of reducing Rochefort. Lauchert's lines were becoming thin, and he needed support; the 116th Panzer had not yet moved into position at Verdenne to cut off Marche from the northwest.

Bayerlein's attack against Rochefort was almost abortive. Scouts entered the town and reported it unoccupied, but when troops actually moved in they were caught under heavy American fire. Bayerlein pulled back, pounded the town with artillery, and found a road and bridge to bypass it to the east and north so that he could continue to attack backing up the 2d Panzer Division.[10]

During the day of the twenty-second the Reconnaissance Battalion, 2d Panzer Division, followed by a panzer grenadier regiment, reached a point only four miles from the Meuse. Here they ran into increasing resistance from American armored cavalry and the advance was stopped. For a while this spearhead was split up, one portion at Foy-Notre Dame and the other between Celles and Conjoux.

That evening Lauchert reported his position near the Meuse. This information went to Model, to Rundstedt, and, on the twenty-third, to Hitler. Hitler offered congratulations. Counting the reinforcements that Hitler gave him that evening (9th Panzer and 15th Panzer Grenadier divisions), Model would have a total of five panzer divisions,[11] if they could be supported, in the spearhead of the attack now so close to the Meuse River.

On the morning of December 24, Private Carroll, in a two-man foxhole, awakened to find his foxhole mate, Eddie Korecki, already alert. I Company of the 334th had been moved to the ridge protecting the Marche-Hotton road three days before. On their left was the small town of Verdenne. Carroll had not liked the position; the foxholes were 50 yards apart. However, the weather was clear and no action had yet occurred.

"Say, Frank," said Korecki, "a bunch of people came through the line early this morning, right through our position over to the left. I thought I'd

---

[10] Rochefort itself was mopped up the next day by the Germans, the American garrison escaping to the west and eventually making its way to Givet on the Meuse River.

[11] 2d, 9th, and 116th Panzer divisions, Panzer Lehr, and 15th Panzer Grenadier.

give the alarm, but then I remembered we had mine-laying crews out last night, so it was probably them. Do you think we'd better check with Lieutenant Seidensticker?"

Carroll thought they should. The platoon leader's foxhole was out of sight over a knoll, so together they scrambled out of their foxhole and slogged their way through the snow to find the platoon sergeant, Ray Owen. His two-man foxhole was empty. The next two-man foxhole also was empty. There were no signs of bloodshed—the four men were just gone. However, the footprints in the snow gave plenty of evidence that a large body of men had come through the positions of I Company without being detected and had picked up the four men.

Carroll sounded the alarm and alerted the company. Soon a patrol was sent to follow the footprints leading down into the woods to the rear. Receiving heavy fire upon their approach, the patrol confirmed what already had been concluded: a sizable body of Germans had come through I Company's position.

Frank Carroll realized that he and Korecki were alone. Their foxhole was located on the right flank of the company, next to an unprotected wood, and it was more than 100 yards to the next manned foxhole. Carroll set out to ask for help at least. Over to K Company he made his way—why K Company he could never recall—and went straight to the company commander. His request for a machine gun or at least an automatic rifle to protect I Company's right flank was met less with scorn than with indifference. No dice. Carroll and Korecki were on their own.

They had the day to think over their situation, while word of the German penetration was hastily passed up to 3d Battalion, 344th Infantry, where the commander soon recognized the precarious nature of I Company's position. Spread uncommonly thin, it was sitting on the Verdenne ridgeline with what were obviously more than 100 Germans behind them and God knew how many still in front. The battalion commander organized a counterattack by K Company and three tanks to hit the woods from the rear, where the Germans seemed to be preparing to spend the winter. At 3:00 P.M., December 24, K Company and the three tanks jumped off.

At the same moment, a major German assault on the front of I Company's position began. Tanks supported by infantry rolled over the extended front. In a short time Carroll found himself with only a few others in the empty woods to the southwest. The company had been shattered by the main attack of the 116th Panzer Division.

Carroll trudged to the rear, hindered more by the thick growth of trees than by the snow. Every so often he found other stragglers from the onslaught, and they all walked together. Finally they stopped and set up a position (fortunately they had K rations and ammunition). Carroll and the 25 men with him surmised on the evidence of some captured Germans that an American counterattack was in progress. After the second night, during which Carroll's band was hit by American artillery fire, they "captured" a patrol. After some grilling they satisfied themselves that the patrol was American—they had made contact with the 335th Infantry.

It was several days before Carroll and his group learned that their original position had finally been restored on Christmas Eve and that what was left of I Company would be reorganized. K Company had rescued Lieutenant Seidensticker and his men, who had been treated well and were none the worse for their capture, though glad the experience was over.

A few days later, Pfc. Frank Carroll was made acting sergeant.

Thus, after several days of hard fighting, Verdenne and the road through it were safe. A pocket around Verdenne had been erased. The 116th Panzer Division had been thwarted once more in its effort to cut the Marche-Hotton highway and open the way northward toward Liège.

The day of December 24 was a bad one everywhere for the Fifth Panzer Army. Not only had Waldenburg's 116th Panzer failed to break through the American 334th Infantry Regiment between Marche and Hotton, but also Marche remained securely in the hands of the U.S. 335th Infantry. Rochefort had been taken, giving room for maneuver on the southern flank, but the 2d Panzer Division was constricted and the lead elements at Foy-Notre Dame were running into American armor. The division was low on supplies and badly strung out, and the threat from the north was becoming more and more serious. During the day American armor had halted the Panzer Lehr Division.

Heinrich Freiherr von Lüttwitz was in a melancholy mood. On the same night as Tony McAuliffe was sending his message to Troy Middleton asking for the "Christmas present" relief of Bastogne, Lüttwitz was concluding the offensive had come to an end. That afternoon he had requested permission from Manteuffel to withdraw spearheads of the 2d Panzer from their exposed position to a line between Marche and Rochefort.

Lüttwitz really knew better. He knew that the surrender of any territory whatsoever was not within the prerogatives of the commander of the Fifth Panzer Army.

Lüttwitz had been commander of the 2d Panzer Division at Avranches. There was something about this situation—a hopeless attack pounded by Allied air forces—that reminded him of the Avranches effort.

However, Lüttwitz's immediate superior, with whom he worked closely and in harmony, was somewhat more optimistic. True, Manteuffel had lost hope for the attack to the west, but possibly he could hold a strong defensive line in a position that would serve as a pivot for a Fifth Panzer Army attack to the north. While he gave no thought to reaching the ultimate objective,

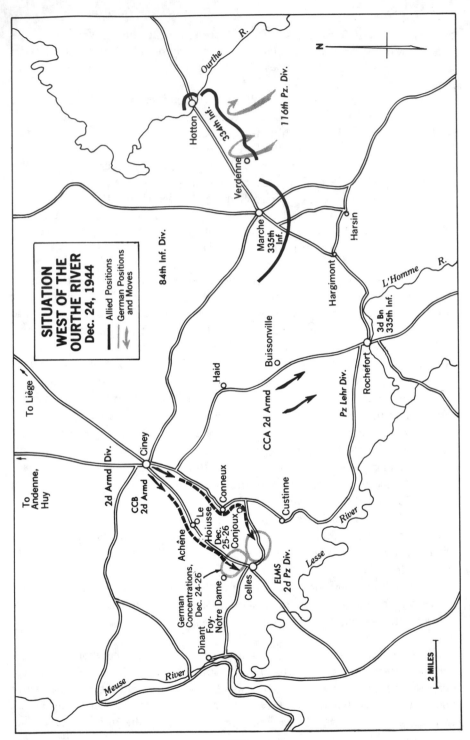

SITUATION WEST OF THE OURTHE RIVER
Dec. 24, 1944

Allied Positions
German Positions
and Moves

Ourthe R.

116th Pz. Div.

Hotton

334th Inf.

Verdenne

N

84th Inf. Div.

Marche
335th Inf.

Harsin

L'Homme R.

Hargimont

3d Bn
335th Inf.

To Liège

Haid

Buissonville

Rochefort

CCA 2d Armd

Pz Lehr Div.

Ciney

2d Armd Div.

CCB
2d Armd

Conneux

Custinne

To
Andenne,
Huy

Achêne

Le
Hoiusse

Dec.
25-26

Conjoux

River

German
Concentrations,
Dec. 24-26

Foy-
Notre Dame

Celles

ELMS
2d Pz Div.

Lesse

Dinant

Meuse   River

2 MILES

366

Antwerp, he did cherish the hope that by turning northward he could achieve a solid tactical victory east of the Meuse.

Manteuffel had several problems: regaining contact with the isolated elements of the 2nd Panzer at Celles, protecting his army on both flanks, and strengthening the slim finger sticking out north of Marche against possible armored counterattack from the north.

On Christmas Eve General der Panzertruppen Hasso van Manteuffel held a telephone conversation with Generaloberst Alfred Jodl, who was at Hitler's headquarters. Manteuffel pointed out that the failure of Dietrich's Sixth Panzer Army had now made his operation the main effort of the German offensive. Neither the OKW reserves nor the available divisions of the Sixth Panzer Army were being delivered to him with sufficient speed. If reserves —with fuel—arrived in time, they would be able to encircle Bastogne and capture it, meanwhile pushing at the same time in the direction of Liège. A battle east of the Meuse, he contended, would be much more promising than a continuation west. Again the "little slam," thinly disguised.

Hitler's adjutant was informed of Manteuffel's views before he left for Berlin on Christmas morning. No answer was ever received.

Major General Ernest N. Harmon of the U.S. 2d Armored Division was like a caged lion this Christmas eve. He was receiving reports of large numbers of German tanks in the vicinity of Celles, many of them immobilized for lack of gasoline. Here was a real opportunity!

On the night of the twenty-second, "Old Gravel Voice" had closed his veteran "Hell on Wheels" 2d Armored into its assembly area some 12 miles north of Marche. The next morning he had sent patrols from the 82d Reconnaissance Battalion to the south and southwest. As he was conferring with some of his commanders, he had been notified that one of his armored cars on a patrol had been shot up at a hamlet near Ciney, a road junction joining the arteries from Marche, Rochefort, Dinant, and Namur.

Harmon had acted promptly. Without awaiting orders, he had dispatched his Combat Command A, under Brigadier General John Collier, in the direction of Ciney. On arrival Collier's men had found the report false. British armored patrols from the 3d Regiment of the 29th Royal Tank Brigade were in the town and no enemy was in sight. However, reports of large forces moving toward Ciney had made it pointless to try to hide the location of the 2d Armored any longer, so Harmon had deployed Collier's CCA from Ciney to Haid and had given Collier the job of pushing southward in the direction of Rochefort.

Attached to his division on his left flank the morning of December 24 was the 24th Reconnaissance Squadron of the 4th Cavalry Group. CCB and CCR, in the rear and still out of contact, were not to be employed without permission of higher headquarters.

As additional reports came in, Harmon took further action. During the morning in the area of Celles, just five miles southwest of Ciney and Conjoux, some British light armored cavalry had been forced back toward Dinant. When two American P-51's had flown over Celles they had received heavy flak.

Harmon did not wait for confirmation. Without delay he ordered CCB, under Brigadier General Isaac D. White, to move westward to back up CCA at Ciney and to secure the town "as a base for future operations." At the same time he sent two battalions of self-propelled artillery into firing positions. In the early afternoon, Christmas Eve, he called headquarters, VII Corps, for permission to wipe out these German tanks in their exposed position.

Harmon's call came in when the corps commander, General Collins, was away from his CP on his daily rounds of visiting his various divisions. Collins' main interest at the moment was the east flank of VII Corps, where word had reached him of a penetration in the 75th Infantry Division's sector. Ordering the 3d Armored to pinch it off, Collins traversed his corps front over icy roads, finally reaching Ciney on the west. Knowing he would be out of communication for part of the time, Collins had authorized his corps artillery commander, Brigadier General Williston B. Palmer, to act in his stead in case of emergency. It was a good thing he had.

General Palmer, known universally in the Army as Willie, was one of its fine soldiers and colorful characters ("Get married, hell!" he once said. "Why should I louse up my military career?"). He drove his subordinates hard, and he drove himself harder. Willie Palmer's lack of tact had become the subject of much good-natured staff officer humor: one of his remarks—"This is an excellent paper! Just insert a 'not' in every sentence"—became celebrated as a "Willie Palmer nit-pick."

That afternoon General Palmer's military career, as well as that of his chief, received a critical test. It was Palmer who received Harmon's phone call urgently requesting permission to attack the German 2d Panzer Division in the general area of Ciney-Celles; the German units, out of gas, were sitting ducks, said Harmon. This, however, would entail a change in major policy, and as such, Palmer judged, would far exceed his authority. He advised Harmon to await the arrival of General Collins, who was on the road to the CP of the 2d Armored Division.

Harmon would not accept Palmer's answer. A few minutes later he was on the phone again, requesting "immediate authority." Sorely tempted, Palmer authorized Harmon to make preparations for the attack but still to hold up pending General Collins' arrival.

In so ordering, General Palmer was well aware of the attitude prevailing at First Army. Across the front some things were looking good; others were not. True, Jochen Peiper had evacuated his position at La Gleize, leaving much booty behind; but the severe attacks against the 82d Airborne and its exposed salient had caused Field Marshal Montgomery to order its withdrawal that day to the line of Trois Ponts and Manhay. Parker's Crossroads had fallen. Elements of the 75th Infantry Division were in trouble at Dochamps. Furthermore, the 116th Panzer Division was beginning to attack at Verdenne, and there was a strong possibility of enemy reinforcement on the First Army front by the German 9th Panzer Division and the 15th Panzer Grenadier Division.

Montgomery that day had visited General Hodges, whose command post had now moved north of the Meuse to Tongres, and relieved his mind somewhat with the news that the 51st British Highland Division was coming across the Meuse into a backstop position and would constitute Hodges' reserve. Moreover, the British 29th Armoured Brigade, with 50 tanks, would cross east of the Meuse, protect Namur, Dinant, and Givet, and make contact with the west flank of VII Corps. But these were defensive measures. Obviously, Montgomery was not yet thinking offensively.

But Palmer, fretting at Collins' CP at Mean, was also impatient. Soon he, in turn, was on the phone with the First Army chief of staff, Major General Bill Kean. Kean had news, although it was somewhat confusing. He notified Palmer that a liaison officer, Colonel R. F. ("Red") Akers, was en route from Tongres to Mean with important oral instructions. Collins, Kean said cautiously, was authorized to use his troops in any way he saw fit. But Palmer wanted something more concrete. Kean tried to comply. In the transparent double-talk that sometimes passes for security, Kean asked Palmer to pick up his map and find two towns whose names began with *A* and *H*. Palmer, looking to the south, found the towns of Achêne and Le Houisse. Palmer was elated; to attack to that line coincided exactly with the axis of advance that Harmon wanted to follow to hit the 2d Panzer. Exultantly he hung up the phone and dispatched a message to General Collins:

241530 December

Gen. Collins,

Bill Kean just called.

Akers will be here about 1700 or 1730 with change in plans based on visit of a fellow you missed today.

Bill was extremely guarded but indicated strongly that new dispositions would call for you to secure your west flank by preventing hostile movement to north or east of Meuse, mentioning a "pivoting move" and inviting attention to an "H" and an "A" (Le Houisse and Achêne?)

Commitment of 2d Armd Div for purpose of anchoring flank appeared to be what he was driving at.

Palmer

Telephone to Ernie out.

P

Palmer called his aide. The message was to be delivered personally at Harmon's command post.

Back at Tongres General Kean was concerned: from the tone in Palmer's voice, just possibly the message had been misconstrued. Kean called again, and repeated that Akers was en route and that Collins was granted complete freedom to use all his troops. But he then said, "Now get this. I'm only going to say it once. *Roll with the punch.*"

Looking at the map for a logical place to fall back, Palmer looked for two other towns beginning with *A* and *H*. To his distress, he found Andenne and Huy, thirty miles north of the other two towns, also on the Meuse River. This completely reversed his previous understanding: VII Corps was to withdraw!

Wasting no time, Palmer took a carbon copy of his earlier message to General Collins and wrote a footnote explaining that he had previously missed Kean's meaning:

> He meant pivot *back*. You can use Ernie any way you need but roll with the punch. Bolling says positive dope that he gets socked tomorrow on his weak left. You better come home!
>
> P

On receipt of Palmer's second message, General Collins took to the road. Before leaving, however, he still gave tentative approval to Harmon's plan to attack the following day, Christmas.

"Look, Ernie," Collins said as his parting words to Harmon, "I'm disturbed about being too cautious here. Unless I direct you otherwise, you go ahead and attack early in the morning."

Colonel "Red" Akers did not arrive at Mean until after the corps commander had had a chance to talk over the situation with his staff: obviously things did not look as bad to VII Corps as they did to First Army. Finally, after a long, hard trip over crowded roads, on a cold, bitter night, Akers arrived. A drink of hot rum seemed to revive him, and he delivered his oral instructions, which differed in two particulars from the tenor of the telephone conversations. For one thing, Hotton, not Huy, was the town whose name began with *H*. This would imply withdrawing the VII Corps flank and giving up Marche and the entire road net east of the Meuse River, including the roads to Givet, Dinant, and Namur. To Collins this was unthinkable. However, Akers' statements also seemed to give Collins more discretion than had been indicated from the guarded conversations between Palmer and Kean.

Now even the aggressive Lightning Joe was in a quandary. His mind went back to the late thirties, when he had been an instructor at the Infantry School in Fort Benning, Georgia. There, as a member of the faculty, it had been his duty to give a series of lectures to reserve officers at Anniston and Birmingham, Alabama. One of the lessons, Collins now recalled, had involved the First Battle of the Marne, when a German liaison officer, Lieutenant Colonel Hensch, had been dispatched from General Helmuth von Moltke to convey verbal instructions to General Alexander von Kluck of the German First Army. These instructions had resulted in a premature retirement of the First Army on September 9, 1914. This action probably saved the French Sixth Army from annihilation, thereby contributing to a French victory. Since the instructions had been *oral,* however, Kluck had since been blamed for losing the battle.

The thought flashed through Collins' mind: *My God, is history repeating itself?*

Determined he would not make the same mistake as Kluck, General Collins requested Colonel Akers to put his oral instructions in writing. This Akers was glad to do, and soon the following message was in Collins' hands:

24 December 1944

SUBJECT: Confirmation of Oral Instructions

To: Commanding General, VII Corps, APO #307, United States Army

1. In compliance with instructions received from Field Marshal Montgomery, C-in-C 21 Army Group, Commanding General, First United States Army is endeavoring to shorten the line now held by First Army units to halt the advance of the enemy and stabilize the line.

2. For the time being, the VII Corps is released from all offensive missions and will go on the defensive with the objective of stabilizing the right flank of First United States Army. Commanding General, VII Corps, is hereby authorized to use all forces at his disposal to accomplish this job. Command General, VII Corps, is authorized, whenever in his opinion he considers it necessary, to drop back to the general line: Andenne-Hotton-Manhay. In the event that the line drops back this far, the bridge at Andenne will be secured. Firm contact on the left will be maintained with XVIII Airborne Corps in the vicinity of Manhay.

By command of Lieutenant General HODGES:

R. F. AKERS, JR.,
Colonel, G.S.C.,
G-3 (Ops)

At the bottom General Collins typed:

Note: The above instructions were typed personally by Colonel R. F. Akers, Jr., at Headquarters VII Corps, at Mean, Belgium, the evening of 24 December 1944. Colonel Akers had been sent by CG, First Army to delivery these instructions orally to the CG, VII Corps.

But even with this authority Collins could not reconcile himself to withdrawal rather than attack. Massed American artillery—11 battalions of it—east of Marche could smash any German attacks up the defile of the Liège road. Ernie Harmon, on the right, should not be denied. The situation was touchy, and the decision was wholly in his hands. He was "authorized," but not ordered.

He decided to attack.

Before Colonel Akers left on his freezing return trip to Tongres, Collins asked him to give General Hodges a complete rundown of the picture as Collins saw it and explain in detail what he expected to do. Unless Collins received specific orders to the contrary from General Hodges, he would attack on Christmas Day as planned. He did, however, assume complete personal responsibility.

That evening Collins was on the phone with both Kean and Hodges. The Akers mission seemed to have caused some confusion, and General Hodges' later personal account says: "It [the instructions sent to Collins] in no way changed his mission or restricted him in offensive use of his troops. In the discussion he was given the authority to push the attack with the 2d Armored Division. This he very much desired to do. . . ." [12]

Collins picked up the telephone, and this time got through to Harmon. With the rasp that had earned him the nickname Gravel Voice, Harmon roared into the phone: "The bastards are in the bag!"

The doom of Lauchert's 2d Panzer Division was sealed.

Brigadier General Isaac D. White's CCB attacked to the southwest from Ciney on Christmas Day. He moved in two task forces—Lieutenant Colonel Harry Hillyard's task force traveled southwest through Achêne and Le Houisse; [13] Major Clifton B. Batchelder's task force went through Conneux and Conjoux, and they converged at Celles, about eight miles from their departure point at Ciney. By the end of Christmas Day they had trapped a substantial part of the 2d Panzer Division.

To the east of this pincer movement the reconnaissance battalion of 2d Panzer came into contact with Harmon's 82d Reconnaissance Battalion and the British 29th Armoured Brigade at Foy-Notre Dame. With the support of Allied air effort, the German reconnaissance battalion was destroyed, the commander and 47 others captured.

Farther east, Collier's CCA, not knowing that the 3d Battalion of the 335th had departed, continued its drive southeast toward Rochefort, cutting off more German forces. The Allied air effort delayed the reinforcement of the 2d Panzer by the 9th Panzer Division. When finally Panzer Lehr, driving northward to Humain and Havrenne, succeeded in taking these two towns and temporarily opening the way westward for the 9th Panzer, the German attack

---

[12] General Hodges' personal account from *The Infantry Journal*, May, 1947, quoted by Hanson W. Baldwin, ed., *Command Decisions* (New York: Harcourt, 1959).

[13] The two towns that had caught Palmer's eye the day before.

against Buissonville, a mile and a half northwest, failed. By the evening all three towns were in the hands of CCA and CCR of the U.S. "Hell on Wheels" 2d Armored Division.

Early Christmas afternoon General Hasso von Manteuffel visited General Heinrich von Lüttwitz. Once again, Lüttwitz proposed that the forward echelons of the 2d Panzer be withdrawn. Since such a decision was beyond the power of Manteuffel, about all that could be done was to send a newly arrived battle group of the 9th Panzer to relieve the rearward battle group of the 2d Panzer, still facing Marche. Hopefully, this battle group would enable Lauchert to relieve his troops.

Just as Lauchert had these orders in his hand, he learned that radio contact with the reconnaissance battalion known to be cut off at Foy-Notre Dame had ceased.

That Christmas Day, when Brigadier General White was surrounding the forward elements of the 2d Panzer Division and the 115th Panzer Grenadier Regiment was being wiped out at Bastogne, Field Marshal Model visited the front. He had delivered an optimistic Christmas Day speech, and now his staff, headed by General Hans Krebs, prepared a report to Rundstedt for Model's signature. Obviously the message would go to Hitler; that evening Model sent the telegram. By this time the Allied plans were apparent to him. He was well aware of the U.S. Third Army's attack from the south approaching Bastogne, and the situation in the area of Marche, with containing action at Elsenborn.

The remarkable thing about Model's message was his airy optimism: the Fifth Panzer Army had pierced the Allied defenses, and its advance units were almost at the Meuse near Dinant.

Model had a reputation for keeping himself well informed, and his chief of operations, Günther Reichhelm (always frank in his evaluation of the Field Marshal), knew that the commander of Army Group B would not send an intentionally incorrect message to Hitler. Model admitted in passing that the Fifth Panzer Army flank was still open, especially to an attack from Marche, and admitted further that Sepp Dietrich had bogged down and the Seventh Army was under attack from the south.

Model suggested that the Fifth Panzer Army should continue to seize "unoccupied" crossings over the Meuse but that the bulk of the Army should go to Ciney and head northeast to roll up the Allied north flank. Bastogne should be taken. The Sixth Panzer Army should continue westward to the Ourthe River. Thus, in Model's view, the Germans could still defeat the main Allied armies between the Ourthe and the Meuse.

Optimism was the watchword in all such messages, since pessimism, in the last days of the Third Reich, was often a court-martial offense. Thus Model had to pay lip service to the possibility of going on to Antwerp and seizing unoccupied crossings over the Meuse. But these things, he suggested subtly, were secondary. His preoccupation now was the defeat of the Allies east of the Meuse in the vicinity of Marche. He urged all reserves be used for this purpose. Finally, he recommended reconstituting a reserve of three or four panzer divisions in the center of Germany.

Model then went on to enumerate prerequisites for all these recommendations—prerequisites that made everything else he had mentioned practically impossible. This peculiarly unrealistic message, one of the few that survived the war, is remarkable in view of the unfavorable reports Model must have been receiving that evening from the front.

Having signed and dispatched the telegram, Generalfeldmarschall Model sat down in front of the fireplace to a good dinner and his usual bottle of Burgundy.

On the morning of December 26 General White's CCB, having closed the pocket at Celles, turned northwest, almost literally beating the bushes to mop up German resistance within the Celles Pocket. American liaison planes were up in force, as were the 37th Fighter Group and Royal Air Force 83d Group. In one area a spotter plane picked up a column of seven enemy tanks north of Celles; all were destroyed. Bayerlein's Panzer Lehr Division, in the meantime, was attempting to relieve the 2d Panzer by an attack from Custinne, southeast of Celles. Again, this attack was foiled by the Allied air power. On the night of the twenty-sixth Bayerlein ordered withdrawal to Rochefort, 15 miles to the rear.

CCB spent two days clearing the thick woods and dense underbrush between Celles and Conjoux. The procedure normally was to shell a given area heavily to allow a slow, methodical advance by the infantry, backed by the tanks.

Some of the 2d Panzer troops did succeed in escaping, including the commander in the Pocket, Major von Cochenhausen, who made his way out on foot. Eventually nearly 600 of his men reached Rochefort. But all the equipment of the reconnaissance battalion of the 2d Panzer, the 304th Panzer Grenadier Regiment, the 2d Battalion of the 3d Panzer Regiment, three artillery battalions, and two thirds of the division flak battalion had to be left behind.[14]

At 3:00 P.M. on the twenty-sixth General Hasso von Manteuffel received approval for the withdrawal of the 2d Panzer Division to the Rochefort bridgehead; by three thirty this authorization was being effected by Lüttwitz's

[14] Cole, *op. cit.,* p. 570.

47th Panzer Korps. The order was transmitted immediately by radio to 2d Panzer Division.

In this duel between correspondingly numbered armored divisions of two armies, so critical to the conduct of the entire campaign, Harmon later reported: "We got in front of the 2d Panzer Division on December 23rd, 24th and 25th, and polished them off. Attached is a list of spoils we took—including 1,200 prisoners. Killed and wounded some 2,500, a great slaughter." Among the spoils, he listed 450 German trucks and 81 artillery pieces. Only 1,500 grenadiers and a handful of surviving tanks escaped to fight again.[15]

Thus, on one day, the twenty-sixth, the lead elements of the Fifth Panzer Army were withdrawn, the Manhay crossroads were restored, and the 4th Armored made contact with the 101st Airborne Division at Bastogne.

The evening General Bradley called General Smith at SHAEF. Though at the time he may not have known all the facts on the northern sector of the front, Bradley was prophetic. To a still skeptical Smith, he said: "As near as we can tell, this other fellow has reached his high-water mark today."

[15] Omar Bradley, *A Soldier's Story* (New York: Holt, 1951), p. 482.

Book V

※※

DECIMATION OF THE WEHRMACHT

CHAPTER 15

❧❧·❧❧

Crisis in the Allied High Command

ON the evening of December 26, 1944, the day of the "high-water mark," General Eisenhower was preparing to leave for Brussels to meet with Field Marshal Montgomery. He had tried to go three days earlier, but air travel had been ruled out, and the lengthy road trip would have kept him absent from his headquarters for several days. The Supreme Commander was fretful. Though telephone communications were satisfactory, Eisenhower wanted to see his commanders personally.

But more frustration was in store: the train scheduled for the trip was bombed by the Luftwaffe that evening, and the trip had to be postponed one more day. At the staff meeting on the morning of the twenty-seventh, Eisenhower heard that Montgomery was now ready to consider definite counterattack plans.

The Supreme Commander's reaction surprised his staff: "Praise God from whom all blessings flow!" For although the First U.S. Army was still sustaining the heavy attacks, Eisenhower was becoming slightly impatient to launch an attack from the north.

The trip to meet Montgomery was a difficult one. Besides the considerable annoyance caused by the elaborate security precautions still in effect, the train had to take a circuitous route that extended the trip to a whole day. It was almost noon on December 28 before Eisenhower met Montgomery at Hasselt.

At 21 Army Group Headquarters Montgomery was once more in the process of disengaging Collins' VII Corps to reconstitute Hodges' reserve. Collins and Hodges both had been trying to convince Montgomery that a counterattack from the north could soon be launched, but he still seemed to feel that another major German attack northward might hit First Army. He was confident he could beat off the attack, but preferred to delay his own until he was sure the German momentum was completely expended.

Eisenhower had some sympathy with Montgomery's attitude. He agreed the best thing to do in this situation was strengthen the front and reorganize units, getting thoroughly ready to launch a strong counterblow. But he set a deadline: If the German attack did not materialize by January 3, on that date First Army was to thrust in the direction of Houffalize to meet with Patton's drive from Bastogne.

That evening Eisenhower called his headquarters from Brussels. Montgomery apparently had sufficient forces to take care of any developments that might be expected in the north. More critical now was the situation around Bastogne, which the German High Command had decided must be reduced at all costs. As a result they had built up an imposing force. In addition to the 26th Volksgrenadier Division, the regiment from the Panzer Lehr, and the 115th Panzer Grenadier Regiment from the 15th Panzer Grenadier Division, the Führer Begleit Brigade was reportedly on its way from the north, and although General Eisenhower could hardly have known it at the time, the remainder of the 1st SS Panzer Division, the 3d Panzer Grenadier Division, and the Führer Grenadier Brigade were also scheduled to arrive in the Bastogne area that day. Before the fighting in Bastogne was over, the 101st Airborne Division, reinforced by the 6th Armored, would be facing also the 9th and 12th SS Panzer divisions and the 340th and 167th Volksgrenadier divisions. Accordingly, General Eisenhower told his headquarters to release the 87th Infantry Division and the 11th Armored Division from SHAEF reserve to General Bradley in the south. Heavy fighting under miserable conditions continued during the days after the dramatic relief of Bastogne by the 4th Armored Division.

After his return to his headquarters in Versailles on the twenty-ninth, Eisenhower drew up an outline plan based on his discussions with Montgomery:

> Basic plan—to destroy enemy forces west of Rhine, north of the Moselle, and to prepare for crossing the Rhine in force with the main effort north of the Ruhr. The several tasks are:
>
> a. To reduce the Ardennes salient by immediate attacks from north and south, with present command arrangements undisturbed until tactical victory within the salient has been assured and the Third Army and Collins' Corps have joined up for a drive to the north-east. Bradley then to resume command of the First U.S. Army. (Enemy action within the salient indicates his determination to make this battle an all-out effort with his mobile forces. Therefore we must be prepared to use everything consistent with minimum security requirements to accomplish their destruction.)
>
> b. Thereafter First and Third Armies to drive to north-east on general line Prüm-Bonn, eventually to Rhine.
>
> c. When *a* is accomplished, 21st Army Group, with Ninth U.S. Army under operational command, to resume preparations for "VERITABLE." [1]

[1] Veritable was the southward attack to clear all territory west of the Rhine in the north.

d. All priorities in building up strength of U.S. Armies in personnel, material and units, to go to 12th Army Group.

e. The front south of Moselle to be strictly defensive for the present.

f. I will build up a reserve (including re-fitting divisions) which will be available to reinforce success.

g. As soon as reduction of Ardennes salient permits, H.Q. 12th Army Group will move north, in close proximity to 21st Army Group H.Q.

h. From now on, any detailed or emergency co-ordination required along Army Group boundaries in the north will be effected by the two Army Group commanders with power of decision vested in C.G., 21 Army Group.

The one thing that must now be prevented is the stabilization of the enemy salient with infantry, permitting him opportunity to use his Panzers at will on any part of the front. We must regain the initiative, and speed and energy are essential.

At conclusion of the battle for the salient, assignment of Divisions to Army Groups and changes in boundaries will be announced.

Dwight D. Eisenhower

This plan was an attempt to blend personal and military considerations. It called for reducing the Ardennes salient by immediate attacks from north and south, with General Bradley resuming command of First U.S. Army when they met. It gave Montgomery one thing he wanted—detailed emergency co-ordination along army group boundaries—while denying him the main thing he had been campaigning for—operational control of both his own and Bradley's army groups.

While Eisenhower was preparing his outline plan on December 30, he received a letter from Montgomery that raised his temper to the boiling point. The following paragraphs from it, in particular, Eisenhower interpreted as an ultimatum:

3. When you and Bradley and myself met at Maastricht on 7 December it was very clear to me that Bradley opposed any idea that I should have operational control over his Army Group; so I did not then pursue the subject.

   I therefore consider that it will be necessary for you to be very firm on the subject, and any loosely worded statements will be quite useless.

4. I consider that if you merely use the word "co-ordination," it will not work. The person designated by you must have powers of operational direction and control of the operation that will follow on your directive.

5. I would say that your directive will assign tasks and objectives to the two Army Groups, allot boundaries, and so on.

   Thereafter preparations are made and battle is joined.

   It is then that one commander must have powers to direct and control the operations; you cannot possibly do it yourself, and so you would have to nominate someone else.

6. I suggest that your directive should finish with this sentence: "12 and 21 Army Groups will develop operations in accordance with the above instructions.

  "From now onwards full operational direction, control, and co-ordination of these operations is vested in the C.-in-C. 21 Army Group, subject to such instructions as may be issued by the Supreme Commander from time to time." [2]

Eisenhower's patience was exhausted. For the moment he set aside his own draft outline plan. Montgomery had to be dealt with first.

On the same day, December 30, Major General Francis de Guingand, chief of staff of 21 Army Group, picked up the telephone and called his friend Bedell Smith at SHAEF. Freddie de Guingand had just had a most disquieting talk with one of the British liaison officers normally stationed at Bradley's 12 Army Group. Feeling at that headquarters against Montgomery was growing by the hour. General Bradley and his staff officers were daily receiving newspapers from the United Kingdom, and they got no pleasure from what they read. The British press was giving the impression that Montgomery had been forced to come to the rescue of an American command that had failed, and this rubbed salt into the wounds of Bradley and his subordinates, who were already sensitive about the temporary transfer of the First and Ninth U.S. armies to the command of 21 Army Group some ten days earlier. Montgomery himself seemed to be utilizing the situation as an additional lever to promote his own appointment as the single, overall land commander.

What Freddie de Guingand learned in his telephone conversation with Bedell Smith increased his alarm. Eisenhower had received Montgomery's "ultimatum" and was contemplating something drastic. Out of loyalty to both Montgomery and Eisenhower—and to the Allied team that had functioned so well from Africa days—de Guingand decided to take matters into his own hands. He knew he had a great asset: he was trusted by both commanders. He would go to see Eisenhower.

Determined to make the flight from Brussels to Versailles that day, de Guingand was faced with some of the worst weather nothern Europe can produce. Nevertheless, he called his pilot, Jack Race, and explained that he had to do his very best to get through.

In the early afternoon Race called back: the weather had cleared enough for them to take the chance. It was a hair-raising ride through fog and snow. For a while it looked as if they would have to give up on Paris and go all

---

[2] Italics supplied.

the way to the United Kingdom to find an open field, but eventually they spotted the Seine River and followed it at treetop level to Paris. With relief, Race landed the plane at Orly Airfield.

In Bedell Smith's office in the Trianon Place Hôtel, Versailles, de Guingand learned that the situation at the High Command was now nearly irretrievable. Eisenhower had decided that either he or Montgomery would have to go. They could no longer work together. In short order, the two chiefs of staff walked to the house in the SHAEF grounds where General Eisenhower was still incarcerated.

They found the atmosphere in the Supreme Commander's office grim indeed. The Deputy Supreme Commander, Air Marshal Tedder, was present, as was Eisenhower's British military assistant, Colonel James Gault. In a somberly lighted room, full of smoke from Tedder's pipe but made somewhat more cheerful by a healthy blaze in the fireplace, Eisenhower explained the intolerable position that General Bradley had been put in, with the very real risk that the British press reports would cause Bradley to lose the confidence of his American troops.

"Does Monty realize," he asked, "the effects of the line taken by the British press? And I wonder if he recognizes the effects of his continual pressing for the establishment of a land commander? I am tired of the whole business and have come to the conclusion that it is now a matter for a decision of the Combined Chiefs of Staff."

So saying, Eisenhower handed de Guingand a message he was about to send to the Combined Chiefs of Staff, through General Marshall. The message was very direct. It outlined the magnitude of the crisis and concluded that one of the two highest ranking officers would have to be relieved. The Combined Chiefs would have to choose between Montgomery and Eisenhower himself.

Freddie de Guingand earned a year's pay in the course of a few minutes. Speaking in deadly earnest, he assured General Eisenhower that the Field Marshal had no idea that things had become so serious. De Guingand was sure that once the entire situation was explained to Montgomery, he would cooperate completely. He implored General Eisenhower to delay sending the wire to Marshall for twenty-four hours. Eisenhower and Tedder were inclined not to agree, asserting that the damage had already been done, but Bedell Smith was on de Guingand's side. Finally, to de Guingand's great relief, Eisenhower agreed to delay his wire for a day so as to give de Guingand a chance to resolve the situation.

General de Guingand left the room mentally exhausted. He could not help reflecting on the fortunate timing that had brought him to SHAEF that day. Once back in Smith's office he sent off a message to Montgomery, telling where he was and saying that he would be flying to Montgomery's tactical headquarters the next day since he had a most important matter to discuss.

But de Guingand's problems were far from over. The next morning, December 31, the weather was again abominable, with fog and snowstorms making air travel impossible, but after a nerve-racking wait and an unpleasant air trip of several hours in the afternoon, de Guingand arrived at Tongres. He immediately drove to Montgomery's headquarters, arriving at his destination at about 4:30 P.M., just in time for tea.

Tea that day was hardly cheerful. It was scarcely proper for two British officers to discuss business during this sacrosanct break in the day, but it was obvious from the disturbed expression on de Guingand's face that something important was on his mind. Montgomery soon left the table saying, "I'm going upstairs to my office, Freddie. Please come up when you have finished your tea."

In a few moments, Major General Francis de Guingand was going through the grim experience of explaining the shocking situation to Britain's most prominent soldier, who was still flushed with the successful role he had played in the stemming of the Ardennes attack. "I've just come from SHAEF," de Guingand said, "and seen Ike, and it's in the cards that you might have to go." He explained the frame of mind existing in the American Command and the Supreme Command; he told a completely baffled Montgomery of the telegram waiting to be sent from Versailles to Washington. "The situation can be put right, I believe," he said, "but it requires immediate action."

Montgomery began to realize how serious the state of affairs was. The mention in the Supreme Commander's wire of Alexander [3] as an acceptable substitute for himself hit him between the eyes. After all, as de Guingand said, if the choice was between Montgomery and Eisenhower, it was inconceivable that Eisenhower would be the one to go—the Americans were now contributing by far the more men and matériel to the war effort. Not even Churchill could save Montgomery under these circumstances.[4]

Montgomery was completely nonplussed. Helplessly he asked, "What shall I do, Freddie?"

De Guingand's advice was to send a message off to Eisenhower without delay. Producing a text he had already drafted, he secured approval, and the following message was sent immediately:

Dear Ike,

Have seen Freddie and understand you are greatly worried by many considerations in these very difficult days. I have given you my frank views because I have felt you like this. I am sure there are many factors which have a bearing quite beyond anything I realize. Whatever your decision may be

[3] Field Marshal Sir Harold Alexander, commander of 15 Army Group during the Tunisian campaign, and Montgomery's former superior.

[4] Churchill and Brooke had earlier assured Eisenhower that they would replace any British officer at the request of the Supreme Commander. Dwight Eisenhower, *Crusade in Europe* (New York: Doubleday, 1948), p. 317.

you can rely on me one hundred per cent to make it work, and I know Brad will do the same. Very distressed that my letter may have upset you and I would ask you to tear it up.

Your very devoted subordinate,
Monty

Montgomery sent off another message to General Bradley. De Guingand, having completed his business at Montgomery's Tac Headquarters, bade his chief good night. Encouraged by news from the Ardennes front, he began the journey over icy roads back to main headquarters in Brussels.

Arriving late in the evening, de Guingand still had one more chore: a press conference with four of the leading British correspondents at 21 Army Group. De Guingand told all and told it frankly. He explained that a major crisis had occurred in the High Command and showed how the press in both England and America were contributing to this situation. Emphasizing that the Americans had borne the major share of the Ardennes fighting, he went on to explain why the Supreme Commander had rearranged the command between army groups on a temporary basis; it was plain that the appointment of a land force commander in Europe would not be acceptable in America, and if the controversy continued, public opinion in the States might bring about a very bad situation.

The correspondents promised to notify their editors in London of the possible consequences of the line they had been taking.

With a good day's work behind him, de Guingand called SHAEF before going to bed. He learned that Montgomery's message had been properly delivered, that Eisenhower had been "most touched," and that the message to Washington was now in the wastepaper basket.

The next day, his temper having cooled, Eisenhower put finishing touches to his outline plan and sent it to all his principal commanders. With the plan he sent to Montgomery a handwritten letter, part of which put to bed the matter of command relationships, at least on a personal basis between the two themselves:

> . . . In the matter of command I do not agree that one Army Group Commander should fight his own battle and give orders to another Army Group Commander. My plan places a complete U.S. Army under command of 21 Army Group, something that I consider militarily necessary, and most assuredly reflects my confidence in you personally. If these things were not true this decision would, in itself, be a most difficult one.
>
> You know how greatly I've appreciated and depended upon your frank and friendly counsel, but in your latest letter you disturb me by predictions of "failure" unless your exact opinions in the matter of giving you command over Bradley are met in detail. I assure you that in this matter I can go no further. . . .

I know your loyalty as a soldier and your readiness to devote yourself to assigned tasks. For my part I would deplore the development of such an unbridgeable group of convictions between us that we would have to present our differences to the Combined Chiefs of Staff. The confusion and debate that would follow would certainly damage the goodwill and devotion to a common cause that have made this Allied Force unique in history.

As ever, your friend,
Ike

While the incident on December 31 settled the issue of command arrangements as far as Eisenhower and Montgomery were concerned, other efforts were being made to assuage feelings all around. On January 5, SHAEF put out an announcement:

When the German penetration through the Ardennes created two fronts, one substantially facing south and the other north, by instant agreement of all concerned that portion of the front facing south was placed under command of Montgomery and that facing north under command of Bradley.

The next day, Prime Minister Churchill wrote to President Roosevelt:

... C.I.G.S. and I have passed the last two days with Eisenhower and Montgomery, and they both feel the battle very heavy, but are confident of success. I hope you understand that, in case any troubles should arise in the Press, His Majesty's Government have complete confidence in General Eisenhower and feel acutely any attacks made on him.

He and Montgomery are very closely knit, and also Bradley and Patton and it would be disaster which broke up this combination, which has in 1944 yielded us results beyond the dreams of military avarice. Montgomery said to me today that the breakthrough would have been most serious to the whole front but for the solidarity of the Anglo-American Army. ...

I most cordially congratulate you on the extraordinary gallantry which your troops have shown in all this battle, particularly at Bastogne and two other places which Montgomery mentioned to me on his own front, one at the peak of the salient, where the 1st and 9th American Divisions fought on and won after extremely heavy losses, and the other in connection with the 7th United States Armoured Division, which seems to have performed the highest acts of soldierly devotion. Also many troops of the First Army have fought to the end, holding cross-roads in the area of incursion, which averted serious perils to the whole armies of the north at heavy personal sacrifice.

As I see there have been criticisms in the American papers of our troops having been kept out of the battle, I take this occasion to assure you that they stand absolutely ready at all times to obey General Eisenhower's commands. I believe that the dispositions which he and Field-Marshal Montgomery under him have made are entirely in accordance with strict military requirements, both as regards the employment of troops in counter-attack and their lateral movement, having regard to criss-cross communications. I have not found a trace of discord at the British and American Headquarters; but,

Mr. President, there is this brute fact: we need more fighting troops to make things move.

I have a feeling this is a time for an intense new impulse, both of friendship and exertion, to be drawn from our bosoms and to the last scrap of our resources. Do not hesitate to tell me of anything you think we can do.

However, the matter was to flare up yet again, even more heatedly, in the press. The difficulty was caused by a press conference given by Montgomery on January 7, 1945.[5]

There is every reason to believe that Montgomery's press conference was given in a sincere spirit of conciliation. For one thing, the Field Marshal made clear what should have been obvious—that the Supreme Commander was the boss:

I am absolutely devoted to Ike. We are the greatest of friends. The other day my plane was damaged. I asked him, "Can you lend me another?" He sent me his own at once.

It grieves me when I see uncomplimentary remarks about him in the British press. I do not think it is right. Mind you, nothing of that sort has ever come from here. It has come from outside—it has raised its head outside.

He bears a great burden. He needs our fullest support. He has a right to expect it, and it is up to us to see that he gets it. Let us all rally round the captain of the team.

Furthermore, Montgomery went out of his way to pay a tribute to the fighting qualities of the American soldier:

He is a very brave fighting man, and he has that tenacity in battle which stamps a first-class soldier. He is basically responsible for Rundstedt not doing what he wanted to do. During this battle, I tried to identify myself very closely with the American soldier, so that I shall take the correct action with these great Allied armies which are now under my command.

I now have an American identity card, which identifies me in the Army of the U.S. My fingerprints are registered in the War Department at Washington —I would sooner have them there than at Scotland Yard.

Saying that he would "never want to fight alongside better soldiers," he singled out especially three stands that had been made in the battle: first, the Monschau shoulder, where American troops had "held the corner so firmly that Rundstedt's northern drive never got started"; then at St.-Vith, from which, Montgomery somewhat erroneously asserted, the 7th Armored Divi-

---

[5] This press conference occurred after the jump-off of counterattacks by VII Corps along a line east of the Ourthe River toward Houffalize, and by Third Army from Bastogne (also toward Houffalize). The German forces were withdrawing, and on that date the vital road from St.-Vith to La Roche had been cut. Manteuffel had finally given up his efforts to capture Bastogne, and the battle of the Ardennes was decided, though much hard fighting was yet to be done.

sion had complained at being withdrawn on December 23; and finally, what he described as "the glorious stand at Bastogne" on the part of the 101st Airborne Division.

The trouble with the Montgomery press conference primarily was one of tone. Undermining the Field Marshal's words of good will was a suggestion that he had come in personally to save the American High Command from disaster. Part of the press conference was particularly distressing to General Bradley:

> When Rundstedt attacked on December 16, he obtained a tactical surprise. He drove a deep wedge into the center of the United States First Army and the split might have become awkward; the Germans had broken right through a weak spot, and were heading for the Meuse.
>
> As soon as I saw what was happening I took certain steps myself to ensure that if the Germans got to the Meuse they would certainly not get over that river. And I carried out certain movements so as to provide balanced dispositions to meet the threatened danger; these were, at the time, merely precautions, i.e. I was thinking ahead.
>
> Then the situation began to deteriorate. But the whole allied team rallied to meet the danger; national considerations were thrown overboard; General Eisenhower placed me in command of the whole Northern front.
>
> I employed the whole available power of the British Group of Armies; this power was brought into play very gradually and in such a way that it would not interfere with the American lines of communications. Finally it was put into battle with a bang and today British divisions are fighting hard on the right flank of the United States First Army.
>
> You have thus the picture of British troops fighting on both sides of American forces who have suffered a hard blow. This is a fine Allied picture.
>
> The battle has some similarity to the battle that began on 31 August 1942 when Rommel made his last bid to capture Egypt and was "seen off" by the Eighth Army.
>
> You have to decide what your design of the battle is going to be before you start that battle. Then you fight your way and not anybody else's way and make the enemy dance to your tune.
>
> If you are going to fight battles in that way you have got to be so balanced that whatever the enemy may do there will be no need for you to react to him.
>
> Having had this hard blow put in and the American Army being parted, it was clear that the battle area must be untidy. Therefore the first thing I did when I was brought into this business by General Eisenhower was to busy myself getting the battle area tidy.
>
> I busied myself getting it sorted out and getting the reserves in the right places and getting balance. I regrouped the American and British Armies, regrouped the whole show.
>
> One of the first things I had to do was to position the Army Corps in what I thought was going to be the line of approach of the German big left

hook up to the Meuse between Namur and Dinant. There was not much there. There was damn little there.

I regrouped an Army Corps under that very fine commander General Collins and had to decide where to put it. I put it in a certain place which turned out not [to] be a bad place so that the Corps I formed took the full blow of the left hook.

It took a knock. I said, "Dear me, this can't go on. It's being swallowed up in the battle."

I set to work and managed to form the corps again.

Once more pressure was such that it began to disappear in a defensive battle.

I said: "Come, come," and formed it again and it was put in offensively by General Hodges.

The enemy was first "headed off" from vital spots, then "seen off."

He is now being "written off," and heavy toll is being taken of his divisions by ground and air action. . . .[6]

Furthermore, the situation was grossly exacerbated by the way in which the British press chose to interpret the Field Marshal's statements. For example, on January 8, 1945, the London *Daily Mail* implied that Montgomery had assumed command of the northern shoulder of the Bulge without authority from Supreme Headquarters. The article, with headlines, ran as follows:

MONTGOMERY FORESAW ATTACK
His Troops Were All Ready to March
ACTED "ON OWN" TO SAVE DAY

Field-Marshal Montgomery's part in stopping von Rundstedt from successfully developing his offensive in its early stages will be described by the Prime Minister, other conditions permitting, in the war review he has promised to give in the House of Commons when Parliament reassembles on January 16.

According to information obtained in reliable political quarters, Field-Marshal Montgomery *took command of all the armies along the whole northern flank of the German salient several days before the idea was confirmed in the highest quarters.*[7]

Apparently the situation was so desperate that Field-Marshal Montgomery, using his own initiative, threw in all his weight and authority and asserted his leadership, which was accepted by those around him. . . .

Finally, the Field Marshal's statement omitted one matter which admittedly also had been omitted from the earlier statement by SHAEF: the adjustment of command was a temporary expedient only.

The press in Britain was quick to pick up the implication that Montgom-

[6] *Daily Mirror,* January 8, 1945.
[7] Italics supplied.

ery's command of the First and Ninth U.S. armies was permanent. On January 9, for example, the *Daily Telegraph* headlined: MONTGOMERY'S NEW COMMAND HAILED IN U.S., CHOICE MADE ON MERIT. With a byline, "Our Own Correspondent," the article stated that the American press had taken the news of Field Marshal Montgomery's new responsibilities in the spirit in which the British press took the appointment of General Eisenhower to the Supreme Command of Western Europe—that "it is a good thing to have the right men in the right places." Quoting the Chicago *Sun* and the *Christian Science Monitor* as representative, the *Telegraph* stated that American newspapers had given much prominence to Montgomery's statement of the day before as "one of the first clear expositions of recent military events on the western front."

The news of the Montgomery press conference and the press reaction to it was received by the American Command, General Bradley and his staff in particular, with dismay and anger. Bradley, by nature a quiet, unassuming man, was highly concerned. He felt the implications were such as to discredit not only himself but also the rest of the American High Command.

The situation was made worse by a clever idea on the part of the German propaganda machine: it rebroadcast a doctored version of the press conference over a station that purported to be BBC.

Something, General Bradley felt, had to be done. Debating it in his mind, consulting with his aides and his public relations officers, Bradley finally decided on an action he had not resorted to previously: issuing a press statement of his own.

In the statement he emphasized one fact: the switchover in command of the First and Ninth U.S. armies to Montgomery's 21 Army Group was always regarded as a temporary expedient only. At the first opportune moment— probably when the northern and southern shoulders met and closed off the Bulge—American troops would revert to command of his own 12 Army Group.

General Bradley's remarks were received bitterly by the British press. On January 12, the *Daily Mail* headlined the report of Bradley's press conference A SLUR ON MONTY:

> It would be unfortunate if the Transatlantic "slanging match," which was showing signs of abatement, were to be revived about the names and achievements of military commanders. . . .
>
> Yet remarks have been made by General Omar Bradley, Commander of the United States Twelfth Army Group, which, we feel, would have been better left unsaid. In justice to a great British soldier, such statements cannot be allowed to pass without comment. . . .
>
> What he stated in effect was that when the Germans broke through on

the Ardennes front and the Allied line was disrupted, Field-Marshal Montgomery at once took command of the northern group of armies and by his "notable contribution" to the battle did much to restore the situation. But his command is only temporary, and when the lines are rejoined the Twelfth Army Group, said General Bradley, will once again take over the whole sector.

This statement bears only one interpretation. It is that Field-Marshal Montgomery is good enough to be given the position of responsibility in an emergency, but when the danger is over and the ravages of the enemy made good his services are no longer required except in a comparatively subordinate capacity.

It can be said at once that the British people would view with dismay the relegation of this great soldier to the somewhat meagre share of the front which he held before Rundstedt's breakthrough. And this is no question of national pride or prestige. It is simply a matter of having the right man in the right place. . . .

Must he again be pushed back into the semi-obscurity which was his lot in the weeks before the Ardennes link was snapped by the enemy? This country will need convincing that his services could not be put to better use. . . .

One of the more unfortunate aspects of the whole furor in the press was that the discussion was entirely academic. Although General Eisenhower later wrote that this incident had caused him more distress and worry than any similar one in the war, there still was no question in his mind that the First and eventually the Ninth U.S. armies would be returned to General Bradley's 12 Army Group.

Montgomery, on his own part, did the best he could to heal the breach between himself and Bradley. He paid Bradley a visit at Luxembourg—a visit that was hardly regarded a success—and in his correspondence seemed to go out of his way to restore a cordial relationship. Bradley responded coolly.

But it remained for the Prime Minister finally to assuage American feelings. With typical Churchill rhetoric he reported to Parliament on January 17, 1945:

> Now I turn to a very different theme and story. I turn from the pink and ochre panorama of Athens and the Piraeus, scintillating with delicious life plumed by the classic glories and endless miseries and triumphs of its history.[8] This must give way to the main battle fronts of the war. In this my chief contribution will be the recital of a number of facts and figures which may or may not be agreeable in different quarters.
>
> I have seen it suggested that the terrific battle which has been proceeding since December 16 on the American front is an Anglo-American battle. In fact, however, the United States troops have done almost all the fighting and have suffered almost all the losses. They have suffered losses almost equal to those on both sides in the battle of Gettysburg. Only one British army

[8] British operations in Greece were under scrutiny in the House of Commons.

corps had been engaged in this action. All the rest of the 30 or more divisions which have been fighting continuously for the last month are United States troops. The Americans have engaged 30 or 40 men for every one we have engaged, and they have lost 60 to 80 men for every one of ours. That is a point I wish to make. Care must be taken in telling our proud tale not to claim for the British Army an undue share of what is undoubtedly the greatest American battle of the war and will, I believe, be regarded as an ever famous American victory.

The members of Parliament responded with approving cheers.

Fortunately, these misunderstandings between close Allies occurred after the crisis in the Ardennes had passed. Furthermore, their importance should not be exaggerated; they interfered very little if at all with the conduct of operations.

The explosion of Allied differences brought on by the German successes in the Ardennes really is significant only because it was the climax of the expression of underlying national viewpoints, and is of interest primarily to the degree it justified Hitler's confidence that the great Allied coalition could not hold up under the weight of adversity. Hitler's hope that he could repeat the exploits of Frederick the Great of Prussia in dividing the alliance facing him proved to contain a germ of substance; but in the end that hope was defeated. Just as Hitler erred in assuming that the Supreme Commander would be required to consult Washington before radically altering his strategic plans, just as he erred in underestimating the competence of the Allied Command and the fighting qualities of the American soldier, he erred in thinking that one powerful attack could split what he regarded as a weak coalition.

The question of the public relations is something else. It does appear that the difficulties could have been much allayed had Supreme Headquarters issued an early statement explaining the change and emphasizing that it was to be temporary. As it was, the statement issued by SHAEF on January 5 was occasioned by a "scoop" in an American magazine.

In defense of SHAEF, however, the Stars and Stripes quoted President Roosevelt on the same date as denying that Montgomery had been made Eisenhower's deputy and stated that Montgomery's new command would be continued "at Eisenhower's discretion."

The fact remains that the SHAEF statement per se mentioned nothing about the arrangement's being temporary.

But with all the noise and ruffled feelings, the rift was patched up. Field Marshal Montgomery and General Bradley continued to cooperate throughout the rest of the war, though they were hardly Damon and Pythias. The threat to Allied unity that Hitler had counted on had not been realized.

CHAPTER 16

❧❧

Friction with de Gaulle

O N New Year's Eve, 1944, Obersturmbahnführer Otto Skorzeny was summoned once again to Hitler's headquarters, still located at the Adlerhorst, near Giessen in Western Germany. His own 150th Panzer Brigade had been relieved from its position south of Malmédy on the twenty-eighth.

Skorzeny was surprised that the officer who greeted him seemed not the least downcast. Nor did the Führer when he received his fellow Austrian. He asked why Skorzeny's right eye was bandaged. Before beginning the conference Hitler sent his protégé to his personal physician, Dr. Ludwig Stumpfecker. Stumpfecker, discovering a suppurating wound and inflamed eye, gave Skorzeny hours of unpleasant and elaborate treatment, including infrared rays and inoculations; Skorzeny later conceded that Stumpfecker had saved his sight in that eye.

In the afternoon Skorzeny was received in Hitler's office. He was astonished by the news the Führer had to offer: "We are now going to start a great offensive in the southeast!"

As was his habit, Hitler took ample time to explain his new operation, code-named Nordwind (North Wind). He talked with great optimism, and Skorzeny, puzzled, could not help wondering whether Hitler was deceiving himself or whether he was under the influence of the injections administered by Dr. Theodor Morell, which other doctors warned contained minute quantities of arsenic that would inevitably prove harmful. Still, Hitler's cheerfulness was so contagious that Skorzeny left him considerably happier than when he had arrived.

Operation Nordwind, which Hitler had described with such gusto, had long been a possibility. Reviving the idea at this time was an attempt to retain some degree of initiative in the west. The target of Hitler's new offensive was Lieutenant General Jacob L. Devers' spread-out 6 Army Group, which was exposed from two directions: Seventh U.S. Army was exposed in the north and the First French Army in the great bulge at Colmar.

393

At the Verdun meeting of December 19, it will be recalled, General Eisenhower had given Devers responsibility for the entire Allied line from Basel, Switzerland, to the Saar, a frontage of about 200 miles.

Facing Devers were two German army groups, although in actual strength these formations comprised little more than one army each. To the south the Nineteenth German Army, under General der Infanterie Frederich Wiese, occupied the Colmar Pocket. This force, along with two SS corps east of the Rhine, came under Army Group Oberrhein, commanded by none other than Reichsführer Heinrich Himmler. (At one point in the war, according to Guderian, Himmler held the titles Minister of the Interior, Chief of the German Police, National Leader of the SS, Commander in Chief of the Training Army, and Commander of the Army Group Oberrhein.[1]) In his capacity as a field commander, in which he was established early in December, Himmler reported not to OB West, Rundstedt, but directly to Hitler himself.

To the north, along the Seventh U.S. Army front west of the Rhine, Army Group G under General der Panzertruppen Hermann Balck had as its principal subordinate unit the German First Army, under General der Infanterie Hans von Obstfelder.

The German First Army consisted of three corps, the 13th SS, the 82d and the 90th, comprising nine divisions, six of which were infantry and three panzer or panzer grenadier. The 89th Korps, not under the command of First Army, was nevertheless in the line, with three infantry divisions and one panzer.

In essence Army Group G had no reserve worthy of the name. Nevertheless, with these understrength and tired troops Hitler hoped to make a strategic breakthrough in Alsace-Lorraine.

General Balck's early preparations for the Alsace offensive were hampered by his being kept in the dark about Hitler's plans until the last minute. True, any competent commander could have sensed during the autumn that a major German attack was pending—otherwise what was the point in taking away Balck's 3d and 15th Panzer Grenadier divisions in November, in stripping all reserves from the army group, in thinning it out to the extent that no new reserves could be formed? Only on December 16, as Model's Army Group B was jumping off in the Ardennes, was Balck allowed to open sealed orders previously received; they briefly announced the beginning of the Ardennes offensive and advised that a relaxation of enemy pressure along the Army Group G front could be expected with the progress of the Ardennes offensive, in which event Balck was to go on the offensive. The Führer's order was given only in general terms, but it did not leave the army group much

---

[1] Heinz Guderian, *Panzer Leader* (New York: Dutton, 1952), p. 383.

freedom of action. Deciding the objective of the offensive and its date was left to Hitler himself.

On or about December 20, Balck concluded that the time for action had come. He pulled two mobile divisions out of the line—the 25th Panzer Grenadier and 21st Panzer—and assembled them in the area west of Pirmasens, that is, just west of the Vosges Mountains and just north of Bitche.

Two objectives for the offensive seemed possible (see map, p. 397). One was the area west of the Vosges Mountains along the Sarre (Saar) River including Metz. By retaking the Moselle sector Balck would shift the front farther away from the all-important industrial area of the Saar Basin. This would have been a bold move, but in Balck's view it surpassed the resources of the army group, including that all-important commodity, gasoline. Furthermore, in this open country Balck would have to contend with Allied air forces whenever the weather cleared.

The alternative was an attack westward through the eastern Vosges, in the direction of Saverne. An attack by the Nineteenth Army northward through the Vosges, linking up with the First Army at Saverne in a pincers action, offered hope of destroying all U.S. forces stuck out in the sharp salient in that corner of Alsace. But again, this scheme depended on the allocation of new forces.

Rundstedt's headquarters shared Balck's view but suspended decision until Hitler would be ready to issue his orders, though Rundstedt did permit Balck to prepare for a major attack on an unknown target. During all the planning, Balck and his staff detected that the American attitude along the front area was becoming increasingly defensive and that the U.S. positions in the lower (northern) Vosges continued to be weak. American movements toward the north and northwest via Saarburg had been picked up.

Planning was made more complicated when, on the afternoon of December 22, General Balck received orders transferring him to "special duties." He was to be replaced by an officer of the highest reputation, Generaloberst Johannes Blaskowitz, a move that indicates further—if this were necessary—that Hitler regarded Nordwind an operation of utmost importance. Until Blaskowitz could arrive on December 24, the acting army group commander would be the commander of First Army, General Obstfelder.

On the morning of December 23, following Balck's departure, Obstfelder received an order to prepare an attack following Balck's second plan. First Army was to attack southward to link up with the Nineteenth at Saverne, and together they would annihilate the U.S. VI Corps in Alsace. While Saverne was designated the objective of the attack, the route of advance was not specified. Obstfelder was told that he would receive reinforcement, one unit, the 6th SS Mountain Division, which was to arrive from Finland between Christmas and New Year's Day. He was given one day to prepare and present his plan of attack to Rundstedt.

On receiving his orders, Obstfelder sat down with the army group's chief of staff, Oberst Horst Wilutski, to view the situation. According to their calculations, five infantry divisions were available to make the attack, plus three mobile divisions, 21st Panzer, 25th Panzer Grenadier, and 17th SS Panzer Grenadier. Artillery support was available, and the 6th SS Mountain Division was on the way. However, the condition of the troops was generally such that they could attack limited objectives only; reinforcements in personnel and matériel were needed. The group also suffered from a lack of self-propelled assault guns in all attack divisions. Only the 17th SS Panzer Grenadier had sufficient replacements in men and matériel. Hardly more than one issue of ammunition could be provided the assault units.

Studying the map, the German officers could see three approaches to Saverne in the lower Vosges Mountains: (a) through the open country to the west; (b) through the American salient at the Lauter River; (c) straight down the lower Vosges.

The first was rejected in view of the air situation: furthermore, the Americans had occupied the Maginot Line [2] in this region in some strength.

The second attack resembled the first, the only additional attraction being the weak forces of the understrength U.S. VI Corps holding the area. However, here, too, the Maginot forts were in U.S. hands, and the area was heavily mined.

What Obstfelder decided to recommend, therefore, was an infantry attack straight down the lower Vosges Mountains, from Bitche to Saverne. Here, he knew, very few U.S. forces held the front, and the mountain range offered protection to the flanks. Moreover, some of the Maginot Line forts in the lower Vosges were in German hands. Thus, Obstfelder's plan became a miniature edition of Hitler's Ardennes offensive to the north, in that it employed the least favorable terrain in order to secure maximum surprise and concealment, hitting the U.S. lines where they were weakest.

The next day, December 24, Colonel Wilutski went to Rundstedt's headquarters to explain the army group's plan to OB West. Rundstedt declared himself in complete agreement and immediately submitted the plan to Hitler at a meeting in which Blaskowitz, the new group commander, was also present.

Hitler intervened. He refused to believe that Saverne could be reached by an attack down the backbone of the lower Vosges, despite the alleged German superiority in winter fighting gained by their experience on the Russian front. He therefore ordered the small diversionary drive west of the Vosges

---

[2] The old Maginot Line ran Saarguemines–Bitche–Lembach–Hatten–Sessenheim.

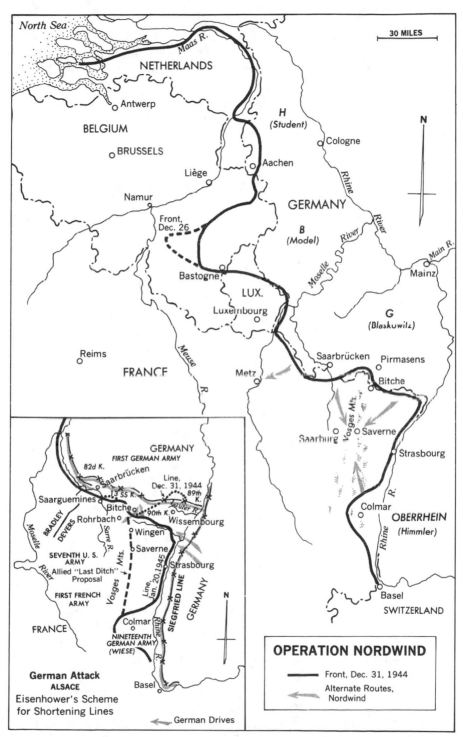

North Sea

Maas R.

NETHERLANDS

Antwerp

BELGIUM

BRUSSELS

Liège

Namur

Front,
Dec. 26

Bastogne

Reims

FRANCE

Meuse R.

30 MILES

H
(Student)

Cologne

Aachen

GERMANY

B
(Model)

Moselle River

Rhine River

Main R.

Mainz

LUX.

Luxembourg

G
(Blaskowitz)

Metz

Saarbrücken

Pirmasens

Bitche

Saarburg

Vosges Mts.

Saverne

Strasbourg

Colmar

OBERRHEIN
(Himmler)

Rhine R.

Basel

SWITZERLAND

N

German Attack
ALSACE
Eisenhower's Scheme
for Shortening Lines

GERMANY
FIRST GERMAN ARMY

82d K.

Saarbrücken

Line,
Dec. 31, 1944

89th
K.

13 SS K.

Saarguemines

BRADLEY

DEVERS

Bitche

90th K.

Lauter R.

Wissembourg

Rohrbach

Sarre R.

Wingen

Saverne

SEVENTH U.S.
ARMY

Allied "Last Ditch"
Proposal

Moselle River

FIRST FRENCH
ARMY

FRANCE

Vosges Mts.

Colmar

NINETEENTH
GERMAN ARMY
(WIESE)

Basel

Line,
Jan. 20, 1945

SIEGFRIED LINE

Strasbourg

Rhine R.

GERMANY

N

German Drives

OPERATION NORDWIND

Front, Dec. 31, 1944

Alternate Routes,
Nordwind

that Obstfelder had planned be expanded and carried out as the main drive (see map, p. 397). The attack from the west was to converge with the attack down the mountains in the Rohrbach area after which the mobile units—the 21st and 25th—could be brought up west of the Vosges and committed as an additional thrust. Hitler insisted that the two mobile units were under no circumstances to be employed—not even elements of them—before the Maginot Line had been penetrated at Rohrbach.

The 17th SS Panzer Grenadier Division was to carry out the main thrust to Rohrbach. All the heavy self-propelled assault guns and antitank battalions, items in short supply in Army Group G, were to be employed in the sector of that one unit, the 17th. Thus Hitler ordered two full-scale attacks, without providing antitank protection to any divisions other than the 17th Panzer Grenadier.

On Christmas Day Blaskowitz, having taken formal command of Army Group G, explained the changes in the plan to Obstfelder, now back with First Army. The division commanders were ordered to report personally to Hitler on December 28. Extremely restrictive security measures were to be taken, and specially selected officers were to reveal the secret to commanding generals, division commanders, and their staff officers only.

The division commanders' conference with Hitler brought out nothing new. Hitler appealed to them to incite the group to a supreme effort:

> The German people have breathed more freely in the last few days. We must make sure that this relief does not fall by lethargy—lethargy is the wrong word, I mean gloom. They have breathed again. The mere idea that we are on the offensive again has had a cheering effect on the German people. . . .
>
> Finally, I wish to appeal to you to go into the operation with all your verve, with all your zest, and all your energy. This is a decisive operation. Your success will automatically bring about the success of the second operation. The collapse of the second operation will automatically bring about the collapse of the threat to the left flank of our Ardennes offensive. We shall then actually have knocked out half the enemy forces on the Western front. Then we will see what happens. Then there will be 45 additional German divisions. I do not believe in the long run he can stand up to those. We will yet be masters of our fate.

In order to achieve complete surprise, Hitler set the time for the beginning of the attack at 11:00 P.M. New Year's Eve.

On December 26, the day of the high-water mark in the Ardennes, Lieutenant General Jacob L. Devers flew to Paris to talk to the Supreme Commander. Seventh U.S. Army intelligence had estimated that the enemy might attack northern Alsace between January 1 and 3.

With the battle between the 2d U.S. Armored and the 2d Panzer in progress only a couple of miles from the Meuse, Devers found General Eisenhower understandably preoccupied with the actions on that front. Furthermore, eying the map, Eisenhower remained convinced that the sharp salient sticking out into the corner of Alsace required too many troops confined to a purely static role. He was of the mind to withdraw voluntarily all the way to the Vosges, releasing more divisions for employment in the main battle and thus insuring more decisive results in the Ardennes. Accordingly, he repeated his instructions that 6 Army Group be prepared to give up ground rather than endanger the integrity of its forces.

On return to his headquarters, Devers ordered both his armies, Jean de Lattre's French First and Alexander Patch's U.S. Seventh, to remain on the defensive. To remedy the offending salient on the northeast corner of the Seventh Army, he ordered preparation of three intermediate positions to which the forces in northern Alsace could fall back. One was to be the Maginot Line, several miles from the advanced U.S. forces that had driven a wedge into the Siegfried Line; another the line east of the Vosges along the Moder River, from Wingen to Haguenau; the final position all the way back at the line of the Vosges. Devers particularly did not relish this third alternative, and he asked his commanders to try if at all possible to hold on to Strasbourg on the north of the Colmar Pocket, and Mulhouse on the south of the Pocket.

A couple of days later, indications of an impending attack increasing by the minute, Devers asked General Eisenhower if he could keep the units earmarked for transfer from 6 Army Group until the threat subsided. On the night of December 31, before Eisenhower could answer, Nordwind jumped off.

The Supreme Commander's plans for Alsace were known to the French, who were kept closely informed. The political significance of Strasbourg was so important to the French that they were willing to go to almost any extreme to prevent its falling into German hands without a fight. At one point General Alphonse P. Juin, chief of staff for the Ministry of Defense, spoke of placing newly organized French Forces of the Interior (FFI) units at the disposal of 6 Army Group for the purpose of defending the Strasbourg area. These hardly could have turned the trick.

General Eisenhower could sympathize with the French view, but his problem was primarily a military one—destruction of Hitler's armies—and the place where maximum destruction could be inflicted was the Ardennes. Despite the French reaction and Devers' reluctance to give up territory, on New Year's morning Eisenhower ordered Devers to hold the Alsace Plain with reconnaissance and observation forces only, withdrawing his main forces to the Vosges.

General Charles de Gaulle protested. The next day, January 2, General

Juin held a stormy session on the subject with Eisenhower's chief of staff, Bedell Smith. There was no change in plans.

The relief and withdrawal in Alsace took some time to organize, and in the meantime the discussion reached its peak. On the morning of January 3 the Supreme Commander discussed the projected evacuation of Strasbourg with his staff. He was still convinced of the wisdom of withdrawing the main forces, particularly VI Corps, from the sharp salient to the line of the Vosges —if this were done, Allied armor might still be able to protect Strasbourg from the north—but withdrawal would have grave political repercussions. Eisenhower was informed that more than 100,000 inhabitants would have to be evacuated from Strasbourg, and 300,000 to 400,000 inhabitants of the area would be subject to possible reprisal by the Germans.[3]

The staff had just learned that Prime Minister Churchill was scheduled to arrive at Versailles that afternoon, and Eisenhower decided to explain his own viewpoint to him as a matter of courtesy. Without notifying Eisenhower, de Gaulle had appealed to both President Roosevelt and Prime Minister Churchill to prevent the withdrawal. Roosevelt had rejected the appeal on the grounds that the decision was a purely military one, but Churchill had decided to come to Paris and talk the matter over, though Eisenhower was unaware that Churchill's visit had this purpose.

Prime Minister Churchill had lunch as planned with General Eisenhower at Versailles, and afterwards they conferred with Field Marshal Brooke and Generals Smith, Whiteley, and Strong. By the time the discussions had finished, Eisenhower had all but made up his mind that Strasbourg should be defended, although it would deprive him of extra divisions and entail some risk.

That same afternoon General de Gaulle, accompanied by General Juin, came to Supreme Headquarters to discuss the matter. Churchill was present as an observer. De Gaulle was persuasive in earnestly explaining his position, emphasizing the symbolic importance of Strasbourg, even while agreeing with Eisenhower that saving troops in the region was militarily correct. Strasbourg was sufficiently important to the French that they would put the whole French force around the city, even at the risk of losing the entire army, rather than give it up without a fight. To evacuate Strasbourg voluntarily would cause bitterness throughout the entire French nation—and probably result in the fall of his own government.

Conversation was frank, but without personal recrimination. At one point, however, de Gaulle produced a letter implying that in the last analysis he might find it necessary to take French forces out from under General Eisenhower's command. At this point Eisenhower's temper, until then known principally only to his immediate staff, flared. He allowed himself the luxury of

[3] Forrest Pogue, *The Supreme Command* (Washington: Dept. of the Army, 1954), p. 400.

informing the Provisional President of the French Republic that if this were done the French Army would get no ammunition, supplies, or food unless it obeyed his orders. He went on to tell de Gaulle pointedly that if the First French Army had previously eliminated the Colmar Pocket, the emergency would not have arisen. In so saying Eisenhower was giving vent once more to his continuing frustration over that thorn sticking in the Allied side on the west bank of the Rhine. It will be recalled that Eisenhower had given Devers a rather curt order to eliminate the Pocket just before Model struck in the Ardennes. Now its reduction would have to be delayed, but its existence would continue to cost the Allies several divisions.

However, the meeting continued, and de Gaulle emphasized that the voluntary evacuation of Strasbourg might well cause unrest in the rear areas, a serious military complication that impressed Eisenhower considerably. Allied forces in Europe were dependent on lines of communication stretching across France from two directions, all the way from Cherbourg and Marseilles. If these lines of communication had to be protected from the French themselves, the whole Allied effort would be weakened. The French divisions were a secondary consideration. Moreover, Eisenhower had realized by January 3 that the situation in the Ardennes differed considerably from that of December 26. The Ardennes battle was now under control, and the question was not staving off defeat but increasing the decisiveness of the Allied victory.

Eventually Eisenhower came up with what he considered a reasonable compromise. It might be possible to pull the VI Corps back, with its left protected on the Vosges Mountains and its right defending some few miles north of Strasbourg. Furthermore, he promised the French leader to take no more troops away from 6 Army Group.

De Gaulle was delighted with Eisenhower's decision. In Eisenhower's words, "This modification pleased de Gaulle very much and he left in a good humor, alleging unlimited faith in my military judgment." [4]

During the meeting the Prime Minister said nothing, but General Eisenhower was gratified that evening when his friend agreed with his action: "I think your final conclusion was absolutely correct. A break with General de Gaulle would have been bad. Could we have a whiskey and soda before we go to bed?" [5]

The miltary operation itself turned out to be unspectacular. The 17th SS Panzer Grenadier Division's attack on the west of the Vosges, insisted upon

[4] Dwight Eisenhower, *Crusade in Europe* (New York: Doubleday, 1948), p. 363.

[5] Pogue states that in the fall of 1945 some French newspapers reported that General Eisenhower had changed his mind under pressure from the Prime Minister. When Churchill informed Eisenhower of his willingness to issue a contradiction, Eisenhower said that no statement was necessary. He recognized that Mr. Churchill, "with his usual confidence," had left the settlement of the matter to the Supreme Commander. *Op. cit.*, p. 401.

by Hitler, was stopped easily, having advanced only a couple of miles. One battle group of the 17th succeeded in penetrating American lines, but it was cut off and temporarily encircled, and only after a long struggle did it succeed in finding its way back. The attack halted when it reached the Maginot Line at Rohrbach and, as had been foreseen by Obstfelder and Rundstedt, had to be discontinued altogether by January 3.

The right attack, that of the 90th Korps down the ridge of the Lower Vosges, met with somewhat more success, and by January 4 one regiment of the 6th SS Mountain Division had moved about five miles to the outskirts of Wingen on the Moder River. Penetrations of the Maginot Line were enlarged. At this point Army Group G felt the lack of self-propelled assault guns, which, by order of Hitler, had been deployed in the western sector in support of the 13th SS Panzer Korps, and the 90th Korps felt the loss of a division that had been switched over to support the 17th SS Panzer Grenadier. But even now Blaskowitz was refused permission from higher headquarters to withdraw the assault guns from the 17th Panzer Grenadier and support the infantry divisions that had met some success in the center. At no time, despite the five-mile penetration, was the center attack group anywhere near the objective, Saverne. For lack of air support, all efforts in the center were abandoned by January 6 and some ground was actually lost.

The large gains in the attack actually turned out to be in the eastern zone, partly the result of the voluntary withdrawal of U.S. forces from the sharp Lauterbourg salient. The 89th Korps, noticing the withdrawals of the U.S. forces on this front, moved forward. Both Blaskowitz and Rundstedt were eager to use the two panzer divisions in an attempt to force a breakthrough to the mountains. This was the maneuver that General Eisenhower had always considered the most dangerous.

The Allied change of orders between the first and third of January had indeed resulted in some hours of uncertainty, and for part of a day Strasbourg was virtually undefended. However, this situation was soon rectified, and though the Germans made secondary crossings of the Rhine at the small towns of Gambsheim and Drusenheim, and though the Nineteenth Army in the south drove some eight miles northward January 7 to 16, at no time were the German lines ever nearer than eight miles from Strasbourg. On January 6, General Devers switched the boundary between the Seventh U.S. Army and the First French Army to give the French the responsibility for the defense of Strasbourg.

Himmler's drive westward to the Vosges never came to fruition, possibly because Hitler himself put higher priority on capturing Strasbourg for political reasons. All major efforts were concentrated north and south along the Rhine.

Thus, aside from the voluntary U.S. withdrawals, Nordwind gained at the most about 15 miles in northeastern Alsace. U.S. troops held handily behind the Moder River all the way from the Rhine River to Saarguemines.

Operation Nordwind was never given resources sufficient to achieve decisive results. Nevertheless, the chief of staff of Army Group G, Colonel Wilutski, writing after the war, felt that the operation might have achieved far greater results had things been better handled on the German side. First of all, he felt that the preparations for the offensive were too late and inadequate. In Wilutski's opinion, Hitler should have authorized Army Group G to begin preparations for the attack on December 1 at the latest and should have provided it in due time with sufficient supplies and personnel. Preparations were further hindered by the elaborate security measures that prevented lower commanders from performing many of the numerous tasks required at the last minute. Wilutski claims that the repeated interference of Hitler and OKW in the planning and execution of operations contributed to the failure. Cases in point were Hitler's order for a two-pronged main effort and, after the deep penetration of the Lower Vosges, OKW's refusal to permit transfer of fire support and reserves to the point of greatest success. Finally, an attack east of Wissembourg, as demanded by OKW (probably on Himmler's insistence), had to be executed by inadequate forces frontally over considerable terrain obstacles.

These arguments seem sensible. They conform to the postwar pattern followed by German generals who blamed all defeats on Hitler and OKW. But they also point up the French concern over the safety of Strasbourg. The discussions at SHAEF in this connection were no mere academic exercise: there was every chance that Strasbourg might have been lost.

One thing can be said for Nordwind. It was successful in tying down Allied divisions General Eisenhower would have liked to use to secure a more decisive victory in the Ardennes. That the price Hitler paid for this diversion was worth it is doubtful.

In early January, 1945, the Supreme Commander and the Prime Minister were concerned over the situation on the eastern front. If the Russians launched an offensive soon, it would eat up whatever reserves the Nazis were holding for reinforcement in the west. To learn what he could of Russian plans, General Eisenhower dispatched Air Chief Marshal Tedder to Moscow, but Tedder was delayed by the weather, so on January 6 the Prime Minister offered to see what he could find out through direct communication with Marshal Stalin:

> The battle in the west is very heavy and at any time large decisions may be called for from the Supreme Command. You know yourself from your

own experience how very anxious the position is when a very broad front has to be defended after the temporary loss of the initiative. It is Eisenhower's great desire and need to know in outline what you plan to do, as this obviously affects all his and our major decisions. . . . I shall be grateful if you can tell me whether we can count on a major Russian offensive on the Vistula front, or elsewhere during January, with any other points you may care to mention. I shall not pass this most secret information to anyone except Field-Marshal Brooke and General Eisenhower, and only under the conditions of the utmost secrecy. I regard the matter as urgent.

Within one day Stalin answered the Prime Minister as follows:

I received your message of January 6, 1945, on the evening of January 7. . . .
It is most important that we should be able to take advantage of our supremacy over the Germans in artillery and in the air. This demands clear flying weather and an absence of low mists, which hinder aimed artillery fire. We are preparing an offensive, but the weather is at present unfavorable. Nevertheless, taking into account the position of our Allies on the Western Front, G.H.Q. of the Supreme Command has decided to accelerate the completion of our preparation, and, regardless of the weather, to commence large-scale offensive operations against the Germans along the whole Central Front not later than the second half of January. You may rest assured that we shall do everything possible to render assistance to the glorious forces of our Allies.

Two days later the Prime Minister expressed gratitude for Stalin's "thrilling" message. He informed the Generalissimo that he had sent a copy to General Eisenhower for his eyes only. "The news," Churchill wrote, "will be a great encouragement to General Eisenhower, because it gives him the assurance that the German reinforcements will have to be split between both our flaming fronts." [6]

Though Mr. Churchill was obviously pleased with this exchange, it remains problematical whether his note had in truth affected the Russian plans. Days before the message was sent, General Heinz Guderian, chief of the German General Staff (OKH), had calculated that the Russian attack would begin on January 12, 1945.

[6] Winston Churchill, *Triumph and Tragedy* (Boston: Houghton, 1953), pp. 278, 279, 280.

CHAPTER 17

❦

Closing the Bulge

A DOLF HITLER's decision, on December 26, 1944, to permit Manteuffel's forwardmost spearheads to withdraw a few miles to stronger defensive positions could well be misconstrued. On the surface it would appear that the Führer, realizing that his offensive had failed, had given up in hopes of saving what forces he could. But this was not the case.

Hitler insisted that Antwerp could still be taken even at this late date. But he had now specified two requisites for victory: one was the capture of Bastogne, the other the destruction of all Allied forces on the northern front between the Ourthe and Meuse rivers—in other words, the U.S. 84th Infantry and 2d Armored divisions. With these accomplished, Hitler still believed he would be able to force crossings over the Meuse and ultimately capture Antwerp.

Hitler has been described as an eternal optimist—to a point where he took leave of reality. This is partially just; but it must be recognized that at that time he was being given much conflicting military advice. A large part he discarded, of course, for by December, 1944, he had come utterly to mistrust the professional military as a group.

Two days before Hitler's decision to turn around and make an all-out effort to take Bastogne, he called a council of war at Supreme Headquarters, at which General Heinz Guderian, chief of OKH (Army General Staff), pleaded for the termination of the Ardennes campaign—which in his view any sensible soldier could see was a failure—and reinforcement of the troops holding the eastern front against the Russians. Confined by Hitler to directing the war in the east only, Guderian understandably had become the protagonist for that front, and he could see that the forces available to meet the expected Russian offensive were pitifully thin. He calculated Russian superiority over the Germans to be 11 to 1 in infantry, 7 to 1 in tanks, 20 to 1 in artillery, and their total superiority in strength approximately 15 to 1 on the ground and 20 to 1 in the air. In Guderian's view, even though the Germans had the advantage of fighting on the defensive—and even though they considered themselves superior to all the other soldiers in the world—this ratio was too heavy even for German soldiers.

The arguments fell on deaf ears. According to Guderian's account, Hitler, declaring that the reports prepared by OKH were based on inflated figures, maintained that a Russian rifle formation had a maximum strength of 7,000 men and that Russian tank formations had no tanks. He literally shouted that these reports were the greatest imposture since Genghis Khan. "Who's responsible for all this rubbish?" he demanded, not stopping to consider that many of his own units also existed only on paper.

Of great comfort to Hitler in his obsession with the Ardennes was the confident attitude of Himmler, who had now become his most trusted adviser. Himmler once said to Guderian that the possibility of a Russian attack was nothing but an "enormous bluff." Also welcome to the Führer was Jodl's optimistic view that the Ardennes offensive, having seized the initiative from the Allies in the west and delayed their timetable, should be continued. "We must not lose the initiative that we have just regained," Jodl argued.

That Christmas Eve, when the issue was being discussed with some heat, news came that the Russians had surrounded Budapest. Nevertheless, when Guderian left the next day, he was admonished that the eastern front would have to take care of itself.[1]

Another factor that undoubtedly influenced Hitler as late as December 26 was the message sent by Model through Rundstedt on Christmas night, in which he recommended that all efforts should be concentrated on defeating the Allies east of the Meuse by heading northeast, dropping also some optimistic hints on the possibility of seizing and later exploiting unoccupied crossings over the Meuse. That same evening Manteuffel was discouraged enough to send a message to Model saying that not even Bastogne could be taken, but it arrived after Model's had been sent.

---

[1] An interesting sidelight on Hitler's attitude to the eastern and the western fronts is given in Guderian's remarks about the birthplaces of the men involved:

> I do not know how much their incomprehension was due to the fact that they both came originally from parts of Germany far from the threatened area. At my last conference I came to the conclusion this fact played a not unimportant part in the decisions they were taking. For us Prussians it was our immediate homeland that was at stake, that homeland which had been won at such cost and which had remained attached to the ideals of Christian, Western culture through so many centuries of effort, land in which lay the bones of our ancestors, land that we loved. We knew that if the assault from the East succeeded our homes were lost. After the examples of Goldap and Nemmersdorf we feared the worst for the inhabitants. But even these fears of ours fell on deaf ears. A request from the generals at the front that civilians be evacuated from the most immediately threatened areas was turned down by Hitler; he said it was just another manifestation of the generals' alleged defeatism and he was afraid that such evacuation would have a bad effect on public opinion. (*Panzer Leader* [New York: Dutton, 1952]. Previous material on Hitler in this chapter also from this source.)

On the twenty-sixth, in compliance with Hitler's concept, Rundstedt turned over the 67th Korps from Dietrich's Sixth Panzer Army to the Fifteenth Army, thus allowing more concentration of effort in the Ardennes campaign. He approved Manteuffel's plan of turning his spearheads around to the northeast to attack Allied forces from the rear east of the Meuse (the attack petered out rapidly, probably from lack of supplies). OKW promised 24,000 replacements, of which 6,000 were to be panzer grenadiers. The days of heaviest fighting for the now famous town of Bastogne still lay ahead.

The next afternoon, Wednesday, December 27, a major general, his driver, and his aide began a journey from Arlon to Bastogne. Maxwell D. Taylor, commanding general of the 101st Airborne Division, had been sent back to Washington on December 10, the "quiet" time, to plead for authorization of greater strength in the airborne units. Taylor had seen General Marshall and succeeded in persuading him that the airborne division, as currently organized, was simply not large enough to perform its missions adequately.

Like many others, General Taylor had been skeptical of the first reports that came back to the United States about the size of the German attack, but when he was briefed in the Pentagon on December 21, he was astonished to learn that his 101st "Screaming Eagle" Airborne Division had been surrounded at Bastogne. He had to get back to Europe immediately. He traveled by cargo aircraft, arrived in Paris on the twenty-sixth, and reported to Bedell Smith (he had to show his dog tag), primarily for the purpose of requesting permission to jump or glide into Bastogne.

"That won't be necessary, Max," Smith said. "We expect the 4th Armored Division to make contact with the 101st today."

Then Taylor traveled by jeep to Luxembourg—and en route was shot at by friendly troops—where he called General Patton on the morning of the twenty-seventh to tell him that he was on the way up to rejoin his division.

At headquarters, 4th Armored Division, General Gaffey did not think it advisable to send a division commander up the narrow corridor to Bastogne. Taylor turned down Gaffey's offer to send him by tank up the Assenois road; he stayed wtih his driver, Staff Sergeant Charles Kartus, and headed straight down the CCB axis for the town.

A very few miles from Bastogne four noted war correspondents huddled shivering, bitterly cold, in a pile of debris, a ruined farmhouse. Joseph Driscoll of the New York *Herald Tribune,* Norman Clark of the London *News Chronicle,* Cornelius Ryan of the London *Daily Telegraph,* and Walter Cronkite of United Press, were hardly there by choice. Trying to reach Bastogne along the Arlon road, they had run into heavy German "88" and mortar fire, and now they had taken refuge in the farmhouse, with no place to go. Occasionally a shell would burst around them.

As they sat wondering what would happen next, they heard the sound of a vehicle coming up the road and peered out anxiously, sure it would turn out to be German.

To the correspondents' amazement, however, it was an American jeep. "Look at that nut!" moaned Driscoll. "When are they going to learn?" Correspondents were seeing so many soldiers killed taking unnecessary chances that they feared they would witness just such a tragic sight once more; but men in a combat zone learn to be philosophical, and they quickly started a pool on the American's chances of making it to the farmhouse. The odds averaged about one chance out of three.

On the stranger came, bouncing and jostling on the shell-pocked road, and the correspondents forgot the pool. The figure in the vehicle was none other than Major General Maxwell D. Taylor. Taylor was oddly dressed for these conditions, wearing Class A uniform (blouse and pinks) garnished with steel helmet and combat boots.

The jeep pulled off the road. Apparently impervious to the firing, Taylor made his way to the building.

The General, the correspondents noted, was in a state of some agitation. He informed his friends that he had just come in from Washington and was hell-bent on getting into Bastogne that night. Vainly they tried to dissuade him. True, a couple of reconnaissance vehicles had made the round trip into Bastogne about an hour before Taylor's arrival, but nobody knew how many vehicles had tried and failed. The trip, they all argued, was not worth the risk.

Taylor would not be dissuaded. As he had space in his jeep, he offered a ride to any of the correspondents who wished to accompany him (he would have been happy to have them along; Cronkite, for one, had jumped with his 101st Airborne Division in Holland).

Cornelius Ryan spoke for the group: "No volunteers today, General." They had none of the extraordinary motivation that spurred Taylor, and until the roads were safe to and from Bastogne, they could not file their stories. Correspondents are of little use without communications.

The four men watched Taylor's jeep continue northward toward Bastogne. None of them expected to see the General alive again.

A short time later Maxwell Taylor was enjoying a cocktail with his comrades of the 101st Airborne Division in Bastogne. His ride from the ruined farmhouse had been hair-raising but brief. During the course of the celebration Taylor told an amazed General McAuliffe that he and the 101st Airborne were worldwide celebrities.

Then Taylor began to inquire about the condition of his division. He learned that since the night before, when the 4th Armored had made contact, 40 truckloads of supplies had already been brought in over the Assenois road and the supply route was open. Twenty-two ambulances, with a total of 652 wounded, had been evacuated.

The town was flattened—ironically, one of the few towns that had been destroyed by German rather than Allied action. Nevertheless, the men's morale was high. General McAuliffe assured Taylor that the division was now ready to attack.

After checking the effective division strength and finding that the 101st had more than 10,000 officers and enlisted men available for duty, Taylor agreed. That evening he radioed General Millikin at III Corps, to which the division had been attached that day, that the 101st Airborne Division was ready for offensive operations.

Despite the dramatic report from the 101st Airborne, the time had not come for Third U.S. Army to launch a full-scale attack toward the north. On the twenty-seventh the situation of the 101st Airborne as viewed on a map resembled a balloon on a string, the string being the tenuous lifeline running from the Third Army positions to what had been the day before an island approximately five miles in diameter. Before an attack could be launched, this corridor had to be widened and indeed protected, for Hitler's orders on the twenty-sixth to cut the lifeline and reduce Bastogne were now making themselves felt through the presence of many new German units.

It will be recalled that on the night of December 28, General Eisenhower called his headquarters from Brussels and released the SHAEF reserve, then consisting of the 11th Armored and 87th Infantry divisions, to General Bradley for further attachment to Patton's Third Army. Since the area to the west of the Bastogne lifeline was largely uncovered, Patton placed the two divisions under the command of Middleton's VIII Corps to the west of the corridor, with the mission of attacking northward, where it was hoped they would come abreast of the 101st. The 87th Division placed on the west, the left, and the 11th Armored on the east, the right. They moved from their former backstop positions behind the Meuse River toward Neufchâteau, and jumped off at 8:00 A.M. on December 30.

The timing was fortunate. When the two divisions attacked, they ran square into the flank of a major German counterattack headed southeast to cut the corridor. The German divisions, the Panzer Lehr and the 26th Volksgrenadier, had seen much action in the area and were weary, and the two new U.S. divisions were able to stop the German thrust and turn it back. At the same time, on the other flank of the Bastogne corridor, the 1st SS Panzer Division and the 167th Volksgrenadier were attacking the 35th and 26th U.S. Infantry divisions; the artillery of the U.S. 4th Armored came to the help of the 35th. Also highly important, despite very bad weather, was the XIX Tactical Air Command's ability to fly most of that day. The German attack was repulsed, with the loss of 55 German tanks.

In General Patton's view, December 30 was the critical day of the operation since this was the most concerted effort on the part of the Germans thus far—made by at least five divisions—to isolate Bastogne. During the action the bodies of 21 Germans wearing U.S. uniforms were recovered.

Patton himself went to Bastogne to inspect its condition that day, decorating Brigadier General McAuliffe and Lieutenant Colonel S. A. Chappuis with the Distinguished Service Cross and admiring the wreckage of the German 115th Panzer Grenadier Regiment, which had been virtually wiped out five days earlier, at Christmas.

The weather continued to degenerate. Snow and sleet made it impossible for even tractors to pull the heavy guns; nevertheless, the Germans continued to counterattack. The Third Army After Action Report counts 17 counterattacks all in one day, December 31. Heavy losses were sustained by both Germans and Americans, particularly by the 11th Armored Division, which was seeing its first combat. On December 31 the 17th Airborne Division, newly arrived, was also released to the Third Army and scheduled for employment later in the same area.

The picture, then, at the end of December and in the early days of January, is both sides attacking under miserable conditions, most of the action being to the west of the Bastogne corridor.

On January 1, at one minute after midnight, all guns of Third Army fired a twenty-minute New Year's greeting at the Germans, inflicting heavy casualties.

That was the day, however, that the Luftwaffe made its last major attack of the European campaign. Early in the morning, 1,035 German planes rose into the air over Holland, Belgium, and Northern France, to assist the German ground forces in their efforts to defeat the Allies east of the Meuse. Many American and British planes were caught on the ground. The German claims included 467 Allied planes destroyed, 66 of which were shot down in aerial combat and 278 reported on aerial photographs. But the days were past when the Luftwaffe was the terror of the skies. Their own losses were excessive. The words of Hitler's diary, kept by Major Percy Schramm, sounded like Pyrrhus reporting a victory: "To be sure, the German losses were so high that continuation of such attacks had to be given up."

While the other divisions of Third U.S. Army were inching their way northward to flesh out the Bastogne salient, the 101st Airborne Division was still fighting for its life. Particularly critical were the days January 1 to 4—well after Manteuffel had decided that taking Bastogne was an impossibility. During this time German prisoners from eight different divisons were taken, although some, such as the 1st SS Panzer, had been reduced to shadows of their former potency.

General Taylor was not overly concerned. For one thing, he was grateful that Hitler was frenziedly throwing in his units piecemeal. Never, during the most critical days at Bastogne, did the Germans mount a completely coordinated attack on the town; had they done so, the position of the 101st would have been much more precarious.

One small item was a boost for morale. Somebody discovered that VIII Corps, in its haste to leave Bastogne on December 20, had left great quantities of liquor in a cellar. General Taylor called General Middleton about this find and, having secured Middleton's agreement, issued a good strong drink to every man in the command as a New Year's Day celebration.

Most encouraging of all was General Taylor's confidence in his people, particularly those in positions of responsibility.[2]

As the Germans were conducting their last abortive air attack on Allied airfields and pounding Bastogne, the ax was about to fall: First U.S. Army, on the north, was poised to launch its January 3 attack toward Houffalize.

The opposing armies were unevenly matched. German losses in the Ardennes had weakened their relative position, and new American replacements were arriving from the United States every day. By January 3, more than 3,700,000 Allied soldiers had come ashore in Western Europe. The casualties totaled greater than 500,000, but many of these men had been returned to duty. Allied forces were organized into 73 divisions, including four in reserve. Twenty of these were armored. Six tactical air commands and a host of heavy and medium bombers backed the armies.

Rundstedt, who was never a supreme commander in the same sense as Eisenhower, nominally controlled 80 divisions, but some of these had been reduced to a mere handful of men. For example, the 26th Volksgrenadier Division had for duty a strength of 5,200, but a combat effective strength of considerably fewer than 2,000. The Germans had almost no trained replacements.

General Eisenhower's plan for a coordinated counterattack to pinch off the German spearheads was practically decided as early as December 19. At the Verdun meeting, the American commanders agreed that Patton's attack toward Bastogne would not stop there but would continue up to Houffalize. This meant that in order to close the pincers an attack from the north would have to make juncture at the same town, which lay close to the center of the maximum German penetration.

Eisenhower's plan was completed at his meeting with Montgomery on the twenty-eighth: the attack from the north would be conducted by Collins' VII

---

[2] Many were or later became general officers. Among them: Anthony C. McAuliffe, Gerald J. Higgins, John H. Michaelis (though Michaelis was wounded at the time), Norman A. Moore, H. W. O. Kinnard, Julian J. Ewell, Robert F. Sink, Joseph H. Harper, and Steve A. Chappuis.

Corps of 100,000 men. It would use as its axis the famous Liège-Bastogne road from Manhay to Parker's Crossroads (Baraque de Fraiture), thence to Houffalize.

This axis was more to Collins' liking than the one previously designated. Although his first preference would have been to move VII Corps all the way east to Malmédy and attack on the axis St.-Vith–Houffalize, the country there was difficult and the distance great. By the twenty-eighth Collins had one of his four attacking divisions already in the line: the 3d Armored, in position just to the east of the Ourthe River, and stretching as far as Grandménil and Manhay, with its left flank protected by the 82d Airborne Division.

The final plan agreed to by Montgomery and Eisenhower on the twenty-eighth was a compromise: Montgomery was to employ British troops to relieve the U.S. 2d Armored and the 84th Infantry divisions west of the Ourthe. These two units would then move to the east of the river. With the 83d Division at the moment out of the line, Collins would have a four-division corps east of the Ourthe.

Collins planned to make a two-pronged attack, with the armor leading, the 2d Armored running along the main Liège-Houffalize road, followed by the 83d Infantry Division. Attached to each armored division was to be an infantry regiment from the infantry division following it. Collins had another division, the 75th, in reserve.

On the east General Gavin's 82d Airborne, of XVIII Airborne Corps, was to push forward, protecting that flank, to positions they had occupied once before between the Salm River and the town of Fraiture.

This scheme meant squeezing the Bulge at the waist—rather than from the shoulders along the Skyline Drive, which any commander would prefer if it were feasible; but the fighting had to be done where the troops were, and the troops were in Bastogne. So Houffalize was actually the only feasible meeting place.

There were plenty of Germans still to be bagged west of the Bastogne-Liège road.

Frank Carroll, of I Company, 334th Infantry, 84th Division, was now a squad leader. After I Company had been reconstituted near Verdenne, it had been moved to the other side of town, farther northwest. Word now came that I Company—indeed the whole division—was being relieved by a British unit so that the 84th could be employed elsewhere. This was welcome news, although the thirty-man 2d Platoon was ensconced in fairly comfortable positions and things had been comparatively quiet for the last few days.

At the appointed time on New Year's Day, a platoon from the 53d Welsh Division came up the hill to take its position. It consisted of eight men—Carroll was glad to see them but wondered where the rest of the troops were. Pointedly he asked this of the British platoon leader, a lean, hard-looking lieutenant. "We've been holding this position with thirty men ourselves, and we still have about thirty yards between foxholes."

The Welshman seemed completely unperturbed. "Well," he said, "I have eight right here, as you can see. And I've got eight more five hundred yards back. Eight are resting in Bourdon, and the rest are back in London. So you can see we're in pretty fair shape."

Acting Sergeant Frank Carroll shrugged and went about the business of getting his men ready to move to the rear.[3]

On the morning of January 3, at eight thirty, the First Army jumped off. The Germans produced few surprises. As had been predicted by Colonel Leslie D. Carter, the G-2 of VII Corps, the Germans' first priority was to stop the Third Army around Bastogne. Some of the divisions that had earlier faced VII Corps had moved south to Bastogne, leaving the 12th Volksgrenadier Division opposite the left wing of VII Corps, the 560th Volksgrenadier in the center, and the fanatic 2d SS Panzer opposite the right wing; the strength of these units varied from 2,500 men in the 560th to 6,000 in the 2d SS Panzer—all of which was as Colonel Carter had predicted.

The severest enemy was the frigid weather. The ground was frozen and covered with snow, the roads were icy, and a foglike overcast sharply restricted visibility. Obviously friendly air support was out; and yet the attack had to proceed, not only in hopes that the air situation would improve but also from a growing feeling among First Army units that the Third Army was going to have to carry the entire burden of closing off the Bulge. Naturally everyone, from Eisenhower down, wanted to catch every German in the bag that he possibly could.

The icy roads made travel difficult for armor, particularly for tanks with steel tracks. Soon the infantry was called on to add more and more support to the armored attack, so that the infantry took casualties substantially greater than those sustained by the two armored divisions. Nevertheless, on the evening of January 3 some two miles had been gained, largely against outposts; the 2d Armored (with 335th Infantry attached) took the village of Beffe, and the 3d Armored Division, hampered by minefields and poor roads, took the villages of Floret and Malempré. On a small-scale map these advances appear trivial, but to the men on the ground, going through deep snow, they represented considerable achievement.

German prisoners taken on January 3 seemed surprised that the attack had been made. Apparently all eyes on the German side had been focused on Bastogne and the continuing attack of Third Army from that direction. Word that the Americans had attacked from the north was passed up the chain of

---

[3] A few days later, on the same day that his rank of sergeant was made official, Carroll was wounded and evacuated.

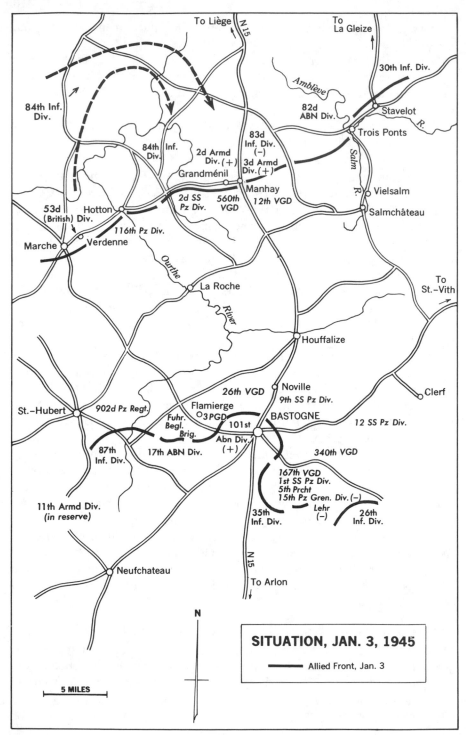

To Liège

To La Gleize

30th Inf. Div.

N15

Amblève

84th Inf. Div.

82d ABN Div.

Stavelot

Trois Ponts

R.

84th Inf. Div.

2d Armd Div. (+)

83d Inf. Div. (−)

3d Armd Div. (+)

Grandménil

Manhay

Salm

R.

Vielsalm

53d (British) Div.

Hotton

2d SS Pz Div.

560th VGD

12th VGD

Salmchâteau

116th Pz Div.

Marche

Verdenne

Ourthe

La Roche

River

To St.-Vith

Houffalize

Noville

9th SS Pz Div.

Clerf

26th VGD

St.-Hubert

902d Pz Regt.

Flamierge

3 PGD

Fuhr. Begl. Brig.

101st Abn Div. (+)

BASTOGNE

12 SS Pz Div.

87th Inf. Div.

17th ABN Div.

340th VGD

11th Armd Div. (in reserve)

167th VGD
1st SS Pz Div.
5th Prcht
15th Pz Gren. Div. (−)
Lehr (−)

26th Inf. Div.

35th Inf. Div.

Neufchateau

N15

To Arlon

N

SITUATION, JAN. 3, 1945

Allied Front, Jan. 3

5 MILES

command until it reached Hitler, who at the beginning of this new year still continued to rationalize his situation: True, he had failed to attain the intermediate objective of crossing the Meuse, and failed even more in reaching the long-range objective, Antwerp. But both these goals had originated in a desire to restore to the Germans the initiative lost since June 6, 1944. The German offensive had prevented the Allies from reaching the Rhine, either in the Aachen area or farther north. On December 16, when the offensive began, there was danger that the Americans would thrust over the Roer at Düren and take Cologne, or force the German troops in the south back to the Black Forest. Or the Americans might have penetrated the Saar Basin and threatened the Rhine south of the Moselle. From this viewpoint, the Ardennes campaign was a success, as all alternate American capabilities had been delayed.

The Americans, Hitler reasoned, had employed practically all their troops available in the west, and several units could be regarded as unfit for battle for a long time; they had even been reduced to employing airborne troops in a ground conflict (he neglected to remember that his own "parachute" units were in the battle up to the hilt). Counting on bad weather, he felt that the Americans would have to employ so many troops to reduce the Ardennes Bulge that he could afford to pull some units out and use them elsewhere.

But when Hitler heard of the American attack, he made a statement significant for a man in his frame of mind: "The originally planned operation is no longer promising of success."

The next day Hitler ordered that the front held by Dietrich against the U.S. First Army be reinforced. Special attention would have to be paid to the extended German flanks in order to prevent an Allied encirclement eastward. The defense of the West Wall was to be continually strengthened. Despite his unrealistic insistence that the attack on Bastogne be continued—he rescinded this order two days later—Hitler was beginning to recognize the realities of the situation.

Major General Ernest N. Harmon had never been known as a slow-moving commander. But Harmon was having his difficulties, which were not unpredictable. On the day before the attack he had warned a press conference that the weather would hold back the rate of advance, and nothing had happened in the meantime to change his mind. The corps commander, General Collins, felt that this time even Harmon had to be pushed a little, but soon Collins was made personally aware of what the 2d Armored was going through: just before his arrival in the 2d Armored sector, a tank had slipped off the road and killed the driver. His body, still partway in the tank, was symbolic enough of the hard going ahead.

Nevertheless, the attack continued. In the zone of Ridgway's XVIII Airborne Corps on January 4, the 82d Airborne Division continued the attack with 325th Glider and the 505th, 504th, 551st, and 517th Parachute regiments, taking more than 500 prisoners in one day. In the center, the 505th beat their way through more than 2,000 yards of heavy woods. Enemy counterattacks during the afternoon were repulsed with heavy losses. Farther east, toward the corps boundary, the 30th Infantry Division improved its defenses so that the U.S. front line in this sector was slightly improved from Stavelot to Malmédy, inclusive. There was no attack planned for Gerow's V Corps.

One hamlet was taken after another. January 7, four days after the jump-off, was a big day. The 84th Division, placed at the front line on the right flank, penetrated more than a mile and a half to secure Marcouray and protect the exposed right along the Ourthe River. The 2d Armored took the important town of Dochamps, and other elements of the division extended the gains south to Odeigne. Most dramatic was the capture of Baraque-de-Fraiture (Parker's Crossroads), a matter of strategic importance to a German army attempting to extricate itself from an ever closing vise.

However, cutting the La Roche-Salmchâteau highway at Parker's Crossroads was not the news of the day. The headlines were given over to Field Marshal Montgomery's explosive press conference, which preoccupied the public for days after.

On the southern flank General George S. Patton, Jr., was feeling jubilant. Blithely forgetting his earlier denunciation of Middleton's holding action at Bastogne, he was as effusive in praise as formerly he had been violent in condemnation. "Troy," he beamed, "holding on that damn town of Bastogne was a stroke of genius."

But Patton had by no means mellowed with success. Impatient to get the attack moving, on December 30 he had insisted, over Middleton's objections, on committing the 11th Armored Division to its first combat without providing enough time for bringing up the rear, for reconnaissance, or for preparation. The resulting attack was a piecemeal affair that fell short of expectations.

Patton's jubilation now gave way to fury. He called Middleton that night, and soon the two commanders were conferring at the 11th Armored command post. Patton stalked out—to stumble over the protruding feet of Middleton's jeep driver, who had stretched out in a small lean-to to catch forty winks. Not knowing who had awakened him, the driver shouted, "You dumb fool, can't you see I'm trying to sleep?"

"Well, you're the first sonofabitch I've seen around this outfit that knows what the hell he's trying to do," snapped Patton in return.

From his position almost due west of Bastogne, Major Morris Anderson, commanding officer of the 3d Battalian, 513th Parachute Regiment, looked across the knee-deep snow to the town of Flamierge almost a mile away, the objective of his battalion's attack launched four days earlier. It was now January 7, and General Patton's effort to bring up the lines on both sides of the Bastogne salient was meeting with the same fanatic resistance that First Army was encountering.

Part of the 17th Airborne Division, the 513th was an unusually select regiment. It was a school troop unit at Fort Benning, Georgia, and many of its members had been chosen from among the best graduates of airborne training. A large number of these men had already been lost; Anderson's battalion, along with the other two battalions of the regiment, had taken heavy casualties even in seizing the initial objective.

Earlier that morning, Major General William M. Miley, commanding the 17th Airborne Division, had visited the command post of the 513th and told the commanding officer, Colonel James Coutts, that the 513th should stop on its initial objective and wait for the 193d and 194th on its flanks to catch up. Colonel Coutts, however, had talked to his three battalion commanders, Anderson among the rest, and they felt they could go on and seize Flamierge. General Miley had given them authority to go ahead.

The mile of terrain from Anderson's position to Flamierge at first sloped gently downward, then rose to the edge of the town, which had been part of the Bastogne perimeter for some days before its voluntary evacuation on December 24. As Anderson's 3d Battalion struggled through the snow, they could see German tanks retreating from the town, perhaps seven or eight altogether. Radio communications had been knocked out, but the battalion stayed together well, Anderson himself giving orders by shouting commands, by hand and arm signals, and by use of runner.

Since the approach to the town afforded neither cover nor concealment, the battalion was moving directly into fire from the remaining German tanks, artillery, machine guns, and mortars; and with no radio, it could get supporting fire only from its own mortars. Snow capes had been issued to key personnel, but they were being discarded rapidly: they identified the leaders and drew special attention from German guns, which concentrated also on men carrying equipment such as radios, bazookas, and machine guns—Anderson's own radio operator carried his damaged set and drew fire throughout the entire advance. The snow was deep and the advance was slow.

As the battalion drew within 150 yards of Flamierge an unexpected heavy friendly artillery barrage struck the town. It had been arranged for by Colonel Coutts, who had figured simply by inspired guessing that Anderson would be getting close to the town and needing support. Grateful for the fire, which forced the enemy to take cover at a critical moment, Anderson paused while the artillery pounded the town and picked a road, sending one company to the left of it and the other to the right. As soon as the artillery lifted, both companies advanced into the town, firing from the hip all the way. The Germans answered with automatic weapons, but the artillery had done a good job and the Americans now had some rubble for protection. Paratroopers with bazookas stalked two German tanks and knocked them out; a third tank miraculously was crippled by a light machine gun, and as the German crew attempted to abandon the vehicle, the paratroopers cut them down. Anderson killed one German by tossing a grenade into a hole in a haystack. The battalion cleared the town handily, throwing grenades into the houses, and the remaining Germans withdrew to the north, the armor leaving in such haste that the battalion captured hot food for 300 men.

During the assault the civilians naturally had taken to their cellars, but as soon as the Germans left they came out to welcome the American paratroopers and help with the wounded. The battalion had gone into the fight that morning with a meager 525 men, and already had suffered 150 casualties. Anderson had only two aidmen, for the others had been wounded or had remained to help at the first objective.

Anderson soon reestablished radio communications and learned that on his left flank the 2d Battalion of the 513th was having difficulty clearing the enemy out of the woods, which were filled with emplaced troops who had to be dug out of their holes.

The 513th had always known this operation was an important one, and this was confirmed when the corps commander himself, General Middleton, sent his personal congratulations to the regiment on their achievement.

Now Morris Anderson could see the Germans begin to infiltrate back into the area his battalion had crossed that day, and he quickly prepared a perimeter defense against enemy armored counterattack. A further source of concern was his inability to contact the 193d Airborne Infantry on the right. A platoon from I Company sent out to find them returned unsuccessful. The 193d simply had not kept up.

By now the 3d Battalion was low on ammunition and needed to be resupplied. In a final blow, early in the evening, communications to the rear again had gone out. Fortunately a captured German ambulance carrying a seriously wounded soldier was being dispatched to the rear, and the request for resupply was given to the two men in charge of the ambulance—Pfc. Roland Bragg, a lightly wounded mechanic from Headquarters Company, and the forward observer from the 466th Field Artillery, Lieutenant McLain. While the mission of the ambulance was a legitimate one, McLain and Bragg would be able to explain the battalion's situation.

They had hardly got beyond the Flamierge perimeter when they took two German prisoners. Knowing the Germans were infiltrating their rear, they placed one of the prisoners between them in the front seat and put the other on the running board. Before long the German on the running board jumped off and ran; McLain cut him down with his tommy gun. A German machine gun opened fire on the ambulance, and Bragg decided the only thing to do was to shove the throttle to the floor and speed through the fire. When the two men reached the regimental command post, they discovered that the German machine gun had damaged the ambulance considerably; the wounded American in the back and the prisoner in the front seat were both dead. Miraculously, neither McLain nor Bragg had been hit, and Bragg was able to return to Flamierge with a supply party later that night.

By the next morning, the eighth, the 3d Battalion surgeon had reached Flamierge with a party to remove the wounded. Ammunition of all categories was now on hand, especially 400 all-important rounds of bazooka ammunition. Early in the morning, after finding Flamierge's location with great difficulty, the regimental executive officer, Lieutenant Colonel Ward Ryon, placed some tank destroyers in position to protect the battalion from armored attack, but by the time he made his way back to the regimental command post, the tank destroyers had abandoned their position and were already at the command post waiting for him. He placed charges against the officer in command, but it was too late to return the vehicles that day.

Many things had been going on during the previous night, however. Communication wire had been laid to all three battalions of the 513th. Every man of Anderson's 3d Battalion manned a post without sleep, and a number of enemy were caught trying to infiltrate the lines. Several wore American uniforms, and one paratrooper had wire cutters. A prisoner wearing a new American overcoat and shirt was vigorously interrogated; at first he said little, but realizing he might be charged with spying, he began to explain in fluent English that he had obtained the clothing from his own organization—they had "bales" of it—and claimed that he wore the uniform only in order to desert the more easily.

The prisoner was useful. He furnished positive locations of German infantry and armored positions, and warned that during the morning of the eighth an attack from all sides would hit the Americans, especially the 3d Battalion.

Morris Anderson was hardly in a sympathetic mood. His first impulse was to execute the spies immediately, but then he had second thoughts. If things did not go well—the possibility had to be considered—his men might suffer if German bodies were found on the spot. He therefore sent the prisoners to the rear, with an explanation of the circumstances to Colonel Coutts and a recommendation that the spies be shot. At dawn he sent a patrol to the 2d Battalion on the left to warn of the coming attack.

Anderson had not long to wait. At 6:00 A.M., 15 or 20 German tanks moved on Flamierge from the north, and five or six, supported by infantry and six self-propelled guns, advanced across the fields between the 2d and 3d battalions. The fog was so heavy that the tanks appeared only as vague forms in the haze, and the artillery forward observer tried using white phosphorous shells in a desperate attempt to detect where the rounds were hitting. One German tank was set afire.

About this time heavy German artillery fire began to pound Flamierge, and it continued throughout the day. Almost immediately, as is so often the case, the wire to the rear went out, and once more Anderson had no communication with any other unit.

The 3d Battalion, well dug in, held off the attacking tanks. German infantry, more vulnerable than tanks, were hit hard as they advanced across the open ground, and the tanks were kept out of the perimeter of the town by the paratroopers' bazooka fire. The tanks withdrew to nearby positions and fired directly at Anderson's men from a distance of only 200 to 250 yards. Even at that range, the paratroopers could drive them back with an occasional bazooka round, but once having located the position of the bazookas, the German tanks fired point-blank into the foxholes. On occasion, enemy infantry wearing American helmets tried to lure Anderson's men into their fire by waving for them to come forward, but they stuck to their positions. Repairmen had been working feverishly on a radio all morning, and at 2:00 P.M. they finally made contact with the regimental command post. The radio was located in a window, the only place where sufficient volume could be obtained. In the storm the artillery forward observer continued to adjust fire, more by sound than by sight, until three German rounds hit the building, sending the walls crashing down on the artillery radio set. The radio operator and operations sergeant were wounded, and three civilians conferring with Major Anderson killed. Anderson himself was nicked.

Now that they were again out of contact with the regimental command post, Anderson's personal radio operator, Pfc. Corley H. Wright, volunteered to run the telephone line through to the rear and make repairs. Anderson could not help admiring him, even though in that battle courage was common. The task seemed impossible, since the line was laid across open fields and enemy tanks were known to be to the rear. Wright himself had his doubts, but he started crawling forward slowly along the line under fire, until he had been wounded three times—through the chest, shoulder, and nose. On a check call he told Anderson that he was going on as long as he could, but Anderson had had enough. "Come on back to Battalion," he shouted.

Wright crawled back and continued to help in the fighting despite his three wounds. He never left the battle.

Firing continued heavily until dark, when all the German tanks withdrew except two, which maneuvered so that they could fire down the main street. At about 9:00 P.M. they too gave up for the day.

The 513th Airborne Infantry Regiment was now too weak to hold off a strong enemy attack. General Miley therefore moved the 507th Parachute

Infantry behind the 513th and ordered Anderson's battalion to withdraw. The 2d Battalion on the left had already gone.

Since no communications existed, the general's order could not be delivered at first so after dark two three-man patrols from Colonel Coutts' regimental headquarters were sent out to 3d Battalion. When the first patrol reached the buildings just short of town and found them occupied by Germans, they returned to regimental command post and reported that the battalion was gone and the town lost.

Unbelieving, Coutts was about to send out another patrol, when a patrol came in from 3d Battalion itself and announced that Major Anderson was holding and hoped to get a radio operational soon. They brought a message from Anderson: open the radio at 9:00 P.M. *exactly* for five minutes and then again every thirty minutes. It was too dangerous to keep the radio going any longer than that, for every time communications were established for any length of time the radio drew fire.

3rd Battalion had been out of communication so long there was no way of encoding a message ordering withdrawal. Colonel Coutts entrusted Corporal Gidley with the job of getting the message to Anderson, as soon as the radio was working.

To fool the Germans, Gidley made ingenious use of American slang. His first message to Anderson told the 3d Battalion to withdraw from Flamierge: "My favorite song has always been 'When the Cowboy Herds His Dogies Back to the Old Corral.'" His next message instructed Anderson to split his men up and come in small groups: "Stray dogies move faster." Finally, an order for an officer to stay in Flamierge to arrange the surrender of the wounded. "A wheel always stays with crippled dogies."

Recalling the incident later, Morris Anderson admitted that this was the most uncomfortable time of his life. He was lying on a snow-covered pile of straw in bitter cold and it took an hour for the three messages to come through.

The orders were quickly given. Every man was on post; a third were to remain until the others moved out. The wounded who could not walk were to be left behind in Flamierge under Lieutenant Charles A. Lewis, who was wounded in the head and foot. All the houses were to be mined or booby-trapped with hand grenades. The battalion moved out in groups of eight to ten men, each under an officer or noncommissioned officer.

By this time nobody knew the current password, and in order to get through American lines, another device was needed. At that time all paratroopers took their airborne training at Fort Benning, and Anderson concluded that no red-blooded man in the regiment could possibly have forgotten the town just across the river from Columbus, Georgia—Phenix City, a rough place then, and the favorite haunt of all the Fort Benning troops. A challenge of "Phenix" ought to bring a password of "City" from every American paratrooper. Sure enough, on passing through the lines to the rear, several paratroopers found it necessary to use this improvised challenge and response.

The return trip in the early morning of January 9 was a bitter one. The men carried out all their weapons and much of their ammunition; they had not slept for two nights; there was no food or water. They made their way on frozen feet, shouldering heavy loads, through knee-deep snow and enemy fire.

The paratroopers of the 513th hated to leave Flamierge and said so, but all who started, including the walking wounded, made the trip successfully. Anderson was in the last party to leave. He had gone only 150 yards out of the town when the Germans began to shell it heavily. He and his party struggled on, carrying one of the men the last lap into friendly lines. In the 513th Regiment area they were given a hot meal and the wounded were evacuated, and the others were sent back into the line by ten o'clock in the morning. In the attack, defense, and withdrawal, the 3d Battalion, 513th Parachute Infantry, had lost more than half its strength.

If the war looked grim to Major Anderson at the end of the first week of January, it looked the same to the High Command of the Third Reich. Viewing Allied successes from the north and northwest on the eighth Hitler realized that the spearheads of his forces would soon be in grave danger if left in position, and so he issued one of his rare authorizations for withdrawal. Manteuffel's Fifth Panzer Army was to withdraw to a north-south line, just west of the Bastogne-Liège highway, between Dochamps and Longchamps. At the same time, in order to make a reserve, he issued orders for withdrawal of the essential elements of the Sixth Panzer Army to areas northeast of St.-Vith and east of Wiltz. Army Group B's mission of defending remained unchanged. The next day, after another hot discussion with General Guderian, the Führer repeated his order that the 2d SS Panzer Korps—comprising the 1st SS, 2d SS, 9th SS, and 12th SS Panzer divisions, plus two werfer brigades and the two Hitler brigades—should withdraw immediately, only this time to the rear of Army Group G in the south for rehabilitation. Rundstedt had strict orders that these units must not be committed to further fighting, which would delay their assembly.

Hitler's order was actually somewhat superfluous, since the Germans had obviously been withdrawing ever since January 3, when the First U.S. Army attack had jumped off. The La Roche-Salmchâteau road had been cut the day before, the eighth. By this time formal order of battle among the Germans was beginning to disintegrate, and U.S. First Army, which had originally started out facing Sixth Panzer Army, was beginning to identify units from the Fifth Panzer. Manteuffel would have liked to withdraw more rapidly, but lack of fuel imposed foot marches and made towing stalled vehicles extremely difficult. In addition, of course, with the pressure of the American troops, the Germans continually were forced to fight rear guard actions. In the confusion, it required 13 days, from January 9 to 22, for the Sixth Panzer Army completely to extricate itself from the Ardennes area and for the Fifth to take over the Sixth's former command functions.

Although they continued to fight fiercely and well, the Germans were now having increased problems with troop morale. When officers and men at the front realized that their efforts to turn the tables on the Allies had failed, physical fatigue and mental anguish became severe. The threat of reprisals against relatives and sweethearts for cowardice and defection was intensified. Conditions deteriorated; rations were reduced. Home leaves were cut—large areas of Germany gradually were becoming closed to men on leave as they became theaters of operations; once on leave—if ever it came—men spent precious time searching for relatives who had been evacuated from the bombing. Mail service to the front deteriorated, and whatever news passed the strict censorship and got to the front was usually bad.

To combat this morale problem Hitler had resorted ever more to the technique of fear. Early in December, even before the Ardennes offensive, he ordered command transferred to the next in rank whenever a troop commander faced with a difficult decision felt he should give up the fight. In such cases, the officer was to ask the officers and men under him, in order of rank, whether one of them wished to carry on with the mission. If so, command authority passed to the man who would accept responsibility, and the former commander joined the ranks. Now in early January, this order was broadened to apply automatically whenever a group was surrounded and whenever a commander was incapable or unwilling to continue fighting, no matter if he had asked the others or not. The Germans' mood, so elated on December 16, was now reversed.

On January 9, the day on which Hitler tacitly admitted defeat by ordering the withdrawal of Dietrich's Sixth Panzer Army, General George Patton knew the time was ripe for attack. Available were eight American divisions, of which four were infantry (the 26th, 35th, 87th, and 90th), two were armored (the 4th and 6th) and two were airborne (17th and 101st). Four of these divisions were attached to VIII Corps on the left and four to III Corps on the right. The main effort was to be made by the 90th Infantry Division attacking northwest through the 26th to reduce the troublesome pocket sticking into the corridor southeast of Bastogne.

The VIII and III corps attack jumped off as planned on the ninth. The 90th Infantry Division made the main effort, receiving heavy casualties from artillery and rocket fire. The 101st Airborne and the 4th Armored Division moved forward in the direction of Noville, where Team Desobry had put up such a gallant fight about three weeks before. The remaining units in the corps made very limited progress.[4]

On January 11, General Patton visited XX Corps to arrange plans for attacking the Germans should they initiate an offensive near Saarbrücken, though in truth he was not personally much concerned over this possibility.

Most encouraging was the morale of U.S. troops. Patton wrote at the time that the troops' attitude was completely changed. Now they were fully confident that they were pursuing a defeated enemy, in spite of the vicious resistance put up by the Germans north and northeast of Bastogne in order to preserve their escape routes.

As the attack northward from the Bastogne perimeter got under way, a staff officer of the 101st Airborne Division at the front lines observing how the action was going came on a sight to which he had become accustomed: rows of German bodies in grotesque positions, discolored from freezing—as this had been contested territory, the Americans had not had a chance to bury the bodies. But as the officer went past, a detail caught his eye: the third finger, left hand, was missing from each of the bodies. The officer stopped, momentarily puzzled. Then, after a long moment, he went on his way.

Meanwhile, in the north, the First Army, with VII Corps making the main effort, continued to fight against the same miserable weather conditions, and over greater distances. On January 9, in view of the marshy ground and impoverished road net leading to the objectives of Chérain and Bouvigny, the 83d Infantry Division took over the main assault role from the 3d Armored on the left wing of VII Corps. It took the 83d two days to break into and clear the village of Bihain, a mile south of the La Roche-Salmchâteau highway, and another day to beat off severe German counterattacks. In this operation the 83d Division lost more than 1,600 men, a high figure, but not excessive in view of the nature of the resistance, the terrain, and the bitter cold.

The British, meanwhile, continued southward on the west bank of the Ourthe, keeping abreast of U.S. VII Corps and generally confining their attacks to brigade strength. As early as January 10, two days after Hitler's order for withdrawal, they reported no contact with the enemy, though some light contact was established on subsequent days.

On January 11, while armored units were regrouping and doing maintenance chores, the infantry elements of the VII Corps continued the attack, making gains of up to two miles against heavy resistance. Finally the cavalry, advancing along the right flank, cleared part of La Roche. Snow fell toward the end of the day, and it remained extremely cold, the temperature again around the zero mark. The German withdrawal was still hardly noticeable in

---

[4] Incidental but noteworthy: On this day Colonel Julian Ewell of the 501st Parachute Infantry received severe wounds in the foot and leg, which ended his combat career for World War II.

front of VII Corps. The report for the day shows that the 2d and 9th SS Panzer divisions, 116th Panzer, and the 12th, 560th and 326th Volksgrenadiers were fighting stubbornly in the general area in which they had all operated up to then. German artillery, mortar, and werfer fire was heavy. VII Corps armored elements received direct antitank fire southwest of Bihain and farther southwest at Langlir. This was the situation that existed in the First Army on the twelfth, while General Patton was planning his big drive on the south for the thirteenth.

On January 12, the long-awaited Soviet winter offensive began. Marshal Ivan S. Konev's First Ukrainian Army broke out of the bridgehead it had been holding at Baranov on the upper Vistula River since December 16. During the next few days, Marshal Georgi K. Zhukov's front on his right, Marshal Konstantin Rokossovski's front on the right of Zhukov, and three other fronts of varying size erupted into an offensive that in some places was to go as far as 200 miles in eleven days. Such a massive offensive exceeded all the fears of the German General Staff, justifying Guderian's black pessimism.

The direct result of this offensive in the east was a directive from Hitler on January 14 that Dietrich's Sixth Panzer Army be transferred from the west to the east. To Guderian's disgust, however, it was to be employed in the direction of Budapest, to protect the Hungarian oil fields, rather than in Prussia. But the difficulties of withdrawing the Sixth Panzer Army units were far from over. Though it will be recalled that the order was given on January 8, it took yet another week before Manteuffel had completely taken over from Dietrich in the Ardennes. Manteuffel got one compensation: at the same time as Hitler ordered the Sixth Panzer Army's removal eastward, he gave Rundstedt permission to bring back the Ardennes salient in line with Chérain, seven miles northeast of Houffalize. This order was to be executed speedily to avoid further serious losses.

By now the German troops were tired from long commitments without breaks. Replacements were of low quality and lacked training; forces were poorly supplied, and rations were being cut. The news from the eastern front and home had reached them. The American forces were far superior on the ground, and every clear day Allied planes were supreme in the skies. After the high hopes at the beginning of the offensive, failure now stared every soldier in the face. Regardless of the prospective destiny of the Sixth Panzer Army, the regular soldier on the western front regarded its withdrawal as preferential treatment for the SS. Manteuffel reported that this situation was not so serious where the troops were busy, but in the rest areas the hopelessness of the entire operation was now obvious.

On January 14, Field Marshal Bernard Law Montgomery wrote a cordial letter to General Bradley:

Dear Brad:

It does seem as if the battle of the "salient" will shortly be drawing to a close, and when it is all clean and tidy I imagine that your armies will be returning to your operational command.

I would like to say two things:

First: What a great honor it has been for me to command such fine troops.

Second: How well they have all done.

2. It has been a great pleasure to work with Hodges and Simpson; both have done very well.

   And the Corps Commanders in the First Army (Gerow, Collins, Ridgway) have been quite magnificent; it must be most exceptional to find such a good lot of Corps Commanders gathered together in one Army.

3. All of us in the northern side of the salient would like to say how much we have admired the operations that have been conducted on the southern side; if you had not held on firmly to Bastogne the whole situation might have become very awkward.

4. My kind regard to you and to George Patton.

Yrs very sincerely,

[signed] B. L. Montgomery [5]

Three days later, on the seventeenth, First Army was to revert to the command of 12 Army Group.

It was still slow going for the American troops from First and Third armies closing in on Houffalize. One example of the difficulty: not until January 15 could the 101st Airborne take Noville, once regarded as part of the Bastogne perimeter. But the time was growing near: the morning of the sixteenth was to see the meeting of First and Third armies.

By January 15 Houffalize had been made untenable to the enemy. At 11:00 A.M. that day, the 333d Infantry from the 84th Division jumped off from Dinet and captured the village of Mont. Tanks, infantry, and artillery renewed their advance to Hill 430 overlooking Houffalize, and in late afternoon it was taken without opposition.

It is difficult to pinpoint the first actual contact between First and Third armies; various patrols were sent out. Typical was a 33-man patrol, representing all the battalions of the 334th Infantry, 84th Division, which left the town of Filly at 11:00 A.M. on January 15. The patrol crossed the Ourthe in two 400-pound rubber boats at 11:45 A.M. and spent the afternoon in an old mill south of the river. Just before dark a small patrol went forward as far as the village of Engreux, about 1,000 yards ahead, where they expected to meet a patrol from the Third Army. The village was free of enemy, but there was no sign of Third Army's patrol.

[5] Bernard Montgomery, *Memoirs* (Cleveland: World, 1958), pp. 276–77.

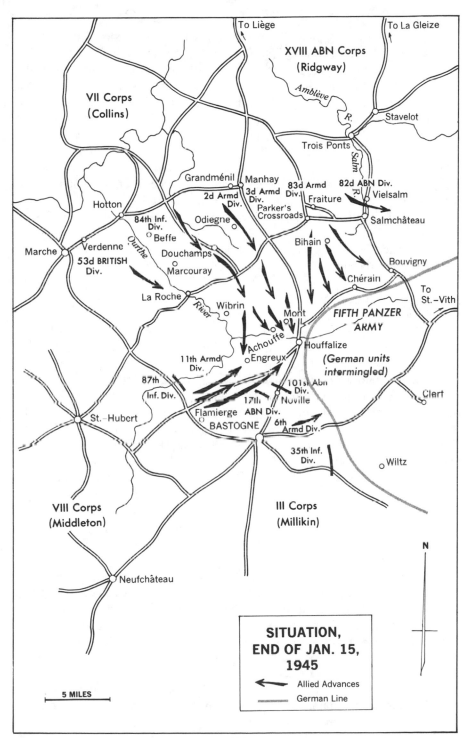

To Liège

To La Gleize

XVIII ABN Corps
(Ridgway)

Amblève R.

Stavelot

Trois Ponts

VII Corps
(Collins)

Salm R.

Hotton

Grandménil   Manhay
             3d Armd   83d Armd   82d ABN Div.
2d Armd   Div.   Div.   Vielsalm
Div.   Fraiture
84th Inf.   Parker's
Div.   Odiegne   Crossroads   Salmchâteau
        Beffe

Marche

Verdenne   Douchamps   Bihain   Bouvigny
53d BRITISH   Marcouray   Chérain
Div.   To
Ourthe   St.-Vith

La Roche   River   Wibrin   Mont   **FIFTH PANZER**
                                            ARMY

                    Achouffe   Houffalize   **(German units**
11th Armd   Engreux   **intermingled)**
Div.
87th   101st Abn   Clert
Inf. Div.   17th   Div.
        Flamierge   ABN Div.   Noville
St.-Hubert BASTOGNE   6th
                              Armd Div.
                    35th Inf.   Wiltz
                    Div.

VIII Corps   **III Corps**
(Middleton)   **(Millikin)**

                                            N

Neufchâteau

┌─────────────────────────┐
│   **SITUATION,**   │
│   **END OF JAN. 15,**   │
│   **1945**   │
│   │
│ ◄───   Allied Advances │
│ ───── German Line   │
└─────────────────────────┘

5 MILES

Late in the evening the 334th Infantry patrol received word that the rendezvous had been changed. The men moved out at midnight, traversed a wooded ridge, and at shortly after 2:00 A.M. on the sixteenth knocked on the door of a small Belgian farmhouse. The whole family—father, mother, son, and daughter—formed a reception committee and provided bread, butter, and hot coffee. The patrol decided that this was the place to stay and await contact.

Nearly seven hours later, Pfc. Rodney Heinz, second in command of the patrol, spied a bedraggled soldier outside the farmhouse. Since all his own men had been ordered to stay inside, Private Heinz decided to give him a good reprimand. "What outfit are you from?" Heinz demanded.

"Troop A, 3d Platoon, 41st Cavalry, 11th Armored Division, Third U.S. Army."

This particular junction took place at 8:45 A.M. on January 16. It is claimed to be the first.

Somewhat later in the morning, a more substantial juncture occurred in Houffalize itself.

On the evening of January 15, Task Force A of CCA, 2d Armored Division, continued the attack southeast. Reaching a tributary of the Ourthe, the engineers, protected by the infantry, built a bridge, and by 8:30 P.M. elements of a task force, commanded by Lieutenant Colonel Hugh R. O'Farrell, were in the woods about a mile northwest of Houffalize, with the east branch of the Ourthe River still south of him. Infantry patrols were sent along the south bank of the river to the road junction two miles north of Houffalize. German infantry and vehicles could be heard in Houffalize, but no contact was made with them.

The next morning Staff Sergeant Douglas Wood, motion picture cameraman from the 165th Signal Photo Company, came into Wibrin at 10:00 A.M. Sure that a meeting of First and Third armies was imminent, Wood had secured permission from CCA headquarters to film the event. With Pfc. Ernest Brown, a still photographer, he drove to Colonel O'Farrell's command post, at Achouffe.

O'Farrell was skeptical. He said he expected no historic meetings with other armies—he was waiting to be relieved by elements of the 82d Recon Battalion. From the vantage point afforded by the high ground in the area, O'Farrell and Wood could see Germans walking around on the highway leading south out of Houffalize. The artillery forward observer from the 92d Field Artillery was bringing fire to bear on the highway, and the Germans were retaliating in kind, shelling tanks of O'Farrell's task force.

A discouraged Sergeant Wood was on the point of returning to Wibrin when the company commander of Company F, 41st Armored Infantry, persuaded him to come to F Company and take some pictures of the dug-in infantry.

A figure came out of the woods. The infantry waved him up, but the soldier turned and called; soon five more men joined him, and all six ran up to Company F. The men identified themselves as a patrol from the 41st Armored Reconnaissance Squadron, 11th Armored Division. The time was about 11:40 A.M., January 16. The cavalrymen were soaking wet from having waded the Ourthe River, and they were cold, hungry, and tired. But everyone shook hands and beamed.

Close on their heels came Lieutenant Colonel Miles Foy, commanding officer of the 41st Armored Reconnaissance Squadron. Foy, also drenched, had left his jeep and come up on foot with his driver and radio operator, leaving his troops in the woods about three miles south of Houffalize. Asking to be taken to some officer of First Army troops, Foy found a ready volunteer in the formerly disappointed photographer, Sergeant Wood.

As they approached O'Farrell's tanks, Sergeant Wood called out, "There's a colonel here from the 11th Armored to see you, sir."

O'Farrell stuck his head out of the tank turret. Foy, startled, blurted out, "Well, Jesus Christ, if it isn't O'Farrell. I didn't recognize you in a tank. Haven't seen you since Fort Knox!"

The Bulge had been closed, although the battle was not considered officially over until twelve days later, when the lines were restored to those held before the morning of December 16.

The hopelessness of the German situation by this time is well illustrated in the diary of a German artillery officer, Lieutenant Behman, written during the days after the capture of Houffalize.

> 20 January: I am ordered to organize a defense in St.-Vith. For the first time since Christmas, I'm in St.-Vith again. The town is in ruins, but we will defend the ruins. We expect the attack on St.-Vith. Only small forces are available for the defense. The "8-balls" in the unit speak of a little Stalingrad.
>
> 21 January: There are no new messages. The battle noises come closer to the town. We can already see the infantry on some of the heights. I am organizing everything for a last defense. Rumor has it that the Tommies have the town surrounded. Some even believe it. At higher commands they believe that we will be forced to yield. These rear echelon men! I am neither optimistic nor pessimistic and I don't give up hope. When the kitchen goes back, I will send all personnel not immediately needed back with it. During the day, it is naturally quiet. Will the enemy surround the town? I'm sending back all my personal belongings. One never knows. I wonder what Heide is doing?
>
> 22 January: Nothing new during the night. At eight o'clock the enemy recommences his saturation fire from the direction of Nieder Emmels.— Exactly one month ago, we took St.-Vith.

On Sunday afternoon, January 23, 1945, the 7th Armored Division attacked and retook St.-Vith. General Hasbrouck gave the privilege of entering first to the combat command that had so heroically defended the town a month before—Brigadier General Bruce C. Clarke's Combat Command B.

The linking up between First and Third armies involved some of the most difficult fighting in the entire European campaign. Almost unbearable weather, difficult terrain, and extremely skillful and desperate defense on the part of the Germans served to slow down the American advance to the point where it took Third Army a week to go the seven miles from the Bastogne perimeter to Houffalize. First Army spent almost two weeks advancing the 15 miles from Grandménil and Manhay to the same objective.

From the soldiers' point of view, some of the units found the fighting all the more difficult because they were new to combat. General Taylor has since said that the 17th Airborne Division, committed on January 4, went into battle under the most difficult conditions for a baptism of fire [6] he had ever seen.

As a result of the weather conditions that slowed the Allied advance, the Germans were able to withdraw many of their forces, largely without their equipment, and prevent the entrapment of a very sizable pocket west of Houffalize. Nevertheless, the linkup operation had been far more costly to the Germans than to the Americans. According to Patton's After Action Report of January 16, the Third Army had utilized 17 divisions, losing fewer than 25,000 men. During this same period the Germans had utilized 20 divisions, losing an estimated 16,000 prisoners, 24,000 killed, and more than 63,000 wounded—a total of more than 103,000 German casualties, a ratio of four to one.

Characteristically, General Patton's report concluded: "We believe that these figures are low."

[6] Interview by author with General Taylor, June 29, 1966.

CHAPTER 18

❧ ❧

Mission Fulfilled

AFTER the failure of the Ardennes campaign, the German military situation had become impossible. North Africa, Belgium, France, Luxembourg, Crete, Russia, most of the Balkans, much of Italy and Poland, parts of the Netherlands, Czechoslovakia, Yugoslavia, and even East Prussia had been lost. The Finnish and Italian allies had gone by the board. The nation's three major industrial regions—the Ruhr, the Saar, and Silesia—were threatened. Germany's reserves had been all but shattered in the Ardennes, and the failure there was all the more disheartening because Hitler had led the Germans to expect so much of that campaign.

But Nazi Germany would not give up. And in some areas her sustaining power was remarkable. German production, for example, reached its peak in the fall of 1944. During September, 1944, Germany produced more than 4,000 aircraft of all types, more than the combined current monthly production of the United States, England, Canada, and Australia. As late as November, 1944, the Luftwaffe boasted more planes than at any other time during the war—more than 8,000, not counting transport planes, more than 5,000 of which were operational. Some 25 new submarines, most of them equipped with snorkel underwater breathing devices, were being completed each month throughout the fall. Tank and assault gun output would hold at a steady monthly level of about 1,600 from November, 1944, to February, 1945. And all this was accomplished with a labor force of nearly 36,000,000 people in September, 1944—roughly 10 percent less than that of 1939.

This only pointed up the wisdom of the Allied air strategy which concentrated on making this production unusable. The strategic air effort was primarily directed against two areas of the German economy: fuel, which had played such a vital part in the Ardennes; and the badly battered German transportation networks. As a result, Germany's situation had now reached the point where OKW was forced, in considering any operation, to ascertain first whether adequate supplies of gas and diesel oil would be available—and

431

at the right time. This fuel shortage forced Hitler to hold the oil fields of Hungary at all costs.

The Germans found themselves in their most desperate straits when it came to trained fighting manpower. Of a prewar population of 80,000,000, close to 13,000,000 men had been drawn into the armed services, and of these 4,000,-000 had been killed, wounded, or captured. To alleviate these losses, Hitler decreed on January 19 that older men, up to forty-five years of age, be shifted from industry to the armed forces. In February he planned to organize eight new divisions, primarily from youths just turned seventeen. Furthermore, as the roles of the Kriegsmarine and the Luftwaffe declined, he was able to transfer substantial numbers of their personnel to the Heer.

In certain types of military equipment the Germans were still superior to the Allies. The American Sherman tank, for example, even the new model with 76-mm. guns, was still outgunned by both the 50-ton Mark V Panther and the 63-ton Mark VI Tiger, each of which mounted a high-velocity 88-mm. gun and boasted thicker armor and wider tracks.[1]

In the air a few of the new German jets had already appeared over the western front. The Germans had made extensive use of their V-1 and V-2 flying bombs and missiles, and it had been reported—inaccurately, it turned out—that the Germans would soon possess an intercontinental ballistic missile. However, German progress in the jet field had caused sufficient uneasiness in high Allied circles for General Carl Spaatz, commanding U.S. Strategic Air Forces in Europe, and General Bedell Smith of SHAEF to agree on January 9, 1945, to elevate German jet production centers to first priority in the bombing program, coequal with oil. On the previous day General Eisenhower had agreed to release heavy bombers from the land campaign in order to intensify the bombing of oil production centers and the new threat, the jets.[2]

On the tactical side, most of the German High Command had long felt that the Ardennes campaign should be given up and the forces moved back to better defensive positions. Manteuffel, for example, has since stated that he and Model agreed on December 29, 1944, that the German forces should be withdrawn entirely from the Ardennes and even fall back behind the Rhine.

Guderian, as we have seen, had had a series of heated discussions with Hitler in an effort to transfer the troops in the Ardennes to the crumbling Russian front. Hitler acceded to this request on January 14. On that same day

---

[1] The 90-mm. Pershing M-26 did not arrive in Europe before the end of hostilities in other than experimental numbers.

[2] Eisenhower had commanded the British Bomber Command and the Eight U.S. Air Force from spring to autumn, 1944. With the lodgment secure, the CCS at Quebec in September assumed direct control of the strategic air forces with the proviso that SHAEF's requirements would have priority. Both Spaatz (U.S.) and Harris (British) continued to give Eisenhower unswerving support. However, use of heavy bombers in tactical role, as in the Ardennes, was an emergency expedient.

Rundstedt and Model recommended that Hitler withdraw the western front to the Rhine; in typical fashion, Hitler turned down this request. He would have preferred to resist along the Sålm and the Clerf rivers, but when the Allied jaws closed at Houffalize even he realized that this forward line could not be defended and agreed to withdraw into the West Wall.

But the German commanders, particularly those of the discredited Army General Staff, were becoming more and more afraid to speak their minds to the Führer. Since he forbade any admission of the possibility of failure, Hitler now acted often on unrealistic estimates. Further, his personality degenerated steadily; those of his utterances that have been preserved from this period vary from reprimands to exhortations to boasts. While distrusting practically everyone about him, he harbored a corresponding overconfidence in a few men, the development of miracle weapons, and the conviction that he and he alone was capable of handling the course of the war correctly.

The men in Hitler's immediate entourage hardly dared do more than plead with him for moderation. Guderian was the exception, even going so far as to carry the day in a few instances. Once Hitler smiled wanly and said, "The General Staff has won a victory today." Nevertheless, Guderian was eventually dismissed, and the trusted Himmler, with his many titles, was sent to the eastern front to save what he could. Göring had long since lost his influence. Jodl, the military adviser and planner, continued a loyal executor of Hitler's wishes and plans. In Rundstedt's opinion, expressed after the war, Jodl was the only person in the High Command, including Hitler, who knew anything about the conduct of military operations.

A clue to Hitler's rationalization of his position remained in his worship of Frederick II of Prussia:

> Not long ago I was reading a volume of Frederick the Great's letters. In one of these letters he wrote (it was in the fifth year of the Seven Years War): "I started this war with the most wonderful army in Europe; today I've got a mulch heap. I have no leaders any more, my generals are incompetent, the officers are no commanders, the troops are wretched." It was a devastating estimate, but nevertheless that man got through the war. What's more, if you read the estimates about the Russian troops, they are wretched, but they carry on just the same. So the important things are the eternal human qualities, the qualities which are really basic to the military profession. Military qualities don't show themselves in an exercise on a sand model. In the last analysis, they show themselves in the capacity to hold on, in perseverance and determination. That's the decisive factor in any victory. Genius is a will of the wisp unless it is founded on perseverance and fanatical determination. That's the most important thing in human existence. People who have brain waves, ideas, etc., will get nowhere in the end unless they also possess strength of character, perseverance and determination. Otherwise they merely ride their luck. If all goes well, they are up in the air; if things go badly, they are down

in the depths and give up everything straight away. One can't make world history that way. World history can only be made if, in addition to high intelligence, in addition to thorough knowledge, in addition to continual alertness, a man has fanatical determination and the courage of his convictions, which will make him master of himself. That's what matters to the soldier in the last analysis, that at the moment of crisis, he feels that those who command him have these qualities. Some don't like it; those are the bad ones. But the good ones feel that they are playing some part; they say: "Why have we had to make all these sacrifices? But we shall only have to go on doing so as long as the war lasts." That's certain. No one can last forever. We can't. The other side can't. It's merely a question of who can stand it longer. The one who must hold out the longer is the one who's got everything at stake. We've got everything at stake. If the other side says one day, "We've had enough," nothing happens to him. If America says, "We're off, period, we've got no more men for Europe," nothing happens; New York would still be New York, Chicago would still be Chicago, Detroit would still be Detroit, San Francisco would still be San Francisco. It doesn't change a thing. But if we were to say today, "We've had enough," we should cease to exist. Germany would cease to exist.[3]

To a large extent the same attitude permeated the German people. In 1918, when the populace had realized defeat was unavoidable, revolutions and mutinies had occurred throughout the Kaiser's realms. But circumstances were different in 1945. Nazism, with all its horrors, had succeeded in establishing a broader base of authority among the people than had the rule of Kaiser Wilhelm, and Hitler supplemented this voluntary support with fear of reprisals against members of the family of a defecting soldier, threats begun during the previous summer and made more severe as time went on. The German people, furthermore, still clung to a lingering hope that secret weapons would be developed. Had not the Germans developed the jet ahead of the Allies?

Hatred of Bolshevism further influenced the German people to fight to the end. In World War I, Russia had been knocked out of the war by 1917. Now the Soviets had set foot on German soil on January 20 and were in the process of overrunning major parts of the Fatherland.

A final incentive for the German people to carry on was the Allied demand, first made at the Casablanca Conference in 1943, for "unconditional surrender." To the Germans, this position precluded any separate surrenders to the Western Allies; the Germans, Goebbels declared, might now expect no better treatment from America and Britain than from Russia.

The attitude of the German people can be summed up: Quit now and all is lost—hold on, maybe something will help. They were now fighting for

[3] Walter Warlimont, *Inside Hitler's Headquarters, 1939–45* (New York: Praeger, 1964), p. 499.

their own homes, in both east and west. Though a few preferred to give up, the great majority continued the battle with stubborn determination.

The military operations which followed the close of the Ardennes campaign were characterized by the rapidity of the advances.

The basic outline plan that General Eisenhower sent to Field Marshal Montgomery at the turn of the year called for several things: the reduction of the Ardennes salient; with that completed, the destruction of enemy forces west of the Rhine and north of the Moselle, with preparations for crossing the Rhine in force with the main effort north of the Ruhr. This phase called for a drive to the northeast by the First and Third U.S. armies on the general line of Prüm-Bonn, followed by an attack south by Montgomery's 21 Army Group. The front south of the Moselle was to remain strictly on the defensive for the moment.

Although Montgomery accepted the plan, its final version, drawn up a month later, caused anxiety to Field Marshal Sir Alan Brooke, chief of the British Imperial General Staff. The feature that most disturbed Brooke was the destruction of essentially all German forces west of the Rhine River before attempting to cross in any one place. Throughout the European campaign Brooke harbored reservations concerning what was loosely called the "broad-front strategy"; he labeled the plan for clearing the Rhineland west of the Rhine a "dispersion of effort."

But General Eisenhower was firmly convinced that the German forces would be most easily defeated west of the Rhine; for an assault crossing of that river, a formidable obstacle, would exact a heavy toll in Allied casualties. Manteuffel and Model, looking from the other direction, had felt the same way.

The Ardennes campaign had strengthened General Eisenhower's convictions. Securing the line of the Rhine and Moselle would enable the Allies to hold great stretches of river with minimum forces and enable them to concentrate in critical areas. Thus it was with some heat that Eisenhower once more insisted 6 Army Group clear out the Colmar Pocket. To insure success he was willing to provide the First French Army, whose job it was, with an additional U.S. corps, Frank W. Milburn's XXI. (Cota's reconstituted 28th Infantry Division participated.) The Colmar Pocket, south of Strasbourg, was finally reduced on February 9, 1945.

Field Marshal Brooke's feelings also remained strong. Suspicious, apparently, that the Supreme Commander's strategy was being dictated partly to assuage General Bradley's feelings, Brooke once said to Eisenhower: "I wish that the 12 Army Group were deployed north of the Ruhr and the British forces were in the center."

This remark hit Eisenhower in a sensitive spot. He retorted: "I am certainly no more anxious to put Americans into the thick of the battle and get them killed than I am to see the British take the losses. I have strengthened Montgomery's army group by a full American army, since in no other way can I provide the strength north of the Ruhr that I deem essential for the rapid execution of my plans. I have not devised any plan on the basis of what individual or what nation gets the glory, for I must tell you, in my opinion there is no glory in battle worth the blood it costs." [4]

In early January, 1945, General Eisenhower learned that Prime Minister Churchill and President Roosevelt, with their respective chiefs of staff, were planning to meet with Generalissimo Josef Stalin at Yalta. On the way they planned to stop at the British base in Malta for preliminary conferences. Eisenhower flew to Marseilles to meet with General George Marshall and explain his strategic plan in detail.

Marshall studied the plan, agreed it was sound, and suggested that Eisenhower send his chief of staff, Bedell Smith, to talk to the Combined Chiefs when they met at Malta. This Eisenhower was glad to do.

Among the issues to be discussed at the meeting was the question of Allied occupation zones in Europe at the termination of the conflict. The issue had already been decided, however. In late 1943 an Allied Control Commission, with representatives from the United States, Britain, and the Soviet Union, had been set up in London to study the future respective occupation of Germany. Ambassador John Winant had served as the U.S. representative.

This commission had come up with three approximately equal zones to be occupied respectively by the Russians, British, and Americans. A major tacit concession to the USSR, however, was the ceding of part of prewar Germany to Poland, thus making Russia's share of the occupied territory really greater than the share of either of the other two.[5]

General Eisenhower had seen this plan for the occupation and noted that the Soviet zone ran approximately westward from the tip of Czechoslovakia to Eisenach along the Autobahn, then northward, including Magdeburg and Wittenberge, but excluding Hamburg and Lübeck (see map, p. 450). Though he had advocated to President Roosevelt a year earlier that Germany be governed without specific national occupation zones, Eisenhower now asked Bedell Smith to emphasize at Malta that Allied forces in the West were going to reach a line farther east than that agreed to by the Allied Control Commission. Perhaps Roosevelt and Churchill would prefer to delay any agreement on postwar occupation zones pending the results of current military operations?

Smith's mission to Malta was partly successful. The outline plan for the

[4] Dwight Eisenhower, *Crusade in Europe* (New York: Doubleday, 1948), p. 371.
[5] France was later given an area sliced out of the western portion.

destruction of German forces west of the Rhine was agreed to, although with some reluctance on the part of the British Chiefs of Staff—and only with the assurance that the main effort over the river would be made north of the Ruhr. The question of the appointment of an overall ground commander was set aside for good. But on the matter of revising the proposed occupation zones of Germany, Smith got nowhere. Apparently Roosevelt felt keenly his obligation to adhere to the recommendations of the Allied Control Commission; he did not choose to reopen the subject of territorial occupation zones with Stalin. The rubber-stamp approval was made at Yalta.

This decision was to have a major influence on subsequent military operations.

Meanwhile General Bradley had been following up his successes in the reduction of the Ardennes salient. Finding minimal forces of Manteuffel's Fifth Panzer Army on his front, he continued his attack with Patton's Third Army into the Eifel, forward of the line of December 16. But when, on February 4, it became apparent that the Siegfried Line was holding firm and Bradley's men were struggling through six-foot snowdrifts, General Eisenhower directed the First Army to sideslip north and resume its attack against the Roer dams. The stage was now set for the major Rhineland campaign.

General Eisenhower's plan for the defeat of the German armies was visualized in three phases: Operation Veritable, Operation Lumberjack, and Operation Undertone.

The first phase, Veritable, was to be executed by Montgomery's 21 Army Group, with Simpson's U.S. Ninth Army under its operational control. Veritable was an unusual maneuver. It consisted of an attack by the Canadian First Army southward up the Rhine River, starting at the bridgehead over the Maas at Nijmegen. This operation would turn the flank of the Siegfried Line and proceed down its rear in front of Dempsey's British Second Army, which would remain in a static position behind the Maas.

Veritable faced the prospect of hard going through the dense Reichswald and certain fortified positions behind it. To assist Veritable, Montgomery was authorized to employ Operation Grenade—in which Simpson's Ninth Army would cross the Roer River at Jülich, drive to the Rhine at Düsseldorf, and turn northward to join the Canadian First Army coming from the north. But before General Simpson could execute Grenade, the Roer River dams had to be taken.

Operations proceeded slowly at first. Leonard T. Gerow's V Corps again began battering the Roer dams as early as February 2; in a week he accomplished what had taken so much time and blood the previous autumn. On reaching the Roer River dams, however, he discovered that the Germans had already wrecked the discharge valves—and the resulting flood would hold up Simpson's Roer crossing for two weeks. But the Canadian attack had jumped off, even though the flooding permitted Blaskowitz (now transferred to the north) to concentrate his forces against the Canadians. The Canadians had traversed the Reichswald and taken Cleves by February 9.

General Simpson was able to launch Operation Grenade on February 23, and in so doing advanced with three corps abreast (left to right, XVI, XIII, and XIX). He attacked earlier than the Germans expected, while the waters were still high, thereby securing complete surprise. By February 28 Simpson had broken loose and was headed toward Düsseldorf, and by March 3 had linked up with Crerar's Canadians at Geldern. The west bank of the Rhine was nearly cleared from Düsseldorf northward by March 5.

The second phase of the Rhineland operation was to be executed by Bradley's 12 Army Group. In this operation General Hodges of the First Army was given two missions. One was to attack in conjunction with Simpson's Grenade operation to the north, protecting Ninth Army's right flank. The other was to drive to the Rhine and turn south, linking up with Patton's Third Army coming north along the Rhine north of the Moselle. This exclusively American pincers movement was known as Operation Lumberjack.

General Patton, in the meanwhile, instructed to remain on the active defense, had chosen to emphasize the word "active" rather than "defense." He crossed the Our River and made it through the Siegfried Line in all points but one near Vianden (so important in Lüttwitz's drive in the Ardennes campaign). He began pushing more aggressively when the attacks began all along the American front on March 5. By that date Collins' VII Corps had crossed the Erft River and, surprisingly, had reached the outskirts of Cologne.

Now things began to happen swiftly. By March 7 Hugh Gaffey's dashing 4th Armored Division (part of Third Army) had driven all the way to Andernach on the Rhine north of the Moselle. Cologne was safely in American hands, and First U.S. Army was closing in on the Rhine River to the north. The pincers of Operation Lumberjack were preparing to close.

On March 1, 1945, General der Panzertruppen Hasso von Manteuffel was summoned once more into the presence of the Führer, this time in the Reichschancellory in Berlin. Manteuffel was shocked by what he saw. Hitler was slumped in a chair behind his desk, and instead of rising and greeting his guest as had been his habit in the past, he contented himself with shouting across the room, "All generals are liars!"

Manteuffel walked directly up to Hitler's desk. Looking his chief in the eye, he demanded, "When have I or any of my officers ever lied to you?"

Apparently shocked, Hitler made an effort to rise. Pulling himself up with difficulty as far as the arm of his chair, a dull-eyed, broken, and weary Führer murmured in a subdued tone, "I didn't mean you or your generals—I just meant the others."

They then went on to discuss a new task Hitler had in mind for his panzer leader. But Hitler's physical deterioration was obvious.

On the evening of March 7, General Eisenhower was hosting a dinner with General Ridgway and other airborne commanders at Versailles when he was called to the phone. At the other end of the line was General Bradley with explosive news. Bill Hoge's Combat Command B of the 9th Armored Division, driving south from Bonn to Remagen, had found a usable railroad bridge. A detachment of his combat command had rushed this Ludendorff Bridge and preserved it against complete destruction, although a small charge had been exploded. Immediately Bradley had sent four divisions across the river—enough to protect the bridgehead against confused German counterattacks—but was calling to make certain that any major diversion of effort at Remagen would not interfere with Eisenhower's overall plan for the conduct of the Rhineland campaign, a possibility that seemed to concern Eisenhower's G-3, Major General Harold R. ("Pinky") Bull, who happened to be with Bradley. There had been no intention of crossing the Rhine in that particular area—but neither had there been any real expectation of such a windfall.

Eisenhower did not hesitate: "Well, Brad, we expected to have that many divisions tied up around Cologne, and now those are free. Go ahead and shove over at least five divisions instantly and anything else that is necessary to make certain of our hold."

The Remagen bridgehead was expanded until by March 9 it was three miles deep. Its seizure and consolidation were to result in a significant shortening of the war in Europe.

By March 10 the Allies held the entire west bank of the Rhine north of the Moselle; only the Palatinate, to the south of the Moselle, remained in German hands. The time had now come for the third phase of the Rhineland campaign, Operation Undertone. It was to be executed by Patch's Seventh U.S. Army, of Devers' 6 Army Group; the Seventh Army up to this time had been ordered to stay strictly on the tactical defensive behind the Moder River, where it had stopped Blaskowitz's Operation Nordwind toward the end of January. The attack jumped off on March 11 under conditions of some difficulty. Before the Seventh Army lay strong fortifications of the Siegfried Line, which caused a modification in the plans for Undertone.

The lightning swiftness of Patton's drive along the northwest bank of the Moselle opened another possibility. To make Devers' task easier, Patton was ordered to cross the Moselle and drive up (southward) the Rhine River behind the Siegfried Line. Within ten days Patton had gone nearly 100 miles along the Rhine River to Mannheim, only about 30 miles from Patch's spearhead at Lauterbourg. In the meantime Patch had traveled approximately 25 miles across his entire front.

By the next day, March 22, the last German bridgehead was reduced. The Allied front was now solid along the entire Rhine River. Adolf Hitler's refusal to evacuate the Rhineland had cost the German Army approximately a quarter of a million prisoners, and possibly an additional 60,000 killed or wounded. To all intents and purposes, the German Army in the west had been destroyed.

General George S. Patton, Jr., possessed a flair for history. He also harbored a highly developed competitive spirit with Field Marshal Bernard Law Montgomery. Aware that 21 Army Group was now engaged in making elaborate preparations to cross the Rhine at Wesel on the north German Plain, Patton's chief concern was to get Third U.S. Army across first, lest he risk losing substantial numbers of troops to Montgomery and be ordered once more to resume a defensive role. Therefore, on March 18, several days before the Third Army had closed to the Rhine at Mannheim, Patton had a conference with General Eddy of XII Corps.

"Eddy," he said, "you've got to get across the Rhine before the twenty-third."

On the morning of March 23, General Bradley was at breakfast at his headquarters, the Château de Namur. A call came from Third Army. "Brad, don't tell anyone, but I'm across."

"Well, I'll be damned—you mean across the Rhine?"

"Sure am," said Patton. "I sneaked a division over last night, but there are so few Krauts around they don't know it yet, so don't make any announcement. We'll keep it a secret until we see how it goes."

Major General Stafford LeRoy Irwin, commander of the 5th Infantry Division in General Eddy's XII Corps, had crossed the Rhine with hardly a casualty.

Late in the day Patton had second thoughts. The Germans had discovered his bridgehead, and there was always Monty. He phoned Bradley, his normally high-pitched voice shaking with emotion: "Brad, for God's sake tell the world we're across. I want the world to know Third Army made it before Monty starts across!" [6]

Once more Hitler turned to his familiar device for attempting to bolster his tottering fortunes. He relieved his old professional, Gerd von Rundstedt, as OB West for a second time. Up from Italy he brought Generalfeldmarschall

---

[6] Omar Bradley, *A Soldier's Story* (New York: Holt, 1951), p. 522.

Albrecht von Kesselring, to assume the post. This move was to make not the slightest difference in the campaign.

The main operational plans for the invasion of Germany, going back to the days before D-Day, had always called for the main effort across the Rhine to be made in the north. Despite the numerous waterways and the low country, vulnerable to flooding, it had been decided early that this was the best route for encircling the vital Ruhr industrial area and for operations thence into the heart of Germany.

As Montgomery's 21 Army Group had remained on the left of the line throughout the entire European campaign, this meant that the major assault across the Rhine River would be made by his force. However, he had only 15 divisions available to him in 21 Army Group and needed reinforcement. General Simpson's Ninth Army, therefore, was to remain under Montgomery's operational control for the crossing. This attachment, plus the two airborne divisions (the 6th British and 17th U.S.), brought Montgomery's force to 29 divisions and 7 separate brigades. Even the Navy was brought into play. Landing craft were brought up by waterway and by trailer to aid in this major assault.

In this operation on the night of March 23–24 Montgomery utilized the airborne troops in an unconventional but effective manner. In Normandy and in Holland the airborne troops had been dropped into their zones of action before the ground troops jumped off. In this instance the Field Marshal elected to assault the river line under the cover of darkness, dropping the British 6th Airborne and the U.S. 17th Airborne the next morning, close enough to participate in the initial tactical effort; linkup was to be rapid indeed.

This crossing of the Rhine—although two others had been made—was an event that attracted numerous visitors, including Churchill and Eisenhower. Montgomery himself retired at 9:30 P.M., on the twenty-third, as on any other night in the war; but the Prime Minister, with Field Marshal Brooke, spent hours walking up and down near the front. General Eisenhower observed the action with General Simpson at a vantage point in an old church tower, where he could witness the gunfire. On the front of the two American assault divisions alone, 2,000 guns of all types were used.

Throughout the night the reports were encouraging, and the next morning Eisenhower went to a convenient hill to watch the arrival of the nearly 1,600 planes and 1,300 gliders, escorted by almost 900 fighters, to execute the airdrops. More than 2,000 other fighters provided cover over the target area.

Throughout the day the news continued excellent. The drops were successful, and General Eisenhower later learned that the two assault units, the U.S. 30th and 79th Infantry divisions, suffered a total of only 31 casualties.

The Prime Minister was overjoyed. When he met with the Supreme Commander on March 25, he exclaimed repeatedly, "My dear general, the German is whipped. We've got him. He is all through." [7] Brooke also offered his warm congratulations.[8]

About noon, General Eisenhower left to visit General Bradley's headquarters. Without Eisenhower's knowledge the Prime Minister clandestinely managed to cross the Rhine in a small boat, finally standing in triumph on the far bank of the greatest barrier protecting the nation that had so threatened his own some five years earlier.

On the day that 21 Army Group crossed the Rhine, Eisenhower's naval aide, Captain Harry C. Butcher, was driving along a French road from Reims toward Châlons-sur-Marne. He picked up three paratroopers from the 101st Airborne Division and, without identifying his own association with the Supreme Commander, asked if they had attended the presentation of the Presidential Unit Citation to the division. He also asked if Eisenhower had made a speech.

"Oh, yes, he made a good one, but I hate to hear him and a speech with 'Good luck and God be with you.' "

"Why?"

"Because every time he has made a speech to us and said 'God be with you,' he has sent us off on a tough job."

The crossings of the Rhine were complete. 21 Army Group, north of the Ruhr, drove eastward and northeastward from Wesel. South of the Ruhr, Courtney Hodges' First Army drove out of the Remagen bridgehead westward to link up with Patton's Third at Giessen. Thence First Army turned north along the great Reichsautobahn to link up with Simpson's Ninth at Lippstadt (near Paderborn), thus encircling Model's Army Group B within the Ruhr.

As First Army drove northward it appeared Model might be able to break out through the thin VII Corps lines. But the lines held, and by the end of March the claws of the pincers were approaching each other. When First and Ninth U.S. armies joined hands, Ninth Army was to revert to operational command of Bradley's 12 Army Group.

In the last days of March, as Allied forces were crossing the Rhine, the Supreme Commander was in the process of formulating his strategy for the final phases of the campaign. Certain events had occurred that had modified

---

[7] Eisenhower, *op. cit.,* p. 390.

[8] "One thing that had given him [Eisenhower] special pleasure was that Field Marshal Sir Alan Brooke, who had once argued heatedly against the plan, had generously told him on the banks of the Rhine as the crossing was in progress that he, General Ike, was right, and that his current plans and operations were well calculated to meet the current situation." Harry Butcher, *My Three Years with Eisenhower* (New York: Simon & Schuster, 1946), p. 792.

the overall situation as he had originally visualized it. The foremost change had been the spectacular gains made by the Russians in their winter offensive, in the absence of German reserves. The Red Army now held a bridgehead over the Oder River at Lubin, 35 miles from Berlin. Here the Russians were assembling a million men, poised to strike.

An article in *Life* magazine, February 5, 1945, provided a typical incident: "One day last week in Belgium an American artillery observer said to his battery over the telephone, 'Don't shoot 'em too far, boys. You might hit the Russians.' Most other American soldiers were thinking about the Russians, too. Men at the front carried frayed little maps of the Russian line torn out of Army newspapers. A frequent remark was, 'I hope the Russians get to Berlin first. They'll know what to do with those Krauts.' "

The Russian populace, aware that Berlin was theirs for the taking, were being whipped into a frenzy: "Six capitals, six countries!" boasted *Pravda*. "But we are thinking about the seventh. . . . Berlin . . . has not long to live!"

In the same article, *Life* reported the temper of the Russians: "Night after night in Moscow, there were two, three, five victory salutes as crowds chanted, 'Berlin! Berlin! on to Berlin!' "

But the Western Allies also were ahead of schedule, and this had a serious bearing on the planned route of advance across the extreme north German Plain, running directly from Wesel to Berlin. The sloppy conditions at this early time of year made the going more difficult than it would have been in May, and made the plain less attractive.

This affected the decision that General Eisenhower had to make: where to draw the line at which the Western Allied forces should halt to make contact with the Soviet forces.

From a strictly military viewpoint the answer was simple: a halt running generally along the line of the Elbe River in the north to the town of Dessau, some 75 miles southwest of Berlin, thence along the Mulde (west of the Elbe) to Sudetenland in Czechoslovakia. From a psychological viewpoint the decision was complicated by the fact that this line left Berlin to be taken by the Soviets, and during the war Berlin had become symbolic for the Western peoples as the heart of Germany, although certainly to a much smaller degree than for the Russians.

The question then became whether, once the Ruhr Pocket was sealed, the Western Allies should make a desperate attempt to seize that symbolic objective—or try to contribute directly to its seizure. With a million Russians virtually at Berlin's gates and the strung-out Western forces 250 miles away (with their center of gravity still west of the Rhine) the prospect seemed highly doubtful. (See map, p. 444.)

Eisenhower consulted Bradley. How many American casualties would it cost, he asked, to make an all-out attempt to reach Berlin? After all, intelligence showed little by way of German resistance until the environs of Berlin. Bradley was hardly encouraging: 100,000 casualties, he estimated, "a pretty stiff price to pay for a prestige objective." [9]

The issue boiled down to the degree political considerations were to be allowed to influence military judgment. Eisenhower's original directive from the CCS had mentioned no authority to set political policy. And furthermore, Eisenhower, from his conversations in Washington, was aware of the existing political climate in that capital. President Roosevelt's attitude, as reflected in directives from the CCS, was that Nazi Germany was the enemy; the Soviet Union was an ally, albeit a difficult one, that could be dealt with later.

But the strongest argument of all was the positive knowledge that no matter who took which territory, the forces of the Russians, British, and Americans

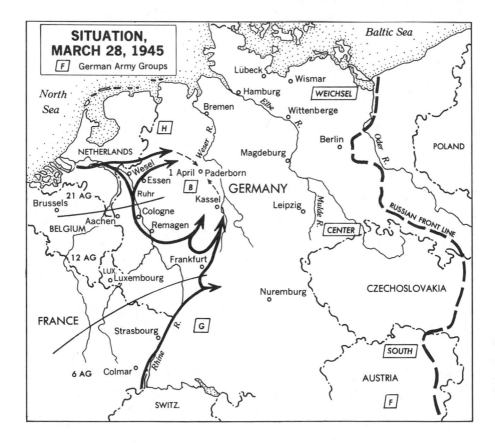

[9] Bradley, *op. cit.*, p. 535.

were all to be withdrawn to the preplanned occupation zones designed by the
European Advisory Commission and rubber-stamped by the powers at Yalta.
The West would abide by this agreement to the letter.

Eisenhower made his decision: until instructed otherwise, he would fight a
military war directed solely against Hitler. He had previously concluded that
the best strategy would be for the First and Ninth U.S. armies to drive eastward from Kassel, after they had linked up, to an area near Leipzig, south of
Berlin. By standing on the Elbe and Mulde rivers, he would be holding, as the
limit of the main thrust, a recognizable terrain feature [10]—and a strong defensive position—along which to join with the Russians. Furthermore this main
thrust to Leipzig would cut the German forces in two and foreclose the possibility of fanatic Nazi remnants retreating to a rumored "Redoubt" in the Alps.
Berlin, whatever its political importance to future East-West relations, was no
longer a significant military objective.

On March 28, 1945, General Eisenhower communicated the essense of
this conclusion directly to Generalissimo Stalin.

When a copy of Eisenhower's message to Stalin was received by the British
Joint Chiefs of Staff, they reacted violently. To their U.S. counterparts in
Washington, the British Chiefs complained about (a) the procedure employed
by the Supreme Commander in communicating directly with the Generalissimo; (b) the substance of the plan itself, which by shifting the main thrust
from the extreme north to an axis somewhat farther south toward Leipzig,
transferred the main effort from Montgomery to Bradley.

The British Chiefs' message was transmitted before the Prime Minister had
a chance to see it. Although Churchill was in essential agreement with his
Chiefs, he felt that their telegram smothered the essential points in too many
details:

> ...6. We weaken our case for a stronger concentration between the sea
> and the Hanover-Berlin flank by suggesting we should like to turn aside to
> clean up matters in Denmark, Norway, and along the Baltic shore....
>
> 7. In short, I see argumentative possibilities being opened to the United
> States Chiefs of Staff by our telegram, on which they will riposte heavily. It
> must be remembered that Eisenhower's credit with them stands very high.
> He may claim to have correctly estimated so far the resisting strength of the
> enemy and to have established by deeds (a) the "closing" [i.e., reaching] of
> the Rhine along its whole length, (b) the power to make the double advance
> instead of staking all on the northern advance.... These events, combined
> with the continual arrival of American reinforcements, have greatly enhanced
> General Eisenhower's power and prestige, and the Americans will feel that,

---

[10] General Eisenhower was only too well aware of many instances in military history in which friendly forces fought each other because of failure of recognition. This
consideration had, in fact, also been critical in Bradley's decision to halt without
completely closing the Falaise Pocket in Normandy.

as the victorious Supreme Commander, he has a right, and indeed a vital need, to try to elicit from the Russians their views as to the best point for making contact by the armies of the West and of the East. . . .

Informed by Marshall of the British complaint, Eisenhower dispatched a complete digest of his plan to the Combined Chiefs on March 30. The message was, incidentally, originally drafted by a British officer in SHAEF.

This is in reply to your radio.

The same protests except as to "procedure" contained in that telegram were communicated to me by the Prime Minister over telephone last night.

I am completely in the dark as to what the protests concerning "procedure" involve. I have been instructed to deal directly with the Russians concerning military co-ordination. There is no change in basic strategy. The British Chiefs of Staff last summer protested against my determination to open up the Frankfurt route because they said it would be futile and would draw strength away from a northern attack. I have always insisted that the northern attack would be the principal effort in that phase of our operations that involved the isolation of the Ruhr, but from the very beginning, extending back before D-day, my plan, explained to my staff and senior officers, has been to link up the primary and secondary efforts in the Kassel area and then make one great thrust to the eastward.

Even cursory examination of the decisive direction for this thrust, after the link-up in the Kassel area is complete, shows that the principal effort should under existing circumstances be toward the Leipzig region, where is concentrated the greater part of the remaining German industrial capacity, and to which area the German ministries are believed to be moving. My plan does not draw Montgomery's British and Canadian forces to the southward. You will note that his right flank will push forward along the general line Hanover-Wittenberge. Merely following the principle that Field Marshal Brooke has always emphasized, I am determined to concentrate on one major thrust, and all that my plan does is to place the U. S. Ninth Army back under Bradley for that phase of operations involving the advance of the center from Kassel to the Leipzig region, unless, of course, the Russian forces should be met on this side of that area. Thereafter, that position will be consolidated while the plan clearly shows that Ninth Army may again have to move up to assist the British and Canadian armies in clearing the whole coast line to the westward of Lübeck.

After strength for this operation has been provided, it is considered that we can launch a movement to the southeastward to prevent Nazi occupation of a mountain citadel. . . .

May I point out that Berlin itself is no longer a particularly important objective. Its usefulness to the German has been largely destroyed and even his government is preparing to move to another area. What is now important is to gather up our forces for a single drive and this will more quickly bring about the fall of Berlin, the relief of Norway, and the acquisition of the shipping and the Swedish ports than will the scattering around of our effort.

As another point I should like to point out that the so-called "good ground" in northern Germany is not really good at this time of year. That region is not only badly cut up with waterways, but in it the ground during this part of the year is very wet and not so favorable for rapid movement as is the higher plateau over which I am preparing to launch the main effort. . . .

Naturally, my plans are flexible and I must retain freedom of action to meet changing situations. Maximum flexibility will result from a concentration of maximum force in the center.

The next day General Marshall, representing the U.S. Joint Chiefs of Staff, replied as follows:

British Chiefs of Staff sent from London to Combined Chiefs today their views on your plan.

They deny any desire to fetter the hand of the Supreme Commander [SCAEF] in the field but mention wider issues outside the purview of SCAEF (U-boat war, Swedish shipping, political importance of saving thousands of Dutchmen from starvation, importance of move into Denmark and liberating Norway) and request delay in the submission of further details to Deane [Major General John R. Deane, head of the military mission in Moscow] until you hear from CCS.

The U.S. Chiefs replied today in substance as follows: SCAEF's procedure in communicating with the Russians appears to have been an operational necessity. Any modification of this communication should be made by Eisenhower and not by the CCS. The course of action outlined in SCAEF plan appears to be in accord with agreed strategy and SCAEF's directive, particularly in light of present developments. Eisenhower is deploying across the Rhine in the north the maximum number of forces which can be employed. The secondary effort in the south is achieving an outstanding success and is being exploited to the extent of logistic capabilities. The U.S. Chiefs are confident that SCAEF's course of action will secure the ports and everything else mentioned by the British more quickly and more decisively than the course of action urged by them.

The battle of Germany is now at a point where it is up to the Field Commander to judge the measures which should be taken. To deliberately turn away from the exploitation of the enemy's weakness does not appear sound. The single objective should be quick and complete victory. While recognizing there are factors not of direct concern to SCAEF, the U.S. Chiefs consider his strategic concept is sound and should receive full support. He should continue to communicate freely with the Commander in Chief of the Soviet Army.[11]

But the wily Prime Minister did not confine his persuasive efforts to government level. On the same day that Marshall was writing to Eisenhower, Churchill was penning his own view:

[11] This message described by General Marshall was considered by Brooke as "rather rude."

31 March 1945

Prime Minister to General Eisenhower

Very many thanks. It seems to me personally that if the enemy's resistance does not collapse, the shifting of the main axis of advance so much farther to the southward and the withdrawal of the Ninth U.S. Army from the Twenty-first Army Group may stretch Montgomery's front so widely that the offensive role which was assigned to him may peter out. I do not know why it would be an advantage not to cross the Elbe. If the enemy's resistance should weaken, as you evidently expect, and which may well be fulfilled, why should we not cross the Elbe and advance as far eastward as possible? This has an important political bearing, as the Russian armies of the South seem certain to enter Vienna and overrun Austria. If we deliberately leave Berlin to them, even if it should be in our grasp, the double event may strengthen their conviction, already apparent, that they have done everything.

2. Further, I do not consider myself that Berlin has yet lost its military and certainly not its political significance. The fall of Berlin would have a profound psychological effect on German resistance in every part of the Reich. While Berlin holds out, great masses of Germans will feel it their duty to go down fighting. The idea that the capture of Dresden and junction with the Russians there would be a superior gain does not commend itself to me. The parts of the German Government departments which have moved south can very quickly move southward again. But while Berlin remains under the German flag it cannot, in my opinion, fail to be the most decisive point in Germany. . . .

The next day the Prime Minister communicated with President Roosevelt. He was distressed, he wrote, that it should be thought that he wished in the slightest degree to discredit the Supreme Commander. Having expressed complete confidence in General Eisenhower, he repeated his strategic arguments, stressing that should the Russians take Berlin, they might be under the impression that they had been the overwhelming contributor to the common victory, an illusion that could bode grave and formidable difficulties for the future.

After one more exchange with Eisenhower, however, Churchill dropped the matter graciously. On April 5—four days after the Ruhr Pocket had been closed and Allied forces were dashing eastward—he sent Roosevelt the final message:

I still think it was a pity that Eisenhower's telegram was sent to Stalin without anything being said to our Chiefs of Staff or to our Deputy, Air Chief Marshal Tedder, or to our Commander-in-Chief, Field-Marshal Montgomery. The changes in the main plan have now turned out to be very much less than we had first supposed. My personal relations with General Eisenhower are of the most friendly character. I regard the matter as closed, and to prove my sincerity I will use one of my very few Latin quotations: *Amantium irae amoris integratio est.*

General Marshall was kind enough to translate this last sentence in a message to Eisenhower—"Lovers' quarrels are a part of love."

For all practical purposes, the issue was settled. Eisenhower's attitude regarding the precedence of political and military considerations, however, was summarized in a message two days later to the Combined Chiefs:

> I regard it as militarily unsound at this stage of the proceedings to make Berlin a major objective, particularly in view of the fact that it is only 35 miles from the Russian lines. *I am the first to admit that a war is waged in pursuance of political aims, and if the Combined Chiefs of Staff should decide that the Allied effort to take Berlin outweighs purely military considerations in this theater, I would cheerfully readjust my plans and my thinking so as to carry out such an operation.*[12]

Eisenhower knew that the views of the U.S. Chiefs generally paralleled his own. He did not know that the U.S. political leader was now near death in Warm Springs, Georgia.

After the war, conflicts of interest developed between the West and East that remain today. Accordingly, the feeling has arisen years later that military considerations in the spring of 1945 were of small importance. This is hardly the case. The German Heer, while shattered in the west, still possessed forces capable of fighting. Furthermore, intelligence reports suggested the Nazis were going to make a desperate stand in the so-called National Redoubt in the Alps. Any such resistance by fanatical troops might have required many months to clear out.

Even more important from a military viewpoint was the avoidance of clashes between friendly forces, Western and Soviet. Had General Simpson been permitted to send three or four divisions into Berlin when he reached the Elbe on April 15, they would have found themselves in the path of the 22 divisions and 2,000 guns with which the Russians pulverized the city, stone by stone. And there is no assurance that the American forces would have gotten past the outskirts of Berlin. The forces that did penetrate the city would have made little contribution—and would have run the risk of heavy losses or, tragically, a battle between Allied troops.

But even political considerations in the matter of Berlin are open to question. At Yalta Mr. Churchill apparently experienced a renewal of his suspicions—suspicions that he had harbored in the thirties—of Communism.

Yet even at Yalta Churchill had agreed to a scheme of German occupation that in the end required the Allies to turn over to the Russians much of the territory captured by the American forces in the last days of the campaign (see map, p. 450).

[12] Italics supplied.

Since the Western Allies were obviously prepared to keep faith with the Soviets, today's map of Germany, Poland, and the U.S.S.R. would not have been affected one iota by an advance beyond the Elbe.

A contributing factor to the tempo of the correspondence that flew between Washington, London, and SHAEF in the spring of 1945 was the historic difference in policy regarding what degree of control should be exercised by the home government over commanders in the field. The British, accustomed to employing small units all over the globe, through the ages have been accustomed to sending detailed instructions from Whitehall to commanders of military expeditions. Montgomery, for example, as senior British commander, was required to submit far more detailed reports to London than General Eisenhower, as Supreme Commander or as U.S. Theater Commander, ever sent to Washington.

But another consideration undoubtedly was a desire on the part of the British Government to retain as much control as possible over the strategic conduct of operations. With British forces being directed by Eisenhower, a supreme commander who was American and could be expected to think like an American, no matter how dedicated he might be to the Allied cause, it

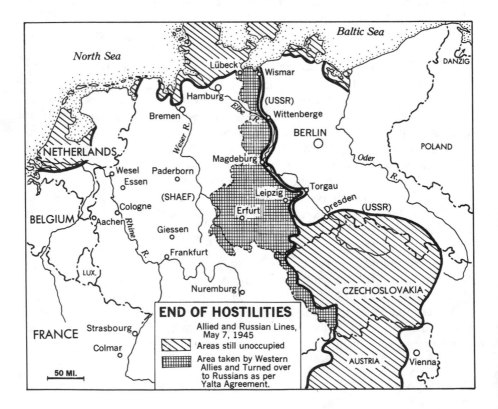

was only natural that the British chiefs favored maximum centralized supervision—in which both nations would have equal say. The Americans, on the other hand, abhorred interfering in a field commander's plans. If a commander was doing well, the American inclination—and especially Marshall's—was to leave him alone as much as possible.

At the government level, the staunchness of two men shines through the documents. One of these was General Marshall, whose support of the Supreme Commander never failed, no matter what the pressure. The other, Prime Minister Churchill, argued long and eloquently to support his often differing views, but his disagreements never descended to a personal level. His support, once decisions were made—even when they opposed his own position—was absolute.

On April 1, 1945, the 3d U.S. Armored Division, spearheading Collins' VII Corps, finally made contact with its sister of the Ardennes, the 2d Armored, spearheading XIX Corps of Ninth Army. The meeting place was Lippstadt. The so-called German main effort, launched over the Rhine at Wesel, had covered a distance of 75 miles. The much-questioned "secondary" effort had advanced 150, although against somewhat less resistance.

Walther Model's Army Group B, with its 325,000 German soldiers, was now surrounded in the Ruhr by the Ninth Army on the north, First Army on the south and east, and Fifteenth Army across the Rhine. (This new Fifteenth U.S. Army was commanded by Lieutenant General L. T. Gerow, whose V Corps had held on the critical Elsenborn Ridge.)

As of that same date other spearheads were beginning the exploitation of the collapsed German front. The Canadian First Army was squeezing Blaskowitz's Army Group H in Holland toward the Ijssel River. Second British Army was developing a bridgehead across the Ems River, driving northwest. Portions of the First and Ninth U.S. armies were proceeding eastward. Third U.S. Army, once more in the hell-for-leather role that Patton relished, was approaching the Thuringian Forest on the east. Patch's Seventh U.S. Army, farther south, having executed the most difficult of all the Rhine crossings, had traveled 75 miles to Würzburg, on the Main River. De Lattre's First French Army was headed southward toward Karlsruhe and Baden-Baden.

The description of the rest of the campaign resembles a geography lesson of Central Germany. Within the Ruhr, an area originally comprising some 4,000 square miles, Model still had supplies for approximately three weeks, provided he could avoid a major battle. Ordered by Hitler to avoid further withdrawals and to destroy the Ruhr's industrial and communications facilities, he tried to hold his lines, but he intentionally disobeyed the order for mass destruction.

General Eisenhower meanwhile adhered to his basic strategy. Carrying the main effort was 12 Army Group, nearing the line of the Elbe and Mulde rivers. On April 11, XIII Corps of Simpson's Ninth Army reached the Elbe River in the vicinity of Wittenberge. Almost immediately Simpson threw two bridgeheads across the river, the northern held by 2d Armored Division and the southern by the 83d Infantry. The northern bridgehead was eliminated by German counterattack—an experience new for the 2d Armored Division—but the bridgehead in the 83d's area was able to hold. Despite the great Allied advances, the Germans still had units capable of fighting.

The day after Simpson closed on the Elbe, Generals Eisenhower, Bradley, and Patton made a tour of the battle areas, inspecting the caches of gold hidden in a cave by the Germans and, to their horror and revulsion, inspecting a Nazi concentration camp near Gotha. General Patton was in bed that evening when he turned on the radio and was jolted to hear that President Roosevelt had died. He notified the two others, and the three friends sat around talking somberly until two o'clock in the morning.

Meanwhile attacks were continuing to reduce the Ruhr Pocket. On April 14 a spectacular assault by XVI Corps on the north and XVIII Airborne Corps on the south met at Hagen, south of the Ruhr River, thus splitting the pocket in two. Four days later, April 18, all resistance ended in that area. The largest mass surrender of German troops up to that time in the war was taken, 317,000 men.

Field Marshal Walther Model died by his own hand rather than surrender.

The last great Soviet offensive of the war was launched on April 16 all along the front. The Soviet masses quickly surrounded Berlin, from which most of the Nazi Government had fled. Hitler himself decided that he would stay and die in the beleaguered city. But when Göring, who had escaped and considered himself successor to the Führer, interpreted Hitler's move as an abdication, the once proud head of the Luftwaffe was stripped of all his positions and powers.

Having closed on the Elbe, Eisenhower now concentrated his efforts in drives to the north and south; the last resistance to his rear, a rather sizable pocket in the Harz Mountains, held by the makeshift Eleventh German Army, was reduced on April 21. By this time Montgomery's 21 Army Group had reached the Elbe on the north, and Patton's Third U.S. Army had turned south to take over part of Patch's Seventh territory, cut off the "Redoubt," and drive as far as possible into Austria, where, in contrast to Germany, no zones of occupation had been designated. Eisenhower informed the Russians that he intended to go as far to the east as Linz—the birthplace, incidentally, of Adolf Hitler.

The Canadian First Army, having cut off German forces under Blaskowitz in Holland, held up further offensive actions in that area to avoid inflicting additional suffering on the Dutch people. Arrangements were made with the Nazi high commissioner, Dr. Arthur Seyss-Inquart, for feeding the population; in exchange for the promise to conduct no more military operations in the area, Seyss-Inquart agreed not to flood the land any further.

Although the Germans still could put up fierce resistance in such cities as Nuremberg, by now the problem was largely administrative and political. Traffic jams held up the vehicles of the driving armies, while the handling of thousands of wandering displaced persons and German refugees became overwhelming. In Stuttgart the French forces occupied the city against the orders of General Devers; apparently feeling their prestige at stake, they remained in the town until pressure from both General Eisenhower and President Truman persuaded them to leave. Eisenhower had to threaten de Gaulle once again that, failing compliance with SHAEF's orders, he would notify the Combined Chiefs that SHAEF "could no longer count with certainty on the operational use of any French forces they might be contemplating equipping in the future." [13]

On April 25 a patrol of the 69th Infantry Division of V Corps crossed the Mulde River and traveled some 20 miles to the Elbe. Here, at Targau near the site of one of Frederick II's great battles, the first contact took place between the Western Allies and the Russian forces.

In Czechoslovakia it appeared that Patton's Third Army, as of April 25, could drive past the Sudetenland, where General Eisenhower had previously announced his intentions to halt, and move on toward Prague. Eisenhower communicated with the chief of staff of the Russian Army, who implored him to hold on the previously understood line of Budjovice-Pilsen-Karlsbad. Eisenhower complied, and large numbers of German troops remained stranded in Bohemia for some time after hostilities ceased.

On April 30, in a bunker in the city of Berlin, Adolf Hitler shared a seemingly routine lunch with a few associates. After lunch Hitler issued some instructions to one of those present and then accompanied Eva Braun, his mistress of twelve years and bride of a day, into the next room. They were never again seen alive.[14]

The bodies reportedly were carried into the courtyard and incinerated in gallons upon gallons of flaming gasoline, as Hitler had specified; those charged

---

[13] Eisenhower, *op. cit.*, p. 413.

[14] The cause of Hitler's death has been variously attributed to self-inflicted pistol shots, poison, and a combination of both. A recently released Russian publication claims that death resulted from cyanide poisoning, followed by a pistol *coup-de-grâce*.

with the grisly task of cremation were forced to take refuge in the bunker from time to time to avoid the heavy concentrations of Russian artillery.

That same day Grossadmiral Karl Dönitz, a professional sailor with no political ambitions, was informed by telegram from Martin Bormann that, a day before, he had been designated Hitler's successor as head of the German State. This was hardly a happy message for Dönitz, but as a military man he was resolved to do his duty to his beloved Reich and try to achieve the best possible terms in closing the war.

Dönitz himself notified the powerful Heinrich Himmler of his appointment, not sure whether he would be immediately arrested by Himmler's SS guards. Strangely enough, even under these bewildering circumstances, Himmler thirsted after the position of head of the German Government. But upon being told by Dönitz that no place existed for him in the fading German Government, to Dönitz's surprise Himmler merely walked away dejectedly.

The one dramatic military move yet to be completed was Montgomery's final drive to Lübeck. Though the province of Schleswig-Holstein had been designated British occupation territory in the agreements at Yalta, the Western Allies were in no mood to test the good faith of the Soviets by allowing the Red armies to overrun this territory. Accordingly, in the last days of April, General Eisenhower attached Matthew Ridgway's XVIII Airborne Corps to Montgomery to bolster the drive in this direction. By May 2, 1945, Ridgway had reached Wismar, only twelve hours before the Russians arrived. Lübeck, a port harboring Nazi submarines throughout the war, had been seized by the 11th Armoured Division of the British VIII Corps the day before. On May 4, forces from the European theater, crossing the Alps at Innsbruck, met the 88th U.S. Infantry Division of Fifth Army coming up from Italy at Vipiteno.

The war was now over except for the surrender negotiations. Dönitz's objective was to prolong the war as long as he could to enable as many prisoners as possible to be taken by the Western Allies rather than by the Russians. On May 5, denied requested permission to surrender to the Western Allies, German Generaladmiral Hans-Georg von Friedeburg signed the surrender of all Nazi troops in northwest Germany, Holland, Schleswig-Holstein, and Denmark to Field Marshal Montgomery.

The Prime Minister was elated. He cabled to his foreign minister, Sir Anthony Eden, who was in San Franciso for the United Nations Conference:

> In the north Eisenhower threw in an American corps with great dexterity to help Montgomery in his advance on Lübeck. He got there with twelve hours to spare. There were reports from the British Naval Attaché at Stockholm, which we are testing, that, according to Swedish information, the Russians have dropped parachutists a few miles south of Copenhagen and that

Communist activities have appeared there. It now appears there were only two parachutists. We are sending in a moderate holding force to Copenhagen by air, and the rest of Denmark is being rapidly occupied from henceforward by our fast-moving armoured columns. I think therefore, having regard to the joyous feeling of the Danes and the abject submission and would-be partisanship of the surrendered Huns, we shall head our Soviet friends off at this point too.

You will by now have heard the news of the tremendous surrender that has been made to Montgomery of all Northwest Germany, Holland, and Denmark, both as regards men and ships. The men alone must be more than a million. Thus in three successive days 2,500,000 Germans have surrendered to our British commanders. This is quite a satisfactory incident in our military history. Ike has been splendid throughout. We must vie with him in sportsmanship.

On that same day German Army Group G surrendered to General Devers.

Admiral Friedeburg proceeded to General Eisenhower's headquarters at Reims, where on May 6 he was joined by General Jodl. Stalling for time on the surrender, the Germans' situation became more and more difficult. Anticipating such a move, Eisenhower had previously arranged for a high-ranking Russian officer, Major General Ivan Susloparov, to be present at the surrender ceremonies.

Bitter at the Nazis on many counts, not the least of which he considered an unnecessary prolongation of the war, Eisenhower refused to negotiate with Friedeburg and Jodl personally. Finally, communicating through Bedell Smith, Eisenhower issued an ultimatum. The unconditional surrender of German armed forces would include all German units everywhere and would be a surrender to all the powers involved.

Furthermore, to stop Jodl's playing for time, Eisenhower told Smith that he intended to close the entire Allied front. He would, by force, prevent any more German refugees from entering Western lines. This would take place in forty-eight hours, whether the surrender was signed or not.

Jodl and Friedeburg, seeing that the situation was hopeless, obtained permission from Dönitz to surrender, and the document was signed in the early hours of May 7 with hostilities due to cease at midnight, May 8.

General Eisenhower was sitting in his office awaiting the outcome of the surrender negotiations. Past the desk of his secretary and into the office came the Nazis, erect and cold. Eisenhower stood up. Rigid, and fixing a cold eye on his enemies, he demanded, "Do you understand all the provisions of the document you have just signed?"

"*Ja!*"

"You will, officially and personally, be held responsible if the terms of this surrender are violated, including its provision for German commanders to appear in Berlin at the moment set by the Russian High Command, to accomplish formal surrender to that government. That is all."

The Nazis saluted and left, and Eisenhower relaxed. A few minutes later he sent a message to the Combined Chiefs of Staff:

"The Mission of this Allied Force was fulfilled at 0241, local time, May 7th, 1945, Eisenhower."

CHAPTER 19

✺⟞⟝✺

The Final Analysis

THE Ardennes campaign of 1944–45 was only one in a series of difficult engagements in the battle for Europe. The landings in Normandy, Operations Cobra and Anvil, the capture of Aachen, the Rhineland campaign, and the overrunning of Germany all required Herculean efforts from troops and commanders alike. Nevertheless, it can be said that the Ardennes campaign epitomized them all. For it was here that American and German combat soldiers met in the decisive struggle that broke the back of the Nazi war machine.

The Ardennes campaign *was* unique in one respect: it was the only time after the Normandy invasion that the Germans held the overall initiative on the western front. That the Germans had successfully surprised the American forces when Allied optimism was so high caused a severe crisis in Allied confidence. The strain on the High Command caused by profound criticism and dismay threatened to disrupt the team General Eisenhower and others had striven so long and so hard to build.

The Ardennes campaign, therefore, became the supreme test of the Western coalition.

There have been two main criticisms of Allied dispositions as they stood in mid-December, 1944. The first can be dismissed almost summarily. In his memoirs, published in 1958, Field Marshal Montgomery claimed that the strategy he proposed in September would have won the war outright during the autumn, thus entirely preventing the Battle of the Ardennes. This is conjecture in the extreme. Most of the officers, American and British, engaged in the campaign disagreed with him.

A far more common criticism of Allied dispositions centers on the U.S. VIII Corps, spread out over a distance of 88 miles and manned by only some 70,000 men. The reason for the thinness of this line lay principally in the nature of the terrain.

No remunerative terrain objective existed in the VIII Corps sector short of the Meuse River—indeed, the French and Belgians in times past had rarely regarded the Ardennes as anything but an outpost line for the real defensive line of the Meuse. General Bradley purposely left nearly all important logistical installations to the west and north of the area. By the same token, the German Eifel, an eastern extension of the Ardennes, held little by way of valuable objectives to the Americans. It seemed almost as though the two antagonists had a tacit agreement to neglect the Ardennes front held by VIII Corps.

The situation boiled down to a basic premise, supported by all Allied commanders, that the Germans should be allowed no respite during the winter of 1944–45. Since it was impossible to attack in full strength on all fronts, the Allies were forced to lessen some part of the line so as to secure enough strength for the main effort north of the Ardennes and for the secondary effort into the Saar. The High Command chose the Ardennes area.

Neither General Eisenhower nor General Bradley have given any apology for the decision to continue the attack through the winter, which necessitated the thinly held Ardennes line. Both commanders support the basic decision with alacrity, in their memoirs and in personal interviews. Either would have accepted the blame had he considered the dispositions incorrect in retrospect, but there is no hint that they would dispose the VIII Corps otherwise, given a second chance.

It is not difficult to understand Hitler's frame of mind during the fall and early winter of 1944. A passionate advocate of the offensive as the only way to win a war, he had succeeded in traversing this territory once before—against the French in May of 1940. The 1940 offensive was executed over the objections of many of his professional military leaders yet culminated in an overwhelming defeat for the Anglo-French forces, which understandably strengthened his determination to make the gamble again.

Hitler's most grievous error was dreaming that the German troops, leadership, and supply situation were in any way comparable to those of 1940. Five years of warfare had taken a grim toll of the Wehrmacht, particularly in trained leaders and trained pilots. In 1940 the Stuka dive bomber and the panzer formation together constituted a terrifying team when pitted against the relatively immobile French and British armies. In 1944, on the other hand, Hitler was forced to depend on bad weather to neutralize the effects of Allied air and ground superiority, and many of his combat formations were now of inferior quality. The panzer divisions were less weak than the rest of the German forces—the four crack SS divisions available to Sepp Dietrich were of excellent quality. However, the new volksgrenadier divisions were made up largely of ill-trained men transferred from the Luftwaffe and the Kriegsmarine, and their officers were less experienced than those who led the German infantry in better days. (This probably accounts for the reckless way in which elements of the German 3d Parachute Division marched blithely down the road to Hünningen on December 16, only to be cut down by fire from the men of the 394th Infantry.)

Probably Hitler miscalculated most on the availability of supplies and fuel. Jochen Peiper later claimed that little was said by his superiors about fueling his panzers from Allied gasoline dumps, though he himself knew perfectly well that this would be necessary. The gasoline that was promised in the forward areas was held too long on the east side of the Rhine, and the fuel needed for the offensive—Manteuffel's estimate was five units of gasoline— was simply not forthcoming.

Hitler's senior commanders, at least those below the level of OKW, were well aware of the deficiencies in the strength of the Wehrmacht and in supply. Rundstedt, an aging man but a military realist, felt he could all but disassociate himself from the campaign. Acting more constructively the German field commanders, apparently with Model in the vanguard, made a counterproposal suggesting a far more realistic employment of German reserves than Hitler's so-called "grand slam," which insisted on a drive all the way to Antwerp. Their "little slam," which visualized cutting behind the rear of the First U.S. Army and driving northward east of the Meuse, might very well have been successful. The penetration through the Losheim Gap did in fact expose the rear of the 2d and 99th divisions on December 16 and 17, and so it seems reasonable to believe that the German panzer reserves would have caused far more damage to the Allied armies by executing the "little slam" than by trying to drive westward.

Of course, U.S. First Army's Courtney Hodges always had in his mind the possibility of his rear's being decimated, and if the German Fifteenth Army on the north had made an iron pincers to nip off a sizable hunk of First Army, they would have made a considerable contribution to the "little slam."

Quite probably Hitler would have best employed the strong reserve he had miraculously assembled by counterattacking as American forces fought to secure a bridgehead across the Roer River. The American Command almost unanimously considered this Model's most logical move, and since Rundstedt, a respected military brain, was nominally Commander in Chief West, the Allies believed that the German reserves would be thus employed.

Hitler's ambitious aim, the seizure of Antwerp, never stood a chance of success. A more limited objective might have wrought great havoc, but it, too, probably would have resulted in the ultimate destruction of the German forces.

Though the Ardennes counteroffensive fell far short of its objective, there is no question that it managed to score some spectacular gains. The distance from Dasburg on the Our River to Celles traveled by Lüttwitz's 47th Panzer Korps is more than 50 miles by air, much farther by road. Advances of this magnitude are enough to disturb any army, particularly one flushed with success like the Allied Army and shocked by an enemy attack of undreamed-of strength.

Therein lies one secret of the early German successes. It was partly luck that brought Hitler his wished-for surprise effect; the six days of bad flying weather that he had "intuitively" predicted did actually come. Perhaps the percentages were on his side at this time of year, but it is safe to say that if the break in good flying weather which occurred on December 23 had come on the sixteenth, the offensive would have died on a line much farther east than it actually reached.

But the competence of the German higher leadership cannot be overlooked. In Rundstedt, Model, Manteuffel, Lüttwitz, and Krüger, Hitler had leaders who, with varying degrees of loyalty to his own person, were dedicated to the cause of Germany and her armies. Honed to a fine edge by bitter experience on the eastern front, they were experts at winter warfare, and knew its devices for deceiving the enemy and how to survive in the bitter snows of Northern Europe. In Manteuffel and Lüttwitz, Model had two aggressive panzer leaders of the first caliber. Even Sepp Dietrich, much maligned by the aristocratic German military hierarchy, had some understanding of tactics; while undoubtedly unfit for the command of an army executing the main effort of a great offensive, he was not so unfit as some of his arrogant colleagues suggest. Dietrich was unswervingly loyal to Hitler and to the Nazi cause.

The failure of the Sixth Panzer Army to secure noteworthy gains lies less in Dietrich's performance than in Hitler's decision to send his crack panzers through the miserable swamps and forests of the Hohe Venne, held in strength by the U. S. V Corps.

There is no gainsaying that Allied intelligence failed regarding German intentions in the Ardennes; despite all the claims made by individual intelligence officers, there is little to support the contention that the Allied High Command was adequately warned. And yet commanders are not accustomed to predictions couched in absolute terms. There are always so many possible courses of action open to an enemy—and so few positive indications of which course the enemy will select—that intelligence people tend to make their estimates only in terms of relative probabilities. Commanders normally find it necessary to take the advice of their G-2's with a grain of salt.

It had been said that the overall psychology of the Western Allies was so geared to the offensive and so firmly expecting a German collapse that they could not imagine the possibility of a great German offensive. This is partially true. While the Americans admitted the possibility of a German attack in the Ardennes—and while General Bradley and General Eisenhower delineated almost the exact line that the German offensive would reach—there still is no question that both commanders were surprised at the amount of strength the Germans were able to accumulate.

Part of this intelligence failure can be laid to the use of Allied air reconnaissance. Uncertain flying weather limited reconnaissance missions to those of top priority, and those missions that could be flown were directed largely toward the area of Cologne rather than the Eifel; German units picked up in the Eifel were thought to be stopping off on their journey between the Cologne Plain and the Saar.

There is little more to be said about the Allied befuddlement. It stands as a monument to the cleverness of the German plans, to luck on Hitler's part, and to Allied unwillingness to believe in the possibility of a large-scale German attack.

However, a related question presents itself: Suppose an omniscient intelligence officer had advised General Eisenhower on December 14 or 15 that an attack by some 20 divisions on December 16 was a certainty. What could Eisenhower, Bradley, and Hodges have done to deal with the situation? Would such measures as could have been effected have denied the initial successes of the German offensive?

One measure that could have been taken was to stop the 2d Division's attack toward the Roer River dams, withdrawing it through the lines of the 99th Division and placing both divisions on Elsenborn Ridge. Another was withdrawing the 422d and 423d regiments of the 106th Division from their exposed positions on the Schnee Eifel; in a tactical position on the high ground to the east, protecting St.-Vith, these regiments would have formed a more formidable obstacle. Moving the 7th Armored Division south from Holland and the 10th Armored Division from Third Army could have begun a couple of days earlier.[1] There seems less that could have been done to help the spread-out 28th Division to the south.

None of these measures could have prevented a penetration.

Basically, the ultimate reason for the failure of the German offensive was Hitler's unrealistic estimate of his capabilities vis-à-vis that of the Allies. But other factors contributed. One, of which he was fully aware, was the effectiveness of Allied air power. (The Allies came ashore in Normandy with fewer divisions in the United Kingdom than Rommel and Rundstedt had in Western France; all the Allied hopes were pinned on the ground-air team, with the air forces denying the Germans daytime mobility.) As Lüttwitz has ruefully admitted since the war, even if the Fifth Panzer Army had succeeded in crossing the Meuse at Dinant, the Allied air superiority over the Luftwaffe would have told eventually, and the German offensive bogged down.

Less predictable, from the German viewpoint, was the speed of the U.S. forces' reaction. Hitler believed that the Supreme Allied Commander would

---

[1] General Bradley is quite positive on this subject, claiming that if we had doubled the number of U.S. divisions located in the Ardennes area at the time of the German attack, the Americans would undoubtedly have slowed down the speed of the attack and limited the extent of its penetration; however, in so doing probably we would have suffered heavier casualties than we did.

be as fettered as Rundstedt, his OB West; that Eisenhower would have to obtain permission from the heads of the two Allied governments to call off Patton's attack into the Saar.

The fact of the matter is that the very night the counteroffensive was launched, Eisenhower suggested to Bradley that 7th Armored Division be moved to the Ardennes from the north and the 10th Armored Division from the south. As we have seen, these two divisions, the 7th Armored at St.-Vith and the 10th Armored at the southern shoulder and Bastogne, proved critical in stemming the German tide. Patton's attack in the Saar was canceled two days after the German offensive was begun, and by the seventeenth, one day after Model's Army Group had launched its attack, the SHAEF reserve, consisting of the 82d and 101st Airborne divisions, were both released to 12 Army Group, to be committed to the critical areas of Werbomont and Bastogne. By the evening of the nineteenth, when Eisenhower decided to split the command between north and south, the Third U.S. Army and First U.S. Army had already begun moving half a million troops toward the Bulge area under General Bradley's command.

A final factor in the defeat of the German Ardennes offensive was the unexpected resourcefulness of the American soldier. His casual deportment, disregard for proper uniform, and general indifference to the outward manifestation of military discipline led the German High Command—this was not confined to Hitler alone—to underestimate him as a fighter. But the American proved to be unusually adept at "going into business for himself," and it was at places such as Trois Ponts, Chevron, Wiltz, and Hotton that the German timetable was upset. Without question his valor and competence under adverse conditions were totally unexpected by Hitler and OKW.

Since the war a certain rivalry has arisen between the American defenders of St.-Vith and those of Bastogne regarding the relative importance of the two actions in frustrating Hitler's offensive. The heroic defenders of St.-Vith have felt that since they were spared the dramatic experience of being surrounded, the action at Bastogne has become associated in the layman's mind with the entire Battle of the Bulge—at their expense. This is partly true. Bastogne has indeed become something of a symbol of the Ardennes battle, not only because of the esprit and heroism of the men of the 101st Airborne Division but also because of the personality of General Anthony McAuliffe and the dramatic relief by the 4th Armored Division of Patton's Third Army. The self-imposed sobriquet Battered Bastards of Bastogne helped make the Bastogne action more newsworthy.

And yet the man who commanded the German forces along both fronts, General der Panzertruppen Hasso von Manteuffel, seems to agree with the protagonists of St.-Vith. "You don't surround and bypass an armored division," he is reported to have said since the war. The retention of St.-Vith by the Americans put the squeeze on the 1st SS Panzer Division supply and resulted in the demise of Kampfgruppe Peiper.

As a matter of fact, there were *five* main pillars upon which the defense against the German counteroffensive was built. Naming them from north to south, the first was the northern shoulder along the Elsenborn Ridge, where the 2d, 99th, 1st, and 9th Infantry divisions fought the Sixth Panzer Army to a standstill. The second was the "fortified goose egg," of which St.-Vith was the easternmost point. The third was Bastogne, and the fourth the southern shoulder around Echternach, held by the 4th Infantry Division with elements of the 9th Armored, 10th Armored, and a regiment of the 28th Infantry Division. The action around Marche, to the west, constituted the fifth.

In these pages, the northern and southern shoulders of the Bulge perhaps have been given less space and have been described in less detail than they undoubtedly deserve—simply because they were defensive actions, where the lines buckled, where cooks and bakers and clerks were thrown in the battle, where men fought for dear life, but where the lines generally held. This should not cloud the fact that holding the Elsenborn Ridge and the southern shoulder near Echternach were elements of the defense as vital as the defenses of St.-Vith, Bastogne, and Marche.

To think of the Bulge in terms of Bastogne and St.-Vith only is a drastic oversimplification that does a disservice to the heroic efforts of the men of the 28th Division, who by holding out in such towns as Vianden, Clerf, and Wiltz, delayed Lüttwitz's drive on Bastogne and enabled the men of the 101st Airborne to reach it before the Panzer Lehr spearheads arrived. It denigrates the actions of such units as the I & R Platoon of the 394th Infantry, that held the German assaults for hours on December 16. It does less than justice to Company C of the 51st Engineer Battalion at Trois Ponts; to the unsung squad who blew the bridge at Chevron; to Major Hal McCown's 2d Battalion, 119th Infantry, which stopped Peiper the night of the eighteenth; to CCA of the 3d Armored Division and the rest of the 119th Infantry that closed in on Peiper in Stoumont and La Gleize; to the heroic defenders of Hotton; to the engineers and headquarters troops from CCR of the 3d Armored; to the defenders of Rochefort—small groups of men who took the initiative in their own hands and fought independently against overwhelming odds. These men certainly deserve their full place in history.

General Eisenhower's decision on the night of December 19 to split the area of the Ardennes penetration between 21 Army Group and 12 Army Group is a move that has caused considerable comment in the ensuing years.

The split seemed totally logical at the time, and it remains so even under scrutiny by the most partisan admirers of General Bradley.

The main disadvantage of this action stemmed from the fact that Field Marshal Montgomery, though a great soldier, was and is a difficult personality. His increased sense of personal prestige that came with his handling of the northern shoulder of the Bulge caused him to renew his agitation for the appointment of an overall ground commander—a position that he obviously coveted himself—while insisting on continuing to command his own army group. This, as we have seen, led to a crisis that was the closest Hitler came to his objective: a breakup in the Allied team.

Even after the Supreme Commander had resolved to make a do-or-die issue of the matter in late December—and after General Francis de Guingand had headed off the rift in the nick of time—Field Marshal Montgomery poured salt in Bradley's wounds with his unfortunate press conference of January 7. Eisenhower has since stated that had he been able to foresee the explosive personality conflict engendered by this action, he probably would have looked for another solution—perhaps placing Hodges in temporary command of the First and Ninth armies as *ad hoc* army group commander.

It was an unfortunate situation all around, for most of the commanders who served on the northern shoulder of the Bulge under Montgomery view his performance with respect. General Collins, who on December 24 assumed the responsibility for violating some of the spirit of Montgomery's directives, has since stated that the split in command was logical and that Montgomery was the man for the job in the north. Generals Hasbrouck and Clarke have shown admiration for Montgomery's grasp of the situation in the north and for his decisive action in pulling the 7th Armored Division out of its precarious position after the division had performed all that could possibly be expected of it.

Generals Ridgway and Gavin do not seem quite to share this feeling. Ridgway reportedly resented the Field Marshal's peremptory action in regard to the 7th Armored Division; and Gavin complained of Montgomery's withdrawing the 82d Airborne Division to a shorter line, thus giving up areas the 82d had paid for in blood.

To the observer some of the disagreements appear to lie in the differing philosophies between officers of armored training and officers of airborne training. On conjecture, it would seem that the armored forces regard the importance of holding terrain less vital than do the airborne. This is understandable. The armored forces tend to think of warfare in somewhat naval terms: desert warfare in North Africa was a tanker's dream. The airborne soldier, on the other hand, not only is inculcated with an unusually fierce pride in his own prowess but also, as usually employed, is in no position to give up much ground once he has been dropped into an airhead.

With all these disagreements—viewpoints which will never come together— it must be admitted that Montgomery made a genuine contribution in assisting the organization of the hard-pressed northern line of the Bulge, the primary target of the Germans. Recognizing this, Eisenhower wrote the Field Marshal on January 17: "Thank you again for the way you pitched in to help out during the German thrust. Some day I hope I can show my appreciation in a more lasting manner."

In regard to the timing of the counterattack from the north, it seems quite improbable, despite the complaints of Bradley and Patton, that Montgomery could have attacked much before January 3. While it is convenient to regard December 26 as the high-water mark—indeed the Germans made no appreciable progress from that day on—the fighting continued bitter. The quality of the resistance put up by elements of the Sixth Panzer Army east of the Ourthe River against the VII Corps attack in January indicates that the German forces still had a great deal of fight in them.

In one respect, however, it seems that General Eisenhower's headquarters made a serious error. In its determination to prevent the enemy from learning of the new, temporary command arrangements, Eisenhower's staff said nothing to the press regarding the changeover in command until January 5. If an announcement had been made earlier, by December 26, or at the latest January 1—and had the announcement specified that the changeover in command was *temporary* only—probably a great deal of ill feeling could have been assuaged, particularly among 12 Army Group.

On the other hand, 12 Army Group headquarters seems to have accumulated a number of officers whose devotion to General Bradley and antipathy to Field Marshal Montgomery fogged their vision (the same was true in Patton's Third Army headquarters). Such partisanship on the part of staff officers is not unusual and is normally harmless unless it affects the thinking of the commander himself. If Ralph Ingersoll's account [2] reflects the prevalent attitude among the 12 Army Group staff, then some of Bradley's advisers were certainly performing their chief a disservice.[3]

Fortunately, though sensitive, Bradley was not a prima donna. He thought his public relations problem through and responded with a press statement— his first. For others it would have been a moderate step. For Bradley it was a radical one.

Though the British press responded vituperatively to Bradley's press statement, the matter later died down and the question of command arrangements was, for all practical purposes, put to bed.

Doubtless it would have been better if SHAEF had made the situation clear in the first place. However, the problem was once again the old bugaboo of secrecy versus public information. We have seen in these pages how keeping Patton "under wraps" while he was dashing across France served a useful

[2] Ralph Ingersoll, *Top Secret* (New York: Harcourt, 1946).
[3] In fairness, little of this resentment was apparent when the author visited Eagle Tac, then located in Namur, in February, 1945, shortly after these events occurred.

purpose; how embarrassment was caused by failure to announce before September the ultimate command setup whereby Bradley, as a tactical commander, would become Montgomery's counterpart; how the appointment of Rundstedt as OB West helped to misguide Allied intelligence chiefs regarding the courses of action the Wehrmacht was likely to follow.

The conflict between security and public information is always present in war. In this case one must conclude that secrecy was overemphasized at the expense of the British public's need for information.

A pertinent question is whether the Allied command took full advantage in subsequent campaigns of the opportunities afforded them by Hitler's blunder in coming out of the fixed defenses of the Siegfried Line. The question has two major parts: (a) Was the strategy of mopping up the entire Rhineland before crossing the Rhine in force a sound one? (b) Did the Allies travel as far east as feasible and proper under the circumstances?

The answer to the first part is yes. Occupation of the Rhineland provided the Allies with a strong defensive line that could be held with minimum forces, thus permitting concentration in critical areas. The swiftness and brilliance of the campaign, once it was launched on February 23, culminated in the seizure of the Remagen Bridge on March 7 and a tremendous number of German losses. Again Hitler's policy of refusal to give ground evolved from mere unwisdom to sheer lunacy. There is no question that the war was won west of the Rhine.

Once the Ruhr Pocket was closed on April 1, few German forces stood between the spearheads of the three Western army groups and the line of the Elbe and Mulde rivers. In recent years much discussion with the advantage of hindsight has taken place about the limits SHAEF set on its advance. Very little was said on the subject at the time.

As for the issue and reasoning behind General Eisenhower's decision to make a central drive eastward to the line of the Elbe and Mulde and subsequent offensives to cut off Schleswig-Holstein at Lübeck and seize Austria as far as Linz—which have been discussed in detail in the previous chapter—one cannot examine this question without paying tribute to the foresight and wisdom of Sir Winston Churchill. He was the first of the Western Allied leaders to recognize that international Communism had not really changed its spots, that to the Soviets cooperation with the Western Allies was a temporary expedient only, to be dropped when the time was ripe. One must sympathize with Churchill's plea that the Allies travel as far east as possible and, if feasible, seize Berlin before the Soviet forces had a chance to enter it. But Sir Winston's arguments bear a strong resemblance to the story of tying the bell around the cat's neck. His attitude toward the eastward advance is interesting and illuminating.

Basically a pragmatist, Prime Minister Churchill was a bold and imaginative man. His outstanding asset in leading the British people was the ability sincerely and masterfully to express deep emotion, particularly regarding the role of the British Empire in world history. It would be idle to expect the doughty Churchill to have been satisfied with anything less than maximum military results in the spring of 1945, despite his pessimism a year earlier. When situations change, so do expectations. Though the peoples of democracies are less prone to expect their leaders to be infallible than people living under despotism, we still expect an unreasonably high percentage of right answers, even when the considerations needed to form a judgment are vague or entirely missing.

In the last analysis Sir Winston Churchill will doubtless be known to history more for his courage than for the acuity of all his military judgments. His espousal of the Gallipoli campaign in World War I hardly earns him a place in history; his defiance of the Nazi war machine in the Battle of Britain in 1940 will make him immortal.

When discussing the feasibility of an attack on Berlin, Churchill's emotional investment in the war, nurtured through five years of bitter struggle at the helm of the British Empire, superseded hardheaded reality. His elation at Germany's impending defeat seems to have marred his military judgment. Even Montgomery, who has a history of disagreement with the policies of the Americans in general and of the Supreme Commander in particular, agrees that an effort on the part of the Western Allies to take Berlin in the spring of 1945 would have been foolish.[4]

It is generally assumed by those who criticize the decision to stop at the Elbe River that taking Berlin would have been an easy matter and that, had the Western Allies done so, today's situation in Europe would be different. For the most part these critics give inadequate weight to the hard problems that the conduct of military operations presents, particularly on the logistical end. They seem to assume that the Soviets, who had become so arrogant that strategy now had to be dictated by political purposes directed against them rather than against the Germans, would stand idly by in overpowering strength at a distance of 35 miles and allow a rather small U.S. force—two to four divisions, say—to move in and occupy the city. It is difficult to believe with the critics that, faced with the Western Allied demand for "unconditional surrender," Hitler would open the gates of his capital city, where he was making his last stand, and invite the Americans in. These assumptions are sheer nonsense.

The fact of the matter is that General Eisenhower had his own share of healthy suspicion of the Russians. Though he had not seen the Soviets' attitude at Yalta, he had had unpleasant personal experiences with the Soviet military while he was chief of Operations Division in Washington under General

[4] Interview with Montgomery by author, October 1, 1966.

Marshall before going to Europe. His suspicions were based not so much on political study of international Communism as on the truculence of individual Russian officers with whom he had come in contact. Basically, he continued to regard the Russians as allies, albeit difficult ones; this was the U.S. political policy at the time, held by the Joint Chiefs of Staff and by President Roosevelt.

General Eisenhower's main concern, therefore, was to occupy a strong military defensive line whereby risk of unfortunate incidents would be minimized, and where, if incidents did occur, Allied forces would hold the advantage. He knew that in any case established political agreements (with which Churchill himself had concurred) would return to the Soviets much of the territory the Western Allies took on the way to the Elbe, as well as any territory taken to the east of the Elbe on the way to Berlin.[5]

Eisenhower felt that to fight a political war *without instructions from his government to do so* would violate the principle of subordinating the military to the political powers in government. It is interesting to speculate—although the answers can never be known—how President Roosevelt, if he had been alive and in good health, would have reacted to Churchill's entreaties to exercise political supervision over the last stages of the European campaign. To do so would mean to direct Eisenhower, through the CCS, to switch emphasis from the swift final defeat of Hitler to political maneuvers designed to thwart the Russians. Such an action on Roosevelt's part, of course, would have been inconsistent with his former attitudes. His backing of the Supreme Commander (through the Joint Chiefs) had been absolute ever since the Normandy landings and manifested itself clearly when Churchill was pleading for a reevaluation of European strategy in late 1944.

The issue at stake during the autumn, however, was a military one. In the spring of 1945, Churchill's vaunted power of persuasion, it can be surmised, would have had a better chance to reassert itself with the issue now one of political versus military considerations. And yet such prospects still seem remote. In view of Roosevelt's attitude toward the Russians throughout the war —and particularly at Yalta—it is logical to conclude that he would have continued to regard Hitler rather than Stalin as the overriding target of military operations.

The debate will probably continue, and there will be those who feel that a desperate effort should have been made to get some Western troops into Berlin. But it is difficult to visualize how Allied participation in taking one city could have changed the basic attitude of the Soviet Government, as Sir Winston seemed to feel it would. Certainly the Soviets' cautious attitude from

---

[5] The Prime Minister's letter to Stalin requesting an early date for the Russian winter offensive has been blamed for the occupation of much territory by the Soviets. This letter was written before Yalta, at which meeting Sir Winston appeared to have hardened his attitude. Further, it is doubtful that his message altered Soviet plans to any degree.

that day to this regarding the power of the United States would seem to belie such a conclusion.

Hitler's decision to form the Fifth and Sixth Panzer armies into a large mobile reserve was undoubtedly correct, since the bulk of his troops was located in strong defenses in the Siegfried Line in the west. As noted, the decision to commit this reserve in a great offensive undoubtedly shortened the war—witness the crumbling of the Nazi armies in the campaigns that followed. His resolve to commit this reserve in a great offensive against the tempting thinly held front of the Ardennes, the scene of his 1940 victory, had one unexpected result: it delayed a planned Allied offensive and thus permitted the Russians to launch their attacks to the Oder River against greatly weakened opposition and advance farther into Germany. Had Hitler sent his mobile reserve to the east rather than into the Ardennes, it is entirely possible that the Western Allies and Russians would have met somewhere in Poland.

But the significance of these facts is military rather than political. In the climate of the times, with the Western Allies and the Soviets acting as partners against the common enemy, occupation territory would in any eventuality have been adjusted *so that the map of Europe would have looked no different from its appearance today.* Had an Allied capture of Berlin affected the attitude of the Russians, as Mr. Churchill predicted, it is the author's opinion that the effect would have been temporary only. Too much has happened since. It is somewhat fatuous to assume that the relations between East and West today would have been affected by the seizure of Berlin, Vienna, Prague, or any other city in 1945.

Given that Hitler's decision to make his last desperate gamble in the west rather than the east had little or no effect on the ultimate political situation in Europe, what then were the consequences?

First, the fighting in the Ardennes proved the mettle of the American fighting man; it reminded the world that the descendants of the heroes of the Alamo could still fight under adverse circumstances.

Second, it established the soundness of the remarkable U.S. Army school systems and the Army's methodical—but still imaginative—selection of persons designated for positions of high responsibility.

Third, and most important, it proved that no strain could destroy or even seriously threaten the vital Anglo-American alliance, to which so many men of great stature contributed.

The world problems of today bear little resemblance to those that faced the Allies in December of 1944. But one solid pillar, vital to any solution, undoubtedly lies in the unity of English-speaking peoples that was so sorely tested in the bitter woods of the Ardennes.

Bibliography

Books

Armored School, "The Defense of St. Vith, Belgium, an Historical Example of Armor in the Defense." December, 1955.

Ayer, Fred, Jr., *Before the Colors Fade*. Boston, Houghton Mifflin Company, 1964.

Baldwin, Hanson W., *Battles Lost and Won*. New York, Harper & Row, 1966.

Baldwin, Hanson W., ed., *Command Decisions*. New York, Harcourt, Brace and Company, 1959.

Blumenson, Martin, *U.S. Army in World War II, European Theatre of Operations —Breakout and Pursuit*. Washington, Office of the Chief of Military History, Department of the Army, 1961.

Bovy, Marcel, *La Bataille de l'Amblève*. Liège, Les Amitiés Mosanes, 36, Place du XX Août, 1947.

Bradley, Omar N., *A Soldier's Story*. New York, Henry Holt & Company, 1951.

Bryant, Arthur, *Triumph in the West*. New York, Doubleday & Company, 1959.

Bullock, Alan, *Hitler, A Study in Tyranny*. New York, Harper and Brothers, 1953.

Butcher, Captain Harry C., *My Three Years with Eisenhower*. New York, Simon and Schuster, 1946.

Churchill, Winston S., *Triumph and Tragedy*. Boston, Houghton Mifflin Company, 1953.

Codman, Colonel Charles R., *Drive*. Boston, Little, Brown and Company, 1957.

Cole, Hugh M., *The Ardennes: The Battle of the Bulge*. Washington, Office of the Chief of Military History, Department of the Army, 1965.

———— *The Lorraine Campaign*. Washington, Historical Division, Department of the Army, 1950.

Columbia Broadcasting System, *From D-Day Through Victory in Europe*. New York, CBS, 1945.

Davis, Kenneth S., *Experience of War: The United States in World War II*. Garden City, N.Y., Doubleday & Company, Inc., 1965.

Draper, Lieutenant Theodore, *The 84th Infantry Division in the Battle of Germany, November 1944–May 1945*. New York, Viking Press, 1947.

Dupuy, Colonel R. Ernest, *St. Vith, Lion in the Way*. Washington, The Infantry Journal Press, 1949.

Eisenhower, Dwight D., *Crusade in Europe*. New York, Doubleday & Company, 1948.

Esposito, Colonel Vincent J., *The West Point Atlas of American Wars*. New York, Frederick A. Praeger, 1959.

Farago, Ladislas, *Patton: Ordeal and Triumph*. New York, Dell Publishing Company, 1965.

Guderian, General Heinz, *Panzer Leader*. New York, E. P. Dutton & Company, Inc., 1952.

Guingand, Major General Sir Francis de, *Generals at War*. London, Hodder and Stoughton, 1964.

——— *Operation Victory*. New York, Charles Scribner's Sons. 1947.

Hart, B. H. Liddell, *The German Generals Talk*. New York, William Morrow & Co., 1948.

Heffner, Richard D., *A Documentary History of the United States*. New York, The New American Library of World Literature, Inc., 1952 (Revised 1956).

Hitler, Adolf, *Hitler's Secret Conversations*. New York: New American Library, n. d.

Horrocks, Lieutenant General Sir Brian, *Escape to Action*. New York, St. Martin's Press, 1961.

Ingersoll, Ralph, *Top Secret*. New York, Harcourt, Brace and Company, 1946.

Jacobsen, H. A. and Rohwer, J., *Decisive Battles of World War II: The German View*. New York, G. P. Putnam's Sons, 1965.

Knickerbocker, H. R., Thompson, Jack, Belden, Jack, *et al.*, *Danger Forward*. Atlanta, Albert Love Enterprises, 1947.

Lame, G. R. de, *La Bataille de la Gleize-Stoumont*. Bruxelles, L'Alliance, n.d.

Leigh, Lieutenant Colonel Randolph, *48,000,000 Tons to Eisenhower*. Washington, The Infantry Journal Press, 1945.

MacDonald, Charles B., *The Siegfried Line*. Washington, Office of the Chief of Military History, Department of the Army, 1963.

Manteuffel, General der Panzertruppen A. D. Hasso von, *Die 7. Panzer-Division im Zweiten Weltkrieg*. Verdingen am Rhein, Josef Broich, 1965.

Marshall, Colonel S. L. A. (assisted by Captain John G. Westover and Lieutenant A. Joseph Webber), *Bastogne: The First Eight Days*. Washington, The Infantry Journal Press, 1946.

Merriam, Robert E., *Dark December*. Chicago, Ziff-Davis Publishing Company, 1947.

Montgomery, Field Marshal, Viscount of Alamein, *Memoirs*. Cleveland, World Publishing Company, 1958.

——— *Normandy to the Baltic*. Hutchinson, London, 1947.

Patton, George S., Jr., *War as I Knew It*. Boston, Houghton Mifflin Company, 1947.

Pogue, Forrest C., *The Supreme Command*. Washington, Office of the Chief of Military History, Department of the Army, 1954.

Rapport, Leonard, and Northwood, Arthur, Jr., *Rendezvous with Destiny—A History of the 101st Airborne Division*. Washington: The Infantry Journal Press, 1948.

Ridgway, Matthew B., *Soldier: The Memoirs of Matthew B. Ridgway (As Told to Harold H. Martin)*. New York, Harper and Brothers, 1956.

Sampson, Chaplain (Major General) Francis L., USA, Chief of Chaplains, *Look Out Below*. Washington, The Catholic University of America Press, Inc., 1958.

Skorzeny, Otto, *Skorzeny's Special Missions*. London, Robert Hale Limited, 1957.

Smith, General Walter Bedell, *Eisenhower's Six Great Decisions*. New York, Longmans Green and Company, 1956.

Stacey, Colonel C. P., and Cloutier, Edmond, *The Canadian Army, 1939–1945*. King's Printer, Ottawa, 1948.

Strachey, John, *On the Prevention of War*. New York, St. Martin's Press, 1963.

Summersby, Kay, *Eisenhower Was My Boss*. New York, Prentice-Hall, Inc., 1948.

Tedder, Lord (Marshal of the Royal Air Force), *With Prejudice*. London, Cassell & Company, Ltd., 1966.

Thone, Georges, *Les Crimes de Guerre*. Liège, Commission des Crimes de Guerre, 1946.

Toland, John, *Battle: The Story of the Bulge*. New York, Random House, 1959.

Warlimont, Walter, *Inside Hitler's Headquarters, 1939–1945*. New York: Praeger, 1964.

Wilmot, Chester, *The Struggle for Europe: World War II in Western Europe*. New York: Harper & Row, 1952.

Magazines

American Legion Magazine, series on The Battle of the Bulge:
    Part I, "Hitler Plans the Impossible" (Jan., 1966).
    Part II, "Disaster and Reaction in the Ardennes" (Feb., 1966).
    Part III, "The Bulge Is Erased" (March, 1966).

Blumentritt, General of the Infantry Günther, "Field Marshal von Rundstedt's On Story of the Battle of the Bulge," *Collier's* (Jan. 3, 1953).

Doherty, John Stephen, "The Battle Babies, Saga of the 99th Division," *Saga* (Jan., 1945).

Endsley, Mark C., "9th Infantry Division Activated—Glories of Past Are Revived," *Army Information Digest* (March, 1966).

Fraser, Gordon, article in *Overseas Press Bulletin* (supplied by "Cy" Peterman) (Dec. 12, 1964).

MacDonald, Charles, "The Neglected Ardennes," *Military Review* (April, 1963).

MacDonald, Charles B., "The Battle for Elsenborn Ridge," *The Johns Hopkins Magazine* (Dec., 1959).

Merriam, Captain Robert E., "Bulgeland Revisited," *Infantry Journal* (Dec., 1949).

Peterman, Ivan H. ("Cy"), "They Took the Nazis' Sunday Punch," *Saturday Evening Post* (Sept. 28, 1946).

Raymond, Captain Allen D. III, "The Battle of St. Vith," *Armor* (Nov.–Dec., 1944).

Official U.S. Government Sources

Official U.S. Government sources consulted in this work break down into two categories. One consists of interrogations of former high-ranking German officers conducted shortly after World War II (see below, "Manuscripts"). These manuscripts are in the possession of the Office of the Chief of Military History, Department of the Army, Washington, D.C.

The other category of source material consists of American reports and interrogations in the possession of the World War II Archives, Alexandria, Virginia. These fall into the following categories: (1) intelligence reports rendered by U.S. headquarters; (2) after action reports; (3) combat interviews. These are differentiated as follows:

1. Intelligence reports prepared by the unit intelligence officer (G-2) consist of:

a. Periodic reports submitted daily and distributed within the headquarters as well as to adjacent, higher, and lower headquarters. A summarization of intelligence interests occurring on the front during the preceding twenty-four-hour period.

b. Intelligence estimates produced at irregular intervals by the G-2 as the situation requires. These estimates are normally rather lengthy documents evaluating the significance of recent enemy activities and attempting to draw reasonable conclusions regarding the course of action the enemy is likely to pursue. At higher levels these estimates constitute the most important influence on the actions of the commander. Unfortunately their worth is often diluted by verbosity and ambiguity.

c. Intelligence summaries (ISUM's). Covering a much wider time frame than the periodic reports, the ISUM is designed to summarize the most important aspects of the daily reports of a given period.

2. After action reports (command reports) are prepared by the operations officer (G-3) in the name of the unit commander. As such they describe the activities of the command—in contrast to the intelligence reports, which concentrate on the enemy. They are prepared daily and distributed to higher headquarters.

3. Combat interviews, prepared not by the units involved in the action but by members of the various historical staff sections. In contrast to the official reports mentioned above, they consist of interrogations of individuals, regardless of rank or position, who have participated in significant actions. Though official documents, they resemble interviews by reporters and are not confirmed by the responsible commanders as to accuracy. They are chiefly valuable as records of individual actions and contribute to this work primarily for their human interest content.

1. INTELLIGENCE REPORTS

12 Army Group: Weekly Intelligence Summary #17 (Dec. 5, 1944); Weekly Intelligence Summary #18 (Dec. 12, 1944).

21 Army Group: Annex 2 to Periodic Report #180, "SHAEF's View of the Enemy Situation."

First U.S. Army: G-2 Periodic Report #36 (Nov. 20, 1944); G-2 (Target Subsection) Study of Enemy Armored Reserves (Dec. 8, 1944); G-2 Estimate #37 (Dec. 10, 1944); G-2 Periodic Report (Dec. 13, 1944); G-2 Periodic Report (Dec. 16, 1944); G-2 Estimate #38 (Dec. 20, 1944); G-2 Estimate #39 (Dec.

21, 1944); Letter of Instructions from Lieutenant General Courtney Hodges, CO, to commanding generals of V Corps, VII Corps, XVIII Airborne Corps (Dec. 21, 1944).

V Corps: G-2 Periodic Report #153, On the Security of the German Prisoners of War.

VII Corps: Inc. 2 to G-2 Periodic Report #8; G-2 Periodic Report, published by VIII Corps (Nov. 16, 1944).

VIII Corps: Order of Battle Notes, translation of two captured German documents; Annex #3 to G-2 Periodic Report #146; G-2 Periodic Intelligence Report (Nov. 8, 1944); G-2 Periodic Intelligence Report (Dec. 1, 1944); G-2 Periodic Report (Dec. 3, 1944); G-2 Periodic Report (Dec. 9, 1944); G-2 Periodic Report (Dec. 10, 1944); Order of Battle Notes, G-2 Section (Dec. 11, 1944); Order of Battle Notes (Dec. 13, 1944); G-2 Periodic Report (Dec. 15, 1944).

4th Infantry Division: G 2 Report (Dec. 16, 1944); G-2 Journal (Dec. 12, 1944).

28th Division: G-2 Periodic Report (Dec. 14, 1944); G-2 Periodic Report #140 (Dec. 14–15, 1944); G-2 Journal, Message 22–25 (Dec. 15, 1944); G-2 Periodic Report #128.

106th Infantry Division: G-2 Journal (Dec. 12, 1944); G-2 Periodic Report #2, Annex #1 (Dec. 13, 1944).

2. AFTER ACTION REPORTS

Eisenhower, Dwight D., Report by the Supreme Commander to the Combined Chiefs of Staff on the Operations in Europe of the Allied Expeditionary Force (June 6, 1944, to May 8, 1945); First U.S. Army (Aug. 1, 1944; Feb. 22, 1945; Third U.S. Army (no specific dates given, but includes Dec. 26, 1944– Jan. 16, 1945, at least); History of VII Corps during Operations in Belgium (Jan. 1–31, 1945, inclusive); XVIII Airborne Corps Summary of Operations (Dec. 18, 1944, to Feb. 13, 1945); 9th Armored Division; 106th U.S. Infantry Division Report of Action against Enemy (Jan. 6, 1945); Rudder, Lieutenant Colonel Earle, CO, 109th Infantry Regiment; 393d Regiment, 99th Division (Dec. 13, 1944); Riley, Colonel Don, CO, 394th Infantry Regiment; 395th Infantry Regiment (Jan. 4, 1945).

3. COMBAT INTERVIEWS

2d Armored Division (include period Jan. 1–16, 1945); 11th Armored Division (Dec. 29, 1944–Jan. 16, 1945); 28th Infantry Division (Dec. 16–19, 1944); 4th Infantry Division (Dec. 16, 1944); Notes on 28th Division (110th Infantry), Colonel Briggs (G-3); 14th Cavalry Group (Mecz), Extensive interviews (shortly after Jan. 1, 1945); 12th Infantry, Regiment Combat Interviews (Dec 16, 1944); 14th Cavalry Group Combat Interviews and Map

(Jan. 10, 1945); Colonel Gustin M. Nelson, CO, 112th Infantry (Jan. 14, 1945); 422d Infantry, 106th Division; 423d Infantry, 106th Division; 513th Parachute Infantry Regiment, 17th Airborne Division (Jan. 2–13, 1945).

Manuscripts, Office of Chief of Military History

The manuscripts pertaining to the European campaign and currently in the possession of the Office of the Chief of Military History (OCMH), Department of the Army, Washington, D.C., consist primarily of five series: A, B, C, ETHINT and R. They are differentiated as follows:

A and B series: Designed to fill gaps in the military information known by American historians from German documents. They were written by prominent German commanders shortly after World War II while those commanders were being held in U.S. custody, aided and supervised by the Historical Section, European Theater of Operations, on behalf of the Office of the Chief of Military History, U.S. Army, Washington, D.C.

C series: Prepared on the same basis as A and B series. It was initiated in 1948 for the purpose of further filling in gaps still existing in desired historical information.

ETHINT *series*: The first manuscripts prepared after World War II. In contrast to the A, B, and C series, the ETHINT's were written by American interrogators on the basis of interviews with important German commanders and staff officers. By and large they comprise interviews with very high-ranking German officials and persons whose status as accused war criminals made it necessary to glean highly important information before those persons should go before Allied tribunals.

R series: In a class by themselves. These were prepared by the Office of the Chief of Military History, U.S. Army, some years after the war. They were designed primarily to assist various official authors in the preparation of the official history—*The U.S. Army in World War II*.

Of these manuscripts the A, B, C, and ETHINT series are soon to be transferred to the National Archives. The R series will remain in the custody of the Office of the Chief of Military History.

A SERIES

A-858, Major Percy E. Schramm, "The Course of Events of the German Offensive in the Ardennes" (Dec. 16, 1944–Jan. 14, 1945); *A-862,* Schramm, "The Preparation for the German Offensive in the Ardennes" (Sept.–Dec. 16, 1944); *A-873,* Generalmajor Siegfried von Waldenburg, "Commitment of the 116 PZ Div. in the Ardennes" (1944–45); *A-877,* General der Waffen-SS H. Priess, "Commitment of the 1 SS Panzer Corps During the Ardennes Offensive" (Dec. 16, 1944–Jan. 25, 1945); *A-924,* Brigadeführer der Waffen-SS Fritz Kraemer, "Operations of the Sixth Panzer Army" (1944–45); *A-925,* Oberst Günther Reichhelm, "Report on Activity of Colonel (GSC) Reichhelm"; *A-938,* General der Panzertruppen Heinrich Freiherr von Lüttwitz, "47th Panzer Corps, Ardennes"; *A-939,* Lüttwitz, "The Commitment of the 47th PZ Corps in the Ardennes" (1944–45); *A-940,* Lüttwitz, "47th PZ Corps in the Ardennes Battle" (Feb. 11, 1945); *A-941, 941a,* Generalleutnant Fritz Bayerlein, "Role of the Panzer Lehr Division in the Ardennes Offensive" (Dec. 18, 1944–Jan. 27, 1945); *A-942,* Bayerlein, "Commitment of the PZ Lehr in First Days of Ardennes Offensive" (Dec. 16–21, 1944); *A-943,* Bayerlein, "Additional Question—Ardennes Offensive"; *A-944,* Bayerlein, "Panzer Lehr Division—Situation Maps" (Dec. 23, 1944–

Jan. 11, 1945); *A-945*, Bayerlein, "Additional Questions—Ardennes Offensive"; *A-955*, Oberst i.G. Hans-Jürgen Dingler, "Report on the Campaign in Northern France, the Rhineland, and the Ardennes"; *A-961*, Generalmajor Carl Wagener, "Fifth Panzer Army—Ardennes (Special Questions)"; *A-977*, Major Herbert Büchs, "The German Ardennes Offensive."

B SERIES

B-024, Generalmajor Rudolf Bader, "560th Volks Grenadier Division" (Nov. 11, 1944–Jan. 25, 1945); *B-027*, Generalmajor Rud. Langhaeuser, "560th Volks Grenadier Division" (Dec. 15–29, 1944), and "12th Volks Grenadier Division" (Jan. 1–28, 1945); *B-032*, Oberst i.G. Werner Bodenstein, "LIII Corps" (Dec. 1, 1944–Jan. 22, 1945); *B-034*, Major Percy E. Schramm, "OKW War Diary" (The West) (Apr. 1–Dec. 18, 1944); *B-040*, Generalmajor Heinz Kokott, "26th Volks Grenadier Division in the Ardennes Offensive"; *B-095*, Oberst Horst Wilutsky, "The Offensive of Army Group G in Northern Alsace in January, 1945"; *B-151*, General der Panzertruppen Hasso-Eccard von Manteuffel, "The 5 PZ Army and the Offensive in the Ardennes" (Dec. 16, 1944–Jan. 25, 1945); *B-151a*, Manteuffel, "Fifth Panzer Army (Ardennes Offensive)"; *B-172b*, Manteuffel, "Requested Expression of Opinion on the Report Written by Major General Wirts" (Aug., 1946); *B-235*, Generalmajor Carl Wagener, "Fifth Panzer Army" (Nov. 2, 1944–Jan. 16, 1945); *B-344*, General der Infanterie Günther Blumentritt, "Three Marshals, National Character and the July 20 Complex"; *B-456*, Oberstleutnant Ruediger Weiz, "The 2 PZ Division (Dec. 21–Dec. 26, 1944) in the Ardennes Offensive (Thrust on Dinant)"; *B-592*, Generalmajor Otto Remer, "Führer Begleit Brigade" (Dec. 16, 1944–Jan. 26, 1945); *B-675*, Oberst i.G. Anton Staubwasser, "Army Group B—Intelligence Estimate" (June 1, 1944); *B-676*, Oberst Günther Reichhelm, "Sixth Panzer Army" (Oct., 1944–Jan. 24, 1945); *B-701*, Reichhelm, "Army Group B" (Oct. 15, 1944–45); *B-767*, Major Kurt Hold, "The First Army in the Winter Battle in the Vosges" (Dec. 20, 1944–Feb. 15, 1945); *B-779*, Oberst der Waffen-SS Rudolf Lehmann, "1 SS Panzer Corps" (Dec. 15, 1944–Jan. 25, 1945); *B-786*, Oberst Emmerich, "The Battles of First Army in Lorraine and Northern Alsace" (Sept. 15, 1944–Feb. 10, 1945), also Part III (Dec. 20, 1944–Feb. 10, 1945); *B-823*, Oberstleutnant Friedrich August Baron von der Heydte, "Kampfgruppe von der Heydte."

C SERIES

C-004, Oberst (W-SS) Jochen Peiper, "Kampfgruppe Peiper" (Dec. 15–26, 1944); *C-020*, Major Percy Schramm, "On Hitler's Directives and Decisions."

ETHINT SERIES

ETHINT *10*, Oberst (W-SS) Jochen Peiper, "I SS PZ Regt." (Dec. 11–24, 1944); ETHINT *11*, Peiper, "1 SS PZ Regt." (Dec. 16–19, 1944); ETHINT *12*, Oberst (W-SS) Otto Skorzeny, "Ardennes Offensive, an Interview with Obst. Skorzeny" (Aug. 12, 1945); ETHINT *45*, General der Panzertruppen Hasso-Eccard von Manteuffel, "Fifth PZ Army, and Interview with Gen. Pz. Hasso von Manteuffel" (Sept. 11, 1944–Jan., 1945); ETHINT *46*, Manteuffel, "Fifth PZ Army" (Nov.,

1944–Jan., 1945); ETHINT 50, Generaloberst Alfred Jodl, "Planning the Ardennes Offensive" (July 26, 1945).

R SERIES

R-12, Charles von Lüttichau, "Ardennes Offensive—Preliminary Planning"; R-13, Lüttichau, "Framework of Wacht am Rhine"; R-14, Lüttichau, "The Strategic Concentration"; R-15, Dr. Magna Bauer, "Key Dates in the Ardennes Offensive" (Part I); R-19, "German Situation in the Fall of 1944" (Military); R-59, Dr. Magna Bauer, "The German Withdrawal from the Ardennes"; R-61, Bauer, "Effects of the Ardennes Offensive"; R-62, "German Commanders on Western Front"; R-66, Günther Reichhelm.

Principal Interviews

Louis M. Bodarwé; Colonel Donald Boyer; Dr. Lyle Bouck; General of the Army Omar N. Bradley; Dr. Frank Carroll; General Bruce C. Clarke; General J. Lawton Collins; Major General Norman D. Cota; Colonel Benjamin Dickson; Colonel William Dwight; General of the Army Dwight D. Eisenhower; Major General Julian Ewell; William F. Cody Garlow; M. Theo Galle; Seymour Green; Robert Hall; Major General Robert Hasbrouck; William James; Major General Alan W. Jones; Lieutenant General Harry W. O. Kinnard; General Anthony McAuliffe; Brigadier General Hal D. McCown; General Hasso von Manteuffel; Lieutenant General Troy Middleton; Erich Moller; Field Marshal Montgomery, Viscount of Alamein; Professor Ernest Natalis; Colonel Oliver Patton; Ivan ("Cy") Peterman; General Matthew B. Ridgway; Colonel Edwin Van V. Sutherland; General Maxwell D. Taylor; Daniel E. Tennow; Major General Sir John Whiteley.

Correspondence

General Creighton Abrams; Harry Butcher; Walter Cronkite; Colonel William Dwight; Major General Julian Ewell; General Leslie Groves; Major General Sir Francis de Guingand; Major General Joseph Harper; Lieutenant General Charles E. Hart; Lieutenant Colonel M. C. Helfers; General John E. Hull; Colonel George Lincoln; Brigadier General Hal D. McCown; General Hasso von Manteuffel; Erich Moller; Jochen Peiper; Dr. Forrest C. Pogue; General Günther Reichhelm; Thomas J. Riggs; Brigadier General William Roberts; Cornelius Ryan; Chaplain (Major General) Francis L. Sampson; Otto Skorzeny; Colonel Howard B. St. Clair; Colonel James Stack; Major General Sir Kenneth Strong; Major General Robert W. Wilson.

Miscellaneous

Bouck, Dr. Lyle J., Jr., Booklet assembled on I & R Platoon, 394th Infantry, Action at Lanzerath (Dec. 16, 1944).
Buenger, Rev. Edward A., "Events Recalled of the Early Days of the Battle of the Bulge, Dec. 16–19, 1944" (pamphlet, Sept. 5, 1966).

Clarke, General Bruce C., *Secret Diary Combat Command B,* 7th Armored Division (1942, 1943, 1944).

Clarke, General Bruce C., Combat Command B, 7th Armored Division, Memo (Dec. 20, 1944).

XVIII Airborne Corps Report of Investigation, CCA, 7th Armored Division, Manhay (Dec. 24–25, 1944).

Eisenhower, General Dwight D., unpublished draft of article for *Saturday Evening Post* (Oct. 26, 1961).

Ferris, Captain Franklin, "The German Offensive of 16 December: The Defeat of the 1st SS Panzer Division Adolf Hitler."

Hasbrouck, Brigadier General Robert W., CG, 7th Armored Division, Letter to General Kean of First Army (Dec. 21, 1944).

Hechler, K. W., *The Enemy Side of the Hill,* Manuscript, U.S. Army Historical Division (July 30, 1949).

Jones, Major General Alan W., Address given at Reunion of the 106th Division, Indianapolis (July 15, 1947).

Kean, William, Diary (Dec. 12, 1944–Jan. 4, 1945).

Kempton, William B., Letter to Lyle Bouck recalling events of Battle of Bulge (June 7, 1966).

Kinnard, Colonel H. W. O., Letter to John Toland (March 19, 1958).

Kriz, Robert L., Letter to Lyle Bouck recalling events of Battle of Bulge (Sept. 14, 1966).

Lambert, Robert L., Recollection of events of December 16–21, 1944 (as recalled on or about April 10, 1966).

McCune, Boyd H., Letter to Lyle Bouck, on actions of December 16–18, 1944, of I & R Platoon, 394th (Aug. 7, 1966).

Palmer and Collins, First U.S. Army Correspondence; Confirmation of Oral Instructions by R. F. Akers (all dated Dec. 24, 1944).

Tennow, Daniel E., *Action at St. Vith: The 106th Infantry Division in the Battle of the Bulge,* Thesis for University of Maryland (Apr. 15, 1966).

Thorne, Corporal Horace M., #32012364, Army General Order #80, awarding Thorne the Congressional Medal of Honor for action at St.-Vith.

Umstatd, Pfc. William (machine gunner, 423d Infantry Regiment, 106th Division), Diary.

Unit Citation of 81st Engineer Combat Battalion, 106th Infantry Division, for Conduct in German Counteroffensive December 16–23, 1944, with supporting narrative supplied by Thomas Riggs.

Unit Journal of 109th Infantry Regiment with map marked by Major Harry Kemp, executive officer, 3d Battalion, 109th Infantry.

Index

Index

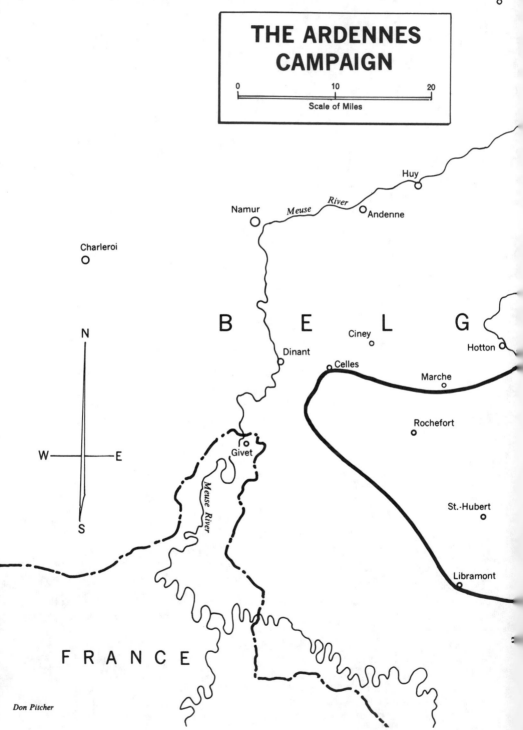

BRUSSELS

Tongres

THE ARDENNES CAMPAIGN

0   10   20
Scale of Miles

Huy

Meuse River

Namur   Andenne

Charleroi

B   E   L   G

Ciney

Hotton

Dinant   Celles

Marche

Rochefort

Meuse River

Givet

N

W——E

S

St.-Hubert

Libramont

F R A N C E

Don Pitcher

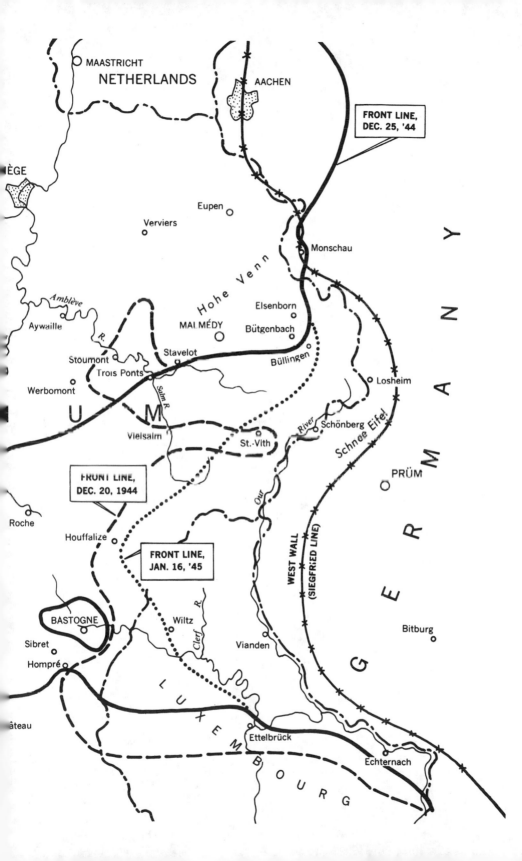

MAASTRICHT

NETHERLANDS

AACHEN

FRONT LINE,
DEC. 25, '44

ÈGE

Eupen

Verviers

Monschau

H o h e   V e n n

Elsenborn

MAI MÉDY

Bütgenbach

Amblève

Aywaille

R.

Stavelot

Büllingen

Stoumont

Trois Ponts

Losheim

Werbomont

Salm R.

Vielsalm

River

Schönberg

St.-Vith

S c h n e e   E i f e l

FRONT LINE,
DEC. 20, 1944

PRÜM

Roche

Our

FRONT LINE,
JAN. 16, '45

Houffalize

WEST WALL
(SIEGFRIED LINE)

Bitburg

BASTOGNE

Wiltz

Clerf R.

Sibret

Vianden

Hompré

âteau

Ettelbrück

Echternach

G   E   R   M   A   N   Y

U M

L   U   X   E   M   B   O   U   R   G

Other titles of interest

THE WAR, 1939–1945
A Documentary History
Edited by Desmond Flowers
and James Reeves
New introduction by
John S. D. Eisenhower
1,142 pp., 20 maps
80763-7 $24.95

EISENHOWER AS
MILITARY COMMANDER
E.K.G. Sixsmith
264 pp., 35 photos, 11 maps
80369-0 $12.95

THE FALL OF BERLIN
Anthony Read and David Fisher
535 pp., 17 photos, 5 maps
80619-3 $16.95

THE GUINNESS BOOK
OF ESPIONAGE
Mark Lloyd
256 pp., 100 photos
80584-7 $16.95

THE LUFTWAFFE
WAR DIARIES
The German Air Force in
World War II
Cajus Bekker
447 pp., 119 photos, 20 maps
80604-5 $15.95

THE MEMOIRS OF
FIELD MARSHAL
MONTGOMERY
508 pp., 61 photos
80173-6 $10.95

THE GI's WAR
American Soldiers in Europe
During World War II
Edwin P. Hoyt
638 pp., 29 illus.
80448-4 $16.95

THE MIGHTY ENDEAVOR
The American War in Europe
Charles B. MacDonald
621 pp., 78 photos, 10 maps
80486-7 $16.95

NUREMBERG DIARY
G. M. Gilbert
488 pp., 24 photos
80661-4 $16.95

PANZER LEADER
General Heinz Guderian
Foreword by B. H. Liddell Hart
New introduction by
Kenneth Macksey
554 pp., 22 photos, 37 maps
80689-4 $17.95

THE PATTON PAPERS, 1940–1945
Martin Blumenson
944 pp., 31 photos, 5 maps
80717-3 $19.95

THE PSYCHOPATHIC GOD
Adolf Hitler
Robert G. L. Waite
512 pp., 20 illus.
80514-6 $15.95

THE ROMMEL PAPERS
Edited by B. H. Liddell Hart
544 pp., 17 photos
80157-4 $15.95

RED STORM ON THE REICH
The Soviet March
on Germany, 1945
Christopher Duffy
415 pp., 14 maps
80505-7 $14.95

Available at your bookstore

OR ORDER DIRECTLY FROM

DA CAPO PRESS, INC.

1-800-321-0050